CATHOLIC RECORD SOCIETY PUBLICATIONS

RECORDS SERIES
VOLUME 87

The Chronicles of Nazareth
(The English Convent), Bruges 1629–1793

Edited by
CAROLINE BOWDEN

PUBLISHED FOR
THE CATHOLIC RECORD SOCIETY
BY
THE BOYDELL PRESS
2017

First published 2017

ISBN 978-0-902832-31-2

A Catholic Record Society publication
published by The Boydell Press
an imprint of Boydell & Brewer Ltd
PO Box 9, Woodbridge, Suffolk IP12 3DF, UK
and of Boydell & Brewer Inc.
668 Mt Hope Avenue, Rochester, NY 14620–2731, USA
website: www.boydellandbrewer.com

A CIP catalogue record for this book is available
from the British Library

This publication is printed on acid-free paper

Printed and bound in Great Britain by
TJ International Ltd, Padstow, Cornwall

Mother Mary Augustina More, 8th Prioress of Nazareth 1766–1807. This last lineal descendant of St Thomas More was Prioress during the troubled times of the French Revolution, and with great courage and determination guided the community to take refuge in Suffolk in 1794 and back to Bruges in 1802. The Chronicles stress 'the admirable manner in which she conducted herself on all occasions' and how she showed herself a worthy descendant of her illustrious ancestor.

(photograph © Jens Compernolle, Bruges, reproduced by kind permission of the Community of Nazareth, Bruges)

CONTENTS

ILLUSTRATIONS

The editor and publishers are grateful to all the institutions and persons listed for permission to reproduce the materials in which they hold copyright. Every effort has been made to trace the copyright holders; apologies are offered for any omission, and the publishers will be pleased to add any necessary acknowledgement in subsequent editions.

ACKNOWLEDGMENTS

A task of this magnitude is made possible only by the contributions of others, whom I am happy to acknowledge here. Firstly, the enthusiasm and support of the Community at Nazareth, who have known all along how important the Chronicles are to increase our understanding of life in the English convents in exile. Next, to Pascal Majérus, formerly of the Archives générales du Royaume in Brussels, who created a digital version of Volume I, transcribed Volume II and started on the footnoting; sadly pressure of work and ill-health prevented him from seeing the project to completion. Victoria Van Hyning contributed her photographs of both volumes to the project and worked with me on establishing a formal style guide and transcription rules. It was good to have a literary scholar on board at that important stage. Together with her husband, Alyn Still, Victoria devised a nifty template for entering members of the community into the volume, for which I was very grateful; they kindly agreed to a version of this citation index being included as an appendix to facilitate referencing the nuns. Amanda Haste was an extraordinary editor for Volume I, fitting it into an already crowded schedule. Hester Higton, as copy-editor, has worked on the text with sharp insights and meticulous attention to detail, which have made a significant contribution the volume.

I am grateful to volunteers who took sections of Volume II, checking text against photographic images with great care. They were: Stephanie Howard-Smith, Diane Hurst, Michelle Meza, Sam Shammai, Hannah Thomas and Tillie Zeeman. One challenge of working on a document created by a community in exile is finding specialist sources to cover the range of contacts, activities and interests of members and I am greatly indebted to colleagues and friends who sent me material: their contributions are acknowledged in the footnotes. I have also realised quite how valuable the team effort in creating the 'Who Were the Nuns?' database was and how far the research of Katharine Keats-Rohan has enabled us to go in finding families and networks supporting communities in exile. I am also indebted to the series editor, Francis Young for his enthusiasm for the Chronicles and his care in the editing process.

I have always found illustrations and maps important to understanding the meaning of documents and I am delighted to be able to include them here. To Brian Farrimond, who made the maps, Katharine Keats-Rohan, who created the family tree, Jens Compernolle, who photographed the portrait of Mother More, and the other photographers, and to Eddie Bohnert for his technical help with the photographic images, my thanks are due.

The illustrations are produced with the generous assistance of a grant from Isobel Thornley's Bequest to the University of London.

The edition is dedicated to Sr Mary Aline, Archivist, and to the Community of Nazareth at Bruges.

Caroline Bowden
March 2017

EDITORIAL PRINCIPLES

Source texts

The Chronicles survive in two manuscript volumes. Volume I, for 1629–1729, measures 16 cm by 20 cm and is bound in dark brown leather. The manuscript appears to have been created as a celebration of the centenary jubilee of Nazareth and was copied from earlier sources by Sister Anne Weston, who died in 1738. Unfortunately the ink has bled through the pages, rendering some portions of the manuscript illegible. A decision was taken for conservation reasons and for legibility to use the typescript made by Sr Agnes Joseph Coppieters in 1997 as an alternative source for this edition. A link to the original manuscript has been retained by using the page numbers from the original rather than the typescript, which appear in bold within square brackets in the text and notes of this edition thus: **[p. 1]**. Very occasionally Sr Agnes omitted the original page numbers in error. She noted a mis-pagination between **[p. 165]** and **[p. 168]**.

Volume II, for 1729–1793, measures 20 cm by 25 cm and is bound in lighter brown leather. The text appears in this edition as it exists from the surviving manuscript written in three scribal hands, discussed in the Introduction. The pagination of the manuscript has been adopted for this edition with page numbers noted in the text. The system of putting the year at the head of each page has been adopted from the original.

Transcription

Spelling is as in the original, with the exception of i/j and u/v, which have been modernised. Missing letters have been added in square brackets if clarification is needed. Capitalisation has been kept as in the original. Common early modern abbreviations have been silently expanded and the letter thorn transliterated as *th*: yt – that; ye – the; wt –what or with; wn – when; yn – then; ym – them; wch – which; F – Father; M – Mother; Rd – Reverend (male); Rde – Reverende (as in Reverend Mother); Sr – Sister (religious); Bd – Blessed.

Names of months have been silently expanded. The distinction between '&' and 'and' has been maintained. Superscripts are transcribed as they appear in the manuscript, for example 1st or Mlle; Sr Agnes did not include superscripts in her version of Volume I. Catchwords are omitted. Latin and other foreign words are italicised and footnoted. Deletions and tears are marked with ~~strikethrough~~ and {tear} as appropriate. Illegible text appears as [*illeg.*]. Crossed-out sections are reproduced thus: ~~strikethrough~~. Added text is indicated ^thus^. The compilers of the Chronicle occasionally omitted words or dates to be inserted later, leaving … in their place; where this occurs in the manuscript it has been retained in this edition.

Place names

Spellings are as written in the manuscript. In footnotes, the spelling of place names is as used by the nuns: e.g. Louvain rather than Leuven; Bruges rather than Brugge; Lierre rather than Lier.

Pagination

Pagination in both volumes follows the manuscripts and is marked thus: **[p. 1]**. Unpaginated text is indicated as **[unpaginated]**.

Footnotes

Every effort has been made to identify individuals, institutions and events appearing in the Chronicles and I am very grateful to colleagues cited in the acknowledgements for their assistance. Nuns' names appear in the text as they were written in the manuscript or typescript and may vary considerably. At Nazareth, names in religion were given at clothing, or earlier in some cases; but for a few nuns it is their name at baptism which was used throughout their convent life. Prioress Lucy Herbert, for instance, hardly ever appears under her name in religion (Teresa Joseph). Name variants such as Austin for Augustine and Stanny for Stanislaus are used in the Chronicles from time to time. Selecting the best form for use in the editorial apparatus became a complex matter. To make identification more straightforward, in the footnotes, the name is given as it appears in the 'Who Were the Nuns?' (WWTN) database, which used a range of sources from the convent, along with the two-letter prefix and numerical code by which that female religious is identified in the WWTN database, now a standard reference guide to English female religious. To avoid too much repetition, full details are not given each time a particular nun is mentioned: they can be checked in the citation index, which appears as Appendix 4.

Family members have been identified from a range of sources, starting with Katharine Keats-Rohan's family trees on the WWTN website (with revised versions available in print in 2017[1]). The genealogy website stirnet.com provided details of many others. Details of any relevant printed family histories have been given in footnotes.

---

[1] K. S. B. Keats-Rohan (ed.), *English Catholic Nuns in Exile, 1600–1800: A Biographical Register*, Prosopographia et Genealogica 15 (Oxford: Unit for Prosopographical Research, Linacre College, forthcoming 2017)

A calendar of saints' days and other religious feasts in the Chronicles appears as Appendix 3.

Biblical quotations

All biblical quotations in the footnotes are taken from the Douai-Rheims translation, *The Holy Bible: Translated from the Latin Vulgate* (London: Burns, Oates and Washbourne, 1914) and on-line.

ABBREVIATIONS

Anstruther 1, 2, 3, 4	G. Anstruther (ed.), *The Seminary Priests: A Dictionary of the Secular Clergy of England and Wales, 1558–1850*, 4 vols (Ware: St Edmund's College, 1969–77)
Bellenger	Aidan Bellenger (ed.), *English and Welsh Priests 1558–1800* (Bath: Downside Abbey, 1984)
Bellenger, *French Exiled Clergy*	Aidan Bellenger (ed.), *The French Exiled Clergy in the British Isles after 1789* (Bath: Downside Abbey, 1986)
Biographie nationale	*Biographie nationale de Belgique*, 44 vols (Brussels: Académie royale de Belgique, 1866–1986)
Chronicle	MS Chronicles of Nazareth, vols 1 and 2, Community of Nazareth, Bruges, Belgium
Corp	E. Corp, *A Court in Exile: The Stuarts in France, 1689–1718* (Cambridge: Cambridge University Press, 2004)
CRS	Catholic Record Society
Dominicana	*Dominicana: Cardinal Howard's letters, English Dominican friars, nuns, students, papers and mission registers*, CRS 25 (London: CRS, 1925)
English Convents	Caroline Bowden (gen. ed.), *English Convents in Exile 1600–1800*, 6 vols (London: Pickering and Chatto, 2012–13)
Foley	H. Foley (ed.), *Records of the English Province of the Society of Jesus*, 8 vols (London: Burns and Oates, 1875–83)
Franciscana	R. Trappes-Lomax (ed.), *Franciscana: The English Franciscan Nuns, 1619–1821 and the Friars Minor of the Same Province, 1618–1761*, CRS 24 (London: CRS, 1922)
Hamilton, *Chronicle*	A. Hamilton (ed.), *The Chronicle of the English Augustinian Canonesses Regular of the Lateran: At St. Monica's in Louvain (Now at St. Augustine's Priory, Newton Abbot, Devon) 1548 to 1644*, 2 vols (Edinburgh: Sands & Co., 1904–06)
Harris	P. R. Harris (ed.), *Douai College Documents 1639–1794*, CRS 63 (London: CRS, 1972)

Holt	G. Holt (ed.), *The English Jesuits, 1650–1829: A Biographical Dictionary*, CRS 70 (London: CRS, 1984)
McCoog	T. M. McCoog, *English and Welsh Jesuits, 1555–1650*, 2 vols, CRS 74–5 (London: CRS, 1994–95)
Mawhood Diary	E. E. Reynolds (ed.), *The Mawhood Diary*, CRS 50 (London: CRS, 1956)
Monasticon belge	U. Berlière *et al.* (eds), *Monasticon belge*, 7 vols (Maredsous: Abbaye de Maredsous, 1890–1993)
ODNB	*Oxford Dictionary of National Biography*, online edition, http://www.oxforddnb.com
OED	*Oxford English Dictionary*
OFM	Order of Friars Minor (Franciscan friars)
OP	Order of Preachers (Dominican friars)
OSA	Order of St Augustine (Augustinians)
OSB	Order of St Benedict (Benedictines)
SJ	Society of Jesus (Jesuits)
Stirnet	http://www.stirnet.com
TNA	The National Archives, Kew
Wood	Martin Wood, *Family and Descendants of St Thomas More* (Leominster: Gracewing, 2008)
WWTN	'Who Were the Nuns?' database, https://wwtn.history.qmul.ac.uk

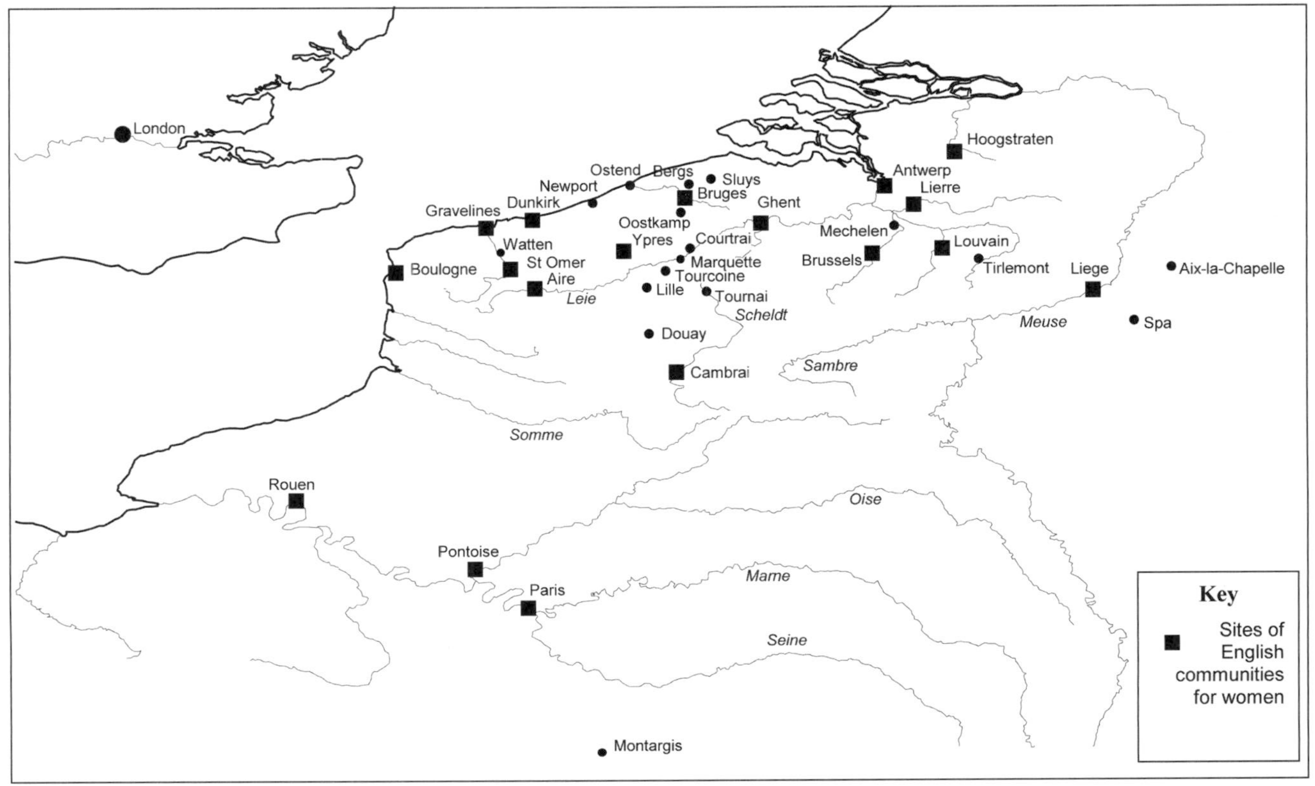

Map 1: Sketch map of Southern Netherlands showing places mentioned in the Chronicles (© Brian Farrimond, created by him for this book)

Map 2: Plan of Bruges identifying communities or places appearing in the Chronicles (© Brian Farrimond, created by him for this book)

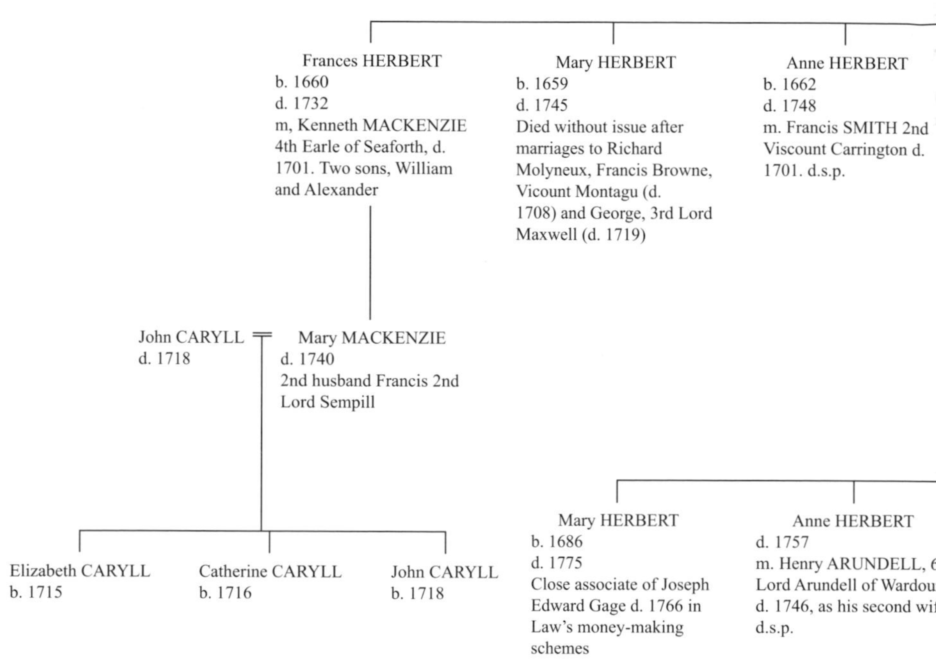

Simplified section of Herbert family tree identifying members of the family appearing in the Chronicles (prepared by Caroline Bowden and Katharine Keats-Rohan)

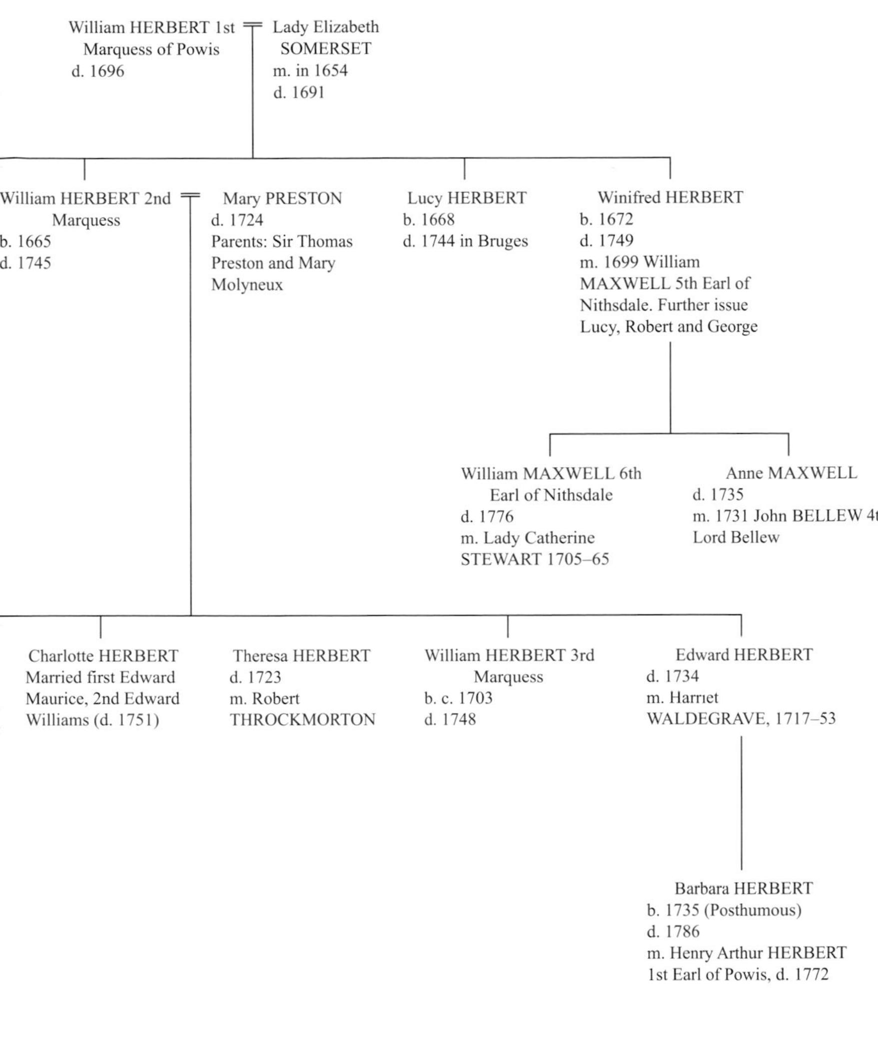
William HERBERT 1st Marquess of Powis d. 1696
Lady Elizabeth SOMERSET m. in 1654 d. 1691
William HERBERT 2nd Marquess b. 1665 d. 1745
Mary PRESTON d. 1724 Parents: Sir Thomas Preston and Mary Molyneux
Lucy HERBERT b. 1668 d. 1744 in Bruges
Winifred HERBERT b. 1672 d. 1749 m. 1699 William MAXWELL 5th Earl of Nithsdale. Further issue Lucy, Robert and George
William MAXWELL 6th Earl of Nithsdale d. 1776 m. Lady Catherine STEWART 1705–65
Anne MAXWELL d. 1735 m. 1731 John BELLEW 4th Lord Bellew
Charlotte HERBERT Married first Edward Maurice, 2nd Edward Williams (d. 1751)
Theresa HERBERT d. 1723 m. Robert THROCKMORTON
William HERBERT 3rd Marquess b. c. 1703 d. 1748
Edward HERBERT d. 1734 m. Harriet WALDEGRAVE, 1717–53
Barbara HERBERT b. 1735 (Posthumous) d. 1786 m. Henry Arthur HERBERT 1st Earl of Powis, d. 1772

INTRODUCTION

These Chronicles were created at the Convent of Nazareth, Bruges (hereafter called Nazareth) by the Augustinian Canonesses. The convent occupies the site of the original foundation and is still familiarly known as the English Convent. There are three separate volumes: the first covers the century from the house's foundation in 1629; the second runs from 1729 to the end of 1793; and the third, from 1794 to 1818. This present edition comprises the first two volumes.[1]

The context

Nazareth was founded in 1629 as a daughter house from St Monica's, Louvain, itself established in 1609 from the Flemish Augustinian convent St Ursula's, also at Louvain.[2] Among the communities for women, only the Bridgettines and the Dominicans from Dartford had survived Henry VIII's dissolution to be revived under Mary Tudor. However, after Elizabeth's accession, when both groups again left the country, the Dominicans failed to recruit in exile, leaving the Bridgettines as the only English community. Two English women joined the Flemish Augustinian convent at Louvain before 1558 but, following the election of Margaret Clement as prioress in 1570, the reputation of the convent spread in English circles.[3] It took some time but, after 1593, 26 English candidates professed before the opening of the new house of St Monica's.[4] The foundation of the first separate English convent in 1598 in Brussels added impetus to the creation of English communities and in 1609 a discrete English Augustinian foundation was opened in Louvain which immediately attracted recruits. By 1629 St Monica's decided to open a daughter house to absorb potential members and avoid overcrowding. The Bruges Chronicles start with an abbreviated version of the foundation of the new community in 1629. The extract below is taken from the chronicle of St Monica's, which considerably expands the account we have in the Bruges manuscript.

---

1 It is hoped that the third volume will be published at a later date.

2 The English nuns always referred to Louvain not Leuven. That practice has been adopted here.

3 Margaret Clement (1557–1612), Prioress of St Ursula's 1570–1605. In the case of the nuns, bracketed dates refer to year of profession and year of death.

4 The figures are drawn from convent lists in the Who Were the Nuns? (WWTN) database. The Dominican community from Dartford was too small to survive the challenges of exile in the Elizabethan period. Only two English women were professed at St Ursula's after 1599, when the Benedictine convent opened in Brussels.

> … we were finding our monastery so burthened with persons that we had not convenient room to receive many more, [so] agreed in our Counsel and yearly consultation to seek for to amplify our Order by setting up of another monastery, whereby sending there ten nuns we should make room here to receive more persons. And hearing that the English Jesuits were willing to sell the house at Bruges, which my Lady Lovel[5] had left them, we agreed to buy the same for to make our cloister there, with the money of some rents of ours that were then laid up at Gaunt at the Mount of Piety,[6] if the house were fit for our purpose. Whereupon our Reverend Father Barnes,[7] who was very desirous to have us increase to more convents, went thither to see it and liked it well, by reason that though it were but little, yet it was commodious to make a cloister … and bought it, giving the same price which my Lady Lovel had given when she bought it. After that we consulted here to send ten nuns, giving them £10 a head every year, which amounted to £100 yearly. But when we came to get the town's goodwill of Bruges, and licence of the bishop there, it was thought too little in respect of the dear time, so that the town would not consent (to receive them) unless we allowed every one £15 apiece yearly, fearing lest otherwise they might become burthensome unto their town, which we were forced to yield unto or else they could not be admitted, although we had procured the Infanta's[8] licence (of happy memory) who then lived.[9]

We have in this paragraph some noteworthy elements also found in other English foundations of daughter houses in Flanders in this period: a successful mother house needing to make space for new recruits; English benefactors facilitating the foundation process – in this case granting advantageous terms for acquiring suitable premises; and concerns expressed locally about the provision of sufficient funds to prevent the new convent from being a burden on the local community. Bruges was one of several English foundations to attract the support of the ruler of the Spanish Netherlands, the Infanta Isabella, who died in 1633; here, as for other convents, her influence would serve to attract other supporters within Flanders.[10]

---

5 Lady Mary Lovell (c. 1564–1628). See *ODNB*.

6 Gaunt: here Ghent. Monts de Piété were approved Catholic low-interest finance houses and served for investing convent income.

7 Fr Stephen Barnes (d. 1653), Confessor at St Monica's, acted as Confessor at Bruges 1629–31.

8 Infanta Isabella Clara Eugenia (1566–1633), ruler of the Spanish Netherlands with her husband, Albert (d. 1621). She was an active sponsor of religious communities, adopting the habit of the Third Order Franciscans on the death of her husband. A licence formed part of the documentation needed to open a convent. The legality of the institution was essential to ensure its standing and to be able to attract candidates for profession and benefactions.

9 A. Hamilton (ed.), *The Chronicle of the English Augustinian Canonesses Regular of The Lateran, at St Monica's in Louvain*, 2 vols (Edinburgh: Sands and Co., 1904–06), vol. 2, pp. 68–9.

10 Isabella and her court were linked to the Benedictine foundation at Brussels in 1598–99, as well as to local houses.

Several of these themes are developed later in the Chronicles. The initial financial arrangements for Bruges failed to provide a sufficiently secure basis for the new house and the early years proved challenging for the new community. They lacked the dowries of the ten founder members from Louvain needed to support the new venture, although they attracted eight professions of their own in the first ten years, which brought significant additional funding.

Other financial accounts from English convents indicate that the substantial dowries of the choir nuns (often more than £300) provided the capital underpinning the convent communities. Without the income from the capital sums invested, carrying out building works and meeting other costs was bound to be difficult. Victoria Van Hyning has commented on the importance of the arrival of Augustina Bedingfield in 1639 from Louvain with accounting experience.[11] Elected prioress in 1640, Bedingfield was able to transform financial management at Bruges, implementing practices that had worked well at Louvain and attracting significant benefactions.[12] She contributed both to the reordering of systems and to the religious life of the convent, for instance by translating the newly agreed statutes from Latin into English, making them more easily read and absorbed by the community. After a second lean decade for entrants, the 1650s saw 21 professions and the convent's future was secured.

The religious life of Canonesses differs from contemplative orders such as the Benedictines in that it combines features of active religious practices with contemplative ones. The contemplative elements of the day at Nazareth were very similar to those followed in Benedictine convents, focussing on prayer, reading and meditation, practised both individually and communally. Active features of the Canonesses' daily life comprised undertakings with a religious purpose which served to bring outsiders within the orbit of the community. For instance, at Bruges the sisters established a school which attracted pupils from the local community as well as the daughters of English Catholics. They also took in paying adult boarders for much of the period of these Chronicles.

These activities counted in the Canonesses' favour when Joseph II closed contemplative religious houses in the Habsburg Low Countries in 1782, with immediate effect on several neighbouring religious houses in Bruges.[13] On the other hand, having lay people within convent property

---

11 V. Van Hyning, 'Cloistered Voices: English Nuns in Exile, 1550–1800', unpublished PhD thesis, University of Sheffield, 2014, pp. 52, 81–2. I am indebted to Dr Van Hyning for providing me with a copy of her thesis and for sharing her expertise on the Augustinian collections.

12 Helen Bedingfield, in religion Augustina (1622 Louvain–1661 Bruges), Prioress of Nazareth 1640–61.

13 For instance, the convent of Bethania (or Bethany) was expecting suppression in the summer of 1783: see Chronicle, vol. 2, **[pp. 268, 280]**. The English Carthusians at Nieuport

seems at times to have caused concerns about intrusion. The Chronicles reveal considerable movement in and out of the community by the extended family of Prioress Lucy Herbert. Following the Revolution of 1688 and associated Jacobite activities attempting to restore the Stuarts to the English throne, four sisters of Prioress Herbert were frequent visitors to Bruges, often with other members of their families.[14] On the death of Lucy Herbert in 1744 the new prioress, Mary Darell, decided to end the practice because she considered that it disturbed community life, and by 1746 Nazareth was entirely without boarders.[15] Thereafter, unless circumstances were exceptional, lay names appearing in the Chronicle lists of pensioners or boarders appear to be those of young girls taken in to attend school or as convictresses who might join the community and were trying out religious life.[16] Names of adult lodgers only appear again during the uncertainty created by the policies of Joseph II from 1783 onwards and are never included in the lists of 'pensioners' at the end of each year in the Chronicles. These lodgers were taken into the convent by the sisters out of charity.[17] It is clear from the Chronicles that the convent leaders were conscious that a balance needed to be struck between the sanctity of the enclosure and looking after their neighbours. All of these activities meant that each year, regardless of the change of policy towards boarders, a surprising number of individuals are mentioned in the Chronicles as passing through the community or becoming benefactors.

The text situates the convent within its local urban context, revealing largely positive relationships with a range of local ecclesiastical and secular dignitaries, tradesmen and professionals over the period covered by the Chronicles. At the same time, it provides evidence of the significance of the convent to wider English Catholic communities on the Continent, in England and even in the West Indies. For instance, it reveals how links between the convent and the expatriate Stuarts changed over time, strengthening when Lucy Herbert became prioress in 1709. Her parents' connections with the Jacobite court in exile at St Germain-en-Laye and her support for her sisters, one of whom was directly implicated in events linked to the 1715 Jacobite rebellion, drew the convent closer to those who attempted to restore the Stuart dynasty.

---

were also suppressed: see Chronicle, vol. 2, **[p. 269]**. The Jesuits had already been suppressed in 1773: Chronicle, vol. 2, **[p. 269]**.

14 For Prioress Herbert and her family in the Chronicles, see particularly Chronicle, vol. 1, **[p. 272]**–vol. 2, **[pp. 104–8]** and the Herbert family tree printed in this volume.

15 See Chronicle, vol. 2, **[pp. 95–6]**. Mary Darell, in religion Mary Olivia (1734–66), Prioress 1744–66.

16 Pensioners were listed annually at the end of the Chronicle from 1783. Exceptionally, a child, Tommy Daly, aged two, and his nurse arrived in 1775; Chronicle, vol. 2, **[pp. 219–20]**.

17 See, for instance the sisters from Bethania, Bruges vol. 2, **[pp. 268–9, 280–1, 326]** and three members of the English Carthusian Priory at Newport, **[pp. 269, 272, 299–300]**.

Prioress Herbert's aristocratic connections, combined with her personal authority and leadership both within the convent and the wider community, significantly raised the profile of the English Convent in the early years of the eighteenth century and brought well-connected visitors, boarders and candidates for profession.[18] However, the Chronicles also reveal that she faced opposition in 1735 to her proposals to build the new church and other works, when the Canonesses feared that the expense would cause them to run into debt and that their numbers were too small to warrant such expenditure.[19] In the end the church created a significant space for worship, drawing visitors and potential benefactors to participate in the liturgy. Lucy Herbert also contributed to religious practice in the convent through her writing and editing of devotional texts in English that became widely popular and are frequently found in monastic and lay libraries of the period.

The Bruges Chronicles give us more insights into the experience of life in the convent than into spiritual and devotional practices, about which we tend to glean evidence only indirectly, for example from the obituaries quoted in the text, comments on celebrations and other observations made in passing. Reports of Chapter meetings provide only short references to discussions; however, these are often revealing about candidates applying to join and attitudes towards them. For instance: how will they fit into the community? Do they really demonstrate a vocation for the religious life? Should they be allowed to try again? Can they be rejected kindly?[20] The Chronicles also demonstrate the connectivity of the Canonesses, particularly within the exile community and its networks. There were occasions when candidates were passed on to different orders, including the English Poor Clares at Gravelines and the Carmelites at Lierre, having shown they were unhappy about professing at Bruges; by the same token, there were occasions when candidates transferred to Nazareth from other houses.

We learn indirectly about illness and medical treatments in the period, music and musicians, and dealing with workmen. Several chroniclers provide evidence of close observation of human foibles and their impact on a closed community, often drawn from discussion of candidates in Chapter meetings. As in other convents, there are several examples of prioresses dealing with challenging relationships with confessors. Such difficulties could be particularly damaging to the reputation of the convent and, as a result, swiftly affect their ability to attract candidates for profession

---

18 For the interconnectedness of the prioress and her family with Jacobite events outside the convent, see H. Tayler, *Lady Nithsdale and her Family* (London, Lindsay Drummond, 1939); also *ODNB* entries for the sisters.

19 See Chronicle, vol. 2, **[pp. 30–1]**.

20 See, for instance, Chronicle, vol. 1, **[pp. 9, 41, 52, 71–2, 101, 106, 131, 149, 199, 285–6, 297–8]**.

or schoolgirls when rumours travelled through the English Catholic communities. Volume II of the Chronicles reports how the last years of Prioress Darrell were clouded by difficulties focussed on the confessor Fr Hinde, who was considered by some in the convent to be too severe and unsuitable to direct women religious.[21] However, since he had supporters in the house, the Bishop of Bruges, the Visitor, would not remove him.

It was left to the new prioress, Mother Augustina More, to resolve the situation and it was finally agreed tactfully that Fr Hinde would withdraw, making it seem as if it were his own choice.[22] The Chronicles state that the account of handling these problems was written by an independent person three years after the affair was finally concluded in order to avoid bias in reporting. It was a difficult situation that lost the Canonesses at least one recruit and impacted on the community, Fr Hinde having a loyal following among the choir nuns.

A rather different problem was resolved quietly in 1782 when the bishop required the confessor Fr Matthew Burgess to attend 'a Spiritual Exercise and a General Confession' at the seminary before being sent back to England, on account of his fondness for alcohol and lack of discretion.[23]

Authorship of the Bruges Chronicles

Given that the exilic English convents were new foundations, they had to develop their own particular 'house styles' of writing. All surviving chronicles (except one) from the English convents are anonymous, with contributors identifiable only from the hands of the scribes and internal evidence.[24] However, given the amount of copying and collaborative

---

21 Fr Francis Hinde arrived at the Convent in 1764 and left in May 1767; Chronicle, vol. 2, **[pp. 182, 190]**.

22 Elizabeth More, in religion Mary Augustina (1753–1807), Prioress 1766–1807.

23 Fr Matthew Burgess (1752–86). According to Anstruther 4, pp. 50–1, he considered himself 'ill-used' by Prioress More. See also Chronicle, vol. 2, [**pp. 265–6**].

24 The only chronicle with an acknowledged author was Abbess Anne Neville, 'English Benedictine Nuns in Flanders: Annals of their Five Communities, 1598–1687', online version at wwtn.history.qmul.ac.uk/publications-static/pdfs/Annalsof5communitiesJan09.pdf, accessed 17 November 2015. Additional full or partial convent chronicles known from the exile period exist as follows: Augustinians, Louvain, partially published in Hamilton *Chronicle of the English Augustinian Canonesses Regular of The Lateran*, complete in manuscript, MS Douai, Box W.M.L.C., MS C2 'Louvain Chronicle' (1535–1836); Paris Augustinians, Paris Diurnal, MS partly published in James E. Kelly (ed.), *English Convents in Exile 1600–1800. Vol. 5: Convent Management* (London: Pickering and Chatto, 2012–13); Carmelites, Hoogstraten, Chronicles 1670–1870, microfilm copy in Maryland State Archives, Annapolis, Hoogstraet Collection of the Carmelite Sisters of Baltimore, MSA SC 5366–6–1, speccol.mdarchives.state.md.us/pages/speccol/results.aspx?keyword=Hoogstraet, accessed 17 November 2015; Carmelites, Antwerp, published in Katrien Daemen-de Gelder (ed.), *English Convents in Exile 1600–1800. Vol. 4: Life Writing 2* (London: Pickering and Chatto 2012–13); Bridgettines, Lisbon, MS in Exeter University Library, Special Collections, Syon MS 262/add.1/B158: Poor Clares, Gravelines, partly published in Nicky Hallett, *English*

projects undertaken in the convents it cannot be assumed that the scribe was necessarily the author of the text. Some convent authors derive their material from a range of sources such as oral testimony and chapter books, and comment on them in their texts. The Bruges Chronicles, however, contain few comments on sources, although the writing shows that a range of manuscripts provided material, including chapter books, obituary notices and benefactors' books. The Chronicles appear to have been drawn up from records which gave outlines of events as they occurred, with additional sources providing the basis of interpretive material for the author to write up some time later.

There appears to be little specific guidance in the Bruges Constitutions on how chronicles or annals should be prepared and what should be included. In essence they stipulated that the prioress should ensure that the Annals of the monastery were kept up to date, and any interesting fact in the life of the community recorded, including the chief benefactors and key business transactions of the house.[25] Victoria Van Hyning's PhD thesis examined writing practices at Bruges and Louvain, which enabled her to identify the chroniclers. Analysing the emphasis of the writing at Louvain, she argued that Sister Mary Copley, the first chronicler at Louvain, had focussed on the families and their individual histories, and interpreted them in order 'to make sense of the nuns' collective exiled present and their purpose as an English community'.[26] She contends that Copley's learning allowed her to create a distinctive personal style of writing while remaining anonymous. Such personal traits are visible throughout both the Louvain and the Bruges Chronicles, although later writers followed their own paths, with changes of emphasis in the selection of material detectable over time.

In spite of the direct connection between St Monica's and Bruges, record-keeping practices did not transfer exactly to the daughter house and the styles diverge. For instance, there is less weight on individual family history in the Bruges Chronicles, although particular families who made significant contributions to the convents either through providing several daughters as candidates or through significant benefactions

---

Convents in Exile 1600–1800. Vol. 3: Life Writing 1 (London: Pickering and Chatto 2012–13); Poor Clares, Rouen, Chronicle published in Caroline Bowden (ed.), *English Convents in Exile 1600–1800, Vol. 1: History Writing* (London: Pickering and Chatto 2012–13); Paris Conceptionists, published in J. Gillow and R. Trappes-Lomax (eds), *The Diary of the Blue Nuns, or Order of the Immaculate Conception, at Paris, 1658–1810*, CRS 8 (London: Catholic Record Society, 1910); Benedictines, Ghent, published as *Annals of the English Benedictines of Ghent* (East Bergholt: privately printed, 1898); Paris Benedictines, partly printed as 'A Sketch History', reprinted from *The Ampleforth Journal* 11–13 (1906–8), copy at St Benedict's Priory, Colwich.

25 Van Hyning, 'Cloistered Voices', p. 83.

26 *Ibid.*, p. 40. Mary Copley (1612–69) was Sub-Prioress from 1638.

do receive some prominence.[27] There are personal touches too: some Bruges chroniclers wrote with greater facility than others when describing major events in the community such as jubilees and celebrations. Others demonstrate a greater willingness to record unfortunate incidents which jarred the equilibrium of a well-managed house. Some elements of the Bruges style remain constant throughout the first two volumes. As at Louvain, the Chronicles contain details of candidates joining, as well as short biographies of members when they died (which in other orders appear in separate obituary or membership books), together with references to confessors and spiritual directors. Throughout, the Chronicles move between historical and biographical writing and between the collective and the individual. The contents are influenced by the personalities, interests, health and skills of the authors, as well as by external events which affected the cloister.

The texts

Volume I (1629–1729) was copied c. 1738 from earlier documents which have not survived by Sub-Prioress Anne Weston.[28] This makes it impossible to deduce authorship from the original hands. The date division indicates that the Chronicle was designed to be a memorial to the first hundred years of the community. Unfortunately Sister Anne used ink that was too rich in iron, resulting in many pages becoming illegible where the ink has oxidised and bled through the pages.[29] In 1997 Sister Agnes Joseph Coppieters prepared a typescript of the volume which has been used as the base text of this present edition, in order to avoid further damage to the original. Transcription issues arising are discussed in the Editorial Preface.

Anne Weston claimed that the original volume was written 'by each successive prioress from 1629 to 1729'. Van Hyning disagrees with Sister Anne, however, arguing from internal evidence. She omits the first two prioresses, Stamford and Pole, positing the origin of the Chronicles with the arrival of the well-educated Augustina Bedingfield from Louvain in 1639.[30] Certainly the first decade of the Chronicles reads more like a retrospective summary than regular contemporary updates and reflections. Bedingfield was skilled at ordering the finances of the convent, which had not been flourishing before she arrived. Financial stability was heavily dependent on a steady flow of candidates bringing dowries.

---

27 Except during the period when Lucy Herbert's sisters paid frequent visits to the convent.

28 See Van Hyning, 'Cloistered Voices', p. 77. Anne Weston (1699–1738) Sub-Prioress 1737–38. Weston also wrote a 600-page volume of collected sermons of Louis Sabran SJ and a copy of the Life of Mother Margaret Clement.

29 See Van Hyning, 'Cloistered Voices', p. 77, n. 2.

30 *Ibid.*, pp. 78–90.

After an initial burst of eight professions up to 1635, numbers had fallen dramatically with only three in the next 15 years, and only recovered to a steady flow from 1651.[31]

Van Hyning argues that 1647 was the first year in which we can be certain that the Chronicles were being written contemporaneously, with Grace Constable the most compelling candidate as author.[32] The style varies considerably over time, suggesting that there were no regular community writing rules being followed at Bruges. Some years comprise little more than lists of events and others include reflections on individuals and events in some detail. For instance, the controversial termination of Fr Francis Hinde's status as confessor in 1766 occupies some 16 pages.[33] Some indication of discussion at Chapter meetings can be deduced from brief references to candidates for profession being sent away rather than accepted for the community or explanations of the character of some nuns who clearly proved difficult to live with.[34]

For two decades between 1670 and 1690 the Chronicles focus more narrowly on brief membership details, providing less commentary on events within the convent or dealings with the outside world. These years coincide with Prioress Mary Bedingfield's time in office (prioress 1661–93).[35] Her long obituary[36] makes no reference to her writing, and the description of lengthy periods of serious illness (alongside her determination to continue with fulfilling her obligations to religious observance) would seem to preclude time for maintaining chronicle writing. From the 1690s extended obituary notices provide more than the life of the newly deceased and form the focus for the annual chronicle for the community. Was the chronicler here consciously building primarily on obituaries written by another member of the community in order to enhance her records?

Volume II still exists in the original manuscript version in three different scribal hands. From the hands Van Hyning identifies Prioress Herbert as author from 1729 until 1742, two years before she died, after which Prioress Darrell takes over to 1766, with Prioress More assuming

---

31 See WWTN, Bruges, 'Profession List', https://wwtn.history.qmul.ac.uk/lists-static/AugustiniansBruges.pdf, accessed 5 January 2016.

32 See Van Hyning, 'Cloistered Voices', p. 89. Grace Constable (1625–73), Sub-Prioress from 1655.

33 Chronicle, vol. 2, pp. **[171–87]**.

34 See, for instance, the case of Mary Bruning (Chronicle, vol. 1, **[p. 72]**) and a Flemish candidate for lay sister, Ann Stevendale, who became Sister Austin before leaving in 1768 (Chronicle, vol. 2, **[p. 195]**).

35 Mary Bedingfield (1652–93), Prioress 1661–93.

36 Chronicle, vol. 1, **[pp. 163–9]**.

authorship shortly before Darrell's death and continuing into Volume III, ending her stint in 1807.[37]

It seems likely that the Chronicles were written for reading within the community, perhaps in the Refectory, alongside other texts generated within the community, as well as printed great lives and other spiritual texts. The Chronicles might also have served to communicate community news indirectly to the outside world. Although none of the Augustinian chronicles was published before the twentieth century, news from the convent leached out through the cloister walls in a variety of ways. A number of historians have pointed out the porosity of enclosure walls in the period. Confessors and chaplains moved on to other posts, taking community news to their own colleagues and contacts. Letters to members of families might serve to spread good news as well as bad. Convent leaders were all too aware of the importance of reputation and its impact on future candidates.[38] The Chronicles from Bruges were unusually frank in their revelation of personal problems among the community: for instance, the attempted suicide of Sister Mary Bernard Forth in 1764, and the dramatic events surrounding the history of Sister Perpetua Errington. Sister Perpetua eloped in 1696, 15 years after her profession, using a skeleton key, only returning to the convent 11 years later to beg forgiveness. She received the welcome of a returning prodigal.[39] Her long obituary in 1739 incorporates evidence of her penitence and her acceptance back into the community.

The latter part of Volume II elucidates the political context of life in the exiled convents. By the end of the eighteenth century, prioresses had to tread carefully in response to the impact of policies enacted by Joseph II as ruler of what had, in 1714, become the Austrian Netherlands.[40] Enclosed contemplative houses of men and women were closed first, followed by those regarded as having insufficient commitment to the neighbouring communities or who challenged the state.[41] The activities of the nuns at Nazareth, taking in local girls for education in the school and women as lodgers, kept them in a favourable position even as Joseph II tightened the rules. The nuns were generous in their hospitality, offering shelter to men and women left homeless when other institutions had closed.[42]

37 Lucy Herbert (1693–1744), Prioress 1709–44; Mary Darell, in religion Mary Olivia, Prioress 1744–66; Elizabeth More, in religion Mary Augustina, Prioress 1766–1807. See Van Hyning, 'Cloistered Voices', p. 78. Darrell takes over on vol. 2, **[p. 81]**.

38 See for example *English Convents,* vol. 5, Convent Management, ed. J. E. Kelly, 'Governance, Leadership and Authority'; C. Bowden, 'Introduction' (pp. 223–8) and 'Letters from Lucy Herbert' (pp. 331–8).

39 For Sister Mary Bernard, see Chronicle, vol. 2, **[p. 161]**. For Sister Perpetua, see Chronicle vol. 1, **[pp. 183–92]**, **[pp. 244–53]**; vol. 2, **[pp. 67–9]**.

40 By the Treaty of Rastatt, 7 March 1714.

41 Rumours began in 1781: see Chronicle, vol. 2, **[pp. 257–8]**.

42 For example, Bethania and the Grey Sisters for women, the English Carthusians for men.

Officials inspected the school in September 1783 and declared themselves satisfied with standards.[43] The prioress was careful to comply with new regulations such as the closure of separate burial places within the convents as part of Joseph II's prohibition on burials in towns.

Concern about the possible impact of the French Revolution and revolutionary wars, added to seven years of anxiety about possible suppression, and combined with lack of security, finally turned the community's eyes towards England.[44] Prioress Mary Augustina More, as recorded in the Chronicles, revealed a strong political sense. She wrote a carefully worded appeal to the Secretary of the Clergy (a body established as part of the religious reforms in the Southern Netherlands to secure state control over the Church), positioning her convent as part of the expatriate English community, drawing members and financial support from outside the local community and therefore not subject to the same laws as local communities. Only twice since their foundation in 1629 had the Canonesses contributed to a gift to the state, and then out of good will. A reading of convent documents, including the Chronicles, would show how far this theoretical position was from reality; yet the foundation documents had set out the basis of the claim for separate treatment. Nothing more was heard in response. The nuns at Nazareth continued to do what they could to support displaced religious, while the external situation grew steadily more threatening. When troops were stationed at the end of the garden, they began to hide precious objects and to plan the detail of their removal to England. As the situation deteriorated further, the sisters took practical steps for packing, sending off the sick and securing the most precious writings, church stuff, some plate and best habits.[45] At the end of Volume II, the community was still in their Bruges home, although clearly it would not be for long.

---

43 Chronicle, vol. 2, **[p. 271]**.

44 Chronicle, vol. 2, **[p. 316]**. For an account of the community's period in England, see F. Young, 'Mother Mary More and the Exile of the English Augustinian Canonesses of Bruges in England, 1794–1802', *Recusant History* 27 (2004), pp. 86–102.

45 Volume III does not explain exactly how the first two volumes of the Chronicles survived the upheavals. While plate was sent away from Nazareth for safe-keeping, some books, manuscripts and other precious objects were secreted under the floorboards. Sister Olivia Darrell (1754–1802) remained behind in Bruges to do what she could to secure the convent property for the community in the long term.

Fig. 1: Watercolour of the convent in 1629. (Photograph by the editor, reproduced by kind permission of the Community of Nazareth, Bruges.)

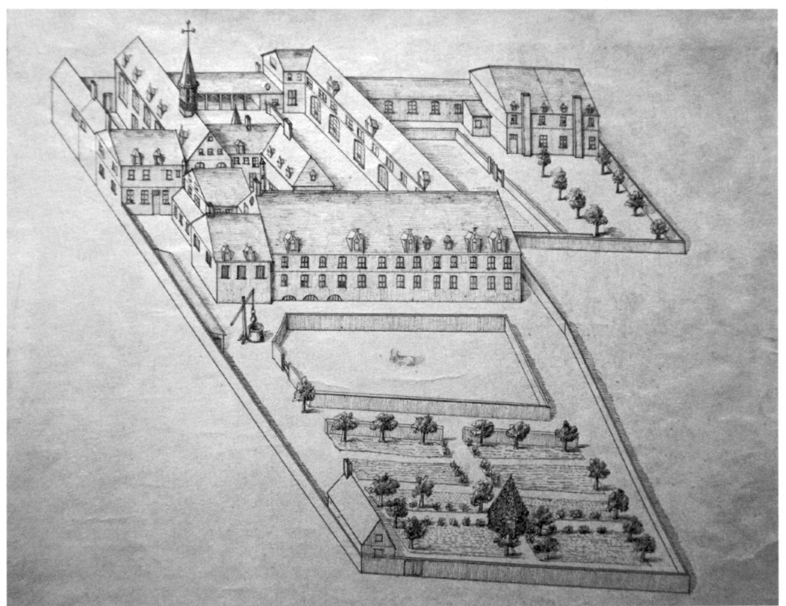

Fig. 2: Modern drawing of the convent as it was in 1691 by an unknown artist, made from Sister Mary Sykes' drawings. (Photograph by the community, reproduced by kind permission of the Community of Nazareth, Bruges.)

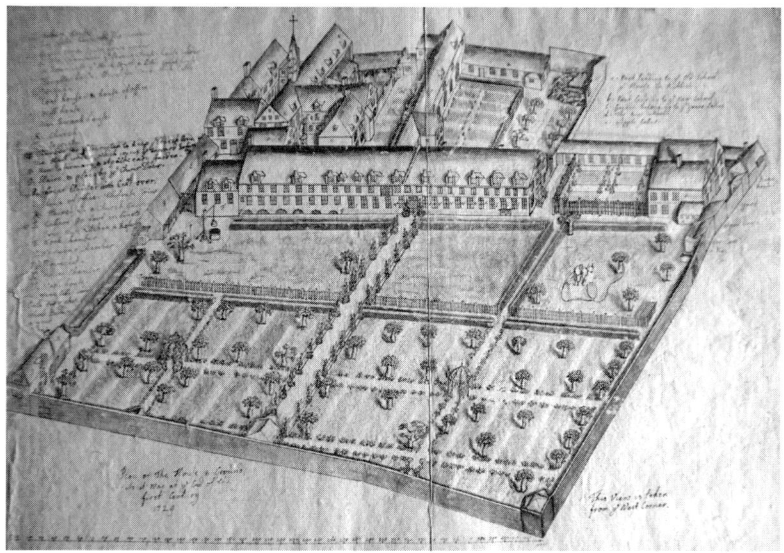

Fig. 3: Drawing by Sister Mary Sykes of Nazareth in its centenary year, 1729. (Photograph by the editor, reproduced by kind permission of the Community of Nazareth, Bruges.)

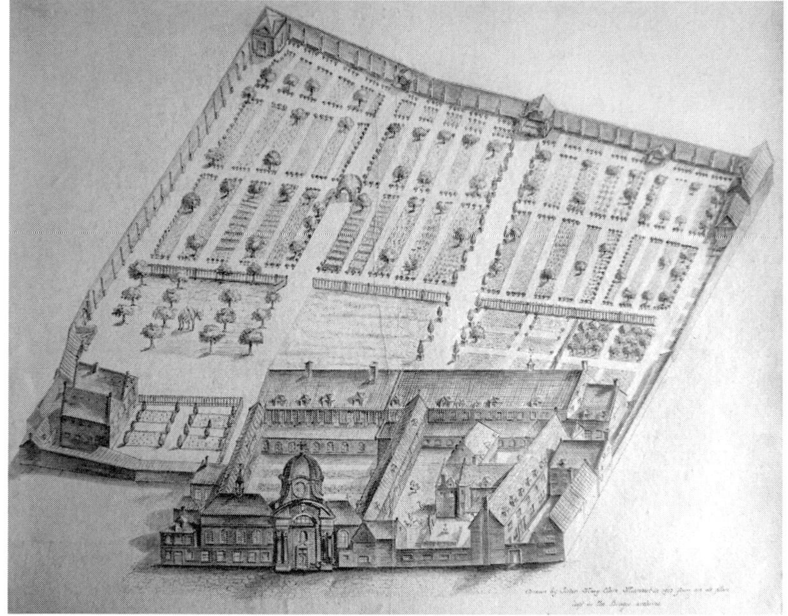

Fig. 4: Modern drawing of the convent, showing the new church completed in 1739, following the building projects of Prioress Lucy Herbert. (Photograph by the community, reproduced by kind permission of the Community of Nazareth, Bruges.)

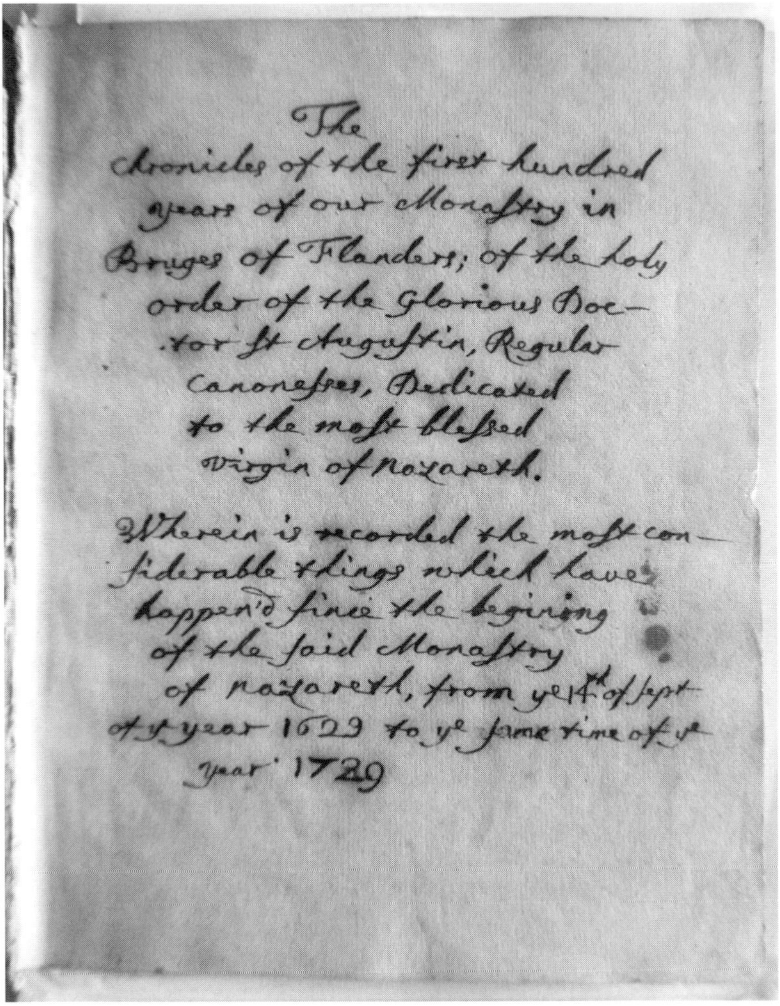

The
chronicles of the first hundred
years of our Monastry in
Bruges of Flanders; of the holy
order of the Glorious Doctor St Augustin, Regular
Canonesses, Dedicated
to the most blessed
Virgin of Nazareth.

Wherein is recorded the most considerable things which have
happen'd since the begining
of the said Monastry
of Nazareth, from ye 14th of Sept
of ye year 1629 to ye same time of ye
year 1729

Fig. 5: Opening of the manuscript copy of Volume I of the Chronicles. (Photograph by the community, reproduced by kind permission of the Community of Nazareth, Bruges.)

The Year
1742 +

in ye 84 of her age & 18 since her holy profession. her disease was
judg'd so infectious yt by orders of doctor & surgion she was to be
bury'd in ye earth & yt as soon as possible for she turn'd black before
was cold, ye next morning she was accordingly bury'd in ye earth in
time of our lauds in our new Church yeard under ye organ left windows.
on ye 15 her mass & all as usuall was perform'd.

Requiescant in Pace.

on ye 11 of Dec: Sister Ann Gladin was cloathed having been two
years Schollar ye reason was because ye number of lay Sisters was more
than we ought to have & ye community was resolved not to cloath any
more till it should please God to take one to himself, but many of our
Religious having compassion of her, beg'd she might be cloathed, she
having comported her self so as to give content to ye community.
she has 60 pound wch mrs Sykes left at her Death, for portion, &
judged not to have sufficient strength, to be either cook or baker
she was dispenced from these two offices not doubting but in other
things she may be very serviceable.
on ye 14 of Dec: mrs Pikering received ye Schoolars kerchief & name
of Cicily.
ye 15 mrs Eliz: Tichbourn & her Brother went for England.

1742

on ye 1st of feb: it pleased God to call to himself our Dear Sister Monica
Strafford a true good Religious woman, & very Serviceable in many imployments, she did not come young to Religion, yet shew'd a great value for ye smallest observances, & was most singularly exemplar in
her zeal for ye common work, & constancy to ye work Chamber, nor
was she less faithfull to ye choir Duties as allso of good Service to ye
she was heartily friendly & of a good nature, but somewhat hott but
it soon past, wch notwithstanding was to her an occation of humility
and to others of patience her love to ye community appeared [illegible]
-ble

Fig. 6: A page from Volume II of the Chronicles, showing the change of hand in 1742, when Prioress Mary Darell took over from Prioress Lucy Herbert. (Photograph by Victoria Van Hyning, reproduced by kind permission of the Community of Nazareth, Bruges.)

VOLUME I: 1629–1729

[Title page]

THE CHRONICLES OF THE FIRST HUNDRED YEARS OF OUR MONASTRY IN BRUGES OF FLANDERS; OF THE HOLY ORDER OF THE GLORIOUS DOCTOR ST. AUGUSTIN, REGULAR CANONESSES DEDICATED TO THE MOST BLESSED VIRGIN OF NAZARETH

VOLUME I

Wherein is recorded the most considerable things which have happened since the begining of the said Monastry of Nazareth, from 14th September of the year 1629 to the same time of the year 1729.

[p. 1]

THE CHRONICLES OF OUR MONASTERY OF REGULAR CANONESSES IN BRIDGES DEDICATED TO THE MOST BLESSED VIRGIN OF NAZARETH FROM ITS FIRST FOUNDATION TO ALMOST THE YEAR 1730

The year 1629

In this year of our Lord, the very Reverende Mother Mary Wyseman, first Prioress of the cloister of Ste Monica at Lovain, a town in Brabant, of the same order of regular canonesses resolved with the consent of her convent, to erect a new monastery of that order; their own cloister being overcharged with religious.[1]

At the same time, the Lady Mary Lovel[2] had bought a house in Bridges with intention to found a monastry there of English women of

1 Jane Wiseman, in religion Mary (1595 St Ursula's Louvain–1633 St Monica's Louvain) LA303, Prioress St Monica's 1609–33.

2 Lady Mary Lovell (c. 1564–1628). Founder of English Carmel, Antwerp with Anne Worsley: see *ODNB*. Lady Mary Lovell was the widow of Sir Robert Lovell and daughter of John Roper, first Lord Teynham. She died in Bruges on 12 November 1628 and was buried in the Church of Our Lady.

the Cistercian order: but death prevented her designe; so by Testament she gave the aforesaid house to the colledge of the English Fathers of the Society of Jesus, in Gant.[1] Upon notice of this, the Reverende Mother Mary Wyseman sent Reverend Father Steven Barnes (their Confessarius)[2] to Bridges to see the House, and to **[p. 2]** treat with the Rector of the English Colledge at Gant, about buying the same. Father Barnes having given his approbation as to the fittness of the Place, with the consent of the most illustrious Lord Jacobus Bonus, Archbishop of Mechelin,[3] the House was bought of the Fathers at the charges of the cloister of Ste Monica. It cost three hundred and forty pounds sterlin and was besides charged with some little rents, as appear'd in the writings.[4]

This cloister was begun in the time of the Infanta Elisabetha Eugenia[5] and also with the consent of the Lord Dionysius Christophor sixth Bishop of Bridges;[6] and of the Magistrates of the same Town, but with this condition, not to be chargeable to the town. Therefore Ste Monica's convent was obliged to allow every Religious whom they should send out to this new foundation, a life rent of a hundred florins yearly: this condition being agreed upon, five Religious were sent forth in this year 1629,[7] upon St Protus and Hyacinthus day in the month of September within the octave of our Lady's Nativity.[8] The eldest of these five was Sister Ann Tremaine who had been Professed in the dutch cloister of Ste Ursula, of the same order in **[p. 3]** the Town of Lovain and came from these with the other English religious, to the foundation of the aforesaid Cloister of Ste Monica, where she had now lived several years.[9] The second was Sister Mary Best, who was professed in Ste Monica's Cloister.[10] The third Sister Mary Altham.[11] The fourth in profession Sister Frances Stamford, whom the Reverende Mother Mary Wyseman judged the fitest for Superior.[12]

1 English Jesuit College, Ghent, founded 1620.

2 Fr Stephen Barnes (d. 1653), Confessor at St Monica's, acted as Confessor at Bruges 1629–31; Anstruther 1, p. 24.

3 Jacob Boonen (d. 1655), Archbishop of Mechelen (Malines) 1621–55; *Biographie nationale*, vol. 2, pp. 699–706.

4 For an account of the foundation from Louvain, see Hamilton, *Chronicle*, vol. 2, pp. 68–9.

5 Infanta Isabella Clara Eugenia (1566–1633), ruler of the Spanish Netherlands with her husband, Albert (1559–1621), and supporter of the foundation of English convents in the region.

6 Denis Stoffels (d. 1629), Bishop of Bruges 1622–29; *Biographie nationale*, vol. 4, cols 103–5.

7 For the background to the selection of this group, see Hamilton, *Chronicle*, vol. 2, p. 79.

8 11 September Saints Protus and Hyacinth, brothers were martyred by the Romans c. 257. Our Lady's Nativity is celebrated on 8 September.

9 Anne Tremaine (1601 St Ursula's, Louvain–1637 Bruges) LA272. According to the Annals of St Monica, they were chosen for different reasons: see Hamilton, *Chronicle*, vol. 2, p. 79

10 Mary Best (1615 Louvain–1631 Bruges) LA031, Procuratrix 1629–31.

11 Mary Altham (1616 Louvain–1661 Bruges) LA004, Novice Mistress from 1629; Sub-Prioress 1635–55.

12 Frances Stamford (1619 Louvain–1635 Bruges) LA242, Prioress at Bruges 1629–35.

The fifth Sister Elisabeth Lovel.[1] The youngest of these had been about eight years professed, and only the three eldest had been of the convent Sisters. With them was also sent from Ste Monica's Cloister Sister Ursula Palmes,[2] a scholar for the order, daughter to Sir George Palmes.[3]

For their guide in this journey they had a religious man of our order, Reverend Father Peter Paris, a canon regular of Grinendal,[4] who was afterwards Prior of the same convent, for Reverend Father Barnes, the confessarius, was gone to Bridges before, to prepare for them. They arrived at Bridges the 14 of September, the feast of the exaltation of the holy cross, which is therefore held the feast of the foundation of our House. Now before these religious arrived to Bridges, the foremention most Reverend Lord Bishop was departed **[p. 4]** this life and, some two days after their arrival, in presence of the Vicariats[5] they made their election, and chose for Prioress Sister Frances Stamfort, who had been before recommended to them by the Prioress of Ste Monica's cloister.[6] Sister Ann Tremaine was afterwards chosen Sub-prioress and the office of Procuratrix was given to Sister Mary Best. The other two were employ'd in other offices: they dedicated the cloister to the blessed virgine, calling her house of Nazareth, because the foundation was begun within the octave of her Nativity.

Before the arrival of these five religious, the Reverend Father Barnes had begun a new building, with intention to make it a Father's house and a Schoole. He gave us then in Almnes twenty pound, and a hundred pound he lent us at rent, to help us with the building.

In the same year with consent of the Archbishop of Mechlin, the Reverende Mother Mary Wyseman sent five more nuns from Ste Monica's to this convent, all younger in profession than the former. Two of them were Sister Barbara Clapton and Sister Lydwina Clapton, who were two of four sisters all professed on a day in **[p. 5]** Ste Monica's, the eldest and youngest stil remaining there.[7] The third was Sister Grace

---

1 Elizabeth Lovell (1621 Louvain–1634 Bruges) LA172, Procuratrix 1631–33; Chantress 1633–34. She was the niece of Lady Mary Lovell (see **[p. 1]** above).

2 Ursula Palmes (1631–79) BA149, Procuratrix from 1655; Sub-Prioress 1673–79.

3 With the group also came a lay sister, Alexia Hobdy (LA131) who later returned to Louvain, and a priest, a Dutch canon regular, Fr Peter Paris from Groenendaal, and an English Gentleman, Mr Fairfax. Hamilton, *Chronicle*, vol. 2, p. 80.

4 Groenendaal, Hoeilart, near Brussels was a house of Augustinian canons founded c. 1356. Their first Prior was Jan or John van Ruysbroek. *Biographie nationale*, vols 19–20, cols 507–91.

5 Vicariats were appointed to administer a see during an interregnum.

6 Frances Stamford (LA242). The Prioress at Louvain in 1629 was Mary Wiseman.

7 Joyce Clapton, in religion Barbara (1622 Louvain–1674 Bruges) LA051; Jane Clapton, in religion Lidwine (1622 Louvain–1669 Bruges) LA052; Mary Clapton (1622–53) LA053; Catherine Clapton (1622–76) LA050.

Constable;[1] the forth Sister Mary Gifford,[2] these two were profess'd on the same day at Ste Monica's. The fifth and youngest in profession Sister Elisabeth Lucy Brereton.[3] They arrived here on the 13th of October, a month after the first; the Reverend Father Barnes being their guide in the journey, who a little before returned to Lovain for the purpose. They promised their obedience to the Reverende Mother Stamford, who gave them all voices in the convent.

The same year and in the same monthe, the 24 of october, came Mrs Mary Hall who was admitted Schollar for a nun.[4]

On the 28 of november Ann' Crafts was admitted Schollar for a lay sister.[5]

On the 3d of december came Mary Atwoode who was admitted Schollar for a lay sister.[6]

The year 1630

In the next year the 29 of May, came Hellen Bowes, who was also received Schollar for a lay sister; but being judged unfit, after more than a years tryal, she was sent back into England, her name in confirmation being changed into Catherine.[7]

This year the Prioress and Convent desiring a Priest from the College of the Clergie at Doway, Mr Doctor Kellison at Doway the President of **[p. 6]** the colledge,[8] sent Mr James Blomfield, who had been made Priest the Lent before.[9] He came not then to be Confessarius, but only to supply in the absence of father Barnes, who as yet was confessor to both cloisters, and came often hither in the beginning of this foundation, for the two first years. This Reverend Priest arrived here in november, and was approved of the religious, by the most Reverend Lord Servatius, 7th Bishop of Bridges, on St Clement's day.[10]

---

[1] Grace Constable (1625 Louvain–1673 Bruges) LA069, Procuratrix 1633–42; Novice Mistress 1642–55; Sub-Prioress 1655–73. On the family, see Hamilton, *Chronicle*, vol. 1, pp. 229–36.

[2] Mary Gifford (1625 Louvain–1675 Bruges) LA107, Procuratrix 1642–55.

[3] Lucy Brereton, in religion Elizabeth (1626 Louvain–1646 Bruges) LA044.

[4] Mary Hall (1632–69) BA093.

[5] Anne Crafts (1631–54) BA068.

[6] Mary Atwoode (1631–40) BA007.

[7] Helen Bowes, in religion Catherine (1633 Bruges; to Louvain 1645–50; returned to Bruges and died there 1679) BA029.

[8] Dr Matthew Kellison (1561–1642), President of Douai College for 27 years until his death; Anstruther 1, pp. 193–4; *ODNB*.

[9] Fr James Bloomfield (d. 1658), Confessor at Bruges 1631–4. I am grateful to Dr James Kelly for identifying him as James Blundeville, alias Bord (1603–58). Anstruther 2, p. 31.

[10] Servaas de Quinckere (d. 1639), Bishop of Bruges 1630–39. St Clement's Day is celebrated on 23 November.

Before his coming, Mr Doctor Weston, doctor of divinity, and canon of our Blessed Lady's church, came every week to hear confessions in father Barnes' his absence.[1]

This year with the expenses of the building, and many other provisions of the house, all place being so extreamly inconvenient we were constrained to take up six hundred florins more at interest, which increased our debts, for we had very few supplies of Almnes, and the officers had yet but little experience. Sister Ann Crafts and Sister Mary Atwoode, were this year clothed for lay sisters.

The year 1631

On the 7th of May our Procuratress Sister Mary Best, departed this life and was buryed at the cloister of Bethania, near the holy water pot, on the left ha[n]d as you go into **[p. 7]** the church.[2] This Sister Mary Best was of catholic parents, and came out of England to be religious in the year 1613 and was received into the cloister of Ste Monica where she was profess'd a Quire nun in the year 1615 on the 16 of November. She was ever a very regular and exemplar religious, and served the convent for several years in the office of Refectress and celaress.[3] She was sent hither by the Reverende Mother Mary Wyseman, to the foundation of this Monastry and was the eldest but one in profession of all that came hither. She was fallen into a consumption before she left Lovain, and being here made Procuratress, the many cares and troubles of that office in the hard begining we had here increased her infirmity very much. She performed that office with great charity and consumed with labours she dyed in the twentieth month after she came to Bridges; making a most peaceable and happy end according to her vertuous life, on the 7th of May. *Requiescat in pace*. Amen.

Sister Elisabeth Lovell succeeded her in the office of Procuratress.[4] This year the town of Bridges was in great danger to be taken by the Hollanders, but God by his sweet providence preserved us, and freed the town, after we had been for some days much frighted.[5] On the 30th of

---

1 Probably Edward Weston, sent to Bruges as Canon of the Collegiate Church, Bruges. He died in Bruges in 1635. *ODNB*; Anstruther 1, pp. 376–7. Mentioned in the book of benefactors for May (Bruges, Archives of Nazareth, C1).

2 Cloister of Bethania: Penitenten van Maria-Magdalena, located in Carmerstraat near Nazareth. *Monasticon belge*, vol. 3, pp. 1123–42.

3 Refectress and Cellaress: see Glossary.

4 Elizabeth Lovell (1621 Louvain–1634 Bruges) LA172.

5 The Dutch army was under the command of the Duc de Vendôme. The town was defended by the Civic Guard and the governor of the city, Paul Bernard, Comte de Fontaine (killed 1643). The siege was raised after a few days.

June Mrs **[p. 8]** Dorothy Chetwin[1] came out of England and was received Schollar for the order.

In this year Reverend father Barnes finding himself not able to make so many journies from Lovain to Bridges, desired to resigne up his title of confessarius here to the aforesaid Mr. James Blomfield,[2] who with the consent of the most Reverend Lord Servatius,[3] was admitted for confessor of this cloister.

It pleased God in this year to visit us with much sickness which was a hard tryal by reason of the great inconveniences and poverty of the house, and our debts encreased much, and we were constrain'd to take up more money upon interest.

On the tenth of August Sister Ann' Crafts and Sister Mary Atwoode were profess'd lay sisters.[4]

On the 17 of September Frances Reading came hither from St Omars in Artois where she had been born, but of English Parents, and very good vertuous catholicks, she was admitted Schollar for a lay sister.[5]

On the 21 of November, the feast of our Lady's presentation, Sister Ursula Palmes made her profession.[6] Her portion was 300 pounds which was all spent upon the building and other expenses and reparations of the house.[7]

The year 1632

On candlemass Eve Sister Dorothy Chetwin **[p. 9]** was clothed. On candlemass day Sister Mary Hall made her profession.[8] Her portion was also 300 pounds but none of it was put out to rent, it was wholly spent in the expenses of the house and reparations. Besides this the debts also encreased, and more money was taken to rent, so that we paid more than twenty pounds a year for the use of money.

On this year, the 6th of July, Sister Catherine Bowes who as unfit for us had been sent away (as tis said before) came over again unexpected, and thro' much importunity was admitted once more Schollar for a lay

[1] Dorothy Chetwin (1633–46) BA173.

[2] Fr James Blundeville. See **[p. 6]**.

[3] Servaas de Quinckere (d. 1639), Bishop of Bruges 1630–39.

[4] Anne Crafts (BA068); Mary Atwoode (BA007).

[5] Frances Reading (1634–72) BA160. Because of the presence of the College, St Omer was a significant centre for Jesuit culture and English Catholics in exile.

[6] Ursula Palmes (BA149) entered St Monica's, Louvain, but left for the foundation at Bruges when a scholar.

[7] Pounds were used widely in western Europe in this period. It is often difficult to be certain which pounds were referred to in the documents. For further details see Appendix 2.

[8] Mary Hall (BA093). Candlemas Day, celebrating the presentation of Christ in the Temple, is 2 February.

sister.[1] But it may be a caution for all communities never to admitt unfit persons for any importunities; for her defect being in her judgment, and being a deep melancholy person, she has proved very troublesome. On the 14 of September she was clothed a lay sister, together with Sister Frances Reading. This year we built a little brew house which was very necessary, the Religious finding great inconveniency and want of health, by the town beer; but this put us farther in debt.

The year 1633

On Candlemass Eve Sister Dorothy Chetwin made her Profession. Her portion **[p. 10]** was 300 pounds of which 250 was left in England as rent in Mr William Stamfordts hands, yielding us twenty pounds a year, and we had his bond for it; the other fifty was spent on her habit and other expenses.[2]

On the 20 of September Mrs Mary Timperly, a young widow was received Schollar for the order;[3] she had before lived some months as a boarder in the father's house,[4] and going into England, returned with three more, who were all received with her: one of them a Schollar for the order, the other two only as convictresses, one of them was her niece.

This month also, Mary Bowes came to our cloister and was received Schollar for a lay sister.[5]

In November, on the Eve of our Lady's presentation,[6] Mrs Timperley was clothed.

On the Presentation day Sister Catherine Bowes was professed.[7]

The year 1634

A little before Lent, Mrs. Timperley not being found able in any sort to undertake a religious course of life, having neither ability of body, nor fit disposition for religious life, she was dismissed, and left the habit, and being put forth, she took away her niece with her; and both the other gentlewomen who entered with **[p. 11]** her went out some time after.[8]

---

[1] Candidates for profession had to meet with the approval of the whole community and be voted on in a Chapter meeting, before being admitted. The admission of Catherine Bowes (BA029) was a matter of some regret to the community.

[2] William Stanford was the brother of Frances Stamford (1619 Louvain–1635 Bruges) LA242; here he was acting as agent for the community.

[3] Mary Timperley, BA201; she left the following year, after clothing.

[4] The fathers' house was one of the first buildings to be erected.

[5] Mary Bowes (1635–80) BA030; see also **[pp. 11, 20, 117]**.

[6] The Presentation of the Blessed Virgin Mary is celebrated on 21 November.

[7] Catherine Bowes (BA029). See also **[pp. 10, 41, 52, 131]**. She was allowed to leave Bruges in 1645 because she could not settle, but she did not settle at St Monica's either and was allowed to return to Bruges in 1650.

[8] See above **[p. 10]**.

In the month of June, the same year, my Lady Babthorp came to Bridges, and boarded with us, she lodged in our father's house, and her little daughter, miss Ursula was received as convictress into the cloister: this Lady was wife to Sir William Babthorp.[1]

On the Eve of the Visitation, the first of July, Sister Mary Bowes was clothed for a lay sister.[2]

On the feast of our Lady's Visitation, Sister Frances Reading was profess'd a lay sister.

About the end of September, the Lady Babthorp fell sick of the Plague, our town being much infected that year. She dyed in the Hall of our father's house on St Michael's day in the morning.[3] We not knowing her disease till after her death, our Reverend Father heard her confession, and two of our lay sisters tended her who went out and came in amongst us as occasion served; and for this reason our house was accounted infected, tho' none fell sick till three weeks after, when those two lay sisters going out to cleanse the room, were struck with the infection. These two falling dangerously sick, Sister Elisabeth Lovell extreamly importuning our Reverende Mother Frances Stamford, at last obtain'd that she might tend those two sick sisters, and was sent **[p. 12]** out to the father's house, where the sick lay, and within a few days was her self struck with the infection and dyed upon St Martin's day.[4] The two lay sisters recover'd.

This religious, Sister Elisabeth Lovell, was profess'd in the cloister of Ste Monica, in the year 1621 on the 6th of June. In her vocation to religion we may see the great providence of God. She came out of England with her grandmother, the Lady Cross, and living with her in these countries she grew perfect in the flemish language. After some time she was courted by an English gentleman of quality, and [the] matche was so far concluded that her wedding gown was made. But afterwards upon some disagreement between her grandmother and the gentleman, about her portion as some say, or else upon some other cause, the match was broken off, at which the gentlewoman was so deeply discontented, having settled her affection that she presently resolved to go to a cloister and become religious. Her grandmother brought her to Ste Monica's cloister at Lovain, where she was admitted Schollar, and after some months clothed. But she had many and great difficulties in her noviship and was often upon the point of leaving the holy **[p. 13]** habit.

When her year of noviship was ended she could not yet resolve to make her profession, wherefore two others who received the habit with

---

1 Lady Ursula Babthorpe née Tyrwhitt, wife of Sir William Babthorpe and mother of Ursula, in religion Monica (1642–62) BA009.

2 The Visitation of the Blessed Virgin Mary was celebrated on 2 July (currently celebrated on 31 May).

3 St Michael's Day is 29 September (Michaelmas).

4 Elizabeth Lovell (1621 Louvain–1634 Bruges) LA172. St Martin's Day is 11 November.

her, profess'd without her, and she remained almost halve a year novice after them. In which time at last, tho' with great difficulty she made her resolution, and after her profession, which she made on the 6th of June, as is said before, nevertheles for several years she had great difficulties, and but smal content. She was employ'd in diverse offices in that cloister, and at the foundation of this, the Reverende Mother Mary Wyseman thought fit to send her hither hoping it would prove to her content and knowing her many natural good parts, with which she might prove very serviceable to this convent, as indeed she did; having an excellent voice for the choir, she was first made chantress, and after Sister Mary Best's death,[1] she was chosen Procuratress, which office she perform'd almost two years, but proving not so fit for Procuratress, as for Chantress, she was freed from that charge, and Sister Grace Constable was chosen Procuratress in her place.[2] She was again employ'd in the office of Chantress which she continued **[p. 14]** till her death, being also grate Sister where with her good behaviour she gave great edification.[3] The great charity where with she exposed her self, to serve her sick Sisters has not only cover'd her small imperfections, but as we may confide, has gain'd her the crown of glory, and she dyed most peaceably: which is rare in that disease, she had her perfect senses to the last breath. She was buryed in the night in Ste Anne's church.[4] *Requiescat in pace*. Amen.

Six weeks after her burial the house was cleansed and we were free from infection. But all this time of sickness proved an extraordinary charge to our convent which put us more in debt; for in all these years we had but little Almnes. Our Reverende Mother Frances Stamford grew this year wholy infirm, being in a consumption, and these crosses and the great debts and poverty of the house, were great sufferings to her in all which she gave us great example of patience.

The year 1635

On the 7th of March, our Reverende Mother Frances Stamford departed this life.[5] She came to Ste Monica's cloister at Lovain in the year 1617, about **[p. 15]** the 22 year of her age. It pleased God to call her to holy religion upon a discontent she took, being cross'd by her father in a mariage she desired, for the young gentleman who courted her, and on whom she had settled her affection, tho' he was of fit quality for her, yet he had no means and therefore her father would not consent to the

---

1 Mary Best (1615 Louvain–1631 Bruges) LA031 died on 7 May 1631.

2 Grace Constable (1625 Louvain–1673 Bruges) LA069.

3 Grate sister: see Glossary.

4 Sint-Annakerk (St Anne's Church), Bruges, was the parish in which the convent of Nazareth was located. The baroque church was completed in 1621.

5 Frances Stamford (1619 Louvain–1635 Bruges) LA242.

match, whereupon she resolved never to marry any other man, but settled her mind to a religious state. She was admitted Schollar in the aforesaid cloister, and so remain'd a whole year, as she at her first entrance desired; for she would not be over hasty in binding herself: yet from the first she gave herself seriously to vertue, and regular observance; and being something hard to learn the latin, and this Quire song, she took great pains to perfect herself, especially for her duties of the Quire. She made her holy profession two years after her entrance, on the second of September 1619. She was ever a very regular religious, and a prudent discreet woman, very much beloved in her cloister. After some years she was chosen Cellaress and continued in that office, till the beginning of this cloister; when the very Reverende Mother Mary Wyseman[1] sent her hither, nominating her for Prioress **[p. 16]** and the four religious who came with her elected her, as 'tis said before. She govern'd this house with great zeal of regular observance, and was very compassionate to all, especially to the sick and infirm, ready to serve them her self, and truly a Mother to every one. Want of experience in the beginning made her somthing fail in the well orde[r]ing of the temporals; which towards the end of her days she perceived and would have amended if life and health had permitted but she grew very infirm, especially in the two last years of her life; yet so zealous of order that she would never absent her self from the Quire or Refectory, but in extremities. Her tryals were many, and her patience great, having had both the afflictions of war and plague, and we may say in some sort of famine also, thro' the extream poverty of the house. The debts of the cloister very much afflicted her, which were near five hundred pounds Starlin, neither in all the time of her government had she any comfort or assistance from any of her friends. She dyed, as we said before, on the 7th of March, having been Prioress five years and half. She was bury'd in the church of the grey Sisters of Ardenburgh, which is right **[p. 17]** over against our cloister: they are now call'd Penitents of the third order of St Francis; she was inter'd before the step of St Francis' altar.[2] *Requiescat in pace*. Amen.

Her death was a great affliction to us. About a fourtnight after our most Reverend Lord Bishop Servatius,[3] put us to a new election which notwithstanding was not so soon concluded, because some desired a Superior from our Cloister of Ste Monica at Lovain, and others rather

1 Jane Wiseman, in religion Mary (1595–1633) LA303, Prioress at St Monica's from 1609.

2 Church of the Grey Sisters of Aardenburg. After the suppression of this convent by Emperor Joseph II in 1784, the body of Frances Stamford was brought back to the graveyard of the English Convent (1786) and four years later buried in the church: see vol. 2, **[p. 300]**.

3 Servaas de Quinckere (d. 1639), Bishop of Bruges 1630–39.

desired one of this convent; yet proceeding on both sides with great peace.[1] In the end all agreed to the election of Sister Mary Poole, a religious of Ste Monica's Cloister.[2] By order of the Bishop our Convent presently sent our servant William Crafts to Lovain with letters to the Prioress Mother Magdalene Trockmorton,[3] and to the convent, with a letter also in particular,[4] to the elected Sister Mary Poole, who made great difficulties to accept the charge, not only for the burden of Superiority, but also by reason of the poor condition of the house and the debts, for which we paid yearly interests. At last she consented with this condition, that we should accept with her another religious of that **[p. 18]** cloister, Sister Augustina Bedingfeld, who was her kinswoman, and also her sister in profession, and one she esteemed very much, and judged proper to be a good help to her in that charge.[5] Our servant was sent back with this answer but our convent would by no means agree into it, yet persevered still in the desire of having Sister Mary Poole Superior. We sent our man the second time to Lovain with a letter signed with all our hands, and a letter also from our Bishop requesting her to come and be our Superior without bringing that other religious with her. At last by advice of Reverend father Barnes, and the Prioress of Ste Monica, and others, she submitted to it, yet ever in her mind retaining an earnest desire to have that religious as will appear hereafter. She departed from Ste Monica's on the 7 of May on a Monday.[6] Reverend father Barnes being her guide, and to attend on her, a lay sister of Ste Monica's cloister, with our servant William Crafts. She arrived here on Saturday the 12 of the same month. And on tuesday, the 15 of that month, our Reverend Lord Bishop Servatius, confirmed her Prioress, and we all promised our obedience to her.

In June the same year, the French and Hollanders having plundered the town of Tirlemont near Lovain,[7] and most inhumanly and wickedly abused the cloister of women, **[p. 19]** this so affrighted the town of Lovain, the

---

[1] Hamilton, *Chronicle*, vol. 2, pp. 122–3, explains that first the community elected Grace Constable (1625 Louvain–1673 Bruges) LA069, then Procuratrix; however, this was not acceptable to the bishop because of her age. After discussion, a second election was held and they elected Mary Po[o]le from Louvain.

[2] Mary Pole (1622 Louvain–1640 Bruges) LA203. She moved to Bruges following her election as Prioress at Nazareth.

[3] Margaret Throckmorton, in religion Magdalen (1613–68) LA267, Prioress at St Monica's, Louvain, 1633–52.

[4] Comment from editor Amanda Haste: 'en particulier' = not only 'in particular' but also 'in private', which is probably the meaning here.

[5] Helen Bedingfield, in religion Augustina (1622 Louvain–1661 Bruges) LA023, Novice Mistress 1640, Prioress 1640–61, moved to Bruges at the request of Prioress Mary Pole.

[6] For additional details, see Hamilton, *Chronicle*, vol. 2, pp. 123–4.

[7] Part of the June 1635 campaign to attack the Spanish army, during the Thirty Years War. The Franco-Dutch army was led by the Prince of Orange, Frederik-Hendrik (1584–1647). The army went on from Tirlemont to besiege Louvain, but it was a costly failure and the Cardinal Infante leading the Spanish army was able to drive the joint forces back for a time.

Army approaching towards it, that many religious fled; amongst whom several of our cloister of Ste Monica, came hither, to the number of 30 persons. We lodged and entertain'd them all, for three days; after that by the great providence of God they were provided of a house in this town of Bridges, lent them by a canon, Mr Blende, where they stay'd about two months, being all that time relieved and maintain'd by the charity of the good people in the town, who daily brought them Almnes, both in money, bread and other things, and lending them bedding and other necessaries. The nuns came often to us, and we had leave of our Bishop to take them into our enclosure whenever they came.

About the middle of August they all return'd to Lovain; but Mrs Agatha Brooke,[1] daughter to Sir Basil Brooke,[2] who had lived some time a convictress in Ste Monica's cloister, and now came out with them, remained here with us, and was admitted Schollar for the order.

After their return, our Reverende Mother Mary Poole, considering the great wants of our house, and seeing with what charity our Sisters of Lovain had been here relieved, having first recommended it heartily to God, she resolved to try their charity **[p. 20]** and coming from her prayers on St Bernard's day[3] (which was about four days after our nuns were gone) she went into the kitchen to our Procuratress and told her she was strongly moved to go a beging, and to begin that day: and presently she sent two sisters to the Abbey of Dunes, where they kept Solemn feast of St Bernard.[4] The sisters were very charitably relieved, and sent home well loaden with flesh and bread. This encouraged our Reverende Mother to persevere a beggar; and she sent our sisters to several other places. Some relieved them, others at first spoke harshly to them, thinking we dissembled and that we were not truly inwant, yet after a while we had many friends, and some advised us to put up a request to the town, declaring our necessities, and craving license to beg. To which the Town giving no answer, we presumed to take silence for consent, and continued beging. Nobody contradicting it. In a short time we had many benefactors who weekly gave us bread sufficient for our whole convent; besides also flesh sometimes, and other things. And at the end of this year we had as much Almnes in money as came to 276 florins.

On the nativity of our Blessed Lady,[5] Sister Mary Bowes was profess'd a lay sister.

---

1 Agatha Brooke (1644–78) BA033.

2 Sir Basil Brooke (1576–1646) of Madeley Court, Shropshire was a metallurgist, farmer and industrialist.

3 St Bernard's day was celebrated on 20 August.

4 Cistercian Abbey, Ten Duine, Bruges. See 'Abbaye des Dunes' in *Monasticon belge*, vol. 3:2, pp. 353–441.

5 The Nativity of Our Lady was celebrated on 8 September.

[p. 21]

The year 1636

In the month of April Sister Agatha Brooke was clothed. Sir Basil Brooke, her father giving fifty pound for that Solemnity, and the charges of her habit, besides he gave forty pound a year for her maintenance. This money was a great help to us, and our Reverende Mother was very careful to begin to pay our debts. And in this year we had other good Almnes in money, about a thousand florins, besides other good things: and to diminish the expences of our house, we this year dismiss'd our man William Crafts, who had served us very faithfully, but we found it too heavy a charge to maintain a servant.

The year 1637

Our holy Father the Pope Urbanus the eight, this year granted as a plenary to our Chapel, for the feast of the nativity of our Blessed Lady.[1] It was for seven years, and there to be renew'd. In the same year his holiness granted a privilege to our high Altar, a plenary for the souls of our sisters departed; to be renew'd in like manner after seven years.

On the 16 of September, our Reverende Dear Subprioress, Sister Ann Tremaine departed this life, having been eight years Subprioress.[2] This religious was profess'd at Lovain in the cloister of Ste Ursula, in the year 1601 **[p. 22]** in which cloister she lived for some years with others of our nation who were profess'd there. When our English cloister of Ste Monica was begun by them in the same town, she came also to that new foundation; and lived several years in that cloister, a very exemplar life, strict in all religious observances, and she served that convent in diverse offices untill at the begining of our foundation she was sent hither by the Reverende Mother Mary Wyseman, and by her nominated and afterwards, here elected our first Subprioress, which office she perform'd with great zeal of regular observances: humble in her conversation, and a great lover of peace. She dyed about the sixtyeth year of her age, and 36th of her profession.

When she lay in her last sickness our Reverende Mother procured a piece of ground to be blessed in the court by our Chappel, to serve for a burying place, being unwilling to have any more bury'd out of our enclosure. She was then bury'd and her happy soul, we are confident, enjoys the reward of her innocent and vertuous life. *Requiescat in pace.*

We were this year relieved with Almnes, especially from those of the Town, and in mercy we had 1120 florins **[p. 23]** with which we lived

---

[1] Pope Urban VIII: elected 1623; died 1644.

[2] Anne Tremaine (1601 Louvain–1637 Bruges) LA272.

without incuring any new debts; and also spared something wherewith our Reverende Mother paid off some old debts.

Upon the death of our Subprioress, our Reverende Mother Mary Poole again renew'd her request of having the fore mention'd religious, Sister Augustina Bedingfeld,[1] taking an occasion upon this to write to the Prioress of Ste Monica's, Mother Magdalene Trockmorton;[2] for she had ever retain'd in her mind an earnest desire of having her here, altho' for some reasons she did not seek to detain her, when with those who had fled from Lovain, she had been here at Bridges two years before. It was then more convenient she should return to her own cloister with the other of her company.

By the answer which was made from Lovain, we well perceiv'd that we should not easily obtain her, wherefore we persuaded our Reverende Mother not to deferr the election of a new Subprioress; so in the month of October, Sister Mary Altham was chosen Subprioress.[3]

The year 1638

We have nothing in particular to record here, but only the providence of **[p. 24]** God towards us, moving good people to continue their Almnes, by which we lived without debts, and had also some overplus, wherewith our Reverende Mother was providently careful to get off some rent, so that in the end of this year there remain'd only a fifty pound debt, for which we gave interest.

Also our Reverende Mother not satisfied with the denyal she had had from Lovain, began her earnest suit again of having Sister Augustina Bedingfeld from the cloister of Ste Monica, where that year she was chosen Arcaria[4] and yet this did not discourage our Reverende Mother, for she now finding that she had the good will and consent of all her own convent, could never be content till she obtained her of the convent of Ste Monica: she employ'd friends and writ many letters, but nothing prevail'd. Wherefore she wrote to the most illustrious Lord Archbishop of Mechlen, unto whose obedience that cloister of Ste Monica is subject.[5] She humbly requested this favour might be granted her by his authority; representing to his Lordship how both herself and convent here that requested it, were also his children. This so moved the Archbishop **[p. 25]** that he was very much inclined to favour her suit, our Reverende Mother also sent him a letter written by us to the Prioress and convent of Ste

---

1 Helen Bedingfield, in religion Augustina (1622 Louvain–1661 Bruges) LA023, Prioress at Bruges 1640–61.

2 Margaret Throckmorton, in religion Magdalen (1631–68) LA267, Prioress 1633–52.

3 Mary Altham (1616 Louvain–1661 Bruges) LA004, Sub-Prioress at Bruges 1633–55.

4 Arcaria: see Glossary.

5 Jacob Boonen (d. 1655), Archbishop of Mechelen (Malines) 1621–55. Both Louvain and Bruges are located in the Archdiocese of Mechelen.

Monica, and signed by all our convent, which she requested might be presented by his officer together with his Lordship's own favorable letter in this behalf. We required no maintainance with her, which pleased him the better. These letters were brought to the Prioress of Ste Monica's by the Archpriest, with order from the Archbishop to take the vote of that convent for the sending this religious to ours. Nevertheless such were the difficulties many there made that it could not be concluded that year.

The year 1639

Our Reverende Mother Mary Poole constantly persevering in her desire, and by means of her sister Mrs Redish[1] (who lived in Bruxelles) often urging and importuning the Archbishop, at last, by his order the Archpriest was sent again to Ste Monica's cloister, to put the convent a second time to their votes, and it was consented that Sister Augustina Bedingfeld should be sent to Bridges, to our convent, but with this condition that the Archbishop of Mechlin should retain his power to recall her **[p. 26]** again to Ste Monica's cloister, and therefore he would not free her of her obedience: as also that it should be in the power of the Prioress, and convent of Ste Monica to call her back again if it should be found necessary for the good of that house. The said religious also had full power granted her to return home to her convent whenever she would, and all these things were recorded for the greater security.

All things thus agreed; upon the 21 of July she set out from Lovain for Bridges; our Reverende Mother having taken care that her sister, Mrs Redish should go to Lovain for her. They arrived here at Bridges on the 30th of July, and she was received into our cloister by our Reverende Mother with no less joy that she had with earnestness been before desired. She promised her obedience in the Chapter house, and was in order amongst us according to her profession: the first of our convent next to our Superioress.

Some weeks after, our Reverende Mother sent for the Archpriest to take the convent's voices for an Arcaria (hitherto we had not had any). Sister Augustina Bedingfeld was chosen Arcaria, and she this year drew out the Procuratresses reckoning **[p. 27]** after the form used at Ste Monica's.[2] This reckoning of our house 1639 is the first that remains recorded in our convent.[3]

---

1 Jane Redish, née Pole, her oldest sister; one of five daughters of Geoffrey Pole (d. 1591 at Antwerp) of Lordington, Sussex and Catherine Dutton.

2 Augustina Bedingfield (1622 Louvain–1661 Bruges) LA023.

3 The Procuratrix was responsible for drawing up the accounts and the Arcaria was responsible for managing all the paperwork of the convent (see the Glossary for further details). Augustina Bedingfield brought the system used at Louvain with her.

In the month of November Mrs Ursula Babthorp was received Schollar for the order.[1]

The year 1640

On the 4th of May the feast of our holy Mother Ste Monica, Sister Ursula Babthorp was clothed, and Sister Augustina Bedingfeld then made Mrs [Mistress] of the novices.[2] On the 18 of June, Sister Mary Atwoode departed this life.[3] She had been profess'd a lay sister on the 10th of August 1631, and lived piously, being very laborious in the service of the cloister; so we may confidently hope she has received her reward in heaven. She was buryed near our old Subprioress Sister Ann Tremaine. *Requiescat in pace*. Amen.

The same year in September it pleased God to visit us with much sickness; several of our Religious having Agues, and some not without danger. At last in October our dear Reverende Mother fell also very ill of the Agues;[4] and after three weeks sickness, suffer'd with great example of patience, it pleased Almity **[p. 28]** God to call her out of this life, to the great grief of all our convent. She departed on the 4 of November at the age of 56, and in the 19 year of her holy profession.

She came to Ste Monica's cloister at Lovain in the year 1620. She was of a noble and catholick family, and Cardinal Poole was her great uncle.[5] She had lived some time in France with her brother, where she became perfect in the french tongue. She was always very pious and having an inclination to a religious life she enter'd a Monastry in France of the order of St Theresia tho' much against her brother's will. She did not persevere in that holy order being hinder'd by sickness, and God having designed her for his service in another. After the death of her Brother she return'd into England to her friends. Notwithstanding she stil held her mind for a religious life, and after some years, obtain'd her desire, coming over into these low countries, and being recommended to Ste Monica's cloister at Lovain, she was there received, and afterwards profess'd on the 19 of June 1622, together with three others who came to the cloister **[p. 29]** before her; one of them was Sister Augustina Bedingfeld, her kinswoman, before mention'd. She was about 39 years of age when she made her holy profession; and tho' she had lived in the world so many years at her own liberty, living with her brother as

---

1 Ursula Babthorpe, in religion Monica (BA009).

2 Comment from editor Amanda Haste: It appears that 'Miss' is used for young girls, and 'Mrs' for older girls, maybe to signify puberty.

3 Mary Atwoode (1631–40) BA007.

4 Reverend Mother was Mary Pole (1622 Louvain–1640 Bruges) LA203, Prioress 1635–40. See also Hamilton, *Chronicle*, vol. 1, pp. 238, 241, 243, 257; vol. 2, pp. 123–4.

5 Reginald Pole (1500–58) was an English Cardinal and the last Roman Catholic Archbishop of Canterbury, holding the office during the reign of Mary I. See *ODNB*.

Mistress of the house, yet from her first entrance into the cloister she apply'd her self with great humility and submission to holy obedience, and was ever very observant of the holy order: and being a very wise and prudent woman, she was employ'd in the office of Grate sister[1] almost presently after her profession. Being elected Prioress of this convent, as we said before, and confirm'd in that office, she govern'd with great prudence and discretion. She was always zealous of regular discipline, and examplar in the observance of order; and both beloved and fear'd in her community; much respected and beloved by strangers and with her prudent and affable conversation gain'd many friends to the cloister, and [by] this means procured Almnes wherewith the great poverty of the house was relieved. And by her careful ordening of things the expenses were moderated, **[p. 30]** and before her death all debts paid. She left also a hundred pound in money in the Arck[2] when she dyed, to be afterwards put out to rent, for she used to say that she could not account all debts paid till she had laid some rent upon Sister Ursula Palmes and Sister Mary Hall, whose portions had been wholly consumed in the expenses of the house and building as it has been said before.[3] She govern'd this monastry five years and half and dyed most peaceably with great signs of content: expressing many times in her sickness how truly willing and resigned she was to die, since God had granted her the comfort to leave here behind her Sister Augustina Bedingfeld,[4] fore seeing as it were that she would succeed her in her office, and also in a manner foretelling the same: for a few hours before she departed, being in her perfect senses, she call'd for that religious, and kissing and embracing her she gave her hearty thanks for the comfort she had afforded her by coming hither from her own monastry. And she recommended this house to her entreating her to be resigned to what Almighty God, after her death, would impose on her, and saying that she dyed most **[p. 31]** resignedly and willingly, leaving her here. She departed on the 4th of November on a Sunday about nine o'clock at night.

The next morning her happy soul enjoy'd the privilege of the indulgence granted by his holyness at her own request, as tis said before in the year 1636, by a Mass offer'd for her at our Altar, by which we may confidently hope she enter'd into the joy of her Lord, she having been so faithfull over her charge, and so zealous a servant of his. She was bury'd in our little piece of hallow'd ground on the Tuesday following, the sixth of November. *Requiescat in pace*. Amen.

---

1 Grate sister: see Glossary.
2 Ark: see Glossary.
3 Ursula Palmes (BA149); Mary Hall (BA093); see **[pp. 8, 9]**.
4 Augustina Bedingfield (1622 Louvain–1661 Bruges) LA023.

The next day being the 7th of November, the Reverend Canon Mr Waghonor, secretary to the deceased Bishop Servatius,[1] was sent by the Vicariats, who were the Reverend Deane Carolus de Bosch,[2] and two other chief canons, to ordain our convent to fast three days, and with silence and prayer to dispose themselves for the making a new election.

On Monday the 12 of November, they came all to our church where they had ordain'd a Solemne Mass to be sung of the holy Ghost, at which all the religious communicated. And after the Vicars, with the secretary, and Doctor **[p. 32]** Weston,[3] an English Canon of our Lady's church, for interpretor, came into the chapter house, and there took the votes of all the nuns, who by these voices elected Sister Augustina Bedingfeld for their Prioress. She was there presently confirm'd in that office, and render'd her vow of obedience there Solemnly to the Bishop of Bridges in presence of the Vicariats, who immediatly caused all the nuns and lay sisters to promise their obedience to her, there in their presence.[4]

When all the Solemnity was ended the Vicariats went all to dinner in the father's Hall, and with the Reverend Dean's leave the Lady d'Eggermont[5] an especial benefactress of our house with two other gentlewomen our particular friends, enter'd the enclosure, and din'd in our Refectory with the new Prioress and our convent. The Vicariats gave the dinner, and when they had dined also enter'd the enclosure again, and visited the house, which the Dean procured, who had recommended it to some of the town. The Burgemesters of the city sent to the new Prioress, and presented her with wine; as the custome is here to persons of quality, and richer cloisters at the confirmation of new superiors, or **[p. 33]** benediction of Abbesses: it having thus pleased our dear Lord to honour his poor servants, and He will not fail to reward the Magistrates of the town, and prosper them for their charity to strangers.[6]

By this example, the Burgemesters of the free, a few days after presented the new Prioress with as much wine as those of the town had given.[7] The next day after the election with an especial leave from the Dean granted

---

1 Hubrecht Waghenaere, Archpriest from 1652. Bishop Servaas de Quinckere died on 3 March 1639.

2 The diocese was then vacant. Karel van den Bosch (1597–1665), Vicar General of Bruges, became Bishop of Bruges in 1651.

3 Probably Edward Weston, sent to Bruges as Canon of the Collegiate Church, Bruges. He died in Bruges in 1635. *ODNB*; Anstruther 1, pp. 376–7.

4 Diocesan Archives, Bruges, MS C/396, fols 10–11.

5 It has not been possible to verify the identity of Lady Egremont.

6 There were two Bourgmestres in Bruges: the 'Burgemeester van de raadsleden', responsible for keeping the peace in the city, and the 'Burgemeester van de schepenen', who supervised city affairs. In 1641–43, the latter was Alexander de Meulenaere. I am indebted to Pascal Majérus for this reference.

7 The Brugse Vrije, or 'Franc of Bruges', was a castellany in the county of Flanders which included the area around Bruges. Since the city and the Vrije were considered as separate, it had its own Burgemeester. I am grateful to Pascal Majérus for this information.

as a singular favour, the Lady of St John's hospital,[1] a great benefactress to our house, enter'd our enclosure, and dined in our Refectory.

The charity of our benefactors continuing, we had good assistances in Almnes, and ended this year without debt; somthing also remain'd which was laid up in the Arck, and reserved with the former hundred pounds to purchase a rent.

The year 1642[2]

In the month of January we made our reckoning, and Sister Grace Constable, our Procuratress having had a long sickness, and being very weak, was released of that office and made Arcaria, and Sister Mary Gifford was chosen Procuratress.[3] After the reckning our Reverende Mother was careful to put out that money to rent, and by counsel of friends, and the convent's **[p. 34]** consent there was a thousand six hundred florins, in January, put to rent upon the new river to Dunquerque, yielding a 100 florins a year, the town of Bridges also being bound for it: as it stands in the writings which are kept in the Arck. This our Reverende Mother (mindful of her predecessor's intentions) apply'd to Sister Ursula Palmes, whose portion had been spent, and so it is yearly accounted in our reckning.[4]

We must not omit in this place to record how the divine Providence this year raised us up a great benefactor one Mr Georges Kenneb, a gentleman of Tournais whose ancestors, as he told us, were of the kindred of St Thomas of Canterbury, who were banished with him in his exile out of England. This gentleman being a Bachelor, and having a good estate in Tournay, came to live in our town of Bridges; and being a great Almnes giver and very charitable, he hearing of our poverty, brought us in the month of June this year, 12 pound flemish, in six english pieces, which Almnes and almost always in the same species, he brought us daily every quarter for several years after, as shal be shew'd hereafter.

In the month of July, on the feast of our Lady's Visitation, Sister Ursula Monica Babthorp was profess'd, having been **[p. 35]** above two years novice, for want of portion.[5] At last there being no hopes, our Convent with the consent of our most Reverend Lord Bishop, the Lord Nicholas de Haudion[6] (who in January this year had been consecrated) agreed to

---

1 Sint-Janshospitaal in Bruges, under the care of the Augustinian Sisters. In 1641, the Prioress was Eleanora Goossens (d. 1654). I am indebted to Sibylla Goegeboer for this reference.

2 Note in the typescript that 1641 does not appear in the manuscript.

3 Grace Constable (1625 Louvain–1673 Bruges) LA069; Mary Gifford (1625 Louvain–1675 Bruges) LA107.

4 Ursula Palmes (BA149).

5 The Feast of the Visitation was celebrated on 2 July. Ursula Babthorpe, in religion Monica (BA009).

6 Nicolas de Haudion (1596–1649), Bishop of Bruges 1642–49. See *Biographie nationale*, vol. 8, cols 772–3.

profess her, having only one hundred pound portion. Her eldest brother gave her 50 pound of it, and the Lady Egremont undertook to make up the other 50, of which she herself gave 25 and she procured the other 25 pounds of a knight of Malta,[1] who then lived in Bridges. This most Reverend Lord Bishop was very charitable to us, and the charity also of our other benefactors continued, so that we lived without debts, and also spared some money which was reserved in the Ark.

The year 1643

In May our Reverende Mother's sister in law brought hither her daughter Mrs Mary Bedingfeld, who was near thirteen years of age.[2] She came out of England with Mr Everard, her second husband, and kept house in this town of Bridges, together with her own mother, Mrs Wyborne: but her only daughter Mrs Mary Bedingfeld, she put into our cloister, recommending her to our Reverende Mother who was sister to her first husband, Mr John Bedingfeld, and aunt to her daughter: she was here received convictress: and at the same time **[p. 36]** came Catherine Bartlett, who was received for a servant, in order to be a lay sister.[3]

In the month of June our most Reverend Lord Bishop made a visitation here; but because our religious had not the language, he remitted the hearing of them to Reverend father Henry More, of the Society of Jesus, an ancient father and very prudent man who had formerly been Provincial.[4] This Reverend father by the Bishop's order, having heard all the nuns, set down in writing such points as the religious desired should be presented to my Lord Bishop, and the next day his Lordship came himself and together with the Archdeacon, the aforesaid father and the secretary, visited the church and house; and giving his benediction to all the religious and money for a recreation, he told us we should expect his answer to the visitation.

It pleased his most Reverend Lordship to change many things in our institutions, and to cause them to be drawn out in a better forme, which

---

1 The Knights of Malta was in origin a religious order whose purpose and fortunes changed over centuries. By the seventeenth century it was a prestigious chivalric order leading attacks on Barbary pirates from its base on Malta. Charles V had awarded sovereignty to the order in 1530.

2 Reverend Mother was Helen Bedingfield, in religion Augustina (1622 Louvain–1661 Bruges) LA023. Her sister-in-law was Susanna née Wyborne, who married as her first husband John Bedingfield. Their daughter was Mary Bedingfield (1652–93) BA019, Novice Mistress from 1655; Prioress 1661–93.

3 Catherine Bartlett (1645–83) BA008.

4 Fr Henry More SJ (1586–1661) was an English Jesuit provincial and missionary, and rector of St Omer. He wrote a history of the English Jesuits: *Historia Missionis Anglicanæ, ab anno MDLXXX ad MDCXXXV* (St Omer, 1660). See McCoog, vol. 2, p. 244; Foley, vol. 7, pp. 518–19.

being a long work we expected till the end of this year before we had any answer to our visitation.

In the mean time in the month of July, Mrs. Elisabeth Young[1] was received here a Schollar for the order.

A few days before Christmass, our most Reverend Lord Bishop sent us our reform'd Statutes,[2] giving the religious **[p. 37]** one year to try them. But they were in Latin and could not be read to the convent till they were translated which was not done till the begining of the next year.

The year 1644

Our Reverende Mother having translated into English the new reform'd Statutes, began to read them to the convent in the month of January; and all the Religious with great submission to the Bishop's will and ordinances, accepted of them upon a years tryal.[3]

Before the end of January they had been all read, and in those constitutions our most Reverend Lord Bishop changed our Midnight hour of Matins to four a clock in the morning. This change had not been desired by any of our convent, and some had difficulty to submitt unto it, the Midnight hour being so ancient a custome of our holy order; but having understood that diverse cloisters of our order had changed it, and seeing it was only ordain'd for a time, we were all content: for our number being small, and several weak persons, it was very hard to keep Mattins at Midnight; and it happen'd very often that we kept Quire with only three at Mattins, one on the one side, and two on the side when the week was kept, nay several times we had many **[p. 38]** in the infirmary or otherways indisposed we have been but one on each side at the longest feria Mattins; and it has happen'd in a duplex feast when the whole community were ill of the cold, that the Prioress and Subprioress have been the only [ones] at Mattins, the Prioress keeping the great week as hebdomadaria, and also the little week, reading the *Venite* and versicles with the Subprioress.[4]

---

1 Elizabeth Young (1646–69) BA231. 'Scholar for the order' suggests that Elizabeth was already considering entering the community.

2 Latin Constitutions given by Nicholas Haudion, Bishop of Bruges, 1645, Nazareth Archives, RM GIV c.

3 This refers to MS translation by Augustina Bedingfield, Nazareth Archives, RM GIV b.

4 The hebdomadaria is the nun who has to lead prayers in choir for a week. The Invitatory is the psalm used to start Mattins in the Liturgy of the Hours, usually Psalm 94, which begins *Venite exultemus* ('O come, let us praise the Lord'). A versicle is the verse said or sung by the versicularian with a response by the rest of the community. Great week and little week: a rota kept by the Chantress with different members of the community chosen to intone the opening of antiphons, prayers, etc. Feasts (feria) with different ceremonies: for instance, Duplex was the feast of a saint; Second Class was for apostles; and First Class was a very important celebration. I am indebted to the Community at Bruges for this explanation.

This difficulty made us more willingly submitt to the changing of the hour and on the feast of the conversion of St Paul we first kept our Mattins at four a clock.[1]

On the same day, Sister Agatha Brooke was profess'd having been novice from the month of April 1631, all these years it was delay'd for want of her portion, her father notwithstanding paying for an Annuity of forty pounds.[2] Our convent was moved to compassion and seeing no hopes of her portion, we requested my Lord Bishop to give leave for her profession.

She was profess'd a veil'd nun but with dispensation from the great office by reason of the weakness of her sight. This my Lord Bishop granted her at the convent's request in consideration she had been so many years novice: nevertheless he **[p. 39]** declared that this should never be an example hereafter, as may be found in the grant kept in the Ark. And altho' she is a nun and obliged to the same statutes, yet she may never have voice in the convent. The same year Sir Basile Brooke her father, was taken prisoner by the Parliament in England, and his estate seiz'd, whereby we fail'd of her Annuity which was a great loss to us.[3] Nevertheless the charity of the town continuing, and Mr Kenneb giving us his Almnes every quarter, we kep[t] out of debt, and what we spared was laid up in the Ark.

About the end of this year my Lord Bishop gave us a new Statute for our lay sisters.[4]

In this year Mr Henry Clifford sent us fifty pound of the money which belong'd to my Lady Lovell, which was presently put out to rent, this was in the month of March.[5]

We must not omitt to record how in the year 1642, our most Reverend Lord Bishop granted us the rent of 230 florins, which the Lady Mary Lovell left by testament to be bestow'd on young maids who should want means to enter into religion; as **[p. 40]** it may be found in our Procuratresses accounts of that year, of which notwithstanding we have

---

1 The Feast of the Conversion of St Paul is celebrated on 25 January.

2 Agatha Brooke (1644–83) BA033.

3 Sir Basil Brooke lost his fortune when he was imprisoned by Parliament in January 1644. His Madeley estate was sequestrated, and he died on 31 December 1646 leaving debts of £10,000. See *ODNB*.

4 *Statute for Lay Sisters*, printed 1717.

5 Henry Clifford had been the secretary to Jane Dormer, Duchess of Feria, and wrote her biography. Following her death in 1613, he was chargé d'affaires for many English exiles in the Low Countries, including Lady Mary Lovell, for whom he bought properties to establish the English Carmel in Antwerp. She had died in Bruges on 12 November 1628. See, for instance, M. C. Questier, *Stuart Dynastic Policy and Religious Politics, 1621–1625* (Cambridge: Cambridge University Press, 2009), p. 146.

as yet no other profit than only the rent of this fifty pound as appears in the same years accounts.[1]

In October our Reverende Mother with the convents consent, laid to rent one thousand six hundred florins of the money reserved in the Ark, which yielded 10 florins yearly; and this for Sister Mary Hall whose portion had been spent:[2] this rent and the changing of it afterwards may be found in the Procuratresses accounts.

On the feast of the Immaculate Conception of the most Blessed Virgin Sister Elisabeth Young was clothed.[3]

The year 1645

In the month of July, our most Reverend Lord Bishop made here a visitation, comitting the hearing of the religious to the same Reverend father Henry More, who assisted in the former visitation in the year 1643.[4] This visitation was chiefly to examin the nuns concerning their new reform'd Statutes; and to hear what difficulties they could propose concerning them; his Lordship resolving how to confirm them; for hitherto he had only given them upon tryal.

The same year in August **[p. 41]** we received from my Lord Bishop a card, containing such ordinances as upon the visitation he judged fitting. And about the month of November we received our Statutes again, alter'd in some points as the religious had requested. And now all the Statutes were confirm'd, and by our most Lord Bishop, commanded to be inviolably observed by all:[5] only the hour of rising at four to Mattins was left still upon tryal, as declared in the card.

In the month of September we sent Sister Catherine Bows to Lovain,[6] having obtain'd of the Prioress there to admit her for a time as a boarder, our convent allowing a hundred florins yearly for her: this our Reverende Mother thought good, with the consent of the Bishop and our convent to try if she could be content there, for here she was very unquiet and most troublesome.

In the same month Sister Catherine Bartlett was clothed here for a lay sister.[7]

We were this year also well assisted with Almnes and lived without debts, and what we could spare was laid up in the Ark.

---

1 For Lady Mary Lovell, see **[p. 1]**.

2 Mary Hall (BA093) professed on 2 February 1632. Her dowry was £300.

3 The Feast of Immaculate Conception falls on 8 December.

4 Nicolas de Haudion (1596–1649), Bishop of Bruges 1642–49. For Henry More, see **[p. 36]**.

5 Latin Constitutions: see Nazareth Archives RM GIV c.

6 Catherine Bowes (BA029).

7 Catherine Bartlett (BA008).

The year 1646

In the month of August our dear Sister Dorothy Chetwin dyed.[1] She had been **[p. 42]** profess'd as is said before, in the year 1633. This religious was ever very regular in the holy order, truly obedient and submissive to her superiors, and a vertuous discreet woman, prudent and very peaceable, and in several offices had done good service to the community; all being sorry to lose her but it was the holy will of God to call her to himself when she had faithfully served him in holy religion about thirteen years after her profession. She was taken with a burning and pestilent feavour upon the feast of our Lady's Assumption,[2] and departed this life on our holy father's Eve,[3] about eleven of the clock in the night: and having been particularly devoted to this our glorious patron, and dying so near his feast, we may hope that by his intercession she feasteth with him in heaven, having ever been of an innocent life in the world, and truly pious in holy religion. She dyed about the age of 40 and was bury'd in our church yard. *Requiescat in pace*. Amen.

On the first of October, Sister Catherine Bartlett was profess'd a lay sister, her portion was about a hundred and twenty pound.

On the Presentation of our Blessed Lady, Sister Elisabeth Young was profess'd, having been **[p. 43]** almost two years novice for want of her portion, which we received afterwards, 2200 florins in money, and an annuity for life of a hundred florins.[4]

On the Eleventh of December, our dear Sister Elisabeth Lucy Brereton departed this life after a long and tedious infirmity.[5] This religious was youngest in profession of the ten who were at first sent tither, tho' she was ancient in years, being almost thirty when she came to religion. She was ever a very zealous observer of the holy order, very diligent and exact to her duties in the divine office, and remarkable for a singular conformity to the will of her Superiors in whatsoever changes or employment: very laborious and profitable in the service of the community and careful to advance the common profit. By which we may be confident (as our holy father says in our rule) that she went daily foward in perfection; till at last it pleased God to compleat her crown by a long and painful sickness; for on the 4th of February this year she was suddenly taken with a Palsie or Apoplex, losing wholy the use of one side, and not being able to move or stir her self but as others help'd her. It pleasing God thus to try her patience, and exercise others **[p. 44]** in charity; for she being a very corpulent and big woman was very unwieldy and hard to be

1 Dorothy Chetwin (1633–46) BA173.

2 The Assumption of Our Lady is celebrated on 15 August.

3 The eve of St Augustine's day is 27 August.

4 The Presentation of our Blessed Lady is 21 November. Elizabeth Young (BA231).

5 Lucy Brereton, in religion Elizabeth (1626–46) LA044.

stir'd or moved. She was very charitably assisted by the religious, unto whom she gave great edification by her patient suffring, and conformity to God's will in this her long and painful sickness: so that every one was comforted to see her, and not only willing, but glad to do her any charitable service. She had her perfect understanding to the last breath, and dyed most peaceably at the age of fifty, on the 19th year of her holy profession. She was bury'd in our church yard. *Requiescat in pace.* Amen.

We were assisted this year with Almnes as formerly, and lived without debt, and what we spared was laid up in the Ark.

The year 1647

In the month of June our Reverende Mother's cousin, Mr Henry Bedingfeld coming hither, and seeing the poor accomodations of our cloister, gave and [*sic*] Almnes of 50 pound, to begin to build cells.[1] This tho' little, that given with that intention, first encouraged our Reverende Mother to think of some way how to enlarge or better our house, either by changing the house or building something. She **[p. 45]** had for the same end carefully reserved what money could be spared in these former years; for when she had now laid to rent as much as sufficed to make an annuity of a 100 florins yearly for those two religious whose portions had been spent, all her care was to get somthing together for the enlargment of the house: in which we had for so many years suffer'd the inconveniency of want of cells, and of a very inconvenient Quire for the divine office.

Mr James Altham also dying about this time, left to his sister our Subprioress, a legacy of a hundred pound, which in like manner we reserved for the same intention.[2] (He had before at the begining of our house, sent us in regard of his sister, near two hundred pound in all, at different times.)

We had also some money remaining this year after our reckoning which was laid up in the Ark.

Our cloister of Ste Monica at Lovain, being in low condition, and not able to continue the payment of those Annuities for our religious who came from thence, this year presented to our convent three hundred pounds to redeem five life rents of ten pounds a year with consent of our **[p. 46]** most Reverend Lord Bishop, we accepted the 300 pounds and from this September, our Cloister was no more to receive any rent

---

[1] Here it is not clear whether the text refers to Sir Henry Bedingfield, 1st Baronet of Oxburgh (1614–84), or to Fr Henry Bedingfield SJ (c. 1582–1659), Provincial of the order from 1647. See McCoog, vol. 2, p. 294; Bedingfield Family in *ODNB*.

[2] James (d. 1647) and his sister Mary (1616 Louvain–1661 Bruges), LA004, were born to Thomas Altham (d. c. 1607) and Magdalen of Mark Hall, Essex. See 'Some Althams of Mark Hall in the Seventeenth Century', Part 2, *Essex Review* 17 (July 1908), pp. 134–46.

from Ste Monica's Cloister. These 300 pounds with the Bishop's and our convent's consent, was also reserved for building.

About the end of September this year, on St Michael's day, Mrs Mary Bedingfeld departed from our cloister for England.[1] This child, as tis said before, was brought hither by her mother, being between twelve and thirteen years of age. Her mother returning into England left her daughter here for education, who at fifteen years of age had a great desire to be a Schollar for the order, and with much importunity requested it of our Reverende Mother, her Aunt; but because her own mother would not consent that she should go forward in the order, her Aunt would not grant her the Schollars habit till she was near sixteen. Then to content her she gave her leave to take it upon St Michael's the Archangel's day in the year 1645. So having been a whole year Schollar, and continuing her earnest desire to go forward in complyance with her true vocation to our holy order, we were forced to send her into England to **[p. 47]** satisfy her mother, tho' to the great grief of all our comunity and much against her own will. This is here recorded for a memory of her, hoping and expecting her return.

In October Grace Eddows was received here a servant, in order to be lay sister.[2]

The year 1648

In March, our Reverende Mother's sister, the Lady Elisabeth Hamilton sent her daughter Lucy a child of eight years old, to have her education here in our cloister, and to be afterwards religious amongst us if God pleases to call her; the child herself being much enclined to it, and her parents freely giving her to God.[3]

In July Mr Mathew Bedingfeld,[4] our Reverende Mother's uncle, came hither to assist her about our house. We were then advised by some friends to get another house more large and convenient, but with better advise in the end it was concluded we should the next Spring begin to build here, and enlarge our house by little and little as we should be able.

---

1 St Michael's day (Michaelmas) is celebrated on 29 September. Mary Bedingfield returned and professed in 1652 (BA019); her mother was Susanna Wyborne: see above **[p. 35]**.

2 Grace Eddows, lay sister (1651–74) BA075.

3 Lucy Hamilton, in religion Laurentia (1656–93) BA095; her mother, Elisabeth Hamilton, née Bedingfeld, BA094, professed at Bruges as a widow in 1674.

4 Matthew Bedingfield of Amersden, husband of Helena Lacon, was the father of three nuns: Margaret Bedingfield (GB017), Mary Bedingfield (GB018) and Anne Bedingfield (AC010). Matthew was living in Brussels in 1646 and subsequently married as his second wife a Flemish lady. See Bedingfield Papers, Genealogical Supplement in *Miscellanea VI*, CRS 6 (London: CRS, 1909). I am indebted to Katharine Keats-Rohan for this reference.

This Summer the french gaining much upon the country,[1] caused great losses to many of our Benefactors, and they **[p. 48]** became unable to continue their Almnes to us. Amongst others our great benefactor Mr George Keneb about this time began also to fail us; this year we had but half the Almnes he used yearly to bestow upon us; and that he gave for his last Almnes till better times, for all his lands were destroy'd by the French. This together with the failing of our rents from Lovain made it go hard with us this year; yet thro' the providence of God we had very little debt at the end of the year, and some smal surplus remain'd after the reckoning which was laid up with the rest in the Ark. Our Reverende Mother kept this money with intention to build, and in the mean time had made some profit of it to the value of 200 florins.

The year 1649

In the month of April our Reverende Mother's uncle Mr Mathew Bedingfeld came again to Bridges about our building, and with the consent of our most Reverend Lord Bishop, we resolved upon building of one hundred foot in length, and thirty foot in breath. In this was build our kitchen, Refectory and Workchamber and under the kitchen and Refectory a vaulted cellar **[p. 49]** of forty foot in length. Above, there was nineteen Cells, and on the side of the building towards the old house was the cloister made like a hanging Pant of equal length with the building.[2] They began to dig the foundation on the feast of our holy Father's conversion the fifth of May. The Platform having been drawn by the Master workman the day before our holy Mother Ste Monica's day.[3] Mr George Arts, a Magistrate of Bridges, charitably undertook to be our Architect, and to oversee the work; and he made the agreements with the workmen, and wholy order'd the work, which was a great help to us.[4]

---

1 A late episode of the Thirty Years War: the French Prince de Condé invaded the South of Flanders in the summer of 1648, taking Ypres and Courtrai. He finally defeated the Spanish troops at the battle of Lens (20 August 1648). This defeat obliged Spain to accept the Peace of Westphalia.

2 Pant: see Glossary.

3 Saint Monica's day was celebrated on 4 May. At this time the feast of the conversion of St Augustine was celebrated at Bruges on 5 May. The date was later changed to 24 April, the date of his baptism in 387. I am indebted to the Community at Bruges for confirming these dates.

4 George Arts (Aerts) was Echevin of Bruges and is mentioned as Churchwarden of Our Lady Church in Bruges in *Description historique de l'église collégiale et paroissiale de Notre Dame à Bruges* (Bruges, 1773), p. 163. His family had been patricians of Bruges since the fifteenth century. Georges Aerts was an alderman of Bruges in 1646, 1648 and 1652 and treasurer in 1649 and 1650. He was Provost of the Confraternity of the Holy Blood in 1656. See F. Van Dycke, *Recueil héraldique* (Bruges, 1851), pp. 5–6. He had received an episcopal authorisation (17 August 1648 and 17 February 1649), to enter the convent to inspect the church. Diocesan Archives, Bruges, 'Acta episcoporum brugensium', B 24bis: fols 127v and 146v. I am grateful to Paul Arblaster and Pascal Majérus for these references.

On the 14th of May it being on a friday the first stone was laid having been bless'd on a Solemn manner, as the first foundation stone of the Monastry: several of the Magistrates and Chief officers of the town being present, and diverse also of the clergie: But our most Reverend Lord Bishop being at that time very ill, could not come to lay the first stone, as he desired and had intended; wherefore the Arch priest did it for him, and laid the first stone, which was bless'd in the name of our holy father St Augustine and his image engraved thereon.[1]

[p. 50] There was also prepared four more stones one for the Abbot of the canon regulars of Eekhout,[2] which had the Abbotts Arms engraved on it, one with the image of St Nicholas for the Abbot of St Andrews of St Benedict's order,[3] one with the image of our holy mother Ste Monica, which was laid by Monsieur St George, General Preston's son and the fourth which was of St Thomas of Cantorbury, was laid by our great benefactor Mr George Kenebb, whom we have mentioned before. We had given us in Almnes by those who were invited to this ceremony, about 300 florins. The enclosure of our Monastery was now broken and so remain'd till the end of our building.

On the 15th of June two of Sir John Webb's daughters, Mrs Frances and Mrs Anne, were received for convictresses.[4]

On the 12th of July, Mrs Frances took the Schollars habit.

On the 13th of July two of Mr John Caryll's daughters Mrs Frances and Mrs Barbara, were received for convictresses.[5]

On the 21 of July Mrs Martha Williscott with her sister Mrs Jane **[p. 51]** were received Schollars for the order.[6]

On the 16th of August, Mrs Elisabeth Brooke daughter to Sir Basil Brooke, was received here for convictress.[7]

In the month of September this year our most Reverend Lord Bishop Nicholas de Haudion, eighth Bishop of Bridges, departed this life whose name is of worthy memory in this our convent of Nazareth, by the reformation he made of our Statutes.[8] *Requiescat in pace*. Amen.

---

1 The Archpriest was Barthelemy de Cridts.

2 The Flemish Augustinian Canons of Eeckhoute in Bruges, like the Canonesses at Nazareth, were also part of the Windesheim tradition. See N. Huygebaert, 'Abbaye de Saint-Trond à Odegem, Bruges et Male' in *Monasticon belge*, vol. 4:4, pp. 1028–31.

3 N. Huygebaert, 'Abbaye de Saint-André à Bruges' in *Monasticon belge*, vol. 3:1, pp. 86–129.

4 Sir John Webb[e] of Odstock, Wilts, and Canford, Dorset. His daughters were Frances Webb, in religion Augustina (1651–70) BA211, and Anne Webb, who later joined the Sepulchrines in Liège, professing in 1656, LS238.

5 John Caryll of Harting, Sussex, was the father of Barbara Joseph Caryll (1656–83) BA045, Sub–Prioress 1679–83, and Frances Caryll (1654) BA046. They were cousins through marriage of Frances and Anne Webb: see the Webb family tree in WWTN.

6 Martha Wollascott (1651–93) BA224, and her sister Jane Wollascott, in religion Mary Magdalena (1652–65) BA223.

7 Elizabeth Brooke, in religion Gertrude (1660–92) BA034.

8 Bishop Haudion died on 24 September 1649.

On the 24 of December Mrs Abigaul Bentol was received here Schollar for the order.

We had this year given us by his highness Leopoldus our Archduke 480 florins, an Almnes for our building.[1] Mr Peter Gifford sent us 200 florins Reverend Mr Zeepe secretary to our deceased Bishop having some money that belong'd to the Bishop to dispose of in Almnes, bestow'd it on us for our building. And from several others we had Almnes for building, about 346 florins.

The year 1650

In February Sister Grace Eddows was clothed for a sister, in our chapter house.[2]

[p. 52] On St Joseph's day the 19 of March, we first began to eat in our new Refectory, and to use our new building. The [*blank*] of March the new work chamber, our Chapel, where we had Mass, and also read and sung our office there till the Quire and church were finished.

On the 16 of May, Sister Frances Webb and Sister Martha Williscott were clothed there.

On the 19 of May Sister Catherine Bowes returned home from Lovain, that convent would not keep her any longer, she having been altogether as troublesome and unquiet there, as she had been here.[3] This is noted that it may be a warning not to send out unquiet spirits to other monasteries, but rather with patience and prudence to keep them in subjection at home: for such as are unquiet in their own cloister are seldom amended by changing place. Her infirmity seeming to be a defect of reason is both troublesome to herself and a continual exercise of patience and charity to those that live with her.

At the same time Elisabeth Bartlett came from Bruxelles, where she had been bred up some years, and perfected in the flemish language.[4] She being sister to **[p. 53]** our Sister Catherine Bartlett,[5] was at her own earnest request admitted into the cloister, yet only as a servant to serve the convictresses, for she had no mind to a religious life, but only for a while to live in a cloister.

On the first of August Mrs Elisabeth Webb[6] Sister to Sister Francis Webb, came hither as a convictress; with her came two others Mrs Mary

---

1 Archduke Leopold Wilhelm of Austria (1614–62) was Governor of the Spanish Netherlands from 1647 to 1656.

2 Grace Eddows (BA075).

3 Catherine Bowes (BA029) had been sent to Louvain in 1645; see above **[p. 41]**.

4 Elizabeth Bartlett, lay sister (1653–91) BA014.

5 Catherine Bartlett (1646–83) BA008.

6 Elizabeth Webb, in religion Winefrid (1652–96) BA212, Procuratrix.

Bruning and her sister Mrs Catherine:[1] also Mrs Mary Wyett who was received a servant in order to be a lay sister.[2]

On our holy Father St Augustin's feast day, our Reverend Dean Carolus de Bosch, who was elected Bishop of Bridges, honour'd us with singing Mass in our new church.[3] This was the first Mass in that church, we had sung Evening song in the Quire on the Eve, and after this our Mass and office was daily sung and read here.

In September Mrs Elisabeth Webb received the Schollars habit for the order at her own earnest request.

In October the 20th of that month, Mr Henri Bedingfeld arrived here, he brought with him our Reverende Mother's niece Sister Mary Bedingfeld,[4] of whom we have made mention; and also his wife's niece Mrs Elisabeth **[p. 54]** Monsey, who was received Schollar for the order.[5] Sister Mary Bedingfeld having now been constant in her vocation three years, and all that time lived with her Mother, thought she had sufficiently shew'd her duty to her; and not being able to obtain her consent to return as yet to religion (for her mother would have her stay in the world till she was twenty one) she without her Mother's knowledge fled from the world finding it dangerous for her, she being now grown tall and handsome. She stole out of her Mother's house at midnight, with only the cloths on her back, and left a letter on her table to secure her Mother from fears by informing her that she was well and gone away to religion. She fled alone with out the assistance of any till she had pass'd the house; then in a lane by her appointment, an honest man waited for her with a horse, on which she mounted behind him, and rid that night fourteen miles to a poor house where she lay conceal'd till she had an opportunity to go to the sea side; there she met Mr Henry Bedingfield who was coming over; and he at his own charges brought her hither to our monastry; where she was most joyfully welcomed by **[p. 55]** all and received Schollar again for the order, and her place was given her as eldest Schollar, she having been in that habit before.

---

[1] Mary Bruning (BA037) was clothed 20 April 1655 and left in January 1656, being dismissed at her own request. Sisters Anne Catherine (OB015) and Catherine Mary Bruning (OB018) professed at the English Benedictine convent, Pontoise, in 1662 and 1658 respectively. They were daughters of Anthony Bruning of Wymering, Hampshire, and Mary Hyde of Pangbourne, Berkshire.

[2] Mary Wyatt, lay sister (1653–84) BA 229.

[3] Karel van den Bosch (1597–1665), Bishop of Bruges 1651–60. The feast of St Augustine was celebrated on 28 August.

[4] Henry Bedingfield; the identity of Mr Bedingfield is not entirely clear here. Mary Bedingfield (BA019): see above **[pp. 46–7]**.

[5] Elizabeth Momsey, in religion Alloysia (1652–91) BA142. Her mother was Frances Wyborne and her father Anthony Momsey: see WWTN.

On the first of December Mrs Dorothy Rows and her sister Mrs Mary Rows,[1] together with their two cousines Mrs Margarite and Mrs Mary Barker,[2] were received Schollars for the order.

We had this year but smal Almnes and great debts by our building wherefore by the help of Mr Arts then Treasurer of Bridges,[3] we presented a request to the Magistrates of the Town for leave to make a common gathering which was favorably granted us: yet for some reasons it was defer'd a while.

The year 1651

On the first of February Mr Arts the Treasurer with eight more of the officers of the Town and free,[4] went round the Town to gather Almnes for us, which they continued four days; in which collection of Almnes we had 570 florins.

The Sunday following we had a Solemn Mass in musick sung in our church **[p. 56]** in gratitude for that charity; and most of these officers were present.

On the 13 of April Sister Mary Bedingfeld, Sister Jane Williscott, Sister Elisabeth Webb, and Sister Elisabeth Monsey were clothed.[5]

The next day, Sister Grace Eddows was profess'd a lay sister.

On the 24 of April, Mr Nicholas Bedingfeld, son to Mr Mathew Bedingfeld, dyed here very piously; having lived some months in our father's house.[6] He lyes bury'd in the vault in our church, which was bless'd for buryal first for him. When his body was laid there, the bones also of our Reverende Mother Poole [d. 1640], and our old Subprioress Sister Anne Tremaine [d. 1637], as also Sister Mary Atwood [d. 1640], Sister Dorothy Chetwin [d. 1646], and Sister Elisabeth Brereton [d. 1646], were taken up out of the church yard, and laid in the vault in our church, where hereafter all our religious are to be bury'd.[7]

---

1 Dorothy Rows, in religion Clare (1654–83) BA166; Mary Rows, in religion Mary Ignatia (1654–83) BA167.

2 Margaret Barker, in religion Agnes (1656–91) BA012; Mary Barker (1656–82) BA013.

3 On Mr Arts, see also **[p. 49]**.

4 Brugse Vrije: see the explanation on **[p. 33]**.

5 Mary Bedingfield (BA019); Jane Wollascott, in religion Mary Magdalena (BA223); Elizabeth Webb, in religion Winefrid (BA212); Elizabeth Momsey, in religion Alloysia (BA142).

6 See above **[p. 47]**. Matthew Bedingfield was a patron and benefactor of the community and in return was able to recommend members of the family to the community.

7 In 1637 a plot of ground in the convent was blessed and became the burial ground. The nuns mentioned above had been buried in this graveyard, but it was decided it would be more fitting to re-inter them in the newly created vaults under the church.

On the 28 of April being the feast of St Vitalis martyr,[1] we escaped a great danger of fire, which by mischance had begun to take in an old room of our house, but by God's holy providence was found out in time and quench'd. In gratitude for this **[p. 57]** preservation, and to beg the protection of the ever immaculate virgin Mary to preserve our house from fire in the future, our Reverende Mother ordain'd that on all Saturdays when we keep commemoration of our Blessed Lady, we should sing Mass in her honour, as it had been an ancient custome in our cloister at Ste Monica at Lovain.

On the 18 of May Sister Frances Webb taking the name of Augustina, together with Sister Martha Williscott, made their holy profession: it being then ascension day.[2] Also on the same day Elisabeth Bartlett received the kerchief of Schollar for a lay sister.[3]

On the 23 of July, our most Reverend Lord Carolus de Bosch was consecrated the ninth Bishop of Bridges.[4]

On the 24 of July, Mrs. Penelope Simons was received here convictress.[5]

This year Mr Arts, Treasurer obtain'd for us an Almnes of the Burgo-mester and Magistrates of Bridges 150 florins for a window in our church, wherein the Arms of the town are painted for a memory of this charity. Also the Burgo-mester of the Free[6] gave us an **[p. 58]** Almnes of 90 florins for a window in our church whereing the Arms of the Free are also painted in memory of their charity.

This year in September we built our Brewhouse and made the cistern for rainwater, both very necessary, tho' very chargeable, by this our debts encreased, but we put our confidence in the divine providence.

The 25 of November, Sister Josepha Bentall, Sister Dorothy Rows with her sister Sister Mary Rows, Sister Margarite Barker with her sister Sister Mary Barker, were all clothed.

On the 27 of November, Sister Mary Wyett was clothed for a lay sister.[7]

At the end of this year we had but few debts, except those of our building, we having as formerly been assisted with some Almnes.

---

1 St Vitalis of Milan, martyred in the third century; 28 April marks the dedication of his church in Rome.

2 Ascension Day commemorates the day that Christ ascended into heaven. It is a moveable feast depending on the date of Easter. Frances Webb, in religion Augustina (BA211); and Martha Wollascott (BA224).

3 Elizabeth Bartlett (BA014). A kerchief was worn by postulants for six months before being clothed.

4 Karel van den Bosch (1597–1665), Bishop of Bruges 1650–60.

5 Penelope Simons, in religion Ignatia (1656–1717) BA175.

6 Burgomaster of Brugse Vrije: see the explanation on **[p. 33]**.

7 Mary Wyatt (1653–84) BA229.

The year 1652

On the ninth of January, five Dames of the English Cloister of the holy order of St Benedict, with a lay sister, passing by Bridges in their journey to their new foundation at Bologne in france, with our Lord Bishop's leave, were entertain'd in our monastery, lodged in our Dormitory and eat in our Refectory, staying **[p. 59]** with us one day.[1]

This year in the lent we had many sick. Our Reverende Mother and two or three Elders, some youngers and novices, and some convictresses, in all to the number of 14, they almost all fell sick together of the Measels, and some not without danger, yet thro' the goodness of God all recover'd, and at Easter the infection ceased.

In April my Lord Bishop coming to our cloister, confirm'd, in our Quire, all our novices and convictresses.

On the 23 of April St George's day, Sister Mary Bedingfeld made her holy profession, her mother having by letter consented to it; but she would not give her portion, nor promise any maintenance. Nevertheless our convent was very desirous to profess her; and my Lord Bishop made difficulty by reason of our poverty, yet at last he consented finding the whole convent requested it.[2] On the same day with her were also profess'd Sister Magdalene Williscott, Sister Wenefride Webb and Sister Elisabeth Aloysia Monsey, who the year before had been clothed with her, and had now changed their names in confirmation.[3]

On the 29 of April Sister Elisabeth Bartlett **[p. 60]** was clothed for a lay sister.[4]

On the ninth of June we were honour'd with a great Solemnity in our church, the consecration of an Abbot of our order. This Prelate belong'd to a convent of Canon Regulars near Ypres, and there being no Bishop then at Ypres, he came to Bridges to be consecrated by our Bishop who perform'd the Solemnity in our church with a Solemn Mass in musick, and several of the chief of the clergie and town were present.

In July we began our speakhouse, and the rooms adjoining to it; but this building was not finish'd this year.[5]

At the end of the year we were not much in debt, except that of our building, we having been assisted with some Almnes as in the past late years.

---

1 [1] For an account of this episode, see English Benedictine Nuns in Flanders, 1598–1687. Annals of Their Five Communities, wwtn.history.qmul.ac.uk/publications-static/pdfs/Annalsof5communitiesJan09.pdf, pp. 37–8, accessed 3 November 2015; and 'The Foundation of Bullogne Written by My Lady Mary Knatchbull' in English Convents, vol. 5, pp. 243–55.

2 Diocesan Archives, Bruges, 'Acta episcoporum brugensium', B 25, fol. 117r.

3 See above **[p. 56]**.

4 Elizabeth Bartlett (BA014). Lay sisters were expected to bring only small portions with them on profession, especially if they brought skills that were valuable to the convent.

5 Speakhouse: see Glossary.

All our novices who were clothed in November the last year had their professions deferr'd because their portions were not pay'd.

The year 1653

On the second of february Candlemass day, Sister Mary Wyett was profess'd a lay sister.[1]

In Lent this year we began to keep enclosure again, our building being **[p. 61]** almost quite finish'd.

On the fifth of May Sister Elisabeth Bartlett was profess'd a lay sister.

On the second of July Mrs Magdalene Kemp was received for convictress.[2]

On the third of July Mrs Ann' Barlow was received convictress.[3]

On the ninth of August two Dames of Gant Monastery of the holy order of St Benedict, passing by Bridges to Bolognia,[4] were with leave of our most Reverend Lord Bishop lodged within our enclosure, and stay'd here a day, supping with us in our Refectory on St Laurence's day[.] from that time forward our enclosure remain'd very strict as formerly before our building.[5]

On the 12 of September little Anne Joscett a child of three years old, was buryed in our vault.

In october my Lady Sands had also a little daughter of hers bury'd there, which was but 3 years old.

On the fifth of November little Anne Smith was received for convictress.[6]

We also ended this year with few debts, assisted by Almnes as before. Our five novices were still kept back **[p. 62]** because their portion was not paid.

The year 1654

About the end of January this year Mrs Josepha Bentall one of our five novices, was forced to go for England for want of her portion; she

---

1 Mary Wyatt (BA229).

2 Magdalen Kemp, in religion Mary Magdalen (1656–87) BA125.

3 Ann Barlow arrived as a scholar at the Poor Clares of Rouen in 1651, but after two years was sent to Bruges 'in hopes she wou'd have been a religious there'. She left and was married, but 'lived a sad life, yet dy'd happily' See 'Rouen Chronicle' in *English Convents*, vol. 1, p. 87.

4 See the reference to the account of the foundation of the Benedictine convent at Boulogne in English Benedictine Nuns in Flanders, 1598–1687, as for **[pp. 58–9]** above: 'His lordship demaunded tow more to make theyr number more compleate and then Dame Lucy Perkins and Dame Francisca Carrington was sent to them'.

5 The feast of St Lawrence is celebrated on 10 August.

6 Ann Smith (1661–99) BA176, Novice Mistress; Procuratrix from 1693.

went by her own desire, but with resolution to return if she could get her portion.[1]

On the 12 of March Mrs Frances Caryll dyed here, who had been about four years convictress with us.[2] She was about sixteen years of age, a most sweet innocent soul, and she had a great desire to be religious here. In her sickness she earnestly desired the Schollars habit, and took great delight in it. Three days before her death she conditionally made the holy vows of religion and we buryd her in our habit in the vault in our church. *Requiescat in pace*. Amen.

About the beginning of April Mrs Lucy Hamilton,[3] and Mrs Barbara Caryll received the Schollars habit, having been long convictresses.[4]

On the 23 of April Sister Dorothy Rows taking the name of Clare, and Sister Mary Rows the name of Mary Ignatia **[p. 63]** made their holy profession.[5]

About this time our Reverende Mother Prioress, Sister Augustina Bedingfeld, having been long infirm, subject to a Palsie, and other cold infirmities, was counsel'd by Doctors and other friends to go to the Bathes of aquisgraine.[6] Her uncle Mr Mathew Bedingfeld judging her life and health yet necessary for this our community, sent one to Bridges to treat with our Bishop about it, who understanding the Doctors opinion, and thinking it necessary to endeavour the preservation of her life, gave order she should make that journey, taking with her two other religious Sister Mary Gifford, our Procuratress, and Sister Mary Bedingfeld. There went also in her company two Scollars, Sister Lucy Hamilton, and Sister Barbara Caryll, the Doctor having order'd Mrs Barbara Caryll to go to the Bath for the recovery of her health, which she had lost thro' grief for the death of her father. Sister Catherine Bartlett a lay sister, went also that journey to serve her.

Mrs Ann' Webb a convictress also went with them, in order to settle **[p. 64]** in the English Cloister at Liege; because she could not be admitted

---

1 Josepha Bentall had been clothed on 25 November 1651. She never returned.

2 Frances Caryll (BA046) professed on her deathbed on 9 March 1654 and died three days later.

3 Lucy Hamilton, in religion Laurentia (BA095), was the daughter of Elizabeth Hamilton née Bedingfield, herself a member of the Bruges community (BA094).

4 Barbara Caryll, in religion Barbara Joseph (BA045); she was sister to Frances Caryll.

5 Dorothy Rows, in religion Clare (BA166) and Mary Rows, in religion Mary Ignatia (BA167).

6 The Baths of Aix-la-Chapelle (Aachen or Aquisgraine). Known for its hot springs since the Roman times, Aachen had become popular again as a spa by the middle of the seventeenth century.

here, having two sisters already profess'd, and my Lord Bishop would not permit three sisters in one house.[1]

On the first of May they began their journey, and our Reverend father went as far as Gandt with them. Our Reverende Mother with her religious lodged in the English Monastry and the next morning they began their journey for Bruxelles, and our confessor return'd home.[2]

They all lodged at Bruxelles in Mr Matthew Bedingfeld's house,[3] uncle to our Reverende Mother, he together with her cousin Mr Henry Bedingfeld undertook the greatest part of the charges of this journey. They having stay'd three days there, went on towards Aquisgraine, Mr Henry Bedingfeld being their guide, and they arrived there on the ninth of May.

After almost a whole months stay there our Reverende Mother in that time taking Phisick and the bath 33 times with very good effects for the desired recovery of her health, they left Aquisgraine upon the sixth of June, and return'd by Liege, where they were most cordially entertain'd in **[p. 65]** the English cloister of Sepulcherians, and there they stay'd three days.[4] From thence they return'd to Bruxelles lodging again at Mr Matthew Bedingfeld's house. After two days they went all to Lovain, the Reverende Mother Magdalene Throckmorton having sent their confessor Mr. Johnson, to meet them.[5] They were most kindly entertain'd at our Monastry of Ste Monica and stay'd there a whole fortnight in which time our father confessor[6] went from hence to meet our Reverende Mother there. Sister Frances Reding went with him having had our Reverende Mother's leave to go thither to see her sister.[7]

This year in May when our Reverende Mother was absent, great part of the town of Gravelin having been blown up with Gunpowder, and the Monastry of English poor Clares much endamaged;[8] the religious were

---

1 Anne Webb joined the Canonesses of the Holy Sepulchre as Anne of St Monica (1656–1711). She entered Liège on 29 July 1654 (LS238). Her two sisters were Frances Webb, in religion Augustina (BA211), and Elizabeth Webb, in religion Winefrid (BA212). It was thought that having several members of the same family in the community might lead to the formation of cliques and hinder the smooth running of the convent. For a discussion of the question, see **[p. 216]** below.

2 The English monastery at Ghent was a Benedictine house, headed by Mary Knatchbull (1628–96) GB118, Abbess 1650–96. See *ODNB*.

3 Matthew Bedingfield had lived in Brussels since 1646.

4 Sepulchrines: Canonesses of the Holy Sepulchre at Liège.

5 The Prioress at St Monica's, Louvain 1633–52 was Margaret Throckmorton, in religion Magdalen (LA267). Fr Richard Johnson was chaplain 1652–87; see Anstruther 2, p. 349.

6 The Father Confessor at Bruges 1630–54 was Fr James Blundeville alias Bord (1603–58). See Anstruther 2, p. 31, and above **[p. 6]**.

7 Frances Redding was Frances Reading (BA160); her sister was Mary Redding (1629–63) LA212.

8 The town of Gravelines was captured several times by French and Spanish armies between 1639 and 1658. In 1654, while under Spanish rule, most of the city was destroyed by the explosion of the gunpowder magazine. It was finally annexed to France in the Treaty of the Pyrenees of 1659. See the account in *English Convents*, vol. 3, pp. 313–17.

forced to disperse themselves, and eleven of them were sent to Gant, who passing by Bridges were entertain'd in our cloister, and lodged in our Dormitory; they stay'd here but one day.

On the 27 of June in our Reverende Mother's absence also, Sister Ann' Crafts dyed here, having been a long time very infirm.[1] **[p. 66]** She had been profess'd a lay sister, as tis said before, in the year 1631, and had been very laborious in the service of the cloister. She had a violent nature which made her often troublesome both to herself and to others for several years; yet she had a good will, and God did reward her endeavours in the overcoming herself and breaking her nature, by giving her much patience in supporting great paines and infirmities some years, and at last with a quiet and peaceable end.

From Lovain they went all with our father confessor to our Blessed Lady of Sicham,[2] and return'd the next day. After a few days stay at Lovain, they went towards Bruxelles by Grunendall Monastry, to which the Reverend Prior father Peter Paris, had invited our Reverende Mother, and there for two days he most kindly entertain'd them all.[3] From thence they went to Bruxelles, and having stay'd there three days at Mr Bedingfeld's, they went all to Antwerp, where Mr James Thomson, an English Marchant, most kindly entertain'd them all.[4] Early the next morning they went all to **[p. 67]** Liere. The Prioress of the English Theresians there, Reverende Mother Downs,[5] our Reverende Mother's near kinswoman, having provided a wagon and sent their confessarius Mr Bedingfeld to Antwerp for them.[6] Our Reverende Mother and the two nuns were entertain'd in the enclosure, Father confessor and the rest of the company with their father, all most cordially for two days. Reverend Mr Bedingfeld, our Reverende Mother's kinsman, conducted them back to Antwerp without any charge to them, the Prioress of Liere discharging all. They lodged again at Mr Thomson's, and the next morning departed for Gant, where they were all entertain'd in the English Monastry by my Lady Mary Knatchbull, Abbess; and our confessarius in their father's house.

---

1 Anne Crafts (1631–54) BA068.

2 Montaigu (Scherpenheuvel in Dutch) is part of the borough of Zichem, Brabant. The baroque church, built by Wenceslas Cobergher between 1609 and 1624, was the site of a major pilgrimage to Our Lady.

3 Groenendaal, near Brussels, was a house of Augustinian canons founded c. 1343. See E. Persoons, 'Prieuré de Groenendael, à Hoeilaart' in *Monasticon belge*, vol. 4, pp. 1067–87. Fr Peter Paris was Prior of Groenendaal 1637–56.

4 James Thomson was a cloth merchant. See P. Arblaster, *Antwerp and the World: Richard Verstegan and the International Culture of Catholic Reformation* (Leuven: Leuven University Press, 2004), pp. 98–9.

5 Margaret Downes, in religion Margaret of St Teresa (1624–82) AC040. She left Antwerp in 1648 to help found another Carmel in Lierre, becoming its first Prioress 1648–55. She was a cousin of Mother Augustina Bedingfield.

6 Fr Edmund Bedingfield, a Canon of Lierre (1625–80), was the son of Henry Bedingfield and his second wife, Elizabeth Houghton. See Anstruther 2, pp. 20–1.

Our Reverende Mother the next day, sent the two lay sister[s] home to Bridges; but all the rest stay'd their [*sic*] three days, and in that time there was solemnised a clothing and a Profession.[1] On the 15 of July they all return'd home to Bridges; Mr d'Ognate[2] did our Reverende Mother the honour to **[p. 68]** send the Barge of the free, in which they came home to Bridges: and our Reverende Mother that evening having visited some cloisters in the town, was joyfully Welcomed home by us, singing *Te Deum* in thanksgiving for her safe return.

On the 17 of July Mrs Margrite Sulyard was received convictress here.[3]

On the eve of our Lady's Assumption, Sister Mary Bruning, Sister Ignatia Simons and Sister Mary Magdalene Kemp, who had been convictresses, as tis said before, received the habit of Schollars for the order.[4]

We ended this year with few debts having been assisted with some smal Almnes.

The year 1655

On the 15 of January, when we now began again to Solemnise the first of the most glorious name of Jesus, Sister Mary Altham[5] our Subprioress having been several years very infirm, neither able to sing nor read with the Quire, yet hitherto kept in that office, by dispensation from my Lord Bishop, now by his orders and her own desire, she **[p. 69]** resigned it; and on this day Sister Grace Constable was by the convent chosen Subprioress, who was before Arcaria, and Mistress of the novices and youngers.[6]

The same day Sister Mary Bedingfeld was by the council sisters chosen Mistress of novices.[7] She being young in profession, our Reverende Mother thought it not convenient to put any of the youngers under her, but with dispensation from the Bishop, took all the young profess'd to her self, and left under the new Subprioress, Sister Margrite and Sister Mary Barker who were novices. Only the Schollars for the order were put under the new Mistress.[8]

---

[1] On 12 July, the clothing took place of Mary Fermor (1655–1711) GB064, and the next day the profession of Catherine Petre (1654–72) GB177.

[2] Marc Albert Arrazola de Oñate (Brussels 1612–Bruges 1674), a member of a Spanish aristocratic family, was Lieutenant-General of the Falconers of Flanders in 1645 and Burgemeester of the Brugse Vrije 1649–59. He was buried at the English Franciscan convent at Prinsenhof, Bruges.

[3] Margaret Sulyard, in religion Alexia (1658–99) BA187.

[4] Eve of the Assumption of Our Lady, 14 August.

[5] Mary Altham (1616 Louvain–1661 Bruges) LA004.

[6] Grace Constable (1625 Louvain–1673 Bruges) LA069.

[7] Mary Bedingfield (1652–93) BA019. This was an unusual appointment for one so newly professed, perhaps explaining the complex arrangements being put into place here.

[8] The Scholars for the Order mentioned here are the postulants: i.e. those who are probationers before being accepted by the community to become novices.

The next day our convent elected a new Arcaria, Sister Mary Gifford, who had long been Procuratress, and now grown very infirm, our convent willing to release her, chose her Arcaria: so as soon as she had made up her reckning, which was in february, she resigned her Procuratressship; and Sister Ursula Palmes was by our convent chosen Procuratress.[1]

On the 24 of January, Sister Lucy **[p. 70]** Hamilton, and Sister Barbara Caryll were clothed.[2]

Mrs Ann' Barlow was in this month sent into England home to her friends.[3]

On the 20 of April Sister Mary Bruning, Sister Imelda Simons, and Sister Magdalene Kemp, were clothed.[4]

In May the aforesaid religious poor Clares, returning from Gant towards Gravelin, were again intertain'd here, in our Cloister, and lodged in our Dormitory: they stay'd but one day.[5]

In the same month, Mrs Mary Heton was sent hither from Antwerp, having been novice there in the English Cloister of Theresians.[6] She having remained some weeks in our father's house, after her own and her friends earnest importunity, with dispensation from my Lord Bishop, requested by our council sisters, was received here Schollar for the order on the 12 of June.

On the 16 of August, Mrs Mary Wright was received here Schollar for the order.[7]

On the feast of our Lady's presentation Mrs Elisabeth Brooke received **[p. 71]** the Schollars habit.[8]

In November Mrs Catherine Bruning return'd home to her friends in England.[9]

---

1 Mary Gifford (1625 Louvain–1675 Bruges) LA107 had been Procuratrix since 1642; Ursula Palmes (BA149).

2 Lucy Hamilton, in religion Laurentia (BA095); Barbara Caryll, in religion Barbara Joseph (BA045).

3 Ann Barlow first arrived at the convent in July 1653; see **[p. 61]**.

4 Mary Bruning (BA037) arrived with her sister (see **[pp. 53, 68]**); both withdrew before profession. This is possibly the Mary Bruning who in 1658 professed at Pontoise as Mary (OB017). Dating evidence in the Chronicle suggests that Imelda refers to Penelope Simons, in religion Ignatia (BA175), who professed the following year; Magdalen Kemp, in religion Mary Magdalen (BA125).

5 The Poor Clares, who had dispersed following the gunpowder explosion at Gravelines in 1654, were able to return home; see **[p. 65]**.

6 Mary Heton (1657–1713) BA102, Sub-Prioress 1699–1710.

7 Frances Wright, in religion Mary (1657–1709) BA228, Novice Mistress; Sub-Prioress 1683–93; Prioress 1693–1709.

8 Elizabeth Brooke, in religion Gertrude (BA034). The feast of Our Lady's presentation (21 November) marked the occasion when Mary, as a child, was presented by her parents in the Temple.

9 Catherine Bruning had arrived in the convent in 1650 (see **[p. 53]**) and was the first of the Bruning sisters to leave.

On the 23 of November, St. Clement's day, our Reverend father confessor kept his half Jubilee of confessarius here, with a Solemne Mass and *Te Deum* sung, the Arch Priest being present.[1]

We ended this year also with some little debts having as formerly been assisted with some smal Almnes.

The year 1656

In January Sister Mary Bruning having been almost nine months, unconstant in her resolution, and pretending want of health, at her own request was dismiss'd. Our Reverende Mother took off the holy habit privately in her chamber, that in presence of the convent sisters who had consented to her clothing.[2] She was then left there to put her soecular clothes her self, and so put out into the father's house where the next day she was examin'd by the Archpriest of the reasons why she left the habit.[3]

[p. 72] This was done upon our Reverende Mother's request who fear'd she having been so long a convictress in our cloister that her friends might believe she had been persuaded to take the habit since she thus changed her mind. But she gave it under her hand to the Archpriest that she had never been persuaded, but took it of her own accord and so left it again, here is to be noted, that when the Archpriest acquainted my Lord Bishop how he had thus examin'd her, he did not approve of it, but wish'd the novice had freely been sent away with out any examin.

This novice's disposition was not fit for religion, and we may esteem it an especial providence of God for the good of our cloister, that she took this resolution of her self; for it is probable our Convent would not have consented to her Profession.

On Candlemass day Mrs Margarite Sulyard received the Schollars habit.[4]

On the 14 of February St Valentine's day, Sister Lucy Laurentia Hamilton and Sister Barbara Josepha Caryll made their holy Profession.[5]

On the 23 of April, St Georges day **[p. 73]** Sister Margarite Ba[r]ker, Sister Mary Barker, Sister Ignatia Simons and Sister Magdalene Kemp made their holy Profession.[6]

---

1 The Confessor was Fr James Blundeville (d. 1658), appointed in 1630. Although the Chronicle always refers to him as Bloomfield, he is more correctly recorded at Blundeville; see **[p. 6]** and Anstruther 2, p. 31.

2 The manner of Mary Bruning's departure was carefully managed by the Prioress and a representative of the Visitor in order to avoid scandal and reputational damage, while at the same time recognising the importance of maintaining communal harmony by permitting candidates who did not wish to remain in the community to leave.

3 The Archpriest was representing the Visitor at the examination of the candidate.

4 Candlemas is celebrated on 2 February. Margaret Sulyard, in religion Alexia (BA187).

5 Lucy Hamilton, in religion Laurentia (BA095); Barbara Joseph Caryll (BA045).

6 Margaret Barker, in religion Agnes (BA012); Mary Barker (BA013); Penelope Simons, in religion Ignatia (BA175); Magdalen Kemp, in religion Mary Magdalen (BA125).

On St Georges Eve Charles the Second King of Great Britany arrived to this town of Bridges, to keep his court.[1]

On the 29 of May, Sister Mary Heton and Sister Mary Wright were clothed.[2]

This Month Dorothy Bernan an English Maid, dying in the town, was bury'd in our vault.

This Summer with the leave of our Most Reverend Lord Bishop, we entertain'd our King in our Refectory with a little colation, for his Majesty, with the Duke of Gloster, and several of his Lords, honour'd us with a visit, and walk'd in our Garden.[3]

The Duke of York also honour'd us this year with a visit, but his highness was only entertain'd at our Grate, not entering the enclosure, that being excused upon expectation of the coming of the Princess his sister, that they might enter together.[4]

This year at the request of some of our friends in the town, we began to **[p. 74]** receive flemish convictresses, and we had seven or eight before the end of the year.

We ended this year also with some little debts, and were as formerly assisted with Almnes.

The year 1657

In January we had the honour to be visited again by our King and his sister the Princess royal, with the Duke of Glocestor who were entertain'd in our Refectory with a smal banket.[5] They had many Lords and Ladies with them: and several press'd in after them, but the Duke of York was then out of Town.[6]

In this month Major Babthorp's Lady being brought to bed in this town and her child dying three days after he was borne, was at her request bury'd in our vault.

---

[1] The exiled Charles II and his court moved to Bruges from Cologne in April 1656. The royal visit in October 1656 to the Schuttershof, home of the Guild of Archers, in Carmerstraat was recorded in a painting by Jan Baptist van Meunincxhove. I am grateful to Sibylla Goegeboer for her advice on this reference.

[2] Mary Heton (BA102); Mary Wright (BA228).

[3] Charles II came with Henry, Duke of Gloucester (1640–60); see *ODNB*. The visits are cautiously treated here. Charles II was conscious of the need to avoid offending potential supporters by favouring Catholic exiles. Although he visited Nazareth twice briefly, he had closer relations with Abbess Knatchbull at Ghent.

[4] James, Duke of York and his sister – probably Mary, the Princess Royal, who did not arrive from France until the end of the year.

[5] The Princess Royal was Mary (1631–60), widow of William II of Orange, who died in 1650. She left Bruges at the end of February to return to Holland; see *ODNB*.

[6] The Duke of York was required by his brother to leave his position with the French army and serve with the Spanish as part of Charles' campaign to recover his throne. W. A. Speck, 'James II and VII (1633–1701)' in *ODNB*.

Also Colonel Whitley whose Lady was sister to my Lord Garrett, had a little daughter of theirs bury'd in our vault, the child being about five weeks old.[1]

Also Colonel Stevens had this year a little child of his bury'd in our Vault.[2]

On the 10 of June Sister Margarite Sulyard was clothed.[3]

[p. 75] On the 11 of June St Barnaby's day, Sister Mary Heton and Sister Mary Wright made their holy Profession.[4]

On the 16 of June Mrs Dorothy Mannock a child of 12 years, came to us from England to be a convictress.[5] We also this year received more convictresses of the town.

We also ended this year with some smal debts, and were assisted with smal almnes as before.

The year 1658

On the 4th of January, our very Reverend dear Father Confessor, father James Blomfield, most happily departed this life,[6] on a friday, about nine a clock in the Morning, at which hour on all fridays, he used on his knees, before his crucifix to read the Passion of our Lord according to St John. He had been above 27 years our Confessor; and our Cloister was most happy in him. He came to us, as we said before, in the year 1630, from the English Colledge at Doway, where his life had been most exemplar in all piety, devotion and innocency. He lived here always most saint like; retired from all conversation with the world; spending **[p. 76]** the greatest part of his time in prayer, except when he was employ'd in what concern'd his charge, as hearing confessions, and assisting the religious: towards whom he had ever a most tender fatherly affection, being most patient and mild, free from all partiality, and most sweet in all his conversation. He was ever most present to himself, united to God in a very perfect recollection, always minding the present, and his usual saying to his children was … Mind the present.

He observed a constant daily practice of vertue in all his exercises, with a continual peace, never disturb'd upon any occasion, but always the same.

---

1 Col. Roger Whitley (c. 1618–97) MP, married Charlotte, sister of Charles, 1st Lord Gerrard. He went into exile with the royalists, returning to England after the Restoration, when he became a gentleman of the Privy Chamber. See P. R. Newman, *Royalist officers in England and Wales: A Biographical Dictionary* (New York: Garland, 1981), p. 409.

2 Colonel Stephens was Col. Sir John Stephens, knighted in 1658. He had Irish connections as a follower of James Butler, who became 1st Duke of Ormond. Like Colonel Whitley, he was in exile with the Royalists. Thurloe noted his presence in Antwerp in 1658. See Geoffrey Smith, *The Cavaliers in Exile* (Basingstoke: Palgrave, 2003).

3 Margaret Sulyard, in religion Alexia (BA187).

4 Mary Heton (BA102); Mary Wright (BA228).

5 Dorothy Mannock, in religion Angela (1662–91) BA134.

6 Fr James Bloomfield alias Blundeville; see above **[p. 6]**.

He fell ill the August before and it pleased God about the same time to exercise him with many interior troubles and bitter desolations for some weeks together: permitting that innocent soul to be afrighted with many representations, and terrified with dreadful judgments of Almighty God in a very extraordinary manner. His infinit goodness, no doubt disposing this for his Purgatory, purifying him by these suffrings to the encrease of his merit, and preparing him **[p. 77]** for his end, which happen'd not long after, tho' he recover'd of that sickness; but his natural strenth was much decay'd, and his shortness of breath encreased, to which infirmity he had been subject many years, and suffer'd much in it; having been all his life very infirm and weak, but ever most patient and resigned to God's holy will. This was most remarkable in him, that in whatever disposition of health he were, or whatever happen'd, he was always chearful and in the same temper. He had a most sweet and peacable death, something sudden indeed, but he was well prepared for it, and in his perfect senses, till he fell into a quiet sleep, in which his happy soul departed without the least motion in any part of his body; and seem'd when he was dead as if he had been in a sweet sleep. He had the extream unction administer'd to him at the very instant of death: but he had communicated in the church on new years day, and heard Mass. His weakness did not permit him to say Mass after St Thomas of Cantorbury's day.[1] On that day he said Mass and communicated the religious. He is bury'd in our Vault **[p. 78]** in a Wainscot Coffin. The Arch Priest perform'd the office of the Funeral. And the Abbott of Eekhoute, and several of the chief of the clergie, were present.[2] His body is bury'd in peace and his memory lives for ever. *Requiescat in pace.*

He has left founded an Annual rent to the cloister, for a perpetual Solemn Anniversary Mass for his soul.

Colonel Witley also this year, had another little daughter bury'd in our Vault, about 3 weeks old.[3]

The sixth of March it being Ash Wednesday,[4] in the Evening by orders from my Lord Bishop, two Lady's, Madame de Vicq and her daughter in law, Madame Theresia Byrhaut upon some disagreements with their husbands, were admitted into our Cloister and lodged in our Convent, to remain there till the end of their Process.[5]

On the 29 of March arrived here Mr Edward Barker, **[p. 79]** a clergie man who by order from Mr Doctor Layborne, President of the English

---

1 The feast of St Thomas of Canterbury is on 29 December.

2 The Abbot of Eeckhoute was Adrien Van Cattenbrouck (1597/8–1664), Abbot 1653–64.

3 For Colonel Whitley, see **[p. 74]**.

4 Ash Wednesday is the start of Lent and a moveable feast depending on the date of Easter.

5 Teresa Lauraine (Byrhaut), in religion Antonia (1662–91) BA127.

College at Doway was call'd out of England to be confessarius here.[1] He had his approbation from my Lord Bishop on the first of April, and was admitted upon tryal confessarius of our cloister.

On the 17 of June Sister Elisabeth Brooke was clothed.[2]

On the 6 of July Sister Margarite Alexia Sulyard made her holy Profession.[3]

On the feast of our Lady's conception the 8 of December Sister Ann' Smith took the Schollars habit.[4]

On the 9 of December Father Edward Barker departed this life after a few days sickness. This Reverend Priest was of Doway colledge, had been both Schollar and Reader there, a man of most exemplar life. He had also lived in England about seven years, where with great zeal he had labour'd in gaining many souls to the true faith. He was invited hither by the President of Doway, as was said before but being of a deep Melancholy humour, he was not fit for this employment. His Melancholy also made him very apprehensive, and his zeal not guided by prudence occasion'd much trouble. The Arch Priest judged him no ways fit for this charge and by our Lord Bishop's **[p. 80]** orders he writ to the President of Doway colledge to remove him. The same President had himself been here at our cloister in October, and found by what he understood here that father Barker was not fit for this employment, yet requested further tryal: promising our Arch Priest that if he found no alteration to the better he would upon notice from him, take care to provide a fitter man. Father Barker was very unwilling to leave this place, and his Melancholy wrought much upon it. As pleased God to permit that one [*sic*] St Andrew's Eve he fell into a great distemper of his head, which he had seem'd much enclined so long before.[5] On St Andrew's day he was furiously mad, and continued so till the Evening before he dyed; then for half an hours space he seem'd to have some understanding and his confessor being by, gave him absolution. The Extream unction he had received the same morning, tho' not in his senses, the Doctor having order'd it finding his strength decay: and the next morning about 3 of the clock being **[p. 81]** Monday the 9 of December, on which day we that year celebrated the feast of our Lady's immaculate conception, he peacefully render'd his soul to God, assisted no doubt by that most Blessed Virgin, his most especial Patroness, unto whom he had ever borne a singular devotion.

---

1 Fr Edward Barker (d. 1658), educated at Douai, ordained 1648; see Anstruther 2, pp. 15–16, where he is incorrectly placed with the English Franciscans at Prinsenhof in Bruges. Dr George Leyburne (1600–77), President of Douai 1652–70; see Anstruther 2, pp. 191–5.

2 Elizabeth Brooke, in religion Gertrude (BA034).

3 Margaret Sulyard, in religion Alexia (BA187).

4 Ann Smith (BA176).

5 St Andrew's Eve was 29 November.

God pleased thus to dispose in his divine providence, calling him doubtless to the reward of his vertuous life, and many labours in his holy service; and preventing hereby many inconveniences, and much unquietness which likely would have been in the cloister, if he either had continued longer here or had heen displaced, as he certainly would have been after a short time more. His happy sould [*sic*] rests in Peace, and his body was bury'd in our vault by the Arch Priest in a very solemn manner, honour'd with the presence of several of the chief of the Clergie of Bridges. *Requiescat in pace.* Amen.

After his death, as also after the death of our Reverend dear father James Blomfield, by the Bishop's order Reverend father Richardus Spyra, a dutch father **[p. 82]** of the society, who spoke English indifferently well heard confessions weekly here.[1] To this Reverend father our cloister has great obligations.

We also this year receiv'd dutch convictresses, and the two Ladies before mention'd still remain'd in our cloister, their Processes not being ended.

The year 1659

On the 2nd of May arrived here Mr William Wall,[2] he went by the name of Marsh and was a Roman Priest, and also had study'd there, and also some time at the Doway Colledge: he was first recommended to us by the Provincial of the English Society, and also by Doctor Layborne, President of Doway Colledge.[3] He was approved by our most Reverend Lord Bishop for confessor here, upon tryal. He was learned, but of a harsh humour: and many difficulties were raised in our cloister, which caused much trouble, and many inconveniences.

On the last of September Mrs Mary Peters arrived here and was received for convictress. She was about 13 years of age.[4]

The two Ladies remained here **[p. 83]** still, their law suits not being ended.[5] The young Lady having a great desire to be religious amongst us, our Reverende Mother at her earnest request proposed it to the convent, being unwilling to admitt her otherways even to the Schollars habit,

---

1 Fr Richard Spyra SJ: Richard Van Spiere (1603–64 Bruges) was ordained at Mechelen. I am grateful to Fr Thomas McCoog for this reference.

2 Fr William Wall alias Marsh entered the English College, Rome 1645, later professed as a Benedictine at Lamspring; see Anstruther 2, pp. 333–4.

3 Dr George Leyburne (1593–1677), President of Douai 1652–70; Anstruther 2, pp. 191–5.

4 Mary Petre (1665–92) BA153.

5 The two ladies were Madame de Vicq and Madame Theresia Byrhaut. See [**p. 78**].

because she was of another nation.[1] The convent being put to votes, all generally consented to admitt her to that tryal, which notwithstanding was deferr'd because her process was not ended.

The year 1660

In January, an agreement being made between the old Madam de Vicq and her husband, and a divorce between them declared by the official of Bridges, this good Lady desiring to end her days peaceably in our cloister, made an accord with us to be maintain'd here all the days of her life; giving us at once the sum of six thousand florins.[2] This, by her, and the consent of our convent, was signed before witnesses, in presence of the notaries on the 13 of January, the octave of the Epiphany. On which day we sung Solemne Mass and *Te Deum* and had recreation and this old Lady had the Summer before clothed her self in a black habit **[p. 84]** like a[s] a Devotaire of St Augustin.

The young Lady, her Daughter in law had her patience try'd still longer, and could not obtain her release so soon.

On the 19 of January Sister Anne Smith was clothed.[3]

In March, the young Lady's case having been sent both to the Doctors of Lovain and Doway, by the sentence of both, but especially that of Doway, she was declared free to enter Religion, and by the Arch Priest's endeavour, the consent of her husband obtain'd; he taking his oath before witnesses that the mariage had never been consummated. The young Lady had also before taken her oath of the same. The official having consented to her entrance into religion; with my Lord Bishop's consent she took the Schollars habit here on St Joseph's day on the 19 of March; and Mrs Agnes Mildmay a young gentlewoman of 19 years of age, who came some few days before to our cloister received that habit with her.[4]

---

1 The community was aware of at least two problems regarding the acceptance of Theresia Byrhaut as a candidate. The first was her Dutch nationality because Nazareth was an English convent by agreement at the foundation. The second was her marital status. Canon law required that the permission of the husband had to be obtained brefore a married woman could enter a convent. In this case, the marriage was annulled by the church courts on the grounds of non-consummation. I am indebted to Fr Luke Becket OSB of Ampleforth for his expert advice on these cases.

2 The separation agreement between Madam de Vicq and her husband was made on the basis of separation mensa et thoro: that is, separation from bed and board. Her case was also different from that of her daughter-in-law, Theresia Byrhaut, because she did not desire to enter the community.

3 Ann Smith (BA176).

4 Agnes Mildmay (1662–91) BA141.

In April our most Reverend Lord Bishop made a visitation here.[1] On the 12 of April his Lordship came and said Mass of the Holy Ghost:[2] after which he call'd for all the Quire **[p. 85]** religious, and laying before them the great importance of an upright proceeding in visitation and commanding secrecy concerning all that should pass in it, he gave us all his benediction, and left the visitation to the Arch Priest; Reverend father Edward Lusher of the Society being interpretor.[3] In two days the visitation was ended. After which my Lord Bishop finding by what had been declared in it, that many difficulties were in the community, and danger of some division; and out of particulars gathering the same to be occasion'd by some imprudent proceedings and indiscretions of the foremention'd confessor Mr Marsh:[4] advising and consulting with the Arch Deacon, Arch Priest and others, his Lordship resolved to dismiss him; and accordingly on the 19 of April sent him his dismission by the Arch Priest. This confessarius having gain'd the affection of several of the Religious, was cause of much disturbance, many of them being indiscreetly passionate and importuning both Arch Priest and Bishop, for his stay: which proved some discredit to our cloister: and no smal grief and affliction to Superiors, who had hitherto found us in all occasions very submissive to their ordinations. That which **[p. 86]** gave most offence was a request presented to my Lord Bishop, signed by the Subprioress, and about 13 or 14 more of the religious, which manner of proceeding seem'd factious, and so it was judged by the Bishop, who has a severe reprehension for it. But this was done by our Religious more out of ignorance than by any intention of resisting the Bishop's will: as it well appear'd afterwards when the said Mr Marsh was gone; for then all submitted peaceably.

Mr Matthew Bedingfield understanding how our cloister was destitute of a confessor, at our Reverende Mother's request, entreated a Priest who lived with him at Bruxelles to come to Bridges and assist us, at least for a time, till we could be provided. This Priest, by name of Mr John Busby, arrived here about the end of April;[5] and recommended by Father Rector of Gant and others, to our Bishop, was by him approved

---

[1] The position regarding the bishopric of Bruges is not entirely clear here. On 15 March 1660 Bishop Karel van den Bosch became Bishop of Ghent. No bishop of Bruges is given until 19 December 1661, when Robert de Haynin was installed. See catholic-hierarchy.org/diocese/db536.html, accessed 8 November 2015.

[2] The votive Mass of the Holy Spirit was often celebrated before visitations to inspire the community.

[3] Fr Edward Lusher SJ (c. 1587–1665); see McCoog, vol. 2, pp. 235–6.

[4] See **[p. 82]**, where the arrival of Fr William Wall alias Marsh in 1659 is described and hints given to explain the problems arising. See Anstruther 2, pp. 333–4.

[5] Fr John Busby (b. 1638) was a member of a family living in exile in Brussels; he remained at Nazareth until 1662, when his health forced him to return to England. See Anstruther 2, pp. 38–9.

for Confessarius to our Monastry on the first day of May. Nevertheless he only accepted of it then for a time. He had study'd with the fathers of the Society, and in their colledge of Validolid in Spain was made Priest.

On the first of May Mrs **[p. 87]** Dorothy Mannock our convictress, receiv'd the Schollars habit.[1]

On the 28 of April Miss Ursula Babthorpe was received convictress here, she was about 8 years old.[2]

On the 28 of June Mrs Theresia Mannock arrived here and was received convictress, she was about 13 years of age.[3]

On the 30 of August, Sister Elisabeth Brooke made her holy Profession, taking the name of Gertrude. She had stay'd all this time for want of her Portion.[4]

We now received no more Dutch convictresses.

The year 1661

On the 8th of January the old Lady Madam de Vicq, having been for some days very troublesome and unquiet, upon pretence of devotion to visit our Lady's of Rosery,[5] went out of our cloister with one of our Lay sisters; and being out, would return no more; but sent the sister home to tell our Reverende Mother that she resolved to live no more in the Monastry. So she lived abroad some weeks at her own charges, endeavouring to raise a suit of law against us to recover the money she had made over **[p. 88]** to our cloister, but not being able to effect it, she made peace with us, upon condition that she should be lodged near our cloister, and have her diet in our father's house obliging us to maintain her in all necessaries as before, and keeping her liberty to walk about as she pleased. It was thought best for us to agree to this, since she would not be quiet any longer in the cloister.

In the mean time her Daughter-in-law, being constant to her resolution, was clothed on the 24 of January.[6]

On the next day, the 25, Sister Ann Smith made her holy Profession.[7]

On the 16 of May Sister Agnes Mildmay and Sister Dorothy Mannock were clothed.[8]

---

1 Dorothy Mannock, in religion Angela (BA134).

2 Ursula Babthorpe (1670–1719) BA010, Infirmarian.

3 Teresa Mannock, in religion Augustina (1665–98) BA135, Novice Mistress.

4 Elizabeth Brooke (BA034) was one of a number of candidates whose profession was delayed by the lack of a dowry. She had been clothed on 17 June 1658; normally profession followed one year after clothing.

5 Our Lady of the Rosary was the site of pilgrimage at Sichem or Montaigu, east of Brussels where a church was founded in 1627.

6 Teresa Lauraine (Byrhaut), in religion Antonia (1662–91) BA127.

7 Ann Smith (BA176).

8 Agnes Mildmay (BA141); Dorothy Mannock, in religion Angela (BA134).

On the 7 of August Miss Ursula Neville, a child about eight years, was received convictress.

On the 26 of July, Ste Ann's day our Reverende Mother[1] laid the first stone of a new buiding for an infirmary, and at the same time enlargement of the Quire, and place by it, with advice of Monsieur Hilverven, a canon of St Donatianus, who had great skill in building.[2] He drew on the designe **[p. 89]** and promised the expense should not exceed 3000 florins.

On the begining of August our dear Reverende Mother Augustina Bedingfeld fell in a continual feavour which for the first three days was judged mortal; yet afterwards it was so moderated that we had hopes of her recovery: but her nature was exhausted with great infirmities, which for several years before her death she had suffer'd with a most Magnanimous patience and courage. She supported the labours of her charge and Government even when her exhausted and dropsical condition scarce permitted her to draw her breath but with excessive pain. She used sweetly to cast her eyes to heaven, where tho' her heart and desires were fix'd, yet she never omitted to perform on earth all that might conduce to the good and profit of our community, or the exact observance of our rules and institutions even to her last. She totally resigned her self to the divine will both in life and death, accompanying both with the true practice of most solide vertues, and rendering her self a true pattern by her example of the **[p. 90]** vertues and regular observances, she always sought the greater glory of God, without humane respects; yet with a true Motherly affection endeavour'd to be wanting in nothing that might conduce to the profit and comfort of her children, by whom she was deservedly esteem'd and beloved, which made them so very sensible to part with her, that she herself in her last sickness sweetly animated us to resigne our selves to God's holy disposition, and cheerfully check'd the complaints and tears of her afflicted children: always exhorting them to a lively confidence in the divine providence which was ever her only support and making frequent and fervent Aspirations to Almighty God when the vehemencies of her feavour permitted her to be sensible. She was often visited by our Reverend Arch Priest who had a high esteem of her most prudent abilities as to government, in her life, and in her most peaceable and pious disposition for death. He gave her the holy oyles himself, and some hours after, coming out of that Agonising fit, she most devoutly received the most Blessed **[p. 91]** Sacrament. She spent the next day in acts of piety and devotion, and in comforting and blessing her afflicted children with a true Maternal affection. She would never declare who she thought fittest or most likely to succeed her, saying that if she could but give a good account to Almighty God of her own time

---

[1] Reverend Mother was Augustina Bedingfield (1622 Louvain–1661 Bruges) LA023.

[2] St Donatus was the cathedral in Bruges at this period.

of Government, she left the future to his divine provide[nce]. All that Sister Mary Bedingfeld, her niece,[1] could any wayes allude to what befell her afterwards, was, that seeing her weep bitterly by her bed side, she exhorted her in a most affectionate and earnest manner not to afflict her self, telling her that whom God loves he chastises, which made no smal impression on the heart of her niece tho' she was not able to answer her. On the l0th of August at night, she fell into her last Agony; and on the 11th of August 1661, amidst the prayers and tears of her children, she render'd her happy soul into the hands of her Creator, to receive the reward of her fidelity to his divine Majesty in the charge he had committed to her: and of her great labours in the settling, and building our Monastery.

She had been Profess'd at **[p. 92]** Lovain, with Reverende Mother Poole,[2] and being called from thence as tis before related, she succeeded her in place of Prioress governing this Monastry the space of 21 years with a most prudent zeal and regular observance, so that she was worthily esteem'd by persons of the clearest judgment, one of the most prudent and exemplar Superiours of her time, both for the spiritual and temporal advancement of our community, which God was pleased to encrease under her, that she profess'd 22 religious for the Choir and four Lay Sisters, and left a good number of novices, and others to go forward. Notwithstanding the great expenses of building of our church, dormitory, and washouse, she endeavour'd to put a competent rent for the maintenance of each religious she profess'd for the Quire. And indeed her provident care and solicitude was admirably bless'd by the divine assistance, for which we have reason to bless his holy name, and next to acknowledge our obligation to so vigilant and prudent a Superior esteeming her as our foundress **[p. 93]** in point of temporals, and much more for spirituals in which she was truly zealous to advance all both by word and example, being ever zealous to uphold the exact observance of our rules, institutions and customs, so that her memory ought ever to live amongst us. She dyed in the 56 year of her age, the 39 of her holy Profession on the 11th of August, the year 1661, and was bury'd in our Vault on the 13 of the same month, our Arch Priest performing the funerailles, and the chiefest of the town being present. *Requiescat in pace.* Amen.

After this, our Vicars (for there was then no Bishop) gave us three days of silence and fasting to recommend to Almighty God, the Elections of a new Prioress.

On the 16 of August 1661, Monsieur de Vicq, the Dean, Monsieur Courtewell official, and Monsieur Scrabeels Arch Priest and the Secretary, all joyned in the Authority of Vicars to Supply the place of a Bishop, came in the morning; the Dean sung the Masse of the holy Ghost, after

---

1 Mary Bedingfield (BA019).

2 Mary Pole (1622 Louvain–1640 Bruges) LA203, Prioress at Bruges 1635–40.

which they came into our Quire together with **[p. 94]** father Spyra, a dutch father of the Society, who having some English, was to be interpretor, and Mr John Busby who then supply'd for our Confessor.[1] The religous being assembled there they made their Election, and Sister Mary Bedingfeld, niece to our deceased Prioress, had two parts of three in the votes and she was confirm'd by the Dean and Vicars.[2] She made to them the ordinary vow of obedience to the Bishop of Bridges, for her self, and community; and all that were profess'd made their vow of obedience to her. The Vicars sent money for two recreations for the religious.

On the first of October came the two sisters Busby for convictresses.[3]

On the 9 of October, Sister Mary Altam departed this life most piously and peaceably.[4] She was a person of an eminent vertue, a most strict observer of our holy rules and institutions, and even of the very least customs of our holy order, most sweetly alluring and perswading the youngers to the like.

She was the second Subprioress of our cloister till thro' her very great weakness and continual indisposition which render'd her unable to keep the Quire[5] **[p. 95]** she desired to be discharged of that office, and Sister Grace Constable was chosen in her place, as we have said before.[6] Nevertheless she remain'd still a most exemplar pattern to our community, and was always present in the Quire at the day office, and in all places of order; and by her exact and sweet conversation edifying all. *Requiescat in pace.* Amen.

At the end of this year our Reverendc Mother and many of the religious had quartern and other Agues.

Our building went on under the care of the aforesaid canon, and Mr Bloemaert a priest: but our enclosure was not broken, nor did any others come in but with leave of the Bishop.

The year 1662

The 25th of January Sister Theresia Lauraine (alias Byrhaut) made her holy Profession, having as tis said before her clothing the approbation of the divine both of the University of Lovain and Doway, and also her husband's full consent and license.[7]

---

1 Fr John Busby: see **[p. 86]**.

2 Elections for Prioress were carried out by secret ballot among the choir sisters and confirmed by representatives of the external Visitor of the convent.

3 Abigail Busby, in religion Thecla (1666–1712) BA041.

4 Mary Altham (1616 Louvain–1661 Bruges) LA004 was one of the founding members of the convent: see **[p. 3]**.

5 'Keep the Quire' refers to full participation in following all elements of the daily rule, including devotions and prayers as well as attending divine office in the chapel.

6 Grace Constable (1625 Louvain–1673 Bruges) LA069. See **[p. 69]**.

7 Teresa Lauraine (Byrhaut) (BA127). See also **[pp. 83, 84]**.

On the 27 of June, Sister Margarite Moss made her Profession for a lay sister.[1]

On the feast of our Lady's Visitation, the 2nd of July, Sister Agnes Mildmay and Sister Dorothy **[p. 96]** Mannock (who took the name of Angela) made their holy Profession.[2]

Towards the end of this Month our Reverend father confessor, Mr John Busby (who was here only for a time as tis said before) finding this air not agree with his health, was perswaded by Mr Mathew Bedingfield to return to England.[3] He served our Monastry these two years for charity, not taking the pension allow'd, and parted from us with a great deal of good will for our community, being a most humble and truly vertuous man; but his being unable to sing or perform our church service, and something in his exterior, made him judged not fit for our confessarius.

Mr Hilleverven, the canon having great compassion of us, as being now destitute of a confessor, apply'd himself very much for the learning of English, and for that effect resolved to go for England: had his lodging prepared at London with the Procurator of the fathers of the Society, where he intended to make the Spiritual exercises and stay some months to perfect himself in our language. On the 22 of July, Ste Mary Magdalenes day, he said Mass in our church and communicated all the religious, having heard their confession the day before. **[p. 97]** He went that day to Ostende, where taking a little boat to carry him to the Packet boat that was going for England, in that short passage, he and several others were cast into the sea by the overturning of that little Boat, tho' non but himself and one more were drown'd. This sad accident caused great affliction to our whole community, and to his friends and church, to whom his great abilities in all their affaires, and his generous and excellent disposition made the loss of him most sensible. He often express'd to our Reverende Mother his serious resolution of withdrawing himself from the press of worldly affaires, in which he was much engaged for the service of others, and of giving himself more entirely to Almighty God, who was pleased to take him in so excellent a disposition. May his divine providence be adored. *Requiescat in pace.* Amen.

Father Spyra supply'd in place of confessor.[4]

In August Mrs Catherine Holland came out of England, whose father Sir John Holland, being a Protestant, her mother, the Lady Sands, a most vertuous **[p. 98]** Catholick had not the liberty to bring up, or instruct her

[1] Margaret Moss (1662–79) BA146.

[2] Agnes Mildmay (BA141); Dorothy Mannock (BA134).

[3] Fr John Busby (b. 1638). See **[p. 86]** and Anstruther 2, pp. 38–9.

[4] Fr Richard Van Spiere (1603–64), a Dutch Jesuit. See **[pp. 82, 94]**.

children in our holy Religion.[1] But this daughter coming to the years of discretion, and applying herself to reading and searching into the errors and confusion of their church, it pleased the divine goodness to give her resolutions of being not only a catholick but also a religious woman, for which intent having often treated with our Reverende Mother by letter; and confess'd with some fathers of the society in England, she stole away from her Parents at London, being unwilling her Mother should have any thing to suffer from her father a severe man: so she found a fit opportunity and came to our Monastry, where she was reconciled, and received the Schollars habit with much joy and satisfaction; we relying upon her honorable Mother for her maintenance.

The 3d of October Sister Ursula Monica Babthorpe departed this life, being about the 40th year of her age, and the 21 of her holy Profession.[2] She was of a most sweet and excellent disposition, and had many good parts very fit for Religion; which she **[p. 99]** employ'd to the utmost of her power in the service of our community: tho' she was ever of a most tender and weak complexion, and very sickly; yet most constant in regular observance as much as possibly she could. She dyed in the office of Mistress of novices and had continually served our community in several employments: suffring her continual infirmities even to her last, in which she happily concluded her vertuous life, by a most pious death. *Requiescat in pace.* Amen.

On the 25 of November Mrs Catherine Petre came to our Monastry to be a convictress.[3]

In the Month of November Sister Bridget Hughs was clothed for a lay sister.[4]

Our building was near finish'd this year, but the expenses of it not paid; it amounting to almost twice as much as was reckon'd upon the begining.

We had Almnes this year about 270 florins, of which 30 florins was a Legacy left by a gentlewoman in town, the **[p. 100]** rest was in little tokens, from Mr John Webb and Mrs Wright to her daughter and besides these, 803 from different persons.

---

1 Catharine Holland, in religion Mechtildis (1664–1720) BA106, Arcaria from 1713. Her father was Sir John Holland MP (1603–1701) of Quidenham, Norfolk. Her mother was Lady Alethea Sandys, née Panton (d. 22 May 1679), daughter of John Panton of Brynkinallt, Chirk, Denbighshire, who married as her first husband William, 4th Lord Sandys (d. 1629) of The Vyne, Hants. Lady Sandys was one of several re-marrying widows in the Chronicle who reverted to their first husband's surname and title from time to time. For an account of Catherine Holland's conversion, see C. S. Durrant, *A Link Between Flemish Mystics and English Martyrs* (London: Burns, Oates and Washbourne 1925), pp. 271–305.

2 Ursula Babthorpe, in religion Monica (BA009).

3 Catherine Petre was the sister of Mary Petre (BA153). She did not persevere and left in 1667.

4 Brigitt Hughes, in religion Margaret, lay sister (1665–82) BA115.

The year 1663

On the 27 of March, Miss Mary Ford, a child of 7 years old was put here to be a convictress.

The … of July Sister Catherine Holland was clothed, her Mother the Lady Sands, paying the charges of her habit and solemnity.[1]

On the 11 of August here arrived Mr Thomas Weedon a Roman Priest, recommended to us for confessor by Reverend father Edward Courtney, Provincial of the English fathers of the Society of Jesus.[2] He was approved by the Ordinary, and placed confessor to our Monastry, about the 28th years of his age, and 2d of his Priesthood.

On the 20 of November Sister Mary Petre, and Sister Theresia Mannock took the holy habit.[3]

On the 25 of November Sister Brigit Hughs was profess'd a lay sister.

We had this year given us in Almnes 381 florins, from Mr Volder Canon, Mr Hilversen **[p. 101]** canon, My Lord Vaux, Mrs Wright, Mr Spanogle and all in Legacies, or little tokens or new year gifts.

The year 1664

Our building was all accomplish'd and paid for, tho' it amounted to near 9000 florins, which was twice as much as it was reckon'd it would come to, when it was begun.

On the 28 of July Miss Mary Crouch came to be a convictress.[4]

About April Sister Anne Busby return'd to England, having been in the Schollars habit for more than half a year, she apprehended she should not be contented in religion and so she went from us: but her sister Tecla took the Schollars habit on the feast of our Lady's Visitation, and proved constant.[5]

The 7th of September Sister Catherine Holland made her holy Profession. Her father was prevail'd with to pay her portion, by the right honorable **[p. 102]** the Lord Henry Howard, who was present at her profession, and dined in our father's house.[6]

---

[1] Catharine Holland (BA106). For Lady Sandys, see **[pp. 97–8]**.

[2] Fr Thomas Weedon alias Williamson (1637–1706) studied at the English College, Rome 1658–63; see Holt, p. 281. Fr Edward Courtney SJ (1599–1677) spent much of his career in Flanders; see McCoog, vol. 1, p. 148.

[3] Teresa Mannock, in religion Augustina (1665–98) BA135; Mary Petre (1665–92) BA153.

[4] She left before profession.

[5] In this period the Feast of our Lady's Visitation was celebrated on 2 July; see **[p. 95]**. Abigail Busby, in religion Thecla (BA041).

[6] The Howard and Holland families had East Anglian connections: Catherine's father became MP for Aldeburgh, Suffolk in 1661 on the Howard interest. See historyofparliamentonline.org/volume/1660-1690/member/holland-sir-john-1603-1701, accessed 12 November 2015. Lord Henry Howard, Earl of Arundel, 6th Duke of Norfolk later had a daughter Ann who professed at Bruges in 1693 (BA107).

We had this year in Almnes 445 florins given by Mr John Webb, Mrs Wright, the Mr Halls, Mr Smith, Mr Palmes, Mrs Heton, Mr Volder the canon, Mr Caryll, and at new year and Mr Moss.

The year 1665

On the 10 of February, Sister Mary Petre, and Sister Theresia Mannock were profess'd. And after the prayers and ceremonies of the Profession were perform'd, the Arch Priest clothed Sister Thecla Busby at the same Mass.[1]

The 17 of April, Miss Sarah van Coulster came here to be a convictress.

On the 5 of May Sister Magdalen Williscott departed this life about the 30 the year of her age, and 13th of her holy Profession.[2] She was ever of a most innocent life, but for some years before her death, grew wholy stupide, and incapable and very infirm. Her death was sudden, yet she received all the Sacraments she was capable of, and her innocent soul was doubtless most acceptable to the divine **[p. 103]** goodness. *Requiescat in pace.* Amen.

The 18 of June, Mrs Mary Watson came to our Monastry to be a religious, tho' she took that resolution upon the discontent of being cross'd in her affections in England, nevertheless she took the Schollars habit, and with her Mrs Catherine Petre and Mrs Mary Ann' Hannoye, a dutch gentlewoman who had lived some years in our house, and was earnest to try if she could make her self fit for Religion.[3] But in a short time she experienced her own want of health and ability, and so resigned her self yet still desired to live a retired life in our cloister.

The 13 of November here arrived the right honorable Lord Stafford and his Lady, with their daughter, Sister Ursula Stafford, who had been profess'd a year before at our cloister of Ste Monica at Lovain.[4] The Lady Mother had lived with her for some Monthes within the Monastery, and out of fondness and tenderness to her daughter in her little infirmities, after she had follow'd her up with Physick and other remedies, her parents got leave of the Bishop of Mechlin[5] for her to change air by going to some Monastry of her **[p. 104]** own order, so they made choice of ours, and the Reverende Mother her Superior requested her admittance for a time to be in our infirmary; it was proposed to our Convent Sisters, and accepted tho' we found many inconveniences therein: but the Countess

---

[1] Mary Petre (BA153); Teresa Mannock (BA135); Thecla Busby (1666–1712) BA041.

[2] Mary Magdalena Wollascott (1652–65) BA223.

[3] None of these three candidates professed.

[4] Ursula Howard (1664–1720) LA241. She took her surname from her father, Sir William Howard, Viscount Stafford of Arundel, Sussex. Her mother was Lady Mary Stafford of Stafford Castle, Staffordshire.

[5] In 1665 the Archbishop of Mechelen was Andreas Creusen (1591–1666), Archbishop 1657–66.

her Mother had not her designe of living with her in our Monastry, so she remain'd about ten days out of the enclosure, and then went for England, leaving her little son who went to Schoole in the Town. And the Lord their father also boarded some time in our father's house, the Daughter remaining in our infirmary.

We had also the Lady Mary Caryll, Abbess of the Benedictin Dames of Dunkirk, with Dame Catherine Savage, for about a Month in our Monastry; they being shut out of Dunkirk in their return from England.[1]

We this year had in Almnes at different times 309 florins from Sir John Webb, Mr Volder canon, Mrs Wright, Mrs Arundel, Mr Edward Hall, Mr Caryll, besides 1,300 florins sent by Mr John Caryll for the seats in the Quire; What Sir John Webb gave was 300 florins for the Tabernacle.

The year 1666

[p. 105] Our most Reverend Lord Bishop Robertus de Haynin ordain'd observances and alter'd some few points in our institutions at the request of our Religious, who were all present when his Reverend Lordship caused them to be read to them in his presence, asking the religious if any one had any thing to say against them. Then he confirm'd them with his Episcopal Seal. Dating his Confirmation of them the 13 of March 1666.[2]

On the 22 of April Sister Thecla Busby made her holy Profession.[3]

On the 18 of June Miss Susan Reynolson came over to be a convictress here, she was about 14 years of age.[4]

In November Sister Mary Watson return'd into England, she wanting health and resolution to go forward in Religion.

We this year received in Almnes 134 florins at different times, from Sir John Webb, Mr Edward Hall, Mr Volder canon, Mr Paston Priest, and given us at new year.

The year 1667

[p. 106] In the begining of May, to our great satisfaction, Sister Ursula Stafford was taken out of our Monastry by her father, in order to return to her Monastry at Lovain. One of our lay sisters accompany'd her to Bruxelles, when hearing that Lovain was likely to be besieged, the Lord

---

1 Mary Caryll (1650 Ghent–1712 Dunkirk) was Abbess of the Benedictine convent, Dunkirk 1663–1712, GB040; Catherine Savage (1638 Ghent–1687 Dunkirk) GB199, Prioress at Dunkirk. In Benedictine convents where the Superior was an abbess, her second-in-command was prioress. The outbreak of the Second Anglo-Dutch War in 1665 rendered the area unsafe for travellers and prevented access. See discussion in G. Rommelse, *The Second Anglo-Dutch War 1665–7* (Hilversum: Verloren, 2006).

2 Robert de Haynin was Bishop of Bruges 1661–68. Diocesan Archives, Bruges, MS 'Acta episcoporum' B 31, fol. 120.

3 Thecla Busby (BA041). See also **[p. 101]**.

4 Susan Reynoldson (1670–1730) BA161.

Stafford wrote to the Reverende Mother Prioress there, that in case Lovain should fall into troubles he might have his daughter out again, which the Reverende Mother refusing, his Lordship carry'd her to a Monastry of our order at Antwerp, where she suffer'd so much hardship that she was very well contented to return to her own Monastry at Lovain.[1] Ours may learn by this occasion never to admit of any religious person, who leaves her own monastry for discontent, or ungrounded pretensions.[2] In September Mrs Susan Reynolson having made her resolution to be religious went into England to see if she could get some advantage in her Portion.[3]

In October Sister Catherine Petre proving unconstant in her resolutions **[p. 107]** for religion, left us and went for England with the Lady Weston, who had lived for some monthes in our father's house.

The 20 of December Sister Ursula Babthorpe and Sister Mary Crouch, took the Schollars habit.[4] So we had then no more convictresses left in our Schoole.

This year we received in Almnes 334 florins in tokens to different religious, as from Sir John Webb, Mr. Edward Hall, Mrs Wright, Mrs Rows, Mr Volder canon, and given us at new year.

The year 1668

On the 25 of May Mrs Susan Reynolson remaning constant in her resolution to be religious, return'd out of England, and took the Schollars habit.

The October this year, Sister Mary Crouch return'd into England, not having courage enough to surmount her unsettled inclinations and apprehensions of religion, nor to overcome her great fondness of her father and her friends.

On the 23 of November Mrs Mary Anne Annoy (whom we mention'd before) dyed **[p. 108]** very piously in our Monastry after a long sickness.[5] She made her Will and left us a legacy of 600 florins, and as much for our silver candlesticks in the church; and 100 florins for the sister that tended her, and the furniture of her chamber etc. And she would have given much more if she had been of age to dispose of her means. She wanted but six weeks of 25. She was bury'd in our Vault with all Solemnity

---

1 The Augustinian convent at Antwerp was either the Convent of the Zwartzusters or the Augustinian Sisters of St Elizabeth; see himetop.wikidot.com/gasthuis-st-elisabeth, accessed 18 January 2016.

2 'Pretensions' then had the sense of 'claims' rather than modern English 'pretensions', from French pretender, to claim. Note the reflective comment here by a convent leader seeking to create harmonious relations appropriate to best practice for the religious life.

3 Susan Reynoldson was able to return to Bruges the following year: see **[pp. 107, 109, 112]** below.

4 Ursula Babthorpe (BA010). Mary Crouch left the following year.

5 See **[p. 103]**.

according to her will which was perform'd by her Brother in Town on the 27 of November. *Requiescat in pace.* Amen.

The 10 of December Reverend Mr Weedon, our confessor, finding the place not agree with his health and inclinations left us, and went for England.[1] We got Reverend Mr. Saxfield an ancient Irish Priest who lived in town, to supply for confessor till we could be provided of one.[2] And we were also assisted by our Reverend Archdeacon, and [by] the fathers of the society.

We this year received in Almnes 1034 florins, 300 of which was the Lady Mary Weston's Legacy paid by the Lord Portland.[3] The rest Legacies and tokens from John Webb, Mr Day, Mrs Annoy, Mr Jenison Priest, a Lady, Mr Volder canon, and for the soul **[p. 109]** of Mrs Woodson.

The year 1669

On the first of April, Sister Elisabeth Young departed this life about the 74th year of her age, and the 25th of her holy Profession.[4] She was advanced in years when she came to religion, and used very great violence to her nature to conform her self to all religious observances, and to break her own will, continuing in this fervour even to her last, by the continual mortification of her self; never accepting the least relaxation in her great age, but for that very reason exciting her self to labour with great fervour, as not having long to live. She had but one day's sickness which the Doctor judged no other than a defailance of nature. She dyed most peaceably and sweetly. *Requiescat in pace.* Amen.

The 17 of May Sister Ursula Monica Babthorpe and Sister Susan Reynolson were clothed.[5]

On the 10 of September, Sister Mary Hall departed this life about the 67th year of her age, and 37th of her holy Profession.[6] She was second profess'd in the **[p. 110]** begining of our house, and with much alacrity went thro' with the labours and hardships of such beginings, being very zealous in all regular observances, fervent and constant in prayer, and sparing no labour to advance the common profit. She finished her course after a very painful and violent sickness. *Requiescat in pace.* Amen.

On the 12 of October it also pleased our Lord to call to himself Sister Lydwin Clapton in the 68 year of her age, and 48 of her profession.[7]

---

1 Fr Thomas Weedon (1637–1706) had been Confessor since 1663; see Holt, p. 281, and above **[p. 100]**.

2 Fr Saxfield: perhaps Sarsfield.

3 In 1668, Lord Portland was Thomas Weston, 4th Earl of Portland, who inherited the title in 1665 on the death of his nephew, Charles.

4 Elizabeth Young (BA231).

5 Ursula Babthorpe (BA010); Susan Reynoldson (BA161).

6 Mary Hall (1632–69) BA093.

7 Lidwine Clapton (1622 Louvain–1669 Bruges) LA052.

She was one of those who came from Lovain to the foundation of our house, and was ever truly zealous in advancing all regular observances. She suffer'd very much in languishing infirmities the year before her death, and that with great resignation, by which our dear Lord prepared her for himself, and entirely took from her that very great apprehension her Melancholy nature had of death. And she most earnestly beseech'd his divine majesty to give her a speedy and happy death. which he was pleased to grant her. *Requiescat in pace*. Amen.

[p. 111] In the month of December, the Lady Mary Caryll Abbess of the Benedictin Dames of Dunkirk, was entertain'd in our Monastry at her return from Antwerp where she had been with a famous surgeon for the cure of her fore breast, which was judged both by that surgeon and several others to be a cancer.[1] She was so very ill of it that she was forc'd to stay here several weeks where it pleased God that she was cured, much of that cure being imputed to the powerful intercession of St Francis Xaverius, whose relick was kept in her chamber, and her Ladyship perform'd devotions to that Blessed Saint.

On the 17 of December Reverend Mr Robert Kent came to our Monastry, and was approved for confessor here.[2]

We this year received in Almnes 554 florins from Mr Walter Gifford, Mrs Hodson, Mrs Wright, Mr John Petre, Sir John Webb, and Mr Volder Canon.

The year 1670

On the 10 of January, Sister Augustina Webb departed this life, the 39th year of her age, and 19th of her holy Profession.[3] She was call'd to religion in a particular manner, by the intercession of the Blessed Virgin who miraculously cured her of a shrinking and contraction of sinews in one of her arms, when she resolved to be religious: and when she entertain'd doubts and thoughts of returning into the world, the pain and contraction most sensibly return'd till she settled her thoughts to religion, in which she lived very exemplary: and tho' of a very weak and tender Constitution, yet most exact in all religious duties: and laborious in all employments obedience imposed upon her; for she did not spare her self in any thing, thereby compleating her crown (as we may piously hope) for a happy eternity. *Requiescat in pace*. Amen.

On the 25 of June, Sister Ursula Monica Babthorpe, and Sister Susan Reynolson, made their holy Profession.

---

[1] Mary Caryll (GB040). See also *A History of the Benedictine Nuns of Dunkirk* (London: Catholic Book Club, n.d.), pp. 24–5. See Glossary.

[2] Fr Robert Kent (1643–78), Confessor 1668–78; Anstruther 3, pp. 121–2.

[3] Augustina Webb (1651–70) BA211.

On the 23 of August here came the Lady Widdrington, her husband Sir Edward Widdrington[1] had lived several years before in this town, and for some time in our father's house a most extraordinary vertuous life; and taking a great affection to our cloister, for the retirement and quiet he observed in it, he **[p. 113]** desired to have his Lady come, who had an inclination to leave the world and to be religious. And he intended himself to take upon him the holy order of Priesthood. The same day she should make her vows of religion. But her Ladyship was much disturbed at her entrance into our Monastry, and that (twas thought) by some of the order of St Francis here in town, telling her it would be a kind of affront to their order (she being of the third order of St Francis) if she left the Monastry of his order to enter ours. So she went towards Paris, but when they came to Dunkirk, the Lady return'd again to Newpoort, and there consulted the Prior of the English Carthusians, and resolved to return hither, which she did and presently enter'd the Monastry, and apply'd her self to learn latin, and but in a few weeks after she fell into a tedious and dangerous sickness, received all her rights, and remain'd sick the whole winter.

There came over with the Lady Widdrington Mrs Mary Charlton, and Mrs Dorothy Errington, who enter'd on the 25 of August, and began our convictresses schoole again.[2]

We this year received in Almnes 358 florins, from Mr Volder Canon, Sir John Webb, Mrs Arundel, a gentlewoman in Town, our official, and given us at new year.

The year 1671

On the 22 of May Miss Frances Farmer was received here for convictress, and three days after Miss Elisabeth Wyburne came for convictress.[3]

On the 13 of June Sir Edward Widdrington dyed in our out house for boarders after long sickness, being exhausted with most rigourous fasting and austerities which he practiced for many years before his death. He began his most extraordinary devout life here in Bridges, by a Pilgrimage which he made on foot to Rome, where having finished in some months his visit and devotions to those holy places, he return'd again on foot to this town where he spent near seven years, rising daily

---

[1] Sir Edward Widdrington (1614–71) of Cartington Castle, Northunberland, was a Royalist colonel and brigadier of horse. See P. R. Newman, *Royalist Officers in England and Wales, 1642–60: A Biographical Dictionary* (London: Garland Publishing, 1981), p. 401. Lady Widdrington was Christina Stuart of Coldingham. They had five children: see Stirnet.com.

[2] Both Mary Charlton and Dorothy Errington were related to Lady Widdrington and had Northumberland connections. The links have not been fully identified. Mary professed in 1674 and Dorothy in 1681. On Dorothy, see also **[pp. 121, 128, 129, 131, 132, 183, 244–52, 442]** and vol. 2, **[pp. 67–9]**.

[3] Neither of these two candidates persevered.

at four in the morning, continuing his prayer and devotions till twelve at noon, then he took for refreshment only the third part of a stiver loaf and some beer.[1] At night his supper was the worst sort of fish, never eating neither Eggs nor **[p. 115]** milk: and on fridays and many other days fasting only with bread and water. He lay continually on the ground or on some bed of straw, and gave to the poor all he spared of his diet and other expenses; which life was the more admirable in him, because he had spent his days before in so much prodigality and pleasure. He intended as we said before, to have consecrated the rest of his time to God, and to be made Priest, but the divine providence was pleased to order otherways and call him to a better life. He made a most pious and happy end, and was buryed in that Capucins habit; in their church.[2] The whole town had a great esteem and veneration of him, and several who recommended themselves to his prayers found great assistance and help in their infirmities: and I hope our community will also find good effects of his intercession for us in heaven, he having had so singular an affection for us upon earth. *Requiescat in pace*. Amen.

About three weeks after Sir Edward's death, his Lady return'd for England **[p. 116]** not being recover'd of her long sickness. And all our hopes in that business failing us, we must still confide in God's providence and learn not to comply too much with secular persons tho' never so vertuous, this having proved so great a trouble to our community.

On the first of August Miss Ursula and Miss Winifred Henage [came] to be convictresses.[3]

We this year received in Almnes 549 florins from Sir John Webb, Mr Havers a devote, Mr Clavering, Yffrow Lambrel, Mr Volder Canon, Mr Palmes, and given us at new year.

The year 1672

On the 8th of June, Sister Frances Redding, a lay sister departed this life, about the 65 year of her age, and 35th of her Profession.[4] She had served our comunity with much fidelity, and even to her last was most laborious in all the works of her profession, and most industrious for the common profit, sparing no pains nor labour, yet very constant in her devotion, and solidly vertuous: which obtain'd of Almighty God **[p. 117]** so pious and happy an end, most singularly edifying to all; she having

---

[1] F. Skeat, *Life of Sir Edward Widdrington, Knt., & Baronet of Cartington, in Northumberland: with an account of his piety in the practice of the Catholic faith* (London: Burns Oates and Washbourne, 1923).

[2] Capuchin Church, formerly in Tzand Square, now demolished.

[3] Neither of these candidates persevered.

[4] Frances Reading (1634–72) BA160.

her senses to the very last, and pronouncing the sweet names of Jesus and Mary to her last breath. *Requiescat in pace*. Amen.

On the third of August Miss Etheldred Mannock was received here for convictress.[1]

The 5th of August Sister Mary Bowes, a lay sister, departed this life the 63 year of her age, and 37th of her holy Profession.[2] She was ever a most innocent vertuous soul and suffer'd much in her latter years by several painful infirmities: yet still she perform'd what she could for the service of the comunity. She had a very long sickness which disposed her to make a most pious and happy end. *Requiescat in pace.* Amen.

On the 7th of November Sister Mary Charlton was clothed.[3]

We this year received in Almnes 1004 florins, 500 of which was left us by Mrs Susan Everard at her death. The rest from Sir John Webb, Mr Caryll, Mr Palmes, Mr Volder canon, Sister Margarite Mosses uncle, and given us at new year. And Mary Lambert at her death, also Mr Ignatius Cuffauld.

The year 1673

[p. 118] On the 3d of May, our Reverende Subprioress, Sister Grace Constable, departed this life in the 67th year of her age and 46th of her holy Profession.[4] She was one of those who came from Lovain for the foundation of this house, of an excellent spirit and very active in advancing the same. She never spared her pains, nor endeavours in several offices; and for 18 years she was our Subprioress, performing that office with much prudence, and zeal of regular observance even to her last. She was for some years before her death much oppress'd with most painful infirmities, yet always cheerful and vigorous; continually employing her self in the service of the comunity, both in edifying it by her vertuous and exemplar sweet conversation, and also by her works and labours, in particular the writing many Antiphon books, and Mass books for the Quire, which may serve for a perpetual memory of her diligence in that kind.[5] Her last sickness and death were most pious and of great edification to all: she speaking to each with such spirit of charity, that it made very great impression in the hearts of many. She received the last Sacrament with **[p. 119]** singular devotion, exhorting all present to charity, obedience and vertue, and speaking the whole time of her sickness in most cheerful and pious discourses, with frequent prayers and desiring all to pray about

---

1 Etheldreda Mannock left before profession.

2 Mary Bowes (1635–80) BA030.

3 Mary Charlton, in religion Augustina (1674–1722) BA048. She was from the Bellingham, Northumberland branch of the family.

4 Grace Constable (1625 Louvain–1673 Bruges) LA069.

5 Some of these have survived and remain in the convent archives.

her till she had passd the last combat of death, which she most happily accomplish'd by sweetly rendering her soul into the hands of her creator amidst the prayers and tears of our whole community about nine in the morning. *Requiescat in Pace*. Amen.

She was buryed in our Vault on the 5 of May.

On the 25 of May, Sister Ursula Palmes was chosen Subprioress by our convent, with a particular dispensation from our Bishop, for her want of voice, she not being able, on that account, to perform the singing on feasts of *secunda* classes.[1] Sister Wenefride Webb was chosen Arcaria in her place.[2]

On the 20 of July, Mrs Anne Andrews was sent hither by her Parents, who had sent her the year before for education to the Irish Dames at Ypres, where their beginings then giving no **[p. 120]** hopes of settlement, she took our Schollars habit in the same month.[3]

The 4 of July came Mrs Mary Bedingfeld to be a convictress, she was about 13 years of age.[4]

On the 25 of July came also Mrs Mary Anne Hamilton, for convictress.[5]

On the 14 of August, the Lady Hamilton desirous to end her days in the state of holy religion, retired to our Monastry, after having lived near 12 years a retired life with the poor Clares of Gravelin.[6] She enter'd our enclosure some weeks after her arrival here, and with dispensation from the Quire and divine office; yet coming to the day service, and to all regular observances (as far as she was able) she received the holy habit on the 13 of November.

We this year received in Almnes 374 florins from Mr Volder canon, Mrs Lomez, Reverend father Mumford, Sir John Webb, Mr Caryll, Mr Palmes, Mr Buck and Mr Rows, and given at new year.

The year 1674

On the 4th of February Sister Grace Eddows departed this life[,] about the 60 year of her age, and 23 profess'd a lay sister.[7] She was a very vertuous sincere creature, but in her later years very weak and consumtive;

---

1 Ursula Palmes (BA149).

2 Winefrid Webb (BA212).

3 Ann Andrews, in religion Ann Joseph (1675–1724) BA003. Ypres was founded in 1665 by Abbess Mary Knatchbull (GB118) from the Ghent community, as an English house. However, it was unable to attract enough recruits to make it viable and it became an Irish cloister in 1682. For the history of the convent, see P. Nolan, *Irish Dames of Ypres* (Dublin: Browne and Nolan, 1908).

4 Mary Bedingfield (1678–1712) BA018.

5 Mary Hamilton, in religion Ann (1682–99) BA096.

6 Lady Elizabeth Hamilton, a widow who was the last of a generation of 11 Bedingfield sisters to enter a convent, professed the following year. Elizabeth Hamilton, in religion Augustina (1674–83) BA094.

7 Grace Eddows (1651–74) BA075.

yet she labour'd in all she could for the service of the **[p. 121]** comunity, even to her last sickness, in which she devoutly received all the rights, and happily reposed in our Lord. She was buryed in our Vault on the 6 of february. *Requiescat in pace*. Amen.

Mr Mathew Bedingfeld sent us his maid Frances Catherine Copland to supply her place in quality of Lay sister, on the 5th of April.

On the 7th of May Sister Josepha Ann' Andrews was clothed.[1]

On the 28 of April, Mrs Dorothy Errington return'd to her father in Northumberland who took no care of her, nor did not pay her Annuity: so we were forced to send our servant Catherine Coplant with her.[2] The said Catherine return'd again on the 16 of August, and brought over her sister, Martha Coplant, to whom she resigned her Place for a lay sister, she being much younger, and judged more able to go through with our work.[3] The Elder [Catherine] went to live with the English religious at Gravelin.

On the 20 of August, Sister Mary Charlton made her holy profession.[4]

On the 22 of September Mrs Frances Farmer, a convictress, return'd to her Parents.[5] She having been at death's door, and being still weak, we were forced to send Sister Catherine Bartlett to conduct her **[p. 122]** to London, who return'd with her little sister Miss Ursula Farmer on the 13 of october.[6]

Mistress Mary Ann' Hamilton went out of our Monastry to live in the town, in the begining of September.

On the 21 of november, Mrs. Keynes came hither with intention to be religious.[7]

On the 25 of november Sister Augustina Hamilton made her holy profession with a dispensation from the Quire and divine office.[8] Her great age of 64 not permiting her to learn Latin, our Bishop and convent admitted her by a particular favour and dispensation; we having been long acquainted with her vertuous life and disposition, and to the respect we bore to her sister Reverende Mother Augustina Bedingfeld, who had so much obliged our community. This Sister Hamilton was the eleventh sister of that family, all religious in several convents of our nation.

On the 26 of november Sister Barbara Clapton departed this life in the 75 year of her age, and 53 of her holy profession.[9] She came from

---

[1] Ann Andrews, in religion Ann Joseph (BA003).
[2] Dorothy Errington, in religion Perpetua (1681–1739) BA076.
[3] Martha Copland, lay sister (1677–1709) BA065.
[4] Mary Charlton, in religion Augustina (BA048).
[5] Frances and Ursula were probably the daughters of Richard Fermor of Tusmore and Frances Brooke of Madeley; neither of them stayed to profess.
[6] Catherine Bartlett (BA008).
[7] Diana Keynes, in religion Mary Joseph (1677–1707) BA126.
[8] Augustina Hamilton (BA094).
[9] Barbara Clapton (1622 Louvain–1674 Bruges) LA051.

Ste Monica's at Lovain, to begin our house; and was a most exemplar good religious woman: very compassionate, and of an excellent sweet nature. She confess'd and communicated the day before **[p. 123]** her death, and the next morning fell suddenly into her Agony, and so in few hours she render'd her happy soul into the hands of her Creator. *Requiescat in pace*. Amen.

We this year received in Almes 688 florins. 150 was from the Lady Carrington, 300 from Sir John Webb. The rest from Mr Volder canon, Mrs Wright, Mrs Oglethorpe, father Richard Babthorpe, Mr Palmes, father Francis Heton, and given us at new year.

The year 1675

On the 19 of March, Mrs Diana Keynes took the Schollars habit, and the name of Sister Mary Josepha.[1]

On the 13 of May, Sister Josepha Andrews made her holy profession.[2]

On the 10 of May Sister Mary Gifford departed this life about the 74th year of her age and fiftyeth of her holy profession.[3] She was one of those who came from Lovain for the foundation of this house, and was very laborious in several offices for the service of the comunity in the begining, tho' always of a weak and sickly disposition; and for many years before her death almost constantly in our infirmary, where it **[p. 124]** pleased God to dispose her for a very happy and pious end by a lingering and exhausting infirmity. She dyed when she was to have kept her whole Jubilee, which (as we piously hope) she went to celebrate in heaven. *Requiescat in pace*. Amen.

On the 8th of September Sister Martha Copland took the kerchief for a Lay sister.[4]

On the 2d of September we received three for convictresses: Mrs Mary Havers and her two little cousines Miss Susan and Miss Dorothy Risdon.[5]

We this year received in Almnes 718 florins, 300 of which was from Sir John Webb, one hundred from Mr Caryll and the rest from Mr Volder canon, father Richard Babthorpe, father Allen: sent to Sister Aloysia Monsey, and Sister Margarite Moss, and given at new Year.[6]

---

[1] Diana Keynes, in religion Mary Joseph (BA126).

[2] Ann Joseph Andrews (BA003).

[3] Mary Gifford (1625 Louvain–1675 Bruges) LA107.

[4] Martha Copland (BA065).

[5] Mary Havers (1681–1733) BA099; Dorothy Risdom, in religion Eugenia (1701–05) BA162. Dorothy's convent history is unusual in that she left the convent, only returning in 1700 to profess in her thirties; see **[pp. 208, 213]**.

[6] Fr Richard Babthorpe SJ (1618–81); see Holt, pp. 23–4. Alloysia Momsey (BA142); Margaret Moss (BA146).

The year 1676

On the 14 of february our Reverend Arch Priest understanding that Sister Mary Josepha Keynes had been baptised by a Protestant Minister, he gave her the baptismal ceremonies and baptised her conditionaly, and on the 16 of the same month she was clothed.[1]

On the 18 of february, Sister Mary **[p. 125]** Bedingfield took the Schollars habit.

On the 28 of April Mrs Ourd, sister to Sir Edward Widdrington,[2] brought hither her niece Mrs Christiane Charlton, who pretended to be a Schollar for the order and she bought her Schollars coat, but would not put it on till another gentlewoman, Mrs Mary Godfrey came to her from our order in Paris.[3] This gentlewoman arrived here on the 10th of July, with the same pretension to be religious: but giving way to vanity and Idleness, they delay'd till Mrs Charlton fell sick. Then she pretended the Air did not agree with her, and that she would return and be religious at Paris: but while she was pretending to get her Mother's leave, they apply'd them selves to nothing but going abroad and keeping company, to the great trouble of our Comunity. Mrs Ourd return'd to England with little hopes of her nieces settlement.

On the 21 of June Mr Francis Bedingfeld brought his little daughter Elisabeth here for convictress. She was about 10 years old.[4]

[p. 126] On the 22 of June, Sister Martha Copland was clothed in the chapter house as usual.[5] And Mrs Christina Charlton enter'd our enclosure that day.

We this year received in Almns 424 florins, of which 250 were given by Sister Susan Reynolson's Brother, the rest by Mr Volder canon, Sir John Webb, Mr Caryll, and given at new year.

The year 1677

On the 14 of March, Sister Mary Josepha Keynes made her holy Profession.

On the 8th of April, Mrs Christina Charlton went out the morning with her companion Mrs Godfrey, pretending some business in town; and they went to a Colonel's house where she met on Captain Talbot with whom

---

1 Mary Joseph Keynes (BA126).

2 Clara Widdrington (d. 1691) married William Orde of Thistlerigg; her sister Mary (d. 1703) married Sir Edward Charlton of Hesleyside (d. 1674/5).

3 Mary Godfrey is not listed in the Paris Augustinian community. For Christina Charlton, see **[pp. 126–7]**.

4 Possibly the sister of Agnes (BA016) and Mary (BA018).

5 The clothing ceremony for lay sisters was led by the Prioress and conducted within the community.

she had contracted an engagement unknown to all her friends.[1] In a week's time she rashly resolved, and was marry'd that morning writing the news of it her self to our Reverende Mother, who was much amazed at it, and our whole comunity in great trouble. By this we may learn what it is to delay with God's grace, and to entertain such unsettled people. She made for excuse of her rashness, that it was the apprehension **[p. 127]** she had of going into her own country, by reason of the censures she might have of being inconstant since she came over with a full resolution to be religious. This made her marry in such haste to repent at leasure.

On the 30th of June, little Miss Ursula Farmer return'd to her parents in England.[2]

On the 12 of July Sister Mary Bedingfeld was clothed.[3]

On the 13 of July Sister Martha Copland was profess'd a lay sister.[4]

On the 10 of August, Mrs Ursula Henage with her Mother's leave, went to live at the French Ursulines at Bulloigne.[5]

We this year received in Almnes 174 florins. 100 of them was given by the Lady Widdrington, the rest by Mr Volder canon and given us at new year.

The year 1678

On the 21 of May Mrs Wenefride Henage return'd to England by her Mother's order.[6] Sister Catherine Bartlett conducted her to London: and return'd the 28 of June with Miss Helen Andrews, and Mrs Mary Wright, the latter took the Schollars habit with **[p. 128]** Sister Mary Havers.[7]

On the last of July the two Mrs Burlow came. About this time Mrs Dorothy Errington return'd.

The 7 of September Mrs de Rope a flemish gentlewoman came to live in our Monastry, as convictress, and after some months return'd home.

---

1 Christina Charlton married Mr John Talbot of Cartington, Northumberland. Their daughter Catherine professed as a Carmelite at Hoogstraten in 1720, HC061.

2 Possibly Ursula, daughter of Richard Fermor of Tusmore, Oxfordshire, and Frances Brooke; see Stirnet.com, family tree, Fermor02.

3 Mary Bedingfield (1678–1712) BA018.

4 Martha Copland (BA065).

5 The French Ursulines had a number of schools where English girls were sent to learn French. The Ursuline school at Boulogne is mentioned quite frequently in the Chronicle and other convent documents. Ursula Heneage is probably the daughter of George Heneage of Hainton, Lincolnshire, and Faith Tyrwhitt, and sister to two nuns, Winifred (PA076) and Constantia (OB060), although she herself did not join a convent. See Stirnet.com, family tree, Heneage2.

6 Winifred Heneage (1685–1719) PA076.

7 Catherine Bartlett (BA008); Helen Andrews (1682–1728) BA004, Procuratrix from 1709, Novice Mistress 1716–17, Sub-Prioress 1717–20, Procuratrix 1720–23, Sub-Prioress from 1723, School Mistress; Mary Wright, in religion Frances (1681–1730) BA227, musician; Mary Havers (1681–1733) BA099.

On the 2 of October Sister Agatha Brooke departed this life.[1] She received all the last Sacraments in her perfect senses, and dyed most piously as she had lived, being ever a most innocent devout creature. She was never idle, but according to her little capacity, always employ'd either in prayer or humble works, so that God's grace was admirable in so weak a creature, and I doubt not but she enjoys his eternal glory. *Requiescat in pace*. Amen.

On the 24 of november our Reverend father Robert Kent[2] departed this life, having been nine years our confessor during which time he was always sickly, yet never omitted his functions, saying and singing his Masses with much alacrity, till some months before his death he lost the use of his arms and suffer'd intolerable pains and sickenesses with very great patience and courage. He was always a great lover of peace, and of our comunity, to which he left better than a hundred pound Sterlin. **[p. 129]** He was bury'd by the Arch Priest in our Vault on the 27 of November. *Requiescat in pace*. Amen.

His place of confessarius was supply'd by father George Janion, an English father of the Society of Jesus, and his companion, they living in town to help the English soldiers.[3]

We this year received in Almns 418 florins of which 150 was from Mr Carvell, 100 from Mr Cary of Antwerp, and 100 florins from Sister Susan Reynolson's brother; the rest from Mr Volder canon, and given us at new year.

The year 1679

On the 2d of february Sister Perpetua Dorothy Errington took the Schollars habit.[4]

On the 10 of May, Sister Margarite Moss a lay sister, departed this life, about the 43 year of her age, and 18th of her holy profession.[5] She had lived a most exemplar pious life, was of a very peaceable fine temper, always present to her self, most careful in the service and profit of the comunity and truly punctual in all religious observances, yet not sparing her self in the most laborious works of the house: by which she perform'd both the parts of Martha and Mary, and happily (as we hope) attain'd to an eternal crown. *Requiescat in pace*. Amen.

[p. 130] On the 18 of September Madame de Vicq[6] whose own name was Petronella la Coste dyed most piously in our Monastry, to which

---

1 Agatha Brooke (1644–83) BA033.

2 Fr Robert Kent (1643–78), Confessor 1669–78; see Anstruther 3, pp. 121–2.

3 Fr George Janion SJ (1646–98), Supply Confessor 1678–81; Holt, p. 129.

4 Dorothy Errington, in religion Perpetua (BA076).

5 Margaret Moss (1662–79) BA146.

6 Madame de Vicq first came to the convent in March 1658 with her daughter-in-law when her marriage was in difficulties; see **[pp. 78, 83, 87–8]**.

she return'd, and lived some years before her death very peaceably and vertuously, disposing her self for a happy end, after a life spent in many troubles and turmoyles: being always enclined to make suits and processes: yet she had constant devotions and fasts in honour of our Blessed Lady who doubtless obtain'd for her so resign'd and pious end, which was very edifying to all. She was bury'd very solemnly in our Vault, and left amongst her other rents, one for a perpetual recreation on her Anniversary day, on which a Mass is to be sung, and she so remember'd with a perpetual. *Requiescat in pace*. Amen.

On the 20 of November, our Reverende Subprioress Sister Ursula Palmes departed this life about the 72 years of her age, and 48 of her profession.[1] She dyed most peaceably and piously as she had lived, being most eminent in obedience and mortification, wherein she seem'd as dead to the world, but ever zealous for all regular observances. She suffer'd a long and painful sickness, and made a most pious end, having been seven years Subprioress. *Requiescat in pace*. Amen.

[p. 131] Sister Barbara Caryll was chosen Subprioress in her place.[2]

On the 17 of December, Sister Catherine Bowes, a lay sister, departed this life in the 71 year of her age, and 47 of her profession.[3] She had had a long sickness, but was not judged by the Doctor so near death, which was so sudden that she had not the last Sacraments, yet according to her weak capacity, we may hope she was piously prepared, having made many good acts. *Requiescat in pace*. Amen.

We this year received in Almns 972 florins, of which the Pope's Nuncio gave 480 florins (the odd 80 is reserved for our Jubilee feast). Mr Caryll gave 500, and the rest was given at new year, and Jonica, our servant.

The year 1680

On the 29 of January Sister Mary Havers was clothed.[4]

On the 12 of february Mrs Mary Constantia Rope came back to our cloister and took the Schollars habit on the 17 of feb:[5]

The 4th of May, Mrs de Mol came to our Monastry with her maid, to live as Boarder.

On the 19 of May, Sister Mary Wright and Sister Dorothy Perpetua Errington were clothed.[6]

[p. 132] On the 25 of May Sister Helena Andrews took the Schollars habit.[7]

---

[1] Ursula Palmes (1631–79) BA149.

[2] Barbara Caryll (BA045).

[3] Catherine Bowes (1633–79) BA029.

[4] Mary Havers (BA099).

[5] Mary De Rope, in religion Constantia (1681–1719) BA165.

[6] Mary Wright (1681–1730) BA227; Dorothy Perpetua Errington (1681–1739) BA076.

[7] Helen Andrews (1682–1728) BA004.

The 2d of June Sister Mary Ann' Hamilton came back and took the Schollars habit.[1]

On the 1st of July, came Sister Clare Johnson to be a lay sister.[2]

On the 5th of August Sister Mary Constantia de Rope was clothed.

On the 22 of August Mrs Ann' Petre was received for a convictress.[3]

On the 2d of September Mrs Susan Rysdon return'd to England.

On the 25 of November Sister Mary Ann' Hamilton was clothed.

We this year received in Almnes only 90 florins. 25 legacy left us by a devote, and 66 [*sic*] given us at new year.

The year 1681

On the 4th of february, Sister Mary Havers made her holy Profession.[4]

On the 20th of May Sister Mary Wright and Sister Perpetua Errington were also profess'd.[5]

The 18 of August Sister Helena Andrews was clothed.[6]

The 20 of August Sister Mary Constantia **[p. 133]** de Rope made her holy Profession.[7]

On the 6 of September Elisabeth Theresia Cook came to be a lay sister.[8]

On the 9th of September came Sister Catherine and Sister Theresia Charlton, and they took the Schollars habit on the 14 of the same month.[9]

On the 24 of September Reverend father Janion and his companion were sent into England by their Provincial, the cause of their living at the colledge here, being removed.[10]

On the 15 of october, Mr John Hawker, a Roman Priest, came to be our confessor. He was recommended to us by some fathers of the Society of Jesus.[11]

The 24 of october Mrs Frances Standish came here to be a lay sister.[12]

We this year received in Almnes 100 florins, 40 given for Mr Paston, and 60 given at new year.

---

1 Mary Hamilton, in religion Ann (BA096).

2 Clare Johnson (1683–1720) BA124.

3 Ann Petre did not profess.

4 Mary Havers (BA099).

5 Mary Wright, in religion Frances (BA227); Dorothy Errington, in religion Perpetua (BA076).

6 Helen Andrews (BA004).

7 Mary Constantia De Rope (BA165).

8 Teresa Cooke (1684–1719) BA064.

9 Catherine Charlton, in religion Xaveria (1684–1731) BA050; Teresa Charlton (1685–91) BA049.

10 Fr George Janion SJ (1646–98), Supply Confessor 1678–81; Holt, p. 129.

11 Fr John Hawker (1650–1707) was Confessor 1681–1707; see Anstruther 3, pp. 95–6.

12 Frances Standish, in religion Mary Theresa (1684–91) BA180.

The year 1682

On the 19 of January Sister Mary Ann' Hamilton made her holy Profession.

The 14 of April the two little Carylls came to be convictresses.

On the 27 of April Sister Clare Johnson was clothed for a lay sister.[1]

On the 21 of June, Sister Brigitt Hughs, **[p. 134]** a lay sister, departed this life in the 49 year of her age, and 19 of her profession.[2] She had been pious and serviceable according to her capacity, for she had a defect in her brain, and at her death only received the holy oyles. *Requiescat in pace*. Amen.

On the 24 of June Sister Frances Standish and Sister Theresia Cook took the kerchief for lay sisters.

The 1st of August came the two Wrights for convictresses

On the 20 of August Sister Helena Andrews made her holy profession.

On the 21 of September Reverend dear Sister Mary Barker departed this life in the 47 year of her age and 27 of her holy profession.[3] She had alwavs been sickly and infirm. She received all the last Sacraments in her perfect senses, and with a full resignation to the divine will, and dyed most piously, as she had lived. *Requiescat in pace*. Amen

On the same day came Mrs Ann' Thirlwall to be religious.[4]

On the 6 of october Mrs Mary Berington, Widow to Mr Schip came to be religious.[5] She being ancient had a **[p. 135]** dispensation from the great office, granted her by our Vicars, but from no other observances. She took the Schollars habit with Mrs Thirtwall upon all Saints Eve: but on the 16 of December, she was against her will, forced to return for England, to dispatch some business which could not be done without her presence.

We this year received in Almnes 330 florins of which Mr Havers gave 100 for the soul of his wife, Madam Cox 100, and the rest given by Mr Henry Bedingfeld, Mrs Ford, and at new year.

The year 1683

On the 4th of January Sister Theresia Cook and Sister Frances Standish were clothed for lay sisters.[6]

On the 2d of April Sister Mary Rows most piously departed this life, disposed by nine days sickness, and receiving the last Sacraments

---

1 Clare Johnson (BA124).

2 Brigitt Hughes, in religion Margaret (BA115).

3 Mary Barker (BA013).

4 Ann Thirwall, in religion Benedict (1684–1739) BA199, Procuratrix 1716–20.

5 Mary Berington, in religion Xaveria (1684–1704) BA022, of Cowarne, Herefordshire. Both her maiden and married names are used in the Chronicle.

6 Frances Standish, in religion Mary Theresa (BA180); Teresa Cooke (BA064).

with great devotion and desire to dye.[1] Her Sister Dorothy[2] praying by her bed side, and desiring her to take her to heaven with her, she told her that she should not stay long after her. She said she had a sense of parting with her Superior, Confessor, and pious comunity; but was glad to go to **[p. 136]** God, and that if she found any power with him her poor blind sister should soon follow. And in effect, the night after her death, Sister Dorothy going well to bed, and most religiously resigned, and even comforted that her sister had dyed so happily, she was found in the morning very ill with a vehement pain in her side, which encreased to that excess that before nine the same morning she render'd her pious soul into the hand of her Creator. She made her confession and immediatly before she received the holy oyls (which could not be administerd to all the parts before she was dead). She had sung a song of the holy name of Jesus, whom she had ever served with much fervour and devotion. For some years before she dyed, she had been blind of one eye, yet she was most constant to the Quire, and was almost in continual prayer before the Blessed Sacrament. She used to say that when it pleased God to take from her the sight of her other eye, she should be still able to sing the *Gloria Patri* etc chearfully to Almight[y] God, which I doubt not but she soon perform'd in a blessed eternity. She died so, that she might have been exposed in the church before the Altar with her sister. When Sister Dorothy was laid out, Sister Catherine Bartlett[3] praying by her corps said aloud, dear Sister Dorothy, I doubt not but ye have as much power with Almighty God, as your Sister; if so, obtain that I may come soon to him: and that day fortnight she was bury'd; whereupon all were forbid such requests. These two sisters came to religion and were profess'd together, and lived about 30 years after. Sister Dorothy was 57 and her sister a year or two younger, and as they lived and dyed most piously and sweetly together, so we doubt not but they now enjoy their heavenly Spouse together in a blessed eternity. *Requiescat in pace*. Amen.

On the 29 of April Sister Clare Johnson was profess'd.[4]

On the 3 of May, Sister Catherine Bartlett, a lay sister departed this life, in her 57th year of her age and 37 of her holy profession. She had served our comunity with great fidelity, and was a very prudent and vertuous person, much esteem'd by all that knew her, giving great edification both at home and abroad, and she had always a true zeal for the credit and profit of our comunity. She dyed most piousl[y], as she had lived. *Requiescat in pace*. Amen.

---

1 Mary Rows (1654–83) BA167.

2 Doroth Rows (1654–83) BA166.

3 Catherine Bartlett (1646–83) BA008.

4 Clare Johnson (BA124).

Our Schoole began again with little **[p. 138]** Mrs Mary Caryll, who came back to us again from Dunkirk where her Parents had plac'd her elder sister with the Benedictin Dames.[1]

On the 26 of May, Mrs Frances Rookwood came for convictress. She was the youngest Daughter of Mr Rookwood of Coldham in Suffolk, and was brought by her Parents to our Monastry from the English poor Clares at Dunkirk.[2]

The two Sisters Catherine and Theresia Charlton, with Sister Ann' Benedicta Thirtwall were clothed on the 13 of June.

Mrs Berrington, widow to Mr Schip return'd from England, and brought her niece with her, Mrs Mary Vaughan, for convictress, then Sister Berrington was clothed on the 29 of July with dispensation from the great office by reason of her age, and because it was impossible for her to learn to read latin.[3]

On the 27 of August Mr Markham of Ollerton, and his Lady brought their 4 daughters to be convictresses.[4]

On the 30 of August Mrs Mary Widdrington, and Mrs Claire Saunderson, came also to be convictresses.[5]

In September the two Wrights took the Schollars habit.[6]

On the 7 of October Sister Augustina Hamilton departed this life in the 74 year of her age, and ninth of her holy profession.[7] She dyed most piously as she had lived, and was the only one of the 11 sisters, who marry'd in the world when after she had gone thro' that state of life with the practice of many vertues, particularly patience in many crosses and afflictions which she bore with true equality of mind (being ever of an excellent temper); God pleased to grant her desire of making the eleventh sister all religious, and having lived nine years in that state, with all true piety and devotion, she render'd her happy soul to her Creator. *Requiescat in pace*. Amen.

---

[1] Mary Caryll was possibly Mary, daughter of John Caryll of Harting and his wife, Catherine Petre, three of whose daughters were members of the Dunkirk convent.

[2] Frances Rookwood, in religion Apollonia (1685–1717) BA164, Sub-Prioress 1716–17. See F. Young, *Rookwood Family Papers, 1606–1761*, Suffolk Records Society 59 (Woodbridge: Boydell and Brewer for the Suffolk Records Society, 2016), p. xxx, n. 116.

[3] Mary Vaughan, in religion Mary Teresa (1687–92) BA208. Mary Berrington (BA022); she was 57 when she was clothed.

[4] Two of these daughters of Mr Thomas Markham and his wife, Ann Nevill, later professed: Henrietta Markham, in religion Melior (1696–1733) BA136; Ann Mechtilda Markham, in religion Ann Matilda (1687–1742) BA137, Sub-Prioress 1732–37. Mary and Ursula returned to England in July 1686; see **[p. 145]**. For a discussion of multiple family members in one convent, see **[p. 216]**.

[5] Mary Widdrington, in religion Ann (1687–1745) BA219, Sub-Prioress 1710–13; Clare Saunderson (1687–1731) BA172, Procuratrix from 1713; Sub-Prioress 1720–23 and 1728–31.

[6] Justina Wright, in religion Barbara (1685–91) BA226; Ann Wright, in religion Ann Victoria (1685–91) BA225.

[7] Elizabeth Hamilton, in religion Augustina (1674–83) BA094.

On the 1st of December our dear Subprioress Sister Barbara Caryll departed this life in the 45 year of her age, and 27 of her holy profession.[1] She was our fifth Subprioress, a person of most exemplar regular life, and of a truly peaceable sweet conversation: a great contemner of the world and all that is in it: and not withstanding the great gift of Almns her father sent her at his death, she would never admitt of the least for her own use, nor have the least particularity but **[p. 140]** still left all to the greater advancement of the common good. Her father and Mother at their death left her more than 350 pound sterling which she desired should be employ'd in the building of the great Pant, as also the 300 florins which her father had settled upon her during her life. But it pleased God to call her to himself which was a very great loss to us in all respects: but her vertuous life and earnest desire of enjoying Almighty God made her ripe for heaven. *Requiescat in pace*. Amen.

In the begining of December Catherine Burdett came to be a lay sister, but return'd again to England.

The 24 of December Mary Holme came and return'd to England the following year.

We this year received in Almns 107 florins, given by a Lady in town, a devote, at her death, and at new year.

The year 1684

On the 4th of January, Sister Frances Standish and Sister Theresia Cook were professed, the lat[t]er was very sick and in danger of death, so our Reverend Arch Priest with his two Deacons came after high Mass into the infirmar[y], where in presence of the whole comunity, she made her vows in bed.[2]

On the 6 of January Sister Elisabeth Brooks **[p. 141]** and Sister Joanna Couchefer took the kerchief for lay sisters.[3]

On the 9th of february, Sister Mary Wyat, a lay sister, departed this life in the 63 year of her age, and 30th of her holy profession.[4] She had served our comunity with much fidelity and great labours, even to the last, puting her self to the hardest and most laborious works of the Monastry, and being very careful of the common profit in all things: she was most sincere in the service of Almighty God, and impartialy charitable in serving all. She dyed most piousl[y] and chearfully, having ever desired to live no longer than she could labour and work for the

---

1 Barbara Caryll (1656–83) BA045.

2 Frances Standish, in religion Mary Theresa (BA180); Teresa Cooke (BA064).

3 Elizabeth Brooks (BA035) was clothed but left afterwards and returned to England: see **[p. 144]**. Johanna Couchefer (1685–1727) BA067.

4 Mary Wyatt (1653–84) BA229.

comunity, which she did to the last notwithstanding her great infirmities. *Requiescat in pace*. Amen.

On the 19 of June, Sister Catherine Charlton and Sister Ann' Thirlwall made their holy Profession. Sister Theresia Charlton stay'd for her portion.[1]

On the 20 of June Sister Justinia, and Sister Ann' Wright were clothed.[2]

In June Mrs Frances Rookwood took the Schollars habit.[3]

The 12 of July Mrs Agnes Bedingfeld and Mrs Mary Lomex came for convictresses.[4]

On the last of July Ann' Cherlicker **[p. 142]** came to be a lay sister.[5]

On the lst of August Sister Mary Xaveria Berington, or Schip, made her holy Profession.[6] The same day Mrs Mary Ann' Williamson came to be convictress.

On the 25 of August, Mrs Catherine Salkeld came as a convictress.

On the 13 of September Catherine Burdett return'd to England, not being fit for a lay sister.

On the 28 of october Ann' Bessbrown came to be a lay sister.[7]

On the 30 of october Sister Elisabeth Barbara Brooks, and Sister Joanna Couchefer were clothed for lay sisters.[8]

On the 23 of november, Sister Frances Rookwood was clothed.

We this year received in Almns 717 florins, of which the Lady Andrews gave 40, Mrs Williscot 200, Sister Berington for her husband 250, Mr Havers 75; and the rest to pray for Mr Farmer, and for Mr Clavering, and at new year.

The year 1685

On the 1st of June Sister Theresia Charlton made her holy profession.[9]

[p. 143] On the 9 of June the two little Nevilles came with Mrs Lane to be convictresses. Mrs Lane return'd to England again.

---

1 Catherine Charlton, in religion Xaveria (BA050); Ann Thirwall, in religion Benedict (BA199). Theresia Charlton was able to profess the following year; Catherine and Theresia were sisters.

2 Justina Wright, in religion Barbara (BA226); Ann Wright, in religion Ann Victoria (BA225).

3 Frances Rookwood, in religion Apollonia (BA164).

4 Agnes Bedingfield, in religion Agnes Genoveva (1687–1725) BA016. Mary Lomax did not profess at Bruges: she may be Mary Lomax who professed as a Carmelite at Hoogstraten in 1688, HC042. If so, the families of both these entrants had Suffolk connections.

5 Ann Cherlicker, in religion Mary Ann (1687–1733) BA051.

6 Mary Berington, in religion Xaveria (BA022). It is interesting to note here that the convent used Sister Xaveria's maiden name, which served to emphasise her English connections, rather than her married surname.

7 Ann Bessbrown, lay sister (1687–1717) BA023.

8 Johanna Couchefer (BA067).

9 Teresa Charlton (BA049).

The 30 of May Mrs Mary Widdrington and Mrs Clare Saunderson took the Schollars habit.[1]

On the 17 of July Sister Justina and Sister Ann' Wright made their holy Profession. And the same day Ann' Cherlicker took the kerchief for a lay sister.[2]

On the 28 of September Mrs Dorothy March, and Mrs Margarite Mountford came to be convictresses, the later after half a years indisposition made a very pious end, being newly converted to the holy catholick faith. She wish'd when she came over that she might die and be bury'd amongst us, as she was, in our Vault. *Requiescat in pace*. Amen.

On the 15 of october Mrs Mary Yates (who came to be religious) took the Schollars habit with Mrs Agnes Bedingfield, Mrs Mary Vaughan and Mrs Mary Lomex.[3]

The 7 of november Mrs Anne Mectilda Markham, and Mrs Ann' Delphina Williamson, took the Schollars habit.[4]

[p. 144] On the 5 of november Sister Joana Couchefer was profess'd a lay sister, Elisabeth Brooks who was clothed with her being gone for England.[5]

On the 19 of november Sister Mary Widdrington, and Sister Clare Saunderson were clothed.[6]

On the 26 of november Sister Frances Rookwood made her holy Profession.

We this year received in Almns 391 florins: of which 200 were given by Mr Thomson at his death, 100 by Count Hamilton, and the rest by Mrs Spanogle and given at new Year.

The year 1686

On the 27 of March Sister Agnes Genoveva Bedingfeld and Sister Mary Augustina Yates were clothed.[7]

The 23 of May Mrs Hill came for a boarder.

---

1 Mary Widdrington, in religion Ann (BA219); Clare Saunderson (BA172).

2 Justina Wright (BA226); Ann Wright (BA225); Ann Cherlicker, in religion Mary Ann (BA051).

3 Mary Yates left the convent in 1688; see **[p. 148]**. Mary Lomax is probably the same Mary Lomax; see **[p. 141]**. Agnes Bedingfield and Mary Vaughan professed at Bruges in 1687.

4 Ann Mechtilda Markham, in religion Ann Matilda (BA137). Ann Delphina Williamson did not proceed to clothing.

5 Johanna Couchefer (BA067).

6 Mary Widdrington, in religion Ann (BA219); Clare Saunderson (BA172).

7 Agnes Bedingfield, in religion Agnes Genoveva (BA016). Mary Yates left in 1688 owing to the lack of a dowry; she professed at the Dominicans, Brussels in May 1690 with a dowry of 2000 guilders (BD076).

On the 10 of June Mrs Apolonia Gibson and Mrs Elisabeth Loveden came for convictresses.[1]

On the 18 of June Sister Ann' Cherlicker and Sister Mary Ann' Besbrown were clothed for lay sisters.[2]

[p. 145] On the 4 of July Mrs Elisabeth Dacres came for convictress, and return'd to England a year and quarter after.

The 15 of July Sister Mary Theresia Vaughan and Sister Ann' Markham were clothed.[3] In the same month Mrs Mary and Mrs Ursula Markham return'd to England.

On the 27 of July Mrs Frances Clough came to be a convictress.[4]

The 2d of August Mrs Sakeld went for Paris.

On the 18 of August Mrs Canning came for convictress.[5]

On the 7 of September Mrs Mary Brown came for Pensioner.

On the 21 of September Mrs Blacket came for Pensioner also.

On the 26 of September Mrs Hill return'd to England.

Mrs Milburge Russell came to be religious and took the Schollars Habit on the 29 of September.[6]

We this year received in Almns 188 florins. 100 of it from Lady Webb, 50 from Mr Thirlwall, and the rest given at new year

The year 1687

[p. 146] On the 7 of January Sister Mary Ann' Widdrington, and Sister Clare Saunderson made their holy Profession.[7]

On the 17 of January Sister Mary Magdalene Kemp departed this life after a most painful sickness of three months which disposed her to a most resigned and pious death in the 50th year of her age and 30th of her holy Profession.[8] The chief motive of her coming to religion was a most serious vow of virginity which she made to the Blessed Virgin in her tender years: who obtain'd her such grace to perform that vow that a very learned man of the Society with whom she had dealt for some years and to whom she had made a general confession before her death, affirm'd that she dyed as pure and innocent in point of chastity as a child of five years old. May she ever enjoy her most chaste Spouse in eternal glory. *Requiescat in pace*. Amen.

---

1 Apolonia Gibson did not persevere; Elizabeth Loveden (1695–1701) BA130.

2 Ann Cherlicker, in religion Mary Ann (1687–1733) BA051; Mary Ann Bessbrown (1687–1717) BA023.

3 Mary Teresa Vaughan (1687–92) BA208; Ann Mechtilda Markham (1687–1742) BA137.

4 Frances Clough, in religion Christina (1689–1735) BA059.

5 Possibly Elizabeth Canning, who professed in 1691 (BA044).

6 Milburge Russell (1688–1730) BA168.

7 Mary Ann Widdrington, in religion Ann (BA219); Clare Saunderson (BA172).

8 Mary Magdalen Kemp (1656–87) BA125.

On the 9 of June Mrs Ursula Mannock came for convictress.[1]

On the 16 of June Sister Milburge Russell was clothed.

On the 3d of July Sister Ann' Cherlicker and Sister Ann' Besbrown were professed lay sisters.[2]

The 15 of July Sister Agnes Genoveva Bedingfeld, Sister Mary Vaughan and Sister Ann Mectilda Markham made their holy Profession.[3]

The lst of July Sister Frances Clough took the Schollars habit.[4]

On the 28 of november Mrs Mary Woolgat came for convictress.

We this year received in Almns 490 florins of which 100 was from the Lady Andrews, 100 from Sir John Webb, 50 from Mr John Thirlwall, 200 from Count Hamilton and the rest given at new year.

The year 1688

On the 2d of May Sister Frances Clough was clothed.

The 21 of June Sister Milburge Russell was professed.[5]

The 2d of July Sister Henrietta Melior Markham took the Schollars habit.[6]

The 29 of August Mrs Theresia Gibson came for a convictress.

[p. 148] On the 15 of August Mrs Elisabeth Canning took the Schollars habit.[7]

The 3rd of September the 4 little Irelands were received for convictresses.[8]

On the 19 of September Elisabeth Heath came to be a lay sister.[9]

Sister Mary Yates not having her full portion went from hence, and was accepted upon tryal at the Spelicains at Bruxelles.[10]

We this year received in Almnes 308 florins, of which 10 was given us to pray for our Prince of Wales, 100 given by Mr Thirlwall, the rest

---

1 Ursula Mannock later left Bruges and professed instead at the Benedictines in Brussels (1697–1746) BB117, Novice Mistress in 1724; see also references to her in her aunt's obituary, **[pp. 198–9]**.

2 Ann Cherlicker (BA051); Ann Bessbrown (BA023).

3 Agnes Genoveva Bedingfield (BA016); Mary Vaughan, in religion Mary Teresa (BA208); Ann Mechtilda Markham, in religion Ann Matilda (BA137).

4 Frances Clough, in religion Christina (1689–1735) BA059.

5 Milburge Russell (BA168).

6 Henrietta Markham, in religion Melior (BA136).

7 Elizabeth Canning, in religion Elizabeth Victoria (1691–1750) BA044.

8 Possibly four daughters (Lucy, Rachel, Frances and Mary) of Thomas Ireland of Albrighton, Shropshire and his wife, Elizabeth Clayton. None of them joined the Bruges convent: Lucy and Rachel joined the Brussels Benedictines and Frances and Mary joined the Lierre Carmelites.

9 Elizabeth Heath; she left before profession and is probably the same Elizabeth Heath who joined the Sepulchrines, in 1694 (LS103).

10 Mary Yates professed at the Dominicans, Brussels (also known as the Spellikens) in 1690 and died there in 1733, BD076.

by a Lady in Town at her death, by Mary Chapman, a maid servant to Mrs Wright, and at new year.

The year 1689

In February little Miss Elisabeth Rookwood,[1] niece to Sister Frances Rookwood, was received for convictress.[2]

On the 14 of february Sister Frances Clough made her holy profession after a long and patient expectation occasion'd by the delay of the payment of her portion.[3]

In April Mrs Mary and Mrs **[p. 149]** Elisabeth Huddlestone eldest daughters to Mr Huddlestone of Sauson, were received for convictresses.[4]

On the 15 of August Mrs Rachel Ireland took the Schollars habit. Her three sisters return'd home to their Parents who lived then at Bruxelles.

We this year received in Almns 130 florins, 50 of them given to pray for the soul of a gentlewoman, 42 Mrs Ford's Legacy, and the rest given us at new year.

The year 1690

On the 30th of March Sister Elisabeth Victoria Canning was clothed.[5]

In September Sister Elisabeth Heath was clothed for a lay sister, tho' she was not very well liked; but she promised, and we hoped great amendment.[6]

Miss Curson came in October for convictress.

This year was very hot and towards the end of it, it pleased God to visit us with the infection of the smal pox of which Sister Ann' Wright fell sick.[7]

We had no Almns this year, only 20 florins given us at new year.

---

1 Elizabeth Rookwood (1684–1759), sole daughter of Thomas Rookwood of Coldham Hall, Suffolk, and Tamworth Martin, later became a central figure of the Catholic community in eighteenth-century Suffolk, marrying John Gage of Hengrave in 1718; see F. Young (ed.), *Rookwood Family Papers, 1606–1761*, Suffolk Records Society 59 (Woodbridge: Boydell and Brewer for the Suffolk Records Society, 2016), pp. xlii–vi.

2 Frances Rookwood, in religion Apollonia (BA164).

3 Frances Clough, in religion Christina (BA059).

4 Elizabeth Huddleston of Sawston, Cambridgeshire, later professed as Angela (1695–1756) BA112, Procuratrix 1723–30. Mary did not profess: she married Sir Francis Fortescue, 4th Baronet of Salden (d. 1729); see Stirnet.com, Family Tree, Huddleston3.

5 Elizabeth Victoria Canning (BA044).

6 The difficulties with Elizabeth Heath continued; see also **[pp. 148, 157]**.

7 Ann Wright (BA225).

[p. 150]

The year 1691

On the 14 of february our dear Sister Ann' Wright dyed of the small pox in the 24 year of her age and 6th of her holy profession.[1] She was ever of a most innocent sweet conversation, and bore her sickness with a great deal of patience. She made a most resigned and devout preparation for death, continually purifying her soul by devout act of contrition for her sins, frequent confession, receiving all the sacraments with much devotion, and entirely resigning her self to the divine will; so that we piously hope she enjoys a blessed eternity. *Requiescat in pace*. Amen.

On the 16 of January, our dear Sister Agnes Mildmay having had a long and most painful sickness for near three months, made a most happy and pious end in the 55 years of her age, and 29 of her holy profession.[2] She was ever of a most Regular pious conversation, sincere in all her proceedings, and very zealous for religious observances. She was particularly devoted to the Blessed virgin, said her Rosary daily, and whilst it **[p. 151]** was recited by her bed side, after she had received her rights, she sweetly gave up her soul into the hands of her creator. *Requiescat in pace*. Amen.

The infection of the smal pox then spread it self extreamly in our Monastry, as it was very much over the whole country. The two other sisters of the Wrights, fell both sick of it on the same day and hour; and dear Sister Justinia Wright[3] was strucken with the worst sort of smal pox; of which few or none ever recovers, which when she saw upon her hands, she presently resigned her self to die; calling for the holy Sacraments, and making a most excellent and pious preparation for death: inviting death to come to her, that so she might soon enjoy the sight and fruition of her heavenly Spouse. She often renew'd her vows, and embracing her crucifix with most amorous affection, she chearfully render'd her happy soul into the hands of her creator on the 4th of february, the 25th year of her age, and 6th of her holy profession. *Requiescat in pace*. Amen.

[p. 152] Our Reverende dear Subprioress Sister Margarite Barker fell sick of the same disease which soon brought her to her last, after she had made a truly pious and happy preparation for death, devoutly receiving all the rights of our holy Mother the Church: and her life had been most regular in all religious observances, ever endeavouring in all her works to advance the common good and profit.[4] She dyed in the 57 year of her

---

1 Anne Wright (1685–91) BA225.

2 Agnes Mildmay (BA141).

3 Justina Wright (1685–91) BA226. Mary Wright, in religion Frances (BA227) survived the epidemic. The fourth sister has not yet been located.

4 Margaret Barker (1656–91) BA012.

age and 35' of her holy Profession, and the 7th of her Subprioressship, on the 25 of february. *Requiescat in pace*. Amen.

The infection still encreased, and the malignity of the disease was such that we had a very great number of our religious in eminent danger of death. It pleased God to take Sister Martha Margarite Clark, a young creature about 17 years of age, who had been with us about a year in tryal for a lay sister, and was judged by her sweet and humble conversation to be very fit for that happy State.[1] She made her vows upon her deathbed, and was buryed in the lay sisters habit in our Vault. **[p. 153]** She dyed on the 16 of March. *Requiescat in pace*. Amen.

On the 17 of March Sister Frances Standish, a lay sister, dyed of a vehement pain in her side which had lasted for some days.[2] She received all the rights, and immediatly after dyed, tho' unexpectedly yet not unprovided. Her life was very religious, and her death pious about the 37 year of her age, and 8th of her holy Profession. *Requiescat in pace*. Amen.

Mrs Rookwood boarding with out in our confessors house, got the infection of smal pox, and being with our Lord Bishop's leave brought into our infirmary to be tended amongst our religious, she made a most christian pious end on the 23 of March, and is bury'd in our Vault.[3] *Requiescat in pace*. Amen.

On the 1st of April our dear Sister Theresia Lauraine[4] departed this life. Some nights before she dyed, she had a particular dream that St Xaverius had obtain'd for her the discovery of a sin or sins, which would have put her salvation in danger if he had not done her that favour **[p. 154]** and that the saint not only order'd her to confess, but also appointed her the father who was to hear her confession. It was the Procurator of the Jesuit's Colledge, he came to town but three davs before and she had never seen nor heard of him, yet could describe him: so he was sent for, and she having made her confession remain'd thoroughly satisfied. She had been ill for some months with a swelling in her legs and such like infirmities, then got the smal pox and most piously and peaceably disposed her self for a happy death which happen'd on the lst of April in the 48 year of her age and 30th of her holy profession. *Requiescat in pace*. Amen.

---

1 Martha Margaret Clarke, in religion Margaret (1691) BA056.

2 Frances Standish (1684–91) BA180.

3 Mrs Elizabeth Rookwood (c. 1629–91), née Caldwell, of Horndon-on-the-Hill, Essex, wife of Ambrose Rookwood (d. 1693), mother of four nuns with the Poor Clares at Gravelines; see F. Young, *Rookwood Family Papers, 1606–1761*, Suffolk Records Society 59 (Woodbridge: Boydell and Brewer for the Suffolk Records Society, 2016), pp. xxix–xxxi. A monument with a Latin inscription commemorating Elizabeth Rookwood was recorded as being at the English Convent in 1732; see ibid., pp. 12–13, for text and translation.

4 Teresa Lauraine (Byrhaut) (1662–91) BA127.

Sister Angela Mannock[1] after she was recover'd of the smal pox, relapsed into a feavour which finding her weak, took her away in a few days; on the 23 of April she dyed most piously, about the 46 year of her age, having lived 29 years in holy religion, a very regular and retired life. *Requiescat in pace*. Amen.

On the 25 of April Miss Judith Markham, a convictress, departed this **[p. 155]** life.[2] She had the smal pox which after wards broke out in ulcers, and she suffer'd incredible paines with great patience for 2 months, then she dyed most sweetly, and lyes bury'd in our church. *Requiescat in pace*. Amen.

Then our merciful God was pleased to take away all infection, and restor'd our family to a perfect health.

On the 5th of May, Sister Elisabeth Victoria Canning, made her holy Profession.[3]

About this time Sister Henrietta Melior Markham having been long Schollar by reason of a sore leg which no endeavour here could cure, she was forced to go to england to seek for remedy there.[4]

On the 30th of July the Lady Anne Howard, daughter to the Duke of Norfolk, came to us, tho' designed by the Dutchess for the third order of St Francis in this Town; therefore she was not received here till the Dutchess had given her consent, and that the third order was satisfied that it was her earnest desire, and not our enticement that brought her hither.[5]

On the 27 of September, Sister Elisabeth **[p. 156]** Bartlett, a lay sister dyed so suddenly in her cell that she could only receive the extream unction, but she had communicated some days before she fell sick and for seven months before seem'd to make devout and particular preparation for death; so tho' the violence of the feavour soon deprived her of her senses and took her away in a short [t]ime: yet we hope she was not unprepared.[6] She was a person truly zealous and laborious in the service of our community, and dyed in the 60th year of her age, and 38th of her holy Profession. *Requiescat in pace*. Amen.

On the 29 September, the Lady Ann' Howard took the Schollars habit.

On the 12 of october our dear Sister Aloysia Elisabeth Monsey made a most pious and happy end, after a very tedious sickness of many years,

---

[1] Angela Mannock (1662–91) BA134.

[2] Judith Markham was possibly one of four girls brought to the convent by their parents in 1683: see **[p. 138]**.

[3] Elizabeth Victoria Canning (BA044).

[4] Henrietta Melior Markham (BA136).

[5] Ann Howard, in religion Dominic (1693–1734) BA107. The convent of the English Franciscans was at Prinsenhof, Bruges. In January 1691, Jane, Duchess of Norfolk placed the hearts of her husband and son in a porphyry urn at Prinsenhof, intending after her death that her own heart should be added. It would have cemented the family relationship with the convent if her daughter had entered: see *Franciscana*, pp. 52–3.

[6] Elizabeth Bartlett (1653–91) BA014.

she being worne out with pains and torments even to her last extremity.[1] She was a person most eminent in self abnegation, and truly exemplar in regular observances. Her death was in the 66 year of her age, and 40th of her holy profession. *Requiescat in pace*. Amen.

[p. 157] On the 26 of November Elisabeth Heath went from our Monastry, she not having the votes of our community for her Profession.[2]

The same day Mrs Mary Weedon came to be religious. She took the Schollars habit on the 28th of November; but not having her health, and being in danger to fall into a consumption, she return'd to England.

On the 6th of december, Sister Theresia Charlton departed this life in the 26th year of her age and 7th of her holy Profession.[3] She had been many months in a continual consumptive sickness which she suffer'd most patiently: and consumed to skin and bone, she concluded a painful life by a most happy death. She had a most excellent voice for the Quire, and was truly regular; so that we may piously hope she got great merit in a little time. *Requiescat in pace*. Amen.

We this year received in Almns 854 florins, of which 200 was given by Mr. Monsey, 500 by Count Hamilton,[4] 50 by Mr. Errington at his death,[5] and the rest by Sister Martha Williscot's friends, for **[p. 158]** her brother's soul, by our Apothecary's wife and given at new year.

The year 1692

On the 22th [*sic*] of February came the Lady Lucy He[r]bert, Daughter to William Duke of Powis, Lord Chamberlain of his Majesty's Household.[6] This Lady being call'd by Almighty God to a religious life, and having seen most of the English Monastries, and read the rules and constitutions of many, made choice of our house to withdraw into: tho' all oppositions were made to her pious resolution both as to the state of life she designed to embrace, and the family she preferr'd. Amongst other instances, it was

1 Elizabeth Momsey, in religion Alloysia (1652–91) BA142.

2 Elizabeth Heath had proved difficult from her arrival; see **[pp. 148–9]**.

3 Teresa Charlton (1685–91) BA049.

4 Probably Anthony Hamilton (1644/5?–1719); see *ODNB*.

5 Mr William Errington, of Errington and Beaufront, father of Dorothy Errington (BA076), died on 12 June 1691. Her sister (no name known) was married to Mr Hamilton of Ireland. Stirnet.com has her mother as Agnes Errington. Her mother's maiden name was Girlington of Thurland Castle.

6 William, 1st Marquis of Powis (d. 1696) and his wife, Elizabeth, accompanied James II and the royal family to France in December 1688, both of them serving in the royal household at St Germain-en-Laye. The title 'Duke' was a Jacobite creation. See Corp, particularly chapter 3. Lucy had been educated with her sister Winifred at the English Benedictine convent in Pontoise from 1674; see Archives départementales du Val d'Oise, Bénédictines anglaises de Pontoise, 68H3, 'Registre abrégé'.

not the least, that our Monastry was in the enemies country,[1] out of all commerce with her relations, and she not acquainted with one person in it; but this difficulty proved a new motive to one that desired to leave the world entirely, and if possible, to be forgoten by it. Her very earnest zeal to be with us, made her not so much as stay for a tolerable season or Spanish Pass, but without either in the midst of a most severe and snowy winter, she happily arrived here, conducted by Father **[p. 159]** Lewis Sabrand of the Society of Jesus, The Queen's Chaplain (and that by her Majesty's orders)[2] and attended only by her woman, and Mrs Mary Burton who came also with desire to be religious.[3]

My Lord Bishop[4] came to visit the Lady as soon as he knew of her being come to town: and as her Ladyship press'd to take the first habit as soon as possible, she received it on the first of March, and would have Mrs Burton take it with her, desiring there should be no difference made between her and any one she resolved to look upon as Sister.

This Lady, by several years application to vertue having all the improvements requisite, was clothed on the 17th of the same month: which was perform'd with all the solemnity the present times would allow of; for her father being then in so eminent a place with our King who was at that time look'd upon as our enemy: this hinder'd the Bishop from performing the ceremony, which he had offer'd to do; and was the cause that the Governor and Chief of the Town were not present at it.

She was clothed so soon with the bishop's and Convent's consent.

On the 26 of March Sister Mary Petre **[p. 160]** departed this life after a short sickness, in the 48 year of her age, and 27 of her holy Profession.[5] She was a person most sincerely vertuous and regular; truly fearing God even to anxiety; yet she made a most peaceable and pious end, made great preparations for a happy death, and wished to die at that very time. *Requiescat in pace*. Amen.

On the 29 of March, Sister Mary Theresia Vaughan departed this life, in the 21 year of her age, and 5th of her holy Profession.[6] She was a most pious regular religious woman, aspiring from her first begining to

---

[1] Flanders is referred to as being in the 'enemies country' as a result of the outbreak of war in 1688 which continued until 1697 (Nine Years' War) between Louis XIV and the Grand Alliance led by William III of Holland. The main fighting occurred in the Spanish Netherlands. The position of Lucy Herbert's family at the English court in exile sheltered by the French king made for some awkwardness: clothing ceremonies were generally occasions of great celebration and invitations were sent to the great and the good locally.

[2] Lucy Herbert, in religion Teresa Joseph (1693–1744) BA101, Procuratrix 1699–1709; Prioress 1709–44. Fr Louis Sabran SJ (1652–1732) was at this time chaplain to Mary of Modena and the Prince of Wales at St Germain-en-Laye. See *ODNB* and Holt, p. 217.

[3] Mary Burton, in religion Mary Alexia (1693–1727) BA040.

[4] The bishop in 1692 was Willem Bassery, Bishop of Bruges 1690–1706.

[5] Mary Petre (1665–92) BA153.

[6] Mary Teresa Vaughan (1687–92) BA208.

the perfection of the religious state: a great lover of holy poverty, exact in obedience, and truly resigned to God's blessed Will in her long sickness: for she had been many months in a tedious consumptive distemper which brought her to her last, and to the last breath she aspired after her heavenly Spouse, may she eternally enjoy him. *Requiescat in pace.* Amen.

On the 21 of April the Lady Anne Howard, Sister Ann' Dominica was clothed.[1]

Our Lord Bishop made a visit to our Monastry this year on the 22 of March. He first said Mass in our church **[p. 161]** then made a french exhortation to all the religious; after that he spoke with every Profess'd nun apart, father Visconti of the Society of Jesus, being interpretor.[2] His Lordship made no alterations, but was very well satisfied with our community.

On the 29 of May Mary Coffee came to our Monastry to be a lay sister.[3]

On the 15' of August our Lady's Assumption, came the two Halsalls, who having lived some weeks in the Monastry, took the Schollars habit on the 7th of September, together with Mrs Elisabeth Loveden, who had long importuned for her admittance.[4]

On the 14 of September Sister Mary Alexia Burton was clothed.[5]

On the 17 of September our dear Reverende Mother Mary Bedingfeld fell into her last sickness which came with the fright and general concern she had when an earthquake made both houses and churches shake; it indeed was a sad omen to us, for her Reverence falling sick to bed never went downstaires more.[6]

On the 13 of October Sister Gertrude Brooke departed this life in the 55 year of her age, and 32 of her holy profession.[7] **[p. 162]** She had been brought up here from a child and was of a sweet pious temper, preventing and willing to oblige. She had a very good voice and did good service to the Quire, helping the musick also by playing on the violin. She had but eight days sickness and dyed most piously. *Requiescat in pace.* Amen.

---

1 Ann Howard, in religion Dominic (1693–1734) BA107.

2 Probably Fr Hermes Maria Visconti SJ (b. 1650 Milan), who moved to the English Province in 1665. He was connected with Ghent and was mentioned as a member of the English Province between 1680 and 1693. See G. Oliver, *Collections towards Illustrating the Biography of the Scotch, English and Irish Members* (Exeter: Featherstone, 1838), p. 195; Holt, pp. 244–5.

3 Magdalen Coffee (1694–1742) BA060.

4 Halsall was the maiden name of Elizabeth Loveden (BA130).

5 Mary Burton, in religion Mary Alexia (BA040).

6 Mary Bedingfield (BA019).

7 Elizabeth Brooke, in religion Gertrude (1660–84) BA034.

On the 20 of October Ann' Devery came to be a lay sister; with her came Mrs Mary Ireland for a convictress who went to see her Aunt at Liège, and then return'd and enter'd our convict on the 24 of November.[1]

On the feast of our Lady's presentation Sister Ann' Devery took the kerchief for a lay sister, being dispensed from the year of tryal which usually the lay sisters have before the first habit.

On the begining of December came the two Mrs Vaughan for convictresses.[2]

We this year received in Almns 236 florins. 200 from Mr John Caryll, and 36 from Mr. Cloysman at his death.

The year 1693

On the 22 of January Sister Martha Williscote departed this life in the 63 year **[p. 163]** of her age, and 42 of her holy profession.[3] She was a good harmless soul, but having been many years from her self she only received the extream unction. *Requiescat in pace*. Amen.

The two Halsalls not persevering in their resolutions for religion, return'd for England on the 12 of May.

Some few days before our Reverende Mother Mary Bedingfeld dyed, Mr Damerin[4] was chosen by her Reverence and her three consultresses, for temporal father, to take care of all our temporal affaires; and this was confirm'd by a publick notary, and signed by father confessor,[5] as wittness and by our Reverende Mother whose hand father confessor guided, she not being able to do it her self; the rest who were present, also signed it.

On the 13 of May our dear Reverende Mother Mary Bedingfeld departed this life at three in the morning, after ten monthes sickness, and an Agony that lasted from ten in the morning till three the next morning, in continual convulsions.[6] This was one of the most mournful days we ever had, since each of us **[p. 164]** lost in her a most loving and tenderly beloved Mother; her own happyness in this occasion was the only comfort, we her afflicted children could be sensible of. Her

---

1 Ann Devery professed as Ann Barbara Devery in 1694 as a lay sister and died in 1733, BA072; after this point, the Chronicles mostly refer to her as Barbara. Little is known about Mary Ireland: she is recorded in the Chapter Book at Liège as having entered in July 1696. The Ireland family of Crofton, Yorks, was linked to the Webb family by marriage in this period.

2 Teresa Vaughan, in religion Teresa Augustine (1709–31) BA209; Ann Vaughan, in religion Mary Joseph (1709–14) BA207. Their brother, Richard (1674–1727), was a Jesuit and Rector of the English College at Ghent.

3 Martha Wollascott (BA224).

4 Antoine Damerin, lord of Hoflande and Heule (d. 1728), married Louise-Dorothée De Groote de Drumez. Listed in F. Van Dycke, *Recueil héraldique* (Bruges, 1851), p. 130. I am indebted to Paul Arblaster for this reference.

5 The Confessor in 1693 was Fr John Hawker; Anstruther 3, pp. 95–6.

6 Mary Bedingfield (1652–93) BA019, Prioress 1661–93.

forty two years in religion were the true pattern of a vertuous life, and the thirty two years she govern'd, may be proposed as the most perfect for her successors to copy. She had been brought up a Pensioner in this house under the care of her Aunt Reverende Mother Augustina whom she succeeded as much by the imitation of her vertues as by filling her vacant place.[1] Three years that a fond Mother employ'd in diverting her in England from the thoughts of being religious, instead of cooling her zeal which carryed her to that happy State of life, so far inflamed it, that perswaded, she had given too much to the obedience she owed her mother, she went from home alone in the dark silence of the night, and tho' naturaly at that age very fearful, pass'd thro' a church yard also, not only leaving what jewels or other things of valu she had, behind her, that the world might see 'twas the only treasure of her soul she was concerned to save, but even forgeting her shooes till a thorne that prick'd her foot minded her of them: and having lurk'd **[p. 165]** some time to escape a very narrow search made every where after her, with such diligence that once she avoided her pursuers by geting out at a backdoor when she saw them enter the house she was conceal'd in; she at last got safe to her long wish'd for refuge, this Monastry, a true Nazareth to her. Thus stock'd at her arrival, she improved to that degree in all vertues that her holy Aunt judged her self oblig'd after four [y]ears' profession, to confide to her that most important employ of Mistress of the novices; and six years after, she was chosen Prioress by the votes of the comunity.

The distracting cares of her employment never interrupted a most tender union with God ever present to her thoughts, and sensibly effecting her heart, over which she strict a guard[2] that the particular papers she had laid up the last [y]ears of her life, coming to her director's hands, he found in 48 distinct papers, an exact account of each month taken at those several reviews in which she constantly spent a whole day; and all the accounts of her particular examen, without the least intermission, with the fruits of each spiritual exercise. For the 7 last **[p. 168]**[3] years of her life she was never free from pain by very sharp humours yet always serene and chearful: during those years tho' the sharp humours work'd several holes in her leg, and pain'd her with violent inflammations which would only allow her to lye in one posture in bed, and often afforded her but few hours of sleep, yet she would constantly rise at four, and never be absent from the choir service: nor did she seem sensible of her pains, except when we forced her to keep her chamber and so deprived

---

1 Augustina Bedingfield (1622 Louvain–1661 Bruges) LA023, arrived in Bruges by invitation 1639, Prioress 1640–61.

2 The meaning is not entirely clear here, but suggests a sense of a nun working ceaselessly to take care of her practical work while attempting to carry out spiritual exercises conscientiously.

3 Pagination jumps in original from **[p. 165]** to **[p. 168]**.

her of the comfort of being at holy Mass, and at the choir duties. Nay tho' confin'd to her bed or couch, she would no[t] omit the duties of her place but wrote her letters till her sight quite fail'd her and dispatch'd all affairs her self then when scarce able to stand she would with great pain get to the choir and read and sing there as if in perfect health. In her most violent pains, she most earnestly beg'd for encrease of patience, but never ask'd any diminishing of her suffrings especialy in her last sickness which lasted from the 19 of September 1692 to the 13 of May 1693. On the first of April she received all the rights of the holy church, after which she seem'd to mend; but on ascension Eve, whilst they were singing Litanies in the Garden, she forced her self **[p. 169]** from her bed to the window, and was taken with so violent a transport of joy at the sight of so many and such vertuous Spouses of Christ, to most of whom she had given the holy veil, that it suddenly sunk her strength. The next day she fell into a convulsion fit, yet received *viaticum* again, and after long and painful Agonies which purified her soul and compleated her crown, she arrived at last to that happy moment so long wish'd for that her continual aspiration for six years in the practice of her particular examen was *Quando veniam et apparebo te*: when shal I came dear Lord and appear before your blissful eyes,[1] in which she render'd her soul into the hands of her beloved Spouse, in the 63 year of her age. The serenity of her countenance when she was dead being a mark of the happiness of her soul, it even comforted the most afflicted for her death, who felt a very great mitigation of their grief while they could stand by her and look on her face. She was bury'd on the 15 in the middle of our church before the high altar. The Arch Priest perform'd the funerals[2] and made a short funeral oration **[p. 170]** amidst the tears of her children, and lamentations of the seculars, she being highly esteem'd by all, and many of the chief of the town being present.

This Reverende Mother, by means of father Sabran[3] (a man eminent for sanctity and learning, and afterwards Provincial of the English Society) establish'd the renovation of vows amongst us, as we annually practice it now with three days recollection and the proper meditations expounded by the Rector. She also introduced the Meditation after Evening song on Sundays for the particular examin.

[*Addition in the margin*] In this Reverende Mother's time was built the great Pant and Dormitory over it, as also the house in the garden; and the house that was our old Schoole was taken into the enclosure. [*end of the addition*]

---

1 Quotation from Psalm 41:2; used in the Office for the Dead.
2 Although the plural is used, there was only one funeral.
3 Fr Louis Sabran SJ (1652–1732); see Holt, p. 217.

After the funerals of our Reverende Mother were perform'd, my Lord Bishop sent the Arch Priest to ordain three days of prayer, silence and fasting, for the happy election of a new Superior. The next day his Lordship came himself to our Grate, call'd for the whole comunity and after a fatherly speech, made us the proffer of chusing a Trianial Superior,[1] insisting very much upon it, and assuring us that if at the three years end we liked our choice he would confirm her for life: but the greater part of the comunity, both Elders and youngers, refused it as apprehending it **[p. 171]** might make a gap for factious spirits to breed some discord, and break that peaceful union which for so many years had been conserved amongst us: therefore it was wholy rejected, and the elections appointed to be on the following tuesday, which was the 19 of May. Then his Lordship came and said Mass of the holy Ghost, communicated the whole comunity, and in the Quire having made a short and most fatherlike speech, recommending the importance of the business in hand, we proceeded to election, the Arch Priest being present, and Reverend father confessor as witness and interpretor. The Subprioress, Arcaria, and Procuratrix were also present as witnesses. The election was most legaly made with the unanimous votes of almost all, for of 31 votes, 27 was for Sister Mary Wright, then Subprioress, who was by his Lordship in presence of the whole comunity, publish'd and confirm'd Superior.[2] She with a most edifying humility and resignation vow'd obedience to his Lordship for her self and comunity. Then after the *Te Deum* had been sung,[3] all the profess'd both nuns and lay sisters, chearfully render'd their vow of obedience to her: and his Lordship **[p. 172]** also caused the novices to come and pay their respects to her. Then by another kind and fatherly speech he expressed how much he was satisfied with the peaceable and religious proceedings of all in this occasion, assuring that he never found a more sensible content than to find so great a unity and concord among us; for he saw that we only sought the glory of God without any humane respects.

The same day presently after the election was past, the Lady Lucy Herbert (whose noviship was out some months before, she having only waited for our Reverende Mother's recovery) went to our new Superior and beg'd she might as soon as possible be permitted to make her publick profession: for she had already made her vows privately on the feast of the Annunciation,[4] a particular day of her devotion. The time then for her profession was prefixt.

---

1 It was the custom for the Canonesses to elect Superiors for life. The bishop perhaps had in mind difficulties caused if Prioresses became incapacitated. The community here stood by the practice previously agreed in order to reject the proposals of the bishop to elect superiors for three years.

2 Mary Wright (BA228).

3 The canticle beginning 'We praise thee, O God'.

4 The Feast of the Annunciation is celebrated on 25 March.

Some few days after the election Sister Alexia Sulyard was chosen Subprioress.[1]

On the 15 of May Mrs Ursula Mannock return'd from England to be religious.[2]

On the 28 of May Mrs Elisabeth Huddlestone also return'd to be religious.[3]

[p. 173] On the first of June Lady Lucy Herbert, Sister Theresa Joseph, made her holy profession.[4]

On the 6th of June Mrs Ursula Mannock and Mrs Elisabeth Huddlestone took the Schollars habit.

On the 8 of June the Lady Ann' Howard, Sister Dominica, made her holy profession.[5]

On the 15 of June came the three Miss Traffords, all sisters; they came with intention to be religious; and Mrs Catherine Smith came with them to be a convictress.[6]

On the 16 of June came the three Hamcotts sisters too, and with them Mrs Bellows, all for pensioners.

On the 26 of June came little Miss Barbara Caryll, for pensioner.

On the 27 of June the three Miss Traffords took the Schollars habit for religion.

Towards the end of July Mrs Mary Ireland return'd to England.[7]

On the 11th of August, Sister Ann' Smith was chosen Procuratress.[8]

On the 18 of August Sister Lucy Hamilton departed this life in the 53 year of her age, and 37 of her holy profession.[9] **[p. 174]** She was dedicated to religion by her Parents when she was but eight [y]ears old, which she at that age also resolved upon as much as such a child could resolve it. She had the happiness to be brought up under the conduct of her Aunt Reverende Mother Augustina Bedingfeld,[10] who cultivated and improved her piety and other good qualities, so that she was a great

---

1 Alexia Sulyard (BA187).

2 Ursula Mannock (1697–1746) BB117. The path to profession for Ursula Mannock was not straightforward and in November 1694 she decided to leave Bruges and join the Benedictines in Brussels, where she remained until her death.

3 Elizabeth Angela Huddleston, in religion Angela (BA112).

4 Lucy Herbert, in religion Teresa Joseph (1693–1744) BA101.

5 Ann Howard, in religion Dominic (1693–1734) BA107.

6 Monica Trafford (1695–1742) BA204; Ann Trafford, in religion Anastasia (1695–1759) BA202. Dorothy Trafford professed at Prinsenhof, Bruges as a Franciscan (1695–1730) BF242. Catherine Smith, in religion Delphine of St Joseph (1695–1721), was the daughter of Thomas Smythe of Walworth Moor, Durham and Catherine Salvin of Croxdale, Durham. She joined the Carmelites at Antwerp as a choir nun, AC113, Prioress 1720–21.

7 One of four Ireland sisters who joined English convents, Mary became a Carmelite at Lierre (1695–1738) LC050; see also **[pp. 148, 149]**.

8 Ann Smith (BA176).

9 Lucy Hamilton (1656–93) BA095.

10 Augstina Bedingfield (1622 Louvain–1661 Bruges) LA023.

help to our late Reverende Mother, animating with an indefatigable zeal all new comers on to the practice of solide vertue, upholding the same by example, prayer, mortification, fasting, and watching. She had been employ'd in most offices, was twice Mistress of novices, and eleven years Procuratress in which she was most laborious, being very charitable, compassionate, indulgent, and tender to all. She had a long and tedious and painful sickness, which she bore with a most chearful patience, and being ask'd if she was not affraid to die? She replied, no more than to fall asleep; at length this infirmity brought her to her end, and she is bury'd close by our late Reverende Mother in our church before the high altar. *Requiescat in pace*. Amen.

On the 15 of September Sister **[p. 175]** Mary Alexia Burton made her holy profession.[1]

On the 17 of november Sister Ursula Mannock, Sister Elisabeth Angela Huddlestone, and Sister Elisabeth Loveden were clothed.[2]

On the 26 of november, Sister Mary Magdalene Coffy, and Sister Ann' Barbara Devery were clothed for lay sisters.[3]

On the 10 of December the Widow Staniars came again, and was admitted to live as a boarder within our Monastry.

We this year received in Almnes 260 florins, all given by Count Hamilton.

The year 1694

In January Sister Monica Trafford and her two sisters beg'd to be admitted to their clothing which being proposed to my Lord Bishop, he refused to give a dispensation for the admitting three sisters, but advised us to write to Rome for it, which was accordingly done; and Reverend father Grymes obtain'd a dispensation for these three sisters only:[4] but in the mean time, the youngest of them Sister Dorothy, upon **[p. 176]** further consideration made her resolution of settling at the English Monastry here in Town, of the third order of St Francis.[5]

On the 20 of April, Sister Monica Trafford, with her sister Anastasia were clothed here, and a few days after their sister Dorothy was clothed at the third order.[6]

On the 8th of May Mrs Mary Curson went for England.

---

1 Mary Alexia Burton (BA040).

2 Ursula Mannock left the convent in 1695 and entered the Benedictine convent in Brussels (BB117) (see **[p. 178]**); Elizabeth Angela Huddleston (BA112); Elizabeth Loveden (BA130).

3 Magdalen Coffee (BA060); Ann Barbara Devery (BA072).

4 Fr Richard Grymes OP (d. 1719); see *Dominicana*, p. 129, and Bellenger, p. 66.

5 Dorothy Trafford (1695–1730) BF24.

6 Monica Trafford (BA204); Ann Trafford, in religion Anastasia (BA202).

On the 18 of June Mrs Elisabeth Langdale, grand child to the Lord Langdale, was received here for convictress.[1]

On the 18 of August Mr Damerin[2] came to live with us, and had a little room prepared for him in our confessor's apartement; he had a little before bury'd his wife, and disposed the affairs of his little children and family, designing to help us in our musick and in the management of our temporal affaires.

On the 7th of october Mrs Henrietta Melior Markham came the second time out of England, it being about four years after she left us, **[p. 177]** during which time she persevered constantly in her vocation and desire of being religious.[3] There came with her Miss Frances Shelly, daughter to Sir John Shelly by his first Lady; she was received here for convictress.[4]

On the 14 of october the Lady Throgmorton and her daughter came hither.[5]

On the 22 of the same month, by this Lady's great desire and importunity, her daughter Mrs Elisabeth Throgmorton, was admitted as a boarder within the enclosure.

On the 16 of november Sister Henrietta Melior Markham was clothed; and the same day our lay sister, Sister Ann' Bessbrown began her journey for England, having the care and charge of Mrs Ann' and Mrs Theresia Vaughan, who by their Parents orders were to return home to them at Courtfield.[6]

On the 9th of December Sister Mary Magdalene Coffy, and Sister Ann' Barbara Devery made their holy Profession for lay sisters.[7]

We this year received in Almns 117 florins given by Mr John Caryll to pray for a Lady's soul, and given at new year 17 florins **[p. 178]**

The year 1695

On the 17 of January Sister Elisabeth Loveden and Sister Angela Huddlestone made their holy Profession; as for Sister Ursula Mannock, it was thought she would do better in another place, and so she went to

---

1 Elisabeth Langdale was the second child of Marmaduke, 2nd Lord Langdale and Elizabeth Savage of Holme, Yorkshire.

2 See also **[pp. 163, 434, 435]**.

3 Henrietta Markham, in religion Melior (BA136).

4 Sir John Shelley, 3rd Baronet of Michelgrove, married as his first wife Winifred Nevill. Frances (c. 1672–1771) was the daughter of this marriage.

5 Probably Lady Mary Throckmorton, née Yate (d. 1722), wife of Sir Robert Throckmorton, 3rd Baronet (d. 1721). They had seven daughters and two sons: one of these married Theresa, niece of Lucy Herbert.

6 Ann Vaughan (BA207); Teresa Vaughan (BA209). They were two of three sisters professed at Nazareth; the eldest, Mary, in religion Mary Teresa (BA208), had died aged 21 in 1692 (see **[p. 160]**). As a lay sister, Ann Bessbrown (BA023) was able to leave the enclosure to escort the girls back to England.

7 Magdalen Coffee (BA060); Ann Barbara Devery (BA072).

the Benedictin Dames at Bruxelles, and was received, and in due time Profess'd there.[1]

On the 27 of March Mrs Elisabeth Baily, a convictress from the third order was by her Parents orders removed from thence hither, and received as convictress here.[2]

On the 21 of April Sister Monica and Sister Anastasia Trafford made their holy Profession.[3]

On the 27 of May Sister Ann' Bessbrown return'd from England, and brought with her Mrs Catherine Smith, daughter to the Lord Strangford, Miss Ann' and Miss Mary Jernegan, daughters to Sir Francis Jernegan of Cawsey, Miss Diana Smith and Mrs Graham, who were all received here for convictresses. Mrs Susan Halsal came also with her to live some time within our enclosure as boarder.[4]

On the 21 of June Mrs Elisabeth **[p. 179]** Rookwood went from hence.[5]

On the 23 of June Mrs Elisabeth Baily went for England.

On the 19 of July Mrs Catherine Smith went from us with designe to settle among the English Theresians, 'tis true she had a very great inclination to be with us, but was convinced that God had call'd her from her infancy to be a Theresian, so she follow'd that vocation, for we had no exception against her, but her want of portion.[6]

On the first of October Miss Frances Shelly was by her father's orders sent to the English Monastry here in town of the third order of St Francis. The Lady Abergeveny, her Grand Mother had sent her to our Monastry, and Sir John Shelly, her father was then very well pleased to have her educated here, but upon some disagreement between him and this Lady, his Mother in law, he wrote a very civil letter to our Reverende Mother assuring her he had no exceptions against our house, but that he would have his daughter removed to the other English Monastry for no other reason but that she might have less dependancy on her Grand Mother and be more entirely under his authority.[7]

---

[1] Elizabeth Loveden (BA130); Angela Huddleston (BA112); Ursula Mannock (BB117). See also **[pp. 172, 173, 175]**.

[2] It seems that Elizabeth Baily was trying both forms of the religious life for English women in Bruges, but failing to settle in either. The third order referred to here is Franciscan.

[3] Monica Trafford (BA204); Ann Trafford, in religion Anastasia (BA202).

[4] Ann Bessbrown (BA023). On Lord Strangford, see historyofparliamentonline.org/volume/1660-1690/member/smythe-philip-1634-1708, accessed 3 October 2016. This is a second Catherine Smith in the convent simultaneously; she left and in 1704 married Henry Roper, 8th Baron Teynham. Ann Jerningham (BA119) and Mary Jerningham (BA118) were both daughters of Sir Francis Jerningham, 3rd Baronet, of Costessey, Norfolk. Susan Halsall returned with her granddaughters in 1735: see *Chronicle*, vol. 2, **[p. 28]**.

[5] Elizabeth Rookwood (1684–1759). See also **[p. 148]**.

[6] Catherine Smith, in religion Delphine of St Joseph (AC113) left Bruges to join the Carmelites at Antwerp. See also **[p. 173]**.

[7] Lady Abergavenny (d. 1687) was the step-mother of Sir John Shelley, 4th Baronet of Michelgrove. These comments suggest a relationship that was less than harmonious.

[p. 180] Father Woodward, a Franciscan fryar (who then was in quality of *confessarius* to Sir John Shelly's family) was the bearer of this letter and had orders to take her from hence, tho' much against her inclinations, and by many tears she express'd how severe and hard this obedience was to her.[1]

On the 13 of october Mrs Mary Hamcots made a most … and pious end.[2] She was of the family of the Hamcots of Bishopric, and God having done her the favour to call her to a religious state of life, she constantly endeavour'd to improve the grace of her vocation by all the practice of piety, her tender age and circumstances would permit. She most particularly mortify'd her self in things the most repugnant to nature, and in this happy disposition it pleased God to visit her with a violent feavour in which she with great devotion received all the rights of the holy church. Then she very earnestly beg'd that she might be permitted to make the vows of religion in presence of the comunity; and tho' her weakness was so great that she could hardly speak to be heard, yet on the feast of St Francis[3] (whom she was much devoted to) she made her **[p. 181]** vows and read them with so clear and intelligible a voice that she seem'd to be renew'd with the strength and vigour which she received by her joy and satisfaction to dye a consecrated Spouse of Christ, as she had resolved to live one in this comunit[y], if the divine goodness had pleased to prolong her life. She render'd her happy and innocent soul into the hands of her divine Spouse on the tenth day after her holy Profession, and in the 14 year of her age. *Requiescat in pace*. Amen.

On the 16 of December Sir John Gifford came, and was lodged in our confessors house.[4]

We this year received in Almns 180 florins. 100 from Sir John Web, and 80 was sent to Sister Web to pray for the soul of Mr John Pitts[.]

The year 1696

Mrs Elisabeth and Mrs Ann' Hamcots procured a marble grave stone for their dear Sister that the happy memory of her piety might ever last. The Epitaph that is engraven on the stone was made by Reverend father Lewis Sabrand, of the Society of Jesus, on whose direction **[p. 182]** she

---

[1] Fr Joseph Woodward (d. 1701) had previously been Confessor at Prinsenhof, Bruges 1684–87. See Franciscana, p. 283; Bellenger, p. 124.

[2] Word missing here. Mary Amscotts (1695–95) BA002. Mary was officially too young to make vows, but an exception was made for her on account of her piety and her terminal illness. She is not included in the community's modern list of the deaths of professed members from the period.

[3] The Feast of St Francis of Assisi is celebrated on 4 October.

[4] Sir John Gifford visited the convent from France, where he lived with the Jacobite court in exile at St Germain-en-Laye. He married Catherine Middleton in 1702.

had depended with great profit in a little time.[1] In this epitaph he calls her Sister Mary Bernard (which was the name she chose for her religious state) and makes a short compendium of her piety and vertue, as may be seen in our church by those who understand Latin.[2]

Not long after Mrs Elisabeth Langdale and Mrs Elisabeth Hamcotts took the Schollars habit, but neither of them persevered.

On the first of September, our Schoole was recruited with a good number of convictresses; for on that day came altogether by one convoy, Mrs Elisabeth Mullineux, grandchild to the Lord Mullineux, three of Sir Rowland Stanley's daughters, Mrs Dorothy, Mrs Elisabeth and Mrs Wenifride, Miss Theresia Strickland, niece to Sister Theresia Mannock and Mr Steven Galloway's two daughters, Mrs Mary and Mrs Elisabeth Galloway, nieces to Sister Susan Reynoldson, all these came in on ship, and were received today for convictresses.[3]

The same day at night came Mrs Ann' and Mrs Elisabeth Weston, daughters to Mr Weston of Sutton, they were that night received for convictresses, **[p. 183]** and Emerentiana Higgonbottom, who came with them, was received as a servant to be a lay sister.[4]

On the 5th of September two of Sir Hugh Smithson's daughters, Mrs Dorothy and Mrs Mary, were received for convictresses.[5]

In this month Mrs Elisabeth and Mrs Ann' Hamcotts went from hence to England.

On the 8th of October Sister Henrietta Melior Markham made her holy Profession, which had been deferr'd by the delay of the payment of her Portion.[6]

On the 27 of october our poor unfortunate Sister Perpetua Errington left her religious habit and stole secretly out of the enclosure by the assistance of John Graunt, a lieutenant of the Army of King William, usurper of the English Crown.[7] She had long lived a most negligent remiss life,

---

1 Fr Louis Sabran SJ (1652–1732); see *ODNB* and Holt, p. 217.

2 All choir nuns had to learn enough Latin to be able to read the liturgy, and many were able to understand Latin.

3 Elisabeth Mullineux [Molyneux] was the daughter of Caryll 3rd Viscount and Mary Barlow (d. 1691), granddaughter of Richard, Viscount Molyneux; Dorothy Stanley (1700–49) BA183; Elizabeth Stanley (1704–41) BA184; Winifred Stanley (1704–42) BA186; Theresia Strickland (b. 1687 in Windsor Castle) was the daughter of Robert Strickland and Bridget Mannock, who went into exile in France with James II and his family. Mary and Elisabeth Galloway have not been identified.

4 Ann Weston (1699–1738) BA215; Elizabeth Weston (1699–1721) BA216; Emerentiana Higgonbottom, lay sister (1700–03) BA104.

5 Dorothy Smithson (1700–37) BA178. Mary later joined St Monica's, Louvain (1700–31) LA240, alongside a third sister, Bridget, in religion Bridget Prisca (1703–06) LA239.

6 Henrietta Markham, in religion Melior (1696–1733) BA136. She spent two years as a novice rather than the usual one year.

7 Dorothy Errington, in religion Perpetua (BA076). For the rest of the account of Dorothy Errington, see also **[pp. 121, 132]** and vol. 2, **[pp. 67–9]**.

but being of a violent temper Superior[s] were forced to tolerate what they most disapproved, especially her extroversion and being often at the Grate with English soldiers and officers, who frequented her as being her country men or particular friends and acquaintances of her brother and Sister Hamilton.

Amongst these, she began her first acquaintance with **[p. 184]** John Graunt, and 'tis really thought by all that this friendship at first was well intended, for his conversion to our holy faith in which our worthy Confessor, Mr Hawker[1] instructed him, and having reconciled him was constantly his confessor whilst he stay'd in these parts, and in all appearance this man lived very well for some years, so that Mr Hawker is of the opinion that his conversion was sincere and true at first: but how long this wicked contrivance had been between them none but themselves can tell. A few days before she got from hence, she had so order'd matters that he came and pretended he was going out of the country, so seeming to take leave of him she appear'd in such an extasie of joy that she could not keep in any moderation, it even look'd like extravigancy or madness, and every one wonder'd what the subject of it could be.

On the 27 of October, St Simon and Jude's Eve, she was seen pass thro' the Dormitory after Compline, in her night gown, night kerchief and veil, tho' nothing was then suspected, yet doubtless she had her soecular clothes on under her night gown, and about nine a clock that night she stole secretly out of the enclosure, tho' she was not miss'd by any of the community till the next day at dinner time, **[p. 185]** for her absence from the Quire was so frequent that no body took any notice of it, and in time of Mass those that observed she was not in the Quire supposed her to be in the lay sisters chappel, but upon her not appearing in the Refectory she was search'd for and enquired after all the house over, every one affirming that they had not seen her that day. They had several times knock'd hard at her cell door which was fast lock'd, so at last our Reverende Mother seeing the great concern of those who were in search of her, went her self with her Emperor key to open the cell door, accompany'd with several of the religious; and there they found the certain proofs of her Apostasy: for the clean habit she should have put on that day (it being both Sunday and holyday) was folded up just as it had been given her, and her foul habit thrown about her cell, at which sight all were strangely surprised and afflicted.

Our Reverende Mother[2] was so seiz'd with wonder and grief that she was ready to swoon in the place, yet being a little recover'd she said: And is it possible that after having 15 years profess'd she should be guilty of such a horrid crime! Her Reverence went then to acquaint

---

1 Fr John Hawker, Confessor 1681–1706; see Anstruther 3, pp. 95–6.

2 Reverend Mother in 1696 was Mary Wright, Prioress 1693–1709 (BA228).

father Confessor with this sad misfortune **[p. 186]** who without further delay immediately went to inform our Bishop of it.[1] In the mean time her night kerchief and night veil were found in the wood stack by the door that opens into the street near our bake house, by which we understood that she was gone out that way. When father Confessor came from the Bishop, he brought orders from his Lordship that none should speak of this misfortune to any out of the house, hoping by this means to prevent further scandal [*blank*] but this unhappy creature as shameless as graceless, to her own greater confusion before God and men, soon made her crime the publick talk all over Holland, that being the Place of refuge for all such guilty persons; there she sought for Protection where such things are applauded and encouraged; nay made it the subject of her diversion to relate the means by which she had so unhappily made her escape out of the Monastry, particularly how she had got the impression in wax of the key of that door she went out at, and so by that means had procured to have a new key made. In this shameless disposition she was publickly marry'd at Sluise[2] to the aforesaid John Graunt. This news was soon brought to our Grate by several, and was related to us in different ways, according to the **[p. 187]** various sentiments of the well disposed or ill affected.

Our Superior sent for her brother in law, and Sister Hamilton, who lived at Ostend, and having inform'd them of all particulars, they undertook a journey to Sluce to try if any means might prevail to bring her back again; but first they imparted their designe to our Bishop who approved of it very much and with a father like affection bid them encourage her to the resolution of returning by the assurance of a favourable reception. This promise was seconded by the letters which our Confessor and Superior writ to her, and sent her by Mr Hamilton wherein was express'd with an affectionate tenderness, the sense they had of the sad and miserable state she was in; assuring her that she might yet by a timely repentance recover the lost favour of Almighty God whose mercies are infinit, and above all his works: and least the apprehension of great penances so justly due to her crimes, should discourage her from the resolution of returning, they promised her that she should be received with all possible favour, that none should reproach her with what was past, nor any hardships nor penance be imposed upon her. These letters were by her brother and sister given into her own **[p. 188]** hands, for they found her at Sluce, but in a very poor condition, yet in appearance better satisfied with that miserable base poverty, than she was here with the engagement of her religious poverty which abundantly supply'd her necessary wants, and her present state could hardly afford that.

---

1 The Bishop of Bruges in 1696 was Willem Bassery, Bishop 1690–1706.
2 Sluce or Sluys.

Her brother and sister Hamilton[1] used all arguments to make her sensible of the miserable state she was in, and of her shamefull and scandalous life, which she might yet in some sort repair, by a sincere repentance and speedy return, expressing how great a satisfaction they should have if she would permitt them to conduct her safe to her Monastry again. Their words seem'd so to move her, that she shed many tears whilst they were speaking to her, which at first gave them some hopes of prevailing; but alas! her obdurate heart was still fixt to her wickedness, which she resolved to continue in, and to which she was much encouraged by the neigbouring people of that unhappy place, who applauded her crimes so much that they even threaten'd to fall upon Mr Hamilton if he persisted to disturb her; nay he even stood in need of her help as a defence against them; and she conducted her brother and sister in **[p. 189]** their return till they were got past this rabble; thus they were forced to leave her having no hopes of success in their charitable undertaking.

Our Reverende Mother has procured many Masses to obtain true repentance for her of the divine mercy, and for this intention had the Carmes[2] for 30 days together to say Mass in our church; besides other devotions which she order'd the whole community to perform and many private devotions have been offer'd for her by particular persons, for this afliction was general to all.

When the convent sisters were to vote for the Profession of this poor unfortunate creature, Sister Wenefride Web[3] (as she has since declared) was much troubled and in doubt if she should vote for her, or against her, knowing how little satisfaction she had given in her time of tryal; at last the motive of charity prevailing: for she hoped her salvation would be more secure in this state, she voted for her profession, tho' much against her sentiment and reason; but when the votes were look'd into, twas found that she had but just enough to consent her, so that if this good religious **[p. 190]** had voted against her, she had been fairly dismissed. This, Sister Wenefride with tears declared after this sad accident, advising all who had votes in such occasions, not to give their votes for any whose irregular lives in their noviships, gave little hopes of their being truly happy religious; yet as the judgments and designes of the Almighty are inscrutable we may still hope and pray for her conversion to that divine majesty who can draw the greatest of goods from the greatest evil.

She stay'd not long at Sluce but before her departure from thence, we heard she had made a publick recantation of her faith that she might

---

1 Stirnet.com includes a sister to Dorothy who married a Hamilton of Ireland; no further details are given. Several Hamiltons are named in J. Parmentier, 'The Irish Connection: The Irish Merchant Community in Ostend and Bruges during the Late Seventeenth and Eighteenth Centuries', *Eighteenth-Century Ireland* 20 (2005), pp. 31–54, at p. 34.

2 Carmelite friars, neighbours living in Carmerstraat.

3 Winefrid Webb (BA212).

receive Almns by way of gathering in the church at Sluce. She went from thence to go for Scotland, and as she pass'd thro' the northern parts of her native country, she was so shameless of her infamy as not to have any difficulty to make her self known, and to excuse her guilt of breaking her vows, by alledging she had not made them but by persuasion and force; tis certain she could not have the least pretence to alledge this in regard of our comunity, we being rather compell'd by motives **[p. 191]** of charity to receive her, she having neither parts nor fortune that could anyway commend her, but as she had been some years a convictress in our cloister, and afterwards had remain'd three years at home with her father, her coming back to us with great expression of her desire to settle in a religious state, was thought a good proof and assurance of a solide vocation. She being then past 20 years of age. And tho' some years after her profession we were inform'd that she had made her resolution to be religious upon her father's crossing her in the designe she had to cast herself away by marrying one of his servants, yet it cannot be doubted but she made her vows and will be accountable to the divine Judgment for the violation of them; and we were so far from persuading her that she was very near being voted out for it was remark'd that no one in this comunity, except her self, had ever been profess'd with so many contrary votes. She has unhappily employ'd her wit and policy to her own ruin, much more than to our prejudice; yet her conversion and **[p. 192]** return is the constant subject of our daily prayers, and we shal omitt no means that can be thought of to move her to it.

This is a sad example which may make us all tremble, since St Paul says: he that thinks himself to stand, let him take heed least he fall.[1]

On the ninth of november the Lady Justina Petre (then lately install'd Abbess of the English benedictin Dames of Gant) return'd from St Omers, and with her, Dame Constantia and the Lady Catherine Howard and a lay sister.[2] They had pass'd by here some time before, and stay'd one day, when they were going to St Omers where my Lady Abbesses brother Reverend father Edward Petre was Rector of the English Colledge, by whose means they expected some relief from the temporal wants of their Monastry.[3] They stay'd three days with us at their return, and then went home to Gant.

In this month Sister Mary Heton was elected Arcaria.[4]

1 1 Corinthians 10:12.

2 Justina Petre (1653–98) GB176, Abbess of Ghent, 1696–98; Catherine, in religion Constantia Howard (1686–1725) GB104; possibly a misreading of the original text here, treating the name in religion as a separate person.

3 Fr Edward Petre SJ (1633–99), Rector of St Omer 1693–7; Holt, p. 191.

4 Mary Heton (BA102).

On the 12 of november Sister Wenefride Web departed this life in the 69 year of her age, and 45 of her holy profession.[1] Her life had been truly pious and painful for she was always of a tender **[p. 193]** weak and sickly disposition, yet was much esteem'd in this comunity for her good judgment and capacity which render'd her very serviceable, especially in the charge and office of Procuratrix, which she had for some years whilst our Monastry was very low in the Temporals. Her Brother, Sir John Web, allow'd her a pension in consideration of her continual infirmities, and out of it she spared so much as was sufficient to procure marble stones for the paving of our church; whilst we daily had only our confessor's Mass, she out of her Annuity procured us a second Mass on Sundays and holy days.

For about two years before her death she was constantly confined to the infirmary, not being able all that time, to lye in her bed by reason of an Asthma which she was continually troubled with, and it was so painful to her to draw her breath when she was laid down in her bed, that for her greater conveniency and ease, we had a large easy chair contrived and made for her, which was placed within a bedstead for her to rest in. Besides this illness she had many other infirmities, particularly violent sharp humour in her legs, all which she **[p. 194]** suffer'd with a most edifying patience and tho' she had a great apprehension of death, yet she daily expected it, and prepared for it, with a perfect submission to the divine will. A few days after she had received the *viaticum* she expired, whilst the sacrament of extream unction was administer'd to her. *Requiescat in pace*. Amen.

We this year received no Almns.

The year 1697

Mademoiselle de Mol, Baroness, having lived some years as a Boarder in our Monastry, it pleased Almighty God on the 27 of March to take her to himself, as we have very good reason to hope, since she had always lived a most innocent, pious life according to her capacity. She in all occasions express'd a sincere affection for all the Religious, and never was troublesome to any, but seem'd much obliged and satisfied in their company when any of them visited her in her chamber, for she seldome went abroad, or about the home. She had her health perfectly well till her last sickness which was not judged dangerous if she would have been perswaded to take the remedies **[p. 195]** prescribed by the Physicians; but her want of judgment render'd her uncapable of comprehending the ease and benefit she might have received, had she taken what was thought necessary for her recovery. We endeavour'd to omitt nothing

[1] Elizabeth Webb, in religion Winefrid (1652–96) BA212. Her brother was Sir John Webb, 2nd Baronet (d. 29 October 1700).

that could be done for her, and she was frequently assisted by one of the Carmes her confessor. She received all the rights of the holy church, and was bury'd in our Lady's church, in the burying place that belongs to her family. She dyed about the age of 59. *Requiescat in pace*. Amen.

As she was not capable of making a will, we had no advantage by her; nay we had great difficulties to get the arrieres of her pension, which for some years had not been paid: but some time after her death we received all that was due to our comunity upon her account.

In April or May, Mrs Elisabeth Langdale went to England, with our Sister Barbara Devery.[1]

In May, Mrs Mary Ann' Woolmar, Sister Burton's niece, was received here for a convictress.[2]

On the 10 of June Sir Francis Jernegan and his Lady came hither from England, and they brought with them Mrs **[p. 196]** Mary Tasburgh, daughter to Mr. Tasburgh of Bodney. She was the same day received for a convictress.[3]

On the 23 of June Mrs Ann' Jernegan took the first habit, and the name of Wenefride.[4]

On the 3d of August Mrs Ann' Weston took the first habit.[5]

In August Miss Teresa Strickland went from us to the Benedictin Dames at Dunkirk.[6]

On the 6 of September two of the Duke of Powis's daughters, Lady Mary and Lady Ann' Herbert were received here for convictresses.[7]

On the 31 of October Mrs Elisabeth Weston took the first habit and the name of Delphine.[8]

On the 2d of December Sister Wenefride Jernegan was clothed.

We this year received in Almnes 40 florins from Mrs Strickland.

---

1 Elisabeth Langdale had arrived at the convent in 1694: see **[p. 176]**. Ann Barbara Devery (BA072).

2 Sister Burton was Mary Burton (BA040). Ann Woolmer joined the Carmelites at Antwerp as a widow, professing in 1712, AC139.

3 The timing suggests that Sir Francis and Lady Ann Jerningham had travelled to Bruges to be present when their daughter took the first habit. Mary Tasburgh, in religion Mary Bernard (1700–15) BA191; see F. Young, 'The Tasburghs of Bodney: Catholicism and Politics in South Norfolk', *Norfolk Archaeology* 46 (2011), pp. 190–8, at p. 195.

4 Ann Jerningham, in religion Winefrid (1698–1741) BA119, musician.

5 Ann Weston (BA215).

6 Teresa Strickland professed at Dunkirk in 1697, taking the name Catherine in religion, DB169. Her brother was the lawyer Mannock Strickland, who acted as agent for several English convents in exile; see R. G. Williams (ed.), *Mannock Strickland (1683–1744): Agent to English Convents in Flanders: Letters and Accounts from Exile*, CRS 86 (Woodbridge: Boydell and Brewer for the CRS, 2016).

7 Lady Mary and Lady Anne Herbert were nieces of Lucy Herbert: see Herbert family tree.

8 Elizabeth Weston (BA216).

The year 1698

On the 23 of January Sister Ann' Weston was clothed.[1]

On the 29 of March, it being then Easter Eve, Mrs Mary Jernegan took the first habit and the name of Mary Teresa.[2]

On the 21 of April, Sister Delphina **[p. 197]** Weston was clothed.

In April or May Mrs Mary Smithson went from hence to our order at Lovain.[3]

On the 23 of June Mr Nicholson a Master of musick came hither, and as he had the character of a vertuous man, and was likely to do us good service in teaching musick, we gave him Lodging and diet in our confessors house; and he had the priviledge of coming into our enclosure to teach the religious and convictresses, being paid for the convictresses, but not for the nuns he taught. He was also engaged to assist at all our musick Masses, and Salües [*Salves*].

On the first of July Mrs Dorothy Smithson took the first habit and the name of Mary Augustina.[4]

In August Miss Catherine Linck was received here for a convictress.

On the 9 of September two more of Sir Hugh Smithson's daughters came hither, Miss Catherine and Miss Bridget. The first was received here for a convictress, and the other by her father's order went to the English Monastry of our order at Lovain, where her sister Mary was Schollar, who got leave to come here to fetch **[p. 198]** Miss Bridget, that she might at the same time have the satisfaction of seeing all her sisters together.

On the 6 of october Sister Mary Teresa Jernegan was clothed.[5]

On the 10 of october Mrs Mary Berington, daughter to Mr Berington of Cowhorn, was received here for a Convictress. She had two Aunts religious in this comunity, Sister Mary Xaveria Berington (or Skip) and Sister Milburge Russel, the one her father's, and the other her Mother's sister.[6]

---

1 Ann Weston (BA215).

2 Mary Jerningham (1699–1757) BA118, Sub-Prioress 1738–48.

3 Four daughters of Sir Hugh Smithson and his wife, Lady Elizabeth Langdale, professed as Canonesses, two at Bruges and two at Louvain: at Bruges Dorothy (BA178) and Catherine (1702–53) BA177; at Louvain, Mary (LA240) and Bridget (LA239).

4 Dorothy Smithson (BA178).

5 Mary Teresa Jerningham (BA118).

6 Mary Berington of Cowarne did not proceed to profession: see **[p. 212]**. Here aunts were Mary Xaveria Berington (BA022), who professed as a widow (her married name was Skippe or Schippe) and Milburge Russell (BA168).

In this month the Lady Mary Herbert went from hence to the Benedictin Dames at Gant; and Mrs Elisabeth Mullineux went to the English Augustins at Paris.[1]

On the 4th of December Sister Wenefride Jernegan made her holy Profession.[2]

On the 10th of December Sister Theresia Mannock departed this life, about the 54 year of her age and 33 of her holy Profession.[3] She was a most regular, good religious; of a very peaceable quiet disposition; her exterior comportment always serene and easy, chearful in times of recreation, and serious at all other times. She was much addicted to interior recollection, prayer and silence, observing an exact regularity in all times and **[p. 199]** places of order; never intermeddling nor so much as speaking her opinion in any concern or affairs of the house, or of particular persons, except in what concern'd her office or charge. She was four years Mistress of the novices, and had her own niece novice under her, which proved an extraordinary tryal to her vertue, for she, not corresponding so well as might have been expected with the example and instructions of her Aunt and Mistress, the comunity judged her not fit to be admitted to her profession; this misfortune was sensible to dear Sister Teresa, yet she would not wrong her conscience by too favorable a judgment of her, but declared her opinion in the matter with great sincerity and calmness, and with an equal serenity bore the separation. And we may justly atribute to her good prayers, that she is now most happily settled with the English Benedictin Dames at Bruxelles. She was as great an example of patience in bearing many infirmities as in supporting other afflictions, for she was always of a very weak and tender complexion, but her last sickness did not confine her to the infirmary above a fortnight. The feast of our Lady's Conception[4] was the first day that the Doctor **[p. 200]** declared her in danger of death, and then he appointed her the last sacraments which she received with great devotion the next day. She had from her infancy a tender devotion to our Blessed Lady, and a few days before her death there was an agreeable fresh smel of violets before a picture of our Lady that had formerly been our Altar piece: what particular devotions she had to it, is not known, but tis certain this smel was smelt at diferent times, by many of the religious, and of the convictresses also in whose Pant the picture hung, and the like has

[1] Lady Mary Herbert probably refers to the sister of Lucy Herbert (see family tree). Frances Molyneux (probably sister of Elizabeth) was professed at the Augustinian convent in Paris on 13 October 1698: perhaps this visit was arranged to coincide with that event. Elizabeth Molyneux had arrived with the group in September 1696; see **[p. 182]**.

[2] Ann Jerningham, in religion Winefrid (BA119).

[3] Teresa Mannock, in religion Augustina (1665–98) BA135. Her niece was Ursula Mannock (BB117). Ursula was clothed at Bruges in November 1693 and left in January 1695.

[4] The Feast of Our Lady's Conception is celebrated on 8 December.

not been smelt neither before nor since. She was bury'd on the 11th of December. *Requiescat in pace* Amen.

On the 19 of December Mrs Loveden departed this life. She had lived for some years with us, as a boarder, and play'd most excellently on the violin by which she gain'd great admiration and esteem in the world; and tho' she was not call'd to a religious State yet she preferr'd a retired and private life before all the advantages she might have got in the world by this art. She was of an ancient Catholick family, but many misfortunes and persecutions for religion had brought them very low; so that she had nothing to depend on for her maintenance but an annuity of about 20 pound a year **[p. 201]** from the Caryll family: she was somthing related to our Reverende Mother Mary Bedingfeld,[1] and was received here by her Reverence and our whole comunity with great satisfaction by reason of her rare musical talent, so she had a chamber within our enclosure, and tabled with our confessor: no pension was exacted of her but her constant help in our musick. She was truly pious and vertuous, of an obliging grateful disposition, so discreet that she never in the least intruded herself into the concerns of the comunity, and was much esteem'd by us for her good sense and judgment. She spared what she could out of her Annuity in consideration of a niece of hers, who was her God daughter and some years after her being here, she sent for her to be amongst our convictresses. This niece after some time, was moved to embrace a religious State, which was a great joy and satisfaction to her good Aunt; tho' there was great difficulty in admitting her, because she had no portion; but our dear Reverende Mother Mary Bedingfeld, upon her death bed, earnestly recommended this act of charity to our comunity, and the divine providence so disposed, that by the help of **[p. 202]** some good friends particularly the Lord Dover,[2] and her Aunt giving all she could. She had at least what was sufficient to maintain her; and her good Aunt had the comfort to see her profess'd three years before she dyed. She often express'd her grateful sentiments of this favour; and was no less sensible of the community's goodness and charity in her own regard, which she particularly experienced some time before her death, she being wholy uncapable of doing any service because her sight and strength fail'd her; and her last sickness and death was chiefly caused by a mere defailance of nature. We do not certainly know her age, but think she could not be less than eighty. She received in due time all the rights of the holy church, had her senses to the last, and was bury'd in our Vault. *Requiescat in pace*. Amen

We this year received in Almns 100 florins for the soul of Mr Havers.

[1] Mary Bedingfield (BA019).

[2] Henry Jermyn, 1st Baron Dover (1636–1708); see *ODNB*.

The year 1699

On the 8th of January Sister Mary Augustine Smithson was clothed.[1]

On the 25 of January Sister Ann' Weston made her holy Profession.[2]

[p. 203] In January Mrs Chamon was received here for convictress, and remain'd about half a year.

On the 18 of March Mrs Barbara Caryll and Mrs Mary Tasburgh took the first habit; the last took the name of Mary Bernard.[3]

On the 23 of April Sister Delphina Weston made her holy Profession.[4]

On the first of June Mrs Dorothy Stanley took the first habit.[5]

On the 9th of July Sister Mary Ann' Hamilton departed this life about the 42 years of her age, and 18 of her holy Profession.[6] She had always lived a most innocent and pious life both in the world, and after she embraced a religious State, in the begining of which she was esteem'd an example of exact regularity and punctuality in the observance of the least custome and duty; but it pleas'd God to deprive her of her Judgment before she was five years profess'd: this misfortune render'd her uncapable of all duties; yet in some favorable intervales she was found capable and piously disposed to receive the sacraments. About half a year before her death she was under the care of the infirmarian, and suffer'd much being brought to an **[p. 204]** extremity of weakness by a consumption. In this time she often had her senses perfectly, and always employ'd those intervale[s] well in practices of piety, preparing her self for a happy death, receiving the last sacraments with great devotion, offering her sufferings and life with many pious acts of submission to the divine will, till the frequent renewings of convulsion fitts deprived her of life. *Requiescat in pace*. Amen.

On the 18 of July Sister Margarite Alexia Sulyard, our Subprioress, departed this life about the 59 year of her age, and 41 of her holy Profession.[7] She had been about five years Subprioress and had perform'd the duties of that charge with great prudence. Her zeal for religious observance was very great, particularly for the divine office, and having a strong voice and skill in the plain song she was very serviceable in our Quire. She had much to overcome in her own natural temper, and the violence she used to her self in many occasions, gave very evident proofs of her solide vertue: and she was always particularly observed to act by the motives of a pious good conscience **[p. 205]** when she was to pass her judgment

---

[1] Mary Augustine Smithson (BA178).

[2] Ann Weston (BA215); sister of Elizabeth.

[3] The following year Barbara Caryll left to enter the Benedictine convent at Dunkirk; Mary Tasburgh, in religion Mary Bernard (BA191).

[4] Delphina Weston (BA216).

[5] Dorothy Stanley, in religion Mary Xaveria (BA183).

[6] Mary Ann Hamilton (1682–99) BA096.

[7] Margaret Alexia Sulyard (1658–99) BA187.

on any thing, tho her natural sentiments seem'd quite contrary. For about half a year before her death she suffer'd much by the frequent renewing of a violent pain in her side; and for three months she was confined to the infirmary by several distempers, and relapses into feavours, all which she bore with great patience, disposing her self most piously for the last Sacraments which she received with great devotion, and dyed in her perfect senses, about 8 a clock on a Saturday morning; she was bury'd on the 19th. *Requiescat in pace*. Amen.

About a week before the death of our Subprioress, Sister Ann' Smith felt sick of a feavour, which daily renewed;[1] and tho' her fits were not very violent, yet her body was weak and indisposed by her long infirmity of a tympany, which began about seven years before, and for the three last years she was swell'd with it to a very great bigness, till she got this tympany. She had always been of a healthy and strong constitution, and ever gave proof of her vertue both in health and sickness: she truly express'd that she loved God with all her strength, since she **[p. 206]** employ'd it all in his service, not only in the exact discipline of a regular religious, but also in the practice of many great austerities which she privately perform'd with the particular leave of her Superiors, being no less exact in all duties of obedience than fervorous in the practice of mortification, both interior and exterior. She had many occasions of humiliation from her own temper which was naturally hasty, and had much to suffer in overcoming the frequent provocations she met in her employments of Mistress of the Pensioners, Mistress of novices, and Procuratress, which offices she had successively one after the other, and acquitted herself of the duties of them with great prudence and discretion; so by the constant and fervorous practice of all vertues, she was happily disposed for the approaching end of her mortal life, and having received all the rights of our holy Mother the church, she departed this life on the 28 of July, about the 56 year of her age and 39 of her holy Profession. *Requiescat in pace*. Amen.

About the begining of August **[p. 207]** our convent Sisters met in order to choose a new Subprioress and Procuratress; in this election Sister Mary Heton was made Subprioress; she was Arcaria before, so now Sister Catherine Holland had that office, and Sister Teresia Joseph Herbert was chosen Procuratress, being but just past six years of profession.[2]

In August Mrs Mary Ann' Woolmar return'd to England.

On the 6th of September Sister Mary Bernard Tasburgh was clothed.[3]

---

[1] Ann Smith (1661–99) BA176.

[2] Mary Heton (BA102); Catharine Holland, in religion Mechtildis (BA106); Lucy Herbert, in religion Teresa Joseph (BA101).

[3] Mary Tasburgh, in religion Mary Bernard (BA191).

On the 10th of September Sister Emerentiana Higgonbottom was cloth'd for a lay sister.[1]

On the 8th of october Sister Mary Teresa Jernegan made her holy Profession.[2]

On the 17 of November Sister Dorothy Stanley was clothed.[3]

We this year received in Almns 200 florins, of which 50 was from Sr John Gage, 50 from Sr John Southcott, and 100 from Mrs Mary Busby.[4]

The year 1700

On the third of February Mrs Barbara Caryll went from hence to the Benedictin Dames at Dunkirk. She had been almost a year in our Schollars habit **[p. 208]** but being very unsettled in her resolutions, her uncle Mr John Caryll had notice of it and gave orders for her removal.[5]

On the 7th of May Mrs Dorothy Risdon came from England, and brought with her, her own niece of the same name, and Miss Dorothy Huddlestone, daughter to Mr Huddlestone of Sauson, and sister to our Sister Ursula Huddlestone.[6] These two last were received into the enclosure for convictresses, and Mrs Risdon and her maid remain'd some time in our Confessor's house to try if this country air would agree with her, she being of a very weak and sickly constitution, yet desirous if health would permitt, to settle in a religious State, and that in this Monastry where she had her first education.

On the 12 of July Sister Mary Augustin Smithson made her holy Profession.[7]

On the 17 of July Mrs Dorothy Risdon (the Aunt) took the first habit and the name of Sister Eugenia.

On the 24 of August Mrs Dorothy and Mrs Wenefride Newton were received here for convictresses.[8]

---

1 Emerentiana Higgonbottom (BA104).

2 Mary Teresa Jerningham (BA118).

3 Dorothy Stanley (BA183).

4 Editing note: this looks like 'Sr' meaning 'Sieur' or Sir, although they are both called 'Mr' in subsequent entries.

5 Probably the same Caryll as the niece of Abbess Mary Caryll (GB040) who accompanied her to stay with the Blue Nuns in Paris from 23 August 1701, where she is referred to as a young gentlewoman. She does not appear to have joined a convent. See J. Gillow and R. Trappes-Lomax (eds), *Diary of the Blue Nuns, or Order of the Immaculate Conception, at Paris, 1658–1810*, CRS 8 (London: CRS, 1910), p. 50; *History of the Benedictine Nuns of Dunkirk* (London: Catholic Book Club, 1957), p. 45.

6 Dorothy Risdom (BA162). Her niece stayed until December 1702, when she returned to England (see **[p. 215]**); Dorothy Huddleston later professed as Laetitia (1706–42) BA111. Ursula Huddleston has not yet been identified.

7 Mary Augustine Smithson (BA178).

8 Neither professed at Bruges, although Winifred joined the Poor Clares at Gravelines, professing in 1707 (GP202).

On the 12 of September Sister Mary Bernard Tasburgh made her holy Profession.[1]

On the 7th of October Sister **[p. 209]** Emerentiana Higgonbottom made her holy profession for a lay sister.[2]

On the 11th of October Sister Eugenia Risdon was clothed by a particular dispensation, which she desired as being advanced in years; for otherways we seldome clothe any till they have been six months in the first habit.

On the 15 of October Mrs Catherine Smithson took the first habit and the name of Sister Lucy.[3]

On the 10 of November Mrs Mary and Mrs Elisabeth Galloway return'd to England.

On the 21 of November Sister Dorothy Stanley made her holy Profession.[4]

We this year received in Almns 200 florins of which 100 was from my Lady Andrews, 50 from Mr Joseph Gage and 50 from Mr Galloway.

The year 1701

On the 12 of March Mrs Plowden and Mrs Obern were received here for convictresses. Mrs Plowden had been sometime convictress at the English Monastry at Liege, and by her Mother's orders was removed from thence to our house.[5]

[p. 210] Mrs Obern lived with her Parents at Bruxelles, who were of the Irish nation.

On the 10 of April Mrs Alice Bracy was received for a convictress, her father was Steward to Mr Sheldon of Weston.[6] She came with a desire to be Religious, but not having the full Portion, we received her as one likely to supply for that by being a good Musician both for the organ and singing, which she had learn'd in England, and still endeavour'd to improve in by the assistance of Mr Nicholson our musick Master.

On the 18 of April Sister Lucy Smithson was clothed.[7]

On the 21 of April Sister Elisabeth Lovedon departed this life in the 39 year of her age and the begining of the 6th year after her holy Profession.[8] From the time she resolved to embrace a religious life, she most seriously apply'd her self to vertue, and often bless'd that happy

---

1 Mary Bernard Tasburgh (BA191).

2 Emerentiana Higgonbottom (BA104).

3 Catherine Smithson, in religion Lucy (1702–53) BA177.

4 Dorothy Stanley, in religion Mary Xaveria (BA183).

5 On the Plowden family and its connections with convents, see Hamilton, *Chronicle*, vol. 1, pp. 221–8.

6 Alicia Bracy, in religion Cecily (1704–39) BA031, musician.

7 Catherine Smithson, in religion Lucy (BA177).

8 Elizabeth Loveden (1695–1701) BA130.

hour in which she enter'd a religious family, tho' at first she had look'd upon it as an uneasy confinement, her head busy full of worldly notions, and she past the years proper for education in a School, but her good Aunt **[p. 211]** having placed her there at her own expenses, it proved a most happy providence for her, since by that measure, she came to be so well settled in religion, where in a short time she advanced to great perfection, and often express'd her ardent desires to enjoy her heavenly Spouse. Her last sickness was a continual distemper, and frequent violent fits of vomiting. She received the news of death with great joy, then in this pious disposition received the rights of our holy Mother the church, and continued in her perfect senses to the last moment of her life. But it pleased God to send her a tryal a few moments before her death, she was apperently seiz'd with a violent fear of the divine Justice, her whole body trembled to the surprise of all present, and being ask'd the cause, she said, who would not tremble at the memory of God's judgments, and soon after dyed in great calmness and peace. *Requiescat in pace*. Amen.

On the 17 of July Mrs Charlot Stanley, one of Sir Rowland Stanley's daughters, came to our Monastry, having left England with a resolution **[p. 212]** to follow the divine call, and settle in a religious State: she is elder than her sister Dorothy who is here Profess'd.[1] Little Miss Mary Petre came with her, who is eldest daughter to Mr Petre of Fithlars, and niece to Sister Hellen Andrews. She was received here for a convictress the same day, tho' not quite six years old.[2]

On the 4th of August the Lady Carrington came out of England to live for some time retired within our enclosure, having not long before had the misfortune to bury her Lord and Spouse. She is sister to the Duke of Powis and to Lady Lucy, our Sister Teresa Joseph. Her Ladyship brought with her Mrs Saunders and Mrs Smiton, who were received for convictresses.[3]

On the 9th of August Mrs Mary Berrington return'd to England.[4]

On the 27 of August Mrs Charlot Stanley took the first habit, and the name of Sister Mary Ignatia.

On the 12 of September Mrs Mary Thirwall, daughter to Mr Thirwall of Newbegin and niece to our Sister Ann' Benedict, was received here for

---

1 Sir Rowland Stanley was married to Ann Paston of Barningham, Norfolk. Their daughters were Charlotte Stanley, in religion Mary Ignatia (1703–25) BA182, and Dorothy Stanley (BA183).

2 Mary Petre was one of three sisters who joined convents. The daughter of Joseph Petre and Catherine Andrews, she arrived at the convent aged five. She was clothed in 1713, but left for health reasons and professed in 1718 at the Poor Clares, Gravelines, where she died in 1724, GP219. See also **[pp. 285, 291, 302, 318–21, 336–7]**. Helen Andrews (BA004).

3 Lady Carrington was Lady Anne Herbert (see Herbert family tree). The convictresses have not been identified.

4 Mary Berrington: see **[p. 198]**.

convictress. And the same day Mrs Obern return'd home to her Parents at Bruxelles.[1]

[p. 213] On the 16 of September our King James the 2d dyed, and we soon after perform'd a Solemne service for him, and had scutcheons, a hearse and other requisites for such a performance.

On the 17 of September Lady Mary and Lady Ann' Herbert, went from hence to a french Monastry, in France.[2]

On the 6th of November Sister Eugenia Risdon made her holy Profession.[3]

On the 29 of November Mrs Smiten return'd to England. This year Miss Lincy went from hence.

We have this year received in Almns 1150 florins, of which 500 was from the Lord Carrington

to Sister Teresia Joseph Herbert,[4] who gave it all for our Mill and Millhouse, 500 from Mr Thirwall which is put to rent for the church, 500 from Mr Havers, and 100 from Mr Weston.

The year 1702

On the 5th of February Sister Mary Ignatia was clothed.[5]

On the 23 of April Sister Lucy Smithson made her holy Profession.[6]

On the 24 of April the Lady Carrington **[p. 214]** return'd to England having left us great examples of humility and charity, so rare in persons of her degree and quality. Several of our religious have received great solaces from her Ladyship in their infirmities, particularly our dear Reverende Mother[7] who had been some time under the surgeon's hands for sharp humours falling violently into her legs so that they broke out in many places, and great quantity of water and humour ran out of them. My Lady was often on her knees to dress them with great charity and tenderness, and by her application and the drinks she appointed, her Reverence found much more benefit than by all the remedies she had used before, and we have reason to hope that the divine goodness has given so great a blessing to this good Lady's charity that our Reverende Mother's life will be happily prolong'd by it.

Her Reverence's sensible grief in parting with my Lady is an evidence of her great esteem and gratitude to so worthy a person.

---

[1] Mary Thirwall left before profession; Ann Thirwall, in religion Benedict (BA199).

[2] Probably the daughters of William Herbert, 2nd Marquess (brother of Lucy Herbert) and Mary Preston, his wife: see Herbert family tree in this volume.

[3] Dorothy Risdom, in religion Eugenia (1701–05) BA162.

[4] She is more usually known in the Chronicle by her name in baptism, Lucy.

[5] Mary Ignatia Stanley (BA182).

[6] Lucy Smithson (BA177).

[7] Reverend Mother here is Frances Wright, in religion Mary, Prioress 1693–1709 (BA228).

On the 12 of August Mrs Plowden went from hence to the English Monastry of our order in Lovain, by her Mother's orders; her family is in such circumstances that we have no hopes **[p. 215]** of getting any pensions for her.[1]

Mrs Alice Bracy being well improved in her musick and constant in her pious desires was admitted to the first habit on the 14 of June and is now call'd Sister Cecily. We shal have at least 100 pound with her.[2]

On the 31 of october Mrs Elisabeth and Mrs Wenefride Stanley received the first habit, and Mrs Elisabeth took the names of Mary Gertrude, and Mrs Wenefride that of Placida.[3]

On the 19 of December Mrs Dorothy, niece to Sister Eugenia Risdon, return'd to England.

About this time we began to have silver spoons in common, for my Lady Carrington gave for all who had them not before.

The year 1703

On the 22 of January Sister Cecily Bracy was clothed.

On the 7th of April Mrs Dorothy Huddlestone took the first habit, and the name of Sister Laetitia.[4]

On the 12 of April Sister Mary Gertrude Stanley was clothed.

On the 15 of April Sister Placida Stanley was clothed. Here is to be noted that these two sisters could not be admitted without a **[p. 216]** particular dispensation, we having already two of their sisters Profess'd here, and tho' our Statutes in 17 chap: and 4 para: seems to require only the Bishop's consent, and two thirds of the votes of the convent Sisters, for the admitting two sisters or more, yet our present Bishop affirm'd that he would answer for no more than the receiving two sisters in our community, but added that if we could procure the dispensation from Rome, he would no ways oppose it. In this occasion our Reverende Mother desired father Lewis Sabran of the Society of Jesus, to endeavour to procure it, and his Reverence recommended it to father John Baker of the same Society, who was then actually at Rome;[5] so he represented this matter to his holyness with such success that he got the dispensation not only for these four sisters but for as many as our Superior and convent were willing to admitt, of this family or of any other family, as it is express'd in the breef father Baker sent from his holyness, which

[1] There is no evidence that she joined St Monica's, Louvain.

[2] Alicia Bracy, in religion Cecily (BA031).

[3] Elizabeth Stanley (BA184); Winifred Stanley (BA186).

[4] Dorothy Huddleston (BA111).

[5] Fr Louis Sabran SJ; see *ODNB* and Holt, p. 217. Fr John Baker SJ (1644–1719); see Holt, p. 24.

our Reverende Mother received before these two Sisters were admitted to the first habit.

On the 17 of May Mrs Dorothy Newton and Mrs Saunders return'd for England.

On the 31 of May Sister Emerentiana **[p. 217]** Higgonbottom most piously ended her mortal life about the 31 year of her age, and third of her holy Profession.[1] Her vocation to a religious life was very particular, for in England she and her three sisters lived together after the death of their Parents, in the practice of religious vertues; their clothing and diet mean and poor; living in perfect unity, with an entire submission to their confessor's orders. The eldest sister had the care and charge of this little family, whom they obey'd as Superior. What they gain'd by their work, more than was necessary for their poor mainte[n]ance, they distributed in Almns to the poor, whom they also succour'd by their spiritual Almns; and their pious instructions, good prayers, example, and charitable endeavours, had such good success by the divine assistance that they converted several. They allow'd themselves but little time for rest, spending the greatest part of the night in prayer, and one night whilst our Emerentiana was employ'd in this pious exercise united to God in most fervent desires of confirming her self perfectly to his divine will and pleasure in all things, it was particularly reveal'd to her, that tho' her present state was **[p. 218]** pleasing to the divine manjesty [*sic*], yet it was his blessed will that she should be more entirely united to him, and by a more perfect sacrifice of her own will be consecrated to him in the state of holy religion. She presently resolved to comply with this divine call, and was confirm'd in her resolutions by her confessor's approving it for a true inspiration. This she imparted to one of our ancient religious, on the very day she made her holy Profession, and added that notwithstanding all the obstacles which opposed her settlement here, she was still constantly assured that this was the place where God designed she should be: for by the secret conduct of the divine providence (as we may suppose for her greater humiliation) the particular character of her pious life in the world was unknown to us before her settlement in our community, which occasion'd her some severe tryals; for the austere and mortified life she had lived had made her so lean and pale that she was judged to be advanced in years, and not able to undertake the labours of a lay sister; and not having been used to such kind of works, her ignorance and awkerdness in all she undertook, provoked the impatience of **[p. 219]** some, and others despised her esteeming her patience and humble simplicity rather a want of sense than the effect of a solide and well grounded vertue, as it realy was found to be by sufficient and convincing proofs.

---

1 Emerentiana Higgonbottom (1700–03) BA104.

Being told that she was entirely unfit for our service and therefore must return to England by the first occasion, she answer'd with great calmness and serenity that tho' it would be a sensible cost to her to go from this comunity yet as she thought it a great happiness to live in a catholick country, she confided that the divine providence would so dispose that at least she might find means of living in this town, being resolved not to return to England. Upon this answer our Reverende Mother was content that she should remain still in the Monastry, yet had no thought of admitting her for a lay sister. After some time, her case being made known to a pious devote in this town, she with a sincere and friendly charity offer'd to charge her self with the entire care of providing for her. To this proposal Emerentiana answer'd that if there was no hope nor possibility of her settling in this comunity she **[p. 220]** was very willing to accept of this kind and charitable offer.

In the mean time, our comunity having had experience for two whole years of her patience and humble submission, never importuning, nor any ways expressing a solicitude for her settlement, but seeming to abandon her self entirely to the conduct of the divine providence and willingly applying her self with a chearful serenity to hardest, most humbling and laborious works; it was resolved that she should be admitted for a lay sister in which state she persevered in a constant evenness of temper and practice of all vertues. She was very healthful all the time of her tryal for almost two years after her profession; but as she said, on her profession day, that she should not live long amongst us, so from after her first two years she fell into a weak and lingering sickness which encreased so fast upon her that in a little time she was confined to the infirmary, and entirely disenabled some time before she dyed. She suffer'd much by violent paines, yet kept herself united to her divine spouse, and often express'd her earnest desire to enjoy him eternally, in which happy disposition she received the last sacraments **[p. 221]** and departed in peace. *Requiescat in pace*. Amen.

On the 28 of october Lady Mary and Lady Ann' Herbert return'd hither from france.[1]

About this time our Bishop made us a visitation; father John Layton of the Society of Jesus, was interpretor, and we all went in our turns.[2] His Lordship was very well satisfied with the peace and union he found amongst us, and granted Sister Catherine Holland and Sister Agnes Bedingfeld the priviledge of keeping their votes as convent Sisters, tho' they were unable to keep their great weeks in the Quire;[3] and order'd that we should have there to a pint of wine every month, whereas we had but a single glass

1 Lady Mary and Lady Ann were nieces of Lucy Herbert: see Herbert family tree. School girls and young women were often sent to other convents to learn French.

2 John Layton was the alias of Fr John Leigh SJ (1639–1703); Holt, p. 147.

3 Catharine Holland, in religion Mechtildis (BA106); Agnes Bedingfield (BA016).

before; but he made not other alterations and seem'd pleased that no complains had been made him of the Procuratrix, which in other places he had generally met with. When all had been with him, his Lordship enter'd our enclosure and let several seculars of our acquaintance enter with him; then in our work chamber he made a very fatherly speech to the religious and another to the novices; and to conclude required **[p. 222]** a catalogue of our Books, which was afterwards sent him, but he did not forbid any of them.

We having this year had the advantage of the Pensions the Lady Carrington gave for her self and attendants, together with some other advantages, have been able with our income to make a new cellar, enlarge, pave and ciel the Refectory, furnish it with new cupboards, tables, and benches. We have also changed and enlarged the work chamber door, and got a new Altar for the same place. All this without taking any money from the Ark.

The year 1704

On the 27 of January Sister Cecily Bracy made her holy profession.[1]

On the 13 of April Sister Mary Gertrude Stanley made her holy profession.[2]

On the 19 of April our dear Sister Mary Xaveria Berrington departed this life about the 78 year of her age and near 20 of her holy Profession.[3] She was daughter to Mr Berrington of Cowhorn, and the most tenderly beloved **[p. 223]** by her father, who after her Mother's death, comitted the care of his house and family to her. From her tender age she always had a great value and esteem for a religious state, and was afterwards so averse to a marry'd life that it was many years before she could be perswaded by her friends to settle in it. Her father and the rest of her near relations earnestly solicited her in be[h]alf of Mr George Skip, a very worthy gentleman; the most reasonable objections she had against him was his being a Protestant which heresie he for some time was very positive in, but at last being convinced of his errors he freely abjured his false religion, and profess'd our holy faith. This happy change was a new engagement to all her friends to espouse his cause, so at last they prevail'd with her to marry him; and they lived many years in great concord and unity, and in the practice of piety, much disengaged from all worldly vanities, and often frequenting the holy sacraments. She was much esteem'd by all, and God particularly bless'd her charitable endeavours to reconcile those who were at variance, comfort the distress'd and afflicted, assist the **[p. 224]** sick, an other such like works of mercy.

---

1 Cecily Bracy (BA031).

2 Mary Gertrude Stanley (BA184).

3 Mary Berington, in religion Xaveria (1684–1704) BA022; see also **[pp. 134–5, 198]**.

She had but two children, a son and a daughter, who both dyed in their infancy; and being so soon disengaged of the care of them, she often used to tell her husband that if she had the misfortune to bury him, she would soon retire from the world to settle in a religious state, as in effect she did for about three months, after his death having made a quick dispatch of her affairs, her constant resolution of concurring with divine grace in so happy a vocation, prevail'd against all the seeming kind perswasions of her friends to the contrary. She chose Father Thomas Farmer of the Society of Jesus,[1] to conduct her to our Monastry, and in her journey reassumed her maiden name. Being then about 56 years of age, she was not judged capable of learning to read latin, so she was dispensed from the duties of the divine office; yet being of a healthy strong constitution, and also very zealous and fervorous, she desired to be engaged in all other duties except the reading in the Refectory; and it may truly be affirm'd of her that her **[p. 225]** primitive fervour never decay'd. She was obedient even to a nicety, and tho' of a timorous and tender conscience, yet her submission to confessors and directors kept her in a constant peace of mind, and easy cheerful disposition which render'd her conversation agreeable to all.

It was apparent that her greatest consolation was to converse with God in prayer, for she seem'd eager to get all the time that could be spared from other duties, to spend in this pious exercise, and our Reverende Mother, to favour her devout inclinations, allow'd her the mornings to her self, and it was wonderful how she could kneel so many hours together as she did without resting, but she esteem'd it the greatest comfort of her life to be present at Mass, and kneeling before the Blessed Sacrament, and thence she drew the treasures of all the vertues which she practised so much to our edification, and to her own advantage for a happy eternity.

About two years before her death her natural strength fail'd her very much, yet as she had constantly conform'd to the common diet, so in the greatest extremity of weakness **[p. 226]** and age, she could hardly be prevail'd with to admitt of any relaxation from fasting or any thing else, but always yielded to obedience. She often express'd her ardent desires to enjoy her God in a happy eternity, but made many heroick acts in resigning her self to live longer in conformity to his divine will. Her last sickness was judged by our Doctor to be a meer defailance of nature. On a friday morning she was found sitting in her cell, so faint and weak that she was not able to dress her self, and it was fear'd that the moving her to the infirmary might hasten her death or hinder her recovery, which we had then some hope of, therefore she was put into her bed in her cell as soon as possible; but the remedies and cordials our Doctor appointed her, seem'd only to encrease her pains and suffrings, which she express'd by

[1] Fr Thomas Fermor SJ (1649–1710); Holt, p. 92.

deep groans, and fervent acts of patience, uniting all her pains with those of our Saviour. On Saturday in the afternoon she received her *viaticum* and the holy oyles, with great comfort and devotion, in which she was lively and sensible, tho' from the time she was first taken ill she seem'd much stupefied to **[p. 227]** all things. The same day about six in the evening, she render'd her happy soul into the hands of her creator, and was bury'd on the 21 of April. *Requiescat in pace*. Amen.

On the 23 of April, Sister Placida Stanley made her holy profession.[1]

On the 5th of May, Sister Laetitia Huddlestone was clothed.[2]

On the 28 of June Mrs Mary Byerley, only daughter to Mr Byerley of Belgrave, arrived here with intention to be Religious.[3] She had been educated at the English poor Clares at Dunkirk, and afterwards lived some time with her Parents. On the 21 of July she was admitted to the first habit, and she took the name of Mary Aloysia.

On the 5th of october Mrs Wenefride Newton went from us to the English poor Clares at Gravelin, desiring to settle in that pious comunity.[4]

On the 25 of october the Lady Mary and the Lady Ann' Herbert parted from hence for England, Sister Barbara Devery had the care of them in this journey, and Mrs Mary Thirlwall went with them as far as Antwerp where she left them and went to the English **[p. 228]** Theresians at Liere.[5]

We this year received five guineas in Almns from Mrs Catharina Stanley, Aunt to our Stanleys.

The year 1705

On the 19 of January Sister Mary Aloysia Byerley was clothed.

On the 29 of April Sister Barbara returning from England, brought with her Mrs Agnes and Mrs Catherine Stanley, Sir Rowland Stanley's two youngest daughters, they were the same day received for convictresses.[6]

On the 17 of September our dear Sister Eugenia Risdon departed this life in the 39 year of her age and 5th of her holy Profession.[7] She was of a very agreeable disposition which unhappily engaged her, whilst she lived in the world, in particular friendships with some who too much affected worldly vanities and by their conversation distracted and diverted her from following the motions of God's preventing grace which enclined her

1 Mary Placida Stanley (BA186).

2 Laetitia Huddleston (BA111).

3 Mary Byerley (1706–38) BA042.

4 Winifred Newton (1707–1738) GP202.

5 Mary and Ann Herbert were nieces of Lucy Herbert. Ann Barbara Devery (BA072) as a lay sister, being unenclosed, was able to act as escort. Mary Thirlwall (b. 1687) later professed at Lierre (1707–71) LC078.

6 Ann Barbara Devery (BA072). Agnes Stanley (1711–23) BA185; Catherine Stanley (bap. 1692) married Robert Blundell of Ince in 1722.

7 Eugenia Risdom (1701–05) BA162.

to embrace a religious state. She had her first education in this Monastry, with her sister Mrs Susan Risdon, for who she had a more tender affection than for any of her relations.[1] Their Parents dying when they were both very young, they depended on the care **[p. 229]** of Mr Havers of Thealton, their uncle, till they were of age; then having got their fortunes into their own hands, they resolved to have no other dependancy than upon one another and to live with as much ease and pleasure as they could without infringing the laws of christian piety: for they always kept an unblemish'd reputation, and gave good example in the practice of many christian vertues. They took lodgings in London and were as they thought very well settled in a pleasant way of living, according to their inclinations: one day as they walk'd out into the fields they met with a girl dress'd very neat like a milk maid, who desired to speak alone with Mrs Susan Risdon, at which she felt a kind of fear, and would not consent to it, the Girl told her she would do her no harm, and her sister and the others did their best to perswade her, but they could not prevail; so the Girl told her she would dearly repent it and went away; then (they say) this Girl met her another time and importuned to speak to her alone; but all to no purpose, for she could not resolve upon it. Not long after, Mrs Dorothy (our Sister Eugenia) fell sick of the smal pox, and was hardly recover'd when Mrs Susan was seiz'd with the same disease, but her danger was not apprehended till about **[p. 230]** half an hour before she dyed, then she ask'd what hour it was, and they having told her, she answer'd, then I have but so long to live, God is just! and so dyed, at the time she had mention'd, before they could get her confessor to her, who was then at the Altar saying Mass. Thus she was unfortunately deprived of the benefit of the last Sacraments, and left her sister in the greatest extremity of grief.

Mrs Dorothy Risdon's friends were very solicitous to comfort her, and invented all the means that they could think of to divert her; but tho' her complaisant humour engaged her by motives of gratitude, to conform to them, yet her deep Melancholy so sensibly oppress'd her that it changed her natural healthy constitution, and she grew very infirm and sickly. One of her chief friends was Mrs Elisabeth Bedingfeld, who had lived with them in this Monastry, and from that time contracted a league of friendship with them. This young Lady thought her constant presence necessary for the comfort of her disconsolate friend, and therefore proposed to join her fortune with hers, and live with her as her sister had done, but her Parents being very fond of her, could not approve of her embracing **[p. 231]** such a kind of life; yet at last by force of continual

[1] The dates of their early time at Nazareth are not in the Chronicle, but their names appear among the schoolgirls for 1675. Their mother was Susanna Havers of Thelton (Thelverton Hall), Norfolk, married to Thomas Risdon of Sandwell, Devon.

importunities, she obtain'd their consent. Scarce were they settled in this way, when their designes were again disappointed, for Mrs Bedingfeld got a violent feavour, and was cut off by death in the flower of her age. Yet God's merciful providence favour'd her with the blessing of a most pious and happy death. She beg'd her Mother's pardon for leaving her so as she had done, received all the Sacraments, and was not only resigned, but desirous to end her life then.

Our dear Sister Eugenia's first affliction being thus sensibly renew'd by the great addition of this second loss, and being again disappointed in this manner of living which she had proposed to her self, seriously resolved to disengage herself entirely from the world, and to settle in a religious state. But she was still continually importuned by her pretended friends to seek some comfort and moderation of her grief, by the diversions they proposed, so they hurry'd her from one place to another, and perswaded her from year to year to deferr the execution of her pious resolution: thus nine years pass'd, her health and strength were much impair'd, and **[p. 232]** greatest part of her portion spent: for her too easy complaisant humour engaged her conformity even with violence to her own inclinations; but she never found any true comfort or satisfaction in any thing of this world after death had deprived her of her dearest sister and friend, which happen'd both in the same year. The first of them dyed on the lst of March 1691 and the other on the 26 of december old stile.

When dear Sister Eugenia was settled in more solide principles of vertue, she was truly sensible of her loss of so much time in the world, and with great regret for the long neglect of her holy vocation she acknowledged God's infinite goodness and mercy in not abandoning her but favouring her still with his assisting grace to compleat her happy settlement in a religious state. She was convinced also that had she endeavour'd to solace and moderate her grief by spiritual means, she should not have prejudiced her health so much by her afflictions, but have found a solide comfort in a due resignation and submission to the divine will, for the greater encrease of her vertue and merit. She often used great violence to her self to conform to the duties of our State, so **[p. 233]** contrary to those natural inclinations she had so much humour'd in the world; but then she encourag'd her self by reflecting that she had often contradicted those inclinations to comply with her friends and the world, and that she could not in Justice do less to comply with her duties in religion, and she realy did conform to all regular duties as much as her health and strength would permitt, supplying for the rest by her patience and submission to the divine will in what she suffer'd; which gives us reasonable hopes that in a short space she fulfill'd much time. She had been long in a lingering weak way, which for some time had confin'd her to the infirmary, and tho' the doctor gave her no hopes of life yet she was chearful, and agreable: at last being consumed with her infirmities and pains, she fell into a long and violent Agony, and expired about six a clock in the Evening.

Those several times when she seem'd to be dead, she again open'd her eyes and mouth and surprised us all with a loud shriek, and the moment after each time she closed her eyes again: no motion of life was at that time in her except in her head and breast. This being so very unusual seem'd frightful to all present, we **[p. 234]** conjectured it might proceed from the strength of her heart, she having taken many fortifying cordials in the time of her sickness. She was bury'd on the 19 instant. *Requiescat in pace*. Amen.

Father Thomas Havers of the Society of Jesus, and cousin germain to Sister Eugenia,[1] was a Missioner in Maryland when she dyed and he affirms that before he heard of her death from any of the living, he had the news of it by an apparition, from her self the very night that she dyed. She appear'd to him in her religious habit and seem'd to weep bitterly; many words pass'd between them, but he could never be prevail'd with to tell any thing that she said; and when his relations at our Grate press'd him for that effect, he said that he would never discover it to any but his confessor, to whom he had told all that pass'd between them; but he assur'd us she was in the way of salvation, and that he had procured many prayers for her.

They say that before this good father went to Maryland, she at our Grate (either in jeast or earnest) told him she would come to him when she was dead, and that he gave her leave.

On the 7th of December Mrs Elisabeth **[p. 235]** Sykes was received here for convictress. She's daughter to Mr William Sykes, by his first wife.[2]

We this year ciel'd the workchamber and the place by the Quire door.

The year 1706

On the 25 of January Sister Mary Aloysia Byerley made her holy Profession.[3]

On the 14 of February Sister Latitia Huddlestone made her holy Profession.[4]

---

1 Fr Thomas Havers SJ (1668 or 1669–1737), son of Thomas Havers of Thelverton, Norfolk and Alice Moore, first cousin of Sister Eugenia (her mother was Susan Havers) and brother of Mary Havers (BA099). He was in Maryland in 1705 and 1706. See Holt, p. 114; Foley, vol. 7, p. 345.

2 Elizabeth Sykes left and later professed at the Poor Clares, Aire in 1710 (AP128). Two other Sykes (sisters) joined the Bruges convent, all with William Sykes as their father, although they may have had different mothers. William Sykes has been identified as a painter and dealer in pictures at the Two Golden Balls in Portugal Row, London. He died in Bruges in January 1724/5: see **[p. 407]**. See artworld.york.ac.uk/personView.do?personUrn=1.00226&br=no, accessed 18 November 2015.

3 Mary Aloysia Byerley (BA042).

4 Laetitia Huddleston (BA111).

On the 18 of June our Reverend Lord Bishop[1] being in the church at the Governor's funerals, fell down suddenly, and from that moment, no signe of life was seen in him; yet tho' his death was so sudden, we have good reason to hope it was not unprovided, for he was a most vigilant and zealous Prelate, and very charitable to the poor. *Requiescat in pace*. Amen.

On the 19 of June we were surprised by an unlucky accident that happen'd to one of our workmen; he was mending the leads or slates on the top of the house and fell down from thence into our Garden; his legs were broken, and his body so bruised that he was a sad object of compassion. We presently sent for the surgeon he desired, and let his wife **[p. 236]** into our enclosure: our Superior and Procuratress with great charity and compassion supply'd them with all that was convenient for the present comfort and ease of the poor man, who was with great care the same day carry'd upon a bed to his own house, and a few days after, he made a pious and happy end. *Requiescat in pace*. Amen.

On the 22 of August we received for Convictress Mrs Ann' Waldegrave, daughter to Mr Waldegrave the Goldsmith.[2]

On the 23 of April Sister Ignatia Simons compleated the 50th year of her holy Profession, and the ceremonies of her Jubilee were perform'd by the Arch Priest in our Quire.[3]

We this year new glaz'd our Quire and made new leaden gutters for almost one side of our Monastry.

We had this year 50 florins in Almns for the sould [*sic*] of Mr John Weston; and a present from Sir Rowland Stanley of 1000 florins in consideration of his not having paid his daughters portions at the due time. **[p. 237]**

The year 1707[4]

On the 21 of January our dear Sister Mary Joseph Keynes,[5] between 6 and 7 a clock in the Evening, was suddenly seiz'd with an Apoplectick fit, while she was at recreation in our Speakhouse with several of our religious, and Reverend father John Baker of the society,[6] who was here to supply for our Confessarius then very ill, while she was talking very

1 The Bishop of Bruges in 1706 was Willem Bassery, Bishop 1690–1706.

2 Anne Waldegrave left the convent because of a lack of dowry, but was able to join the Sepulchrines at Liège in 1711, LS234. Mr Edward Waldegrave was active as a goldsmith and banker at the Anchor, Russell Street, Covent Garden, London 1690–1721. See artworld.york.ac.uk/personView.do?personUrn=1.04876&br=no, accessed 18 November 2015. He was one of three Catholic bankers in London identified in this chronicle. It was important for the convent to have access to sympathetic bankers to assist in the transfer of funds from England and to handle other transactions.

3 Penelope Simons, in religion Ignatia (1656–1717) BA175.

4 The typescript erroneously heads this section 1710.

5 Mary Joseph Keynes (1677–1707) BA126.

6 Fr John Baker SJ (1644–1719); Holt, p. 24.

pleasantly, on a sudden her speech failed her, to the great surprise of all present. She was immediately carry'd in a chair to our infirmary, and express'd her suffrings by lamentable groans, but from that time never spoke a word, nor gave the least signe of any sense. Our Doctor was sent for with all speed, and in the mean time father Baker gave her the holy oyles whilst she was held up in her chair. As soon as the Doctor came, all the remedies that could be thought of, were apply'd; she was put to bed, and from that time seem'd as in a Lethargie, continually sleeping, yet sometimes took and swallowed what was put into her mouth. She bit her tongue till she made it bleed, so that we were forced to keep a spoon, or a key in her mouth to hinder that. In this manner she lived till the 23 of January, then expired about **[p. 238]** three a clock in the morning. The vertuous and regular life she had lived amongst us, gives us good assurance that tho' she was so suddenly deprived of her senses yet she was happily prepared for death. She was very serviceable to this comunity by her good talents, being perfect in the french and flemish tongues, and very ingenius in several sorts of works, she had a strong voice both for musick and the plain song, and fervorously employ'd her talents in the offices of chantress, Mistress of the Pensioners, and Portress. The manner of her death we may hope was particularly designed for her by the most favorable and merciful providence of God, since she had always a very tender and timorous conscience, and often express'd a great fear and apprehension of death. She was of a very pious disposition, compassionate and charitable in assisting others; and most particularly devoted to our Blessed Lady and St Joseph whose names she took in religion, and we may reasonably hope she particularly experienced their powerful assistance at her death, which was on the feast of their Espousals. She was about 58 years of age, and near 31 of her holy Profession **[p. 239]** *Requiescat in pace*. Amen.

On the 24 of March our Reverend father confessor, Mr Hawker, most piously departed this life.[1] He had been for some years very infirm and sickly, and was thought much enclined to a consumtion, but from the begining of the January before he dyed, he was constantly confined to his chamber by a lingering feavour which was some time very violent. On the 20 of January, by our Doctor's order, he received his *viaticum*; and he then made his will having obtain'd our Reverend Mother's leave that Sister Mary Charleton might be his Executrix.[2] He left the greatest part of what he had to his niece Mrs Mary Clifton who had been some

[1] Fr John Hawker (1650–1707), Confessor 1681–1707; see Anstruther 3, pp. 95–6.

[2] Mary Charlton, in religion Augustina (BA048).

time a convictress here, but was then settled in York amongst those pious Ladies de *l'institute de Ste Marie*.[1]

After this pious preparation for death, and settlement of his affairs, he was sometimes much better, but never in any hopeful way of recovery, not able to say Mass, nor hear confessions. *In fine* the Doctor dispair'd of him, and then a German officer's Lady undertook him, and at first we had some hopes of good success, he being a little revived **[p. 240]** with what she gave him, but he soon relapsed and we had reason to suspect that what she did was not in God's name, nay she said her self that her remedies had not their usual effect because he, or we were too holy; so she was soon dismissed. His long continual suffrings were a very severe affliction to our comunity which had a great esteem and respect for his Reverence, as he justly deserved by his prudence and vertue. He was naturally of a Melancholy disposition, but acted by the rules of prudence and vertue, and not by his own humour, chosing rather to suffer in silence than to express his resentments, and tho' he was most exemplar in all vertues yet he was most zealous in point of charity, and gave great edification to all that conversed with him by his great caution in avoiding all occasions of hearing or speaking ill of others. He was so humble as to prefer the advice given by any spiritual Director before his own; and both approved and commended any ones dependancy on our extraordinary or other spiritual Directors, often affirming that each one ought purely to regard what was most advantagious for **[p. 241]** her spiritual profit and advancement in perfection. In the time of his sickness he frequently received the most Blessed Sacrament with great devotion and having received all the rights of our holy Mother the church, he happily ended his pious life on the Eve of our Lady's Annunciation about 11 a clock in the morning while we were singing Vespers it being the time of Lent. The next day he was exposed in the church, and we said a long dirge for him. On the 26 of March he was bury'd in our Vault with all the usual ceremonies, our Arch Priest singing the Mass and performing the funerals. He was about 58 years of age, and had been near 26 years confessor to this comunity. *Requiescat in pace*. Amen.

On the 13 of May Mrs Catherine and Mrs Ann' Caryll came here from England and were received for convictresses. They are daughters to Mr Philip Caryll of North.[2]

---

[1] Mary Clifton (1680, entered 1697–1720 York) MW047. The Mary Ward Sisters opened a house in York, known as the Bar Convent, in 1686. Her time as a convictress at Bruges is not recorded in the Chronicles.

[2] Catherine Caryll left before profession. Ann Caryll, in religion Mary Ann (1712–36) BA047.

On the 17 of June Mrs Henrietta Browne, niece of the Lord Montague of Cowdrey, was received her [*sic*] for convictress.[1]

About this time we having no Bishop, the Reverend Lord Bishop of Gant[2] came to **[p. 242]** this town, and confirm'd here Sister Catherine Holland, and the two Miss Carylls.[3]

On the 10 of July, our Reverende Mother Mary Wright[4] celebrated her whole Jubilee having completed the fiftyeth year of her holy profession on the 11 of the June before, which fell that year on the Eve of Pentecost, and therefore the publick celebration of her Jubilee was deferr'd till this day. The musick Mass was sung by the Abbot of our order, assisted by six of his Monks, our Reverende Mother had a place prepared for her in our church, and two of our ancient religious attended her till the ceremonies were over.

Sister Mary Heton, our Subprioress,[5] having made her holy profession on the same day with our Reverende Mother, her whole Jubilee was celebrated a few days after: our Arch Priest sung the musick Mass, and she had a seat prepared for her in our Quire where the usual ceremonies were perform'd. We had recreation for eight days together, and also in the Refectory during those days at dinner and supper, except Saturday night. Our religious acted three plays for our Reverende Mother's diversion, and one for our Subprioress, but her Reverence would not permitt **[p. 243]** any one to enter our enclosure, tho' she was much press'd to it by the importunity of her friends; nevertheless they were all hansomly entertain'd in our Confessor's house, and at the Grate.

After the death of our worthy confessor Mr Hawker, our Reverende Mother took great care to have his place supply'd by a proper and fit person, so address'd her self to the Society of Jesus, and particularly to father Sabran,[6] and the person they Recommended was Mr Augustin Pointz[7] who had been educated by the English Clergy at Doway, but upon some occasion of dissatisfaction in that Colledge, he left it, and went and ended his studies at the English Colledge at Rome where he was ordain'd Priest, and from thence came to our Monastry on the 15 of July; then on the first of August he was examined and approved for our Confessor.

---

1 Henrietta Browne, daugher of Henry, 5th Viscount Montagu and Barbara Walsingham. She never professed and later married Richard Harcourt. Her uncle Francis, 4th Viscount Montagu married Mary Herbert, sister of Prioress Lucy Herbert: Stirnet.com, family tree, Brown 01.

2 The Bishop of Ghent in 1707 was Philips Erard van der Noot, Bishop 1694–1730.

3 Catharine Holland, in religion Mechtildis (BA106). The two Miss Carylls were Catherine and Ann, as above.

4 Mary Wright (BA228).

5 Mary Heton (1657–1713) BA102.

6 Fr Louis Sabran SJ (1652–1732); Holt, p. 217.

7 Fr Augustine Poyntz (?SJ) (1679/80–1723); Holt, p. 204. Holt queries whether Poyntz professed as a Jesuit on his deathbed.

On the 29 of August Mrs Ann' and Mrs Teresia Vaughan[1] came hither with a resolution to settle in a religious state. They had been educated in this Monastry, and went from hence about 14 years before, but were then too young to fix their resolutions, and afterwards met **[p. 244]** with obstacles which hinder'd the more speedy execution of their designes; but their desires of not deferring it any longer being very much approved of by our Reverende Mother and comunity, they were admitted to the first habit on the 7th of September, and the eldest of them took the name of Mary Joseph, the youngest of Teresia Austin.

Our new Confessor Mr Pointz fell dangerously ill of the spoted feavour, his recovery was so much dispair'd of that by the doctor's orders he received his *viaticum* and was very piously disposed for death. Our comunity had had but little acquaintance with his Reverence, but by the character given of him, we were very sensible that his death might prove a great loss to us, therefore we were willing to undertake that ten fridays devotions for him in honour of St Francis Xaverius, if it pleased God to restore his health;[2] this offer being made he grew better by degrees, and as soon as he was in a hopefull way of recovery we began the devotion about the 11th of november.

On the 14 of november, our unfortunate fugitive, and now most happy Penitent, Sister Perpetua Errington[3] came back to us again.

[p. 245] It was eleven years compleat the october before, from her unhappy flight: in which time many prayers and particular devotions had been offer'd for her conversion and some in our community writ to her but all seem'd in vain. About five years after her departure we heard that she was gone to her brother's house in a miserable poor condition, and not long after one of her younger brothers, who was then there, writ to our Reverende Mother to inform her Reverence that his sister Dorothy was dead and that he hoped she dyed a true penitent; upon this we were sensibly moved, and out of great but indiscreet compassion, resolved to hang our church in white and perform her obsequies as we do for the rest of our religious at their buryal: but before this was put in execution our father confessor was perswaded to go to the Bishop, and understand from him what we were to do. His Lordship sent us word that we were not to perform any publick service for her, nor to pray for her, except we were assured that some Bishop had taken off the excommunication; and that if her body could be got it must be dragged about the streets by

1 Ann Vaughan, in religion Mary Joseph (BA207); Teresa Vaughan (BA209) (see **[pp. 162, 177]**).

2 The devotion of Ten Fridays to seek improvement in health was particularly associated with Fr Louis Sabran who also recommended it to the Carmelite, Catherine Burton. I am indebted to Nicky Hallett for this footnote.

3 Dorothy Errington, in religion Perpetua (BA076); see also **[pp. 113, 121, 128, 129, 131, 132, 183, 442]** and vol. 2, **[pp. 67–9]**.

a horse and whips for the scandal she had given. In the mean time, she was alive in Scotland; tho' tis certain **[p. 246]** there was a woman who came to Mr Erring's House and perswaded the younger brother (for the elder was not at home) that she was his sister Dorothy; she even told him several things that he had said to her and she to him, at our Grate; and took notice of several alterations in the house, so that he truly thought it was his sister; the root of her mouth was eaten up by the french disease, and she really dyed there, having first desired she might be buryed in a dress like Sister Perpetua's picture, which they had got drawn in our habit before she left us. Who this woman was God only knows, Sister Perpetua thought it might be one whom she was familiarly acquainted with in the camp, but who or what she realy was, we have no certainty. So to return to our dear penitent.

Some time before she came our Reverende Mother received a letter from a Catholick Bishop in Scotland, who affirm'd that he had several times spoken with her, and found her very sensible of her unfortunate state, and well disposed to return to us again, if money could be procured for her journey. Our Reverende Mother answer'd this worthy Prelate's letter expressing a sensible gratitude to his Lordship, and great satisfaction in **[p. 247]** the good news he sent her, assuring him that whatever he thought necessary for the expense of her journey, should be return'd to his Lordship by our Agent at London; to whom her Reverence writ and order'd him to return to this Bishop without delay whatever sum he should demand of him.[1] After this, several months past but nothing more was heard of her, and we understood from our Agent that he had neither heard from his Lordship, nor no money had been demanded of him which made us almost hopeless of any good success in this affairs, till she unexpectedly came to our Grate with Reverend father Skilton, a benedictin Monk.[2] They call'd for our Reverende Mother, and as soon as he had discover'd who she was, she on her knees with abundance of tears beg'd of her Reverence admittance again in our community. This was a most agreeable surprise to our Reverende Mother, who had a sensible joy and comfort to see at her feet so great an object of God's infinit mercy and goodness; her Reverence encourag'd her, and with all speed gave notice of her arrival to the Vicars, who order'd that she should be

---

1 The role of agents for the convents has been little studied. Being in exile meant that the communities needed contacts in England who could assist in arranging passages to the continent, advise on suitable convents for particular candidates, arrange for the transfer of funds and liaise with families. Three bankers with businesses in Covent Garden are mentioned in the Chronicle acting in some capacity for Nazareth: Sir Francis Jerningham, Edward Waldegrave and Anthony Wright. Mannock Strickland acted for a number of convents: see R. G. Williams (ed.), *Mannock Strickland (1683–1744): Agent to English Convents in Flanders: Letters and Accounts from Exile*, CRS 86 (Woodbridge: Boydell and Brewer for the CRS, 2016).

2 Probably Fr John (Gregory) Skelton, OSB (d. 1721); see Bellenger, p. 108.

taken into our enclosure that night, promising to meet the next day and **[p. 248]** conclude what was further to be done.

The chief of the Vicars, Monsieur Bourré, came to our Monastry and spoke with her at the Grate both before and after their consultation, and was very well satisfied with her entire submission and sincere repentance which appear'd in the many difficulties she had gone through to come back again; particularly in the so long and troublesome journey from the Highlands of Scotland, which is above four hundred Miles from London. She own'd that during the eleven years of her absence she had constantly been uneasy with bitter remorse, yet she could never come to a resolution of seeking any means to disengage her self from her unhappy slavery till after the unfortunate death of Grant, who was accidentally drowned about a year and half before she came hither; his dead corpse being laid before her, struck her almost dead with grief and at the same time moved in her a lively sense of what his soul might suffer and terrifying reflections how far she was accessory to the misery she might so justly fear he suffer'd. From that time, she resolved to return, tho' violently opposed by her pretended friends **[p. 249]** and frighten'd by the apprehension of great penances. In these conflicts she had not the comfort of a Priest nor any catholick near her whom she could speak to: at last she found the means of writing to this Lord Bishop N. who shewed a most singular kind preventing charity in seconding the motions of divine grace and facilitating all her difficulties. He found the means to inform her brother Mr John Errington, of her good dispositions, and he prevented his Lordship's accepting of our Reverende Mother's offer of money, and most worthily act the part not only of a kind brother, but also of a most tender father, freely allowing her a sufficiency for the expenses of her journey, and offering her whatever might be necessary to settle her in any other Monastry, but upon her assurance that she would rather return to her own again, he sent his Priest with her.

The good Priest brought with him a letter from the Bishop to our Reverende Mother wherein he inform'd her in very obliging terms, what promises he had made in her Reverence and comunity's behalf to **[p. 250]** Mr. Errington, and all her relations, engaging for us that we would give her a most favorable and kind reception; and indeed we all endeavour'd to make good his Lordship's assertion; for as soon as our Arch priest had assured us we might freely speak to her, tho' she was not yet absolved, we joyfully embraced her with tears of tenderness and compassion, and were very sollicitous that our Vicars should be favorable to her, as indeed they were, even more than we could have expected; for on the thursday after, they came into our Quire, our whole comunity being present. She came before them in her soecular clothes, and kneeling down by their orders made a profession of her faith which she read in french. Then she was absolved from the excommunication, and they enjoyn'd her no other penance but to be separated from the comunity for one month, yet she was to be present in the Quire, and to sit by the novices in time of the divine office. The Vicars exhorted her to endeavour to repair the scandal of her past life, by exactness in all regular observances, and **[p. 251]** expressly order'd that at the end of the month she should be placed in the rank and order of her Profession, and that none should ever reproach her with her past misdemeanours.

On the Sunday following she again received our holy habit, and our Superior and whole comunity (of nuns) being all together in our work chamber she humbly prostrated at our Reverende Mother's feet, and with many tears beg'd pardon of all for the scandal she had given, then after her Reverence had made a short speech of God's infinit mercy and goodness, she was received amongst us as a reunited member of our comunity, with the kiss of peace from every one, and we sung *TE DEUM*, she joining with us, standing in the last place. From that time she began to prepare for confession, the Vicars gave her leave to chose any confessor she would which privilege was large to her, since she could speak both the french and Flemish tongue; but she desired no other than Reverend father John Baker, who was still here to supply for our Confessarius, who was not yet able to perform his duty. On St Andrews days [*sic*][1] she made her first communion, after **[p. 252]** her return to us; and the month being ended on the 20th of december she was placed in her rank and order of Profession, and has the freedom of the house, and of conversation with us. We hope God's infinite mercy will compleat the work he has so happily begun, and that our humble penitent will be an example of vertue and Regular observances, as she had been of scandal to the whole world.

On the 24 of December we received four sisters for convictresses, Mrs Elisabeth, Mrs Constantia, Mrs Mary and Miss Anne Blount, all daughters to the late Mr George Blount, and nieces to Sir Walter Blount, who sent them hither.[2] They are cousine germains to the two Sister Jernegan's and to Sister Tasburgh.

We this year new boarded the work chamber, paved the two Pants with marble and the speak houses with black and white stone, and ciel'd the Dormitory.

---

[1] The Feast of St Andrew is celebrated on 30 November.

[2] George Blount of Mawley Hall, Shropshire (d. May 1702) and his wife, Constantia Cary, had five daughters: Constantia, Mary, Anne, Elizabeth and Catherine. His brother Sir Walter Blount, 3rd Baronet (d. 1717) had no children. See Stirnet.com, family tree, Blount 02. Two of the daughters professed at the Ghent Benedictines: Elizabeth (GB019) and Anne (GB020).

The year 1708

On the 20 of January the two Sister Vaughans were clothed.[1]

On the 16 of May the four youngest daughters of Sir William Gage of **[p. 253]** Hengrave, were received here for convictresses, to wit Mrs Julia, Mrs Penelope, Mrs Catherine and Mrs Ann';[2] there came also with them Mrs Judith Bond their cousine Germain and daughter to Mr Thomas Bond, who at the same time came over himself with several other gentlemen to conduct the Lord Dover's body which was to be bury'd in the Carmes church.[3] That Lord left us a hundred pound sterlin, and we sung a Solemn Mass for his soul, and made an entertainment for those who came out of England to assist at this funeral.

On the 8th of August our King James the third enter'd our enclosure with all his attendancy and a crowd of other people rich and poor who got in with them. His Majesty touch'd several in our infirmary and that in a most edifying devout manner, tho' he was then but a young Prince.[4] We prepared a hansome table with coffee, tea, etc., but his Majesty would not accept of any, being just come from dinner, at Count La .. ..., the general of the French in these part.

Three of those our King touched were of our Religious, Sister Clare Saunderson, Sister Henrietta Markham and Sister Mary Bernard Tasburgh.[5]

On the 20 of Aug., Miss Charlot Hacket, a Merchant's daughter of Rotterdam was received here for a convictress.

On the 10th of September Mrs Elisabeth Sykes went from hence to the Poor Clares at Gravelin, with a desire to settle in that holy order.[6]

On the 4 of November, three sisters Mrs Anne, Mrs Mary and Mrs Margarite Compton, were received here for convictresses.[7]

---

1 Ann Vaughan, in religion Mary Joseph (BA207); Teresa Vaughan, in religion Teresa Augustine (BA209).

2 They were the daughters of Sir William Gage, 2nd Baronet of Hengrave, Suffolk and his wife, Mary Charlotte Bond (see F. Young, *The Gages of Hengrave and Suffolk Catholicism, 1640–1767*, CRS Monograph 8 (Woodbridge: CRS, 2015), pp. 82–3). Only Penelope professed, taking the name in religion Stanislaus (BA085). For complications surrounding her profession, see also **[pp. 291–2, 294–5]**.

3 Henry Jermyn, Lord Dover (d. 6 April 1708) asked to be buried at the Carmelites' church in Bruges; see *ODNB*. Judith Bond was the daughter of Thomas Bond, brother of Mary Charlotte (d. 1732) of Bury St Edmunds and Henrietta Jermyn of Bury St Edmunds.

4 James III (b. 10 June 1688); he left England in December 1688 with his mother, after James II fled to France, where they were provided with a home by Louis XIV at St Germain-en-Laye; *ODNB*. For the medieval origins of the practice in France and England, see F. Barlow, 'The King's Evil', *English Historical Review* 95(374) (1980), pp. 3–27. Barlow states that the practice died out suddenly in 1714 with arrival of the Hanoverian monarchy. It had declined in the early part of the seventeenth century, but rapidly expanded under Charles II.

5 Clare Saunderson (BA172); Henrietta Markham (BA136); Mary Bernard Tasburgh (BA191).

6 Elizabeth Sykes eventually professed at Aire (1710–47) AP128.

7 None of them professed; it has not been possible to identify them further.

We had no Almns this year, but what the Lord Dover left us.

[p. 254]

The year 1709

On the 2nd of January we received for convictress Mrs Margarite Bedingfeld, eldest daughter to Mr Francis Bedingfeld of Redingfield Hall, and niece to Sister Mary and Sister Agnes Bedingfeld.[1] We had then 21 convictresses, which was a greater number than we had ever had at a time.

On the 30 of January happen'd the wonderful cure of Mrs Mary Blount.[2] She had had a quartan Ague for about six weeks in the year 1708, and on the 16 of November the same year being indifferent well after her fit the night before she in the morning went with the rest of her companions to practice their writing: and suddenly she surprised them all by falling into a strange fit, rouling her self on the ground, screaming and crying out in a most frightful manner. The Doctor and Surgeon were presently sent for, and father confessor came to her; all stood amaz'd and thought her seiz'd with violent convulsions. Remedies being apply'd she came to her self again, had no more Ague fits, and continued very well for about **[p. 255]** eight or ten days, then she fell into such another fit, and seven or eight persons could hardly hold her in these fits, having one or two a day, or more; sometimes they were but short, and sometimes long, and she always fell suddenly into them, and came suddenly out of them, and after several of the first fits, she was very well the moment they left her. When her fits began to be so frequent, she was removed from the Schoole and lodged in our infirmary where the religious constantly tended her night and day, for we could not be secure of her being any time free from these fits; and sometimes she would come to her self two or three times in the same fit, and immediatly fall into it again. On the 30th of December, she had a fit that lasted seven hours, and after that she was like a changling, and knew no body. On new years day she entirely lost her speech, tho' her senses came again by degrees, and by signes she could make us understand her: our Doctor and several experienced persons, affirm'd they had never seen, nor heard of any **[p. 256]** one in so strange a way, and as we apprehended there might be somthing of witchcraft or what was not natural in the matter, we got a Bernardin Monk to come to her who was appointed to exercise and pray over possess'd persons; and he came several times whilst she was in her fits, and pray'd over her, but

---

[1] She left in 1710. Her aunts were Mary Bedingfield (BA018) and Agnes Bedingfield (BA016).

[2] Mary Blount; see above **[p. 252]**. On this and other exorcisms in English convents, see F. Young, *English Catholics and the Supernatural, 1553–1829* (Farnham: Ashgate, 2013), pp. 175–6.

this spiritual remedy had no more present effect than the corporal ones had which our Doctor had prescribed her.

She continued in this manner till the 24 of January, then coming out of a fit, she complain'd by signes of a violent pain in her side, which by all the simptoms was judged to be the stone; she continued in great pain with stoppage of urine till the 29 of January, her fits being more frequent than ever, which brought her to so great a weakness that she could not struggle in them as she used to do. The next day she fell so frequently into these fits, that they seem'd to be but one continued fit, for she only somtimes came to her self for the space of an *Ave Maria*; this made the Doctor appoint her the extream unction, not thinking her capable of receiving her *viaticum*, but our Reverend father confessor being **[p. 257]** well acquainted with the child's innocency and piety which had moved her before to desire his Reverence to give it to her when she should be judged in danger; therefore not to deprive her of so great an advantage, he brought the most Blessed Sacrament into the infirmary, resolving to comunicate her at the first intervale after her fit. The moment he enter'd the chamber she came to her self, and received the Blessed Sacrament with as great signes of devotion as her weakness would permitt, she had no sooner swallow'd the Blessed Sacrament but she immediately fell into another fit; father confessor and the comunity remain'd still in the Room praying before the Blessed Sacrament and saying the Penitential Psalms;[1] at the end of the 4th Psalm, she came to her self again which those who were by her bed side, gave father confessor notice of; and he immediately gave her holy oyles. Presently, after she fell into another fit, then father confessor carryed back the B.S. and came into the enclosure again to pray by her as a dying person, but being desired to warm himself in the infirmary before he went to her chamber, she in the mean time came out of her fit, which had not lasted **[p. 258]** above a quarter of an hour; and to the great surprise of all present suddenly set her self up in her bed, said she was perfectly cured, and spoke as plain as ever she had done in her life.Then she arose and as soon as she was dress'd, went downstairs and was conducted by father confessor and many of our religious to adore the Blessed Sacrament with thanksgiving for so wonderful a cure. That night she walk'd about from one place to another without any difficulty being free from all pain and finding no weakness nor inconveniency by the many violent remedies that were used to her, as bleeding, blistering, cupping, Physick, etc, but enjoying a perfect health. This happen'd on thursday the 31 of January, between 3 and 4 of the clock in the afternoon. On the octave day of her recovery we had a Solemn Singing Mass, and

[1] Penitential Psalms: seven psalms sung in time of trouble, expressing sorrow and begging forgiveness; see further details in the Glossary.

Te Deum sung in thanksgiving, at which she was present. She was then about 14 years of age.

As soon as her Uncle Sir Walter Blount had notice of her illness, he gave orders she should be sent to her Mother, when she was able to undertake the journey; and the first night of her recovery, she earnestly desired that those orders might be comply'd with **[p. 259]** which was accordingly done, for a few days after she went from hence for England.[1]

On the 27th of February our most Reverende and venerable Mother Mary Wright, departed this life, and left us in great affliction for so sensible a loss.[2] But her happy memory will ever live amongst us. Before she was Superior she gave great example of exact regularity and of all vertues; but her humility was singularly remarkable above all the rest, by which she for many years avoided the offices of Subprioress and Procuratress, both being offer'd her, but her prayers and tears prevail'd; yet by an obedience very contrary to her inclinations she twice submitted to the office of Mistress of the novices, and that for several years each time; but she own'd she could resigne with much more ease and natural satisfaction to meaner offices tho' more laborious and painful, and of this she gave sufficient proof in different employments, particularly in that of Vestarian in which for many years she labour'd much with great zeal for the common profit. Her conversation was so generally agreeable to all that in difficult occasions most had recourse to her for comfort and advice. She was remarkable for her constant chearfulness in time of recreation, and serious recollection at all other times. To comply with her duty to her Mother, she writ her once a year, but avoided all unecessary correspondance, and all acquaintance at the Grate, or with soeculars, in so much that when she was first elected our Superior, it was a great wonder amongst them who we had made choice of, they being entirely ignorant that we had such a person in our Monastry, tho' she had been Subprioress for about two years before the death of her worthy Predecessor, which we may believe the divine providence disposed that she might more easily submitt to the charge of Superior; tho' her resignation to it was with so great difficulty, that she afterwards declared in her usual sincere and humble manner of speaking: that she thought she pleased God more in submitting to be Superior, than she did in leaving the world to enter a religious state; since this sacrifice was far more apposite to her natural inclinations: yet with **[p. 261]** a chearful submission to the adorable will of God, she entirely abandon'd her self to his divine providence, and in many occasions she declared that her dependance on it alone was her only ease and comfort in all difficulties, and it evidently appear'd how

---

1 Sir Walter Blount, 3rd Baronet of Sodington, sent Mary to her mother, Constantia Cary (of Torre Abbey, Devon).

2 Mary Wright, Prioress 1693–1709 (BA228).

pleasing to God this humble confidence was; for our community never enjoy'd a more constant prosperity, than during the time of her government.

After her death we found some fine papers written in her own hand; for she had taken care to have the rest burnt; and those we found contain'd in short some fruits of her spiritual exercises, and renovations, with two particular entertainments she had with our Lord after communion. All this was writ after she was Superior, and all tended to confidence in the divine providence and abnegation of her self with humility, silence, solitude and prayer. In one of her entertainments she said to our Lord: "Dear Lord, I fear I have offended yu[1] in taking upon me this charge of government." To which our Blessed Saviour interiorly answer'd: "Do yu believe yu have received me in the Blessed Sacrament, true God and true man?" She replyed: "I firmly believe I have received the **[p. 262]** very self same God and man who lay nine months in the womb of his sacred Mother." To which our Lord seem'd to answer: "Then believe yu have not offended me in the least by taking this charge upon yu. I designed it in eternity, and fear not, what is wanting I will supply; confide in me, and take my words (as true as yu have received me this day) that heaven and earth shal pass, but my word and promise shal not fail yu." In another place she says that after communion our Lord in a particular manner assisted her with his graces, in order to reform her life and make her self an example to her subjects in silence and solitude. In another place she thus expresses her self. "I purpose to unite my heart often in the day with that of my divine Jesus who has enlighten'd mine with what my pen cannot express. I shal ever confide in him, living and dying." And again: "Considering the excess of God's love to me which is known to none but him and my self, I cannot but redouble my wishes and endeavours to return the most ardent love I can comprehend, by often uniting my heart with that of my divine Jesus, and avoiding all occasions of offending him."

By this we may judge of the **[p. 263]** sanctity of her interior, and her exterior comportment was answerable to it. In all occasions she seem'd wholy to depend on, and confide in God alone, and in tryals of the greatest difficulties, she would say with great sweetness and serenity: "This business will end well", and so it always happen'd even when there was least appearances of good success. In her practice of humility, she seem'd to abase the authority of Superior rather too much, by the difficulty she had in submitting to the respect due to her in that charge. She constantly supported the weakness and frailties of others with an edifying meek and humble patience, and was most zealous to animate and encourage the most regular both by words and example. The weak and infirm always

---

[1] Evidently the polite form of address (ye, you) rather than the intimate form (thee, thou); viz. tu, toi/vous, vous.

experienced in her the compassion and care of a most affectionate Mother, but she was most vigorous to her self without any consideration of her age and infirmities, not taking any relaxation from regular observances even when she was a Jubilarian. She constantly came to Matins, and so accustomed her self to it from her younger days that **[p. 264]** she would come for several months together without once sleeping and hardly could be prevail'd with to stay from the Quire when it was judg'd absolutely necessary on account of her infirmities, by which she suffer'd very much some years before her death, particularly by sharp humours which fell into her legs, being also much troubled with a dropsie and Asthma. The last winter of her life was most severely sharp, more than had been experienced for many years, yet she would not admitt of reasonable solace, till both our doctor and surgeon declared they could not hope to do her any good if she would not take convenient rest, and have a constant fire in her chamber, which she consented to a few days before her death, but could lye in our infirmary, for she never would lodge in the Superior's chamber. Our Archpriest hinder'd by some affairs, from giving her the holy *viaticum*, she received it on her knees from the hands of Reverend father confessor, who made a very edifying speech in commendation of her vertue and fervent devotion to the adorable Sacrament; and it was much to her Reverence's satisfaction **[p. 265]** that she was assisted by him, and not by the Archpriest since she could not understand the french, nor flemish tongue. She was perfectly her self all the time of her illness and having received the holy oyles she soon after expir'd sitting in her chair, between nine and ten a clock in the morning, on a wednesday. The next day being the feast of our holy father's translation,[1] we sung the Mass of Requiem for the repose of her dear soul. She was 72 years of age, and 52 Profess'd, and near 16 years Superior during which time she Profess'd 23 Religious for the Quire and three lay sisters. She was bury'd on the 29 of february by our Archpriest with all the usual ceremonies.[2] *Requiescat in pace*. Amen.

Our Reverende Vicars having ordained the three days of fasting and silence for the happy success of the election of a new Prioress, we perform'd the same with the prayers as our institutions appoints; and on tuesday the 5th of March (which was the day designed for the election) our Reverend father confessor sung a Solemn Mass of the holy Ghost, and communicated all the religious. Monsieur Bouré, the official, sent us word that some unexpected business obliged him that day to go **[p. 266]** to Gant, so there was only present Monsieur Brookman, and the Archpriest, the

---

[1] The feast of the translation of the relics of St Augustine has been associated with two dates; here it is placed on 28 February, which marks the removal of the relics from Africa to Sardinia. They were later moved a second time, to Pavia.

[2] Here a complication with dating arises, since 29 February refers to the leap year in 1708, rather than following the custom in the Chronicles of starting the year on 1 January.

secretary and Mr Pointz, our confessor[1] who distributed to the religious the schedules which were all printed; and he declared to us the Vicars by a particular favour allow'd the younger Sisters to have active votes in the election: so that with them there was just 42 Electresses, and the Lady Lucy Herbert[2] was legaly chosen for Prioress, which the Vicars declared, and confirm'd. Her Reverence was daughter to that Duke of Powis who was in france with our king James the Second after his abdication; and her Mother, the Lady Dutchess was Governess to the then Prince of Wales and now (by right) King of Great Britanny, James the third.[3] In religion she took the name of Sister Teresa Joseph (as we said before) and had been ten years Procuratrix when chosen Superior. As soon as the Election was confirm'd she made before the Vicars her Solemn vow of obedience to the Bishop of Bruges,[4] for her self and comunity; after which being conducted to her place, all the religious came to her in order, according to their Profession, and each render'd her vow of obedience to her. Then we had recreation that day, and also in the Refectory both at dinner and **[p. 267]** collation, for it was in the holy time of Lent.

On the 7th of March Sister Hellen Andrews was chosen Procuratrix.[5]

On the 6th of April Mrs Penelope Gage was admitted to our first habit and took the name of Stanislaus.[6]

On the 22 of May Ann' More came out of England and was received for a servant, in order to be a lay sister.[7]

On the 13 of June Sister Mary Joseph and Sister Teresa Austen Vaughan made their holy Profession.[8]

On the 16 of June Mrs Ann' and Mrs Frances Trafford (nieces to Sister Monica and Sister Anastasia Trafford) were received for convictresses.[9]

In this month of June we by means of Mr Roulof bought the further most part of the garden which belong'd to Waterman, but he bought it as for him self it being thought best that we should not own it till we could buy the other garden that joynes to it.

---

1 Fr Augustine Poyntz (?SJ) (1679/80–1723) Confessor 1707–23; see Holt, p. 204.

2 Lucy Herbert, in religion Teresa Joseph, Prioress 1709–44 (BA101).

3 For the court in exile in France, see Corp. For William Herbert, 1st Marquess of Powis (c. 1626–1696), see *ODNB*.

4 Between the death of Bishop Bassery in 1706 and the appointment of Bishop van Susteren in 1716 there was a vacancy, so Lucy Herbert swore her oath before the Vicars as representatives of the diocese.

5 Helen Andrews (BA004).

6 Penelope Gage (1712–72) BA085, Sub-Prioress 1748–69.

7 Her health problems prevented her joining: see below.

8 Mary Joseph Vaughan (BA207); Teresa Augustine Vaughan (BA209).

9 Anne Trafford, in religion Francis Borgia (1711–70) BA203. Frances did not join the convent. They were daughters of John Trafford and Katherina Culcheth. Their aunts were Monica Trafford (BA204) and Anastasia Trafford (BA202). A third sister, Teresa, had joined the Franciscans in Bruges (BF242).

On the 3d of August, Ann' More return'd to England by her own desire, she being unsettled in her resolution, and not fit for us.

On the 19 of August Mrs Anne Waldegrave went from us to be religious at the English Sepulcherians at Liege.[1] She had a mind to settle here, but not having the portion we require, our Reverende Mother **[p. 268]** writ in her behalf to that Monastry where she was accepted.

Mrs Agnes Stanley having been some years a Convictress here, most earnestly desired to settle amongst us in a religious state, but having four sisters already profess'd in this Monastry, to prevent all difficulties that might be alledged against her, and to be more secure of her further advancement, our Reverende Mother thought fit before she admitted her to the first habit, to have the consent of the convent.[2] So it being put to votes, she fairly had two parts in three, and took the first habit and the name of Mary Xaveria on the Eve of our holy father St Augustine's feast.[3]

On the 5th of September we were all surprised and frighten'd by a sad accident which happen'd that morning about nine a clock. Sister Martha Copland,[4] one of our lay sisters drowned her self in the great Well in our Garden, but we have reason to hope that this action was no ways criminal in her, she having been some months before quite from her self. The beginning of her distemper was a strange melancholy frenzy which strongly possess'd her imagination and continually oppress'd her with dismal apprehensions and fears, which was a disposition she never seem'd naturally enclin'd to. She had all the spiritual and corporal helps that could be used to **[p. 269]** one in her condition. The Doctor from the begining affirm'd that her disease was a mere frenzie, which at last turn'd to a rageing madness; and in these fits she broke the windows and many could hardly master her, yet by the help of some remedies she recover'd so far as to have some intervales of sense, and a few days before her death she made her confession very sensibly. She was carefully lock'd up every night in the house in the Garden, tho' in the day time when she was found best disposed, she had her liberty and was sometimes employ'd in some little things about the house.

On the day this accident happen'd, the lay sister who had care of her had been with her but some few moments before, and left her alone to rise and dress her self, but unfortunately did not lock the door after her when she came out. About a quarter of an hour after, the same sister returning with some others into the Garden, saw her old night gown with

---

1 Anne Waldegrave, in religion Mechtilda (1711–39) LS234. Her dowry at Liège was 300ll, here referring to livres tournois.

2 Agnes Stanley, in religion Mary Xaveria (BA185). Unusually, all five sisters remained at Bruges. See **[p. 216]** for a discussion regarding the profession of sisters.

3 The Feast of St Augustine is celebrated on 28 August.

4 Martha Copland (1677–1709) BA065. Martha Copland had been recommended by Matthew Bedingfield from Brussels. See also **[pp. 121, 124, 127]**.

her scapular and relicks lye close by the well, and coming nearer to their great surprise and affliction, saw her in the well.[1] Father confessor[2] was presently call'd who gave her absolution conditionally, but tho' she was taken up with the greatest haste and care that could be, yet there was no signes nor hopes of recovering life by any endeavours which were used.

[p. 270] Father confessor went presently to give an account of this sad accident to the Vicars, and having inform'd them of all particulars, they judged her innocent from any crime in this action, and gave orders she should be privately bury'd that night in our Vault and to prevent all trouble and further examination into the matter by soecular powers, they also by an express comand obliged all the religious not to discover the manner of her death to any; and they forbid us to own her death for some time, or to have any publick prayers for her, tho' several Masses were said privately for her soul: and she was recommended to the private devotions of every one; and about a month after her death we said a dirge for her in our Quire, and two Solemn masses were sung for her, all which we hope, has been to her advantage and benefit. She has served the comunity with great fidelity, and was always very laborious in the hardest works, even to her latter days, as much as her strength would permitt. Her frequent failings in the observances of silence and interior application to recollection seem'd in her rather a want of sense and capacity than a defect of piety and devotion. She was always of a charitable compassionate disposition **[p. 271]** and by her words and actions express'd a true affection and concern for this comunity in all occasions. She dyed on a thursday about the 60th year of her age, and 33 of her holy Profession. *Requiescat in pace*. Amen.

After this accident the Well was carefully cleansed before any use was made of the water.

On the 22th [*sic*] of october Sister Stanislaus Gage was clothed.[3]

On the 2d of November Mrs Henrietta Brown (whose father is now the Lord Mountague) went from hence to a french Monastry at Roan where her sister was a Benedictin Dame.[4]

In this month of november, Reverend father Sabran,[5] Provincial of the English Society of Jesus, being here, accompany'd our Reverend father confessor to the Vicars in order to give them information of the strange case of Mrs Mary Blount, by means of the most Blessed Sacrament, the

---

[1] The scapular was a sleeveless tunic worn over the habit.

[2] Fr Augustine Poyntz (?SJ) (1679/80–1723); see Holt, p. 204.

[3] Stanislaus Gage (BA085).

[4] Henrietta Browne. She arrived in 1707: see **[p. 241]**. See W. Berry, *County Genealogies: Pedigrees of the Families in the County of Sussex* (London: Sherwood, Gilbert and Piper, 1830), pp. 354–5. Her sister Elizabeth (OB014) left the convent at Rouen and in 1721 arrived at Bruges, before moving through several English convents, ending her life at the English Benedictines at Pontoise.

[5] Fr Louis Sabran SJ (1652–1732); Holt, p. 217.

particular of which are mention'd before in the month of January: the Vicars came to our Monastry, and at our Grate examin'd those religious who were most with her, and assisted her in the time of her illness. The account they gave being affirm'd by oath (which was required of several of them **[p. 272]** the Vicars declared the case miraculous, and ordain'd a Solemne Mass to be sung every year on the day it happen'd, and that the Blessed Sacrament should be exposed in time of the Mass, and the benediction before and after it in grateful acknowledgment of the miraculous favour. And besides this Annual acknowlegdment, they also ordain'd that every thursday in time of the Convent's Mass, the Blessed Sacrament should be exposed and the blessing given before and after, which advantage we joyfully embraced.

On the 20 of november Mrs Mackenzie was received into this Monastry.[1] She was of a younger family to the Earl of Seafort. She was converted to the catholick faith by a particular providence, and fled from her Parents on the account of religion, they being Protestants. Her first designe was to be a lay sister amongst the English Teresians at Antwerp, and there she pass'd some months in the tryal of her noviship; but her continual want of health would not permitt her to comply with her pious inclination in that place, tho' she continued very desirous to be settled in a religious state.

On the 7th of December Mrs Julia and Mrs Catherine Gage began their journey.[2] **[p. 273]** We this year received in Almns 70 florins, 60 from my Lady Web, and 10 from an unknown hand.

The year 1710

On the 4th of January Mrs Ann' Trafford was admitted to the first habit and took the name of Frances Borgia.[3]

On the 20 of January Sister Mary Xaveria Stanley was clothed.[4] On the same day Mr Nicholson happily departed this life. He was a musick Master, and had lived about 11 years in our father's house, coming frequently into the enclosure to teach several of the religious and Pensioners. He received the last Sacraments with great piety and devotion, and by a due resignation to the divine will he was disposed for a happy death, and was bury'd in Ste Ann's church. *Requiescat in pace*. Amen.

On the 24 of february Mrs Vanderwall, one of this town, was received here for a convictress.

---

[1] Like Henrietta Browne, a connection through the Herbert family: Frances Herbert, a sister of the Prioress, was married to Kenneth Mackenzie, 4th Earl of Seaforth. See also **[pp. 283, 298–300, 414–16]** and Herbert family tree.

[2] Neither of these daughters of Sir William Gage, 2nd Baronet of Hengrave professed; scc also **[p. 253]**.

[3] Anne Trafford (BA203).

[4] Mary Xaveria Stanley (BA185).

On the 9th of April Mrs Mer brought her daughter Mrs Bell, who was very desirous to be religious, and she being much commended for her voice which was likely to prove very serviceable both for our musick and Quire, our Reverende Mother admitted her to be one year in **[p. 274]** our schoole for her further improvement and to have a more certain proof and tryall of what she might be capable of.

On the 11th of April Mrs Ann' Compton went from hence to the English Dominicanesses at Bruxelles.[1] She having been very sickly, her father order'd her to be thither to try if that Air would contribute to her better health.

On the 4th of May Mrs Margarite Bedingfeld return'd for England.[2]

After many difficulties we this month purchased the other Garden, of Mr Crets; but he refused to leave it upon reasonable termes, alledging that many years before, we had refused to admitt one of his family to be religious amongst us, upon which disgust he held his Garden at a very high rate, and made us pay considerably more for it than it was worth; which being judged a very great exaction in him, he offer'd to return the whole sum, and take back his Garden again, but that we would not consent to, nor would he return that the overplus of the due value, tho' several divines assured him that he could not in conscience retain it: this gave him some disturbance and as he had the character of a just and honest man we are in hopes that he will at last make due restitution. On the 20th of May came the letters of Amortisation[3] by vertue of which the said inheritance was made saleable, being signed by the King and his **[p. 275]** counsell: we having also the consent of the Magistrates of this Town to take possession of the Garden, began to build up the walls round about it, in order to take it into the enclosure; but none came into our enclosure till the old wall that parted the new Garden and our's was almost quite down, then for some days we had the continual distraction of people's coming in, to see our Monastry.

On the 4th of June, Frances Montock, one of these countries, being recommended to us for a lay sister, we received her for a servant in order to it.

On the 17 of June Sister Frances Borgia Trafford was clothed.[4]

On the 20th of June whilst our enclosure was open, some of the chief Magistrates coming in, our Reverende Mother conducted them into our infirmary, together with Mr James Crets, Mr. Cornelius Roolof and their wives, and our Lawyer being also present, and there the letters

---

1 Her sister Margaret professed as a Dominican in 1717 (BD023) but there is no record of Anne professing.

2 Margaret Bedingfield had arrived in January 1709: see **[p. 254]**.

3 Special permission had to be obtained from the crown for the sale of the land by Mr Crets to the nuns because it would be held in mortmain: that is, in perpetuity.

4 Anne Trafford, in religion Francis Borgia (BA203).

of inheritance were made over before the Magistrates of this Town, by Mr Roolof and Mr Crets to the profit of this convent, and signed June the 20th 1710.

Whilst Mr Crest [*sic*] was in the Monastry he ingeniously owned to our Reverende Mother and father confessor that when he sold the Garden he did not think it unconscionable to exact so much, but understanding now by some divines that he had proceeded unjustly in that occasion, he would more **[p. 276]** seriously reflect on his obligation, and if he found no other means to satisfie his conscience he would return with he had unjustly exacted, if not in his life, at least at his death.

On the 26 of June Sister Mary Heton, our Subprioress, resigned her office, she being very ancient and so infirm and lame, that she was uncapable of all duties, for she could not so much as move from her chair to her bed without help.[1] She had been about eleven years in the place, and was put into it by the favour of a dispensation from my Lord Bishop, not being capable of Singing in the Quire nor of performing the office of Hebdomadarian, but she now desired to be discharged; so Sister Mary Widrington was chosen Subprioress by the votes of the convent.[2]

On the same day, which was the octave of Corpus Christi,[3] we understanding that the Procession of the most Blessed Sacrament was to pass from the Carmes church by the Gate of our new Garden, and our enclosure being still open, we were all very desirous it should go round our Garden, but not having had timely notice to make due preparation, we sent to the Prior of the Carmes to beg the favour that we might at least have the benediction at the Gate for which effect we all went into the Garden;[4] but the Gate being open they unexpectedly entered with the most Blessed Sacrament; and the walk being all in disorder, they could not **[p. 277]** well pass any other way than close by the Well where our great misfortune happen'd the fifthe of the September before. There the Father who carry'd the Blessed Sacrament stop'd and gave the blessing, which we hope was the particular providence and designe of Almighty God to evidence this by his Sacramental presence and blessing, that he will for the future mercifully preserve us from any more misfortunes in that kind.

The same day there was another Procession of the Blessed Sacrament from Ste Ann's church, that was to pass thro' the street next our Garden, about five a clock in the Evening; and we took care to be prepared for

---

1 Mary Heton (BA102).

2 Mary Widdrington (BA219).

3 Corpus Christi, celebrating the real presence of Christ in the Eucharist, is a moveable feast, falling on the Thursday following Trinity Sunday. In some countries it falls on the Sunday after Trinity Sunday.

4 The presence of the Carmelite friars gave the name to Carmerstraat; they had property adjacent to Nazareth. The nuns' concern was that they had not had time to mark a route for the parish procession to pass through their gate in an orderly fashion, and there was as yet no full enclosure to keep the people out.

it; the Pastor being willing, at our request, to bring it round our Garden; so the walks were all decently prepared, and an Altar erected for the Blessed Sacrament to repose on: we all met, and follow'd it with lighted candles in our hands, and whilst it reposed on the Altar, *O Sacrum*, etc was sung in musick by our religious, then after the benediction had been Solemnly given, all the seculars (who were in great numbers) follow'd the Blessed Sacrament out of the enclosure.

The wall round our new Garden being sufficiently built for enclosure, our Reverende Mother sent to the Vicars for leave to esteem it as our enclosure, that **[p. 278]** we might have the liberty of walking in it which we had not yet done. The Vicars came themselves to see it on St Peter and Paul's Eve[1] and they gave us all leave to enter it whenever our Reverende Mother pleased, so that night after Compline our Reverende Mother and Subprioress went first, and the rest of the religious follow'd in order, they began the litanies at Our Lady's Altar in the old Garden, and we continued it round the new one, our Reverende Mother all the time carrying Our Lady's image; from this time our enclosure was no more open to any.

Mrs Elisabeth Blount, one of our Convictresses, being by her Parents orders sent to Deynes, a Monastry in Gant, to perfect her self in the french tongue; after she had been there some little time, she declared her vocation was to be a Benedictine and made her resolution to settle her self with the English Dames in the same town: and having obtain'd leave from her friends, she took the first habit on the 10 of July.[2]

On the 24 of July, by the desire and express orders of the Vicars, we received a boarder within the enclosure, one Mrs Tereway (or Pricket) who had a great fortune left to the care of her Grandfather, and her Uncle, but she being very young had indiscreetly **[p. 279]** disposed of her self, and was marry'd with out their consents, which they were much displeased at, especially her Uncle who was very active in this matter, and resolving to punish her for her disobedience, began a Process against her. The new marry'd couple were parted for some time, and he sent to the carthusians, she to our Monastry, till things could be adjusted. We were not much enclined to receive her but could not well avoid it. So we admitted her into the enclosure and she had a chamber to her self in our convict, and she had her diet apart and particular.

On the 3d of August Mrs Catherine Stanley went from hence for England.[3]

Sister Delphina Weston having been five years subject to Rheumatick humour in all her joints, by which she suffer'd much and was sometimes

1 The Feast of St Peter and St Paul is celebrated on 29 June.

2 Elizabeth Blount, in religion Justina, professed at Ghent 1712 and died sometime after 1725, GB019. She had arrived at Nazareth in 1707 with her three sisters; see **[p. 252]**.

3 Catherine Stanley had arrived in 1705; see **[p. 228]**.

so ill that she was not able to go about the house nor perform any duty tho' ever most fervorous to force her self to the utmost of her power, we had a consult of Doctors for her, and many remedies she try'd, but all in vain.[1] Our Doctors affirm'd that the Bathes were the most likely remedy to do her good; which her Mother being inform'd of, was very solicitous for her recovery, and earnestly press'd by letter, that all **[p. 280]** endeavours should be used to procure leave for her to go out of the Monastry in order to make tryal of this remedy; offering to be at the whole expense of her journey. This being a remedy very strange and new amongst us, many difficulties were at first alledged against it; and she her self often declared that she had rather suffer any pain than go out of her enclosure to seek a cure. She writ to father Sabran[2] expressing her reluctance and scruples about it, being of a very pious and timorous disposition, to which he answer'd thus: "I truly think no religious should go out of her Monastry to save her own life, but Judge each ought to be willing to go any where to save her community the burden of a useless body; to be willing to prevent the becoming so by any remedy, not of proper choice but appointed; so if the bathes abroad be order'd you, I conceive yu may feel a great reluctance, but in that as in all other things, keep all the indefferency possible."

This made her calme and resigned to do what should be judged best.

Whilst this business was in suspense, Sister Mary Teresa Jernigan[3] was in a sad condition with a kind of King's evil or excessive scurvy which broke out **[p. 281]** all over her body, and the Doctor feared it might be of ill consequence if not speedily remedy'd, but judged the bathes a certain cure for her, and the only remedy he could propose since those she had try'd were ineffectual. These motives were pressing yet our Reverende Mother would not act by her own authority, nor resolve on any thing till she had had the opinion of all her convent Sisters: after which father confessor went to propose their going to the bathes to the Vicars, who judged it very reasonable, yet required that the necessities should be affirm'd by a consult of Doctors, which was procured; they met in our infirmary, where the two infirm religious were present, together with our Reverende Mother and her three council sisters. The Doctors affirm'd that the bathes would be a speedy and certain cure for Sister Mary Teresa; but fear'd that Sister Delphina's disease had already impower'd it self too much, and that her cure would not be so easily effected, yet they assured that no remedy but that could be thought of, or was likely to do her good; and that she must either hope for help by this means, or never expect it, tho' **[p. 282]** she was young, and might live many years

---

1 Delphina Weston (BA216).
2 Fr Louis Sabran SJ (1652–1732); Holt, p. 217.
3 Mary Teresa Jerningham (BA118).

a cripple. This they affirm'd by writing and set their names for it; our Reverende Mother also signed it, as did the three aforesaid religious, then the paper was carry'd to the Vicars who freely consented and gave them their obedience, so they began their journey on the 18th of August. Sister Barbara Devery, a lay sister went with them, and father confessor accompany'd them to Liege.[1]

As soon as it was resolved that Sister Mary Teresa should go to the Bathes, she writ to Sir Francis Jernegan, her father, and we afterwards received his answer, in which he express'd a kind and tender concern for his daughter, and promis'd not only to be at the whole expense of her journey to the Bathes, but if that fail'd of the desired effect, he would also pay for her going into france to be touch'd by our King.[2]

On the 26 of August, Mrs Verbeeck, one of these countries, was received here for convictress.

On the 30 of August Mrs Ann' Caryll received the first habit, and took the names of Mary Ann'.[3]

On the 4th of September Mrs Teraway went from hence; her affairs being almost settled, and she quite sick of confinement, her grandfather and uncle were **[p. 283]** prevail'd with to give her her liberty. She paid a patacoon a day for her board here, which we demanded having been inform'd that it was the ordinary rate, when persons in her circumstances were taken into Monastries, and her friends willingly paid it in permission money, reckoning the day she came, and the day she went away.

Mrs Mackenzie[4] persevering in her desires to be religious, and not having our portion for a nun, nor being judged fit for a Sister, our Reverende Mother (who had a particular concern for her) recommended her to the Benedictin Dames of Spermaille, where she was admitted on the 13 of September to make her tryal for a Quire nun, tho' all her Reverence could promise for her portion was fifty pound Sterlin, which had been left to my Lady Carrington for some lay sister or religious.[5]

On the 21 of September Mrs Mary and Mrs Margarit Compton went from hence to the English Dominicanesses at Bruxelles.[6]

---

[1] Ann Barbara Devery (BA072). Father Confessor was Fr Augustine Poyntz (?SJ) (1679/80–1723), Confessor 1707–23.

[2] Mary Teresa Jerningham (BA118). She was the daughter of Sir Francis Jerningham, 3rd Baronet of Costessey, Norfolk. For more discussion of touching for the king's evil, see **[p. 253]**.

[3] Ann Caryll (BA047).

[4] Mrs Mackenzie is probably Anne Mackenzie, sister-in-law of Prioress Lucy Herbert's sister Frances. She is recorded in Stirnet.com as dying unmarried in 1734. She first arrived at Nazareth in November 1709; see **[pp. 272, 298–300, 414–16]**.

[5] Lady Carrington was Anne (1662–1748), sister to Prioress Herbert.

[6] Margaret Compton professed in 1717 as Margaret Joseph (BD023) and died after a distinguished career in 1768. A third sister, Ann, is mentioned on **[p. 274]**.

On the 29 of October little Miss Gifford was brought to our Monastry by her nurse; she was then about four years old, and Sir John Gifford, her father, had promis'd her to my Lady Lucy **[p. 284]** our Superior as soon as the child was born. Soon after Sir John dyed, and his Lady being marryed again, her Mother, the Lady Middleton, took care to send her, and return'd fifty pound Sterlin for her.[1]

We having heard several times from our two religious at Aix-la-Capelle, understand that Sister Delphina is something better since she has taken the waters and used the bathes, and that the Doctor there gave great hopes of her cure if she does but stay another season. This being, our Reverende Mother thought fit to procure the Vicars' leave for her staying there till the next May, rather than to put her friends to the charges of another journey; so by her own choice and desire she was placed in a Monastry of Sepulcherians in the same town; where she was very kindly received by the Superior and Religious; and our Monastry resolves to pay her Pension whilst she is there, and not desire that of her friends, who have promised to pay the rest.

As for Sister Mary Teresa,[2] she has not found the benefit by the bathes which the Doctors gave her hopes of for her breaking out; but as she has **[p. 285]** many years been troubled with the stone, and has had some violent fits of it at Aix-la-Capelle, the bathes and the other remedies she used there have done her a great deal of good, and we hope by this means she will be wholy freed from that torment and being duly resigned to God's will for the cure of her other disease, she began her journey homewards with Sister Barbara, having first seen Sister Delphina placed in the Monastry. In both going and coming they received great kindness and civility from the English Monastries at Liege, Lovain, Bruxelles and Gand; and by the particular providence and goodness of Almighty God, they met with no parties nor any misfortune in all their journey, but came safe home to us, on the 7th of november.

On the 22 of november Mrs Mary Petres went for England in hopes to get her pension paid, and some security for her portion that she may be religious here.[3]

On the 27th of December Sister Mary Havers went from us to live in a dutch Monastry at Bruxelles, for her health and content and for other reasons known only to the Vicars and her self; for which they gave her leave to go to another Monastry, and declared it **[p. 286]** necessary and

---

1 Sir John Gifford of Burstall, Leicestershire, married Lady Catherine Middleton at St Germain-en-Laye in 1702. He was Groom of the Bedchamber. After his death in 1707, against the wishes of her family, she married the Irish soldier Lieutenant-General Michael Rothe.

2 Mary Teresa Jerningham (BA118); see **[pp. 80–1]**. Sister Barbara is Ann Barbara Devery (BA072); Delphina is Delphina Weston (BA216); see **[pp. 279–80]**.

3 Mary Petre returned and was clothed; however, she was unable to continue without a dowry and withdrew in October 1714 following a health crisis: see **[pp. 291, 302, 318–20, 336–7]**.

expedient for the common good of our community, and for her own in particular.[1] She had the consent of our Superior and convent Sisters who voted her out according to her desire, they being informed that she was advised to it for our good and hers, by Reverend Father Sabran Visitor and Vice Provincial of the English Society of Jesus, and other Spiritual Men; for otherways we knew no reason for her leaving us, but her own uneasy temper.[2] The Vicars gave express orders that Reverend father confessor should go with her and see her in a dutch monastry of our order at Bruxelles, where they obliged her to remain one year under the obedience of the Superior of that house, yet they did not think fit to disengage her from her obedience to our Reverende Mother, who with the Convent, consented to pay the pension that was required for her. She was in the 30th year of her holy Profession, and about the 49th of her age. She had been some years one of our convent Sisters, which when the Vicars understood, they seem'd displeased, and disapproved of our way of always making up the number of them by taking in the next eldest in profession. And on this account gave express orders that for the future the convent Sisters should be chosen by votes **[p. 287]** in the manner our institution appoints.

The year 1711

On the 25 of January, Sister Mary Xaveria Stanley made her holy Profession.[3]

The purchase of the Gardens having enlarged our enclosure, our Reverende Mother's next care was now to enlarge the house by making more cells and other conveniences suitable to the number of our Religious, we having a large community, and the prospect of encrease.[4] Her Reverence consulted several Master workmen and other persons capable of judging what might be the expense of such a building as she proposed and having calculated what it might come to, and contrived the whole designe of it, she proposed it to the convent Sisters on the first of february, and when they had given their votes, there was only three against it, tho' when it had first been spoken of many seem'd averse to it.

On the 2d of february Frances Montock was admitted for a tryal and took the Schollars kerchief in order to be a lay sister.[5]

On the 25 of February Mrs Vanderwall return'd home to her father.

The building being resolved upon, our Reverende Mother made choice of Mr l'Epée **[p. 288]** as overseer of the whole work, he being

---

1 Mary Havers (BA099).
2 Fr Louis Sabran SJ (1652–1732); see *ODNB* and Holt, p. 217.
3 Mary Xaveria Stanley (BA185).
4 Reverend Mother in 1711 was Lucy Herbert (BA101).
5 Frances Montock had entered as a servant but she did not go forward to profession.

generally esteem'd an experienced and understanding man in all such affairs, therefore to his care her Reverence recommended this business; then the agreement being made with the Mason and carpenter for the whole building, and the writings drawn and signed, the workmen began it on the 27 of february.

On the 10th of March Mrs Grillion, one of this town, was received here for convictress.

On the 23 of March whilst the workmen were digging the foundations, one of our Vicars, with another Gentleman and father confessor, enter'd the enclosure to see and understand the designe of the building, our Reverende Mother desiring to know their opinion of it. They very freely spoke their different thoughts upon this subject, yet after all, by a general approbation of the designe, they affirm'd that it was very well contrived.

On the 18 of April, our Reverende Mother laid the first stone of the building, at the further end of the designed new Pant, the second stone was laid by our Subprioress, the third by the Arcaria, the fourth by Sister Procuratress, and the fifth by Sister Ursula Babthorpe who had the care of the workmen.[1] Our Reverende Mother laid money upon her stone for her self and **[p. 289]** those that follow'd her. This new building contains a warming room, a noviship, a musick room, and a walk[2] house, with cells over them on both sides, and a hansome hanging Pant bigger than that we had before, but not so large as our great Pant, tho' near as high.

On the 21 of April Miss Charlot Hacket went from hence.

On the 27 of April Sister Mary Ann' Caryll was clothed. Father confessor perform'd the ceremonies of the clothing by the Vicars orders, because the Arch Priest had lately broken his arm by a fall.[3]

On the 3d of May Mrs Mary Vaughan, daughter to Mr Vaughan of Courtfield, and niece to our Sister Vaughans, together with Miss Ann' Sykes, were received for convictresses.[4]

On the 15 of May Mrs Verbeck return'd home.

On the 21 of May Elisabeth Sales and Mary Taylor arrived here, and were received as servants in order to be lay sisters.[5]

---

1 Ursula Babthorpe (BA010).

2 Here the typescript clearly gives 'walk house'; however, the building contains a work house, which is the more likely reading.

3 Ann Caryll, in religion Mary Ann (BA047). Normally for choir nuns, clothing ceremonies were performed by representatives of the External Visitors. There was still a vacancy for the bishopric of Bruges.

4 Mary Vaughan was the daughter of John Vaughan of Courtfield. She left the school on 6 April 1714 (see **[p. 314]**). She was niece to Mary Joseph Vaughan (BA207) and Teresa Augustine Vaughan (BA209), who professed in 1709. Ann Sykes professed in 1726 (BA188).

5 Elizabeth Sales (1713–24) BA169; Mary Taylor, in religion Agatha (1713–15) BA198.

On the 28 of May Mrs Catherine Caryll went from hence.[1]

Sister Delphine Weston having made use of the baths the second **[p. 290]** season, and thereby entirely complyed with all that either doctors and friends could judge necessary for her cure, she earnestly desired to come home.[2] So Sister Barbara Devery was sent for her, and brought her safe to us on the 17 of June.[3]

We found her much better in health, but still very lame with the stiffness in her joints, which nevertheless did not hinder her from employing her time well there, she having learnt embrodery and petit Métier,[4] and embroder'd a hansome veil for the chalice: but she regreted that so much trouble and expense had been bestow'd upon her, since her amendment came short of our wishes, however she was very brisk and we mutually rejoyced for her return. her brother paid the whole expense of her journey, which was thirty pound sterlin.

On the 21 of June Sister Frances Borgia Trafford made her holy Profession.[5] Father confessor perform'd the ceremonies, our Arch Priest not being recover'd.

Mrs Mary Bell[6] having had very ill health from the time she came to this Monastry, and we not finding her voice according to our expectations, our comunity was not disposed to admitt her, tho' she was very constant in her pious desires of being religious, **[p. 291]** therefore her Mother, Mrs Le Mer took her from hence on the 26 of June, and went with her to the English Benedictin Dames at Bruxelles, where tis hoped she will be received.

On the 4th of July Mrs Mary Petre return'd to us again, she having procured her father and brother's promise for the payment of a hundred pound sterlin, the february after for pension, and four hundred pounds before her profession.[7]

On the first of August Mrs Mary Petre was admitted to the first habit.

---

1 Catherine Caryll was probably the sister of Mary Ann Caryll above. She returned to the convent briefly in 1721; see **[pp. 378, 383]**. A third sister attended school at Nazareth in 1720–21; a fourth sister, Mary Benedict, professed at the Benedictines, Dunkirk (DB032).

2 Delphina Weston (BA216).

3 Ann Barbara Devery, lay sister (BA072).

4 A petit métier can mean a craft, occupation or skill (all small or lowly ones) creating textiles, such as using a hand loom. I am grateful to Amanda Haste for this reference.

5 Francis Borgia Trafford (BA203).

6 Mary Bell was accepted by the Benedictines and professed in Brussels as a choir nun 1715 (BB011). Her small dowry payment suggests that the convent made allowances because of her singing.

7 Mary Petre was the daughter of Joseph Petre Esq. Of Fithlers, Essex, and Catherine Andrews. She was unable to proceed without a dowry and left after a health crisis in 1714; see also **[pp. 291, 302, 318–20, 336–7, 438–9]**. She attended the profession of her younger sisters at Gravelines and decided to enter there, professing in 1718 (GP219).

On the 10th of August Mrs Judith Bond went from hence.[1]

On the 12 of August Mrs Dorothy and Mrs Elisabeth Hurst were received for convictresses.

On the 20th of August Mrs Ann' Gage and Mrs Frances Trafford began their journey for England.

On the 8th of September Elisabeth Sales and Mary Taylor were admitted to the Schollars kerchief.[2]

On the 25 of September Mrs Hellen and Mrs Mary Hodgson were received for convictresses.

Sister Stanislaus Gage having been very near two years novice, and her **[p. 292]** father, Sir William, delaying to pay her portion, our Reverende Mother was advised by those who knew her father's circumstances very well, to send her into England that by pleading her own cause she might more speedily get possession of her portion, than could be expected by her longer stay here.[3]

The Vicars were acquainted with this designe, who at first made great difficulties, alledging it was a case that had never before been proposed to them, for a novice to go out, and returning again to make her Profession without another noviship; but after some consideration, they gave their consents, for three months. It was then thought fit to propose to the convent Sisters the consenting of her, that she might be assured of her Profession at her return; and she having apply'd her self to all the duties of a good novice, was by the convent consented for her Profession, if she return'd with security as to her portion. She went from hence on the 27 of September much against her own inclinations, and with an earnest desire to return speedily again. Mrs Constantia Blount went to England with her, both under the care of Mrs Le Mer.[4]

On the 18th of october Mrs Grillion **[p. 293]** return'd home to her father.

On the third of november Mrs Mary and Mrs Catherine Brinkhurst were received here for convictresses.

---

1 Judith Bond had arrived in 1708 with Gage relations as part of a group escorting Lord Dover's body to Bruges for burial; see **[p. 253]**.

2 Both continued to profession: Elizabeth Sales (BA169); Mary Taylor (BA198).

3 She was professed the following year as Stanislaus (BA085). Around this time Sir William was engaged in a protracted financial and legal dispute with his eldest son, Thomas, which may explain why he was unable to pay Stanislaus' portion. Thomas' death in 1716 put an end to the dispute; see F. Young, *The Gages of Hengrave and Suffolk Catholicism, 1640–1767*, CRS Monograph 8 (Woodbridge: Boydell and Brewer for the CRS, 2015), pp. 79–80.

4 Mrs le Mer was the mother of Mary Bell, who had just left the convent to try the Benedictines at Brussels.

The year 1712

On the 13 of January Sister Mary Bedingfeld departed this life in the 52 year of her age, and about 34 of her holy Profession.[1] She had been an humble good religious woman and very zealous for regular observances. Some time before her last sickness, she was perswaded in her own thoughts that she should not live long, therefore she perform'd a *novena* to St Joseph to obtain a happy death, which she ended the day before she felt sick; and we have reason to believe her prayers had the desired effect, since she was so happily disposed, and received the news of her approaching death with so much content and satisfaction, that she declared nothing but conformity to the divine will could make her resigned to live. She often express'd how sensible she was of all her little past failings, yet at the same time she found her self so moved to confide in the infinit mercy and goodness of God, that she said she thought she was uncapable of the least impression of fear. She was **[p. 294]** bury'd on the 15 of January upon which day we kept the feast of the sweet name of Jesus, in whose infinite goodness and merits she had placed her entire confidence. When her cell was visited after her death, all in it was so very poor, that it visibly appear'd how much she valued her vow of poverty: having been contented with the barely necessary; yet with her usual sincerity, she told Reverende Mother, in her sickness, that this was the only of her vows she had any scruple about, as for the rest she was satisfied she had done her best, and God's particular mercy to her in so pious and calme a death gives us reasonable hopes that she had not been considerably deficient in any, and that he has rewarded her humble confidence in him with eternal bliss. *Requiescat in pace*. Amen.

On the 4th of February Sister Frances Montack was clothed for a lay sister.[2]

On the first of June Sister Mary Ann' Caryll made her holy Profession.[3]

Sister Stanislaus Gage having been three months in England, and her affairs not yet ended, the Vicars leave was again renew'd. Fifteen hundred pounds Sterlin was the portion she was to have after her father's death, according **[p. 295]** to his marriage settlement; but during his life she had no hopes of it; therefore if Sir William would have paid down 500 pounds for her portion in religion, and have paid the arrieres of her sister and her pension, she would have resigned the rest of her fortune to her youngest brother; but Sir William not being then in circumstances to do this, offer'd our Reverende Mother to pay 30 pounds a year for 5 years, and to the end of the fifth year to pay down the 500ᵗᵗ, and if he

---

[1] Mary Bedingfield (1678–1712) BA018.

[2] Frances Montack was not found suitable as a lay sister and left the community later in the year, after receiving insufficient votes of support in Chapter. See also **[p. 297]**.

[3] Mary Ann Caryll (BA047).

fail'd of his word either in duely paying the Annuity, or that portion at the time appointed, then she might exact the 1500 after his death. Our Reverende Mother made these proposals to the convent Sisters, which by their votes they accepted of, and on these conditions, she was a second time consented by them to her holy profession. The writings being drawn and signed in security of this, she without further delay left England, and again took the novices habit here on the third of June. Her cousine Germain Mrs Charlot Bond, came out of England with her, but Mr Thomas Bond, father of the young Lady, living in this town, he kept her with him till the 23 of June, and then she enter'd our enclosure, **[p. 296]** received the first habit and is call'd Sister Teresa Joseph.[1]

Tho' Sister Stanislaus Gage had the consent of the convent before, yet she was not excused from beging her Profession of each convent Sister, and by their votes she was a third time consented, then after the usual preparation and penances, she made her holy Profession on the 12 of June.

On the 20 of July Mrs Dorothy and Mrs Elisabeth Hursts return'd for England.

On the 12 of September Sister Elisabeth Sales and Sister Mary Taylor were clothed for lay sisters.[2]

On the 13 of September Mrs Anne Blount was by her uncle to Mother's orders, sent to the English Benedictin Dames at Gant, where her eldest sister was profess'd.[3]

On the 17 of September the Lady Carrington (sister to our Reverende Mother) came out of England with designe to remain here some months as a boarder within our enclosure.[4] Her Ladyship brought with her Mrs Mary Fairfax whose Parents being Protestants, she was brought up in that perswation, but her Mother's second mariage being to a Roman Catholick, she was well inclined **[p. 297]** to our religion and desirous of her daughter's conversion, which we hoped would be soon effected, she being young and well disposed, so we received her as convictress.[5]

Sister Frances Montack having pass'd some months of her noviship, and being found unfit for this comunity, we had thought of dismissing her, but tho' many were against her, yet there were some to much concern'd for her and thought her unjustly dealt with; she had also many relations and friends in Town who took her part, and by whose means her case was represented to our Arch Priest who came to our Monastry, but having

---

1 Stanislaus Gage (1712–72) BA085. Charlotte Bond, in religion Teresa Joseph, left the Augustinians in 1713 and joined the Carmelites, professing in Antwerp in 1715, AC015.

2 Elizabeth Sales (BA169); Mary Taylor, in religion Agatha (BA198).

3 Anne professed in 1718 aged 17 (GB020). Her elder sister, Elizabeth, had professed in 1712 (GB019).

4 Lady Carrington was Lady Anne Herbert, who had married Francis Smith, 2nd Viscount Carrington. He died in 1701.

5 Her mother moved her to the English Benedictines at Ghent in June 1714; however, there is no record of her having professed there. See **[p. 314]**.

spoken to our Reverende Mother, he was by her so fully satisfied, that he told her she might freely dismiss her as soon as she pleased, without puting it to the votes of the community, but the novice thinking the number of her friends much greater than it proved, earnestly desired it might be voted by the whole comunity, if she should go or stay till the end of her noviship. Our Reverende Mother yielded to give her this satisfaction which proved quite otherways than she had expected, for there was only eight votes for her, the rest were all negative, so to her grief she **[p. 298]** was obliged to take her soecular clothes again, and she went from hence on the 30 of September.[1]

The Superior of the Monastry at Bruxelles where Sister Mary Havers was,[2] having writ several letters to our Reverende Mother, to desire her removal from thence, her Reverence employ'd many friends to procure another Monastry for her, offering any reasonable pension they should require with her, but finding no place to accept of her upon any termes, our Reverende Mother was obliged to yield to her desires of returning to us again, which by several letters she had very earnestly requested, promising a due submission to whatever Superiors should order, concerning her; Her Reverence assembled the convent Sisters and acquainted them with her desires and submission, laying before them the necessity of receiving her again, which none could appose; so one of our lay sisters was sent for her, and she again was received into our enclosure on the 30 of october.

Tho' Mrs Mackenzie was not one of our religious, yet she having relyed on the care and charity of our Reverende Mother, who recommended her to the Bernardines **[p. 299]** of Spermaille, and procured her the little she had in order to a settlement; it may be convenient on several accounts, to take notice here on what termes they received her, and the liberty our Reverende Mother gave them to dismiss her before her clothing if they judged her unfit for them.[3] And I mention it in this place, because they profess'd her on the 26 of november this year.

They accepted her upon these termes: she was to have fifty pounds Sterlin for her portion, her cell furnish'd, sufficiency of habit both linnen and woolen; money for the recreations at clothing and Profession; all this was faithfully perform'd.The Lady Carrington (sister to our Reverende

---

1 Frances Montack; see also **[p. 294]**.

2 Mary Havers (BA099); see also **[pp. 285–6]**. The Chronicle refers only to a Dutch monastery in Brussels: the identity of the Superior is unknown.

3 Prioress Herbert had made arrangements on Mrs Mackenzie's behalf to join another convent as she considered that she would not fit into the community at Nazareth, nor did she have enough dowry. However, the Prioress was prepared to do her best to find Mrs Mackenzie a suitable community locally. See also **[pp. 272, 283, 414–16]**, and Appendix 1.

Mother) paid the fifty pounds for her portion, and the Lady Seafort (another of her Reverence's sisters) paid another fifty pound for all the rest.[1]

At her first going thither, whilst she was in their Scholars kerchief, she not understanding their language and being naturally somthing rough in her ways (tho' a very good woman) they were much disatisfied with her, and many complaints were made to our Reverende Mother, who fearing they would not be mutually happy in one **[p. 300]** another, and understanding that their circumstances were very low; her Reverence by letter freely gave them their liberty to dismiss her; at which both the Dames and the Schollar were much offended, as having no mind to part at least, her Reverence thereby justified her self that she put no restraint upon either side; so in a short time after, they understanding one another better, all went well, and she was profess'd at the due time by the Abbot of the Dunes which was a favour our Reverende Mother obtain'd to save the great expense of having their Abbot come from Antwerp.[2] Her Reverence promised upon her account to be kind to their monastry, when it was in her power, but made no other promise. And considering they could afterwards only afford her lodging and very mean diet; and had in her a substantial ingenious woman; I think they had no very hard bargain of it.

On the 18th of December Sister Tecla Busby departed this life in the 65 year of her age, and 46 of her holy Profession.[3] About half a year before her death she lost her senses which rendered her a most sensible object of compassion to all, for her raving fits ran most upon dismal melancholy subject, and she took a fancy from the begining of her madness, that whatever she eat or drank would make her deaf or blind, so that tho' she suffer'd much by hunger and **[p. 301]** thirst yet she could not even be forced to take sufficient nourishment to maintain her natural strength; all care was taken, and some remedies forced upon her, but none had any effect. The extremity of weakness she had brought her self to by fasting, gave evident signes of her approaching end, which moved Reverend father confessor and our Reverende Mother's charity so much that on the octave day of our Lady's conception[4] they gave a comunicating day to the whole comunity that all might join in their devotions to obtain for her the blessing of a happy death, which we may reasonably hope she had, since she had been disposed for it by the pious life she led before this misfortune happen'd to her, in which she was not capable of offending, and therefore her death may be esteemed innocent and good. She had been many years our organist, and whilst she had her eye sight she cut green parchment most curiously, and was

[1] Lady Seaforth was Frances Herbert (d. 1732), married to Kenneth, 4th Earl of Seaforth, who died in January 1701: see Herbert family tree.

[2] The Abbot of the Dunes Abbey in 1712 was Luc de Vries, Abbot 1699–1723.

[3] Abigail Busby, in religion Thecla (1666–1712) BA041.

[4] The Feast of the Immaculate Conception is celebrated on 8 December.

very serviceable to our comunity in many things; nay when her eye sight failed her she would sweep the house, shell peas and beans, wind thread, or do any thing rather than be idle.

The holy oyles were administer'd to her and she had the advantages that could be procured by good prayers, father confessor constantly assisting her, gave her absolution just as she expired. *Requiescat in pace*. Amen.

[p. 302] We this year received in Almns 50 florins from Mr Bond to pray for the soul of his daughter.

The year 1713

On the 2d of January Sister Mary Petre and Sister Teresa Joseph Bond were clothed.[1]

On the 7th of March Margarite Linny, a young Girl about 15 years old came out of England being recommended to us for a servant.[2]

On the 16 of March we sent Mrs May Brinkhurst to England.

On the 7th of April Sister Mary Heton departed this life in the 87 year of her age, and 56 of her holy Profession.[3] She had been a good regular Religious woman, and was for some years our Subprioress, till about three years before her death, it pleased God to visit her with most painful infirmities which so deprived her of the use of her limbs that she could not help her self nor stir out of her chair without the help of many, she being a fat woman, yet by the contrivance of a chair with wheels she was daily carry'd to our lay sisters chappel where she had the comfort of hearing holy Mass, and of receiving the most Blessed Sacrament. She bore all her sufferings with an incomparable patience and conformity to God's will; and lay for many months on a bed pan that she might not distress the Sister who lay by her, in the night. A few days **[p. 303]** before her death she was wholy confined to her bed, and received the last Sacraments with great piety and devotion, having her senses to the last moment, which she exprest when she could not speak by the signes she made that she understood the good things which were said and read to her, and by her attention to what she heard her affections seem'd to be sensibly moved to God into whose hands she peaceably render'd her soul, and was bury'd on Palme Sunday the ninth of April. *Requiescat in pace*. Amen.

On the 7th of June Mrs Vanderwall return'd to us again after having been about 15 months away: she being a considerable fortune, her father free himself from all fears concerning her, desired to have her live in some Monastry, and she very willing to comply with his inclinations, preferr'd our Monastry before any of her own nation.

---

1 Neither of these two candidates proceeded to profession.
2 Margaret Linny, lay sister (1717–65) BA128.
3 Mary Heton (1657–1713) BA102.

On the 9th of June Sir Francis Jernegan and his Lady came out of England designing to table with our confessor. They brought with them their little niece Miss Ann' Blount, the youngest daughter of Mr Edward Blount.[1] She was the same day received here for convictress.

On the 10 of June Mrs Hellen and Mrs Mary Hodgson return'd for England.

On the 29 of June Mrs Mary Elliot, niece to Sister Canning, was received here for convictress.[2]

On the 30 of June Mrs Mary Sykes was received for convictress.[3]

On the 10 of July all our convent Sisters were assembled in order to chuse three council Sisters, to wit Subprioress, Arcaria and Procuratrix, the former having laudably perform'd those offices for three years, which in the terme our present Superior has designed her for the change of all offices, when no particular inconveniency, or consideration of the common good, opposes it. In this election Sister Hellen Andrews was chosen Subprioress, Sister Catherine Holland confirm'd Arcaria, and Sister Clare Saunderson made Procuratrix.[4]

Our novice Sister Teresa Joseph Bond,[5] from her first entrance was somtimes in doubt and uncertainties concerning her settlement, having some reasons to believe she was moved by a particular call from God to the order of Ste Teresa. Her first thoughts of being religious was to settle in this house, but before she was received into our enclosure, making a visit to the English Teresians at Antwerp, she found her self **[p. 305]** sensibly moved by the piety of those good religious, to make her resolution of settling there, but being just of age to take possession of a considerable fortune which she had independant of her father, she was obliged to go into England, tho' first she declared her resolution to her father, who not approving her being a Teresian, would have her rather comply with her first purpose of settling here, which she was easily enclined to, owning it to be much more according to her natural inclinations, and being assured it was so absolutly her father's will, she dispatch'd her affairs with all speed, resigning her fortune to her father, only taking 500 pound Sterlin for her portion, which she paid into the hands of our corespondent at London, and immediatly began her journey for Bruges. After some stay here in Town with her father, he brought her to our Monastry, and resigned her into the hands of our Reverende Mother: who admitted her to our first habit. Soon after, her former doubts

---

1 Sir Francis Jerningham, 3rd Baronet of Costessey, Norfolk, was married to Anne Blount of Sodington. Mr Edward Blount of Blagdon Devon and Anne Guise were probably the parents of Ann Blount (d. 1769): see Stirnet.com, Blount 02.

2 Sister Canning was Elizabeth Victoria Canning (BA044).

3 Mary Sykes, in religion Mary Michael (1717–73) BA189, Procuratrix 1749–51.

4 Helen Andrews (BA004); Catharine Holland (BA106); Clare Saunderson (BA172).

5 See **[pp. 295–6]**. Teresa Joseph Bond (AC015), professed at Antwerp in 1715.

renewing again, she consulted some spiritual persons who thought they were very like temptations; in this concern, to be better assured of God's will she was advised to perform the ten fridays devotion and comunions in honour of St Francis Xaverius which she very **[p. 306]** exactly did, but was still in great perplexities and doubts, tho' she had free liberty given her both by her own father, and our Superior, to make the resolution which she thought would be most to her content and happyness both in this life and the next, and none that knew of her doubts did any ways perswade her either to go or stay; this she could not determine having nothing to except against this house and order, but being in great solicitude to know what God's will and designe over her, not thinking it so secure to depend on the revelation and Prophecy of Reverende Mother Burton,[1] Superior of the English Teresians at Antwerp, who was a person very renown'd for her great piety and sanctity, and had declared from the first time she saw her, that she would be Profess'd in her comunity whilst she remain'd in this uneasyness, earnestly desiring to know the will of God by a positive and clear assurance which none would give her; till at last Mr. Pointz, our confessarius,[2] freely told her that her thoughts of removing from hence seem'd a mere temptation, since she had all the means of attaining perfection here which she could expect by the observance of any other Rule. Upon this she fixt her resolution of settling here and **[p. 307]** beg'd to be admitted to her clothing. So she was clothed about a month after and apply'd her self with great chearfulness, fervour and zeal to the exact observance of all duties, tho' the great defect she had in her speech render'd her uncapable of reading any thing alone either in the choir or Refectory, but her healthy, strong constitution, and truly good natural disposition, and pious inclinations, made amends for that defect.

For about three or four months after her clothing, she seem'd very easy and well settled, tho' as she afterwards confess'd, she was never thoroughly convinced it was the will of God she should be here, yet she sincerely intended it and was very well satisfied that she had used the most secure means of knowing and practicing the divine will, by the entire submission of her own judgment. Reverende Mother Burton after she heard of her clothing did stil affirm that she would be profess'd in her House, and the effect proved the truth of her revelation; for divine providence presented an extraordinary motive of charity to further its designes. Sister Teresa Joseph had a near relation very desirous to be religious, but wanted both means and health to recommend **[p. 308]** her to any place; as Reverende Mother Burton being inform'd of, her Reverence promised to receive her into her comunity with her cousine Sister Teresa

---

[1] Catherine Burton, in religion Mary Xaveria of the Angels (1694–1714) AC020, Prioress 1700–14.

[2] Fr Augustine Poyntz (?SJ) (1679/80–1723); see Holt, p. 204.

Joseph.[1] This motive of charity, tho' it was not judged sufficient of it self, yet it gave full weight and balance to her other motives and reasons, and by wise and prudent counsell she fixt her resolution of going to Antwerp on the second of July, having just past half a year of her noviship here. That she might not put soecular clothes again she earnestly requested our Reverende Mother to permit her to go from hence in our first habit, which she put on a second time on the 18th of July, and the same day began her journey to Antwerp. On Ste Anne's day[2] she and her cousine were clothed there; and a few days after she sent for her portion which was in our Reverende Mother's hands, who return'd it to her all together, at her first demand.

On the 4th of August we received Mrs Catherine and Mrs Rebecca Pigot, for convictresses. They were daughters to counsellor Pigot.[3]

On the first of September the Lady Carrington (Sister to our Superior) went from hence, having left us most edifying examples of piety, humility **[p. 309]** and charity.

On the 14 of September Mrs Griffith came to our Monastry, and brought with her Margarit Conyers, grand-child to Sir John Conyers of Stroughton;[4] we received her the same day for convictress, and on the 7th of october Mrs Griffith entered our enclosure designing to board with us for that winter: she had been woman to the Princess of Powis (our Superior's Mother) and was afterwards cabinet keeper to our Princess, at St Germain's;[5] but an early death having deprived our English nation of all the advantages that might be hoped for in so accomplish'd a Princess, Mrs Griffith obtain'd leave of the Queen to go into England to see her relations there, and in her return from thence, she came to us, desiring to stay the winter within our cloister.

On the 14 of october Mrs Anne Markham, daughter to Mr Markham of Ollerton (and niece to Sister Ann' and Sister Henrietta Markham) was received here for convictress.[6]

Our Queen having notice that Mrs Griffith was come to our Monastry, sent orders of her speedy return to her at **[p. 310]** St Germain's, which

---

1 The name of Sister Teresa Joseph Bond's cousin is not certain.

2 The Feast of St Anne was celebrated on 26 July.

3 Counsellor Pigott was Nathaniel Pigott, the last Catholic called to the bar until 1791, and a well-known Catholic conveyancer of the Inner Temple. Catherine Pigott returned to England in 1716, and Rebecca decided to enter the Poor Clares at Gravelines, professing in 1718 (GP222). For Nathaniel Pigott (bap. 1661–1737), see *ODNB*. See also **[pp. 326–7, 328, 329, 334–5, 337]**.

4 Margaret Conyers, in religion Alipia (1717–58) BA063. The Conyers property was Great Stoughton, Huntingdonshire. Sir John died on 14 September 1719.

5 Princess Louise Marie, daughter of Mary of Modena and James II, born in 1692, died in April 1712. See Corp, p. 315.

6 Ann Delphina Markham, in religion Christina (1717–45) BA138. She was the daughter of Thomas Markham (d. c.1720) of Ollerton and Catherine Constable of Houghton, Yorks.

disappointed her of remaining here the whole winter. She presented our Reverende Mother with black velvet enough to make a complete suit for our church; she also gave 20 pound Sterlin for the making it up; and having fully discharged the two months pension for her self and servant, she went from hence on the 27 of november, having some hopes of returning to us again if she could easily disengage her self from our Queen's service.

On the 6 of December Mrs Ann' Cannying, niece to Sister Victoria Cannying, was received here for convictress.[1]

On the 7th of December Mrs Vanderwall return'd home to her father.

We this year received in Almns 100 florins from Mrs Williscot.

The year 1714

On the 19 of January Sister Mary Joseph Vaughan departed this life in the 34 year of her age and 5th of her holy profession.[2] She had been always infirm but about the middle of last January she fell into a lingering distemper, and on the 25 of the same month, to our great surprise, fell suddenly into raving fits which our Doctor affirm'd to be no **[p. 311]** effect of her present illness. We sent for an extraordinary Doctor who said it was a feavour upon the spirits, and gave great hopes of her cure in a short time, but notwithstanding all his endeavours and the prescriptions of a council of Doctors, she continued her raving, tho' by the violence of their remedies she was brought to a very great weakness, and judged to be in a deep consumption. She had been an examplar good religious woman, and one that constantly apply'd her self to an exact regularity as much as her health would permit, being very zealous in her endeavours to attain perfection, nay her very ravings were much on the subject of piety and devotion: and she told us (which we took for raving also) that she had offer'd her senses as a sacrifice to Almighty God for Sister Tecla's soul, when she was in the sad condition we have related in the year 1712.[3] And since Sister Mary Joseph's death, Mr. Pointz, our confessarius, has affirm'd this for truth; she ask'd him once if he would not approve of such an oblation of charity, and he answering that by no means he would not approve of such a thing; she then told him that she had already made it on the octave day of our **[p. 312]** Lady's conception, when all the comunity join'd in offring their comunion to obtain the blessing of a happy death for Sister Tecla. Almighty God seem'd to accept this oblation, since about a month after Sister Tecla's death she fell into this way, and continued so the whole year.

---

[1] Ann Canning was probably the daughter of Elizabeth Victoria Canning's brother Francis. See WWTN family tree.

[2] Mary Joseph Vaughan (1709–14) BA207.

[3] Abigail Busby, in religion Thecla (1666–1712) BA041. See **[pp. 300–1]**.

We perform'd the devotion of the ten fridays comunions in honour of St Francis Xaverius for her; and confide in the infinit goodness of God it had a happy effect tho' not in the restoration of her senses; for she often with a great sense of piety and devotion desired to comunicate, and some spiritual persons who had spoken to her, join'd with father confessor in the opinion that it might with great security and advantage be given to her; so on the feast of our Lady's Assumption was the first time she received the holy communion after the defect of her senses, but after this feast she communicated several times before her death and was always found well disposed by an earnest desire and a great sense of piety. She was not apprehended to be in danger of death till the morning she dyed, and father confessor being call'd to her, she humbly desired to receive her *viaticum* and the extream unction, which she did receive with great **[p. 313]** content and joy, expressing her sentiments of piety by such devout and fervent aspirations that all who heard her were moved to tears. She humbly ask'd pardon of all expressing a grateful sense of their charity, and tho' her weakness did not permit her to speak much, yet all she said that morning was very sensible and rational; she yielded up her happy soul about eleven a clock in the morning, and was bury'd on the 21 of January. *Requiescat in pace*. Amen.

About this time Mr James Crets[1] being dangerously ill, he sent his confessor to our Reverende Mother, desiring her to resigne and forgive the overplus of the money he had exacted and received for that part of the Garden we purchased of him in the year 1710. Her Reverence prudently answer'd that it was not in her power to resigne what was due to her comunity, and what in his own conscience he thought himself obliged to restore. Two days after his Executors came to our Monastry and told our Reverende Mother that Mr. Crets was happily departed this life, and had discharged his conscience of this debt having in his will left a 100 and 40 pound grote[2] **[p. 314]** permission to our Monastry, which doubtless was what he judged our due both as to the overplus, and the interest of it, he having had it four years in his hands, and since by law we could not have exacted it, we acknowledged this act of justice by praying for the happy repose of his soul, which our Reverende Mother recommended to the private devotions of each; and on the 22 of January his relations were all invited to a Solemn Mass that we sung for him. *Requiescat in pace*. Amen.

On the 6th of April Mrs Mary Vaughan return'd for England.

---

1 Mr Crets was the previous owner of the garden, sold in 1710 to the nuns at a very high price. See **[pp. 274–6]**.

2 By this time the Flemish pound grote was a basic unit, which had different values for wholesale (1 pound = 240 grote) and retail (1 pound = 40 grote).

On the 23 of June Mrs Mary Fairfax went from us to the English Dames at Gant.[1] She was here instructed and happily converted to our holy religion to her own great content and satisfaction, but she being enclined to greater liberty than we allow our convictresses and understanding that at the Dame she might have a chamber to her self and other little conveniences, she wrote to her Mother for leave to remove, and her Mother coming over carry'd her to Gand, tho' she seem'd more inclined to have her daughter remain here.

On the 24 of June Mrs Mary Sykes return'd for England.[2]

[p. 315] On the 27th of June we were all surprised and frighten'd with a strange accident; it was hot but fine clear day, when on a sudden between eleven and twelve a clock at noon, there was a great flash of lightening and a terrible clap of thunder; and at the same instant a thunder bolt pierced through the church wall on the side of our Sisters' Chappel; and made its way thro' the cupboard at the end of our church, split the boards of it, and rent the cloaths that cover'd the guildings and other ornaments of the church which were kept there. The window by the cupboard was broke in several places, some of the guildings tarnish'd, and one of the marble stones that paved the chappel was broke in four pieces, leaving a round hole in the earth just in the place that stone had cover'd. This accident happen'd immediately after our first Refectory, and there was only three nuns in the choir; they saw the lightening flash in at the windows like a great sheet of fire, and sparks of fire flying about. A thick smoke and sulferous smel remain'd for sometime in our church and chappel. **[p. 316]** The slates fell from the house a great distance off, some into the Magdalenes Gardens, and some as far as the Shooters Hof;[3] the greatest part of the ornaments of our steeple were also beat down, and after all, a little shower of rain concluded this violent tempest, and a fine clear day ensued.

In the midst of this storm, Sister Mary Alexia Burton[4] was kneeling just before the chappel Grate, and one of our Lay sisters behind her about two yards distance; the flash of lightening came between them, and the Sister with the sudden fright ran shreeking out of the chappel where she left Sister Burton kneeling up right with her head circled round with the flames: she declared her fright and how she had left good sister Burton.

---

1 Mary Fairfax is not included in the surviving history of Ghent, where the account focusses on candidates who proceded to profession.

2 Mary Sykes (BA189). This was a temporary stay only, which she used to improve her skills in painting and other such talents: she returned in 1716. She was responsible for the drawings related to the expansion plans for the convent by Prioress Lucy Herbert and for supervising the works; her drawing of the convent in 1729 appears in this volume.

3 Magadalene's Garden was that belonging to Bethania, adjacent to Nazareth. The Schuttershof in Bruges was the house of the guild of archers in Carmerstraat. I am indebted to Sibylla Goegebuer for this reference.

4 Mary Alexia Burton (BA040).

Immediately some had courage enough to run to her assistance, and found her fallen down on her side with her feet just at the place where the marble stone was broken. She was in convulsions, and being carry'd to the infirmary, father confessor was call'd to her, we having reason to apprehend her present danger; but in less than half an hour she came perfectly to her self complaining very much of her **[p. 317]** head, and of her eyes which for some time were blood shot, and her sight so weak that she could not bear any light. She has since affirm'd that she does not remember that she had seen the lightening or heard the thunder; and therefore was not in any fright or fear: but whilst she was very serious at her devotions she suddenly felt somthing like a great blow upon her head, and presently seem'd to be press'd and crush'd down with great violence; and she remember'd that she thought and said as she was falling: "dear Lord that I be crush'd quite down into the earth, and die all alone!"

The chief in our Town and several others have been here since to enquire into all particulars of this accident, and many judicious persons esteem our preservation a very wonderful effect of God's merciful providence and favorable Protection, in gratitude for which we sung a Mass the next day in honour of the most blessed trinity, and said our Lady's Littanies[1] for nine days all together in the choir, and on the eighth day after, Sister Burton ask'd and obtain'd a particular leave to communicate in **[p. 318]** thanksgiving for hers and our comunity's wonderful preservation, she also got leave to comunicate Annually on the day for the same intention.

In July the Lady Butler Abbess of the Irish Benedictin Dames at Ypres with two of her Dames being come out of their Monastry upon some business in their return, stay'd three days with us, and were lodged in our infirmary.[2]

In September Sister Catherine Holland celebrated the feast of her whole Jubilee being fifty years profess'd.[3]

On the 25 of october we were obliged to part with our novice Sister Mary Petre[4] tho' with great regret, she having persevered constantly in her vocation and in the earnest desire and patient expectation of her Profession, and had so well comported her self that none could alledge any thing against her, except the want of Portion which her father's ill circumstances deprived her of, yet at last we were in hopes of getting it, he designing to sell some part of his estate but that money was all disposed of for the payment of debts and therefore Mr Petre gave express orders **[p. 319]** for her returning home to him till providence should so

---

1 Our Lady's Litanies: see Glossary.

2 The Abbess at Ypres was Dame Mary Joseph Butler (1657 Boulogne–1723 Ypres) OB019, Abbess 1686–1723.

3 Catharine Holland (1664–1720) BA106.

4 Mary Petre; see also **[pp. 285, 291, 302, 438–9]**. Mary Petre professed at Gravelines (1718–24) GP219.

dispose that he could pay her portion, upon this, our Reverende Mother designing to propose more favorable termes to him, would not let the novice know of this ill news till she heard from her father again, and the community having consented her upon condition he paid her portion, tis thought they would have taken her for little or nothing if another accident had not happen'd; but on the 10th of october in the Evening, this poor novice was strangely seized with such dismal Melancholy fancies, and so obstinately fixt on such unreasonable and groundless apprehensions, that father confessor as well as her Mistress, was surprised to find her in such an unusual disposition so contrary to her natural temper, which they had always found easy and submissive, but now nothing that was said either by confessor or Superior, to appease her fears, could satisfie her, nor were those fears only interior, for every little noise was a new surprise and fright to her, so that she could not be left a moment alone either night or day. **[p. 320]** Alle remedies were used both spiritual and corporal, but without any sensible effect for nine days; but on St Luke's day[1] she being with her Mistress alone in the noviship, suddenly burst out into tears (which before she could not shed). And kneeling down before the Altar, she said aloud, what strange thoughts have I had, so injurious to the infinit mercy and goodness of God, I now disavow and detest them from my heart, and continuing some time in such most pious and affectionate acts, she desired to go before the most blessed Sacrament saying to her Mistress as they were going to the chappel (for it was in time of Vespers): "Sure these frightful thoughts I have had come from the devil, I never had such in my life before. I found myself in them so violently moved by an obstinate disposition, not to believe whatever you or any one else said for my comfort and satisfaction, that I could not so much as endeavour to resist it, believing it not in my power, but now I am most willing to submitt to any penance that shal be imposed upon me, I desire to ask everyone of the religious pardon for the disedification I have given."

[p. 321] After Vespers her Mistress went with her to Reverende Mother and her Aunt, and we all rejoiced to see her so perfectly come to her self. The next day being friday, our Reverende Mother gave her leave to begin then the ten communions in honour of St Francis Xaverius, which permission she most gratefully accepted, and earnestly desired to return again to all regular duties which her Reverence promised she should begin the next day; but in the morning at her first awaking we found her in the same way she had been the nine days before, and seeing no hopes of her recovery, we sent Sister Barbara Devery with her into England.[2] In this we may adore the secret and incomprehensible designes of the

---

1 St Luke's Day is celebrated on 18 October.
2 Ann Barbara Devery (BA072).

divine providence, and comfort our selves with the assurance that God never abandons those who entirely depend upon him as this truly pious novice did, and as many prayers and devotions have been offer'd for her, we have reason to hope that God will gratiously hear them to his greater honour and glory, and the good of her soul.

On the 10th of november Mrs Catherine Brinkhurst, and Mrs Anne **[p. 322]** Cannying began their journey for England.

We this year received in Almns 50 florins for the soul of Mrs Petit.

The year 1715

On the 7th of April, Sister Mary Bernard Tasburgh departed this life in the 36 year of her age, and 15th of her holy Profession.[1] She had a dropsie which began about 12 years before her death and went on encreasing till her body was swell'd to a great bigness, tho' she was very lean and of a lively active disposition. She suffer'd much by this infirmity, yet was as exact in regular observances as could be expected from a person in her condition, and in occasions, she express'd the great value and esteem she had for her holy State of life.

About the begining of lent this year she fell into her last sickness and suffer'd with great patience and submission to the divine will, continually offering her pains, and accepting them in the spirit of penance, and expressing great sorrow for the least fault or transgression of our holy rule. Nothwithstanding her long infirmity she had a very strong and violent Agony, and cry'd out so **[p. 323]** lamentably that those who watch'd with her that night were very much frighten'd, yet for about two hours before her death she was in a quiet peace and calme, expressing great ease and security of her salvation by our Lady's intercession. She dyed on passion Sunday about two in the morning, but before she could be exposed or put into her coffin we were force to send for the surgeon to open her corps as far as it was necessary to let out the water that had swell'd her so prodigiously, and about 16 stope of water came from her. She was bury'd on the Monday in our Vault. *Requiescat in pace*. Amen.

On the 24 of April Mr Edward's Lady came from England, and brought her eldest daughter whom we received for convictress. After a short stay Mrs Blount return'd for England with Sir Francis Jernegan and his Lady.[2]

On the second of May the Lady Knatchbul, Abbess of the English Dames at Gant, with Dame Constantia Howard, and another young Dame,

---

[1] Mary Bernard Tasburgh (1700–15) BA191.

[2] Edward Blount was married to Anne Guise. Sir Francis and Lady Jerningham had been staying in the confessor's house since June 1713; see **[p. 303]**.

passing thro' this Town to go for England, call'd at our Monastry, but stay'd no longer than to take a breakfast at the Grate.[1]

[p. 324] On the 13 of May Mrs Ann' Sykes went for England.[2]

On the 17 of June the Lady Mountague, sister to our Reverende Mother, came hither, her Ladyship and her woman were lodged within our enclosure.[3]

On the 22 of June our man Thomas Dath departed this life having served us about 16 months. He was born in Maryland, and was but newly baptised and converted to our holy faith when he came to live with us. Those who knew him gave him the character of one who had always lived an innocent and moral good life; but after his conversion he seriously apply'd himself to the knowledge and practice of piety and vertue. He fell sick of the smal pox in the begining of June, and could not be removed out of our house in the Garden, so we hired a woman to tend him, and he was often visited by our Doctor, and an English Carme, his confessor. With great devotion he received all the rights of our holy Mother the church, and as soon as he was departed we rung our Bell and said the commendations for him in our choir. He was bury'd at Ste Ann's and was about 33 years of age. our Reverende Mother caused some Masses to be said for the happy repose of his soul. *Requiescat in pace*. Amen.

[p. 325] The same day Mary Green came out of England and was received within our enclosure for a servant, being recommended to us for a lay sister.[4]

Also on the same day, Sister Mary Taylor,[5] one of the last profess'd of the lay sisters, fell sick of the smal pox; they came out very well, and our Doctor in several visits did not apprehend her in any danger, no not even in his last visit which was on St Peter and Paul's day in the morning; but that afternoon about four a clock she fell suddenly from her self, and into convulsions, so that she could not receive her *viaticum*; Father confessor was call'd to her to give her the holy oyles, and she expired about six a clock in the Evening. Tho' her death was sudden and surprising yet we have great reason to hope she was happily disposed for it, since she had always lived an innocent and pious life, and after she had a habit on, did seriously apply her self to religious perfection. Her age and capacity gave very promising hopes that if it had pleased God to prolong her life she would have been a very serviceable member in our community. She dyed on a saturday **[p. 326]** the 29 of June in the 24 year of her age, and

---

1 Mary Knatchbull, abbess at Ghent 1711–27 (GB119); Catherine Howard, in religion Constantia Howard (GB104).

2 Anne Sykes (1726–73) BA188.

3 Lady Mary Herbert married Francis Browne, 4th Viscount Montagu: see Herbert family tree.

4 Mary Green, in religion Mary Agathe, lay sister (1717–68) BA091.

5 Mary Taylor, in religion Agatha (1713–15) BA198.

second of her holy profession. On the Sunday after Compline she was privately bury'd, and on Monday the Solemn Mass was sung and funeral ceremonies perform'd for her. *Requiescat in pace*. Amen.

Many of our young people being now in great apprehensions of the smal pox, our Reverende Mother promised that if the infection ceased, all those in our community who had not had the smal pox should in october perform the devotion of the 10 fridays communions in honour of St Francis Xaverius, and in thanksgiving for our preservation.

On the 13 of July the Lady Knatchbul, Abbess of the Benedictin Dames at Gant, Dame Constantia Howard, and Dame Hockens, return'd from England, and brought with them two other soecular gentlewomen.[1] They were all lodged in our infirmary, and went from hence to Gant on the 16 of the same month.

On the 25 of July the Lady Mountague departed from hence, having highly raised our esteem for her Ladyship by her piety, affability, and eagerness in all.

On the Eve of our Lady's Assumption, Mrs Margarite Conyers, and Mrs Rebecca **[p. 327]** Pigot were admitted to our first habit; the first took the name of Sister Alipia, and the other of Sister Eugenia.[2]

On the 4th of october we began the devotions of the ten fridays in honour of St Francis Xaverius and the leave was extended to all that desired to perform this devotion.

On the 17 of october Mrs Edwards, the Lady Carrington's houskeeper, came hither, she being newly converted to our holy faith, her Lady thought that living some time in a Monastry would confirm her more and settle her in good principles of vertue. She had a chamber in the convictresses Schoole.

On the 21 of october Mrs Ann' Markham was admitted to the first habit, and took the name of Sister Christina.[3]

On the 21 of november Mary Green received the Schollars kerchief.[4]

The year 1716

On the 25 of March Margarite Linny received the Schollars kerchief.[5]

---

1 Dame Hockens has not yet been identified; possibly Hawkins.

2 Margaret Conyers, in religion Alipia (BA063). Rebecca Pigott, in religion Eugenia, clothed May 1716, left in January 1717 to become a Poor Clare at Gravelines, professing as Mary Benedict (GP222); see **[p. 334]**.

3 Ann Delphina Markham (1717–45) BA138.

4 Mary Green, in religion Mary Agathe (1717–68) BA091.

5 Margaret Linny (1717–65) BA128.

About this time our new Bishop[1] being settled in his Episcopal Palace **[p. 328]** Father confessor made him a visit in behalf of our Reverende Mother and community, and presented him from her Reverence with a very hansome pendalum English clock. His Lordship was very much pleased, and obliged by this visit, and as ours was the first Monastry which had sent to compliment him after his installation, he said he would come to visit our Reverende Mother before he went to any other Monastry, and would at the same time confirm those of our family who had not received that Sacrament. On the 3d of April his Lordship came and said Mass in our church, after which he confirm'd two of our Schollars, Sister Eugenia Pigot, and Sister Alipia Canyers, and also the little Lord Maxwell, nephew to our Reverende Mother, Mrs Catherine Pigot and Mrs Edwards.[2] His Lordship this time enter'd no further into our enclosure than our Choir, where all the religious were assembl'd to receive his blessing. He in a most obliging manner assured us of his fatherly care and assistance, and that day presented our Superior with several bottles of excellent claret sufficient for portions for the whole community, which we had that night **[p. 329]** at collation being in Lent.

This was the Lord Henry Joseph van Susteren. The Bishoprick had been ten years govern'd by Vicars, there having been no bishop till this year from the death of the Lord William Bassery, who as we said before fell dead in the church, in the year 1706.[3]

On the 7th of April, the Lady Mountague return'd to us again.[4]

Mrs Mary Sykes who went from us with a desire to return again, having improved her self in painting and other works which she had a genius to, and being constant in her desire to settle here, our Reverende Mother proposed to the convent Sisters the taking her with an under fortune, and it was decided in her favour; upon which she was sent for, and arrived here on the 30 of April.[5] She was admitted to the first habit on the ninth of May, and took the names of Mary Michael.

On the 10 of May Sister Eugenia Pigot and Sister Alipia Conyers were clothed, Reverend father Lewis de Sabran of the Society of Jesus,

---

[1] The Bishop of Bruges since 25 January 1716 had been Hendrik Jozef van Susteren (1668–1742), Bishop of Bruges 1716–42. Father Confessor was Fr Augustine Poyntz (?SJ) (1679/80–1723), Confessor 1707–23. Reverend Mother in 1716 was Lucy Herbert, Prioress 1709–44 (BA101).

[2] Sister Eugenia Pigot: see **[pp. 326–7]**. Her sister Catherine did not join the convent either. Margaret Conyers, in religion Alipia (1717–58) BA063. Lord Maxwell was William, son of Lady Winifred Maxwell, née Herbert, Countess of Nithsdale, and the nephew of Prioress Lucy Herbert: see Herbert family tree.

[3] Bishop Willem Bassery died on 18 June 1706, from which time the see had remained vacant.

[4] Lady Montagu, sister of Prioress Lucy Herbert.

[5] Mary Sykes, in religion Mary Michael (BA189). See also **[p. 314]**.

examin'd them by the Bishop's orders, our Arch Priest being newly dead;[1] he also sung the Mass, and perform'd **[p. 330]** ceremonies of the clothing.

On the Eleventh of May the Lady Mountague went from hence, and took Mrs Edwards with her.

On the 17 of May Sister Christina Markham was clothed, and father Sabran officiated for her.[2]

On the 18 of May Mrs Catherine Pigot went for England.[3]

On the 3d of June which was wednesday in Whitson week,[4] our Bishop made us another visit, and after having said Mass in our church, and confirm'd some of our pensioners, he enter'd our enclosure, and having seen our cells and all the Monastry, he came into our work chamber where all the religious and novices were assembled, the religious in their surplices. His Lordship made us a very fatherly kind speech, expressing how well satisfied and pleased he was with the character he had heard of us, exhorting us to a happy perseverance in the exact observance of our holy rule and institutions. He told us that he had read our Statutes, and finding them so comformable to our holy rule he thought no means would help us more, and secure our constant observance of them, than to have **[p. 331]** them printed to the end that each religious might always have a copy by her, and by frequent reading the same retain in mind and heart that most secure means to acquire the perfection of our State. His Lordship in this visitation only spoke with our Superior in private, and afterwards with her Reverence and the three council Sisters together.

Before the rule and Statutes were printed, his Lordship sent up his Pastoral letter by which he approved, and recommended our institutions to our Superior and Community, and as they had been form'd by different visits made by precedent Bishops, they were by his orders and authority put into due order, such things cut off which in one place contradicted another, or the constant practice; in two or three paragraphs the sense was more fully explain'd, and some little alterations were made which seem'd reasonable and regular to his Lordship, at the request of our Superior and her Council Sisters.[5]

On the 12 of August our Convent Sisters met together for the election of a Subprioress, a Procuratress and an Arcaria. Sister Frances Rookwood was chosen Subprioress, Sister Ursula Babthorpe Arcaria, and Sister Ann Benedict Thirlwall, Procuratrix.[6]

---

1 Alipia Conyers (BA063).

2 Christina Markham (BA138). Father Louis Sabran SJ (1652–1732); Holt, p. 217.

3 Catherine Pigott (1697–1747) later married Edward Caryll (1695–1766).

4 Whitsunday or Pentecost celebrated the day 50 days after Easter when the followers of Christ were visited by the Spirit and enabled to speak in other languages.

5 The Constitutions were printed the following year: see **[p. 339]**.

6 Frances Rookwood, in religion Apollonia (BA164); Ursula Babthorpe (BA010); Ann Benedict Thirwall (BA199).

[p. 332] On the same day the Lady Nithsdale (sister to our Reverende Mother) with her little daughter Lady Anne Maxwell, and her two women, arrived here from England.[1] This Lady has gain'd great renown for having undertaken and so ingeniously contrived her Lord's escape out of the Tower of London, just the night before they designed to execute him with the Lord Derwentwater. This Lord was made Prisoner in the Tower upon the unhappy defeat of all our King's friends at Preston, and as soon as his Lady (my Lady Nithsdale) had news of it, she undertook a long and tedious journey on horse back from Scotland to London, in the sharpest time of winter, when the snow was very deep. She presented her self on her knees before King George to beg her Spouse's life, but her petition was most roughly rejected by him, and finding no means to prevail with him, her Ladyship with only the help of her women contrived his escape, disguising him in women's appareil and painting his face, then sending him away with her woman by the favour of the Evening, and remaining in his chamber till she thought they were got safe away, after which she follow'd, and the divine providence so favour'd her endeavours, that under another **[p. 333]** disguise he was soon convey'd into the french dominions. Then this heroick Lady return'd into Scotland to secure what she could of the personal estate, but the King's anger threatening her most severely, she absconded for some time, till meeting with a conveniency she came over, and stay'd here till the 14 of September, then went to her Lord in france.

On the 17 of September Mr Edward Blount and his Lady came, out of England, and brought with them the Lord Falconbury's three daughters, Mrs Mary, Miss Ann and Miss Penelope Bellasses, and also two of their own daughters, Mrs Mary and Miss Henrietta.[2] They were all five received for convictresses, but Mr Blount having taken a house in this Town intended to have one or two of his children be always with them; and our Bishop gave leave that they might come into our enclosure in their turns, as their Parents thought fit.

On the 9th of november Sister Mary Michael Sykes was clothed by our new Arch Priest.[3]

On the 22 of november Sister Mary Green and Sister Margarite Linny were clothed.[4]

---

1 Lady Nithsdale was the youngest sister of Prioress Lucy Herbert. See *ODNB* and H. Tayler, *Lady Nithsdale and Her Family* (London: Lindsay Drummond, 1939).

2 Edward Blount (1643–1726) married Anne Guise. Their daughters Mary (b. 1702) and Henrietta (b. 1710) did not enter the convent. Their daughter Ann came separately in 1713. Mary, Anne and Penelope were the daughters of Thomas Belasyse, 3rd Viscount Fauconberg (d. 1718) and his wife, Bridget Gage. None of them entered the convent, although three of their cousins joined the Benedictines at Dunkirk.

3 Mary Michael Sykes (BA189).

4 Mary Green (BA091); Margaret Linny (BA128).

[p. 334] On the 29 of December we received Jean Collingwood as a servant upon tryal for a lay sister.

The year 1717

Our novice Sister Eugenia Pigot[1] about a month after her clothing began to think that God call'd her to a more austere order, and she fixt her resolution to be a poor clare some months before she discover'd her thoughts to any, so that when she first declared her mind upon this subject it was not to ask counsell but to manifest what she had so long before resolved upon; being already convinced (as she affirm'd) that it was with God required of her: therefore without any further counsell, she desired to depart as soon as she could obtain her Parents' leave. The first letters she received from them upon this subject, they refused their consent, and express'd themselves very much displeased at her proposals and thoughts of removing. Upon the receit of these letters she was prevail'd with to take advise and counsel, that better to secure her future content and satisfaction, which could never be well grounded if her motives and reasons had not the approbation **[p. 335]** of learned spiritual men, who are most capable of discovering what is truly inspired by God, or suggested by the common enemy. Father confessor, and father novice Rector of the English Colledge at Gant, were by her consulted in this affair, and after due consideration of all circumstances, they approved her motives of subjecting her self to a more austere rule. They both writ their opinion of the matter to her Parents, as did our Reverende Mother, and by this means her friends were satisfied and gave their consent for her removal; so she reassumed her soecular clothes, and went from hence for Gravelin on the 14 of January.

On the same day Sister Ignatia Simons[2] received her *viaticum* being most happily disposed, and resigned with great ease and chearfulness to depart this life which was particularly noted in her because she had always been very apprehensive and fearful of death. She had been very serviceable to our comunity in the care and charge of the woolen habit, which office she had perform'd about 30 years **[p. 336]** labouring in it with great diligence, and constantly helping to fold the wet linnen in wash weeks, till her age and infirmities render'd her uncapable of that labour. She had a very mean conceit of her self, and a high value for obedience saying in occasions of the greatest difficulty: "This is Superiors orders", and that thought was sufficient to make her easy and well satisfied.

On the 15 of January she received the holy oyles on which day we kept the feast of the adorable name of Jesus, and this day she had chosen for her hour of prayer, from three to four in the afternoon, for the association

---

1 Eugenia Pigott professed as Mary Benedict (GP222) at the Poor Clares, Gravelines in 1718.

2 Ignatia Simons (1656–1717) BA175.

of the perpetual adoration of the Blessed Sacrament; by her solicitude and care one was appointed to keep this hour of prayer for her, and just at the end of the first half hour, she expired; the last motion of life was seen in her tongue with which she pronounced the sacred name of Jesus with her last dying breath. She was about 78 years of age, near 61 profess'd, and 11 from her whole Jubilee. On the 17 of January she was bury'd. *Requiescat in pace*. Amen.

Mrs Mary Petre (who had been novice here, and of whom mention is made before) having perfectly recover'd **[p. 337]** her health, and had some experience of the continuance of it, she had several times by letters express'd her desire to return to us again, but seem'd very much doubt of her being so welcome to us as before, apprehending the reflections which might be made upon the condition she was in when she went from us. Her fears were not altogether groundless, for some in our comunity were very much against her return upon that account. Yet she had been so exact a novice that her vertue, good humour, and parts, had gained her many friends here, who desired to have her a member of our body, so that she had very kind invitations to return to us. But last october she went from England to the English poor clares at Gravelin, to be present at the Profession of her two younger sisters, whose example encouraged her soon after to fix her resolution of settling there with them: so on the 6th of february she and Mrs Pigot (our other novice) were clothed there.[1]

On the 9th of March Jane Collingwood parted from hence, being of a sickly and infirm constitution. She was judged unfit for us.

[p. 338] On the 22 of March Sister Ann Bessbrown, one of our lay sisters departed this life in the 52 year of her age and 30th of her holy Profession.[2] She had been always infirm and sickly and from the September before her death was confined to the infirmary; for she being a person full of humours they gather'd in several parts of her body, for which she suffer'd many painful incisions, and bore her infirmities with great patience and submission to the divine will, thereby, we hope atoning for her frailties which she seem'd very sensible of, and in disposing her self to receive her *viaticum* she desired father confessor to beg pardon in her behalf of the whole community for the disedification she had given in not having lived so regularly and conformably to her holy State as she ought to have done. She confided much in the infinit goodness of God, and expected her last moment with great chearfulness ease and peace of mind, in which happy disposition she expired about one a clock in the morning, on Monday in holy week. *Requiescat in pace*. Amen.

---

[1] Mary Petre professed at Gravelines as Mary Xaveria (1718–24) GP219; her sisters were Bridget, in religion Clare Stanislaus (1716–1747) GP217, and Helen, in religion Mary Felix (1716–79) GP218. Rebecca Pigott (known as Eugenia at Bruges), in religion Mary Benedict (GP222).

[2] Ann Bessbrown (1687–1717) BA023.

[p. 339] In April our Rule and Institutions being printed,[1] the later were read to us in the work chamber; as the alterations of them had been read before they were printed, and now our Superior desired we should try them for one month the better to comprehend the advantage of the change or by experience, be better able to offer more reasonable objections.

On the 20 of April the Lady Carrington, and Lady Mary Herbert, sister and niece to our Reverende Mother, came from France to our Monastry.[2]

On the 25 of April, the Lady Carrington went for England designing to return soon again, and Lady Mary Herbert remained.

On the 10th [of May] the Lady Falconburg brought ..... Bridget Bellasses, niece to her Lord and soon after her Ladyship took her Eldest daughter to live with her, designing to settle with her family for some time at Bruxelles.[3]

On the 20 of May Sister Frances Rookwood our Subprioress departed this life in the 50 year of her age and 32 of her holy profession.[4] For the last twenty years of her life she had **[p. 340]** particularly apply'd her self to the two solidest helps to vertue, Prayer and mortification; as also to retiredness to solitude, and that even more than the common regular observances generally allows of; because she had a great weakness and defect in her eyes which made her less able to apply her self to the common work. She was naturally very stiff in whatever way she took, and it was very visible in her, that grace does not destroy nature, but only gives us light to discover and strength to overcome the violences of it; so tho' Subprioress truly tended to perfection, yet when nature was guided by a mistaken zeal she ...tily gave scope to it; this chiefly [appea]r'd when our Reverende Mother by the [Bishop's] orders (as was said before) resolved to have our institutions printed, and some alterations made in them for the better; tho' the work had been duly examin'd, approved and recommended by our Bishop, and had been dilligently review'd by the person who for thirty years had directed her conscience, yet upon a fancy that the community had not been sufficiently **[p. 341]** consulted in the matter, she as Subprioress conceived her self as obliged to receive the difficulties and complaints of a few dissatisfied persons, and being a kind of a head to them, might have occasion'd great disturbances in the comunity, tho' not disignedly. When God's providence ever attentive

---

1 *The Rule of S. Augustin as also the Statutes & Constitutions of the English Regular Canonesses of the Order of St Augustin Established at Bridges in Flanders*, printed with permission in the year 1717. *The Statutes or Constitutions of the Converse-Sisters commonly called Lay-Sisters* were published in the same year. (The titles are taken from title pages of copies in the Nazareth Archives.)

2 Lady Carrington, sister of the Prioress. Lady Mary Herbert was the daughter of William Herbert, 2nd Marquess of Powis and Mary Preston; see Herbert family tree.

3 Lady Bridget Falconberg, née Gage (d. 1738) was married to Thomas Belasyse, 3rd Viscount Falconberg (d. 1718).

4 Frances Rookwood, in religion Apollonia (1685–1717) BA164.

to the protection of such as serve him with a sincere and right heart, visited our Subprioress with many sharp infirmities, in which contrary to all expectations she remain'd most easy and free from the anxious scruples she had been troubled with for most part of her life, and after the practice of many edifying vertues, she dyed in an entire peace, and the dissatisfied were in a short time fully calm'd. By this Superiors may learn, when they have settled with due consideration and consultation any thing for the Glory of God and good of their communities, not to be startled at the oppositions of some even otherways pious souls, but to expect with humility and patience the moment in which God will never fail one way or other to protect what he has moved them to establish for **[p. 342]** his honour and by the same all subjects are taught not to relye easily upon their own judgment in the least opposition to what the lawful authority of their Superior had ordain'd.

The Subprioress had been confined to the infirmary from the be[gi] ning of last october by the encrease of a dropsie, violent fits of the stone, and the frequent renewing of a feavourish distemper which brought her to an extream weakness; yet recovering a little in the intervals of these fits, it was hoped that by the advancement of the Spring and Summer season, she would get above it, the Doctor assuring us from time to time that she was not in any danger. During the whole time of her sickness, our Superior exprest her charitable concern for her with great tenderness, and took care that nothing should be wanting that could be thought of for her ease and comfort. On Whitsonday she was suddenly seiz'd with convulsions, and that day received all the rights of our holy Mother the church, being in her perfect senses when she received her *viaticum*, as she **[p. 343]** always was in the short intervals between these convulsions, which frequently renew'd, and in one of those intervales she desired to speak with our Reverende Mother alone, with designe (as tis thought) to acknowledge and ask pardon for her mistaken zeal; but when her Reverence came to her she falter'd so in her speech that our Reverende Mother could not understand what she said; nevertheless we doubt not but that Almighty God accepted of her good intention. On thursday in Whitson week between 6 and 7 in the evening she render'd her soul to God, in one of those convulsion fits, and was bury'd on the 22 of May. *Requiescat in pace.* Amen.

We having made tryal of our new regulated Statutes some were dissatisfied at two points: the first that the second half hour of Meditation should be kept every day immediately after Vespers, and the second that in ordinary chapters seven only were to speak their faults; though both are so express'd in our Statutes that our Superior may determine the 2d half hour either after Vespers **[p. 344]** or after Compline, and allow only seven or the whole side choir to speak their faults; yet rather desiring her communities satisfaction, than to decide these things by her own judgment and authority, she let all the professt religious have the liberty to vote for either as they thought best according to conscience and reason: and on the 28 of May the votes of all being given for each of these articles separate, it was consented by the far greater number that the half hour should be after Vespers, and that only seven should speak their faults in ordinary chapters, there was very few votes for the contrary.

On the first of June Sister Alipia Conyers and Sister Christina Markham made their holy Profession,[1] three days before our Archpriest came to examine them; but being call'd out of town upon pressing business he gave leave that the ceremonie should be perform'd by Reverend father Sabran who was then here; and his Reverence began with a very fine sermon.

[p. 345] On the 8th of June Mrs Powdrel who had boarded in our father's house, went for England, and took her niece with her, Mrs Mary Elliot.

On the 10 of June our Convent Sisters were assembled for the election of a Subprioress, and Sister Hellen Andrews was a second time chosen for that office;[2] and it was also resolved by our Reverend Mother and the Convent Sisters, that she should not then be discharged of the office of Mistress of novices (which was given her the november before) til more young ones took the habit, we having at that time only one novice, who had just past seven months of her noviship.

On the 29 of June the Lady Carrington return'd from England, and on the 3d of July her Ladyship, with Lady Mary Herbert her niece, went from hence to France.

On the 12 of August Margarite Aspinal was received here as a servant in order to be a lay sister.[3]

On the 15 of September Mrs Anna Maria Hyde arrived here from England, being desirous to settle in our family.[4] She is of a younger family to the Hydes of Pangburn.

Miss Penelope Bellasses being **[p. 346]** seized with a Palsical humour which she had also had in England, the Lady Falconburg her Mother came from Bruxelles and carry'd her thither where that family lived then.[5] Her Ladyship took with her Mrs Anne Belassis her second daughter, and her niece Miss Bridget Bellasis assuring our Reverende Mother that she intended to send these two last to us again when she had given them a little diversion and fited them with new clothes. They went from hence on the 15 of September.

On the 24 of September Mrs Anna Maria Hyde received our first habit, and then our Subprioress Sister Hellen Andrews was discharged of the

[1] Alipia Conyers (BA063); Christina Markham (BA138).

[2] Helen Andrews (BA004).

[3] Margaret Aspinal, in religion Catherine (1720–86) BA006, was a convert from Protestantism.

[4] Anne Maria Hyde, in religion Maria (1719–33) BA116.

[5] For the three Belasyse sisters, see **[pp. 333, 339]**.

office of Mistress of novices and Sister Delphina Weston was appointed to succeed her in that employ.[1]

On the 9th of november Sister Mary Michael Sykes made her holy profession. Her father allowed her what was very sufficient both at her clothing and Profession, for recreations, habit, and all other expenses, besides what was agreed upon for her Portion.[2]

[p. 347] On the 22 of november Sister Mary Agatha Green and Sister Margarite Ling made their holy Profession.[3]

The year 1718

On the 9th of february our Reverende Mother[4] proposed to the convent Sisters the building a new schoole for our convictresses, our old one being much decay'd, and judged so unfit to be inhabited that we were blamed for keeping them in so poor a place, and advised for God's greater glory (in the pious education of youth) and the advantage of our Monastry, be at the expense of building a new house. These motives and reasons being proposed by our Reverende Mother our convent Sisters approved of them and voted for the building.

On the 25 of March Margarite Aspinal received the scholars kerchief and took the name of Catherine.[5]

On the 25 of April the workmen enter'd our enclosure to begin the building, Monsieur l'Epee being the overseer of the work.

On the 11th of May the first stone **[p. 348]** was laid by Miss Gifford, daughter to the deceased Sir John Gifford.[6] She was then the only Pensioner we had, Mr Blount having carry'd his two eldest daughters to a Monastry at Marguette[7] in order to learn french, and taken the other two home for a time at least.

On the 30 of July our Reverende Mother sent Miss Gifford to the Ursulines at Lille, that she might be perfected in the french tongue.

A true account of the strange sickness and sudden cure of Sister Cecily Bracy.[8]

---

1 Helen Andrews (BA004); Delphina Weston (BA216).

2 Mary Michael Sykes (BA189).

3 Mary Agathe Green (BA091). Margaret Ling probably refers to Margaret Linny (BA128).

4 Reverend Mother was Prioress Lucy Herbert (BA101).

5 Margaret Aspinal, in religion Catherine (BA006).

6 Miss Mary Gifford was the daughter of Sir John Gifford and Catherine Middleton, who lived at the Jacobite court in exile at St Germain-en-Laye. Sir John died in 1707. See **[pp. 283–4]**. Mary Gifford died on 23 April 1759 and her heart is buried at Nazareth: see vol. 2, **[pp. 128, 132, 140–3]**.

7 Marquette-lez-Lille, France.

8 Cecily Bracy (1704–39) BA031.

On the 15 of last August Sister Cecily fell ill of a little feavour, having been some time before weak and indisposed: this feavour lasted about a week, and left her so extreamly weak, that she was confined to her chamber, was not able to stir without help, even from her bed to the couch, had very restless nights, and was subject to frequent vomiting fits, so that she hardly retain'd any thing she eat. Our Doctor gave her the greatest cordials and the most strengthening medecines **[p. 349]** he could think of, but finding they were ineffectual, he changed his method, and appointed her a glass of cold water every day after dinner. This seem'd so contrary to her that she apprehended it would be her death, tho' in submission to the Doctor's orders, and obedience to her Superior, she took it for some days, and her vomiting ceasing she stil continued very weak, and had no appetite, slept but little, was not able to walk like another, but crept from place to place by the help of a staff in each hand; nor could she kneel up for the space of 3 *pater noster*'s without being ready to swoon which she was often subject to it. She forced her self to move faster than her ordinary pace; yet she was never sensible of any particular pain in her limbes but only a great weakness and defailancy: and when she moved her body seem'd to her rather a heavy logg of wood than a living thing. Our Doctor after the tryal of several remedies without effect, often declared that tho' he had with great diligence study'd her case, yet he could not find out the nature of her disease, nor could he think of **[p. 350]** any other means to help her. Besides these corporal remedies several devotions were offer'd for her recovery, yet the divine providence so disposed that she found no exterior effects of them, but stil continued in the same way, somtimes worse, and then a little better; but we had perceived no amendment since last January, about which time the Doctor gave over his remedies, advising her to stir as much as she could, and to go somtimes into the Garden, which she daily did when the weather would permit, tho' she could only creep slowly along with the help of her two sticks, and having no hopes of a cure, she forced her self to do all she was able, and obtain'd leave to lye in her cell, and to sit up somtimes in the choir at the two last hours and Vespers; and she being our organiste, she play'd on the organs when she could, but was somtimes so spent and tired with such sort of exercises, that she seem'd in a dying condition till she had taken a glass of wine or a cordial in which she always found a present relief.

She had always had a most particular devotion to the sacred **[p. 351]** name of Jesus, and on the 31 of July, which was Sunday, and the feast of St Ignatius, she was present in the choir whilst the introit of the Mass was sung; it begins: "*In the name of Jesus let every knee bow*" and which words renew'd the fervour of her devotion to this Sacred name; and at the same time she felt a tender affection for Blessed St Ignatius who did so much to glorifie this Sacred Name. She purposed to say that Antiphon, verse, and prayer in his octave for his honour; and if in that space of time she was cured of her infirmities, she promised to take him for her special Patron, and to perform such devotions in his honour as superiors should approve of.

During this octave our Doctor appointed a plaister to be laid all along her back bone, tho' in effect she found no good of it, but rather thought it made her worse. On friday night she was very ill and so restless and uneasy that she could not sleep. The next day she found so great weakness in her legs that she could hardly move **[p. 352]** at all, and the whole day found her self in such extremity of weakness that several times she was ready to swoon away. In this condition being laid down upon the couch in the infirmary, she lifted up her mind and heart to Almighty God, offering her self to suffer thus as long as he pleased, adding that if it were his blessed will, she should be glad to know what her illness was, or the cause of it. After this she had a mind to try if she could find out where her greatest weakness was, and found that by bending her knees and inclining her body she could more easily move her legs. This experience made her think that perhaps the motion of her legs was hinder'd by the shrinking of some sinews, and at the same time she thought that some oyl of camomill mixt together with brandy and warm'd, might do her some good: this remedy she had never try'd before, but after she had rub'd her limbs with it for about the space of a *miserere*, the very next moment she found she could go very **[p. 353]** well without the least impediment, but it being then after Compline, a time of strict silence with us, she said nothing of it, but went to bed and rested very well. The next day was the octave day of the feast of St Ignatius,[1] and in the morning we were all surprised to see her come walking into the choir without any support or uneasyness, remaining there on her knees both before and after holy communion, without any rest, for the space of about two hours. After which she affirm'd to our Superior and others that spoke to her, that she found no difficulty neither in kneeling nor walking; nor was she sensible of any weakness but seem'd to have recover'd her natural strength and health as perfectly as ever. And being animated by this sudden cure in a great transport of joy and fervour she spent that afternoon till Vespers in walking and kneeling, not allowing her self any rest. It was that day violently hot, and having walk'd so much, she was in an excessive heat all the time of Vespers (at which she assisted) and at the end of it, we were **[p. 354]** again surprised by her falling suddenly into a swoon, but being revived in the space of a quarter of an hour she was very well again, after which tho' she found her natural strength not so entire and perfect as formerly, yet she had not the defailancy in her limbs, but continued in good health, to the greater glory of the Sacred Name of Jesus and Blessed St Ignatius.

---

1 The Feast of St Ignatius is celebrated on 31 July.

Several spiritual men who have had the relation of this cure affirm it to be miraculous; tho' some persons dispute the effects which the plaister or the oyl and brandy might have had. Yet persons of good judgment and skill affirm that the plaister could have done no good since she had it but two days, and in that time she was worse than she had been before, and that the oyl and brandy could not in so short a time affect such a cure so sudden and entire. She her self attributes her cure to the favorable intercession and merits of St Ignatius. and as all the particulars of her sickness and cure are here faithfully related, all that read it may judge of it by the light of faith and reason to God's greater glory.

[p. 355] On the 11th of December Miss Elisabeth Willis,[1] a Marchand's daughter was received here for Convictress and was the only one we had then.

We this year caused the great Altar to be new painted; and got pictures for the upper part of the church.

This year the Lady Mary Caryll,[2] niece to our Reverende Mother, gave us a 100 pound Sterlin for the foundation of an Annual Solemn Mass for her Spouses soul.

By the death of Mrs Petit, sister to our Sister Bedingfelds, we had 65 pound Sterlin, part of which was laid out for the Altar in the noviship.

And Mrs Vaughan left her sisters here a legacy of forty pounds Sterlin, but seven of it was spent in geting it.

The year 1719

On the 30 of January Sister Catherine Aspinal was clothed for a lay sister.[3]

On the 9th of february Sister Anna Maria Hyde made her holy profession.[4]

On the 31 of May Mrs Frances and Mrs Elisabeth Conyers, grand-children to Sir John Conyers of Strougton and sisters to Sister Alipia Conyers were **[p. 356]** received her for convictresses, together with Mrs Frances Wright, eldest daughter of Mr Wright the Goldsmith, and little niece to our late Reverende Mother Mary Wright.[5]

On the same day Sister Barbara Devery went from hence for England.[6]

[1] Elizabeth Willis, in religion Mary Xaveria (1730–35) BA222, musician. She returned in 1728.

[2] Daughter to the Earl of Seaforth and Lady Frances Herbert, and niece to the Prioress: see Herbert family tree.

[3] Catherine Aspinal (BA006).

[4] Anne Maria Hyde (BA116).

[5] Frances Conyers professed as Clementina (1724–41) BA062; her sister was Margaret Conyers, in religion Alipia (BA063). Their sister Elizabeth did not profess. Frances Wright left for Dunkirk on 29 August 1720; see **[p. 370]**.

[6] Ann Barbara Devery (BA072).

On the 6th of June Reverend father Slaughter, Rector of the English Colledge at Gant,[1] bless'd our new schoole, which our Reverende Mother has particularly recommend to St Joseph's protection and has caused the image of that great saint to be placed in the front of the house.

On the 8th of June it being then the feast of the most Blessed Sacrament,[2] our four convictresses enter'd their new house, it being sufficiently furnish'd for them, and our Reverende Mother received them there, and gave them her blessing.

On the 5th of July Sister Barbara Devery return'd from England, and brought with her Mrs Catherine and Mrs Ursula Chichester,[3] the two eldest daughters of Mr Chichester of Arlington in Devonshire, they were received for convictresses, and Mary Hilton[4] who also came at the same **[p. 357]** time, was received as a servant in tryal for a lay sister.

In this month several of our community got feavours and Agues, which were then very much not only in these countries but also in England and other places.

In August Sister Constantia de Rope[5] fell sick of an intermitting feavour, yet somtimes we were in hopes of her recovery till the 20th of the same month, she suddenly swooned away as she lay in her bed, and tho' she soon came out of this swoon yet from that time we had little hopes of her life; our Doctor affirming that she was much consumed by an inward feavour; this cause[d] her a continual long and painful time of suffring, which was the more sensible to her because she had so many years been favour'd with the blessing of a constant good health, and a little before she fell ill, she was saying how perfectly well she was, tho' past three score years old. What she most complain'd of was a continual sickness and thirst, yet she had great difficulty to drink, or take any thing, not finding any refreshment or solace by it; **[p. 358]** tho' all that could be thought of for that effect was offer'd her. She abandon'd her self entirely to the divine will either for life or death, and by many fervent acts united her painful thirst and all she suffer'd, to our Saviour's bitter death and passion, and as she had been particularly devoted to the Sacred heart of Jesus, and to our Blessed Lady, we confide that Jesus and Mary mercyfully disposed her for a happy eternity. What she suffer'd by the entire deprivation of all solace and refreshment from any thing she took, she humbly received

---

[1] Fr Edward Slaughter SJ (1655–1729), Rector of the English College, Ghent 1719–22. See Holt, p. 230; Foley, vol. 7:2, p. 715.

[2] The Feast of the Blessed Sacrament was Corpus Christi.

[3] Catharina Chichester, in religion Teresa Joseph (1724–69) BA052; Ursula Chichester, in religion Frances Xaveria, professed 10 July 1723 and died three days later, BA053.

[4] Daughter of Richard Hilton of Longford, Ireland. She took the first habit on 19 March 1720 and the name Mary Joseph **[p. 363]**. She left and professed later as a lay sister at the Poor Clares of Gravelines (1723), under the name Mary Bonaventure, and died there in 1736, GP153.

[5] Constantia De Rope (1681–1719) BA165.

as a merciful and favorable chastisement from the paternal hand of God, for having been too nice in her diet, and too solicitous in pleasing her palate. On the 24 of August she received her rights, and from that time lived a lingering, painful and dying life, continuing in her perfect senses, and expecting each moment would be her last, till the 10th of September when she fell into her Agony, and expired on the 11th of the same month between 3 and 4 a clock in the morning.

[p. 359] She was about 66 years of age, and just enter'd the 39 year of her holy profession. She was bury'd on the 12th of September. *Requiescat in pace*. Amen.

On the 3d of october Sister Teresa Cook departed this life in the 79 year of her age, and 36 of her holy profession.[1] She was one of the first that fell ill of the feavour, and by reason of her great age was apprehended to be in danger. So by our Doctor's appointment she received her holy *viaticum* on the 12 of August. Soon after the feavour left her, but she never recover'd her strength, remaining so weak and feeble that she could not help her self. She had always been of a very weak health, and the great charity of our comunity was very apparent in admitting her to be a lay sister; but her piety supply'd for her want of strength to perform the most hard and laborious works. She had been chosen by God's special providence to be a child of the true Catholick church, for tho' her Parents being hereticks she had the prejudice of that unhappy education, yet coming to the years of discretion, and having a good natural wit, the divine grace concurring, she was the more easily convinced of the errors of her **[p. 360]** false religion, and the better disposed to receive the good principles of solide vertue which she endeavour'd to improve, especially after her happy settlement in a religious state. She had a very good memory to relate what she had heard or read of vertue, which made her discourses very edifying and profitable, particularly to the younger Sisters, and some of them acknowledged they received great benefit by her pious advices and entertainments. Her great value and esteem for holy obedience particularly appear'd in her submission and respect to superiors, and also to all the religious, nevertheless she had often the sensible humiliation of finding less tenderness and compassion shew'd to her than to others, in her infirmities, because they were thought to proceed chiefly from lowness of spirit, which she had always been subject to, and not to foment the disease, less regard was had to her, but she being particularly devoted to our Saviour's passion, made her advantage of this and of all her sufferings by patience and submission to the divine will. Tho' from the time she first fell ill we had little hopes of her recovering, yet we **[p. 361]** did not apprehend her death so near, as to our surprise and sensible concern we found it; so that she had not the advantage of

[1] Teresa Cooke (1684–1719) BA064.

receiving her *viaticum* a second time tho' she had frequently communicated in time of her sickness, and her last communion was on the feast of St Michael, four days before her death. She expired in receiving the Sacrament of extream unction just as her eyes were touch'd with the holy oyles, about 8 a clock in the morning. She was bury'd on the 4th of october. *Requiescat in pace*. Amen.

On the 1st of november, the feast of All Saints, our Reverende dear Sister Ursula Babthorpe departed this life.[1] She was born in these countries, but her Parents were English of very ancient famillies, tho' by misfortunes reduced to such low circumstances that they had not [*blank*] sufficiency to maintain and settle their children; nevertheless God's special providence provided for each in turn the most honorable and happy settlement in the State of holy religion, and there is now none of the family left but one of the Brothers who is now an ancient father of the Society of Jesus, **[p. 362]** and a sister who is Supream Superior of an order in Germany call'd *l'Institute de Ste Marie*. Our comunity has always thought their charitable admittance of Sister Ursula Babthorpe very well recompensed in her person, she having proved a very serviceable member. The divine goodness had favour'd her with a very strong and healthy constitution which she employ'd with much zeal and fervour for the common good, particularly in the office of infirmarian. Her charity in helping the sick was fervent and laborious, as well as tender and compassionate to all that needed her assistance. The most humbling employments seem'd always the most agreeable to her, and she would often labour with the lay sister in the washes and other hard works. But about three years before her death she was much disenabled by several infirmities, in particular the Rheumatisme, Gout, and Dropsie. The last 15 months of her life she was entirely confined to a chamber in the infirmary, and for several months could not lye by reason of **[p. 363]** a cancerous humour that afflicted her particularly in her legs, by which she suffer'd continually with the violent pains of the sores and frequent incisions which the surgeon made in hopes of giving her remedy or ease. Nothing was omitted that could be thought of for her solace both spiritual and corporal. She frequently received the most Blessed Sacrament, and between the 20th of last March and the day of her death, she communicated three times by way of *viaticum*, and twice received the holy oyls. The last time she received her *viaticum* and the holy oyles was on the Eve of all Saints, and the next morning she expired about two a clock. Both living and dying she gave us great examples of courage, patience, and submission to the divine will, and we have reason to hope that by the pious use she

---

[1] Ursula Babthorpe (BA010). Her brother was Fr Albert Babthorpe SJ (1646–1720); see Holt, p. 23. Her sister was Anna Barbara Babthorpe, superior of the Institute of Mary in Munich 1683–97 and General Superior of the Institute 1697–1711, MW010.

made of her long and painful infirmities, she has had the advantage of a meritorious Purgatory before her death, and pass'd from that purgatory to the enjoyment of her divine Spouse, and to share in the glory of all the Saints. She was just enter'd into the 69 year of her age, and was in the 50th **[p. 364]** year of her holy Profession. She was bury'd on the 2d of november, and the same day in the afternoon we said the long dierge for her in the choir, which could not be said the day before because of the dierge we sung for their souls. *Requiescat in pace*. Amen.

Soon after her death Sister Agnes Bedingfeld was chosen Arcaria.[1]

On the 19 of november Lady Mary Herbert brought us Miss Mary Sackville.[2]

Towards the end of this month we were put to great confusion by a dutch Girl whom we had taken to look after the cow, and wash dishes. She had been ill for some time, and we very innocently gave her remedies which we hoped might do her good, but at last an old widow woman whom we kept for charity (and call'd Aunt Betty) discover'd that she was with child upon which we soon got her out of the Monastry, and three days after she was brought to bed of a Boy, she laid the child to a Man of ours whom we had dismissed the July before.

[p. 365] This year we received in Almns 31 florins: twenty of them were left us by Mr Clifton at his death; and the rest given us by Mrs Chafts for her Husband's soul.

The year 1720

On the 6th of January Sister Catherine Holland departed out of this world about nine a clock in the Morning.[3] She had experienced God's special grace and favorable providence in her conversion to the true faith, the history of which she has left written in her own hand, being engaged to do it by the express orders of her spiritual Director, and she has therein most humbly and sincerely express'd her grateful sentiments of the divine goodness, particularly for her conversion, and vocation to a religious State, in both she faithfully concurr'd with the divine grace, tho' being of a high spirit, and a quick wit, she had much to overcome in her nature; and the struggle between nature and grace was somtimes very apparent, twas also very edifying to see the victories **[p. 366]** which grace gain'd over her natural humour and inclinations. Her conversation was pleasant and diverting with her merry conceits jeasts; her genius to Poetry was also an innocent subject of diversion; but that which made more to her advantage was that she so well employ'd her pen as to

1 Agnes Bedingfield (BA016).

2 A convictress who left on 30 September 1724: see **[p. 405]**.

3 Catharine Holland (1664–1720) BA106.

perpetuate her pious memory in this community by several pious books and saints lives which she translated from french and dutch into English.

About four months before her death she had frequent ague fits, of which she recover'd so well between times that we often hoped the worst was past till her fits renew'd again, which were very severe, and tho' her courage always surpass'd the strength of her little body; yet her weakness and great age assaulted by an intermitting feavour could no longer resist. She was four days confined to her bed, and on Epiphany Eve received the last Sacraments with great devotion and submission to the divine will. She had her perfect senses to the **[p. 367]** last moment being heard to pronounce the Sacred name of Jesus with her dying breath. She was 85 years of age, and in the 56 year of her holy profession. She was bury'd on the 8th of January. *Requiescat in pace*. Amen.

On the 12th of January Lady Charlot Herbert, youngest daughter to the Duke of Powis, and niece to our Reverende Mother, came hither from Paris, and was received into our inclosure being to remain here till the Duke gave orders for her going into England.[1]

On the 3d of february Sister Catherine Aspinal made her holy Profession.[2] Our Reverend father confessor perform'd the ceremonies, the ArchPriest being hinder'd that day.

On the 11th of february Lady Charlot Herbert went from hence under Sister Barbara Devery's care,[3] in order to go to England, but being on the sea they were assaulted by a furious storm, which lasted for the space of 23 hours; and they were in eminent danger of being cast away. **[p. 368]** Nevertheless by the particular conduct of the divine providence they landed safe at Ostende, and return'd back to us on the 14 of february, and Lady Charlot was again received into our inclosure, and having been much frighten'd with her danger her Ladyship resolved not to venture again till a more favorable time and season.

On the 19 of March Mary Hilton received the Schollars kerchief, and the name of Mary Joseph.[4]

On the 5th of April our convent Sisters met for the election of a Subprioress and Procuratrix. Sister Clare Saunderson was chosen Subprioress, and Sister Hellen Andrews was discharged of the office of Subprioress, and made Procuratrix.[5]

On the 28 of April Sister Barbara Devery parted from hence again with Lady Charlot Herbert in order to conduct her Ladyship to England.

---

[1] Lady Charlotte Herbert was the daughter of William Herbert, 2nd Marquess of Powis and Mary Preston. Charlotte married Edward Williams in 1732.

[2] Catherine Aspinal (BA006).

[3] Ann Barbara Devery (BA072).

[4] Mary Hilton; see **[p. 356]**.

[5] Clare Saunderson (BA172); Helen Andrews (BA004).

On the 23 of June Sister Barbara return'd out of England, and brought with her Mrs Severn,[1] who having a mind to be religious, but not being fully determin'd as to the place (being a new convert), our Reverende Mother let her be within **[p. 369]** the enclosure, that she might a little see the manner of Religious people, and be the better able to make her resolution.

On the same day Mrs Faith Barlow, Daughter to the late Sir George Barlow, came out of England and was received here for a convictress. Her Uncle Mr Thomas Henage sent her to us.[2]

On the 15 of July we took Dorothy Comby for a servant in the Schoole: she was of English Parents, but had been brought up in these countries.

On the 20 of July we admitted Anne Tremaine (a flemin) for a servant in order to be a lay sister.[3] She had lived with us some time before, and from that time constantly persevered in her desire to settle here.

On the 21 of July Mrs Severn went from us to the English Benedictin Dames at Gandt, where she desired to settle, so our Reverende Mother sent Sister Barbara to conduct her tither.[4]

On the 12 of August Mrs Clark, a Scotch gentlewoman, was sent hither by Lady Mary Herbert; she had been recommended to her Ladyship's charity, as a person well enclined to embrace the **[p. 370]** holy Catholic faith, and she was received into our inclosure, and had a chamber in our convict.

Mr Edward Blount and his Lady designing to return for England, Miss Ann' Blount was by her own desire placed in a flemish Monastry at Antwerp, that she might be perfected in her musick; and Miss Hariot, the youngest sister, was a second time received here for convictress.[5] She re-enter'd our Monastry on 21 of August, together with her two elder sisters who were to stay here till they went with their Parents into England.

On the 29 of August Mrs Frances Wright by her Parents orders, went from us to the English Benedictin Dames at Dunkirk where she had two Aunts who desired to have her with them.[6]

On the 30 of August Mr Blount and his Lady began their journey for England, and their two eldest daughters went from hence to go with them.

---

1 Rebecca Severn left Bruges and professed as a choir nun at the Benedictines, Ghent in 1723, GB203.

2 Sir George Barlow (d. 1726), 2nd Baronet of Slebetch, Pembrokeshire, MP married Winifred Heneage, daughter of George Heneage of Hainton: see Stirnet.com family tree, Barlow 01.

3 Ann Tremaine, in religion Ann Teresa (1722–29) BA205.

4 Ann Barbara Devery (BA072).

5 Edward and Anne Blount, with two daughters, Mary and Henrietta, had first arrived in 1716. Their daughter Ann had arrived separately in 1713. None of them professed at Nazareth. See also **[pp. 304, 324, 332, 333]**.

6 The events here are not clear; there was a Frances Wright as a lay sister at Dunkirk, but she died in 1673 at the Ypres convent. Further family research is needed for confirmation.

On the 25 of September Mrs Catherine Salkild arrived here from England. She being desirous to settle in religion and was recommend to Lady Mary Herbert's charity; who order'd her to come here, and promised to pay her portion if she persevered.[1]

[p. 371] On the 25 of September Mrs Clark went from us, there being no hopes then, of her conversion which she seem'd very averse to; and even was unwilling to be inform'd of the principles of our holy religion, tho' due care was taken to bring her to it, especially in a dangerous fit of sickness, which she had but newly recover'd when she went away: during the time of it she declared she would live and dye in her own perswasion, tho' she seem'd to know but little of any religion, and could not oppose any reasonable Arguments against those which were proposed to her. But we afterwards heard that she being return'd into france, was then converted.

On the 19 of october, Sister Clare Johnson, one of our lay Sisters, departed this life in the 71 year of her age and 37 of her holy Profession.[2] She was a native of Ostende, and proved a very serviceable member in our community, expressing in all occasions **[p. 372]** a great zeal for the common profit, which she endeavour'd to advance by her continual labours, particularly in the charge of Market Sister, which she had for about 27 years; and notwithstanding the great fatigue of that employment she also did much service within doors, and was even solicitous to seek occasions where her help was most necessary, saying that she did not do her duty by doing only what she was order'd to do, if there was any thing undone, that her assistance could any ways forward or advance. She was not only laborious, but very devout especially to our Saviour's Passion, and if by reason of her continual business she forgot a communicating day (as it somtimes happen'd when they were not holydays by the church) she would weep and complain that no body had put her in mind of it. She had several times had the misfortune of accidental falls, and suffer'd much by the prejudice she received by them, but as well in these occasions as in her other infirmities, her patience was very edifying, for she would never complain or speak **[p. 373]** of what she suffer'd as long as she was able to go about, or could do any thing. She had escaped many accidents wherein the danger of death was apprehended, and God's special providence appear'd most particularly in the last which happen'd on the 15 of this month. She having some business for the Monastry, at one of our customer's in Town, went to the house and just as she was opening the door a Dog surprised and frighten'd her by sudden and furious barking at her; she started back, and fell from the threshold of the

[1] Catherine Salkeld was the daughter of Thomas Salkeld of Whitehall, Cumberland; the connection with Lucy Herbert has still to be established. See WWTN website and **[pp. 376–7]**.

[2] Clare Johnson (1683–1720) BA124.

door upon the stones in the street which wounded her head very much. A surgeon of our acquaintance chanced at the same time to pass that way, and seeing her fall, he by the help of others took her up, at the first sight believing her to be quite dead, but finding her alive, they carry'd her into the house, and the same surgeon immediately dress'd her wounded head, not apprending the wound to be mortal, and she found her self so well recover'd that she ventured to go further, and dispatch'd all her business before she came home, nay when she was come home she said nothing **[p. 374]** of the accident till we heard it from others: soon after she fell into a feavour, yet for some time our surgeon and the other with whom he consulted had hopes of her recovery, but at last her feavour was so great that it hinder'd the effects of their remedies, and prevented what they further designed. She received the last Sacraments in her perfect senses, after which she had but short intervales of sense and dyed on a Saturday about one a clock in the afternoon. We endeavour'd to conceal her death because we heard that the Magistrates thought themselves obliged to examine accidental deaths, and to require a certain fine for the King when such things happen'd; so tho' our Bishop had disputed the case with them, and would not allow that they had any thing to do with religious people, yet they insisted in the matter; and notwithstanding our precaution to keep Sister Clare's death secret, the Magistrate heard of it and some of them came to our Superior and told her that they had heard of Sister Clare's accidental death, and that they desired to come in to see the body: her Reverence answer that she was dead of feavour which she might have had if she had had no fall, and that as to **[p. 375]** their entering our enclosure twould be an honour to us, but that it was not in her power to let them in without the Bishop's leave; upon this they parted very civilly. This was on the 20th of October, and on the same day in the Evening we bury'd her, both to prevent their further solicitation, and because her head and face were so swell'd and disfigured that she could not be exposed after her death, nor be well kept longer above ground. We inform'd my Lord Bishop[1] of all that had pass'd, and his Lordship said we had done very well to bury her and bid us not fear the Magistrates for that the cause was his and not ours.

On the 21 we sung high Mass for her and perform'd the usual ceremonies, during which the Magistrate came again, and having call'd for our Superior, they desired to see the corps, which they supposed we were then burying. Her Reverence told them that we had bury'd her the Evening before, because she having dyed of a feavour we could not well keep her longer above ground, at which they seem'd dissatisfied, and ask'd her if she did not know the **[p. 376]** King's orders, to which her Reverence prudently reply'd that we were ignorant of such things, and

---

[1] The Bishop of Bruges in 1720 was Hendrik Jozef van Susteren, Bishop 1716–42.

only thought it our duty to know our Rules and institutions; they could not disapprove so religious an answer, nor compass the end they came for, so they civily took leave, and afterwards spoke very advantagiously of our Superior's prudence and discretion. *Requiescat in pace*. Amen.

On the 4th of november we received for Convictress Mrs Elisabeth Caryll, daughter to Mr Phillip Caryll of North, and sister to our Sister Mary Anne Caryll.[1]

On the 12 of november Mrs Markham of Ollerton (Mother to Sister Catherina Markham) having a little before bury'd her spouse, she came for retirement to our Monastry and brought with her Mrs Mary Ursula Markham, her youngest daughter, and Miss Ann' Poulton, who were both received here for convictresses.[2] Mrs Markham and her maid, Mrs Catherine Train had chambers in our convict.

On the 20th of november Mrs Catherine Salkild received the first **[p. 377]** habit and took the name of Mary Bernard.[3]

On the first of december we received Mrs Elisabeth Lloyd[4] for a convictress. Her father was a captain, and being dead, his wife and children were in great distress, having had nothing to depend on but his office. Our Reverende Mother had great compassion of them and not only gave the Widow some present relief (who was of the Bedingfeld's family) but also promised her that if she could procure ten pound a year pension for her eldest Daughter, she should be educated amongst our convictresses; so Mrs Lloyd having found means to make her case known to the right noble Lady Petre of Ingerstone, her Ladyship promised to pay the pension for 4 years.[5]

On the 8th of December Ann' Tremain was admitted to the Schollar's kerchief, and she took for names Ann' Teresa.[6]

We this year received in Almns 200 florins, of which 50 was for the soul of Mrs Ann' Weston, 100 for Mr Williscot, and 50 from Mrs Powdrel.

---

1 Mary Ann Caryll (BA047). Her parents were Mr Philip Caryll of North, in Catherington, Hampshire, and his wife, Mary.

2 Mrs Markham was the mother of Anne Delphina Markham, in religion Christina (BA138), so this may be a misnaming. The younger daughter was Mary Ursula, who later married Benedict Conquest of Imham. She was probably Catherine née Constable, d. 1730, of Houghton, Yorks. The dates of death for two Thomas Markhams (father and son) have been variously given, Catherine's husband died c. 1720. See K. S. B. Keats-Rohan (ed.), *English Catholic Nuns in Exile, 1600–1800: A Biographical Register*, Prosopographia et Genealogica 15 (Oxford: Unit for Prosopographical Research, Linacre College, forthcoming 2017).

3 Catherine Salkeld left the convent in 1721 because Lady Mary Herbert was unable to fulfil her promise to pay her dowry because of her own financial problems; see also **[p. 383]**.

4 Elizabeth Lloyd, in religion Mary Joseph (1726–48) BA129, Cellarer in 1748.

5 Lady Petre of Ingatestone was Catherine Walmesley (1607–1785), widow of Robert Petre, 7th Baron Petre (d. 1713), widely known for her commitment to charitable causes.

6 Ann Tremaine, in religion Ann Teresa (BA205).

[p. 378]

The year 1721

On the 6th of January Mrs Catherine Caryll, sister to Sister Mary Ann Caryll, came to our Monastry. She had lived some time in a dutch Monastry at Poperingue where she had been very ill of a feavour, and being desirous to try if change of air would recover her quite; our Reverende Mother condescended to her request, and appointed her a chamber in our convict.[1]

On the 4th of March Sister Elisabeth Delphina Weston departed this life in the 42 year of her age, and 22 of her holy Profession.[2] She had been about 16 years a continual sufferer by a Rheumatisme and Gout settled in her limbs, for tho' she was somthing better by the Bathes yet she never perfectly recover'd her limbs, and they afterwards grew worse, so that she had a continual exercise of patience, and her constant practice of that vertue, was admirable; as was her fervour to comply with all regular observances, from which she was never willing to be dispensed, saying that she could never hope to be cured whatever relaxations she took, and therefore she desired to do her duties, as far as she was able; which she **[p. 379]** really did, and somtimes more: for being of a timorous tender conscience, our Reverende Mother often yielded to her pious importunities for fear of giving her any uneasiness in mind, and because it was evident that her whole delight was in the observance of religious discipline, and particularly in being before the Blessed Sacrament, where she spent many hours besides the Regular times, tho' she was forced to sit in her seat, not being able to kneel so long.

She had a swelling or wen upon her knee, which growing still bigger and bigger was at last so extreamly troubelsome that she desired leave to consult our surgeon about it, who having seen it said that he could cut it if she was willing. She ask'd him how long he thought he should be in curing it; and he answer'd about three weeks: this was great encouragment, so with our Reverende Mother's leave, the day was appointed and the surgeon and his two men came, and she was seated in her bed, where he cut the wen open, and took out a great bag like a crop, of a turkey. She bore all the pain of this operation with so **[p. 380]** great patience that the surgeons were amaz'd at it. When they left her she was not distemper'd but soon after an inflamation fell into the smal of the same leg, and she fell into a violent feavour which put her quite from her self, then she got several mortifications in her body and leg for which she was frequently cut and slash'd by the surgeon. Several times she had convulsions and was thought to be in her Agony, and it was a daily subject of admiration both to Doctor and Surgeon that she still lived. In this extremity she

---

[1] Catherine Caryll was sister to Mary Ann and Elizabeth Caryll: see above **[pp. 241, 289]**.

[2] Elizabeth Delphina Weston (1699–1721) BA216.

continued many weeks without any hopes of recovery, and she had the advantage of communicating more than once by way of *viaticum*, when she was come to her self. Our Reverende Mother and whole comunity were particularly kind to her and solicitous for her, and her Reverence gave her leave, and even advised her to make a vow that if it pleased God to recover her, she would communicate on the 25 of each month as long as she lived (if Superiors gave leave) and that in honour of the infant Jesus; and also that she would fast on the eve, and comunicate on the feast of St Francis Xaverius.[1] This obligation she was very willing to accept of, and as soon **[p. 381]** as she had made her vow she began to recover by degrees, and came at last to be much in the same way she had been some years before her knee was cut. Then she again apply'd her self to her duties with her former fervour tho' still with much pain and difficulty by reason of her gouty limbs and a sore foot which the surgeon could not heal. Thus she lived eight years more, and tho' her fingers were stiff yet she did a great deal of work for the common, particularly the Tapistry hanging for the church, in which she had the largest share; and for the last three years of her life she was Mistress of the novices, but ever since last Easter she has been constantly confined to the infirmary, and on the 3d of last September she received the rights of the church, after which tho' she continued alive yet we had never any hopes of her recovery, always in pain, and not able to remain long in one posture, nor to help her self; so that she had two or three to turn her in her bed, or to move her in her chair, for even to the last day of her life she was daily taken out of her bed, and set in a chair, tho' the least motion increased her pains, and all her former **[p. 382]** sore were renew'd again; in this extremity she used to say that she had still three natural joys, to wit, *she was glad when she was got up, she was glad when she was put in bed again, and she was glad of a good pot of beer*, for she had a continual distemper, and towards the last was swell'd like a dropsie: but Almighty God was pleased to give her for solide comfort, peace of mind, and conformity to his will; for tho' she had always been chearful, yet she was naturally anxious, and fearful of death, but in this sickness she was in a quiet calme abandoning her self entirely to the divine will by a perfect conformity, and saying that she was willing to suffer in this manner even till the day of Judgment if it was most pleasing to God. Her pious aspirations were fervent and frequent, and she had a great sense of gratitude to our Reverende Mother and the community for all their care of her, and kindness to her. On the 25 of february she again received the last Sacraments and tho' she was in a great extremity of weakness, she desired to have all the prayers read to her which she used to say in honour of the **[p. 383]** infant Jesus, attending to them with

---

[1] The Feast of St Francis Xavier is celebrated on 3 December.

great devotion. On the first tuesday in lent, which was just eight days after she had received the rights, she communicated again by way of *viaticum*; and on the same day just as the clock struck three in the afternoon she peaceably render'd her dear soul into the hands of her creator. The next day (the 5th of March) we celebrated the feast of all the saints of our order, and we have more than ordinary reason to hope that we kept her feast with the rest of that blessed company. She was bury'd on the 6th of March. *Requiescat in pace.* Amen.

On the 10 of March Mrs Catherine Caryll went from us to a dutch Monastry at Gandt, being advised to change air for the cure of her Ague.

On the 13 of March Sister Mary Joseph Hilton was clothed for a lay sister.[1]

On the 27 of April our Schollar Sister Mary Bernard Salkild began her journey for England; the unhappy turn of fortune have disenabled Lady Mary Herbert from complying with her charitable inclinations in her favour **[p. 384]** and Mrs Elisabeth Caryll went with her into England.[2]

On the 31 of March Mrs Elisabeth Clough,[3] sister to Mr Clough of Minttown, and Mrs Frances Berrington,[4] Daughter of Mr Berrington of Mote Hall, were received her for convictresses; the first of them is niece to our Sister Frances Clough, and the other her cousine Germain's daughter.

On the 8th of July Sister Susan Reynoldson celebrated her whole Jubilee, the ceremonies were perform'd by the Archpriest in our choir; it was a year the 25 of last June from the time she compleated the fifty year of her Profession.[5]

In the evening of the same day Mrs Elisabeth Browne, sister to the Lord Mountague, arrived here and was received as a boarder within our enclosure, for she is a benedictin Dame profess'd in a french Monastry at Roan [Rouen], but that Monastry being reduced to extream poverty, her relations obtain'd leave of the Archbishop of Roan that she might leave that house and she being a near relation to our Reverende Mother, earnestly desired to **[p. 385]** live for some time (at least) under her

[1] Mary Joseph Hilton left the following year; see **[p. 386]**.
[2] See **[pp. 376–7]**.
[3] Elizabeth Clough, in religion Ursula (1724–89) BA058. Her mother was Elizabeth Berrington of Winsley Hall, Herefordshire.
[4] Frances Berrington of Moat Hall, Shropshire, took the first habit as a choir nun and the name Mary Xaveria on 17 June 1724 (**[p. 401]**), but left for the Flemish monastery of Spermalie, in Bruges, before finally professing at the Poor Clares, Gravelines (1726–47) GP033.
[5] Susan Reynoldson (1670–1730) BA161.

obedience which her Reverence condescended to, and appointed her a cell in the Dormitory.[1]

On the 12 of August Miss Harriot Blount went from hence to the Ursulines at Antwerp, where her sister Mrs Ann' Blount was soon to begin her noviship.[2]

On the 9th of october Mrs Dorothy Salvin, niece to the Lord Mountague of Cowdrey, and daughter to Mr Salvin of Tudo, came here to see her Aunt (the aforesaid Dame Browne) before she went to be a convictress at the English Dames at Gandt.[3] But her Aunt took the freedome to retain her here, and by my Lord Mountague's means got Mr Salvin's leave that we might have her for convictress; so we are entirely obliged to that Reverende Dame for her dear niece, since if she had not procured her for us, we should not have been so bold as to have offer'd at it, she being designed for another place.

On the 20th of october the Lady Carrington came to us again, and **[p. 386]** lodged within our enclosure where her Ladyship furnish'd a chamber for her self.[4]

On the 18 of november Sister Ann' Teresa Tremain was cloth'd for a lay sister.[5]

On the 30 of December, the Lady Carrington went from hence to france, and took Dorothy Comby with her for a servant.

We this year received in Almns 50 florins for the soul of Mrs Powdrel, Sister Cannyng's sister.

The year 1722

On the first of April our novice, Sister Mary Joseph Hilton went from us to the English poor Clares at Gravelin.[6] Her first vocation was to that holy order, but they having then their full number of Sisters, could not admitt of her; and after she had past her tryal and noviship here, tho' she was very willing to make her profession yet upon due examination she sincerely confess'd that her earnest desire was still to be at Gravelin, if

---

[1] Born in 1686, Elizabeth Browne was the daughter of Henry, 5th Viscount Montagu. She had a peripatetic convent career: she professed as a Benedictine in a French convent in Rouen, taking the name Pelagia. As a relative of Prioress Herbert she came to Bruges, but failed to settle. In 1724 she obtained permission to go to Pontoise, where she remained until her death in 1745, OB014.

[2] The Ursulines at Antwerp were a local foundation which had established a well-known school for girls.

[3] Dorothy Salvin, in religion Mary Baptist (1728–40) BA170. The emphasis here on the recommendation of Nazareth as the destination for the candidate shows the importance of connections and networks to maintain a flow of suitable candidates to sustain membership over the long term.

[4] Lady Carrington was the sister of Prioress Herbert. See **[pp. 212, 83, 296]**.

[5] Ann Tremaine, in religion Ann Teresa (BA205).

[6] She professed at Gravelines as Mary Bonaventure (GP153).

there was any possibility that she **[p. 387]** could be admitted there. Our Superior understanding this found means to procure her admittance into that holy community.

On the 12 of May, Miss Mary Montack (one of this town) was received here for a convictress.

On the 2d of June the Lady Mountague (sister to our Reverende Mother) came hither with her two women, and they were lodged within our enclosure.

On the 27 of June a devote[1] call'd Juffrouw Catline, was taken into our enclosure for some months, to teach and work embrodery.

On the 7th of July Mrs Mary and Mrs Frances Huddlestone were received her[e] for convictresses. They are daughters to Mr Huddlestone of Sauson and nieces to Sister Angela and Sister Latitia Huddlestone.[2]

On the ninth of July Mrs Catherine Chichester and Mrs Elisabeth Clough were admitted to the first habit: the first of them to the name of Teresa Joseph, and the other that of Ursula.[3]

On the 10 of July, Sister Mary Charleton **[p. 388]** departed this life in the 60th year of her age, and 48 of her holy profession.[4] She was always esteem'd a woman of very good sense, but being of a high spirit and too active a temper, she somtimes overshot her self and gave exercise of patience to Superiors and others, nevertheless when she was sensible of a fault in this kind, she would very humbly ask pardon, and she was certainly a most agreeable person when in a right temper. For the greatest part of her life she suffer'd much by headackes and ill health, which was a great hindrance to her regular observance of order, and we may charitably conclude that the relaxations she admitted in her spiritual duties and the liberty she gave to her high spirit, we [*sic*] most excusable in the sight of God, than they seem'd to the eyes of many; since she had just reasons to fear that a more serious application, and greater restraint, might have endanger'd the loss of her senses, which misfortune had happen'd to several of her very near relations. But tho' an apprehension so well grounded, may be just and excusable in her, yet it is certainly more commendable to abandon **[p. 389]** our selves to the divine providence, and to keep faithfully to the duties of our State, then whatever God permitts will be sure to turn to our greater advantage, and eternal glory. In her last sickness she was for several months confined to our infirmary, suffering much by inward paines which were often very violent in which her patience was very edifying. Our Doctor gave her

---

1 Devote: see Glossary.

2 Mary Huddleston, in religion Mary Barbara (1725–57) BA114, musician; Frances Huddleston, in religion Mary Justina (1727–87) BA113, Novice Mistress. Their aunts in the convent were Angela Huddleston (BA112) and Laetitia Huddleston (BA111).

3 Catharina Chichester (BA052); Elizabeth Clough (BA058).

4 Mary Charlton (1674–1722) BA048.

several remedies but in reality he did not understand her disease, nor think her so ill as in effect she was, therefore he would somtimes make slight of it, and tell her she was in no danger but would recover if she had but more courage; this was very sensible to her, nevertheless she bore it very well, and the Doctor was at last convinced that her illness was no fancy. She received the last Sacraments, and by her frequent aspirations express'd her submission to the divine will, and seem'd to have her perfect senses to the last moment of her life, which was about a quarter after three in the afternoon on a friday. She was bury'd on the 12 of July. *Requiescat in pace*. Amen.

[p. 390] On the 15 of July the Lady Mountague went from hence to France.

On the 9th of August Mrs Faith Barlow began her journey for England.[1]

On the 19th of August Mrs Mary Markham and Mrs Ann' Poulton parted from hence to go to two different Monastries at Namurs, in order to be perfected in the french tongue.

On the 11th of november Miss Joanna Poulate, one of this Town, was received here for a convictress.

On the 22 of november Sister Ann' Teresa Tremaine was profess'd a lay sister.[2]

On the 23 of november Mrs Elisabeth Conyers began her journey for England.[3]

On the 23 of December Mrs Frances Conyers received the first habit and took the name of Clementina.[4]

This year our Reverende Superior caused a very profitable book to be printed for her community: her Reverence had collected her self from many good Authors. It contains several excellent methods for holy Mass, and pious **[p. 391]** practices for religious duties.[5] Most of the English Monastries were very desirous of them, and had several; but her Reverence could not spare so many as they desired for fear she should not have enough for her own Religious. Lady Teresa Throgmorton (niece to our Reverende Mother) presented her Reverence with 22 pound Sterlin for the printing of them.[6]

We had this year 50 florins in Almns for the soul of Mr Mannock.

---

[1] See above **[p. 369]**.

[2] Ann Teresa Tremaine (BA205).

[3] She had arrived at the convent with her sister, but decided not to continue.

[4] Frances Conyers (BA062).

[5] *Several excellent methods of hearing Mass* (Bruges: John De Cock, 1722); *A daily exercise and devotion for the gentlewomen pensioners* (Douai: M. Mairesse, 1712). These two books of devotion were republished together for the use of the school at the end of the eighteenth century: *Several Excellent Methods of hearing Mass ... collected together by the Right Honourable Lady Lucy Herbert of Powis, Superiour of the English Augustin Nuns, At Bruges* (Bruges: C. De Moor, 1790; reprinted 1816).

[6] Theresa Throckmorton, née Herbert: see Herbert family tree.

The year 1723

On the 18 of January Sister Teresa Joseph Chichester and Sister Ursula Clough were clothed.[1]

On the 9th of february Mrs Ursula Chichester received our first habit and took the names of Frances Xaveria.[2]

On the 7th of June Mary Ford came to us from England and was received as a servant in tryal for a lay sister.[3]

In June Sister Hellen Andrews was chosen Subprioress, Sister Ann' Markham Arcaria, and Sister Angela Huddlestone Procuratrix.[4]

On the 30th of the same month Miss **[p. 392]** Joanna Poulate return'd home to her Parents.

On the 9th of July Mrs Browne,[5] the Benedictin Dame went from us to the English Dames at Bruxelles, tho' her inclinations were to remain here, she having great esteem for our Reverende Mother, and a real kindness and esteem for our community, which she testified in all occasions; and left us her niece tho' she could not have the satisfaction of staying her self; for tho' her wit and good humour render'd her agreeable to all yet it being thought more conformable to her profession to live in a Monastry of her own order. She submitted to what the rigid zeal of some of our good people had privately promoted by geting the case represented to the Bishop according to the notions that zeal gave them.

My Lord Mountague her Brother paid thirty pound sterlin a year for her while she stay'd here; but then we were to find her in habit.

Sister Barbara Devery attended her to Bruxelles; and our Reverend father confessor[6] went with them as far as Gant, in hopes that the Air of that Town might contribute to his recovery; for from the April **[p. 393]** before, his Reverence had been very ill of several diseases at once being much enclined to a dropsic, a Lethargie, and an Asthma. On the fifth of May, by the Doctor's orders he had received the last sacraments by the hands of our Arch Priest, and he had also made his vows and Profession to die a member of the Society of Jesus, which vows were received by Reverend father Saltmarsh, Rector of the English colledge at Gandt who was then here.[7] After this his Reverence seem'd so much better that we began to have some hopes of his recovery, but it was much hinder'd by

---

1 Teresa Joseph Chichester (BA052); Ursula Clough (BA058).

2 Ursula Chichester (BA053).

3 Mary Ford, in religion Mary Bernard (1725–64) BA081.

4 Helen Andrews (BA004); Ann Mechtilda Markham (BA137); Angela Huddleston (BA112).

5 Elizabeth Browne, in religion Pelagia (1707 Bellefonds, Rouen–1745 Pontoise) OB014. See also **[pp. 384–5, 401–2]**.

6 Fr Augustine Poyntz (1679/80–1723), Confessor 1701–23. This account of his death suggests that he was admitted to the Society of Jesus on his deathbed: elsewhere it is questioned.

7 Fr Edward Saltmarsh, SJ (1656–1737), Rector of the English College, Ghent 1722–5; see Holt, pp. 218–19.

frequent little relapses; nevertheless he was well enough to undertake this journey; which our Reverende Mother the more willingly condescended to, being assured that no spiritual or corporal assistance would be wanting to him in that place, and her Reverence sent our man with him to take care of him.

On the 10th of July our young Schollar Sister Frances Xaveria Chichester, being ill of a violent feavour, received the last Sacraments.[1] She had but short intervals of sense, and in one of **[p. 394]** them she desired to make her vows which our Reverende Mother granted her; and she made them on the same day that she received her *Viaticum*. She was always a most pious innocent good child, and agreeable to all by her constant mild, even temper. In the short time of her tryal, she apply'd her self to learn and practice the duties and vertues of a religious State, so that we have good reason to hope she in a short time fulfilled God's merciful designes, and now enjoys him in eternal glory. She dyed on the 13 of July, in the 16th year of her age, and three days after she had made her vows, having been but six days ill. She was bury'd in our habit on the 14th. *Requiescat in pace*. Amen.

On the 13 of July Mrs Catherine Henique [Henick] one of this town, was received here for convictress.

Whilst we were singing the high Mass for the burying of Sister Frances Xaveria, the Doctor appointed our dear Sister Mary Xaveria the last Sacraments, which she received as soon as the funeral ceremonies were over, her immediate danger being apprehended **[p. 395]** by reason of her extream weakness, she having been about nine days ill of an intermitting feavour.[2] She was the youngest of five Sisters profess'd in this community, and we may affirm that in religion she never lost her primitive fervour, but still went on encreasing it to the last. She gave to solitude, silence and prayer all the turns she could lawfully get, and her exterior comportment at such times, manifested her interior recollection and serious attention; yet that she might not be taken notice of for being so long at her prayers, she would change her place, and go from the choir to the Chappel, and from the Chappel to the choir, especially on sundays and holy days when the time was her own, for otherways at the first signe to any duty of obedience, she went to it so readily and perform'd it so chearfully it was very edifying. Her mortification was constant and general, but especially in her diet, eating the veryest scraps she could find in the dishes, and pretending she liked them best, what she suffer'd by the cold in winter was very apparent, her hands being all swell'd **[p. 396(1)]** and the skin broken with chill-blanes, and when obedience obliged her to go to the fire, she would sit and scorch her self a little, and then go away. She

---

[1] Ursula Chichester, in religion Frances Xaveria (1723) BA053).

[2] Mary Xaveria Stanley (1711–23) BA185.

had from her infancy a weakness on one side from her hip downwards, which made her limp, yet she would never complain of any difficulty or pain in laborious exercises, but would always give great assurance they were easy to her. Her charity was so universal and obliging to each one, that none could judge it particular to any, and when any favour was ask'd of her, she express'd so great a contentment in the performance that she seem'd more obliged in doing the service, than the person could be who received it; this gave great freedome to all, to have recourse to her whenever her assistance was wanted in any kind: and when her charity had engaged her in the service of one so that she could not at the same time comply with the desires of another, she was not less obliging in the concern she express'd, desiring if it could be, that the business might be put off till she was at leisure; yet she would never **[p. 396(2)]** engage her self so as to omitt the least duty of obedience. Never was the most remiss religious so ingenious to seek occasions of relaxation as she was to excuse her self from it, even when judged most necessary for her by reason of her tender constitution, or real illness, and when she thought her sisters care of her prevailed with our superior to indulge her in any kind then (in their regard) it appear'd she had a high spirit, which otherways she so tamed by vertue that she rather seem'd of an even mild disposition. This want of submission in such cases, and too great fervour in concealing her illness, were the only failings which were observed in her; and in this her last sickness she particularly endeavour'd to make atonements for such faults by an humble acknowledgment of them, beging our Reverende Mother's pardon for having so often opposed her will by her wilfulness (as she term'd it), and earnestly desiring her Reverence to manifest her frailties and even vilifie her to the whole comunity, that their charity might be the more moved to pray for her. It was surprising to see how quiet and still she lay, even in the **[p. 397]** very height of her feavour, keeping constantly in the same posture, and complaining of nothing, but by her sweet and chearful countenance expressing the interior peace she enjoy'd, tho' she had the mortification of being very deaf in this sickness, so that she could not have the comfort of perfectly hearing the good things which were said or read to her. She had her other senses to the last moment of her life, and expired on the 20th of July about eight a clock in the morning, being in the 33 year of her age, and 13th of her holy profession. She was bury'd on the 21th [*sic*]. *Requiescat in pace*. Amen.

On the 20th of July Mrs Markham with her priest Mr Horton, and her servant Mrs Catherine Fraine, went from hence to live some time at Lille.[1]

[1] Possibly Robert Edward Houghton OSB (d. 1751), professed 1710, ordained 1720; see Bellenger, p. 73.

On the 2d of August Sister Clementine Conyers was clothed.[1]

On the 12th of August Mr Pointz our confessor, departed this life at Gand in the English College. He was in the 45 year of his age, had been about 18 years Priest and 16, our confessor. On the 13th, instant as **[p. 398]** soon as we had the news of his death, we rang our Bell and said the recommendations for him all together in the choir. On the 16 we said the long dierge for him and the funeral ceremonies were perform'd for him here by our Arch Priest, with a herse and the same Solemnity as if he had been bury'd here. And we rang 3 hours for him.

His Reverence's death was a great loss to us, for he was a worthy good man, very learned, and orthodox in his doctrine, yet he had an humble conceit of himself and was ready to submitt to the learned when reason or cause required it. He was very nice in point of charity, and would never say, or countenance any thing to the prejudice of others; and tho' he was naturaly a little hot, yet by his vertue and discretion, he overcame himself, and for the generality gave satisfaction to all. His charity to the poor was constant and generous, relieving many with money, and not suffering his clothes to be much mended for himself, saying when they grew old, they belong'd to the poor, to whom he gave them, as a due; yet he would havc his shoes mended, before he gave them away, that the poor might have the greater **[p. 399]** benefit by them. He edified us particularly in one occasion, for when as we said before, Sister Clare Johnson was brought home in a coach after one of her falls, she not being able to set her foot to the ground, we thought to make our man carry her from the coach to the infirmary, but he not being tall enough to carry her easily, Mr. Pointz like the good Paster, carry'd her cleaverly upon his back to our sickhouse, and in all occasions he truly deserved that title, so that we have reason to hope he now enjoys the reward of his labours and fidelity.[2]

He dyed of the infirmities he carry'd with him to Gandt, where they so encreased upon him, that he was not able to return hither, tho' he much desired it, and by letters express'd great gratitude, and affection for our community, most humbly beging pardon if in any thing he had given us occasion of offence. He had made his will some time before, and left us three score pound Sterlin for an Annual Mass. *Requiescat in pace*. Amen.

On the 25 of August we received Mrs Dorothy Reynolds for a convictress.

[p. 400] On the 26 of August Mrs Yallop (under the name of Edwards) was received here as a boarder within our enclosure.

On the 12 of September Mary Ford was admitted to the Schollar's kerchief in order to be a lay sister. She took the name of Mary Bernard.[3]

---

[1] Clementina Conyers (BA062).

[2] Clare Johnson (BA124).

[3] Mary Ford, in religion Mary Bernard (BA081).

On the 12 of november Mrs Montock went from us to her friends.

On the 20 of november Mr Caryll Gerard, son to Mr Thomas Gerard of Highfield, arrived here from Rome, he being a Roman Priest was recommended to us by father Sabran, for a Confessor.[1] And on the 25 of the same month he was examin'd and approved.

We this year received in Almnes 107 florins, 60 for the soul of Mrs Gerard and 21 for the soul of Canon Egleson.

The year 1724

On the 9th of February Mrs Yallop went from hence.

Ou the 5th of March Mrs Mary Huddlestone was admitted to our first habit, and took the name of Mary Barbara.[2]

[p. 401] On the 20 of March Catherine Simner (a Lancashire young woman) was received here for convictress; on the same day Isabella Vendo and Ann' formby (who came with her) were received as servants in order to be lay sisters.[3]

On the 18 of April Sister Teresa Joseph Chichester, and Sister Ursula Clough, made their holy profession.[4]

On the 5 of May Mrs Ann' Sykes, sister to our Sister Mary Michael arrived here from England, and being desirous to settle amongst us, she received our first habit on the 24 of the same month, and took the name of Ann' Augustine.[5]

On the 30 of May Elisabeth Bambridge[6] was received here for a servant.

On the 17 of June Mrs Berrington and Mrs Lloyd were admitted to our first habit. The first took the name of Mary Xaveria, and the other that of Mary Joseph.[7]

On the 22d of June Miss Henique return'd home.

On the 13 of July Mrs Browne, the Benedictin Dame return'd to us again, she being of a very tender weak constitution, and always used to good fires in winter, was not able to pass without **[p. 402]** not to make use of the stoves; and the Dames at Bruxelles having no common fire, not being willing to let her have one in particular (tho' her brother my

---

[1] Fr Caryl Gerard alias Wright (1695–1779). He trained at the Venerable English College, Rome and arrived intending to stay 'a year or two' but remained 56 years; Anstruther 4, p. 110. Fr Louis Sabran SJ (d. 1732) acted as Spiritual Director in the 1690s; see Holt, p. 217.

[2] Mary Huddleston, in religion Mary Barbara (BA114).

[3] Catherine Simner, in religion Frances Xaveria, lay sister (1726–62) BA174; Isabella Vendow, in religion Mary Joachim, lay sister (1726–45) BA210; Ann Formby, in religion Ann Clare, lay sister (1726–58) BA082.

[4] Teresa Joseph Chichester (BA052); Ursula Clough (BA058).

[5] Anne Sykes (BA188).

[6] Elizabeth Bambridge, in religion Martina, lay sister (1729–74) BA011.

[7] Mary Xaveria Berrington decided to leave Nazareth: see **[p. 403]**. Elizabeth Lloyd, in religion Mary Joseph (BA129).

Lord Mountague would have paid for it) she desired to return hither;[1] so our Reverende Mother having a tender concern for her, got leave of our Bishop that she might be here for six weeks, till she could get her Brother's consent to return to her Monastry at Roan [Rouen], when the Superior and Religious most kindly invited her and would willingly have made her their Abbess, but she resolved not to accept of that honour, and would much rather have remain'd an inferior here for the rest of her life.

On the 23 of July we began to say every Sunday in honour of the most Blessed Trinity, the Benedictus Antiphon and prayer of that feast, as a soveriegne remedy to preserve us all from madness. It was a devotion recommended by a religious man at Bruxelles who affirm'd that by means thereof their convent had been preserved from such misfortunes for above three hundred years.

On the 2d of August Mrs Elisabeth **[p. 403]** Bedingfeld, niece to our Sister Agnes, was received here for convictress.

On the 7th of August Sister Clementina Conyers made her holy profession.[2]

On the 13 of August Sister Mary Bernard Ford was clothed.[3]

On the 17 of August Sister Mary Barbera Huddlestone was clothed.[4]

On the 29th of August Miss Alexander was received here for convictress.[5]

Our Schollar Sister Mary Xaveria Berrington after having with difficulty obtain'd leave of her father to settle here, and then worne our first habit near three months, remember'd that she had made a vow to be a poor clare, some time before she received that habit. Her youth must excuse so odd a proceeding, and tis thought her vow might easily have been dispensed, but since she seem'd desirous to comply with it, we had no reason to diswade her: therefore she again put on her soecular clothes, and being unwilling to return to our Convict we sent her to Spermaille, that she might remain there till her friends should give orders for her removal.[6]

On the 24 of September Sister **[p. 404]** Ann Joseph Andrews departed this life in the 71 year of her age, and near 50 of her holy Profession.[7] She was always of a quiet pious disposition, and from the begining of her religious life, most fervorously tended to perfection, being exact to a nicety in all that regarded the vows, rules and institutions, and most

---

[1] Elizabeth Browne, in religion Pelagia (OB014). See also **[pp. 384–5, 405]**.

[2] Clementina Conyers (BA062).

[3] Mary Bernard Ford (BA081).

[4] Mary Huddleston, in religion Mary Barbara (BA114).

[5] Anne Alexander left Bruges in 1726 and became a Benedictine in Ghent under the name Romana (1728–90) GB002.

[6] Spermalie: see Appendix 1. Mary Xaveria (in baptism Frances) Berrington eventually professed as Clare Frances at Gravelines (1726–47) GP033. She had arrived at the school in 1721; see **[pp. 384, 401]**.

[7] Ann Joseph Andrews (1675–1724) BA003.

humble, charitable, and patient; so that we may justly hope she in her first 25 years attain'd to an eminent degree of sanctity, when by the inscrutable judgment of Almighty God, he was pleased to deprive her of her senses for the rest of her life; nevertheless her raving was all pious, and she was often judged capable of the Sacraments, and when she was not she was continually overcoming her self in the frequent occasions her fancy gave her. Not long before her last sickness, her sister who was then our Subprioress, fell dangerously ill, so that she received all her rights, and we had no hopes of her, this being told to Sister Joseph, she answer'd that her sister would not die then, for she her self was to die first; this we then look'd upon as raving, but in effect it proved true, for soon after **[p. 405]** she got a feavour and dyed when her sister was just upon recovery; but she did not come to her self before she dyed, so only received the extream unction, nevertheless we doubt not but is a most happy soul. She departed between 10 and 11 at night, and was bury'd on the 26. *Requiescat in pace*. Amen.

My Lord Mountague being determined not to consent to his sister's returning to her own Monastry at Roan,[1] chusing rather to maintain her in an English Monastry than in a french one; his Lordship got leave of the Arch Bishop of Roan that she might go to the English Benedictines at Pontoise where she was accepted of; so she having been here above the six weeks which our Bishop at first granted her (because Sister Barbera Devery fell sick, who was to go with her into france) our Reverende Mother send Sister Margarite Linny to attend her, and at the same time Mrs Sackville, one of our convictresses went into France to her friends.[2] They began their journey on the 30 of September.

On the 9th of october Mrs Berrington went to the English poor Clares at Gravelin, with her Parents consent.[3]

[p. 406] On the 21 of november Catherine Simner, Isabella Vendo and Ann' formby were admitted to the Schollar's kerchief in order to begin their tryal for lay sisters. The first is called Sister Frances Xaveria, the 2d Sister Mary Joachim, and the 3d Sister Anne Clare.[4]

On 31 of December Sister Elisabeth Sales, a lay sister, departed this life in the 42 year of her age, and 12 of her holy Profession.[5] She was pious and good humour'd being ever willing to oblige the religious when it lay in her power, which made her be generaly beloved: and tho' she had her little failings, yet she did us very good service, particularly in

---

[1] For the negotiations surrounding Elizabeth Browne, in religion Pelagia (OB014) see **[pp. 384, 385, 401–2]**.

[2] Margaret Linny (BA128).

[3] Frances Berrington professed at the Poor Clares, Gravelines in 1724; see above **[pp. 401, 403]**.

[4] Catherine Simner (BA174); Isabella Vendow (BA210); Ann Formby (BA082).

[5] Elizabeth Sales (1713–24) BA169.

the employ of cook which she perform'd very well, and in that regard we have particular reason to regret the loss of her, it being a talent so rare among our Sisters.

She had been ill for some time before her death, tho' we did not apprehend it to be any great matter; and she continued to do her work, till she was suddenly seized with a violent pain in her leg, which being accompanied with a feavour soon brought her to her end. She not only **[p. 407]** resigned to death, but even rejoyced at the news of it, and in her pious preparation for the same, she gave more marks of solide judgment than ever she had shewn in her life before. She received all her rights, and dyed between one and two a clock in the afternoon. She was bury'd on the 2d of January 1725. *Requiescat in pace*. Amen.

We this year received in Almns 76 florins, to wit, 26 for the soul of Mr Mannock, and 50 for the soul of Mr Chichester.

The year 1725

On the 11th of January, Mr Sykes, father to our two Sister Sykes, dyed at the House over against our Gate; he had received all the rights of our holy Mother the Church, and was we hope well disposed for a happy death.[1] We immediately said the commendations for him in our choir; and the next day, we sung Solemn Mass, as we do for all the fathers and Mothers of our religious, if they die after the Profession, and before the death of their children. He was bury'd in the Carmes church on the 14 instant. *Requiescat in pace*. Amen.

On the 30 of January, Sister Ann' **[p. 408]** Augustine Sykes, and Sister Mary Joseph Lloyd were clothed.[2]

On the 20 of March we received a french gentlewoman for convictress and some days after she went away again, finding she could not confine her self to the orders of a Schoole.

On the 17 of April Mrs Dorothy Reynolds went from hence for England.

On the 12 of July the Lady Mountague (sister to our Reverende Mother), and Lady Ann' Maxwell, her niece, with Mrs de la haye, Lady Mountague's woman, came hither from france and lodg'd within our enclosure.[3]

On the 7th of August Sister Frances Xaveria Simner, Sister Mary Joachim Vendo, and Sister Ann' Clare formby were clothed.[4]

On the 18th of August Sister Agnes Bedingfeld departed this life in the 56 year of her age and 38 of her holy Profession.[5] She was a woman

1 William Sykes: father of Mary Michael Sykes (BA189) and Anne Augustine Sykes (BA188); see **[p. 235]**.

2 Anne Augustine Sykes (BA188); Mary Joseph Lloyd (BA129).

3 See Herbert family tree.

4 Frances Xaveria Simner (BA174); Mary Joachim Vendow (BA210); Ann Clare Formby (BA082).

5 Agnes Bedingfield (1687–1725) BA016.

of good sense, very virtuous and regular, and tho' naturally she was apt to resent any thing that seem'd less kind or considerate **[p. 409]** of her than of others (as was discovered by some writings of her reviews and exercises which were accidentally seen) yet she never complain'd or desired particulars, tho' she frequently saw them given to her neighbours. She had for many years before her death been almost blind, and tho' that might reasonably have excused her from the divine office; yet her fervour was so great, that she learned by heart most of the proper Psalms, and got the proper Responsaries writen in a large print hand, so that she generally assisted at the choir, or could say her office with another (or in Summer by her self) when she was to sleep. Once there came a famous oculist to this Town whilst her eyes were so very bad, and with our Reverende Mother's approbation, she consulted him about them: he having seen them undertook to couch them, giving great hopes that she would recover her sight. She with great courage bore the painful operation, and saw better as soon as it was over: then the oculist order'd she should for five days be kept blindfold least too much light at first, might hinder the perfect cure; but when she **[p. 410]** was unblinded she saw no better than she did before her eyes were couch'd; this was a hard tryal, nevertheless she bore it with a chearful resignation to the divine will. Many months before her death she had been confined to the infirmary by violent pains like the stone, of which she used to have fits somtimes, but this fit never entirely pass'd nor did she find any benefit by the remedies she used; at last she fell into convulsions, upon which the Doctor appointed her the rights of the holy church. She received the extream unction in one of those convulsions, and being come perfectly to her self again, she with great devotion received her *viaticum*, and most peaceably expected her last hour which was some days after, about eleven a clock at night, so that she could not well be bury'd before the 20th of August; and that day was designed for the Profession of Sister Mary Bernard Ford, nay we knew not how to deferr it without disobliging the Arch Priest, he being to go out of Town the next day; therefore the funeral was perform'd in the morning as early we could, at which we sung the commendations and the burial, but had only a low Mass **[p. 411]** then we sung the high Mass next day; by this means the Profession was the same morning, but we could not be merry at that recreation, it being preceded and follow'd by the most melancholy transactions, for in the afternoon Sister Mary Ignatius Stanley received her rights.

Sister Agnes was bury'd about 8 a clock in the morning. *Requiescat in pace*. Amen.

On the 20th of August (as we said before) Sister Mary Bernard Ford made her holy Profession.[1]

---

1 Mary Bernard Ford (BA081).

On the 23 of August Sister Mary Ignatia Stanley departed this life in the 47 year of her age, and 23 of her holy Profession.[1] She had been a most fervorous, laborious, good religious woman, having for many years labour'd to the utmost of her strength in several offices, never sparing nor favouring her self in any thing, tho' she was preventingly kind and charitable to others. About two years before her death she got a cancer in her breast, which after some time broke, and mortified, by which she suffer'd extreamly, but all with an incomparable courage and patience; generally standing whilst the surgeon **[p. 412]** cut, and dress'd it, tho' he was often forced to cram flax or lint hard into the sore to stanch the bleeding; yet she was not impatient nor dishearten'd; nor did she bemoan her case nor complain of the many tedious hour and night which she suffer'd with that breast; but seem'd to make her real advantage of her suffering, and of her temper, which was naturally hot; so that we have reason to hope she had her Purgatory in this life, and now enjoys the crown of her labours, pains, and victories, in a happy eternity. She dyed between two and three a clock in the afternoon, having received all the rights of our holy Mother the church. She was bury'd on the 25th. *Requiescat in pace*. Amen.

On the 27 of August Mrs Frances Huddlestone was admitted to our first habit, and took the name of Justina.[2]

On the 28 of August my Lady Mary Caryll (niece to our Reverende Mother) with her three little daughters, and her two servants, enter'd our enclosure and lodged within till the 3d of September, when they went away.[3] Her Ladyship's little son also had leave from our Bishop to come into our enclosure in the day time **[p. 413]** as long as they stay'd.

On the 9th of September Sister Mary Barbara Huddlestone made her holy Profession.[4]

On the 30th of September my Lord Maxwell, nephew to our Reverende Mother, came out of England with his gentleman Mr Robinson and they boarded in our confessor's house.[5] At the same time came Mrs Lindsay governant to Lady Ann' Maxwell, and she enter'd our inclosure and lodged with her young Lady in our Convict.

On the 2d of october the Lady Mountague and Lord Maxwell began their journey for England; her Ladyship also took with her Miss Willis one of our Pensioners, but being come to Ostende the wind being set against them, her Ladyship and the rest return'd to us again on the 6th of october.

---

1 Mary Ignatia Stanley (1703–25) BA182.

2 Frances Huddleston, in religion Mary Justina (BA113).

3 Lady Caryll was one of the sisters of the Prioress: see Herbert family tree.

4 Mary Barbara Huddleston (BA114).

5 Lord Maxwell was the son of Lady Winifred Maxwell, née Herbert and nephew of Prioress Lucy Herbert; Lady Anne Maxwell was his sister.

On the 18th of october Miss Willis again went from hence for England. She had a vocation to be religious, and a very good voice; therefore her father was willing to be at the expense of Masters for her in England, that her voice might in part supply for a portion, if his circumstances would not allow him to give her another, he being then brought very low by the South Sea contrivance;[1] **[p. 414]** nevertheless our Reverende Mother and community were willing to admitt of his daughter if she persevered in her pious inclinations, and got her musick perfectly for which effect she went into England, and her father's repeated grateful acknowledgments of our kindness to his child still more excites us to assist him in this occasion; he having the character of a most patient, grateful, industrious good man, and the daughter has many good qualities.

In november Melle Cunning one of this Town, was received here for convictress.

This year we made a new burying place in form of ovens, our Vault being full.[2]

Mrs Mannock gave us also this year 26 florins for her husband's soul and we gave 50 florins to the English Jesuits towards repairing their church at Gandt.

The year 1726

On the 31th of January Sister Justina Huddlestone was clothed.[3]

On the 3d of february Mrs Mackenzie[4] the Bernardin Dame at Spermaille, departed this life, after long suffering **[p. 415]** by continual infirmities in her later years, yet till about half a year before her death, she kept up, and comply'd with the regular observances, tho' she had a dropsie, was subject to excessive bleeding at the nose, and had such violent cramps in her limbs, that night after night she could not sleep nor lye down in her bed; nevertheless she bore all with great patience, and never complain'd to the Dames, when she could conceal what she suffer'd, and they were then in very low circumstances so that the infirm had no consideration from the common; all the relief she had was the three pound a year which our Reverende Mother procured for her from my Lady Caryll; and the charities she received from her Reverence and this comunity; for which she was ever most grateful, and ready to serve in any thing, being very ingenious and handy at many trades, and we had our Bishop's leave to let her come into our enclosure when she had leave to go abroad, so that

[1] The South Sea Bubble: the ripple effects of the catastrophic collapse in the value of the company in 1720 were felt widely. The reference here suggests that the author of the Chronicle had at least a basic understanding of the probems caused.

[2] Ovens were created to bury individual bodies; see Glossary.

[3] Mary Justina Huddleston, in religion Mary Justina (BA113).

[4] Mrs Mackenzie had arrived at the convent in 1709. See also **[pp. 272, 283, 298–300]**.

we sometimes had her here for months together, and we almost look'd upon her as one of us. The last time she was here was when we had a breach to make the door of the burying place into our church; then she came with her Abbess and all that community, but as it was soon after **[p. 416]** a great fit of bleeding, she was very weak, and full of pains in her joynts, from that time she never recover'd, but her blood being exhausted she fell into convulsions, yet she lived some months after in a dying way, but sensible till towards the last she seem'd stupified, yet would give a reasonable answer when roused up. She received her *viaticum*, but the Doctor affirming she was in no present danger the holy oyles were deferr'd, and she dyed without that advantage, being about 44 years of age, and in the 14 year of her holy Profession.

She was a convert, and in her conversion and all the course of her life, God seem'd to have a particular providence over her, but he was pleased to lead her by the way of the cross, and tho' she was naturally hot yet she was a very patient sufferer; she was also humble, charitable, and gratefull. May divine mercy crown his own gifts with everlasting bliss, and give her eternal rest. Amen.

As our Reverende Mother promised to be kind to Spermaille on account of this good Dame, they having accepted of her with an under fortune, so her Reverence was most faithful to her promise, and at different times gave them in all full 25 **[p. 417]** pounds sterlin, which was money her Reverence had to dispose of, for prayers for the deceased, besides this she frequently lent them money when they were in great distress, once in particular she lent them 30 pound grote,[1] and as it would have been very hard for them to repay it in ready money, her Reverence sent them all our Pensioners that the debt might be more easily acquited by their board, tho' it was indeed necessary to send them out, we having then the smal pox in the house. She also gave them the value of their two great candlesticks, and the liberty to redeem them again, provided they did it in a year after their old Abbess Ververa's death, which being almost expired, at their request her Reverence allow'd them another year for the Redemption of them; but they not being able to do it in that time neither, the candlesticks are ours very fairly. All this is here mention'd to justifie our Reverende Mother, it having been reported by mistake (since Dame Ann' Teresa's death) that her Reverence had promised more for her, than she had perform'd, which was certainly a very gross error.

On the 14 of March my Lord Maxwell went from hence.[2]

---

1 For pound grote, see **[p. 313]**.

2 This could refer to William Maxwell, 5th Earl of Nithsdale, who was married to Winifred Herbert, sister to Prioress Lucy Herbert, or to George, 3rd Lord Maxwell, the third husband of Mary Herbert (m. 22 August 1716), or to the young Lord Maxwell referred to on **[p. 413]**, although we are told that he had already left the convent. As a close member of the family, one might have represented the others. See Herbert family tree.

On the 14 of february Sister Anne **[p. 418]** Augustina Sykes and Sister Mary Joseph Lloyd made their holy professions.[1]

On the 18 of April the Lady Mountague, and her woman, went from hence for England.

On the 23 of May Miss Alexander went from hence to the English Benedictin Dames at Gandt.[2]

Our Reverende Mother being very desirous to have our Quire song in the greatest perfection, to God's greater glory, by the performance of the divine office in the most solemn and moving manner, proposed to our Lord Bishop the changing our plan song into a more harmonious manner, by cutting off superfluous notes, and adding such graces as in ancient times were not used. His Lordship answer'd we might freely do it provided we did not change the words, and could be at the expense of it: nevertheless many of our Religious seem'd dissatisfied at the novelty of the thing, therefore tho' our Reverende Mother could have **[p. 419]** concluded the matter by votes of our Convent Sisters, yet for the more general satisfaction, her Reverence put it to the votes of the whole comunity, on the 21 of June, and it was consented by the plurality of voices, there being but two against it.

This being done our Reverende Mother found means not long after, to get the consent of the Lady Fleetwood Abbess of the English Dames at Dunkirk,[3] to let us have a book of their pla[i]n song, which they had reduced to the form we desired, and which was generally admired by all that heard it.

My Lady Abbess very obligingly lent us a book, and our Reverende Mother order'd one of our religious to copy it, designing to have books printed for our choir; but it is a work that will require some time.

On the 28 of June the Lord Maxwell came hither again for a visit to our Reverende Mother (his Aunt), and to Lady Ann Maxwell his sister.[4]

On the 2d of July Miss Newlin, daughter to a Protestant Minister was received here for convictress, she was sent hither by the Lady Mary Caryll.[5]

On the 5th of July Mrs Elisabeth Bedingfeld went from hence for England.

[p. 420] On the 9th of July The Lord Maxwell and his Sister Lady Ann' Maxwell, went from hence for France.

---

1 Anne Augustine Sykes (BA188); Mary Joseph Lloyd (BA129).

2 Anne Alexander professed at Ghent in 1728 taking the name in religion Romana (GB002).

3 Anne Fleetwood, in religion Benedicta (1686–1748) DB061, Abbess 1712–48.

4 See Herbert family tree.

5 Elizabeth Newlin, in religion Teresa Austin (1737–86) BA147. According to the archpriest who interrogated her before her clothing, she had intended to become a lay sister as a sign of humility, but was convinced to take the black veil of the choir sister instead. Her father, a Church of England parson, required her to leave and go home. However, she returned much later to profess. See also **[p. 429]** and vol. 2, **[p. 21]**.

On the 21 of July Miss Lelia Huddlestone, daughter to Doctor Huddlestone, was received here for convictress, she is niece to our two Sisters Huddlestone, by the father's side, and to Sister Stanislaus Gage on the Mother's side.[1]

On the 25' of July, Mrs Sykes, Mother to our two Sisters Sykes enter'd our enclosure within for a month or two.[2]

In this month of July, our Reverende Mother had notice from her sister the Lady Mountague of a Legacy of above 100 pound sterlin left to her Reverence by one Mrs Orick, whose maiden name was Longfort, in consideration of the kindness her nephew had received from her Reverence when he was a student. But this Legacy is not to be paid here till after the nephew's death; nevertheless that her soul might not be so long be deprived of the benefit of our prayers, her Reverence presently order'd that each of us should here a Mass and communicate for her; and soon after appointed each to offer for 30 Masses and a **[p. 421]** *trentum* of our three a clock's indulgence which is 100 days pardon granted by the pope to all of this Diocese who shall with their arms extended in form of a cross, say 5 *Paters* and *Aves* in honour of our Saviour's death; at three in the afternoon, or sooner or later when lawfully hinder'd from performing it at three.[3]

When the money is ours, this good gentlewoman is to be written in the dierge book as a benefactress, and more prayers offer'd for her as reason shall require.

On the 3d of September Mrs Dorothy Bedingfeld of Reddingfield, arrived here and was received for a convictress.

On the 4th of September Miss Winy Willis a child of about seven years old, was received here for convictress.[4]

On the 9th of September Sister Frances Xaveria Simner, Sister Mary Joachim Vendo and Sister Anne Clare Formby made their holy Profession.[5]

On the 10th of September Mrs Sykes went from hence for England. The same day our Archpriest bless'd our **[p. 422]** new burying place, and little church yard, this church yard is the same piece of ground which at the begining of this Monastry was bless'd to bury our religious in, but after we had a Vault in our church it was neglected and misused, so that we were fain to send for hollow'd earth from St Annes church yard, when our religious were to be bury'd; therefore our Reverende Mother

---

[1] Leila Huddleston was the daughter of Dr Henry Huddleston of Durham and Mary Gage of Hengrave. She left before profession.

[2] Mary Dovery (d. 1738), widow of William Sykes (d. 1724/5), became a benefactor of a number of institutions. See also vol. 2, **[pp. 19, 53–5, 66, 86, 128]**.

[3] These are the Cross Prayers referred to on a number of other occasions in the Chronicle: see Glossary. I am indebted to the Community for the explanation.

[4] Winefrid Willis later professed as Mary Catherine (1742–97) BA221.

[5] Frances Xaveria Simner (BA174); Mary Joachim Vendow (BA210); Ann Clare Formby (BA082).

having caused this piece of ground to be dugg up, and decently enclosed with rails, got it bless'd with our new burying ovens, that we might have holy earth at home, and a place to bury the bones in when they should be taken out of those ovens.[1]

The ceremonies of blessing such places are very particular. Our Arch Priest was vested in an Alb and cope, and father confessor in a surplice, a little blewcoat boy brought fifteen yellow wax candles, and carry'd the holy water. Five of our religious were order'd to come with every one a crucifix, and they stood one at each corner of the church yard, and one in the middle. The rest of our religious were also present, as many as could enter the place without the rails. **[p. 423]** The Archpriest sat in a chair without the rails, between the church yard and the new burying place, so that he could conveniently give his benediction to both places. After he had read some prayers and Psalms, he order'd three of the wax candles to be stuck lighted upon each of the crucifixes which the religious held; one upon each arm of the cross, and one at the top, so the five crosses held the fifteen candles. The Arch Priest walk'd several times round the church yard, and father confessor after him, holding up his cope, he sprinkled it with holy water, and said many prayers, verses and Psalms, which father confessor and we answer'd as well as we could; tho' this ceremony, not being in the common Pastoral, but in a book call'd an Episcopal, the Arch Priest was forced to say the greatest part himself, because none but his Reverence had such a book. Our Reverende Mother, Subprioress, the Arcaria, and two other elders, held the crucifixes and candles.

On the first of october Madelle Cunning went from hence.

On the 6th of october Mr Willis, father to our little Miss Willis, dyed **[p. 424]** in town of a feavour. He had been over here the year before about an estate that was fallen to his wife in these parts; and from that time was so replenish'd with a sensible devotion, that his zeal, prayers and tears, were most edifying to all that saw him, and it visibly appear'd that the change was from the right hand of the highest. He then return'd into England again, but never lost his fervour, and coming over this year upon the same account, with his wife and one of his chidren, and some friends, he got this feavour, and having received all the rights of our holy Mother the church, he beg'd that he might be bury'd in our church, which our Reverende Mother and the community condescended to, and on the eighth of october about seven in the Evening, he was bury'd at the mouth of our old Vault in the church. We sung the burying in the church and next day sung a Solemn Mass for him. *Requiescat in pace*. Amen.

This gentleman was an attorney at law, by his practice he gain'd about three hundred a year, but as that dyed with **[p. 425]** him, his widow was uncertain what her circumstances might be, therefore she only

---

[1] Ovens: see Glossary.

acknowledged she had great obligations to us, and went into England by the first occasion, but left her little one with us.

On the 14th of December Mrs Dorothy Salvin received our Schollars habit, and took the names of Mary Baptist.[1]

On the 21 of December: Elisabeth Bambridge received the kerchief for a lay sister, and has the name of Martina.[2]

This year the English Colledge at St Omars was burnt down by casual fire, and as from the begining we have been much obliged to the English father of the Society, therefore our Reverende Mother and comunity were desirous to shew their gratitude in this their distress; for which effect her Reverence assembled the Convent Sisters, and by plurality of votes we gave a 100 pound sterlin towards the rebuilding of the colledge.[3]

We this year received in Almns two guineas from Mrs Mannock for her husband's soul. and 94 guilders 13 stivers from Mr Simner. in all 119 gilders, 3 stivers. **[p. 426]**

The year 1727

On the 2th [*sic*] of february Sister Justina Huddlestone made her holy Profession.[4]

On the 17th of May Sister Mary Alexia Burton departed this life in the 69 year of her age, and 34 of her holy Profession.[5] She was own Sister to that venerable Superior of the English Teresians at Antwerp,[6] who dyed some years before her in great repute of sanctity, and as their whole family (even in the world) was remarkable for piety and goodness, so I may affirm that our dear deceased Sister did not degenerate. She was most fervorous and exact in all religious observances from the begining of her noviship to the end of her life, stil aiming at the highest perfection but never thinking she had acquired the least, which humble conceit of her self join'd with her fervour, made her even [*sic*] importune to hear and know good things; for she always esteem'd her self a learner in point of vertue, and was willing to learn of any, even the youngest in the house. She came to religion in her riper **[p. 427]** years and not having learn'd to read latin before, she was never perfect in it, nor could she say much of the divine office by heart when her eyes fail'd her, which was some years before her death, nevertheless she came constantly to Matines

---

1 Dorothy Salvin (BA170).

2 Elizabeth Bambridge (BA011).

3 St Omer suffered badly in the fire of October 1726, which destroyed much of the building and contents. A major fundraising campaign was initiated and much had been restored by the end of 1727. See G. Holt, *The English Jesuits in the Age of Reason* (London: Burns and Oates, 1993), Chapter IX.

4 Mary Justina Huddleston (BA113).

5 Mary Alexia Burton (1693–1727) BA040.

6 Catherine Burton, in religion Mary Xaveria of the Angels (1694–1714) AC020.

and the rest of the office, supplying for her defects by the vehemency of her fervour which sometimes broke out in a tone so different from the rest of the choir that it gave an edifying distraction to her neighbours. The october before she dyed, being to sleep Matins, she distinctly heard part of the long Litanies said aloud, a little before the peal to Matines and during the time of the ringing; this she imagin'd to be the indiscreet fervour of a young nun who lay next door to her, and as it disturb'd her rest she endeavour'd to cover her self up that she might not hear it, but the same continuing she sat up in her bed and plainly heard: *Sancte Michael, sancte Gabriel, Ste Raphael*. Soon after it ceas'd, and afterwards upon enquiring it was found that neither that young religious nor any one else had been so **[p. 428]** loud in their devotions at that strict time of silence; therefore she concluded it was a warning for her death and that she should die the following october. Some time after this her legs began to swell, and she found a great oppression on her stomach, for which she was taken to the infirmary where she remain'd a considerable time, yet she did not keep her bed till the very day she died. Her death was most pious and peaceable on the 17th of May, about six in the Evening, and she was bury'd in the lowest oven next the church in our new Vault, on the 19th which happening to be one of the rogation days, the long Litanies was sung in our choir whilst her corps lay in the church, which made us reflect that the Litanies she had heard in october might reasonably be taken for a notice of her death about this time, since we were to sing the same Litanies so near to her buryal. *Requiescat in pace*. Amen.

On the 26th of May Sister Mary Baptist Salvin was clothed.[1]

On the 28 of July Miss Newlin **[p. 429]** went from us for England, her Father the Parson, having a scruple to let her stay longer because he found we would make her a Papist, which we always thought was his tacite intention, since he left her education to the Lady Mary Caryll (our Reverende Mother's niece) who intended to have her wait on her eldest Daughter, the Minister having desired as much of her Ladyship; but now all those designes were broken, and he made the child go to church the very next Sunday, after she came home.[2]

On the 13th of December the old woman dyed here whom we called Aunt Betty; she was an old widow who had had three husbands, and several sons, one of her sons having lifted himself for a soldier came over into these countries and afterwards marry'd a woman of this town, and was converted; then being very zealous he with much importunity perswaded his Mother to come over, and tho' she was a fierce Protestant, yet he **[p. 430]** had the comfort to see her converted and soon after it he dyed: when her son was dead his wife treated this old woman very

[1] Mary Baptist Salvin (BA170).

[2] Miss Newlin: see also **[p. 419; vol. 2, p. 22]**.

unkindly and unjustly, so that she had not a house to put her head in, nor scarce bread to eat; which being, the good Priest who had converted her fearing she might return to England and lose both her religion and her soul; he over perswaded us to take her into the Monastry both for charity sake, and for her talent, she having skill in chirurgery, stilling etc. We received her then upon these motives, and as for the charity it remains permanent, but her talents were soon obscured by her years and her ill humours, nor could we expect (had we consider'd the matter) that a woman of past threescore, should improve upon our hands, nevertheless she was pious after her manner, and did several cures both at home and abroad, and for the latter she received money for her own use, and a year or two before she dyed, we allow'd her a fire and a Sister to serve her, she being quite blind, and very infirm. She departed this life in the 86th year of her age **[p. 431]** and was bury'd in Ste Ann's church yard on the 14th of December. *Requiescat in pace*. Amen.

This old woman left about 12 pound sterlin which on her death bed she told our Reverende Mother should be for the community; and in reason it ought to have been so, she having gain'd it by her chirurgery, which was in great part at our expenses, besides the trouble and charges she put us to in her latter year. Nevertheless after her death, the good Priest her confessor, produced a deed signed with her name, whereby she gave ten of the twelfe pound to him, to acquit part of a debt he had to this Monastry, and as her buryal cost above five pound grote, we had only our labour for our pains in this world; but have the solide comfort that God will duely reward our charity in the next.

On the 20th of December Sister Johanna Couchefer departed this life between eight and nine in the morning.[1] She was of Ostende and being admitted here for a lay sister she was very laborious and served us most faithfully and diligently about forty years, but in her latter years she was very infirm and had such unaccountable ailments and pains within her, that neither Doctor nor Surgeon could comprehend them: this **[p. 432]** made her often desire that she might be open'd after her death for the benefit of others, since she could find no remedies for her self. A year or two before her death she was almost constantly in the infirmary, yet between times when she was a little better, she would weed in the garden, or sweep or do any thing she was capable of; at length worne out with her strange pains, Almighty God was pleased to take her to himself in the 64 year of her age, and 43 of her profession. When she was dead (according to her desire) we had her open'd, and it was found that the passage of her stomach was almost quite grown up, which had caused her being in such a violent way after eating, for she either brought up her victuals, or if it forced down, her whole body suffer'd by it. The

[1] Johanna Couchefer (1685–1727) BA067.

surgeon and Apothecary affirm'd that had they known before the cause of her illness they could not have help'd her, and by consequence if the like happens to any of us, it is to be fear'd there will be no remedy but patience; nevertheless we are obliged to her for her good intention. She was bury'd on the 21 in our new burying place, in the first oven of the 2d row from the bottom next Sister Burton.[1] *Requiescat in pace.* Amen.

[p. 433] We this year received in Almns ten pound sterlin, to pray for the soul of Fr Peter Miglioruche.

The year 1728

On the 29th of January Sister Martina Bambridge was clothed.[2]

In february Sister Frances Xaveria Simner's friends sent tend [*sic*] pound for prayers and our Reverende Mother order'd us to hear three Masses which were said for that intention, and each of us to offer up one communion and also to offer for the same intention one indulgence every day for the space of three months.[3]

On the 24th of April, Mrs Markham, with her Daughter and her servant, return'd to us again, and they were lodged within our inclosure as before.[4]

On the first of June Sister Mary Baptist Salvin made her holy Profession.[5]

On the third of June Miss Mary Chichester was received here as convictress, she is sister to Sister Teresa Joseph.[6]

About this time we had news that the Lady Dover[7] had left us fifty pound sterlin without **[p. 434]** any other obligation upon us but to pray for the souls of her Lord and her self, for which intentions our Reverende Mother appointed a Solem Mass, and that each of the Religious should offer one communion, hear ten Masses, and for the space of thirty days offer some indulgence for their souls they are besides writen in our Month book to be pray'd for as Benefactors for ever.

On the 18th of June Mrs Dorothy Bedingfeld went from hence for England.

---

1 Mary Burton, in religion Mary Alexia (1693–1727) BA040.

2 Martina Bambridge (BA011).

3 Frances Xaveria Simner (BA174).

4 Mrs Catherine Markham (née Constable), widow of Thomas Markham of Ollerton. Her daughter Mary Ursula and her maid Catherine Train accompanied her; see **[pp. 376, 390, 397]** and vol. 2, [*unp.*] at beginning of volume. See K. S. B. Keats-Rohan (ed.), *English Catholic Nuns in Exile, 1600–1800: A Biographical Register*, Prosopographia et Genealogica 15 (Oxford: Unit for Prosopographical Research, Linacre College, forthcoming 2017). I am indebted to Dr Keats-Rohan for sharing her new research with me.

5 Mary Baptist Salvin (BA170).

6 Mary Chichester was daughter to Giles Chichester, Esq, of Arlington, Devonshire, and Catherine Palmes. Teresa Joseph Chichester (BA052).

7 Lady Dover was Judith Pooley, widow of Henry Jermyn, Lord Dover; see **[pp. 202, 253]**. She died in 1726 leaving no children.

On the 4th of July, The Lady Mountague return'd to us again. She brought with her two servants, and at the same time her Ladyship brought us a little Convictress, Miss Anne Howard, Daughter to Mr Bernard Howard's Eldest Son.[1]

Mr Damerin having been long infirm and growing still worse, his son (who was marry'd, and kept house in this town) used all his endeavours to get him to his house, and at last he prevail'd;[2] but the good Gentleman being no where so easy as with us, return'd here again as soon as he grew a little better; nevertheless he soon grew worse agin, with the gout, a shortness of breath, and a kind of dropsie which in a short time made us fear he could not recover it; then his son again importuned him to go to his house, which he did on the 13th of July.

[p. 435] On the 21 of August the Lady Mountague and her two servants, went from hence for England.

On the 6th of october Mr Damerin departed this life about five in the morning. He was in the 71 year of his age, and in the 33 of his Priesthood. This good gentleman in his youth was one of the Spanish Embassador's Pages in England, after that he marry'd a Lady of this town who had a good fortune, by her he had four children, but two of them dyed young; the other two (a son and a daughter) lived to bury their father, and behaved themselves most dutyfully all the time of his sickness and death. His wife dyed many years before, and then for his own devotion he desired to be a Soecular Priest, for he had not learning enough to assist his neighbor by preaching, or hearing confessions, etc. when he was made Priest being desirous to live retired, and having a kindness for our Monastry, he was admitted to board in our Father's house tho' he paid nothing, but found his own washing, and sheets as long as his stock lasted. He had also bed and beding of his own, and was a great help to our musick, for he play'd on the violin. When Reverende Mother Bedingfeld lay on her death bed **[p. 436]** undertook the management of our affaires in these countries, as is said before page 163. but we paid him no particular pension, only gave him his board and somtimes a present, not money, something out of England, that might be hansome for his children, or himself, and that very seldome.

When we heard of his death we toled and rung our Bell as we do for our own Religious, and said the commendations for him all together in

---

1 Anne Howard was the daughter of Bernard Howard and Anne Roper; she later professed at the Conceptionists, Paris and was twice elected abbess before her death in 1794, PC051.

2 Mr Damerin's son was Guillaume-Antoine Damerin (d. 1761), who married Jeanne-Constance Jaquiere. In 1716 he became provost of the Confraternity of the Holy Blood. For Damerin father and son, see J. Gailliard, *Recherches historiques sur la Chapelle du Saint-Sang à Bruges* (Bruges, 1846), p. 297; F. van Dycke, *Recueil héraldique* (Bruges, 1862), p. 130. I am indebted to Paul Arblaster for these references. See also **[pp. 163, 176, 437, 450]**.

the Choir. On the seventh we said the long Dierge for him, and the same day about eight in the Evening he was bury'd in our new burying place as he had desired; he lyes in the upper most oven next the church. On the eighth a Herse being prepared, the funeral ceremonies were performed for him by the Archpriest, our Bishop was present and two Abbots, with some of the chief of the Town whom his son had invited. We rung bell three hours for him, and our Reverende Mother ordered each of the Religious to offer a communion for his soul, and to hear three Masses, or say six short dierges for him; this was in some sort his due, he having punctually said three Masses for every one of our nuns who departed this life while he lived here **[p. 437]** besides we were obliged to him for his kindness to our house, and must be so just to his memory, as to affirm he was a pious, worthy good gentleman. *Requiescat in pace*. Amen.

Some little time after Mr. Damerin's death, our Reverende Mother proposed to his son the taking care of our affairs on these countries as his father had done; and he accepted of it because his father had desired him to do so if we ask'd him; but as he could not have the advantage of boarding here, having a family of his own, our Reverende Mother mention'd a salary, and he (having been misinform'd) hinted at a very considerable one which our house had formerly given to one Mr Meulinar; but that being proved a mistake, and our Rents being but ill paid; he was willing to accept of twenty pound grote a year, and now he fully supplys his father's place in our temporal concerns of these countries.

On the 9th of December Mrs Elisabeth Willis return'd from England in order **[p. 438]** to receive our Schollars habit, she having improved her self in singing, and learn'd the italian manner.[1]

On the 12th of December our dear Subprioress Sister Hellen Andrews, departed this life between 7 and 8 in the Evening in the 64 year of her age, and 47 of her holy Profession.[2] She was from the begining a most exemplar good religious woman, and all her life she was a patern of regularity, humility, patience, submission, zeal and fervour. Adorn'd with these vertues she in process of time worthily acquited her self of the chief offices of the House as Subprioress, Procuratrix, and Mistress of novices and Pensioners: besides the tryals these offices might afford her, Almighty God gave her most heavy crosses in her nearest and dearest relations, for her own sister was many years from her self in this Monastry, and dyed so, as we have said before page 403 and her niece[3] a hopefull young woman after having been a considerable time novice here, had a strange turn of her head, for which we were force to send her into England, and **[p. 439]** tho' she perfectly recover'd it yet she would not return to us,

---

1 Elizabeth Willis, in religion Mary Xaveria (BA222).

2 Helen Andrews (1682–1728) BA004. Her sister was Ann Joseph Andrews (1675–1724) BA003.

3 Mary Petre (GP219) was her niece. See also **[pp. 291, 319, 438–9]**.

but went to be a poor clare at Gravelin where she ended her happy days a few years after her profession. All this our dear Subprioress bore with an incomparable resignation and silence, and having compleated her crown by an almost continual mortification and prayer, she had a fore knowledge of her happy death, for some months before she fell ill she told a friend of hers that she should not live till Christmass, and so it was, for being seiz'd with a feavour and violent pain in one of her breasts she was brought to the infirmary where in a short time she ended her pious days having received all the rights of our holy Mother the church. She was bury'd on the 14 in the 2d oven from the ground next the church. *Requiescat in pace*. Amen.

On the 22th of December Sister Clare Saunderson was chosen Subprioress.[1]

On the 23 of december Mrs Elisabeth Willis received our Schollars habit, and is call'd Sister Mary Xaveria.

This year in the summer, we had **[p. 440]** all our House whiten'd for it[s] Jubilee. It was done by a man of Bruxelles very expert in the trade. We bargain'd with him to whiten all within the enclosure for 472 florins. At the same time we had the little house at the end of the new Dormitory stop'd up because the stink of it was insupportable.

This year we have received in Almns 50 poun Sterlin which the Lady Dover left us for prayers for her soul.

The year 1729

On the 22th [*sic*] of february Sister Martina Bambridge made her holy profession.[2]

About this time Sister Frances Xaveria's neighbours sent 20 shillings for prayers, and our Reverende Mother had 3 Masses said for them, and order'd each of us to hear a Mass for the same intention.

Her friends also sent five pounds for prayers for a woman and her son; and our Reverend Mother had five Masses said for them, and order'd each of us to hear **[p. 441]** five, and to offer one communion for the same intention.

As last year we made a kind of remote preparation for the Jubilee of our House, by having it all whiten'd; so this year as soon as the season would permit we began to prepare more immediately for the same. And first our Reverend Mother express'd her kindness to every one of her subjects in particular, giving to each a little book of Meditations on the passion and of our Lady; a pound of coffee, and the choice of either a little bed gown or a short cloak; but to the lay Sisters in place of the bed

---

1 Clare Saunderson (BA172).
2 Martina Bambridge (BA011).

gown or cloak, her Reverence gave two shifts a piece. Thus our dear Superior rejoyced our sould and bodies to prepare for the great Jubilee.

And to prevent our solicitous gratitude which would naturaly have inclin'd us to a return of some little present to her Reverence, she declared that she did not desire it; but that those who were able would oblige her more by doing somthing for the conveniency or adornment of the house. This was sufficient to move those **[p. 442]** who had any thing to spare of their little allowances, to bestow it according to our Reverend Mother's inclinations; and to excite the rest to pray more particularly for her Reverence, and for the common profit, the good of the House. Therefore Sister Perpetua Errington gave the picture at the great crucifix in the Garden.[1]

Sister Ann' Markham gave the boarding of the warming room.[2]

Sister Victoria Cannying gave two guineas for her Reverence to bestow as she pleased, and our Reverend Mother intends to lay it out upon a hansome image of our Lady's dolours, for a chappel in the Garden.[3]

Sister Ann' Weston gave the step with the little silver Angels for our Lady's Altar in the Dormitory, and new bed curtains, and coverlets for the inner sickhouse.[4]

Sister Mary Austin Smithson gave the boarding of the choir.[5]

Sister Mary Teresa Jernigan gave her Reverence a hansome Garden of all sorts of silver work'd flowers, of her own work.[6] +

Sister Lucy Smithson gave the blew curtains for the choir.[7]

[p. 443] Sister Mary Ann Caryll gave the guilding of the little Altars by the choir door.

Sister Teresa Joseph Chichester gave the great picture at the end of the great Pant.

+ Sister Dorothy Stanley and her sisters gave two Lessonaries in the middle of the choir.[8]

This year our new organ was finish'd. It was begun the last year, and is esteem'd a very good one. It was made by a Factor of Liege, the father began it but dyed before he could finish it, so his son completed the work it is a double organ and set lower than our old organ, for the Advantage of our new plain song, the printing of which, three of our

---

1 Dorothy Errington, in religion Perpetua (BA076).

2 Either Ann Mechtilda Markham (BA137) or Ann Delphina Markham (BA138).

3 Elizabeth Canning, in religion Elizabeth Victoria (BA044). Our Lady's dolours refers to Our Lady of the Sorrows.

4 Ann Weston (BA215).

5 Mary Augustine Smithson (BA178).

6 Mary Teresa Jerningham (BA118).

7 Lucy Smithson (BA177).

8 Mary Ann Caryll (BA047); Teresa Joseph Chichester (BA052); Dorothy Stanley (BA183), whose sisters at Bruges were Winifred (BA186), Elizabeth (BA184) and Charlotte (BA182).

Religious daily labour at so that in a year or two we hope our choir will be wholy reform'd without any vast expenses.

Our great organ cost a hundred Pistolles, and 30 crowns for its carriage from Liege, and two Guineas to the Factor for his journey, when he came to take his measures for this organ. The little organ within the great one, cost **[p. 444]** three score pound Sterlin: all money well spent since for the performance of the divine service in a more Solemn and moving manner.

On the 30th of May Sister Mary Xaveria Willis was clothed.[1]

On the first of July Almighty God was pleased to visit us with smal pox. Sister Mary Joseph Lloyd fell ill of it, but within a month was perfectly recover'd.[2]

On the 7th of July Miss Mary Chichester went from hence for Paris.

On the l4th of July our Reverend Mother's sister, the Lady Mountague, and her two servants, came to board for a time within our inclosure.

On the 31 of July, Dame Mary Benedict Caryll, a Benedictin Dame of Dunkirk, enter'd our inclosure.[3] She is own Sister to our Sister Mary Ann Caryll, and having had very ill health in her Monastry for many years, her father Mr Phillip Caryll of North, procured leave for her to go to the Baths at Aix La Chapelle, and he conducted her thither, and was at all the expenses. **[p. 445]** Now at their return (she having received some benefit by the Baths) Mr Caryll desired she might be here some months before she went back to her Monastry: the Doctors judging this delay necessary, therefore our Reverend Mother admitted her and she lay in the Schoole, because the smal pox had lately been in the infirmary, and we were still in fear of having more as in effect it happen'd for on the 7th of August Sister Ann' Teresa Tremaine (a flemish lay Sister) fell ill of the smal pox, and dyed on the l2th of the same month about 3 in the afternoon in the 33 year of her age, and 7th of her holy profession.[4] She fell so unexpectedly into her Agony that she only received the extream unction, tho' she had been at confession the day before in order to go to communion, but did not communicate because she could not swallow some bread we try'd her with (upon this accident and the like which had happen'd in town) our Doctor order'd that if any more fell ill of the smal pox, they should have their *Viaticum* at the begining of it. She was pious and laborious, and **[p. 446]** tho' always sickly, yet being strong and handy, she did us good service.

The Doctor said she dyed of the worst smal pox, and we having no burying place but our ovens, the old Vault being full, it was judged

---

1 Mary Xaveria Willis (BA222).

2 Mary Joseph Lloyd (BA129).

3 Mary Benedict Caryll (DB032), sister of Mary Ann Caryll (BA047). Their father was Philip Caryll the younger, of Catherington, Hampshire.

4 Ann Teresa Tremaine (1722–29) BA205.

prudence for fear of infection, to bury her in our little church yard, so on the 13th at the begining of Matins, she was bury'd there under the Rails next the street. *Requiescat in pace*. Amen.

On the 14th of August Sister Alipia Conyers fell sick of the smal pox. She received her *Viaticum*, and had them very much, but recover'd.[1]

On the 22th of August Mrs Trowers and her daughter enter'd our inclosure, the Mother as a boarder, the daughter as a convictress, but they both lay in the Schoole and eat with our Pensioners.[2] On the 31 of August Miss Ann' Jernegan, daughter to Mr. Henry Jernegan, was received here as convictress.[3]

[p. 447] On the 9th of September we received Miss Henick (a fleming) for convictress.

The Jubilee of our House, the hundred year since our foundation in this place being now very near, the work men belonging to our House requested of our Reverend Mother that on the Jubilee day they might enter our inclosure and shoot off little canons in the Garden, as they usually do in these countries at great Solemnities. Our Reverend Mother did not relish the noisy kindness they proposed, so she civilly refused it; but they would not be so put off; then her Reverence told them that it was not in her power to let them in upon such an account without a particular leave from the Bishop; hoping that might dash their designe; but in place of that they went in a body to our Bishop, and beg'd the favour of him, his Lordship, because not long before he being to bless a Bell in the country, a man was accidentaly kill'd in time of his Mass, as they were shooting off such canons: but our workmen esteem'd **[p. 448]** themselves more expert at it than the Boors,[4] and therefore insisted that there was no danger: so My Lord Bishop yielded to their importunity upon condition they should not shoot while he was at our Monastry. This being concluded they prepared 150 canons to gunpowder accordingly at their own expenses. There were above 20 men of them, of all the Trades that ever work'd within the Monastry.

On the 13th of September the Jubilee Eve, some of the workmen came and adorn'd our Steeple with Boughs, and a silk flag, which they placed on a Pole a vast heighth above the weather cock, and so it remain'd tille after the octave.

In due time our Reverend Mother took care to invite my Lord Bishop to sing Mass here, and also desired his Lordship to do us the honour to dine in our father's House, but he absolutely refused the last, and said that he intended to have a good dinner that day at his own Palace, and to have all our father's house and those we intended to invite, dine at

1 Alipia Conyers (BA063).

2 They only stayed for a month; see vol. 2, [*unp.*] at beginning of volume.

3 Ann Teresa Jerningham (1735–96) BA120.

4 Defined in *OED* as peasants or countrymen, particularly of Dutch or German origin.

his Table. This was so **[p. 449]** uncommon and unexpected a piece of kindness that our Reverend Mother humbly refused it alledging that we had invited some of the best of the Town, and prepared a dinner for them, which could not be put off, and that if we changed the designe, it would look as if we either wanted power or will to effect it. His Lordship then civilly told our Reverend Mother that since he could not obtain that favour, he would invite all the Pastors of the Town to his dinner to drink our healths, and rejoice with him for our Jubilee.

Our Altar was dress'd in so beautiful a manner that the whole Town admired it. The Antependium was of Japan made by Sister Mary Michael Sykes who was at the expense of it.[1] The back and pedestals of the Altar were of the same work, and made by the same hand, but given by Sister Teresa Austin Vaughan.[2] There was many candles, but few flowers, because they would have hid the Japan which so agreeably adorn'd the back of the Altar.

On the 14th of September the feast of the exaltation of the holy cross, we **[p. 450]** Solemnised our hundred years Jubilee.[3] The Bishop in his *Pontificalibus* sung a Mas of the Blessed trinity, at which we had none but our own musick and voices.[4] His Lordship was attended at the Altar by six Priests who came with him. The Lord Abbot of the canon regulars of Eeckhoute was present with some of the chief of the town whom our Reverend Mother had invited;[5] The Governor Count Allen had promised to be one, but was hinder'd by some business. After the Mass the Bishop gave us a Solemn blessing and entoned the *Te Deum* which was sung in musick. When all was done his Lordship and his six Priests went away, And my Lord Abbot of Eeckhoute, Major d'Ognate, Mr Damerin, and some other gentlemen dined in our Father's House.[6] They had a hansome dinner prepared by a cook of the Town, who dress'd most of it in our kitchen without any trouble to us: but that hinder'd our having so good a dinner in the Refectory as we should otherways have had.

We had for recreation in the **[p. 451]** Refectory, Pasties, and Beef baked in plumb Puddin. The little canons in the Garden play'd briskly at the begining, middle and end of dinner; and when they drank healths in the father's House.

---

1 Mary Michael Sykes (BA189).

2 Teresa Augustine Vaughan (BA209).

3 The first sisters arrived from Louvain on 14 September 1629.

4 The Bishop of Bruges in 1729 was Hendrik Jozef van Susteren (1668–1742), Bishop of Bruges 1716–42. Masses sung in Pontificalibus were celebrations where the best vestments were worn by the celebrants and special music was sung.

5 The Abbot of Eeckhoute in 1729 was Baudoin de Witte (1676–1731), Abbot 1721–31.

6 Major d'Ognate was probably Jerome Nicholas Arrazola de Oñate, captain of a cavalry regiment in the service of Spain, d. 1749 in Bruges, buried in the crypt of the Roper family. For Mr Guillaume-Antoine Damerin (d. 1761), see note on **[p. 434]**.

We gave all the workmen a good dinner, and wine and beer enough. And our neighbours without any encouragement adorn'd the whole street with flags and Boughs.

There was a rumour in Town before the Jubilee, that any one that would, might come into our inclosure at the Jubilee but thank God that was a mistake, for our good Bishop would not permit any of the Town to enter, he only gave leave for those of our Father's House to come in once, which they did afterwards.

In the afternoon, my Lord Abbot of Eeckhoute officiated at Salüe [*Salve*], and was attended with as great ceremony as the Bishop had been at Mass.

At Supper we had recreation again, and the canons went off as at Dinner. In time of Supper we had a little **[p. 452]** pious representation. The Angel Guardian of the house adress'd a speech in verse to our Reverende Mother, and invited her Reverence and the community to go and meet the Angel Guardians of our ten Foundresses, at the great crucifix in the Garden. Her Reverence presently rose up, and was led thither by that Angel, the whole community following. When we came to the Garden door, we were forced to stop till the workmen had shot off the canons, after that salutation we went on; and found at the crucifix ten of our best voices dress'd like Angels. Each Angel said some verses which gave a brief account of his Pupil according to what we find written of our foundresses at the begining of these Annals; exciting us to imitate their vertues that we might partake of their crowns. Then all the Angels together sung the hymnes of the holy cross and the *salve Regina* in English: after that the Angels distributed to each of us a crown and a heart of March-pan:[1] these were given us by our Reverend Mother, the heart as an emblem of her affection to each **[p. 453]** of us, and the crown as a symbole of those we may hope for in heaven if we happily finish our course upon earth.

After this we return'd to the Refectory where we had half pints of burnt wine[2] and my Lady Mountague being here, her Ladyship was so obliging as to give every one of us a two pound of sugar, which was surprisingly agreeable we having never had the like before; tho' we were accustom'd to my Lady's kindness and benevolence to us. While we remain'd in the Refectory our young people acted a little diverting Gambol.

We said Compline after Vespers and had leave to sit up till nine a clock; but as the work men when it grew dark, began to throw squibs and to repeat their canons, which they continued till after nine, our Reverend Mother gave leave to any that would to sit up longer:

We gave the workmen a supper, and they departed very well satisfied.

---

[1] Marzipan.

[2] Brandy. I am indebted to Hester Higton for this reference.

As soon as it grew dark our neighbours set up lights, and made bonfires in the street, and there was great noise **[p. 454]** and rejoicing tho' we had not then given them any thing; my Lord Bishop having advised our Reverend Mother not to give them drink for fear of a noise and tumult, and our Reverend Mother's inclination was to have this Jubilee only a festival of devotion and merriment amongst our selves and some few friends but finding our neighbours so kind without encouragement, her Reverence order'd two Barrils of beer which were placed at different houses in the street on the octave day; and then they set up lights again on our walls, and drank and danced, and sung till late at night. The Beer was distributed by the neighbours at whose houses it was placed, so that we had not the trouble of it.

We also gave two hundred pen'orth of bread privately to poor neighbours.

Our Lady's Altar at the end of the Dormitory has an image of our Lady upon it, which is said to have been brought from Lovain by our Foundresses. At this Altar we therefore sung our **[p. 455]** Lady's Litany in musick on the Jubilee Day, and every day of the octave we sung *Sancta Maria succurre miseris*,[1] etc. at the same Altar.

Our church was dress'd all the octave as on the day, and we had three musick Masses within the octave, and three Recreations in the Refectory, and it did not ring to work all the octave.

Our neighbours the Religious of Bethania[2] set up lights and made bon fires to rejoice with us. And the Grey Sisters sent us a religious compliment, the assurance of their prayers and congratulations. Our Reverend Mother return'd their civilities in a manner most agreeable to them.

For the Procuratresses expenses at this Jubilee, our Reverend Mother allow'd her 50 pound grote permission.

[p. 456] Thus ended the first hundred years from our foundation, but our Reverend Mother do's not think the Annals compleat without a grateful Memorandum of all our benefactors, therefore (as near as we can find out) here follows a catalogue of all the presents made to this House since the begining of it, such things only omited which are set down in their proper places of these chronicles.

---

[1] 'Holy Mary, help the unfortunate': words of Bishop Fulbert of Chartres (c. 952–1028), widely set to music.

[2] The Bethania and Grey Sisters of Aardenberg: see Appendix 1.

A catalogue of the presents which have been made to this house since the foundation, both by our religious and their soecular friends

To the church

Reverend Father Steven Barnes gave the least chalice, 2 corporal cases and veiles, some pictures, and 260 florins.[1]

Reverend Father Blomfield gave some Almns to the church, as also a hansome Mass book and other things; and left us a rent of 30 florins a year.[2]

Mr Richard Smith, a Priest, gave us 240 florins and several books of his translating.

Reverend Mother Bedingfeld gave us a suit of red silver taby, with cope and Deacon's coats.[3]

Our Reverend Mother Lucy Herbert gave a suit and Deacons coats of blew Damask so thick of silver lace that it serves for a white suit, her Reverence also gave that two side steps which are silver upon **[p. 457]** copper.[4]

Sister Barbara Caryll got the gilt leather hangings, and the great silver crucifix.[5]

Sister Wenefride Web paved the church with marble, and she and her sister got the great silver crucifix and the great silver cruets and plate.[6]

Sister Gertrude Brook gave a suit of a rich silver stuff.[7]

Sister Mary Heton gave a cope of a silver stuff with blew flowers.[8]

Sister Susan Reynoldson's friends having given her at least a hundred pound, Reverend Mother Bedingfeld had it put out, and allow'd her the interest of it to provide her self with things necessary for her continual infirmities; this money she never spent that way, but at different times bought for the church, three pairs of silver candlesticks; six pair of silver flower pots; a silver holy Ghost, a silver Bed, 2 silver sconces. the great step for the Blessed Sacrament, which is silver upon black, and the silver ciborium.[9]

---

1 Stephen Barnes (d. 1653), Confessor at St Monica's, acted as Confessor at Bruges 1629–31; Anstruther 1, p. 24.

2 James Blundeville alias Bord (1603–58). See Anstruther 2, p. 31, and above **[p. 6]**.

3 There were two Bedingfield Prioresses: Augustina Bedingfield, Prioress 1640–61 (LA023); and Mary Bedingfield, Prioress 1661–93 (BA019).

4 Lucy Herbert, Prioress 1709–44 (BA101).

5 Barbara Caryll, Sub-Prioress (BA045).

6 Winefrid Webb (BA212).

7 Gertrude Brooke (BA034).

8 Mary Heton (BA102).

9 Susan Reynoldson (BA161). The ciborium was a receptacle to reserve the Eucharist (*OED*).

Sister Ursula Babthorpe[1] gave the two gilt shrines which are usually placed upon the Pedestals of the Altar.

[p. 458] Sister Constantia gave a suit of silver Taby with gold flowers in it.[2]

Sister Berrington gave a suit with red flowers and silver ground.[3]

Sister Ann' Dominica Howard gave a cope of silver Taby.[4]

The two Sister Traffords having between them a 100 pound above their portion, it was by their desire put out for a little rent for the church. They also gave a hansome white scarf.[5]

The two Sister Jernegans gave a suit and cope, Deacons coats, and scarf of red velvet with raised embrodery and gold galoons.[6]

The two Sister Westons gave a suit and Deacons coats, of a white silk with gold flowers, trim'd with gold lace and galoons.[7]

Sister Mary Austin Smithson gave the Turkey work carpet.[8]

Sister Mary Ignatia Stanley gave a suit of purple Damask with silver galoons and fringe.[9]

[p. 459] The two Sister Vaughans gave the great Silver Remonstrance, the silver compass, the Doors to the Tabernacle which are silver upon gilt copper, the little silver step, and the red silk scarf embroder'd.[10]

Thc two Conyers gave a suit and cope, Deacons coats and scarf of a rich red silk trim'd with gold lace.[11]

Sister Salvin gave a suit with two vestments and a scarf of a very good red and white silk, trim'd with gold.[12]

Lay Sisters

Sister Anne Grafts, and Sister Mary Bows beg'd money to buy the silver gilt remonstrance.[13]

---

[1] Either Ursula Babthorpe (BA010) or Ursula Babthorpe, in religion Monica (BA009).

[2] Constantia De Rope (BA165). Sister Constantia here gave a mass suit for a priest made from watered silk taffeta (taby). As we can see from this list, it is one of a number of similar bequests. It is not certain whether these items were adapted from clothing gowns.

[3] Xaveria Berington (BA022).

[4] Ann Dominic Howard (BA107).

[5] Anastasia Trafford (BA202) and her sister Monica Trafford (BA204).

[6] Mary Teresa Jerningham (BA118); Winefrid Jerningham (BA119). Galoons were narrow trimmings of gold, silver or silk thread (*OED*).

[7] Paula Weston, in religion Ann (BA215); Elizabeth Weston, in religion Delphina (BA216).

[8] Mary Augustine Smithson (BA178).

[9] Mary Ignatia Stanley (BA182).

[10] Ann Vaughan, in religion Mary Joseph (BA207); Teresa Vaughan, in religion Teresa Augustine (BA209). The remonstrance is more usually known as the monstrance.

[11] Frances Conyers, in religion Clementina (BA062); Margaret Conyers, in religion Alipia (BA063).

[12] Dorothy Salvin, in religion Mary Baptist (BA170).

[13] Anne Crafts (BA068); Mary Bowes (BA030). Both were lay sisters.

The two Sister Bartlets gave the little silver cruets, and the little silver crucifix.[1]

Sister Martha Copland gave the velvet Mass book that is plated with silver[2]

Sister Clare Johnson gave the pictures round the upper part of the church.[3]

Sister Johanna Couchefer by selling old rags and candle grease, got money enough to buy a little silver cup for the Priest to wash his fingers in; the communicating silver candlestick, 6 half flower pots of silver, a silver **[p. 460]** crown, and a compass, a step and two little Angels of silver gilt wood, besides a silver soap spoon for the father's house.[4]

Soeculars

The Lady Carrington gave the silver salver that is used in the church for the Brides crowns at clothing and professions.

The Lady Nithsdale gave a suit of silk Tapestry which we use on our holy fathers day.[5]

My Lady Dover gave the great Silver lamp with a foundation for oyl to maintain it.[6]

Lady Mary Herbert gave a suit and cope and Deacons coats of white silver stuff finely embroder'd.[7]

Sir John Web gave the Tabernacle and another 40 pound for a chalice and cruets and 50 pound.

Mrs Griffith gave a suit and Deacons coats of black velvet with raised embrodery on the Antependiums and at her death she left our Reverend Mother Lucy Herbert, about 100 pound Sterlin, which her Reverence gave to the common[8]

[p. 461] To the Choir and there about Sister Magdalen Kemp gave the great crucifix with the images under it.[9]

Sister Helena Andrews gave the red curtains.[10]

Sister Ann' Benedict Thirlwall gave the silver holy water pot for the Choir door, and her father left at his death a 100 pound sterlin to the

---

1 Catherine Bartlett (BA008); Elizabeth Bartlett (BA014). The cruets were small vessels for wine or water during the Eucharist.

2 Martha Copland, lay sister (BA065).

3 Clare Johnson (BA124).

4 Johanna Couchefer, lay sister (BA067).

5 Both Lady Carrington and Lady Nithsdale were sisters of Prioress Lucy Herbert.

6 Lady Dover was Judith Pooley, widow of Henry Jermyn, Lord Dover (see **[pp. 202, 253]**).

7 Here, probably Prioress Lucy Herbert's niece.

8 Lucy Herbert (BA101); 'gave to the common' here means for general use in the community rather than for herself. Antependiums were alter frontals.

9 Magdalen Kemp (BA125).

10 Helen Andrews (BA004).

Monastry, part of it was spent in Masses for his soul, which were said at Namur, and for some years we had a yearly Mass said for him here.[1]

Sister Babthorpe gave our good Angels picture.[2]

Sister Henrietta Markham gave the little Altar in the organ House.[3]

Soeculars

Mr Caryll, Sister Barbara Carylls father, gave the wainscot and seats of the choir[4]

Mrs Magdalen Altham gave the two great Antiphonaries.

[p. 462]

To the Chappel

Sister Henrietta Markham gave the great Altar, and Sister Susan Reynoldson the silver candlesticks.

To our Reverend Mother's Chamber

The Lady Carrington gave the blew bed and hangings of the great Room, and my Lord Carrington (her Spouse) left our Reverend Mother[5] at his death 50 pound Sterlin, which her Reverence gave to the Common

+ our Queen Mary, King James the Second's Queen, gave her picture to our Reverend Mother Herbert.[6]

The Lady Mountague gave the purple bed and hangings for our Reverend Mother's little chamber.

Sir John Gifford gave our Reverend Mother his own and his Lady's picture. He had boarded in our father's house before he was marry'd, and was always very kind to us, giving us frequent **[p. 463]** recreations, and wine twice a week in Lent. He did not live above 4 or 5 years after his mariage to my Lord Middleton's daughter, and as he always retain'd a kindness for us, he had promised his little daughter to our Reverend Mother; after his death my Lady Middleton sent her to us, as we have before remark'd in page 283.[7]

Our Reverend Mother Herbert's Relations, partly at her own half Jubilee and partly at the Jubilee of the House, gave her at least a hundred pound Sterlin, which she most hansomely bestow'd upon our community.

---

1 Ann Benedict Thirwall (BA199).

2 It is not known to which Sister Babthorpe this refers: either Ursula Babthorpe, in religion Monica (BA009) or Ursula Babthorpe (BA010).

3 Henrietta Markham (BA136).

4 Sister Barbara's father was John Caryll (c. 1603–79) of Harting, married to Catherine Petre (1607–82).

5 Lucy Herbert (BA101).

6 The queen was Mary of Modena. The gift was probably related to Lucy Herbert's mother's service to the Jacobite court in exile at St Germain-en-Laye.

7 Sir John Gifford of Burstall, Leicestershire, married Lady Catherine Middleton at St Germain-en-Laye in 1702. See **[pp. 283–4]**.

To the Dormitory

Sister Mary Austin Smithson gave St Joseph's Altar with the rails and wainscoting of the place it stands in.[1]

My Lady Andrews gave the great clock.

To the work chamber

Sister Susan Reynoldson gave to **[p. 464]** the Altar 2 pair of silver candlesticks and 2 pair of silver flower pots.[2]

Sister Ann' Markham gave the red velvet suit.[3]

The Lady Nithsdale gave the silver heart that hangs on our Lady's arm.[4]

Sister Mary Havers gave the chairs.[5]

Sister Helen Andrews gave the two great Landscips of our holy father's life.[6]

Our Reverend Lord Bishop Henry van Susteren gave us his picture.[7]

Mr Sykes gave us the great picture of the descent of our Lord from the cross, and the picture of our holy father at length.[8]

Mrs Sykes gave us the great picture of our Lord's Resurrection.

Four of our confessors, to wit, Mr Kent, Mr Hawker, Mr Pointz and Mr Gerard gave us their pictures.[9]

To the Infirmary

Sister Barbara Caryll gave bedsteads **[p. 465]** and green bed curtains to the great Room above stairs. Cupboards and chairs to the other rooms.[10]

Sister Susan Reynoldson gave the great screen, and the great cupboard for linnen.[11]

Sister Ann' Markham made the little closet.[12]

Sister Henrietta Markham gave the great Altar that has the picture of a crucifix, and the little Altar that has the picture of our Lady's visitation:

---

1 Mary Augustine Smithson (BA178).
2 Susan Reynoldson (BA161).
3 Either Ann Mechtilda Markham (BA137) or Ann Delphina Markham (BA138).
4 Lady Nithsdale, one of Prioress Herbert's sisters: see Herbert family tree.
5 Mary Havers (BA099).
6 Helen Andrews (BA004).
7 Hendrik Jozef van Susteren (1668–1742), Bishop of Bruges 1716–42.
8 William Sykes, painter and dealer, father of Anne and Mary; see **[pp. 235, 407]**. His wife was Mary née Dovery.
9 Fr Robert Kent (1643–78), Confessor 1669–78; see Anstruther 3, pp. 121–2. Fr John Hawker (1650–1707), Confessor 1681–1707; see Anstruther 3, pp. 95–6. Fr Augustine Poyntz (?SJ) (1679/80–1723); see Holt, p. 204. Fr Caryl Gerard alias Wright (1695–1779); see Anstruther 4, p. 110.
10 Barbara Caryll (BA045).
11 Susan Reynoldson (BA161).
12 Either Ann Mechtilda Markham (BA137) or Ann Delphina Markham (BA138).

she also wainscoted the chimney in the inner sickhouse, and that of the little Room above stairs.[1]

To the speak houses

Sister Mary Charleton ciel'd the little speakhouse and the Lobby, and wainscoted the Lobby.[2]

Sister Ann' Markham gave chairs to the great speakhouse.[3]

To the Refectory

Sister Clare Johnson got the Refectory Matted round, and gave the Brass sconces.[4]

[p. 466]

To the Warming Room

Sister Ann Markham gave the chairs.[5]

To the Noviship

Sister Agnes Bedingfeld gave the Altar and the great table.[6]

Mrs Charlot Bound gave the chairs.[7]

To the Musick Room

Sister Wenefride Jernegan gave the great Cupboard, the table, and the chairs, and the best pair of Spinets.[8]

To the Schoole

The Lady Carrington gave the damask bed.[9]

Sister Ann' Weston gave the stones to pave the Refectory; and she and her sister paid for the parting the great Room into three chambers, and for the hangings, Wainscot and chairs of the best of these Rooms, and for the blew Bed in the little room.[10]

---

1 Henrietta Markham (BA136).

2 Mary Charlton (BA048).

3 Either Ann Mechtilda Markham (BA137) or Ann Delphina Markham (BA138).

4 Clare Johnson (BA124).

5 As above (note 3).

6 Agnes Bedingfield (BA016).

7 Charlotte Bond (AC015) left the Augustinians in 1713 and joined the Carmelites in Antwerp.

8 Winefrid Jerningham (BA119).

9 Lady Carrington is probably Anne Herbert, sister of Prioress Lucy Herbert: see family tree.

10 Ann Weston (BA215); Elizabeth Weston, in religion Delphina (BA216).

[p. 467]

To the Garden

Sir Rowland Stanley sent our Reverend Mother three Guineas, and her Reverence bestow'd it in an image of our good Angel, and a little chappel for it in the Garden.[1]

We find in Reverend Mother Bedingfeld's hand that Mr Caryl gave to this Monastry 260 pound Sterlin besides the 100 pound he gave for the seats in the choir, and the yearly good tokens he sent to his Daughter.

This 260 pound we suppose went towards the building of the great Pant for the accounts do not mention that he gave more.

[p. 470] That there may be no mistake in the opening our burying ovens, when necessity of more place obliges us to it, we will here set down in order when and where each of our dear deceased were bury'd in those ovens.

Remark that we reckon the Rows from the top to the bottom, or from the bottom to the top, begining from the side next the church.

Sister Burton was the first we bury'd there. She dyed on the 17th of May 1727, and lyes in the lowest oven of the first Row.[2]

Sister Johanna Couchefer dyed on the 20 of December 1727. She lyes in the lowest oven of the second Row.[3]

Mr Damerin dyed on the 6th of october 1728. He lyes in the first oven from the top of the first Row.

Sister Hellen Andrews dyed on the 12th of December 1728. She lyes in the 2d oven from the ground of the first Row.[4]

Dame Mary Benedict Caryll **[p. 471]** dyed on the 13th of october 1729. She lyes in the second oven from the top, of the first Row.[5]

---

1 Five daughters of Sir Rowland Stanley professed at Bruges between 1700 and 1711.

2 Mary Alexia Burton (BA040).

3 Johanna Couchefer (BA067).

4 Helen Andrews (BA004).

5 Mary Benedict Caryll, of the Benedictines, Dunkirk (DB032), died at Bruges on her journey back from the baths at Aix, where she had gone in search of a cure: see **[pp. 444–5]**.

VOLUME II: 1729–1793

[unpaginated]

J + M

The Chronicles of the secound hunder'd years of our Monastery in Bruges in flanders of Regular Chanonesses of the order of St Augustin dedicated to the Bless'd virgin of Nazareth
where in is recorded what happen'd since september 1729 which concluded the first hunderd years

we ended the first hunderd years of our monastery with a pious jubilation, & we begun the secound with a continuation of the same, for we keept an octave of the jubilee & our Reverend mother invited severall friends at different times to dinner in our Fathers house.[1]

On the 21 of september M[rs] Trowers & her daughter went for england being oblig'd by business to leave us, but she resolved for return again as soon as possible.[2]

On the 26 of september Sister Clementina Conyers fell ill of the smalpox,[3] she was the forth who ^had^ it & they all had it succesively one after another, as soon as one was up or departed, another fell down which made it the harder. but God knows what is best for us his blessed will be done, she received her viaticum & recover'd.

M[rs] mary weston Aunt to Sister Anne weston,[4] having left her neece a legacy of fifteen pound sterlin, ten of it was put into the common & therefore a solomn mass was sung for her & our Reverend mother order'd each of us to hear two masses, & to offer one Communion for her soul.

[unpaginated] on the 12th of october M[rs] Markham with her Daughter, and her sarvant went from hence for england.[5]

on the 13th of october Dame Mary Benedict Caryll a benedictine Dame of dunkirke, departed this life in our Cloister a bout ten in the morning in the 40 year of her age, & 22 of her holy profession.[6] she had been at the

---

1 The Prioress in 1729 was Lucy Herbert (1693–44) BA101, Prioress 1709–44.

2 Mrs Trowers and her daughter entered Nazareth in August 1729; see vol. 1, **[p. 446]**.

3 Clementina Conyers (BA062).

4 Ann Weston (BA215). Her aunt, Mrs Mary Weston, née Copley (of Sutton Place, Surrey), came from a family with many connections to the English convents in exile.

5 Mrs Markham of Ollerton (formerly Catherine Constable) of Houghton and her daughter Mary Ursula returned to the convent several times; see also vol. 1, **[pp. 376, 390, 397, 433]**. Her daughter Anne Christina (BA138) professed in 1717. See K. S. B. Keats-Rohan (ed.), *English Catholic Nuns in Exile, 1600–1800: A Biographical Register*, Prosopographia et Genealogica 15 (Oxford: Unit for Prosopographical Research, Linacre College, forthcoming 2017)

6 Mary Caryll, in religion Mary Benedict (1708–29) DB032. Her father was Philip Caryll Esq of Catherington, Hants, and her mother was Mary Fettiplace. Her sister Ann (BA047) professed at Bruges in 1712.

bathes of Aise la Chapell, as we have said before in the Annals of the last century pag: 444[1] & remaining here in hopes to recover more strength & health in order to go her journy for dunkerke, it pleas'd allmighty to call ^her^ to himself, she was a woman of good sense, pious & of an agreable sweet temper. she received all the rites of the Church & was present to her self to the last moment of her life. she dy'd of a deep Consumption. We bury'd her on the 14th in our new burying place. she lyes in the secound oven[2] from the top of the first row next the Church. we said the Commendations & the long Dierge for her, & we sung mass & burying & rung three hours, as we do for our own Religious. *Requiescat in Pace*

this good Dame in time of her sickness, express'd a great sence of gratitude to our Superiour & all our Community for the kindness she received amongst us, her father was eye wittness of it, for our Bishop gave him leave to come in every day to see her, so that he both heard from her & saw with his own eyes that nothing was omitted which could be thought of for her recovery or solace.

On the 22 of october Miss Charlot Conyers went from hence for england.[3]

about the same time we had notice of Mrs mannocks death she was neece to sister Susan Reynoldson, we had five pound for to pray for her soul, we sung mass for her.[4]

On the 17 of november we received mary Cook for a sarvant in order to be a lay sister.

Mrs Pole Sister to Sister Anne & Sister Henrietta Markham[5] sent us a hundred pound starlin for an Annuall Requiem mass for her spouse Mr Pole of spinkel. & as her desire in giving it here was kindness to our monastery as well as to her deceased spouse, our Reverend Mother ordred that each of us should offer for Mr Poles soul one Communion, & some indulgence every day for the space of a month, & to offer a Communion & hear three masses for Mrs Pole.

---

1 See vol. 1, **[p. 444]**.

2 Oven: see Glossary.

3 Charlotte was the sister of Teresa Conyers and the daughter of Sir Baldwin and Lady Margaret Conyers: see **[pp. 9, 10, 11]** below.

4 Susan Reynoldson (1670–1730) BA161. Mrs Mannock has not yet been identified.

5 Mrs Pole, in Stirnet, Family Tree Markham 01, is Ursula (b. 1668), who married as her second husband John Pole (d. 1724, will TNA) of Spinkhill, Derbys. Her sisters were Ann Mechtilda Markham (BA137) and Henrietta Markham (BA136).

[p. 1]

J + M

1730

[*Two lines crossed through, illeg.*] we sung immediatly a solemn mass, & an annuall mass is to be perform'd for him & his name to be writ as a benefactor & hers allso when dead, besides this each all so was order'd to offer some Communions & masses for both the deceas'd & her.

the 10 of january Mrs Picard daughter to the factor that made our new organ was received for convictress.

the 24 of january my lady Montaigue & her two sarvants parted from hence for England, their comportment whilst here was very edifying; they ware very carefull not to cause the least disorder.[1]

the 30 of january Sister mary frances wright departed this life.[2] She was sent Convictress about 16 years of age, & at 18 took the kercheif. from her first coming she was an innocent pious soul, she had a very good voice for the choir & was not less constant & diligent, whilst in health then servissable: she was one eassely drawn by those she thought past for witt, which unhappily engag'd her in a conversation less regular, by which her first fervour for some years was deminish'd but they dying before her, she return'd to what she had been & before her death made ample satisfaction by her most ediffying patience, for a bout six months she had spook [spoke] of a swelling she had on her side below her hip, but in such a manner that non could imagin ^it^ any great matter till a bout three weeks or a month before her death. the surgeon being sent for found not only the flesh but even bone corrupted, which must have given her a great deel to suffer, & when he drest it he took out both pices of flesh & bone, all which she bore with so great patience as never to complaine, or give any signe of the violent paine she sufferd **[p. 2]** except by pressing ~~the hand~~ their hand that held her, the surgeon selldome Drest, the sore with^out^ tears of compassion knowing what she endur'd, he was so edified with her patience that he said sure she was a most holy soul that could suffer so much with out complaint. her gratitude was not less exemplare being most thankfull for the least sarvice that was render'd her in this her illness; still expressing their charitable goodness & her obligations to them which gave a sensible pleasure to all: she dyed the 30 between 9 & ten in the morning perfectly sensible to the last, the 68 of her age & the 49 of her profession, she was bury'd the 31 in the secound oven of the secound row in our new burial place. *Requiescat in Pace.*

---

[1] Lady Montagu, was Mary, sister of Prioress Lucy Herbert (BA101); she retained the surname of her second husband, who had died in 1708.

[2] Mary Wright, in religion Frances (1681–1730) BA227.

the 3[d] of march Mary Cook parted hence her health & strength not being sufficient for a lay Sister.

M[r] Markham sent five pound for his wifes soul for the which three masses & one Communion was order'd to be offer'd by all.[1]

the 4th of aprill Sister Susanna Raynolson departed this life.[2] for some years she had been wholly confin'd to the infirmary. she allways had been a sickly woman yet very labourious in what ever imployment she had been in, & zealous of the Common profitt, in her younger years very fervourus, but still t'was all in a particular way not so advisable in religion; all superiours was forced to condesend to her having the misfortune of a very odd temper, which often gave her self as well as others much to suffer, she was sensible of it & in her latter years would sometimes say t'was her unhapiness not to have it brook [broke] when young, for that not t'was to late, the humiliation which this must have given her we hope atton'd for many faults, she suffer'd much with her continuall infirmitys & with patience. she was sensible to the last & dy'd about 4 in the morning **[p. 3]** the 81 year of her age & neer 60 of her holy profession she was bury'd upon the 5 in the third oven of the secound row. *Requiescat in Pace.*

the 26 of aprill Elizabeth moady was received a sarvant in tryall for a Lay Sister.[3]

the first of may mis Lilia Huddleston went for england to her friends who sent for her.[4] [*marginal insertion vertical*] 20 of may mis Pention was received for a convictress.

The first of june Sister mary Xaveria Willis made her holy profession.[5] Mr weston at his death left his sister 30 pounds, ten of which was given to the procuratrix for the present use of the house & the other twenty his sister was desirous to imploy in some conveniences for the benefitt of the imployment she was in, there was a solemn mass sung for him & each order'd to offer a Communion & othere prayers for him.[6]

the 17 of july Mis teresa Conyers went for england her parents having sent for her.[7]

---

[1] Thomas Markham was the father of Ann Delphina Markham (BA138). His wife was Catherine Constable of Houghton, Yorkshire (d. 1730).

[2] Susan Reynoldson (1670–1730) BA161.

[3] Ann Moody later returned and professed as Elizabeth (1734–49) BA143.

[4] Possibly Leila (or Laelia) Huddleston, daughter of Henry Huddleston, a doctor in Durham, and Mary Gage of Hengrave. She married James Farril of Bury St Edmunds, Suffolk; see Stirnet, Family Tree, Huddleston 03.

[5] Mary Xaveria Willis (1730–35) BA222, musician.

[6] Mr Weston was probably John Weston (d. 1730) of Sutton Place, Surrey, brother of Paula, in religion Ann (BA215); their sister Elizabeth (BA216) died in 1721.

[7] Teresa Conyers was the sister of Charlotte and the daughter of Sir Baldwin and Lady Margaret Conyers; see also **[pp. 9, 10, 11]** below.

Mademoisell Picard, having had hopes given her before she came of a probability of being admitted here for a nun in the account of her voice & musick: some of the community being for it & otheres not, t'was judg'd proper to deside it by votes which was done, & the suffrages being taken she was cast out: upon the 24 of july she parted hence for Liege.[1]

the 6 of aug: Elizabeth moody not having her health returned to england with a promiss if she recover'd it, to be againe received.

the 5 of sep ^Sister Angel Huddleston^ having been procuratrix about 7 years, was chang'd & Sister Dorothy Stanley was chosen in her place.[2]

the 11 of sep Mademoisell Henick parted from hence to her friends in twone.[3]

thc 20 of sep Mademoisell Grisper one of Ostend, was received for a pentioner.

the 27 of sep Sister Milburge Russel departed this life about 3 in the morning the 65 of ^her^ age & 43 of her holy profession.[4] From her first coming she was very pious & from her puttin on the **[p. 4]** habitt she was very observant of all her religious duties & a very good religious woman. the three last years of her life God was pleas'd to try her with cattracts on both her eyes so that she could scarce see her way, which she bore with much resignation tho a most sencible cross to her. She had the misfortune of a very resentive temper, which often we doubt not proved as great a subject of merit as of suffering & humiliation to her, for it render'd her less agreable to others, inconsideration of this her weakness our superiour did not only make her her chapelin but continu'd her tell her death tho so blind as not to be capable in many things of sarving her & in time of recreation after supper she walk'd with her, which condesension she judg'd a necessary solace for her, & there fore tell her death she would not admitt of what was desir'd by severall of the community of walking with her by turns. Upon the 6 of this month she was seiz'd with a fevour, which soon proved dangerous she received with much piety & devotion all the last sacrements being perfectly her self till falling into convelsions she had a long & violent agony. She was bury'd the 20 in the uppermost oven of the 2[d] row in our buryall place. *Requiescat in pace*

1 There is no record that she professed at the Sepulchrines at Liège.

2 Elizabeth Angela Huddleston (BA112); Dorothy Stanley (BA183), Chantress; Procuratrix 1730–49.

3 The Chronicler uses 'Mademoiselle' to distinguish young women from the locality from English boarders or entrants.

4 Milburge Russell (1688–1730) BA168.

The 28 of sep: mis mary floyd was received for a convictress.[1] Sister Frances Xaveria Simners friends sent a guinea for prayers for her sisters soul, for which we all heard a mass & offered a Communion.[2]

1731

The 4th of feb: Sister mary Havers celebrated her wholl jubilee.[3] The 27 of aprill Sister Catherin Charlton departed this life a bout 8 in the morning the 68 of her age & 47 of her profession.[4] there was great hopes when she was first received of her proving a serviceable religious, but God disposs'd othere ways for she was seiz'd with madness the 2d year after her profession & continu'd in that afflicting state tell death, but was so much herself then as to confess & receive extrem unction. She dy'd of a fevour & mortification in her leg & was bury'd the 28 in the first oven from the ground & third row in our buriall place. *Requiescat in pace.*

[p. 5] the 28 may mr Tasbrough & his Lady with their two little daughters came, the eldest which was mary gest past 13 year old & the other was past ten, they ware both taken in for convictresses.[5]

this year one Mr Baker left us at his death a hunder'd guineas for the which every one of the Community was order'd to hear eight masses, & offer one Communion, & to say the Cross prayers or the scapular pardon for 30 days for his soul & there was a solemn mass sung for him.

the 30 of may Mis Margret Taclock was received for a convictriss & Helen Blevin as sarvant in tryall for a Lay Sister.[6]

One Mrs grifith a relation of sister Helen Andrews left her at her death a legacy of five pound, but she being dead before it came the Community was order'd to hear one mass & communicat for the soul of her that left it.[7]

---

1 Mary Floyd: the surname variant Lloyd was widely used. Mary Lloyd was the sister of Elizabeth Lloyd, who professed at Bruges in 1726 (BA129): see vol. 1, **[pp. 401, 417–18]**. Mary left Bruges and was sponsored by the Duchess of Norfolk to join the Conceptionists in Paris, where she professed in 1736, PC070. See J. Gillow and R. Trappes-Lomax (eds), *The Diary of the 'Blue Nuns', or Order of the Immaculate Conception, at Paris, 1658–1810*, CRS 8 (London: CRS, 1910).

2 Frances Xaveria Simner, lay sister (1726–62) BA174. Her sister has not been identified.

3 Mary Havers (1681–1733) BA099.

4 Catherine Charlton, in religion Xaveria (1684–1731) BA050.

5 They later professed: Mary Tasburgh, in religion Maria Frances (1741–93) BA192; Margaret Tasburgh (1748–81) BA193. Their parents were Francis Tasburgh of Bodney, Norfolk, and his wife, Mary Symonds.

6 Margaret Tatlock, in religion Mary Alexia, lay sister (1736–73) BA194; Helen Blevin, lay sister (1734–88) BA026.

7 Helen Andrews (BA004). Mrs Griffith has not been identified.

my Lady Abbess of the Benedictins at Gant having been for some time Elected but for want of a Bishop (he being dead)[1] could not be bless'd, & tell that was done she could not performe some functions therefore was oblig'd to go out of her monastery to some towne where there was one, which we hearing invited ^her^ very kindly to come to our house. which offer was with gratfull acknowledgments accept'd of, & the day by our Bishop apointed to be St mary magdalin.[2] she with two of her Religious, Dame flavia tempest[3] & dame Ildefonsa Clifford,[4] came on the 19 of july with their Confessor & one M[rs] Haggerson which ware intertain'd as long as they stay'd in our Father house, but my lady & her two dames lodg'd & eate with in.[5] on the day apointed by our Bishop[6] he with six priest that attended him, & the Arch D[e]acon & Arch priest came about ten & the serimony was perform'd with great solemnity. he sung the mass & would have sent us his musick but we did not exept it, but performed it all ourselves. our Church was as fine as we could dress it & all our house with in doors in the best order that possibly we could, both to honour & shew our kindness to her. after mass my Lord Bishop invitted to his table in his own palace our Confessor[7] & all the Company that was in our fathers house & treated them very nobely, & gave them all leave to enter our inclosure which they did. after vespers, our Community assembled in the worke Chamber, at the upper ^end^ of which was lay'd a Carpit & an **[p. 6]** armd chair set for my Lady Abbess & an intertainment of musick was made in prayes of her, & a Coppy of verses to the same effect was presented her, made by our Confessor & printed on white sattin. her Ladyship seem'd much oblig'd for the sevilitys & kindness that was shown her, & press'd to pay the expences we had been at on her account & likeways to have given a recreation to the Community but both was generously refuss'd. her ladyship & all those that came with her return'd to gant the 24 of july.

on the 6 of august our dear Sister Teresa Vaughan departed this life.[8] she had been sent by her parents a Convictress at ten year old, & at twelve by her father who was very antient recal'd home, he being desirous to

---

1 The Abbess of Ghent was Anne Tyldesley, in religion Cecilia (1707?–1736) GB234. She was elected in July 1730. The Bishop of Ghent, Philips-Erard van der Noot, died on 2 March 1730 and was not replaced until June 1731, by Jan-Baptist de Smet. Abbess Tyldesley was confirmed by the Bishop of Bruges, Hendrik Josef van Susteren.

2 St Mary Magdalene's day is celebrated on 22 July.

3 Frances Tempest, in religion Flavia (1710–after 1749) GB219.

4 Roda Preston Clifford, in baptism Ildefonsa (1724–after 1748) GB048.

5 The Confessor at the Benedictines, Ghent in 1731 was Fr James Whetenhall 1728–73; Anstruther 4, p. 297.

6 The Bishop of Bruges, Hendrik Josef van Susteren, Bishop 1716–42.

7 The Confessor at Bruges in 1731 was Father Caryl Gerard, Confessor 1723–79; see Anstruther 4, p. 110.

8 Teresa Vaughan (1709–31) BA209.

see his Children before he dy'd. she left us at that tender age with an arnest desire of being religious, in so much that being in sight of her fathers house those that was sent for her said in gest now mis you see your fathers house will you go to it, or return back from whence you came, she without the least demur turn'd her horce to go back, tho found [*sic*] of her relations would have left them unseen to have Comply'd with her vocation, but after some time that she was with them those generous sentiments grew cold, tho the resolution of being religious never left her, but vaine pleasurs & divertions stiffled the motion of divine grace for some time. but the death of her sister in law who dy'd in Child bed, revived againe in her those pious thoughts, but not withstanding the love for her brother retain'd her for about 13 years, during which time she suferd a great conflict between nature & grace, the later prevailing she fixt her journey & her sister which went over with her made the same resolution but each ignorant of the others designe tell a few days before ~~before~~ it was executed, having broke through that great obsticle of parting with her brother, she expected no more conflicts but God permitted her to under go another, for making a vissit to the Teresians at Lier,[1] where she had a relation, there contemptable habit[2] & the solitude of the place together with their kind invitation moved her inclination to have remained there, but was unwilling to determin by her self a thing of that consequence, she apply'd herself to Reverend Father Roper,[3] who told her that the place where she received the first grace was the place in which she should comply with it, from this answer she no more doubted of the place then of her vocation & from the first putting on the habit she practiss'd the same submission to all that God placed over her, & was a most exact good religious **[p. 7]** woman she never spar'd her self in any imployment. she had a mighty deffidence in her self & therefore had a great difficulty to be cheef in any imployment, but to be put as help she had non, how ever labourious it was. she was a woman of good sence & faithfull to the attracts of God's grace, by which he lead her to an exact obsarvance of order. for about two years before her death, she had an open sore in her leg, which she own'd was some times extremly painefull, yet she obsarved order as much as if she had it not, nor would admitt of any relaxation nor even sleep matins. all she desir'd was to go some times from Complin & of that she all so had some remorce as to much indulging nature. tho one less fervoress would have thought much more to have been but necessary. these two last years she in a particular manner prepared herself for death, persuaded that she should not live long. upon the 24 of july being as well as usuall she said to the

1 Teresians: another name for Discalced Carmelites, after their foundress, St Teresa of Avila.
2 'Contemptible habit': reflects the austerity of their monastic rule.
3 Probably Fr Thomas Roper SJ (1654–1716); see Holt, p. 215.

religious that was her Companion in the Church that she had a mind that day to go to confession before vespers, which was before her turn. God so permitting, othere ways she would not have gone at all, for she was taken very ill before it came to her turn, it proving a fevour the next day the[y] apprehended it would seize her head & render her uncapable, so the same religious advise'd her to go again to Confession to which she answer'd she had nothing more to say then what she had said. soon after she was taken wholly from her self & for many days so raging that with out tying her no two in the house had strength to hold her, & with all she had conveltions so could only receive extremunction [*sic*] & the last absolution & so expier'd a little after midnight the 50 year of her age & 23 of her profession, the doctor & surgeon declaring that she dy'd of the spoted fevour, we ware not permitted to read the Psalter ^by her^ nor was she expos'd nor bury'd in our ovens but in the Church yeard & the deep in the ground because of the infection which was done the same day at noon, the next day the solemn mass & funerall was performed as if expos'ed in the Church. *Requiescat in pace*.

on the 31 of August we sent sister Anne Formby for England to conduct mis Howard[1] who had been ill from the 3d of november, on which day she was seiz'd with convultions, both doctor & surgeon did their utmost but without success, she was by both judg'd in danger & on the 16 she received her *viaticum* which was the first communion she ever made tho she had a most earnest desire to have communicated before ^but^ was thought to young. she communicated with so great a sense of piety & devotion that it moved to tears those that ware present. she continu'd for the space of about six weeks to fall into convultions every 3 or 4 hours, & during those six weeks how little norishment **[p. 8]** or sleep she took is not to be belived, according to human reason it seem'd not sufficient to sustaine nature. the frequent convultions took a way her eye sight so as not to distinguish on[e] thing from another, & from her hips to her feet she had no feeling, they remain'd allways stretched out & her heels so drawn in that she appear'd to have non & they lay'd hollow from the bed, the doctor & surgeon finding all this pro[s]criptions to have a contrary effect for when they gave her any thing to make her sleep, she would not sleep a wink & when they gave her phisick tho never so strong she would not go so much as once to stool, & so of everything ellce, which made them think her illness some^thing^ more than naturall. the surgeon say'd if it was his Child he would have her excercis'd,[2] which could not be done without my Lord Bishops leave, which he granted to our Confessor, ordering him to fast three days before, & four of our

[1] Ann Formby, lay sister (1726–58) BA082. Miss Anne Howard: possibly the same Miss Howard who arrived with Lady Montagu on 4 July 1728: see vol. 1, **[p. 434]**.

[2] Here the meaning is 'exorcised'.

religious to do the same, which was done & upon the 16 of january he performed the serimonies as the church ordaines for posses'd or bewitch'd parsons. finding no amendement we lost hopes, the Child whose piety increas'd with her illness earnestly desired to go to Communion that she might gaine the jubilee it being time of it, which was granted her the 25 of feb: her mistress bid her be sure to beg of God her health it it ware his will & she promist she would. having pray'd for about half a quarter after Communion with much recolection & devotion her mistress took a book to read some prayers to her, she told her she had some feeling in her legs for she felt the sheet which she had not felt before & could move them a little which for a considerable time she could not do, her mistress could scarce believe it but making tryall found it as she said. she rais'd her up a little in her bed which for some three months she could not do with out her swooning away. the next day with help she got up & walk'd a little but her limns was stiff & continu'd so tell the 22 of march which was maunday Thursday,[1] on which day it was granted her to communicated a gaine, to return thanks & to beg a more perfect recovry, after which she walk from the lay Sisters Chapel to the scool with out any help & seem'd only now to want an increase of strength to perfect her recovery. at whitsonty'd[2] she fell ill a gaine, but not in the same manner upon ^which^ we resolved to send her for england her native air, hoping it might recovery her. she went the a bove mention'd day, much a gainst her will her petition during her sickness was that she might dye rather then go for england, her comportment during the wholl time of her sickness was more like a woman advenced in vertue then like a Child. She neither ask'd for any thing, nor refuss'd to take any thing they gave her what ever relunctance she had, how bad the medecin was she would over come herself by a motive of vertue & take it. she was never seen to be out of humour or pivish the wholl time, her discource was commonly of piety seaming to be a Child prevented by God, with his mercys designes her the event will show.

[p. 9] on the 4 of september about 9 in ^the^ morning our dear subprioress Sister Clare sanderson departed this life the 63 of her age & 45 of her holy ^profession^.[3] from her first begining a religious life was very exact in her religious obsarvance, & of a most peascable mild temper, & very desirous to consarve it in the Community which made her often to put up not only with silence some most sensible reflections made of her, but even with out shewing more feeling of them then consisted with meekness in which vertue she was eminent. which no doubt render'd her dear to God as well as to us all. for some years before her death she was

---

1 Maundy Thursday: in Holy Week just before Easter, celebrating the Last Supper.

2 Whitsuntide: see Glossary.

3 Clare Saunderson (1687–1731) BA172.

infirme & did dayly preceptable decay & grew weaker. yet still observant of order, she dy'd as she lived, patient, gratfull & quiet. gest after we had ended the prayers of the association for a happy death, having receiv'd all the sacrements the fiftenth day of ~~her~~ her sickness, which was a smale fevour & decay of nature. & was bury'd the next day in the 2^{d} oven of the third row in our buriall place. *requiescat in pace*

on the 5 of september mis willis, sister to our Sister mary xaveria willis came to see her before she enter'd at the benedictins Dames at dunkerke[1] where she was upon our recommendation taken for her voice. but having been ill for some time & not perfectly recover'd we took her in, tell she was, that it might be no obsticle to her reception there.

We begun this year to sing the new plain song upon the solemn feasts but not having a sufficience of books printed we could not begin~~g~~ it for good till the 8 of september which is the feast to which our house is dedicated having then compleated a sufficient number we begun it.

on the 10 of september my Lady Conyers with her two daughters mis Charlot & mis Teresa & a sarvant designing to stay here for a considerable time was taken into our inclosure & lodg'd in the apartement which is in our pentioners school & tabled in our Fathers house.[2]

the 17 of september Sister Anne Markham was chousen subprioress & Sister Angela Huddleston Arcaria.[3]

on the 17 of september Sister Anne Formby returned from england & brought with her Anne Moody a sarvant in tryall for a Lay Sister.[4]

five pound was sent for prayers for the soul of m^{r} wright brother to our deceased Sister mary Frances, for whom all was order'd to hear three masses & offer one Communion.[5]

the 20 of september mademoiselle de Grisper went from hence to her friends at ostend.

the 27 the above mention'd mis willis went from hence to dunkerke.

[p. 10] one m^{rs} Errington Cousen to our Sister Perpetua Errington, sent ten pound for prayers for her self, her father & brother & for Lady Baltamour her friend, which was newly deceas'd,[6] for the Lady we sung mass & for her self & the others each was to hear five masses & one

---

1 Miss Willis: Joanna Willis, finally professed at the Conceptionists, Paris (1742–73) PC128. Mary Xaveria Willis (BA222).

2 Margaret, Lady Conyers (née Neville) of Horden, Durham, widow of Sir Baldwin Conyers (d. 1731), was the mother of six daughters. These two, Charlotte and Teresa, were sisters of Frances, in religion Clementina (BA062) and Margaret, in religion Alipia (BA063).

3 Ann Markham (BA137); Angela Huddleston (BA112).

4 Ann Formby, lay sister (BA082); Ann Moody (BA143).

5 Mary Frances Wright (1681–1730) BA227; her brother John died in 1731. See WWTN, Wright of Elvdeon family tree.

6 Dorothy Errington, in religion Perpetua (1681–1739) BA076. Lady Baltimore: possibly Charlotte Lee, wife of the 4th Baron Baltimore, who died in 1721.

Communion On the 17 of november mis Catherin Caryll daughter to Lady Mary & neece to our superiour was received for Convictress.[1]

1732

Sister Frances xaveria friends sent four pound for prayers for their famile that was living & for those that was dead, for the which each was order'd to hear two masses for the living & two for the dead & the Cross prayers for five days.[2]

on the 14 of june my Lady Conyers with her two daughters & sarvant went from hence for the spa.

july the 22 the Governess of newport with the Baroness de Mol[3] & a nother lady obtained leave of the bishop to see our enclouser, they ware only in it for two hours. we treated them with tea & sugar cakes & a little musick & they seemed extreemly oblig'd with our sivility.

my Lady Gerard left us at her death five pound, we sung a solemn mass for her & all was order'd to hear a nother & offer a Communion for her.[4]

the 12 of august mis joana Willis sister to our Sister mary xaveria Willis was received for a Convictress.[5]

on the 14 my Lady Fortescu & her maid & her priest & nephew & Mr Bodenham & his Lady came here, the two latter went to brussells to the profession of his daughter, during which time my Lady Fortescu & her maid remain'd in our enclousur.[6]

on the 30 they being return'd from Brussells, they all parted from hence for england.

on the 7 of september M[rs] Dorel daughter to my Lord Strangford[7] came here with eldest son & three daughters, the youngest of which having had for some years a desire fixt her resolution of being here upon the Characture she had of our house. They remain'd in towne for about fifteen

---

1 Catherine Caryll (1716–48) was a grand-daughter of Prioress Lucy Herbert's sister Frances Herbert.

2 Frances Xaveria Simner (BA174).

3 The Governess was the wife of the Governor of Nieuport. Baroness de Mol: a connection to the Digby family in the seventeenth century through Diana Digby, who married Rene de Mol in 1667.

4 Lady Gerard: either Mary Cansfield, widow of William Gerard, 5th Baronet, or Elizabeth Clifton, wife of William Gerard, 6th Baronet.

5 Joanna Willis: a convictress at Bruges, but later professed at the Conceptionists in Paris, PC128; Mary Xaveria Willis (BA222).

6 Lady Mary Fortescue was probably Mary, née Huddleston (d. 1744), widow of Sir Francis Fortescue, 4th Baronet of Salden, Bucks (d. November 1729). Mr Bodenham and his wife: Charles Bodenham of Rotherwas, Herefordshire, and his wife, Anne Stonor, were the parents of Mary Bodenham, who professed at the Benedictines, Brussels (1732–92) BB023.

7 Mrs Olivia Darell, née Smythe, was the daughter of Philip Smythe, 2nd Viscount Strangford; three of her sons became Jesuits. She was also the sister of Catherine Smith, who joined the Carmelites at Antwerp (AC113): see vol. 1, **[p. 178]**.

days during which time they dinn'd in our Fathers house, on the 23 they all parted hence for england except the youngs [*sic*] daughter mis Oliva Darel, which on the same day enter'd the enclosure & beg'd the habitt.[1]

[*these two lines pasted in*] M[rs] willis having desir'd us to send her daughter winefrid to a relation of hers at dunkerke we sent ^her^ with m[rs] Darel she going that way for england.[2]

[p. 11] on the 27 m[rs] Oliva took the first habit & is call'd sister mary Oliva.[3] on the 25 my Lady Conyers with her daughters & sarvant return'd from the spa[4] & lodgs as before in our enclosur.

on the 15 of october mis pention by her parent's orders went for england, much against her inclination, she having a desire to be religious.

upon the same day allmighty God was ^pleas'd^ to work a most surprising change in our dear Sister Teresa Joseph Chichester,[5] who for some years seem'd tanted with madnesss she had allways been a pious good creature, & from her first taking the habitt truely apply'd herself to vertue perticularly to a most exact observance of order & to correct her own naturall temper which was prid, sloth & willfullness not failing to humble herself when she had transgress'd. she was never esteem'd a woman of particular good parts, yet of sufficient to give hopes she would prove a serviciable member till of a sudden she fell into a melancholy dejected way, & severall times told one of the religious that prid was her prodominant passion, & that God would humble it, & make her an example to others, for that she should be imprison'd for it, the religious to whome she said it, invain indevour'd to put those thoughts out of her head but could not, for she grew perceptable worce. the advice of our Phisician being ask'd, he judg'd to proceed from lowness of spirits, all possible remedys ^was^ used but with out effect, after which she fell into great fitts of laughing & would burst out at all times of choir & refectory, grew more willfull & heady & refused to do humble duties. but in all others was very exact & went constantly to the sacrements tell about two years agoe her judgement was so gone as refuse all subjection to superiours thinking her self not oblig'd there unto & would never go to confession, yet would go to communion. so that on those days that they [*sic*] religious went to communion she was bolted up in her cell tell after communion was over. after this upon the least conterdiction she would strick who ever oppos'd her, for the which she was severall times confin'd to her cell, but by the tenderness of our superiour s[t]ill releas'd with out being able to make her promiss amendment which by

1 Mary Darell, in religion Mary Olivia (1734–66) BA071, Prioress 1744–66.
2 Winefrid Willis, in religion Mary Catherine (1742–97) BA221. See **[pp. 71, 75, 135, 147, 199, 340–1]**.
3 Mary Olivia: probably Mary Darell (see above).
4 They had been taking the waters for her health at Spa near Liège.
5 Teresa Joseph Chichester (1724–69) BA052.

no indeavours kind or sever could she be made to do. in october last finding she still grew worce & apprchending that her being at liberty might be dangerous because of her striking & the community being affraid of her for which reason it was thought fitt to confine her in the house in the garden which was in her present circumstances the properest place for her, where she remain'd about a year **[p. 12]** or more, in a sullen manner, & seldome would speak except to give ill languish or in veigh against our superiour, against whome she had particular spight. many ^prayers^ was perform'd for her & masses say'd for her, yet we found no a mendment, hearing of the severall miracles that had been latly wrought by the venerable mother Anne of St Bartholomew,[1] some of our religious propos'd making a novena[2] to her & getting some of the dust of her coffin for to take inwardly those days, which being procur'd severall begun the devotion for her which being ended had in appearance no othere effect then that she became more sevil so as to answer those that spoke to her & to shew some sence of her confinement, yet would not hear of the least submission in order to her releasement, tell upon Saint Teresa's day[3] Father Confessor[4] going to her (as he had often before done in vain) found her intierly chang'd, being very willing to ask pardon & submit to what ever should be require'd upon which Reverend mother[5] went to her & she behav'd herself in so humble a manner as to draw tears from all present. after this she sent for others & most humbly ask'd them pardon. but the community being still afraid of her she was ^not^ releas'd tel the Sunday following which was St Peter of Alcanteras day.[6] then she having been at confession & Communion, after dinner, the Community being assembled together in the work chamber Reverend mother brought her in, where she most humbly accus'd herself of all her misbehaviour & beg'd pardon of all, & not content with this which was only requir'd of her, she went to severall of the Lay Sisters to whome she had been abusive & ask'd them pardon, kneeling, this being done she went to her duties & perform'd each with the same exactness as before her misfortune. she goes constantly to the sacrements & shews in all an humble obedient & sevil disposs[it]ion, to the no less surprize then comfort of us all.

---

[1] Mother Anne of St Bartholomew: Anne Downes (1622–74) AC039, had been professed at the Antwerp Carmelites. Thirty-two years after her death her body was found to be incorrupt, which was seen as a sign for potential beatification. See Nicky Hallett, *Lives of Spirit: English Carmelite Self-Writing of the Early Modern Period* (Aldershot: Ashgate, 2007), pp. 63–6.

[2] Novena: see Glossary.

[3] St Teresa's Day: 15 October.

[4] Father Confessor in 1732 was Fr Caryl Gerard, Confessor 1723–79; Anstruther 4, p. 110.

[5] Reverend Mother in 1732 was Prioress Lucy Herbert (BA101).

[6] The feast of St Peter of Alcantara was celebrated on 19 October.

on the 25 of november Sister Margret was sent to conduct mis Caryll to dunkerke, who had~~ving~~ a most Earnest desire to be religious here.[1] Lady mary Caryll her mother, [~~*illeg*~~.] thinking [her] to young for such an undertaking & for othere reasons, order'd she should go to dunkerk to vissit her two aunts & there to remaine for some time.[2] but before she went she beg'd the habit both to put a stop to the importunitys she so much apprehended in going to her aunts, as allso to advance her taking the habit at her return.

[p. 13]

The Year
+
1733

Allmighty God was pleas'd to begin this year with an allmost universall sickness through all parts of Europe of which vast numbers tho of different diseases dy'd.[3] great colds, fevers & plurecis[4] was the shere which fell to our town, we heard continually of the afflictions & sufferings of other monasterys, both in our neighbourhood & distant towns, who had not sufficient well to tend the sick or able to keep choir or refectory. yet still we continu'd pritty well, tho scarce one escap'd a great cold tell about the end of january, we then begun to pertake of the universal affliction, so many falling ill each day that upon that purification of our Blessed Lady which is the 2[d] of feberary we was forced to leave of singing, & could sing neither mass nor no part of the office tho the choir was still keept, yet it was by the sick for we ^had^ non well. in this suffering condition no care was wanting for our solace, both by better diet, & all other helps. Reverend Mother appointed one each morning to goe at four o clock to all that rise to go to mattins, to give them a bit of ginger bread, & a little dram that they might not come fasting to mattins. tho it was with extreme difficulty that the choir service was maintain'd yet prayes be to God it was.

On the 5 of feberary sister Oliva Dorel[5] was Cloathed which was design'd to have been on the 3[d] but she & many more of the Community being ill it was defer'd but finding no hopes of things growing better more

---

[1] Sister Margaret: Margaret Linny (1717–65) BA128, a lay sister and able to leave the enclosure. Miss Caryll is as yet unidentified; no Carylls are listed in the professions at Dunkirk in this period.

[2] Probably Lady Mary Caryll, née Mackenzie, daughter of the Earl of Seaforth and Frances Herbert, who married John Caryll in 1712. They had two daughters, Elizabeth and Catherine, born in 1715 and 1716. The two aunts at Dunkirk were Mary Caryll (d. 1760) DB031, and her sister Arabella (d. 1759) DB026.

[3] References are made to epidemics of influenza and smallpox across Europe in 1732–3.

[4] plurecis: pleurisy.

[5] Mary Darell, in religion Mary Olivia (BA071).

still falling ill & the first not recovering, the seremony was perform'd by the Arch Priest with only a reading mass & no Deacons nor no musick. & the bride her self being ill, was forced to go to bed after dinner, all the recreations was deffer'd tell Community was in a better state of health.

upon the 9 of feberary Sister Mary Havers departed this life the 70 year of her age, & 52 of her profession.[1] she had allways been a very infirme woman & much troubled with the gaul[2] which was cheefly cause of that unease fretfull humour she was so lyable too, which frequently appear'd by some cross peevish words, which gave each one in their turn much to suffer. but we look'd upon it as the effect of her indisposition & naturall misfortune rather then a fault, for she selldome or ever fail'd after having said a pivish thing to seek some occation either to say or do some thing kind to the parson, nor was she so troublesome after her return from the **[p. 14]** dutch monastery as she was before she went. She had allways been piously inclin'd & much devoted to our Blessed Lady, of which we now hope she feelds the happy effect. On the 2 instant she was seiz'd with the cold & a fever on the 3[d] in the evening she was carry'd to the infirmary yet continued dayly to rise & sett up the greates part of the day & contrary to her usall temper was ease & content with all things & afraid of giving trouble. She continuing to grow worse on the 9 the doctor appointed her viaticum which she received with much piety & devotion. Sister Anna Maria Hyde & Sister Ann Charlicker being all so judg'd in danger received theirs at the same time.[3] Sister Havers continuing still to grow worce, between one & two in the afternoon received the Holy oyls. she was sensible & continued so to the last moment, & seemingly with out any Agony or even sigh expir'd about half an hour after eight. she was bury'd upon the 11 in the third oven of the 3[d] row of our buriall place. *requiescat in pace*

her funeral was sung & perform'd as usual tho with great difficulty by reason of the number of religious that was sick for which reason the Psalter could not ^be^ said in publick in the quir, so each said ^it^ privatly by them selves & was order'd to finish it in seven days & in consideration of its not being said in publick, there was a mass said for her soul, & all was ordained to hear it for her.

on the 13 of february our Dear Sister Anna Maria Hyde[4] departed this life the 45 of her age & 14 of her Holy Profession. she was bread up by her Grand mother with whome she lived tell her death & took care

[1] Mary Havers (1681–1733) BA099.

[2] It is not clear from this passage whether the writer is referring to illness connected to gall-bladder problems or to gall sickness.

[3] Anne Maria Hyde (1719–33) BA116; Ann Cherlicker (1687–1733) BA051.

[4] Anna Maria Hyde, lay sister, was the niece of Dorothy Risdom (1701–05) BA162; the family was from Standlake, Oxfordshire. Her father, William Hyde, died in 1717; her mother, Mary, in 1733. Mary Hyde's will mentions two sons, Richard and Charles.

of all her affairs, she had long had a desire to be religious, but duty & gratitude to her grandmother could not permitt her to leave her, as long as her presence was so necessary to her, but as soon as freed from that charge God having taken her out of this life she immediatly writ here to offer her self, & being excepted of, she soon came over conducted by her Eldest brother, who offer'd her to go & see othere monasterys but she refus'd it & would not go any where tell she had been here for fear as she after wards own'd it might might cause wayvering thoughts as probabily it would, since it pleas'd allmighty God to permitt her to have a dislike at her first comming to almost all she saw, but being convinced t' was the place God call'd her to, she was resolved to stay, & to secure her doing so, she made then her vows, which would not have been permitted her to have done if known. so tho we remain'd free to dismiss her, yet she on her side was oblig'd to **[p. 15]** be what ever we would make her, which generous sacrifice of hers was rewarded by an intier content & satisfaction which was not only more then ever she expected, but all so more then she was persuaded she should have found any where ellce, for the which she express'd a great gratitude to God, & to the community which in love & esteeme, she prefer'd before all others. this moved her still to be more liberall to God & to make a sacrifice to him of her reluctances, & from the time she did so, she found no difficulty in those things which before she had a great one. as she own'd she had in the smell of all phicicall drugs. but no sooner had obedience imploy'd her there in, but allmighty God for whose sake she evercome her reluctance was pleas'd to take it so interly a way that she had after no difficulty in such things. she was not less ready to sacrifice to God what ever satisfaction she thought he requir'd of her, she was a great taker of snuff but thinking it might be pleasing to him to make a sacrifice of it, she made a promiss of never taking it more, & from that time tell her death which was a bout nine years after, she never took so much as one pinch. she had a great skill in surgery by which she not only saved the Community many a pound, but all so freed the religious from many a great mortifications, the cures she wrought both with in & with out has been very great. she was a woman of a solid judgment, but of a rough & unpolished education which was sweeten'd by an honist sincerity & good will of each, which made that her rudest speeches was not taken ill. as she came advanced in years to religion it gave her much more difficulty to larne her little duties & serimonys, in which she frequently made great blunders, which was a subject of humility & confussion to her. she had so great an esteeme of obedience that she would be derected by it in all she did, which caus'd her to go to our superiour upon all communicating eves to know of her for what intention she should offer her communion, & so of any indulgence that was to be gain'd, to whome she would have her apply it. her cheef devotion was to the infant Jesus & to the adorable Eucharist she never omitted holy communion nor for many years before her death approched it with out being allmost the wholl morning disolved in tears. she could not make a greater sacrificc then to be call'd away but by unforseen accidents, she often was, which gave her much confussion because it discover'd to others that sensible devotion which she would not have had seen by any, tho she was compationat of others she was not so of her self as apear'd by the diciplins she took when order apointed them the place she took them in being ever discover'd by the quantity of blood she sheed **[p. 16]** the beginning of her illness was a quartern Ague,[1] which took her a bout last autem which some thought was stopt to soon by the bark. how ever towards the end of january it return'd againe, to which was added a great Cold, which was the distemper of the year, with a paine in her side. yet upon the purification[2] she came to choir & received her Candle, & communicated with the rest. the paine of her side continuing to grow worce, on the 9 when the doctor appointed Sister Mary Havers her *viaticum* he order'd she should receive hers all so, tho we were surprised at it, yet we lost not hopes, but believed God had permitted that unnecessary precation of the doctor that she might have the advantage of going to communion it being her profession day. but she growing still worce, on the 12 he ordered the Holy oyles as he all so did to Sister Anne Charlicker, & both receved them that same day after supper, & on the foll[ow]ing which was the 13 a little before 3 in the after noon she expir'd perfectly sensible to the last, making aloud most tender acts of love, confidence, & humility, even all most to the last moment. she neither shew'd a fear of death nor a desire of life during her wholl sickness, but abandonn'd her self intierly to the divine will. she dy'd upon a friday just time enough to have the Cross prayers[3] said for her before we begun the commendations. she had a perticular devotion to these prayers especially on fridays, & we hope she immediatly found the effect of them. *Requiescat in pace*.

on the same day to witt the 13 of february Sister Annc Cherlicker[4] departed this life gest three hours after Sister Anna Maria Hyde. she came young to the monastery & was ever very pious, & in her younger days had been very labourious & serviciable to the Community, not sparing her self. but for these last eight or nine years of her life, she was able to do but little, & was good part of it confined to her bed, by reason of a sore ledg [*sic*], which ever now & then mortify'd, & put her to extreme paine. what she suffer'd by it can not easely be express'd, & what added yet more to her suffering was the thought she had that she was neglected,

1 Quartern ague: defined in Hooper's Medical Dictionary (1820) and earlier as an intermittent fever whose paroxysms came on during the afternoon at 72-hour intervals; occurring more frequently, as here, in the autumn.
2 Here the Feast of the Purification on 2 February, also known as Candlemas.
3 Cross prayers: see Glossary.
4 Ann Cherlicker, lay sister (1687–1733) BA051.

& a resentment if she saw one have any thing of which she had not part, which we look'd upon but as an effect of her illness which she discover'd ^more^ by her tears then by her words, which was no less an humilation to **[p. 17]** her then a trouble to those that sarved her, which sufferings may have been her purgatory she having beg'd of God to have it here, or ellce a smal punishment for some secreet prid or vaine complicence she may have taken in her self whilst she had her health. having been a very regular religious woman, but apt to be disedify'd with others, & offended if any one should think she would admitt of any indulgence. at the begining of february she got this cold with the rest, which soon ended her suffering life which would have been much encreas'd had she long surviv'd her charitable & compassionat surgeon Sister Anna Maria who with her skill & charitable endevours presarved her life, but God permitted not this cross to hapen to her. she was perfectly sensible to the last & dy'd most piously the 65 of her age & 46 since her holy profession. *Requiescat in pace*

having two corps at once & the greates part of the comminity ill, not withstanding tho one solemn Mass & Dirige[1] would have sarved for both, yet we performed two, because that on the 30 day there will be but one for both. that we sung on the burial day was both & likways the Dirige, the secound was sung on the 3^{d} day after, for both, & the Dirige in the afternoon was said for both. the watching & ringing was the same as for one, they being both together they ware carry'd out to gether & lay exposs'd in the Church to gether, but in place of puting only 4 candles round the herese we put 6 which sarve for both. Sister Anna Maria Hyde was bury'd in the upper most oven of the third row,[2] & Sister Anne Cherlicker in the lowermost of the forth row. the Community being something better, the Psalter was begun & said in the Choir as usual for Sister Anna Maria.

on the 22 of february our Community being now much recover'd tho far from well, & it being the first sunday of lent, we begun to sing our office as usual in the Choir.

Mr Canningh left his Sister twenty pound, which being given to the Procuratrix for the Common use, Reverend Mother order'd every one to offer for his soul five Masses & one Communion & to say for 30 days the Cross prayers.[3]

the 13 of aprill Mis Lloyd went from hence for england.[4]

---

[1] Dirige: from the first word of the antiphon of the Office of the Dead and here used as the name for that service (OED).

[2] The ovens were the equivalent of a vault for burial: see Glossary.

[3] Elizabeth Canning (1691–1750) BA044; her brother, Francis Canning of Foxcote, Warwickshire, made his will on 10 July 1732. See J. O. Payne (ed.), *Records of English Catholics of 1715* (London: Burns and Oates, 1889), p. 174.

[4] Mary Lloyd had arrived in September 1730; see **[p. 4]**.

this 19 of may tis a year since we changed our veils which that year was Rogation Monday,[1] we put them on for the first time to go the prossession **[p. 18]** the reason why we changed them was first because they reguir'd much mending & the best eyes to be imploy'd in do them, which did very much prejudice their eyes, & secoundly because they were thought even by seculars not to have a religious air ^&^ tho our superiour could have done it by her self the statu[t]es allowing her the power, yet knowing that severall was unwilling to change she would not do it unless she was satisfy'd that two parts of three was for it, which could not be known but by voting it, which was done & the votes being collected there proved yet more for it.

Sister Frances Xaverious [Simner] freinds sent 20 shillings for prayers for them selves & for their friends that were dead for the which all was order'd to hear two masses.[2]

on the 23 of june Mis Weston with her sarvant enter'd our inclousure, leave having been obtained of my Lord Bishop that she should lodg with in whilst she staid, she came to see her aunt[3] & was lodg'd in the little musiek rome in the School my Lady Conyers having the othere appartment.

on the 25 of june Sister Helen Blevin & Sister betty moody was cloathed.[4]

on the 5 of july it pleas'd allmighty God to call to him self our dear Sister Heneretta Markham[5] a perfect good religious woman; her piety & fervour never seeming the least to have been decay'd from her first putting on the holy habitt to her death. so great & constant was her exactness & zeal for each point of order that she would never be excus'd from any not even from such as by the extreme weakness she had in her limbs seem'd above her force for her fervour supply'd this defect of nature so that it only served for her sufference & humiliation & consequently her increase of merit but never for dispensations. towards her latter years the weakness of her hands so encreas'd, that she was scarce able to work yet non more diligent & constant in that duty, never refussing what was given her to do, supplying with her teeth the defect of her poor fingers which had not strength to pul out her needle. & in winter when the least cold her fingers were so benum'd that she could not even stick a pin in her cloaths, without the help of another she could not get dresst for matins, yet would come tho she had leave for the contrary to sleep. she was a good mortify'd religious & very **[p. 19]** charitable & compationat yet not so well beloved as esteemed in our Community. for which no

---

1 Rogation Monday: rogation days were set aside to ask for mercy and to seek blessing on fields for planting at the end of April and just before Ascension.

2 Frances Xaveria Simner (BA174).

3 Possibly Elizabeth Weston (BA216).

4 Helen Blevin, lay sister (BA026); Elizabeth Moody, lay sister (BA143).

5 Henrietta Markham (1696–1733) BA136.

othere reason can be given then God's permission for the excercise her vertue, being of a very sensible & resenting temper & over solicitous & desirous of pleasing all. a few days before her death she found the rose a coming in her leg which she was very subject to & did not speak of it, on fryday she found her self a little ill, yet did not break her fast nor even sleep matins next day, to which she was call'd as usual & rise to have gone. her Sister not seeing her in the Choir went out at the last Lesson to see what was the matter with her, she found her flat upon her face in her cell with out apperance of life.[1] she with much difficulty rais'd her up & brought her a little to her self, what she complained of was of a great oppression on her breast, & an indispossion all over her. the doctor being sent for found her very ill & order'd her some thing to be taken each hour & said he would come next day, but we finding that she continued to grow worse sent for him againe that night & when he came he found her so ill as to order her the Last sacrements, which was immediatly administr'd to her, tho she had but short intervals to prepare for them, being the most part in a dosy sleep. yet we have the Comfort to think she was not unprepar'd for besides a most pious & religious life which is the best preparation for death, she made it her practiss frequently to prepare to prepare [*sic*] herself for it, by doing then what she ought to do at the hour of death. on sunday which was the fifth, at five in the afternoon she render'd her pious soul to God, the 60 of her age & 37 of her holy profession. she was carry'd out the following day but could not be expossed neither in the pant nor Church because she purged so much both by her nose & mouth & smelt so strong that we could not keep her tell the next day & there fore after the Dirige was said she was bury'd & the next day we sung the mass & funeral for her as usual which was on the 7th. she was bury'd in the 2d oven of the last row. *Requiescat in pace.*

on the 9 of july mis Mary Greenwood came & was received for a Convictress which was turn'd of 13 years of age.[2]

on the 15 of august we begun to sing the masses in the new plain sung.

the . . of september: Madamoiselle Montack, which was a wine Marchands daughter was received for a convictress by the Arch priest desire.

on the 20 of september Mrs Sykes[3] & a maid sarvant enter'd our in closure she having bury'd her husband & all her children except the two that are religious here & settled all her affares in England was desirous

---

1 Her sister was Ann Mechtilda Markham (BA137).

2 Mary Greenwood/Greenward was great-niece to Elizabeth Canning (BA044); see WWTN family trees, Sheldon.

3 Mrs Mary Sykes, née Dovery, mother to Anne (BA188) and Mary (BA189). Mrs Sykes offered £1000 to fund two free places for boys to be educated at St Omer; see G. Holt, *The English Jesuits in the Age of Reason* (London: Burns and Oates, 1993), p. 138. See also Chronicle, vol. 2, **[pp. 53–5, 66, 86, 128]** and vol. 1, **[pp. 421, 422]**.

to end her days here[.] she brought with her mis Eliz: Smithson **[p. 20]** & mis Gage who was turn'd of ten, & mis Smithson was turned of 13 years of age for Convictresses.[1]

the 22 of september: mis Weston & her sarvant returned for england.

on the 11 of october: Lady Conyers with her two daughters[2] & sarvant went for england

on the 15 of october: Mis Willis whose Christen name was jonny went to her friends in england.

on the 9 of november: Mrs Frances Gasling[3] came hether from gant where she had been some time but could not be ease nor resolve to settle amongst them, her inclination leading her to be here where she was proposs'd before she came over, but we refuss'd to take her both on account of her age & for that we had our number of lay Sisters & she no capable of much labour. how ever compassion made us yeild to her importunity & we permitted her to come. but to our satisfaction after a few days she resolved to return back to gant which she did on the 15 of november:

upon the 26 of november Sister Barbara Devery departed this life,[4] she was advanced in years when she came to religion & had lived for severall years a servant in the Duke of Powis's family & had even then a desire of being religious. one of his daughter promist her if ever she was so her self she would send for her & accordingly she did. she was then housekeeper to the Marquise of Seaford[5] sister to our present superiour who unwillingly parted with her she being a most faithfull & disinteres'd sarvant & one of a good judgment & understood perfectly well house keeping & having been much us'd to the charge of under sarvants it had begot in her an ordering way a mongst the lay Sisters her companions which was not so well taken by them as ment by her, tho she had not strength to under go heard works notwithstanding tell she grew in years she was not exempt from wash, scour & cleaning the house with the rest nor from any employ but cook & beaker which she had not strength for, she call'd to mattins for a bove 25 years & was very serviciable to the Community ^in^ the severall journys she went, both to france & england. m^r^ Galloway which was then our agent,[6] said she was a fitt parson to be sent about business being very capable of it. God not having given her

1 Elizabeth Smithson is not yet identified; Catherina Gage later professed as Mary Xaveria (1740–63) BA084.

2 Lady Margaret Conyers; see also **[pp. 9, 10, 11, 38]**.

3 Francisca Gostling professed at the Ghent Benedictines in 1736 (GB088); date of death unknown.

4 Barbara Devery, lay sister (1694–1733) BA072.

5 Prioress Lucy Herbert's sister Frances (d. 1732) was married to Kenneth Mackenzie, 4th Earl of Seaforth; see Herbert family tree.

6 Agents carried out a range of tasks on behalf of the convent, including arranging for the passage of potential candidates, transfer of funds and other tasks.

the gift of prayer she endevour'd to make amends by imploying those times that ware at her own dispossall in working for the Common profitt for the which she had a great zeal & all her works tended to it. she was of a tender concience but not the least [s]crupulous. she had good health tell a bout a year before she dy'd the want of which & her age render'd her **[p. 21]** uncapable of any more sarving the Community, which made her very desirous to dye that she might not be a burden to it & it pleased allmighty God to grant her, her desire for after a few months illness in which she was reduced to the infirmary she dy'd on the before said day about 3 in the morning at the age of 77 & 39 of her holy profession & was bury'd on the 27 in the third oven of the last Row of our new valt. *Requiescat in Pace.*

the 2[d] of december: madamoiselle Van Asta who was of our towne was received for a convictress.

Mr Philip who formerly had some acquantance here left us at his death five pound for prayers for his soul. all was order'd to hear two masses & to offer one communion & to say once the Cross prayers

1734

upon the 20 of january mis newland[1] returned to us from england by the name of Smith that her parents might not find her out during the six years she had been with them tis all most impossible to say the various endevours they us'd to make her return to the prodestant church but young as she ^was^ being but eleven when she went from hence nothing had force to make her stager in her faith or gaine her concent to ^any^ thing contrary to what she had been taught here; amongst the many Conflicts she was dayly assaulted with, the most sencible was the constant prayers, tears & persuassions of her mother, but grace still render'd her victorious. she often (tho in vain) made atempt to escape from them. at length the divine mercy bless'd her endeavours & she got safe to London. she gave us notice as soon as she was there & beg'd leave to return which, by the same post was granted, & she received, to the satisfaction of all. she was then about 18 years old.

on the 9 of february: Sister Oliva Darell made her holy Profession.[2]

on the 5 of march our Reverend Mother[3] solemnised her half jubily of being superior which hapened this year to be the Friday before shrove Sunday[4] which day & time did not favour our mirth not withstanding it did not hender in the motive of it being to rejoyce & prayes God

[1] Elizabeth Newlin (BA147), daughter of Rev. John Newlin of Harting, Sussex; see vol. 1, **[pp. 420, 429]**; vol. 2, **[p. 43]**.

[2] Mary Darell, in religion Mary Olivia (BA071).

[3] Lucy Herbert, Prioress 1709–44 (BA101).

[4] Shrove Sunday was the Sunday before the start of Lent.

according to that, let the just rejoyce & be glad in the sight of our Lord, & so indeed all seem'd to be a more universall mirth I have never seen every one giving all the testimonys they could of it & of their love to our Reverend mother & she all so to us, expressing how glad she was that non of her relations or any on[e] was here which might have hender'd her from injoying the Comfort of being with her Community whose company was more dear to her then that of any of her relations would have been. she seemed to take **[p. 22]** extreemly kindly the markes that each one gave her of their affection which they exprest not only in the presents they made her which was according to each ones ability but much more in the kind manner they made it in which was far more agreeable to her, then any thing they could have presented her with.

the manner of our solomnising this day was as follows: after the half hour after Communion (it being all Saints of our order) our Reverend mother having given the signe for going out of the choir she went first & all the Community followed her to the refectory, where there was prepar'd for all crame coffe & white bread & butter (for tho it was fryday we did not fast my Lord Bishop[1] having given leave for the contrary) our Reverend mothers place was adoarn'd with a Canopy & crown & in it was represented the 25 years she had been superiour & the number of those she had profess'd a live & dead by so many stars for those that ware dead & so many hearts for those that ware living. when all were seated our musiciens sung & the crowne prepar'd was placed on her head, during our breakfast which all took in the refectory together each one in their place we ware exceeding merry. at ten a clock there was a mass in musick & the Abbot of our order[2] attended by five of his monks sung it, with as many serimoneys as the Bishop himself, at the end of which the *te deum* was solemnly sung when finish'd the first peal to dinner was rung, the recreation both at dinner & supper was very hansome, the Community besides those two recreations gave all so three more very hansome ones. after dinner our Reverend mother was obliged to go to the grate to receive the complements from them that was invited to dine in our Fathers house which was besides my Lord Abbot & his five monks the arch Deacon & Arch Priest & 3 or 4 seculare parsons, after which we went to the Choir & read our vespers & complin & a short *salve* then we made our accustom'd meditation after which we went down to the worke chamber after a little musick which was made the curtaine was lifted up & there apeared two quires of angels consisting of four of a side & between the quires of Angels stood upon a high stand the frame of a Crowne of beaten silver & be hind it was a high seat, every Angel had in

[1] Hendrik Josef van Susteren, Bishop of Bruges 1716–42.

[2] Abbot of Eeckhoute: Leon van Male (d. 1742), Abbot for around nine years. Eeckhoute was an abbey of Augustinian Canons Regular in Bruges.

his hand a flaming heart of silver & in the meddle of it was written one of the gifts of the Holy Ghost each Angel in their turn made a speech to our Reverend mother concearning the gift writ in the heart he carry'd & then he stuck his heart in the frame of the crown, the Angels were all of our best voices the last Angels had the name of Jesus which he stuck in the **[p. 23]** midle of the pinacle as soon as the crown was finished two of the Angels took the crown & two others lead our Reverend mother to the high seate & all of them sung as the[y] went *veni sponsa Christi accipe coronam*[1] when they had crown'd her with the crown they had composs'd of the hearts with the gifts of the Holy Ghost, there entered another Angel as sent from our Blessed Lady with her name in silver, which he placed on her breast then all the Angels sung the hymn *Jesu Corona virginum*[2] in english & between each verse two lines alluding to the gifts they had given her which both choirs sung together, then one of them shaked a tree which was planted at the front of the stage & said *now holy virgins you shall pertake from the tree of life these fruits I shake* then fell down papers in which was written the fruits of the Holy Ghost, & a proper verse upon each which the nuns scrabling to get caus'd us all to laugh, then two Angels brought our Reverend mother back to her place & musick concluded the action. from whence we went all to supper. after grace those in the vestery[3] in disgize handed her up to the great garret where they had prepar'd a seat with a canopy over it for her to seet in & they did their best to devert her dancing in wooden shoose which made great merith. from whence we went down to the fire to warme us & all had leave to sett up & devert them selves tell nine a clock which was the hour that concluded that joyfull day.

the fire works & shutting which all our workemen had designed to have made & had prepar'd all things for it, & had been at some expence in order to it, was prevented by my Lord Bishop, who disaprouved there of as well as our Reverend mother, who desir'd no noise should be made abroad, yet could not have hender'd them for doing it had she not told them that my Lord Bishop forbid it, which was a great disapointment to them who designed there by to have shown their love to the Community. all assurances was given them that we took it very kindly of them & was as much obliged to them as if they had done what so kindly intended. they ware all invited to dinner in the fathers house on a day that our Confessor dinned abroad & ware very hansomely treated, wine as much

---

1 Underlined in original: 'Come, bride of Christ, receive the crown …' Antiphon: *Veni sponsa Christi, accipe coronam quam tibi Dominus praeparavit in aeternum pro cujus amore sanguinem tuum fudisti et cum Angelis in paradisum introisti. Veni, electa mea, et ponam in te thronum meum quia concupivit Rex speciem tuam.*

2 'Jesu the virgins' crown': office hymn for the Common of Virgins from the fourth century, attributed to St Ambrose and traditionally sung at Vespers and Lauds.

3 Vestry: place where habits and other garments were made.

as they would drink. they all came to return ^thanks^ to the grate & seemed very well pleased & very gratefull.

our Reverend Mother gave us three hansome recreations of the best & most acceptable things she could get, the last was after Easter on which day was acted a play of the Convertion of our Holy Father[1] she all^so^ rebuilt a little summer house in the Garden for the Comfort of the Community in which, & in other things for the advantage of the house she spent a hunderid pound english or there abouts her relations having sent her for a present at her half jubile. severall little imbelishments both in house & garden was made to **[p. 24]** solomnis this day & new puter both poringers plates & portion dishes infine nothing that the Community could think of was wanting which might express their kindness & love for her.

the 16 of may mis Tacklock took the schollers kerchar in order to begin her tryall for a lay Sister & is called Sister Mary Allexia.[2]

the 4th of june Mrs Henry jernegan[3] came to bruges in order to go to the spa[4] that she might be fully satisfy'd of the sincerity of her daughters vocation we sent her out to her to remaine with her whilst in town she strikly examend her about it & was convinced it was her own desire & no persuation so gave her her consent & she took the kerchar on the 7th of june & is called Sister Anne Teresa.

the 20 of june we solemnis'd the wholl jubilé of Sister Anne Benedict Thirwell.[5]

the 25 of june Sister Helen Blevin & Sister Betty Moody maid their Professions.

the 14 of july mis Mountack parted from hence to her friends in town

the 16 of august mis Mary Wyrill came, brought ^by^ one Mrs smith which brings children over, we had no notice of her coming, neither did we know her parents, who ware protestants, her Father sent her because her Mother who was of an odd temper did not love her.[6] she was about 14 years old.

the 31 of august Mrs Henry jernegan returned hether from spa & entered our enclosure in order to stay sometime.

---

1 The date of celebration of the feast of the Conversion of St Augustine changed from 5 May to 24 April. There is insufficient evidence here to know which date is implied.

2 Margaret Tatlock, in religion Mary Alexia (BA194). In her obituary it is written that, 'not being able to learn her latin and so could not be a Choir Nun, [she] chose rather to be a lay Sister here …'. See **[pp. 212–13]**.

3 Mrs Henry Jerningham was Mary Jonquet de l'Epine, mother of Ann Jerningham(1735–96) BA120, Procuratrix 1751–56, 1760–66, 1782–?88; Chantress.

4 Mrs Jerningham's intention was to take the waters at Spa, near Liège.

5 Ann Benedict Thirwall (1684–1739) BA199.

6 It was most unusual for the community not to be advised of the arrival of any aspirant. See also **[p. 26]**.

one Frances Kelly who had been a sarvant in Sir Rowland Stanleys family[1] left his three daughters here 15 pound which they resigned to the Common[2] for the which a mass was said for her & the Community order'd to hear it & five more for her soul & for five day to say the cross prayers & offer one communion for her

Mrs Dorothy Risdon[3] who had formerly been a pentioner here at her death left us five pound desiring that 20 masses might be said for her which was done & besides in consideration of the severall relations which ware religious amongst us & herself having ^been^ pentioner the Community was order'd to hear three Masses & one Communion & for 3 days to say the Cross prayers.[4]

thc 3[d] of october M[r] Henry Jernegan came & his wife left our enclosure & went to him & on the 9 they both went for england.[5]

the 22 of november Sister Anne Teresa jernegan was cloathed.[6]

the 28 of November Sister Anne Dominick Howard departed this life the 61 of her age & 42 of her profession.[7] for some years before she dy'd she suffered much with an extreme unwelldy bulk being very fatt which occation'd her **[p. 25]** body to be most miserably gall'd & allso shortness of breath, the night be fore she dy'd finding herself in danger of sufficating she went to the religious & lay in the cell next to her & call'd her up & with much difficulty got down to the infirmary her legs being grcatly swell'd tis very apparant that she must have suffer'd more then was thought or apprehended. but her manner of living & discription of her illness madc us not have so much regard to it, so that she might not have had all the assistance & solass as her present condition requir'd, for all she complain'd of was a shortness of breath which was judg'd to proceed but from her being so very fatt, neither doctor nor surgeon seem'd to think it any thing ellce when their advice was asked some time before. but ^being^ again now sent for, to our great surprise he order'd her without delay all the Rights of the Church, accordingly was done, & Father Confessor[8] to our Comfort seem'd very well satisfy'd with her

---

1 Sir Rowland Stanley, Baronet of Hooton, Cheshire (d. 1737). Five Stanleys professed at Bruges, between 1700 and 1711, but Agnes died in 1723, followed by Mary Ignatia in 1725, leaving three still alive in 1733. Frances Kelly has not been identified.

2 Here meaning that the money was handed over for communal use, rather than being kept for use by the individual recipients.

3 Mrs Dorothy Risdom (1701–05) BA162.

4 Cross prayers: see Glossary.

5 Mr Henry Jerningham and Mary Jonquet de L'Epine were the parents of Ann Teresa (BA120). For more on Henry Jerningham, goldsmith and banker, see archive.thetablet.co.uk/issue/7th-october-1911/8/52232, accessed 8 February 2016.

6 Ann Jerningham, in religion Ann Teresa (BA120).

7 Ann Howard, in religion Dominic (1693–1734) BA107, daughter of Henry Howard, 6th Duke of Norfolk, and Jane Bickerton.

8 Father Confessor in 1734 was Fr Caryl Gerard, Confessor 1723–79; Anstruther 4, p. 110.

present disposition, he say'd that for these last six weeks he had found her better disposs'd then usuall, she having heard that our Bishop made difficulty for us to admitt one to be religious that was uncapable of larning Lattin tho othere ways fitt & lik'd by the community she begun upon that to apprehend the divine office to be of a greater obligation then she had imagin'd for tho our Confessor was of that oppinion[,] yet others she had consulted ware not on account that her embracing a religious life was not her own choice having no other motive but the will of her mother whome she fear'd if she did not tho her being in this house was her own choice, having stoled a way from M^rs D'Ognate with whom she came over & who had orders from her mother to carry her to the third order in town,[1] where her mother designed she should be. unknown to us in ^time^ of our Refectory she got in to our enclosure by the Communicating door in the choir. yet the Comunity would not receive her, tell the Dutchess her mother & the monastery of the third order had concented to it, as she wanted the grace of a real vocation. tis no wonder that her religious duties was as burdensome & disagreable to her, as her irregularitys was to us. some time before her death she told one of our religious that she did not now repent her being a religious, & if it ware againe to do, it should be her own choice. that it was not so [at] her first coming was wholly unknown to the comunity tell after her profession or she would never have been professed here, as her obligation could not be equal to those who call'd by God & with their own free will embraces a religious life, so we doubt not but it much lessen'd her faults in Gods sight & it made superiours more ease in tolerating what they could not amend nor with a safe conscience othereways have permitted. besides her example was not of ill consequences to others, for **[p. 26]** through a week judgment & an odd temper her wholl Conduct was such as moved more to dislike it then to the least inclination of following it even in the most remiss; she could not but see that it render'd her Contemptable & of no esteeme, which humiliation might in some measure attone for her faults & move Gods mercy to bestow his grace on her at her death which he seemingly did by granting her a perfect resignation to dye, & a peacefull dispossion, so that how ever troublesome she had been during life, non ever gave less in her sickness & death then she which was the time we most apprehended. she was sensible to the last & thankfull to those that sarved her, she received all the rights up, for she had a great difficulty to ly down in her bed notwithstanding some hours after she was put to bed & before eleven at night she expired, she was bury'd on the 30 in our little churchyeard because the ovens ware not large enough for her coffin

---

[1] English Franciscan convent at Prinsenhof, Bruges. A key problem over Anne Howard's profession here is the question of freedom of choice regarding entry. Every candidate underwent an examination before clothing and profession where the questions included one to ascertain that they made their decion to join a convent of their own volition.

& her dear soul, we realy hope is in a fair way of injoying Allmighty God. *requiescat in pace*.

five pound was left us by Mrs Frances Trafford[1] at her death for prayers for her soul she having two Aunts & a Sister in our house & having been a pentioner here herself, we ware order'd to offer the hearing of three masses & one Communion & five days the Cross prayers for her.

the 21 of december mis wyrill was baptis'd,[2] the Bishop order'd our confessor to ^do^ it conditionatly there being no sertainty of her having been baptis'd & some reasons to fear she had not, it was perform'd at our organ house door, she made there her profession of faith & was received into the Church to her unspeakable Comfort, she came as is mention'd before on the 16 of august the occation of her fathers sending her was because her mother not loving her took no care of her, he seeing the miserable life that this child lead by reason of her mothers unkindness & fearing she might be ruin'd for want of good education sent her here, desiring we would be kind to her & educate her as we did the rest, he being told we should cartainly bring her up a Catholick to which he shew'd no concerne provided she was well used. As to the poor girl she had no notion of any religion except a horror of a papist & by consequence would do nothing that **[p. 27]** was required of her. she had no knowledg of what it was to sarve God nor did she know evil from good, to curce or swear an oath seemed no harme at all to her, she heated the name of a Roman Catholick & all the perverce & spitfull things she could think of she say'd against them she continu'd in this obstance & perverceness for some two months notwithstanding all she had seen & heard of good example nothing of which had any influence upon her, nor had our best endevours the least effect tell the beginning of october, at which time was given the spirituall excercise to the Community she being present at the expounding with the rest of her companions, the first day she begun to reflect a little upon ^what^ she had heard & the 3^d day her heart was so touch'd with a desire of her salvation that she earnestly beg'd to be taken into the Catholick church, but this was not immidiatly granted it being thought proper to try if she continu'd constant which she did nor could her tears be stop'd but by the promiss of it. she was taken into the Church & made her profession of faith & baptis'd on St Thomasses day[3] as is said before. the day following she made her generall Confession from which time her temper which before seem'd as bad as her principles

---

[1] Frances Trafford (d. 1734), daughter of John Trafford of Croston, Lancashire, and Katherina Culcheth. Her sister was Francis Borgia Trafford (BA203); her aunts were Anastasia (BA202) and Monica Trafford (BA204). She had a third aunt, Teresa Joseph, at the Franciscans, Prinsenhof (BF242).

[2] Miss Wyrill; see also **[p. 24]**.

[3] The feast of St Thomas was celebrated on 21 December.

begun to change & to be as pious as she was before perverce, which instance of Gods mercyfull providence in her regard concluds this year

+

1735

on the 19 of january ther arrose so violent a wind that vast damages was done in towne, the wind lay full against the weest part of our house yet we had only the window at the end of our dormitary blown down, which was carryed by the wind a good way into our dormitary & some few tills blown of, where as the workmen assured us that 2000 pound flemish would not repaire the damages it had done in towne, in thanks giving for our presarvation we sung mass in honour of our Lady.[1]

the 28 of aprill Sister Mary Alexia Tacklock was cloathed for a lay Sister.[2]

the 30 of aprill the two mis Tanckerds with their sarvant came the eldest which was mis Anne being design'd for our house we took in to our enclosur, she was about 13 years old, her sister with the sarvant went for Lieg the 4 of may.[3]

the 9 of may M[r] Tasbourgh with his lady & one m[rs] Theodorick came here which gentlewoman had been newly converted & came over to see **[p. 28]** a monasticall life we took her into our inclousur & lodg'd her in the pentioners appartement & she eate in our Fathers house.[4]

the 17 of may mis spellabeen one of this town was received for a pentioner in our childrens school.

the 18 of may mis mary & mis fanny Tasbourgh went from hence with their father & mother the eldest they took with them to the Spa & the other not being well they left at the dames at Gant.[5]

the 24 of may M[rs] Tancker'd sarvant went for england having been here some days in her return from Liege.

the 31 of may M[rs] Lloyd arrived here with the two mis Beddingfields, which she had obtained for our house & came a purposs to bring them & therefore was admitted into our enclosure during her stay, the eldest of mis Beddingfields was 12 years old & the other eleven.[6]

---

1 2000 Flemish pounds were roughly equivalent to £200.

2 Mary Alexia Tatlock (BA194).

3 Ann left the convent in May 1737 without professing; see **[p. 39]**. Elizabeth Tancred professed at the Sepulchrines, Liège in 1741 aged 18, LS219.

4 Mr and Mrs Tasburgh were Francis Tasburgh of Bodney, Norfolk, and Mary Symonds.

5 Two daughters returned and professed: Mary as Maria Frances in 1741 (BA192) and Margaret in 1748 (BA193). Sources do not agree on baptismal names, but it is likely that they are these two girls.

6 Mary and Margaret Bedingfeld of Coulsey Wood, Suffolk, daughters of Henry Bedingfield and Mary Havers of Norfolk.

the 21 of june M[rs] Eyers who formerly lived here (as may be seen in the year 1695) her maiden name was Susan Halsell[1] brought with her two of her Grand Children mis Lucy & mis mary Tichborn the Eldest was past 12 & the youngest 11, & with them all so their father M[r] Tichborn, the two children was for our school & she designed to have ended her days here.[2] the first of july M[rs] Lloyd went from hence for england.

on the 9 M[rs] Eyers having changed her mind to our great satisfaction went for england together with m[r] Tichborn.

the 11 of august mis jonny willis (sister to our religious mary xaverius) she being very desirous of being religious & hoping we might have taken her for such, come under pretence of a visit to her sister whose death was dayly expected, she was taken into the enclosure but no hopes could be given her of being religious, for besides that she had nothing she was very sickly so was adviced by all to return to england to her parents[3]

on the 24 of august: mis Smithson parted from hence to go for england. her parents requiring her to return to them having been here for about two years.

the 20 of september: M[rs] Theodorick returned for england with a seeming desire soon to dispatch & settle her affaires in order to come here again by the following spring mis jonny willis finding no hopes of being admitted allso returned with her.

[p. 29] the 21 of September: our dear ^Sister^ mary xaveria willis departed his life about ten a clock in the morning.[4] she had been a convictriss here from the age of 9 years old tell 15 during all which time her friend never pay'd but one years pention, not for want of good will but means, they own'd towards the latter end, that their circumstances would not permitt them to pay for her but when ever it did, they would with gratitude do it & therefore they said we might send her over to them since they could ^not^ pay for her being here which we did, but knowing she had a vocation to be religious & that she had an extraordinary fine voice, which would be a great advantage both to choir & musick, we offered her father to take her with out portion provided he would be at the expence of an italian master to teach her during her stay in England which propossion he with gratitude excepted off. upon which we sent her no ways doubting of her perseverence in her vocation for according to human reason, she was not like to meet with what might move her to the contrary, in order to better herself, for the circumstances of her famile did not permitt them to keep a maid, so she was forced to be both nurce

---

1 Susan Halsall: see vol. 1, **[p. 178]**.

2 Mary Tichbourne, in religion Mary Ignatia (1741–81) BA200; daughter of William Tichborne and Lucy Eyre. See also **[pp. 69, 71, 256–7]**.

3 Joanna Willis remained determined to become a nun and was eventually professed at the Conceptionists, Paris in 1742, where she died aged 56 in March 1773, PC128.

4 Mary Xaveria Willis (1730–35) BA222.

& maid, their being for most part of the time she stayed some sick in the family. not withstanding she had not been long in the world but her pious inclinations to a religious life begun to cool & she lost the desire of returning. she was from time to time put in mind of it by one of our religious who wished her to writ if she continued in ^the^ same thoughts & desires as when she went from hence, othere ways we should conclude she did not pretend any more to our state of life, & so might take a nother in her place, there being severall that would with great gratitude accept of the offer made her, her father was advertised of the same upon which he urged his daughter to return, but this was unknown to us tell after her profession, tho we perceived in her at her first coming a great coldness, & that she did not seem sensible of the happiness she was a going to posses, nor of the Communitys great goodness to her, her scoolership seem'd but little better, but during her noviship it was very apperant that she apply'd her self to vertue & seem'd truly sensible of the happiness of a religious state, & expressed a great sense of Gods goodness in calling her to it. she owned in confidence to one of our religious that after she had been in the world some time, she lost the desire of being religious but that when ever she went to communion it returned again, & she found herself quit chang'd & the things of the world appear'd not only with contemptable but even disgustfull, which change was visible to those that saw her exteriour, who took notice to her of it, but it lasted not long, for a few days after wordly sentiment took their place in her again; she say'd that she never before nor sence, experienced so sensibly Gods grace, as she did in those communions **[p. 30]** from the time of her profession we had the Comfort to see she truly tended to vertue & to all her religious obsarvances, & was excus'd from non on account of her voice which was judg'd by those even that had been in Itally to be one of the best they ever heard; two years before her death the musick depending much on her, as well as the choir song, we thought it proper to free her from being in the garret, having to do with weet linnen she being under refector,[1] which might occation her to get colds, so she was taken out, as allso freed from some duties appertaining to that office which was thought might prejudice her voice, which precaution our Lord seem'd not to bless, for a little after her health fail'd her, & she complained of a pain in her stomack, & a continuall working, which wore her a way so much, that we apprehended a Consumption, because her family was inclined to it, & severall of them dy'd of it, we ware very solisitous for to procure her recovery, besides our own doctor which is esteemed the best of the towne, we sent her cace for england, & had the best advice we could get from thence, but without effect, & hearing there was a doctor in great esteeme at ostend, we sent for him, & she follow'd his

---

[1] Under refector: assistant to the Refectress.

prescriptions, but without any good effect, he judg'd her illness in great part to be histericts, & not what is called a right consumption, but being so far gone, what he did availed her nothing, she was so weasted a way, that she was nothing but skin & bones: she received all the Rights of the Church some time before her death, because we expected she would not have held it out so long. she expressed a great desire of death, & sometimes a great fear of it, however perfectly resigned to Gods will, she had violent convoultions before she dy'd, she dy'd the 26 of her age & 6 of her profession & was bury'd the 23, in the uppermost oven of our new vault. *requiescat in Pace*

on the 19 of October my Lord Bishop, with the Arch priest, & the Architect[1] came into our inclosure to see a bout a fitt place for the building of a new church, which our Religious from the beginning had designe of doing, when ever able, ours being a poor little one, but for want of sufficient means, was forced to lay a side the thought of doing it, tell it should please God in his mercifull providence to afford us where with all. which he having now done by our receiving fifteen hunder'd pound from Sister Stanny Gages friends,[2] which we had little or no hopes of, she having been about 23 years profest & no portion pay'd her, her father not willing, or not able to pay it, after his death she had an equal share with the rest of his Children, which was the before mentioned sum, much a bout the same time M[r] Marckham[3] pay'd us a thousand pound, which ^he^ ow'd us for his sister & Aunts account, which with what we had in our Arke,[4] made us assume the designe which had so long been lay'd **[p. 31]** aside for want of sufficient means, which we esteem'd ourselves to ^now^ have our Reverend Mother propos'd it to the Community, who tho formerly had been eager for it, many of them now by the permission of God, was chang'd, & against it, for fear of runing in debt, & for the inconveniences they should suffer during the building, the distance of place from some offices, & as we had not sufficient Religious to fill the old choir there was less want of a new one. The reasons which our Reverend mother propossed to the Community when she assembled them, was, that since God had sent unexpectedly means sufficient she thought we could not better imploy them, then in building a Church or temple for his honour, since that he now has, is the very worce part of our house, & it ought to be the best, 2[dly] because

---

1 The Bishop in 1735 was Hendrik Josef van Susteren, Bishop of Bruges 1716–42. The architect for the project was Hendrik Pulinckx or Pulinx (1698–1781). Trained as an artist and gifted at sculpture, he was not a trained architect. The priory church of Nazareth has been described as his most important building.

2 Stanislaus Gage (1712–72) BA085, Sub-Prioress 1748–69.

3 Mr Markham: George Markham (1698–1760) had one sister, Christina (BA138), and two aunts, Henrietta Melior (BA136) and Ann Mechtilda (BA137), at Bruges. The Chronicle does not specify whether these were Flemish pounds or pounds sterling.

4 Ark: see Glossary.

it would be a great help & in a manner a necessary one for our vo[i]ces, which are but few & smale, where as a vaulted choir & church would be a great addition to them, & more than the addition of ten or twelve parsons, 3dly that standing not in need of the money neither for increasing our Rents, of which prayes'd be to God we had sufficient, for maintaining as many as our house could conveniently admitt of, nor yet for making any addition to our house or garden, both being large & convenient ^& ^ as to the objections which was made; our Reverend mother said that the fear which they had of running in debt there was no liklywhood of it, & as to its being more distant from some offices, it would be neerer to others, & would prevent the pentioners from coming through the house as they now are obliged to do, when they come to Mass or choir, which is both a distraction, & a henderence to the freedome of the religious, which motives changed the minds of so many of the convent Sisters, as that they pluriall number to witt seven voted for it, & five against it, which being done my Lord Bishop was informed, that the Convent had consented to it, so my Lord came as is said before, & the platforme drawn for it was approved by my Lord, all the religious being gethered together in the work chamber, his Lordship made a fatherly speach to us, & wished us all prosperity & succes in the undertaking we ware a going a bout, & with his blessing gave free leave to begin. His Lordship allso vissited the pensioners school, & granted to their Alter 40 days pardon, for saying five *Paters* & *Aves* before it.[1]

on the 4th of desember Sister Anne Teresa Jernegan made her holy profession[2]

on the 15 of desember our dear Sister Frances Clough[3] departed this life, she ^had^ been ill, in a languishing condition ever since the universall great coldes, which she got three years before, & was so ill with ^it^ that we had little hopes of her life, which it pleased God to prolong, for her encrease of merit, she having been in a suffering condition ever since, she had from time, to time **[p. 32]** some intervals of being better & when ever she found her self so she returned to the obsarvuances of order being ever a regular good religious woman the last five months of her Life she was wholly confined to the infirmary where she gave not less edification by her patience not asking but accepting with gratitude what ever was given her, concerned for the trouble she gave to others, & was as ready to help those that ware sick with her in the infirmary as she was when in health to labour for the Communitys sarvice so that she was often called the druge of the house, rather out of prayes then contempt of her. the sunday before she dy'd find^ing^ her self much worce than

---

1 The *Pater Noster* (Our Father) and *Ave Maria* (Hail Mary) must be said before the altar.
2 Ann Teresa Jerningham (BA120).
3 Frances Clough (1689–1735) BA059.

useall, the doctor was sent for, he apprehended no present danger but he order'd her some thing to take, which had so good an effect that she thought her self much better, nay the very day she dy'd, she say'd to our Reverend Mother,[1] I begin now to doubt what our Lord designes to do with this old woman, meaning her self, but the event soon appaer'd for a bout six a clock in the evening & one of our religious ^went^ to see her, & she said the broth she had taken had made ^her^ sick, & but a little before she came to call some body to help an old jubilarian that lay in the same rome with her. the religious call'd the infirmarian to give her some thing to take she being inclin'd to vomit, & as she gave it her she perceived her head to bend down & a great change in her looks upon which she call'd for Father Confessor who immediatly came & gave her absolution, & then run out to fetch the Holy Oyles, but before they could be wholly apply'd she was dead, tho not as those that ware neer her says when he begun to give them & tis sufficient for the benefitt of them if apply'd but to one of her senses, great part of the Community was ignorant of her being neer dying for it was so speedy that no notice could be given them, so that they heard of her death before they knew of her dying, but we have the Comfort to believe that tho her death was sudden that her vertuous & innocent life made it in noways unprovided, she was in the 63 of her age & 46 since her profession, she was buryed on the 17 of December in our little Church yeard because there was ^no^ place in the vault. *Requiescat in Pace*

on the 22 of desember my Lord Bishop entered againe our enclosure with the Arch Priest, & the Architect who brought with him the perfect moddel of what we pretended to. the building being now concluded on, was a Church & choir, & a cloister to layd to it, & under our choir; a Choir or chapel for our Lay Sisters, a Chapter house, & under that, a burial place which containes 45 ovens. we not having sufficient place to make the Choir of the length we wanted to have it ^we^ was **[p. 33]** forced to bye two poor houses that joy[n]'d, the value of both was not judge to be above 300 florence,[2] but seeing the necessity we had of them, they would not sell them us under 1100 florence, which we were forced to consent to, because we could ^not^ do with out them, which being a larger spot of ground then we stood in need of, for the choir & stair case, both in breadth, & length we built a rome by the choir for our Reverend Mother & under it conveniences for our great Sisters,[3] & the procuratrix for to receive & give out such things as might come during the time of divine office & mass, & on the other side of the stair case, a wash house because the other being under the cells, it was a hendrence to

[1] Reverend Mother was Prioress Lucy Herbert (BA101).

[2] Florins. Ten florins were equivalent to one Flemish pound.

[3] Here 'great' refers to the grate which marked the division between the enclosure and the world; see Glossary.

the religious for taking their rest, with a little kind of court by it, which affords us all wc stand in need of for our conveniences.

1736

we begun this year as we ended the last with the afflicting distemper of the smale pox: on the first day of it Sister margrit, our market Sister fell ill of them, on the 8 Sister Oliva Darel, & on the 17 Sister Mary Anne Caryll got the infection,[1] the smale pox was very fatal to her ^famile^ which made us the more concerned for her having them, but we were put in hopes that it would not prove so to her, both by the doctor & surgeon who ware both with her but few hours before she dy'd, & said they thought it would go well with her; ^but^ between ten & eleven she fell into a violent purging, with out any signes of sence, & expir'd about midnight, having received the Holy Oyles; she had received the *viaticum* (as all the rest had done) at the first begining of the distemper. so malignant was her distemper, & so violent was the stench of it, that her body was forced to be sunk, as soon as they could get the Coffin & the grave ready, & even the bed on which she dy'd bury'd with her. all was over before ~~by~~ mattins so that the Community was not appriz'd of her danger tell inform'd of her being dead & bury'd, for over night both doctor & surgeon thought it would go well with her, so that our surprise was not less than our affliction. we say'd the Commendations & long D[irige]: for her as usual, but we did not ring the bell, not to give notice of her death to the pentioners, for fear of stricking a terror in them, several of them not having had the smale pox, & therefore it was judg'd proper for some time to conceal her death. On the 30 day after her death her funeral was solomnly perform'd, & some masses & prayers apointed to supply for the delay, & for not ringing. her family formerly ^had^ been **[p. 34]** benefactors to this house, in consideration of which she was in part taken, for her fathers circumstances did not permitt him to give her any portion, but her uncle in France, Lord Caryll,[2] gave her 1000 Livers french, at her profession, which was a bout seventy pound english & settled upon her for life 300 Livers a year, her father came to see her, some few months before she dy'd, & told her that she should ^not^ continu under the notion of being taken in part upon Charity, for after his death she ^should^ share his estate with her Sister, who was the only that was left a live of all his children, but he was no sooner dead

---

[1] Sister Margaret was probably Margaret Linny (BA128), who was a lay sister and carried out a number of different tasks for the community outside the enclosure; Olivia Darell (BA071); Mary Ann Caryll (1712–36) BA047.

[2] Her father, Philip Caryll, died in 1735 in Dunkirk. One sister, Mary, had been a Benedictine nun at Dunkirk, dying in 1729 (DB032); the other, Frances, married Lieutenant Walker of Lord Clare's Irish Brigade. Sister Mary Ann's uncle, John Caryll, 1st Baron Caryll of Durford (d. 1711), had been Secretary of State to the Jacobite court in exile at St Germain-en-Laye.

but her Sister seiz'd all his estate, which had our deacesed liv'd to have known, it would have been the heardest cross she had ever meet with, which allmighty God was ^pleas'd^ to free her from, by taking her out of this ^life^. She was a very regular good religious, & had severall good parts, besides her voice which was usefull both to the choir & musick, & render her very serviciable. She was of a sweet temper, & wittily pleasent yet innofencive in conversation which indear'd her to all. she was bury'd in our little church yeard the 42 of her age & 24 of her holy Profession. *Requiescat in Pace*

the infection of the smal pox continu'd to go on, & after that all the religious that had not had them had got them it did the same amongst the pentioners so there was not one that escaped except an old jubilarian. but by the end of February it was all over, & to our great Comfort & satisfaction having lost but one of the number that had them, which was 13, in thanks giving for which we had a Mass said & *te Deum* sung.

on the 7 of march the foundation was begun to be digg'd for our new Church, & upon the 12 of march St Gregorys the day the first stone was lay'd; the serimony was nigh two hours long & perform'd with great order, we had 4 scalleters to hender the mob from crowding in, many came to see the serimony with hopes allso of seeing our house the enclosure being broke, but my Lord Bishope[1] to our great satisfaction hender'd them from entering the house, & gave him self the example by walking through the street after the serimony was done to come to the grate in place of coming through the house. & there before the Company he repeated the orders he had before given to our Reverend Mother of not letting any enter our inclouser, which prevented any from taking ill of us, our refusing them entrance.

On the eve my Lord Bishop gave orders that our Confessor should plant **[p. 35]** a Cross which was 9 or 10 foot long, it was painted red & adorn'd with Laurels but no crucifix upon it gest in the middle before where the high Alter was to be, which was accordingly done. the next morning there was a kind of Alter prepar'd on one side in the open air, & kind of tents made to secure the assembly from the weather, there were three square stones lay'd, the first by the Bishop, the 2^d^ by the Abbot of our order,[2] the 3^d^ by Mr Damerin[3] who takes care of our temporalls, on the first stone which my Lord Bishop lay'd was ingraven the image of our Holy Father & the Bishops arms on the 2^d^ which the Abbot lay'd

---

1 Hendrik Josef van Susteren, Bishop of Bruges 1716–42.

2 The Abbot of Eeckhoute in 1736 was Leon Van Male (c. 1684–1742), Abbot 1733–42.

3 Mr Damerin is Guillaume-Antoine Damerin, Lord of Hofland, former city Councillor and Treasurer of Bruges, who agreed to look after external financial affairs (temporals) for the convent on the death of his father in 1728. I am indebted to Dr Paul Arblaster for this reference.

was that of St monica[1] with his arms, & on the 3[d] which the gentelman lay'd was St Gregory whose day it was, & the gentelman's arms. there was a bout 10 or 12 stepes made for them to go down to the bottom of the foundation with a Carpit lay'd upon them. the Community was placed on the othere side seperated with boards from the seculars. the Bishop & his Clargie said & answerd all the prayers & Psalms that were said. he came with several priests & due attendants. the serimony begun about 3 a clock, the Bishop vested him self in the open air there being only a shade over his head, he put on an alb a stole & a Cape, & his mitter on his head, he begun by blessing holy watter & then he bless'd the three stones & said a great many prayers, & thurified them,[2] after that, he desended with his crosier carry'd before him into the fosse,[3] attended with the priests, when he was come to the place, he said more prayers & Psalms after which with a little instrument or pen knife he cut a cross at each Corner of the stone he was to lay, & on his knees he placed the stone & with morter fixt it, when that was done, he ascended up a gain & said the long Litanies & *Veni Creator &c*:[4] after which he & the priests that attended him went round the place where the Church was to be saying Psalms & sprinkling it with holy water, when all that was done he unvested him self & the Abbot of our order & the othere gentelman mention'd before Laid their stones, all being finished my Lord Bishop with the Abbot & the rest came to the Grate to wish us much joy & congratulate with our Reverend Mother for it. not withstanding the breach we had of our inclosier, thanks be to God such care was taken that non enter'd it, my Lord him self on that account would not come through the house, but went by the street, to the place where the Church was to be.

the 22 of march a dicission was made between the pastor of St Anne[5] & our Confessor, a bout some privileges of our monastery, the first **[p. 36]** occation of it, as there is reason to think, was our Confessor[6] baptissing Mis Wyrell which the Bishop had order'd him to do, they ware very moderate on both sides, & the Bishop being not in town then it seem'd to drop, but our new church having a very sumptuous door to the street they fear'd it would with draw from the parish, & that allso we might pretend to have a gathering to their Loss, which was never our thoughts, a memoriall was made of the grivances they apprehended, by the Pastor of St Anne's & others that joyned with him, as allso of their

---

1 St Monica was the mother of St Augustine and of particular importance to Augustinian convents.

2 The thurifer was responsible for incensing during Mass and other services by swinging the thurible at the appointed moments.

3 Fosse: here a ditch or trench, perhaps dug for the foundations.

4 *Veni Creator Spiritus*: 'Come creator Spirit', a hymn used on many occasions but particularly associated with Pentecost.

5 St Anne's church was the local parish church.

6 In 1736 the Confessor was Fr Caryl Gerard, Confessor 1723–79; Anstruther 4, p. 110.

pretentions which was presented to the Bishop which was as follows first that all our Convictresses borders & sarvants with in our enclosure should be his parishioners, both for making their Easter in the parish Church & for the last sacrements & burial 2dly that we should pay an Annual tribute to the Pastor & 3dly that we bye neither house nor Land in their parish with out their Consent. as there never was a president of such demands from our first establishment tell now, our Confessor stood briskly for maintaining the rights of our house, & he was strengthed in it by severall monasterys which he consulted which said we had right on our side & even the present Archpriest who had been him self Pastor of St Anne's say'd a Custom of a bove a hunder'd years was an inpregnable wall, my Lord Bishop seem'd to be on our side & the Abbot of our order wish'd our Confessor not to yield, but our bishop desirous of an acommendation & that an agreement should be made it was agreed upon in this manner that all our Convictresses that was english should be under the Confessors juridictions but that the sarvants & boarders with in our enclosure should be the pastors Parishoners: both for making their Easter in the parish (unless they had his leave for the Contrary) for the administering the last sacrements our Confessor was to do it, but was to send to the Pastor each time for his consent, & we were to [pay] an Annual tribute of three florence. which agrement was signed by my Lord Bishop, the Pastor of St Anne our Confessor & our Reverend Mother & put into our Arke to be keept.

the 6 of aprill mis Anne Harcourt, not seven year old was receiv'd for a convictriss.[1]

on the 9 of aprill mis Newland took the schoolers habit & is call'd Teresa Austin.[2]

[p. 37] the 29 of Aprill Sister mary Alexia Tacklock made her holy Profession.[3]

on the 25 of may Madamoiselle D'hofland was taken in to our enclosure in notion of a pentioner eating with them but no othere thing was requir'd of her she being a women it was in consideration of her father m^{r} Domerin that takes care of our temporalls that we were willing to receive her.

The 2^{d} of june mis Gage was sent out to larne French, near to the place where her cousin Bond lives to whose care she was recommended.[4]

---

1 Anne Harcourt, daughter of Richard Harcourt, a merchant of Boulogne, and Henrietta Browne, daughter of the 5th Viscount Montagu.

2 Elizabeth Newlin, in religion Teresa Austin (1737–86) BA147.

3 Mary Alexia Tatlock (BA194).

4 Miss Gage and her cousin Bond: the link to Bond family was through the 1675 marriage between Sir William Gage, 2nd Baronet (d. 1727) and Mary Charlotte Bond (d. 1708), and the marriage between Mary Gage (d. 1719) and William Bond (d. 1696). See F. Young, *The Gages of Hengrave and Suffolk Catholicism, 1640–1767*, CRS Monograph 8 (Woodbridge: Boydell and Brewer for the CRS, 2015), p. xii (family tree).

On the 10 of june Mademoiselle Van Asta, which was then pentionere in our schoole, departed this life, she was one of this towne, & had been convictriss here from December 1733, she was recommended to us by the Archpriest, her father & mother being dead her uncle & Aunt who had care of her, fearing she might marry, she being very rich, had a mind to have her ^for^ their son & thought she could be no where so secure as here, where she was not to go out, unless they sent for her, we perceiv'd when they did, that it was with some relucktance that she went to them, & with joy that she return'd to us, by reason of their continually importuning her to marry their son which she could not bare to hear of, which brock her heart, & in all appearance was cause of her sickness & death, she had been with [them for] eight [*blank*] & they would have had her remaine with them for good & all but with much a do she obtain'd their consent to return to us & remaine with us three months longer. she exprest at her return here a more then usall joy, & said she should spend here her days with joy hoping no more to go away, & so indeed it prov'd, she had actually a fevour upon her which she said she had had three days before but would not let her uncle & Aunt know it for fear they should have hender'd her from coming to us, her distemper encreasing, we gave to her friends who procur'd a Consult of doctors for severall days to come to her, but all in vain. she had rather dye she said, than to marry her Cousin Germain tho they got leave for it, our enclosure being open by reason of our building he now & then came in, but she would not see him. her Aunt & her uncle came frequently to see her which gave her much to suffer they persuading her to make her will & give away what she ought not to have done having two Sisters to whome it belong'd, which as soon as she was sensible of, she was greatly proplex'd & troubled & desir'd with all speed the Archpriest who was her Confessor to come to her, by whose help & advice all was againe rectify'd & another will made, he administer'd her the last sacrements, which she receiv'd with great devotion. he was with her by night as well as by day, but the last night **[p. 38]** he not being able to be with her, the[y] sent for the Pastor of St Anne[1] which assisted her the last night, she was present to the last moment she left us a hunder'd florence permission.[2] as soon as she was dead we said the Commendations for her in the Choir. on the following day she was carry'd to our Church & we sung mass & the Funeral as if she had been burry'd here[.] the following day they took her body from our Church with great seremony, & carry'd it to the burrying place of her friends. *Requiescat in Pace*

---

1 St Anne's church; see Map of Bruges.

2 The revised version of the Constitution granted permission for money received to be shared among the community or applied to community projects rather than remaining in the hands of the recipients.

the 7 of august mademoiselle Landscarp on of this towne was received for a Convictriss.

on the 18 mis Patty Smithson about ten years old was received for a Convictriss her Sister who had been here before came with her to make us a vissit & on the 5th of september return'd againe for england.

on the 14 of september Mr Williscot with his lady & his two Children & two sarvants arrived here, business calling mr Williscot further in the Country he left his Lady (which was Sister to [*blank*] of our religious)[1] with her two Children & her maid, for all which we got leave to enter our enclosur & lodg in our pentioners appartement tell his return, which was the first of October then they all lodg'd in towne as before.

the 30 of October mademoiselle D'hofland daughter to mr Damerin return'd to her friends much against her will she having been but a bout half a year where as she pretended to have stay'd at least a year, to render her going more ease & to prevent our disobliging both her & her friends, we assur'd them she should be wellcome to come a gain after Easter & stay a nother half year.[2]

on the 26 of november Sister Teresa Austin newland was Cloath'd

by the end of this year the head of the Church, the Choir, the staircase & Cloister had all the out walls built & the Roofe on, & all the windows stopt with straw, & the Doom[3] all so cover'd with it to secure it from receiving damage from the weather, & that they might be able to continu working with in durring the winter.

1737

The winter proving favorable the dead vault & the vault of the choir made & finished by the time that the season permitted to remove the straw & work again in the air.

On the 7 of january our dear Sister widdrington celebreated her **[p. 39]** whole jubily of fifty years of profession with all the serimonys appertaining to it.[4]

the 20 of feberary mademoiselle spellbeen return'd to her friends in ^towne^.

the 4th of march mademoiselle Prolli went from hence to her friends ^some^ at brussells we having desir'd them to send for [her] she not having her health here.

---

[1] Thomas Wollascott married Henrietta Maria (Harriet) Conyers, daughter of Sir Baldwin Conyers, 4th Baronet (d. 1731). Two of her sisters were professed at Nazareth: Frances Conyers, in religion Clementina (BA062); and Margaret, in religion Alipia (BA063).

[2] For the Damerin family, see **[p. 35]** above.

[3] The dome of the priory church.

[4] Mary Widdrington, in religion Ann (1687–1745) BA219, Sub-Prioress 1710–13.

the 16 of aprill mademoisell Lanen one of Antwerp was received for a Convictriss

the 24 of aprill mademoiselle D'hofland came again to remaine with us tell winter according to the promiss we made her, but no ways to the satisfaction of the Community, yet it could not be avoided.

the 22 of aprill mis Beddingfields[1] went to lille to larne French, & mis wyrill went to douay at the same time.

Sister Anne Markham being near her jubily & having been subprioress six years made continual intercession to be released saying she could not solomnise her jubily tell discharg'd of her office she being infirme so upon the 14 of may a new ellection was made & Sister Anne Weston chosen in her place.[2]

the 22 of may mis Anne Tanckerd went for england to her mother who sent for her her father being newly dead.[3]

the 26 of may, Mrs Harcourt with her sarvant came over & lodg'd in our pensioners appartement, with her sarvant, we having obtain'd leave for the time she stay'd, which was tell the 5th of june & then she went.

Mr John Stanfort left us at his death 20 pound starlin we sung mass for him, & each was order'd to hear three more & to offer three Communions, & for three days the Cross prayers.

Sister Mary Barbara Huddelston[4] having been long in a very ill state of health, & allmost a whole year in the infirmary & by spitting of blood which she did in great quantity was brought to such weakness that we had no hopes of recovering her or even of prolonging her life for all the remedies & advices we got from england as well as these parts had no effect[.] our Confessor propos'd to our Reverend Mother to make trial of the spa watters & change of air her Reverence unwilling to omit any possible remedy, sent for the parson that hed her cure in hand tho not a profest'd doctor yet one that was knowing in that art, & of which Sister mary Barbara had more esteeme then of the doctor of the house[.] they asked his advice who seem'd to have no doubt of the desir'd effect if she could reach the place but he believed she was to weak for the journey[.] the next day the doctor of our house was sent **[p. 40]** for & consulted who incourag'd our hopes of success & said she had sufficient strength provided they went slowly & rested as she found necessary, our Reverend Mother then proposs'd it to the Convent who were willing on account of her voice, which was much wanted both for the quire musick, my

---

1 The Miss Bedingfields were daughters of Henry Bedingfield and Mary Havers; see also **[p. 49]**.

2 Ann Mechtilda Markham (BA137); Ann Weston (BA215).

3 Anne Tancred was daughter to Thomas Tancred (d. 1737) and Frances Guizaine of Covent Garden, London. She later married Thomas Webbe of London. See Katherine Keats-Rohan, *Biographical Register* (2017, forthcoming).

4 Mary Barbara Huddleston (1725–57) BA114.

Lord Bishop being by our Confessor inform'd gave leave & as no time was to be lost, three days after the leave was granted which was the 6 of june she begun her journey with a lay Sister which was Sister Anne Clare[1] our Confessor could not then be spar'd nor she thought fitt to be without one, so Father Rector of gant[2] was desir'd to send a father with her as far as Liege which he did, she arrived at the spa[3] on the 17 & by a letter from her the 25 she said the watters agreed very well with her & that found her self allready much better & that the doctors there gave great hopes of a perfect cure.

the 13 of july Mrs Mannocks & Mrs Thorold with a sarvant came from Brussells to Sister Anne Markhams jubily being invited by her they enter'd our enclosure & lodged in the schoole.

the 15 of june Sister Anne Markham selebreted her jubily of fifty years of profession.[4]

the 23 of july Mrs mannocks return'd to Brussells & six days after Mrs Thorold, that came with her, went away.

the Archdutchess[5] last year demanded a subsidue or tenth from all the Clargi & monasterys under her government in order to raise a sum to assist the Emperour in his war against the Turks, we excus'd ourselves by reason of our building which excuse was admitted of but this year the same demand being made again to all such as had not pay'd we was advised by my Lord bishop to do it, so we gave 20 pound Starlin which was graciously receiv'd.

the 8th of august Mrs Hartcourt & her maide enter'd our enclousure & lodg'd in an partment in our schoole.

the 26th Mrs Blundel & maide came & a leave was obtain'd for them to enter & lodg in apartment in the same schoole she having two Cousen germains religious amongst us,[6] these frequent leaves would neither have been ask'd, nor yet granted, but that on account of our building we having so many workemen with it may be said to be in a manner open.

the 2^d^ of September mis Greenwood went for england her friends having sent for her.

---

1 Ann Clare Formby (BA082). Lay sisters were not bound by the rule of enclosure.

2 The Rector of the Jesuit College, Ghent in 1737 was Fr Percy Plowden SJ; see Holt, p. 197.

3 They travelled to Spa near Liège.

4 Ann Mechtilda Markham (BA137) was the jubilarian in question because she professed in 1687.

5 Archduchess Maria Elisabeth of Austria (1680–1741) was appointed governor of the Austrian Netherlands in 1725 by her brother. She arrived in October 1725 and spent the rest of her life in the country.

6 Mrs Blundell here is probably Frances, daughter of Marmaduke, 3rd Lord Langdale of Holme, married to Nicholas Blundell, 'The Diarist', who died in April 1737. She had two Smithson cousins at Bruges: Lucy Smithson (BA177) and Mary Augustine Smithson (BA178). Their mother was Frances' sister, Elizabeth Langdale: see WWTN, Langdale family tree, and Stirnet, Family Tree, Langdale01.

the 23 of September our Confessor Mr Gerard[1] went for england for change of air he not being very well, & all so to see his friends promissing to be back by Christmass, his place was supply'd by Father James Darel[2] **[p. 41]** one of the society which was of the Coledge at Gant which was recommended to us by the Rector of the same Coledge.[3]

the 2^d of october Mrs Harcourt & her sarvant went from hence to settle at St Omers.

Sister Frances Xaverious friends sent 20 pound for prayers for her relations that were living & for those were dead, for which all ware order'd to hear three masses & one Communion for the living & the same for the dead.[4]

the 21 of october Sister mary barbara Huddelston with Sister Anne Clare Formby return'd from spa not so perfectly recoved as we hop'd for yet a vast deal better then when she went, it was judg'd fitting that she should remaine in the infirmary tell spring & not sing. care was taken not to give her any conterdiction, not to render fruitless the great expence the Community had been at for her recovery, her illness being judg'd in great part hysterical.[5]

the 11 of november Mademoiselle D'Hofland return'd home to her friends to our great satisfaction.

the 19 of november our dear Sister Mary Austin Smithson[6] departed this life she was a very pious good religious woman but by nature very passionat [.] she had but a shallow capacity & through weakness of nature was so mastter'd by her imagination which made her continually suspicious of her things being taken from her, or changed for worce, it was not in the power of any to convince ^her^ of the contrary & it did but sarve to provock her to endevour it, there was no remedy to be had, but patience, she her self suffer'd infinetly by it, as much as if it were real & done as she thought out of unkindness, which occation'd her to make many an heroick acts of patience & resignation. her acts of vertue was (as her Imaginary injurys continuall) & as her sufferings by it was real, so no doubt her merrit was allso. in her noviship she was so sickly as to apprehend she would not live, & therefore not judg'd fitt to under take a religious life, but she was persuaded that as her vocation was from God, she should recovere her health through the intercession of Sister Frances Xaverius for which intention she was allow'd to performe the

1 Fr Caryl Gerard, Confessor 1723–79; Anstruther 4, p. 110.

2 Fr James Darell SJ (1707–85), buried in the church of the English Canonesses, Liège; see Holt, p. 76.

3 Jesuit College, Ghent, founded in 1585.

4 Frances Xaveria Simner (BA174).

5 See **[pp. 39–40]**.

6 Mary Augustine Smithson (1700–37) BA178.

ten fridays[1] in his honour which was attended with such success that she recover'd, & remain'd healthy ever after, tell some years before she dy'd, which health she faithfully imploy'd in an exact obsarvance of order, she was very just, & a great lover of it, in all the imployments she has been in, she neither gave nor refuss'd but in that vew, she was very Charitable & it was sufficient to be sick or in affliction to pertake of her best assistance. few dy'd, that she did not get many masses say'd for them, to procure them a happy death; she was ever very carefull **[p. 42]** that what ever assistance she gave to any should not be known, which she desir'd of Reverend Mother when she asked leave for it. her little prayers & devotions seem'd to be accompan'd with simplicity & great confidence which render'd them more powerfull with God. some years before she dy'd, she was much inclined to a lethargi & had great difficulty to keep her self aweak even time of the divine office & she complain'd of a cold flemetick humour on her stomack & shortness of breath, but as she had complain'd of it for some time, & there appearing no sings [signs] of death we did not apprehend her, so that she was not in the infirmary, but the doctor being sent for, & he finding her worce then we thought, order'd her severall remidies which were try'd but without success he appointed her the Rights which she receiv'd with great piety & even with joy, she had prepar'd herself for that happy hour for a long time before being persuaded that she had not long to live. our Confessor being not return'd from england, she had a mind to have the Confessor of the 3d order,[2] accordingly we did our endevours to have got him leave of the bishop to have heard her confession. but he thought not fitt to grant it, we having one of the society which was sent us from gant to supply fathers Confessors place, but if it would not content her she might have ^he said^ Mr Morphy or some jesuite from the Coledge,[3] but this did not satisfy her, her mind being bent upon having the Fryer confessor to the 3d order,[4] tho at the same time she own'd that what she had to say, was what she might dye safly with out saying, but that it would be a great comfort to speak of it to the Fryer, & she thought that comfort could not be refuss'd to a dying parson, we sent ^therefore^ to him to come to her, but at the same time, desir'd him not to let her know that we could get no leave for him to hear her confession. he came & heard what she had to say, & spook very Comfortably to her, which as he found was only necessary, when he was gone she said all was well over, & she had nothing more say or to do then to prepare herself for death, which she truly endevour'd the best she could to do: she not having rested the

1 Frances Xaveria Simner (BA174). Devotion of Ten Fridays: see Glossary.

2 Third Order Franciscan, already connected to the English Franciscans at Prinsenhof as Confessors.

3 Possibly Fr Richard Murphy SJ (1716–94); Holt, p. 174.

4 Probably Lewis Middlemore OFM, Confessor Prinsenh of 1737–9: see WWTN.

whole night, one of the religious that watched by her pitt[i]ed her for not resting, she said I am going to rest, I meane eternally. then she lay for some time quiet, the watchess thought she slept tell hearing a little noise they look'd & found her a dying[.] Father Dorel[1] being but in the next chamber came time enough to give her the last absolution, she expir'd as we were going to mattins the 60 of her age & 38 of her Holy profession & was bury'd the 20 of november in our little Church yeard next to the sick house windows *Requiescat in pace.*

the 4th of desember Sister Teresa Austin newland made her Holy profession.[2]

on the 6 Mrs Lloyd came & a leave was ask'd for her to lodg within our enclosure whilst she stay'd

[p. 43] both our buryall places being quit full t'was judg'd now a proper time to empty them it being a frost, so the 9th of desember a great pit was dig'd in our little Church yeard sufficient to containe the bodys that were bury'd in the ovens which was 16 in number amongst which was Mr Damerin & Dame Caryll a benedictin Dame of Dunkerke,[3] whilst they were doing it, our Reverend Mother with one or two of our Religious stood by to see that it was perform'd with decence & respect & said the *de profundis* for each. The day after, as soon as Mass was said, the most Blessed Sacrement was remov'd out of the tabernacle into the Sacrestin in order to empty the vault[.] all they religious was forbid to come to the Choir or lay Sisters Chapel (except two that was appointed to be present) for fear of infection t'was thought that the stench would have been very great. but to our great surprise it had little or no smell, from eight a'clock in the morning tell six at night, three men were imploy'd in empting ^it^ & then a nother man was added, & they labour'd tell two in the morning in hopes to have finish'd it, but finding it was impossible, they shut it up, & made the Church as decent as they could for mass, after Mass they begun again & wholy clear'd it, all that was remaining of their bodys was bury'd in our little Church yeard, & their souls as we may piously believe in joys God & will I hope pray for our Community where in they sanctify'd themselves.

on the 17 of Decenber Mr Gerard our Confessor return'd from england pleas'd with his journey, & mended as he thinks in health.

being inform'd that the Altar which was makeing at Rome for our new Church could not enter the Emperour's dominions with out paying great duties we apply'd our selves to Arch Dutchess Governess of these Conterys at Brussells by means of a friend there, that had some intress in

---

1 The Jesuit assistant confessor was Fr James Darell SJ (1716–94); Holt, p. 76.

2 Teresa Austin Newlin (BA147); see also vol. 1, **[pp. 419, 428–9]**; vol. 2, **[p. 21]**.

3 Mary Benedict Caryll (DB032) had left her convent in Dunkirk to go to the spa for her health. She remained for some months at Nazareth, but died there on 13 October 1729; see vol. 1, **[pp. 444–5, 471]**.

the Court to present our petition to her highness which she received, & very Graciously granted us a full exemption from all duties in whatever part of the Emperours dominions it should pass. in acknowledgment of which favour Reverend Mother sent a box of the best silver flowers & a Reliquary, being informed that such things would be acceptable to her, she received very Graciously & seem'd very well pleas'd with it.

Mrs Chichester being dead without a will & having a daughter here, we were inform'd that she had an equal clame to share with the rest of the Children, in the parsonal estate of her mother, & therefore was advis'd to demand her due.[1] our Reverend Mother wrote to Mr Chichester & told him the advice that had been given her of suing for what was due to his Sister & at the same time assur'd him that she had no inclination to dispute with him her right & chouse rather to be depriv'd in part of it than to risk loosing his friendship by gaining the whole, tho at this time of our **[p. 44]** building it would be most wellcome to us, she moreover assur'd him that what ever he should bestow we would consider as a gift from him, & accordingly should pray for him: his answer to this letter shew'd, he took very kindly our proceeding after that manner, he said since we did not require any thing as due, but left it to him he would send us five hunder'd pound, which we were very well pleas'd with, tho more might have been her due, yet rather, chouse to have that with the good will of the family than to have disoblig'd them, by going to law & perchance have got nothing according to the Laws in england. some little time after hearing that we were procuring an Altar from Rome he presented us thirty pound towards it & his lady with twenty, so that in all we received five hunder'd & fifty pound which was dubly agreeable to us because with out the least breach of friendship but the contra[r]y.

we having the exposs[it]ion of our Rule (which our customes requires should once a year be read in the refectory) but in a writen hand, & not well done neither, our Reverend Mother proposs'd to Loven to joyn with us to have that printed which was translated out of french, & much more to our liking which they consented to, we got a hunder'd printed, fifty for them, & the same for our selves, which was printed the year before last but forgot to be put down, Reverend Mother gave to each of the religious one, & sent fifty to Loven.[2]

---

1 Teresa Joseph Chichester (BA052); her sister Ursula (BA053) had already died in 1723, aged 15. Their mother was Catherine Chichester, née Palmer (d. 1730), a widow when she died (Stirnet, Family Tree, Chichester 03). She inherited estates in Wales. Mr Chichester was her son John; he was not Catholic.

2 Loven here is St Monica's, Louvain, the mother house of the Bruges convent. *The Rule of the Great S. Augustin Expounded ... now Publish'd in English for the use of the English Augustin Nuns at Bridges*, printed by John de Cock [1737]. Several copies survive in the library at Nazareth.

I can't end this year with out some account of our building we were deceiv'd in the promiss they made us of its advance for insteed of the Doome[1] being finish'd, tis a gaine cover'd with straw to prevent its receiving damage from the weather, & our dead vault by ignorance or neglect of the masson letts in watter so that the ovens[2] must all be taken down a gaine & a new built. & for a neglect in not specifying in the articles that if not well done they work man was to repaire it at their own expence we were forced to be at expence of it, which was very unreasonable & a great addition to our expences.

1738

the first of january Mrs Lloyd return'd back againe for england

the 21 of january mademoiselle Law return'd to her friends in towne.

the first of feberary Mrs Blondel & her sarvant enter'd our enclosure & a leave was got for them to lodg in Childrens apartement whilst they stay'd.

an Aunt of Sister Catherin' & Sister Ann Clare'[3] sent us a seven pound for prayers; for the which each of the Community was order'd to hear six masses, & to perform for three days the Cross prayers, & to offer two Communions.

[p. 45] Mademoiselle D'hofland being reduced to a very ill state of health & pining to return again here, her friends pleading for it, we could not without disobliging them refuse it tho unwellcome to all, so on the 17 of march she enter'd againe our enclosure.

on the 8 of Aprill all mighty God was pleas'd greatly to afflict our Community by depriving us of dear Sister Weston which was then our Subprioress,[4] she was esteem'd by all for her vertue & good parts, & as God had bless'd her with a constant good health she faithfully imploy'd it for his sarvice & the good of her nighbour & benefitt of our Community, the spare times she had at her own dispossal she employ'd in writing & translating sarmons & such like things as might be of use & a benefitt for the Community there are severall volumes of her writing in which she imploy'd the time that was at her own dispossal & to mortify her naturall eagerness when imploy'd about such things, & to testify her love to God, & keep herself in a continual disposition of fullfilling his will she would from time ^to time^ interrupt what she was about, as at every half hour, & kneel down for the space of an *Ave maria*, & renew her

---

1 The dome in the new church.

2 Ovens: see Glossary.

3 Sister Catherine and Sister Ann Clare: probably Catherine Simner (BA174) and Ann Clare Formby (BA082). Both were known to be from Lancashire and they arrived at the convent together in 1724 to become lay sisters. It is not currently known whether or how they were related.

4 Ann Weston (1699–1738) BA215.

intention of doing it for God by her fidelity in doing this she keept her self in a dispossion of punctuall obedience to the will of God signify'd either by a bell or the inclination of a superiour. her application to an interiour life & union with the divine will was very appeearent [in] the papers she writ which came to light after her death confirm'd what her behaviour shew'd of it in her life, as allso her obedience to the advice of her derector in making her monthly revew, & it noting down each month how often she fail'd in the vertue she was to make ^it^ upon, & how often she committed the fault contrary to it, which ~~she~~ went greatly against her inclination to do as she expresses in the same papers. nothing but to please God could make her do it, with which desire of pleassing him in all she dos, she begings each day, & frequently renews the same during the day as her monthly revews shows, & says she hopes she is not mistaken in thinking she truly desires to please God. tho allmighty God was liberall of his talents to her, having given her a good capacity, yet she seem'd not to value her self for it nor to make use of it for her own honour but his, she had a generous heart that sought not her own interest but the Glory of God & good of her neighbour, ~~in all her prayers she petitions~~ which was the motive she aimed at in what she did, she took greatly to heart those two great precepts the love of God & of her neighbour & in all her prayers she petitions for her neighbour as well as for her self, as her papers shews, & begs God to give her a disposition of goodness & sweetness towards her neighbour that she might compassionate their little humours & assist them in all she could, & defend the absent, & humble her self to the present, & never presume to make her self a jud[g]e of their proccedings, or treat them with her natural blountness, but consider each as his spousses & carry her self towards ^them^ with kindness & respect, grieving & rejoyceing with **[p. 46]** each as reason or cause requir'd it, & with a maternal tenderness even to the most disagreeable. all which God was pleas'd to grant her the grace to make her practiss, as was apparent to us ^but^ towards her self she was annimated with the spirit of penna[n]ce, sensible that all sin's must be satisfy'd either in this life or the next, & tho a Religious life, if constantly comply'd with is judg'd to be the best of pennances yet she was not content to obsarve what was most strick & heard in it, but she more over obtain'd leave to add two disiplins ever week.[1] she had a great esteeme for indulgences & was carefull to do what was requir'd for to gain them, & when she vissited the sick she would informe them of those that were in their power to gain. she had a very good genius to poetry & for the divertion & to comply with the desire of some of they ^religious^, she made severall playes, poems & such like things as

---

[1] Disciplines: the use of disciplines as a form of penance was monitored by senior members of the convent, who were concerned that they should not be used excessively.

well for instruction as divertion being intermixt with solide maximes of Christion & religious vertues in which apear'd her good judgment, she was indued with a great deal of good sence, & of a sharp witt, which her darling vertue Charity keept inoffencive othere ways she was by nature inclined to be blunt & sharp, & ruff in her way, not having that agreeable sweetness which is taking in conversation, how ever each receiv'd such proufes of her tender compassion & good will when they stood in need of it as indear'd her to all. upon the 16 of march she was taken ill with a shortness of breath & swelling in her stomack & sharp choliks[.] the doctor was sent for & he found her pulce much distemper'd but both he & we all hop'd it would soon pass, but we were deceiv'd, for in place of growing better she grew worce & worce, all possible means was us'd for her recovery but in vain; on the 29 which was the eve of Palme sunday the doctor order'd her to receive her *viaticum*, which she received with great piety & devotion. she was perfectly sensible the whole time of her illness, & did not less edifye by her patience chearfullness & gratitude to those that tended her than she had in her life by her constant & [un] interrupted obsarvance of order. on easter munday she had a great desire to make her Easter & pascal communion which was granted her she desir'd one of the religious to read to her what she her self had writ to prepare her self for it, she express'd what a Comfort it was to her to have communicated, her countence shew'd the serenity & content of her mind, even to the last moment, between 2 & 3 ^a clock^ of the following day ^she^ apear'd to draw nearer her end; Father Confessor[1] being by her, said to her, Child offer your self to lay down your life for love of Him that dy'd for love of you. to which she answer'd I do puerly for his ~~sake~~ love[.] a little after she inclin'd her head towards him for absolution, & said some thing but they could not hear **[p. 47]** what & a bout two or three minites after, she expier'd, keeping still a smilling countenance. the 62 of her age & 40 of her Holy profession, she was bury'd the day following which was the 10 of oprill [*sic*]. *Requiescat in pace*.

the 17 of aprill our Community was afflictedly surpriss'd & terify'd by the sudden death of Dear Sister Byerly,[2] who was found dead, she had been many years very infirm, & not able to keep quire, & othere religious duties she was allso exempt from. she had a fistula for which she had been cut which caus'd her to suffer violent pains, which she bore patiently & couragiously, yet this was the lest part of her sufferings, for besides her being of an anctious scrupulos dispossition, she was of unhappy temper that allow'd her no rest, seeming to have a peculare art to turn all things to her own uneaseness so that she was never with out some subject to torment her self & others with, in so much that there was not one in the

1 Father Confessor: Fr Caryl Gerard, Confessor 1723–79; Anstruther 4, p. 110.
2 Mary Byerley, in religion Mary Aloysia (1706–38) BA042.

Community to whome she did not give an occation of merit by baring with her temper which with a great deel of Charity each one did for Gods sake who permitted it for the encrease of her merit as well as ours for she suffer'd by it more then she gave others to suffer which was nothing to what she indur'd her self. our late superiour Mother Wright[1] made difficulty to have admitted her to her Cloathing but finding the Elders for it she yielded to them it had been much to the ease & peace of the house had she not (as experience has shown us), by which we may see that it is better to follow the sentiments of a superiour in such matters then our own. ware such another put to the votes of the wholl Community, tho with a thousand pound & more they would not accept of her for peace & quiet is preferable to all things which it could be not be [*sic*] said we perfectly injoy'd as long as she lived for tho she was of a pleasent ready witt & when disposs'd to be deverting none could exceed her, yet in her Company there was a constant restraint least some look or word should be by her misinterpreted which could make to her un eassiness, which happen'd very frequently, it was a dayly subject of Combate to her, the bardoning of imaginary or mistaken injurys, which was as difficult & consequently as meritorius as if they had been real. she was pious & of a Compationat temper & had a great feeling of any that she thought wanted & would give them for their solace what even was necessary for her self tho sure next **[p. 48]** moment to want it, & that even to those who at that present was most out of favour with her, it was obsarved that the day she dy'd, she spook in prayes of them she had no naturall liking to, & intertain'd the religious in the sickhouse with what she had read of severall sudding deaths & show'd a fear of hers being such which indeed it was, & in all appearance so sudden that she was dead before she could be sensible that she was dying, she was ~~heard~~ seen by severall in the dormitery towards the end of silence, & in time of vespers she was heard strongly to cough by one whose cell was near hers[;] t'was then most sertainly that she dy'd & in all appearence with out the least struggle, for she was not wholly falen from of the Chair she sat on. her head was all most to the ground which made the blood to settle in her face so that it was thought not expose her but next morning she was a fine corps[.] we sent imediatly for the surgion who was of oppinion she must have been dead well three hours before we found her, the surprise & terrour was so great that two of [*sic*] three of our religious was forced to be blooded & t'was long before many others recover'd it, & it being towards night made it more dreadfull. had the like happen'd to any of the othere religious it would have been sooner perceiv'd, but her absence from choir was in a manner constant because of her infirmitys, & from the first refectory some times that it gave no cause of looking after her,

[1] Mary Wright (1657–1709) BA228, Prioress 1693–1709.

but not seeing [her] at later table search was made & they found her in the cell where they keep the books & where she us'd to read her office, & the book for reading her office open, which either she had begun to read or was a going to read, she had a good custome of compossing her mind by quieting all unease & resenting thoughts before she begun the divine office which was a good preparation for death, & no smale comfort to us that seeing her death was so sudden it was in the performance of so holy a duty, our Confessor who was throughrowly acquanted with her concience & temper assur'd that he look'd on the suddenesse of it as a perticular mercy of God to her. she was bury'd the 19, & of her age the 5[2d] of her Holy profession. [the 32d] she [was buried in] our little Church yeard with the rest of our religious. *Requiescat in Pace.*

the 21 of aprill Mrs Blundell with her sarvant maid, parted from hence & went to Gant. **[p. 49]** on the 28 Sister Mary Teresa Jarnegan was chosen for subprioress.[1]

the 12 of may the two Mis Bedingfields came back from Lille.[2]

the 19 of may Mrs Blundell return'd here again, & remain'd here tell june, & then to dunkerke.

the 24 of may the two Mis Titchborns went from hence to St Omers by order of their friends, to larne french.[3]

the 29th of may Mademoiselle D'hofland ~~went~~ from hence to her friends.

the 31st of may Mis Catherin ^gage^ took the Schooler's kerchif, & is call'd Sister Mary Xaveria.[4]

the 7 of june mis mary & mis Margrit Bettam, was received for confictrisses, the one was 17, & the other 16 years old.

this month the superiour at Loven keept her whole jubily,[5] our Reverend mother ^thought^ it a necessary civility, to writ to her, to assure her of the prayers of our Community, & of the share we took therein looking on our selves as Children of their house. she presented her with three books printed by one of our Religious, one was the masses through out the whole year, the othere two, was the *Antiphons*, they ware all three hansomly bound in spanish leather, & silver cla[s]pes, which was most kindly receiv'd, & that our Community might drink her health & be merry, she sent us for that effect three pistols which were accordingly imploy'd.[6]

---

1 Mary Teresa Jerningham (BA118), Sub-Prioress 1738–48.

2 See also **[p. 39]**.

3 The Miss Tichbournes were daughters of William Tichbourne and Lucy Eyre; see also **[p. 28]**.

4 Catharina Gage, in religion Mary Xaveria (BA084).

5 The Superior at Louvain was Mary Cecilia More (1690–1755) LA186, Prioress 1733–55. There appears to be a discrepancy in the dates here, since her date of profession in the Louvain Chronicle is given as 1690. It is possible that they counted from her year of entry rather than profession.

6 These books do not appear to have survived.

the 29 of june mis Belon Ancker one of this towne was receiv'd for a convictris she was about 12 years old.

the first of july my Lady Montaigue with three women sarvants enter'd our enclosure with a designe to end her days amongst us, some time before Lord Duke of Powis writ to our Reverend Mother, that his Sister Lady Montaigue,[1] was resolved to retire in a monastery to end her days, & as she was not able to walk but ^must^ be carry'd, was resolved to go where she could have the benefit of hearing Mass dayly with out sturing out of her Chamber, & as she knew she could not have that conveni[e] nce here, she intended to go to paris where she knew she could have it, which was a trouble to our Community, both on account of the love & esteeme they had for her, as all so because it would give occation to the world to think she must have seen what displeas'd her when she was here before, othere ways having a Sister ^here^ superiour she would sartainly have prefer'd this house before any othere. Sister Weston **[p. 50]** which was then our subprioress, wished our Reverend Mother to get my Lord Bishops leave that she might have mass said in her Chamber, which accordingly she did, & my Lord very obligingly granted it, Reverend mother immediatly ^writ^ to the Duke of Powis to informe his Sister Lady Montaigue of it, at which news she was over joy'd, desiring nothing more then to be here, preferably to all othere places, as having a sincere love & esteeme for our house, nothing but being depriv'd of the advantage of dayly hearing mass could have made her resigne to have gone ellce where. that difficulty being removed she resolved immediatly to come, which news was very agreeable to our Community. she arriv'd here as is said before, the first of july, & with her came the two mis Blundells, the eldest of which was 15 year old, & the othere 12 & a half, & allso the two mis Fair Childs the Eldest 13 & a half & the other 11 & half.

the same day about an hour after came mis Anne Jernegan & mis Darill,[2] both past 10 year old they were all receiv'd for convictrisse.

on the [*blank*] of july mass was said for the first time, in Lady Montaigues Chamber by the Carmes,[3] & is to continue to be said there as long as she lives.

on the 2d of august the two mis Beddingfields parted from hence to go for england.

on the 3d of august Mrs Lloyd enter'd our enclosure in order to carry the two mis Beddingfields for england, which went the day before to dunkerke to expect her, & she parted from hence the 7 of august.

---

[1] Mary Herbert, Lady Montagu (1659–1745) was the sister of Prioress Lucy Herbert (BA101). Their brother was William Herbert, 2nd Marquess (1665–1745); see Herbert family tree.

[2] None of this group appears to have professed.

[3] The Carmelite friars of Bruges in Carmerstraat were assisting Fr Gerard, the Confessor at Nazareth, because of his health problems and the additional demands placed by the presence of Lady Montagu, who had Mass said daily in her rooms.

the begining of august our fine marble Altar arrived here in 32 casses, so nicely pack'd up, that neither by the length of the voyage nor different manner of carage was the least indamag'd, much about the same time my Lady nitchdail,[1] Sister to our Reverend Mother writ to her, to give her notice that the Cannon which she had imploy'd at Rome to see it well done according to the Agreement made was gone from Rome to take possestion of his cannonry at Castel not far from S[t] Omers & designed to come here, which he did soon after & brought with him a young italian man that had work'd at such things at Rome[.] we differ'd opening the Casses tell they came that they might be present both at the openning them **[p. 51]** & at the errecting the Altar to prevent all accidents & to see it done as it should be. we found their assistance very necessary, but some of our workmen wear so sett in doing their own way that we could not make them do as they would have them. The table of the Altar was scarced fixed but we perceiv'd it was placed so [far] back that a third part of the tabernacle behind would have been bury'd in the nitch upon which we requir'd to have it advanced forward 14 inches that the beautifull turn of [the] Altar might be seen which othereways could not, the Cannon & his man press'd mightily for the same, but the work men opposs'd it, & the over seere that was consulted sided with them, finding that we could make yield they complain'd to my Lord Bishop that we intented to spoil the simitry of the Church with bringing more to vew of the fine marble[.] my Lord who was charm'd with what he had seen of it as it lay in our work chamber before it was set up was very desirous to have it well fix'd, but [not] thinking him self a sufficient judg of the dispute between our sentiments & thers, sent his secretary with the Arch dacon to forbid our going on tel the Architect at Rome that made the Altar had been consulted ordering we should stand to his judgment[.] this stop was no smale disapointment on both sides, our Reverend Mother writ imediatly to her Sister Lady Nitzdail & inclos'd the plan with all the reasons pro & con desiring her to procure & send the Architects decision.[2] the Cannon & the italian his man shew'd more concerne in this affaire then we knowing that the best Architect & abelest work^man^ had been imploy'd in making it, besides they had seen it in its beauty, for it was errected at Rome. that they virtuosees might pass their judgment upon it & it receiv'd from them their unanimous approbation, regreting its going from Rome as to find a pice of work for any place but there. the Cannon & his man finding nothing could be more done tell we heard from Rome, which we could not well ^do^ under about two months, took leave of us & return'd to Castel. when the letter came it was with

[1] Lady Nithsdale (1672–1749) was Winifred Herbert, sister of Prioress Lucy Herbert (BA101). She was married to William Maxwell, 5th Earl of Nithsdale; see *ODNB* and Herbert family tree.

[2] The architect of the church was Hendrik Pulinckx (1698–1781).

orders to advance it out of the nitch 12 or 14 inches as was needfull, but those here of a different sentiment, could not be prevailed upon to yield more than seven inches, which was all we could obtaine; & to prevent what we could the rest from being hide & bury'd in the nitch, we had it inlarg'd 4 inches of each side, & fifteen in higth, to make as much be seen of it as we could **[p. 52]** it being too late in the year to work at setting it up, we were forced to lay side the thought of it tell spring. the whole Altar is what they call crusted marble, that is marble of the thickness of crown pice lay'd upon rustick stone, they make them so at Rome so that except four or five of the old standing ones, there is non of solid marble. such marble is very scarce, most of it come ^from^ Egypt, & persia, our Altar is composs'd of two or three & twenty sort of the finest marble. the guilding of the Capitalls & basses was done upon marble, & so beautifull that it was not less admir'd than the marble, but by the ill useage of ^they work men^ & damptness of the place was intierly spoilt. the Altar with the caces & packing up cost five hunder'd & two & twenty pound english, which was thought exceeding cheep, even those at Rome judg'd it to have cost as much again the carrige from Rome hether cost a hunder'd & eight & twenty pound english. had the parson to whouse ^care^ it was commitd sent it as we desir'd to ostend, which he might easely have done, it would not have cost us by a great deel so much, because we had obtain'd of the Archdutchess an ample exemption of all the duties. where as comming by Holland we were forced to pay all the duties which ware very great, which expence coming at a time that we ware less able to bare it made it very heard, for the money we receiv'd from m^r^ Chichester & his Lady was but five hunder'd & fifty, & the Altar with the carrige came to six hundred & forty eight pound, but not to inflame the Arke Reckoning which was very high on account of our building, our Reverend mother pay'd, all that was over the money that Mr Chichester gave, out of her exchange money, & presents given her.

the 5 of September Mrs Blundele & her sarvant return'd again here.

we had notice that Mrs Trafford at her death had left us five pound for prayers for her soul,[1] each was order'd to heare five masses for her & to offer one Communion.

Lady Hungate sent us a guinea desiring the prayers of the Community.[2] Reverend Mother order'd all to hear a Mass for her.

Sister Frances Simner[3] mother sent ten pound five for prayers for her husband soul & his friends, & five for her self, & friends living, we

[1] Frances Trafford (d. 1734); she had a sister (BA203) and three aunts (BA202, BA204, BA242) in the convent.

[2] Probably Lady Mary Hungate, née Weld (1677–1749), widow of Sir Francis Hungate, 4th Baronet (d. 1710), leaving one daughter of the marriage, Mary (b. 1709).

[3] Catherine Simner, in religion Frances Xaveria (BA174); no details are currently known about her parents.

were order'd to hear five Masses & five days the cross prayers for him **[p. 53]** & five masses & one Communion for her & her friends. the same sum was sent us a year before but forgot to be writ downe, as all so the prayers we perform'd

The first of October mis Salvin came & was receiv'd for a Convictriss she was about 13 years of age.[1]

the 31 of desember it pleas'd allmighty God to call Mrs Sykes[2] to a better life as we may piously belive from the vertuous life she had lay'd in the world, she had been about six years & a half with us to her great content & satisfaction, God by it seem'd even in this life to recompence her patient suffering of the Crosses & afflictions which her former life had been in vould in by a peasefull retierment very conformable to her inclination. she was a woman of few words but of a solide good judgment of a great courage & presence of mind, & ever mistress of her self by an eveness of temper, she was a great lover of truth & a heatred of all disimulation, & so just that she ow'd to her Children that she could injoy no Comfort whilst any debt remain'd unpay'd, & she only wish'd to live to see each have their due which having now done she experienced more content then ever she had done from her first being a wife, she was a prudent good wife & a kind mother she was not one of much prayer but had ever a singular devotion to our Blessed Lady putting her trust & Confidence in her as mother of mercy & selldome fail'd going to Communion on her feasts tho other ways it was selldome that she went under a falce notion of respect thinking it a priviledg only fitt for religious, she remain'd all day long in her chamber & went out but to mass, if they religious vissited her she took it kindly & if not she shew'd no concerne[;] for the most part she never saw any tell evening not so much as her own daughters for she did not desire they should omitt any duty on her account[.] she was neither a trouble nor a distraction to our Community, her maid did all that appertain'd to her, in her last sickness she was not only no trouble, nor any ways **[p. 54]** burdensome but the contrary for she made her maid that watched with her go & assist them that were in the sickhouse which prevented a lay sister from setting up or rising in the night to them. the three last months she was constantly watch'd with our religious offer'd to have done her that sarvice, but she would not permitt it[;] she hyer'd a woman to spare her sarvant but for want of languish made it inconvenient to her so her maid sleept in the day & watched in the night, at the beginning of her illness she was seas'd with some speces of an appeplix, & soon after with a defiance of nature which perceptably encreas'd, on the day of our Blessed Ladys

---

[1] Miss Salvin was the daughter of Bryan Salvin of Croxdale and Anne Haggerston.

[2] Mrs Sykes, née Mary Dovery, was mother to two choir sisters at Bruges, Anne (BA188) and Mary (BA189), and a benefactor to Catholic institutions on the continent. See also **[pp. 19, 66, 86, 88]**.

conception[1] she was communicated by a Carme at midnight & some days after receiv'd the last sacrements which Father Confessor[2] administred to her, the surgion which she made use of as her doctor for she would consult no othere said she suffer'd greatly yet never complain'd, neither did she shew a desire of life nor a fear of death it seemed as if her cheerfull submission to Gods will was by a long habit become naturall. on Christmas night she fell into her agony which prevented her communicating as designed after our midnight mass from which time there was intervals in which her judgment failed, the last day & night ther appear'd no signe of life but by breathing. she expir'd about six a clock in the morning the 77 of her age in arms of her Eldest daughter & the other by her all so, the Carme that assisted gave her the last absolution for our Confessor having difficulty in helping the dying & not judging this his obligation desir'd to be excus'd. from her death to her burial a Carme attended & pray'd by the Corps not to burden our Community which other ways must have done it, we rung our bell & said the Commendations that same morning. the 2[d] of january we carry'd her out as we do our own religious & say'd a long Dirige for her, the next morning we sung the Commendations mass & burrial, after which they Carmes came & fetched the body to burry it in their Church by her husband according to her orders *Requiscat* [*sic*] *in Pace*.

She appointed her Eldest daughter, Sister mary michael[3] to be the executrix to her will who knew her inclinations & was to dispose of all she left accordingly, she was by my Lord Bishop & our Reverend **[p. 55]** Mother concent impowerd to act, she gave a hunder'd & twenty pound for the joins in the Choir & organ loft, & thinking the best sarvice she could do the Community was to procure the recovery of Sister barbary Huddlestons health on account of her voice which was much wanted for the Choir & musick she gave fortty pound for a secound journey to the spa[.][4] Mrs Sykes left us a rent of which the Capital is five hunder'd pound starling for a perpetual education of a Convictrix which is accepted of for that use the Conditions are put into our Arke & are signed by our Reverend Mother & her three Councel Sisters, but this rent for some time will be necessary to discharge other parts of her will so is not to be apply'd to that use tell that be done, she furnish'd the Chamber she lay in & made it convenient in so much that our Reverend Mother has chouse it for her Chamber it being near the infirmary kitching & great door which will render more ease to sarvice her when sick. in consideration of what

[1] Otherwise known as the feast of the Immaculate Conception, 8 December.
[2] Fr Caryl Gerard, Confessor 1723–79; Anstruther 4, p. 110.
[3] Mary Michael Sykes (BA189), Procuratrix 1749–51.
[4] Mary Barbara Huddleston (BA114).

Mrs Sykes has left us ther is another solomn mass to be sung for her & her name to be placed amongst the benefactors.[1]

to conclude this year with the account of our building is as follows it wants much of being finished, the dead Celler[2] is once more to be pav'd to secure it from the watter coming in, all tho it has allready 12 or 14 pavements where as four would have been sufficient had they workman understood the manner of doing it, which is a great addition to our expence & besides we loos two ovens of each side for what goes under the Chapter house would bear but two ~~ovens where~~ rows of ovens, in place of three, because the pavement was rais'd, so, that we have in all but 42 to burry in, where as we should othere ways have had 56. the sacristin is yet to be done, & the Altar, organ & portal to be errected, besides much of the plastering work that is wanting which has partly been our own fault, in sending our master workman to Louvain, but we have a fair promiss that all shall be finish'd by Easter.

1739

the 8 of january mis Elizabeth Smithson came over to fetch her sister,[3] she having been pentioner in our School & her sister being so, a leave was ask'd for her coming & lying with^in^ whilst she stay'd to expect mis Tan^c^kerd coming from Liege, which by her mothers desire was to return with her for england.

[p. 56] the 18 mis Tanckerd came from Leige for whom we all so got leave for her to lodg with in both because she had no acquaintance nor any to take care of her in towne & all so to oblige her family we having had her sister for two years pentioner in our School.

on the 19 of january it pleased allmighty God to take to himself dear Sister Cicely Bracy[4] which was a most perfect good religious woman she answer'd the advantagious Charactur that her Confessor gave of her before she came who said that he could say a great deel of her vertue & favours she receiv'd from God but that it was not proper to be told whilst she was living, & as he dy'd before her that has been conceal'd from us, but we might in some measure judg of it by the perfect life she lay'd from her first putting on the habitt, which was such, that no one could accuse her of what might be a volontary imperfection. she seem'd to have no will but that of God made known to her by the duties of her religious state which she performed with cheerfullness whatever it was, as

---

1 In 1733 Mrs Sykes had planned to leave a scholarship for boys to St Omer, but she was turned down. For other benefactions to Nazareth, see also **[pp. 66, 86, 128]**.

2 The dead cellar contained the vaults or ovens. See Glossary, under 'burial practices'.

3 There were four Smithsons in convent in this period, two of whom professed at Bruges. Catherine Smithson, in religion Lucy (1702–53) BA177; Dorothy Smithson, in religion Mary Augustine (BA178).

4 Cecily Bracy (1704–39) BA031, musician.

sweeping & the other duties which apertaine to the young profest, & tho it took the time from her musick which was necessary for her to practiss to answer what was requir'd of her, she being taken for that having but one hunder'd pound portion, yet she was never seen to be troubled or concernd for being hender'd from practising & improving herself in it as long as it was not through any fault of hers othere ways she said she should have had a great scruple of not imploying all the time she had in it, judging that she Committed a sin by ravaging the community of what was to be her portion, but when imploy'd in any thing by order she was ease & said to those that was concern'd that whilst God imploy'd her in that he could not require any thing ellce, & that she was content with what ever was his will. as she was faithfull to God in endevoring allways to keep her self united to his will so allmighty God was liberall of his favours to her[.] Father Wright[1] which was then Rector at Gant & our extrodinary to whome she discover'd her interiour told our Reverend mother that she was an eminent sarvant of God & much favour'd by him, but for fear she might take any complisance in her self, he said he made slight of what she told him, as if they proceeded more from nature then grace, tho at the same time he had a high esteem of her, & told our Reverend mother for her Comfort that she had a great sarvant of God under her care, Mr Poinz our Confessor[2] had a like opinion of her & acted with her after the same manner telling **[p. 57]** her that humility self abnegation & labour was what he esteem'd much more then those favours, & therefore wish'd her to give her self to the studdy & practiss of them which she did. it pleased allmighty God after many years spent as I said before, in which she truly ^was^ a shining example of all regular obsarvances, never entermedeling her self with any thing, private, or publick, but tending to God & to her self, allways ease peacable & cheerfull he permitted to ^her^ obscure the high esteeme which all had for her before by an undiscreet tenderness for one of our religious that was gone from her self, & so was seperated from the Community & confin'd, her motive was Charity but it was a mistaken one, & made for think others wanting in Charity, that was not of her sentiment, which was to have had her with & like the rest, which was not fitting[.] she being from her self, this greatly afflicted her, &, as we all thought impaired her judgment, which made the stiffness in her opinion the less fault, & perhaps non in Gods sight, she was not like the same parson she was before, she own'd to our Reverend Mother that

---

1 Fr Philip Wright SJ (d. 5 November 1737), Rector of Ghent 1734; Holt, p. 272 (though not listed as Rector there). Jesuits were not permitted to become confessors to convents of women, although they did serve both as extraordinary confessors assisting the confessor and as spiritual directors to individual nuns.

2 Fr Augustine Poyntz SJ(?) (1679–1723); Holt, p. 204. Poyntz's case is complicated by the fact that his place in the Society of Jesus rests on a ceremony carried out on his deathbed. He appears in Holt with a question mark.

it was a constant grife to her, & a dagar to her heart, which made our Reverend mother indevour what she could to have got the Community to have consented to her coming amongst them, promissing them that she should be bolted up at nights, but finding so many to be apprehensive of her, fearing she might do them harme if she was permitted to go about[.] she could not therefore cure the wound which it made in dear Sister Cicelys heart which tho perfectly resigned in the superiour part of her soul to Gods will yet could shake of the concerne she felt, which we have reason to think was the cause of her falling into a Consumtion of which she dy'd. allmighty God may have permitted it as a temporall punishment for her hollding too stifly to her own opinion & blaming others that was not of the same, as allso perhaps for her greater sanctification by the humiliation it drew on her for it lessen'd the esteeme which all had before for her & indeed her life desarved it, had not this happen'd her death would have been infinetly regreeted & her memory in greater esteem. for besides her vertuous example, she had the perfect skill of musick & a good voice for the Choir, & play'd on the organ, & let blood which [*blank*] was very usefull & of great sarvice to our Community & she never refuss'd nor made difficulty to be imploy'd in them when wanted but with pleasure she did what ever might [be] beneficiall or of sarvice to the Community, or to any in it, she taught those talants to others & was glad to have them out do her in them which shew'd how much she sought the Common good before her own, which with reason gain'd the love & esteeme of all, & tho allmighty God permitted it to be deminish'd as a **[p. 58]** temporall punishment for we can look on it as no othere having all reason to believe, that the perfect life she lay'd has acquir'd her a crown of imortall Glory which we confide she now injoys, she received all the rights of the Church, after which she told our Confessor that she had a mind to have the Bishop & desir'd him to come along with him & to be her interpret which according was done some days before she dy'd[.] she was present to her self to the last, & render'd up her happy soul to her creator the 19 of january, & 61 of her age, & 35 of her profession she was bury'd in the little buryall place amongst the rest. *Requiescat in pace*.

1739[1]

the 26 of january Sister Mary Xaverius Gage was cloathed.[2]

the 31 of january mis Tanckerd & they two mis Smithsons parted from hence for england to go to their friends.

The 3d of February mis Landscop went home to her Friends in towne.

---

[1] No explanation is given for the repetition of the year in the heading. The events follow sequentially without a gap or overlap.

[2] Mary Xaveria Gage (BA084).

this spring as soon as the wether permitted we went about setting up our Altar but did not desire the Cannon nor his man to come for fear of disputs with our work men[.] it was erected & all finish'd by Easter but not with out some damage, especially ~~of~~ the guilding the Capitalls & basses of the pillows[1] ^which^ were most beautifull when they came but by the ill usage of they workmen in errecting the Altar & the great damps of the new walls intierly spoilt, but we are put in hopes of obtaining the knowledg how to repaire it by my Lady Nitchdails[2] means who with the Altar sent us pices of all the sorts of different marbles with derections for repairing it if necessary for fear that the carrige might have indamag'd it, & all so the manner how to clean it, not withstanding the harme it received in putting it up, tis to our Comfort esteemed one of the greatess curriosity in these countrys, there comes dayly numbers to see it even from a far off, so that the portress & lay Sister that is with out which is forced to be call'd to open the Church door, are tired of their legs & thinks there never will be an end, those that understands such curiositys seemes to lament greatly that so much should be bury'd in the nitch & not seen which we could not hender tho we did our best to have done it.

on the 28 of march our dear Sister Anne Benedict Thirwall[3] departed this life at 3 in the after noon the 84 of age & 55 of her Holy **[p. 59]** profession being five years past her jubily, about six weeks after she had solomnisd it, she was by lamness confin'd to the infirmary, which lamness caus'd her vastly to suffer it proceeding from the shirnking [*sic*] of her sinews which was so shrunk that she could not stand nor even ~~go~~ strecth out her legs neither up nor a bed. she was forced to be carry'd in a Chair which was made with wheels in which she was rowl'd every day to mass in the lay Sisters Chaple & it was [on] communicating days Father Confessor came in there to communicat her as she sat in her chair which continu'd about three or fore years, some months before she dy'd ^she^ was confin'd to her bed & turn'd Child & by fitts seem'd to have lost senses yet a habit of piety in all she did & said. from her first coming to religion tell the loss of her judgment one might say her life was an interrupted sean[4] of fervour zeal & piety & all other religious vertus which most justly gain'd her the esteeme of all, yet God so permitted, that tho each look'd on her as a Saint, yet not one I can say naturally lov'd her, the same may be said of all spirituall men with whome she converc'd, they express'd no less a dislike to her company then high value for her vertue. one of our Rectors with a Sister a nun amongst us declar'd to her that tho by a motive of gratitude he shew'd as if she was wellcome,

1 Here meaning pillars.

2 Lady Nithsdale: Winifred Herbert, sister of Prioress Lucy Herbert (BA101).

3 Ann Benedict Thirwall (1684–1739), Procuratrix from 1716, BA199.

4 Meaning here not clear: the implications of the sentence seem rather to be that her life was rather an uninterrupted seam or perhaps scene of fervour, zeal and piety.

to him. yet when ever she came to him he said to consarve his patience he was forced to take his crucifix in his hand, & yet affirm'd he judg'd her so holy a soul that he was persuaded she would be in Heaven before her bones were cold on earth. tis heard to say what it was that render'd her so disagreeable[;] the only reason to be given was Gods permission to purify her by it since the strongst natural inclination she seem'd to have was to be belov'd & tho she was not ignorant that she was not yet appear'd not troubled at it, for besides Conformity to Gods will she was blest with a chearfull gay heart which render'd her scarce suseptable of malancoly tell her judgment by age fail'd her. she receiv'd the Holy oyles but was not capable of more & dy'd on holy saturday & was bury'd in our little Church yeard where all the bodys of the rest was translated & bury'd. & as we could keep the Corps tell a convenient day for burial so after vespers on Easter day we carry'd her out as usuall, & our pentioners being all in their best dress it look'd more like a profession of a Saints body then a funerall. the corps being sunck we perform'd no more on that day but the wednesday following we had a herse plac'd in the Church & perform'd all as if the **[p. 60]** body had been there[.] in the after noon we said the Dirige & the next day we begun the Psalter which we read twicc a day that we might end it before we entred our new Church but we could not ring our bell as we are us'd to do in during time of the Dirige because it was in the steeple of our new Church in place of which our Reverend Mother got some masses said for her soul, it seem'd as if divine providence would have the last duties we perform'd for this our dear Sister to have some resemblance with her life, which was not naturally agreeable, but I hope with as much addition of merit as it was heard & inconvenient to us. *Requiescat in Pace.*

on the 7 of Aprill which was Tusday after low sunday on which day this year was keept the feast of our Blessed Lady's anuntiation[1] our new Church was consecreated by my Lord Bishop,[2] tell which serimony was perform'd he would not permit us to make use of it, which othere ways we had design'd to have done on Easter eve that the first thing we should have sung in it should have been <u>Lumen</u> <u>Christi</u>[3] but we were forced to lay a side that thought & in obedience to his Lordship to be resigned to remaine in the old one tho to our great inconvenience for the pavement was taken up some time before towards paving the new one[.] the grave stoons all so was taken away, to be made use of, & tho boards put to cover in place of it, & the vault where we bury'd our religious which was before empted yet not so close but there came a great wind, the inward doors was all so taken a way & the wenscoat behind the seats which made it

---

[1] Feast of the Annunciation, celebrated on 25 March unless it falls in Holy Week. Low Sunday is the Sunday after Easter.

[2] Lord Bishop: Hendrik Josef van Susteren, Bishop of Bruges 1716–42.

[3] Light of Christ: sung at the Easter Vigil as candles are lit.

both very cold & frightfull to see, yet we was oblig'd to keep our Easter there. the weather being sharp our Reverend Mother fearing if we left of our mantels (as allway on Easter eve we do) the Community would get colds gave leave to all to continu wearing them tell the weather was warmer or that we went into our new Church which accordingly we did tell the above mention'd day that our Church was consecreated, which serimony begun about nine a clock but as we were made to believe it would have begun an hour sooner to the end we might be ready we rise half an hour sooner & went to mattins in like manner[.] we read of all our hours before mass we could sing no part of our office which on that feast we are us'd to do, nor even mass for fear of not having done before the Bishop came[.] half an hour after Communion we all took our breakfast, not **[p. 61]** expecting to go to dinner tell very late for we were told that the seremony would not be ended before twelve.

An account of the dedication of our Church, which was as follows[.] two days before the dedication the Arch deacon & master of serimonys came to acquant us from my Lord Bishop that we were all to fast the eve of the dedication which father Confessor all so did[.] the next day in the after noon the master of seremonys & the Bishop Chaplen came to see if all was prepar'd right in order for the seremony & the day following Father Confessor was to go fetch the relicks from the Bishop which was to be placed in the Altar which accordingly he did, & brought them into the sacristy & placed them in the shrine ^that^ was put apon a table for that porpose with lighted Candels on each side[.] after that was said the office of many martyrs according to my Lord Bishops appointment, which was perform'd by Father Confessor in the sacristin & nine or ten of our religious which our Reverend Mother appointed to say it with him in the pant, the door being open'd.

next morning about eight & half his Lordship came to perform the seremony attended by six priest he went into the sacristin & put on his Alb & cope,[1] after which the Bishop & all the priests that attended him went all out of the Church. Father Confessor which was appointed to be the Deacon that was to remaine a lone in the Church lock'd up the Door having first turn'd every one out. on the outside of the Church near the door there was a Carpet spread with a desk hansomly cover'd, a great couching & an harm'd chaire, a silver Cistern full of watter & a solver with salt. the first thing the Bishop perform'd at the Church door was the blessing of the Holy watter, after which he knelt down & said the seven penetential Psalms[2] & long litanies[.] when that was done the Bishop with his attendance went in prosession wround the Church saying some vercis

[1] Alb and cope: the alb is the white linen robe covering the whole body; the cope is generally semicircular and worn over the alb, and often highly decorated with embroidery.
[2] Penitential psalms: see Glossary.

of the *miserere* & bless'd the walls with holy watter & the Church yeard[.] when he came to the church door he knock saying that verce of the 23 Psalme *Attollite portas principes vestras* & the Deacon that was with in the Church answer'd *Quis est iste Rex gloriae*[1] then they went a secound time round the Church performing the same as they did the first time & when he came to the door of the church he knock'd againe saying the same verce & the Deacon **[p. 62]** answer'd the same. the third time they Carry'd the relicks with them round the Church in prossesion, two priests carry'd the Relicks in the shiren[2] between them on their shoulders the Bishop, & the rest of the Company follow'd after with some lighted torches[.] when they came to the Church door his Lordship knocked a gaine saying the same verce & the Deacon answer'd & then open'd the doors & the Bishop with all those that attended him came in the Relicks was repossed upon a table that was prepar'd near the high Altar on the Gospel side.

the Bishop went to the place prepar'd for him, which was in the meddle of the Church with a desk cover'd with a hansome Carpet & a chair behind him, on his left hand was placed a table cover'd with a Carpet wher all the things stood that was to be made use of for the blessing of the Church & Altar, which things were a great holy watter pot full of watter, a silver Ewn[3] with wine in it, a salver with salt & a nother with ashes, of this mixtur was the Holy watter made for blessing the inside of the Church & Altar, the sprinkler was made of hysope.[4] besides this there was a silver salver with five cross candels upon it, which was made of a wax book cut into little pices & put to gether in forme of a cross & turn'd up a little at the ends, in each of these was put five grains of incense[.] there was all so a salver with lime & brick dust which was to make the mortor for to fasten the marble that was to be put over the little silver boox of relicks which was placed in the Altar stone.

after my Lord Bishop had said the Long Litanies which he begun as soon as he came into the Church he made the Holy watter & then blest the above mention'd things[.] whilst that was doing the master of the ceremonys & Father Confessor made a Cross with Ashes from on[e] side of the Church to the other upon the ground[.] then the Bishop went three times round the in side of the Church & bless'd it with the Holy watter he had made at each time he stood at the door of the dead valt & bless'd it, as he went round he & the priests that attended him repeated verses out of the *miserere* after that he went to the Church door & made three

1 Psalm 23:7–8, *Attollite portas* … ('Lift up your gates, O ye princes, and be ye lifted up, O eternal gates: and the King of Glory shall enter in'); *Quis est iste rex gloriae?* … ('Who is this King of Glory? The Lord who is strong and mighty: the Lord mighty in battle').

2 Shrine.

3 Probably ewer.

4 Hyssop: a plant associated with cleansing rites; it gave its name to the holy water sprinkler or aspergillum (OED).

Crosses upon it from top to bottom with his cro [*blank*] saying a prayer between every cross that he **[p. 63]** made[.] after that he writ with the end of his cro[zier] on the Cross made in ashes on the ground down one ^on^ side the Alphabet in Lattin & down the other side the Alphabet in Greeck, when he ^had^ performed that, he took the Holy watter he had made to sprincle the crosses ^&^ with the Holy oyles he went to the first cross on the Gospel side (there was in all twelve all of them reed) which was by his orders painted upon the walls the day before. each had a Candle lighted over them, these crosses was in memory of the 12 apostles, in the meddel of these Crosses the Bishop anointed them with the Holy Oyles, & at each cross he said as he annointed them this Church is deducated to the Father Son & Holy Ghost, & to our Blessed Lady & to St Augustin. then he took the Thurible[1] & incenseth'd the Cross[.] when he had been round & finish'd all this, he went to the Altar to bless it. then he with the rest of his attendance begun to say at the steeps of the Altar the prayers ordain'd, then the Bishop went three times round the Altar & bless'd it with the Holy watter he had made in the Church after which he took the little boox made of silver for the relicks & placed it in the little sepulker which was cut in the middel of the Altar stone & with morter fasten'd down the piece of marble that was to cover it[.] when he had done that, he did all over with red wax & put the Holy oyles into the five crosses that was upon the Altar stone upon which was placed five cross Candles which were all lighted & when they were all most burnt out the master of ceremony put chips upon them to burne out the Holy oyles, after which they scrap'd the Altar stone with a wooden knife, & wiped it with Cotton as cleane as they could, & then with lenning Cloaths,[2] then they bless'd all the three cloaths that was to ly on the Altar, then the master of ceremonys put the Crucifix & Candles upon the Altar for tell then it was intierly bear. the ceremonys being ended my Lord Bishop went to the place prepar'd for him in meddle of the Church & kneelt there tell the end of mass which was said by Father Confessor for my Lord Bishop was too much fatigue, & there fore it was not sung, othereways it should have been a sollom singing mass.

when mass was ended the Bishop went to the steeps of the Altar & inton'd the *te Deum* which was taken of by the quire at the end of which his Lordship sung the prayer of the Bleased Trinity & then gave us an indulgence of {on scrap of paper pinned in the bottom margin} ^n.n. days, & he told the people ~~there present~~ that from hence forward the dedication would be keept upon the 2[d] sunday after, & those that visseted the Church devotly on that day ~~might gain~~ be granted 40 days indulgence to[.]^

---

[1] The thurible is a metal censer in which incense is burned. During services it is swung by the thurifer to spread incense.

[2] Linen cloths.

[p. 64] after which my Lord Bishop went away with all the Priests that attended him. & Father Confessor with several of the Chief Gentelmen ^went^ to the old Church & took the most Blessed sacrement out of the tabernacle & carry'd it to the new Church these Gentelmen follow'd the most Blessed sacrement with torches in their hands through our Pants to our new consecrated Church & the Religious follow'd after.

tis to me noted that upon the spot of ground, that the Bishop Bless'd for a burial place for our religious (when wanted) there stood a prive[1] which we have sence taken away so we look upon that space of ground on which it stood as not bless'd & therefore will obsarve not to burry where it [was], tho others are of opinion that tis all so bless'd, because that is according to the intention of him that bless'd it which was to bless all that we design'd for a burial place, & we design'd the whole for it intending to take away the prive as soon as conveniently we could[.] but least any should make difficulty, tis fitt it should be known where it stood which is the window that is opposit between the noviship & musick rome from whence went the passage that went to the prive which was eight foot broad & nine foot long, & the prive it self was 13 foot square. we begun from vespers on the day of the Consecration to performe the office in the Choir[.] we read our Complin that day imediatly after our vespers not to interrupt the recreation of the Community which were allow'd to recreat tell nine we had recreation both dinner & supper on that day, & severall more in the octave.

the weather being very cold & the Choir & Church very damp our Reverend mother gave leave to us all to ware our short mantells provided they were white from mattins tell mass for fear of cat[c]hing cool which we did tell the weather was a little warmer.

about the end of aprill we begun to turn our old Church & choir into such places as we stood in need of, which was speakhouses & beyand that a Convenient rome for our Confessor to lye in with a Closet Libarary & press for his closes all in the same rome & a confession house by it which with a rome, before the speakhouses on our side, & a passage to go to the Confession house, [which] took up the whole choir & uper part of the church. the under part of the Church & the Lay **[p. 65]** Sisters Chapel with the old rowle house[2] was made into a convenient apoticary shop & still house, a rowle house & a little rome for our men sarvants to dinne in when on sundas & holy days that they dinne not in the enclosure & a hansome dinning rome for our Confessor, out ^which^ is a little alle, that lay'ds him to the Church under Cover, & a door out of the same passage when any lys under the Rights of the Church to come to

---

[1] Privy or earth closet.

[2] Rowle house refers to the wheel or turn which allowed goods to pass from outside into the enclosure without compromising the rules relating to the separation of the convent from the world.

the sick in extremity which key must be keept by the superiour. the old sacristy is made into a lardar for the Sister with out to keep the things for the Fathers house with a conveniency for a considerable number of bottles to stand in. the vault which was under the Church in which we bury'd our Religious is now a prity little seller which will be very usefull for the keeping of many things[.] a door goes downe out of the inward rowle house to it.

tho the expence of making these altarations was not great, yet too great to have made them now, having been at so great an expence for our Church, but for these two reasons[:] first the need we had of those conveniences, which we could not well be with out, & ^the^ reason was to bring to pass all ^that^ was belonging to the old Church & Choir, which had we not now done, half would have been embecil'd[1] & lost, & ^as^ it was nothing was lost, but all came to pass & saved us the expence of buying abundance of things. the wenscoat behind the seats in the Choir was imploy'd in the new sacristin & for the rome below in in [*sic*] our Father's house, the seats was placed part in the Lay Sister's chapel & Chapter house, & what was more then could stand there was put in the passage that goes into the great garden. the pavement of the old Church & sacristin was us'd for our new staire case & Lay Sisters Chapel. the gravestoons which was in all five was thus imploy'd, Mother Austins[2] was taken for our Altar stoon. & the other four which ware all so marble were cut for Steeps to go up to the Altar on both sides so in a manner all was brought to pass, even the rails that parted the old organ house was taken to make the seperation of the new one, between the seculars & the religious, & the rails that was at the uper end of the old Choir was placed in our new speakehouses to make the separation there.

the 21st of may Sister mary Barbara Huddleston & Sister margarit Linny a lay Sister set out for spa.[3] from her last being there, she was told by severall that a secound journy there would effect her perfect cure, which made her very desirous of going but our Community by the late **[p. 66]** great building was uncapable of being at the expence of it, & her friends not well able neither, afflicted her & made her dayly loos ground as to her health for which reason Mrs Sykes which had a kindness for her said if her going was judg'd necessary the expence should ^not hinder^ it, for she would concurr to it[.][4] upon which our Reverend mother sent our Confessor to ask leave of his Lordship which he was pleas'd to grant, & Sister mary Michael[5] daughter to Mrs Sykes which she left her executrix

1 Embezzled.

2 Mother Austin was Prioress Augustina Bedingfield, who died in 1661 (LA023).

3 Spa, not far from Liège, was a town famous for its healing waters. Mary Barbara Huddleston (BA114); Margaret Linny (BA128).

4 Mrs Sykes had been a boarder in the convent; see also **[pp. 19, 53–5, 86, 128]**.

5 Mary Sykes, in religion Mary Michael (BA189).

gave her some thing above forty pound, & to the lay Sister that went with her where with all to pay for such helps as she might want, without being an expence to the other for those things

the 16 of june mis margarit Tasbourgh was received for a Convictris; she was past twelve years old.[1]

The 22 of june mis mary Tichbourn ^returned^ from the french monastery to us againe.[2]

the 19 of july mis mary & mis margrit Bethams having neither of them any inclination to a religious state return'd home to their friends

the 24 the two mis Blundells went to a monastery at Lille to larne french

the 27 M[rs] Lloyd passing this way made us a short vissit we obtain'd her leave whilst she stay'd to be with in our enclousur which was tell the 2[d] of august then she parted for england.[3]

the 2 of september mis Bellinda Ancker return'd to her freinds in towne

the 7 mrs Gage came & on the same day mrs Bamber with her sarvant entred our inclousure as Borders.

the 22 the two mis FaireChilds went to Lille to larne french.

the 25 M[rs] mary Tasburgh which for a Long while had indevour'd to get leave of her parents to be religious having their consent enter'd our in clousure for that effect to the great satisfaction of the Community[4]

the 2[d] of october M[rs] Gage went from hence for the french quarters.

the 10 M[rs] Mary Tasbourgh took the first habitt & the name of mary Francis.

the 25 Sister mary barbara Huddleston & Sister margarit return'd from spā hethere[.] both seemes to have recover'd so much their health by it as to give cause to hope that the time & money was well spent notwithstanding that the money that M[rs] Sykes gave, & ten pound which Lady Fortescu sent did not suffise[.] their expences came to a bove 13 pound ten shillings more which our Community pay'd.[5]

[p. 67] the 4th of november M[rs] Bamber & her sarvant parted from hence for to go live at doway.[6]

the 8 of desember Ann Gladin[7] which was sarvant to M[rs] Sykes took the Kercher for a lay Sister & is call'd Sister Anne she had an ernest

---

1 She later professed as Margaret (1748–81) BA193.

2 Mary Tichbourne (BA200).

3 Mrs Lloyd paid a number of short visits to Nazareth in this period, bringing aspirants or possible schoolgirls to the convent or escorting them back to England if they decided not to enter. It has not yet been possible to identify her.

4 Mary Tasburgh, in religion Maria Frances (BA192).

5 Lady Fortescue was probably Mary Huddleston of Sawston (d. before 1744), who married Sir Francis Fortescue, 4th Baronet of Salden (d. 1729). She had four sisters who were nuns: Angela (BA112) and Laetitia (BA111) at Nazareth; Anne Justina (LS118) at Liège; and Placida Francisca (LB093) at Lisbon. See Stirnet, Family Tree, Huddleston 03.

6 Douai.

7 Ann Gladin, lay sister (1742–56) BA087.

desire to be a religious long before her mistress dy'd & from that time has continu'd in the sarvice of the Community but we having a bove the number of lay sisters could not then encrease them; but her behavioure having been such as to gaine the good will of the Community she was admitted to the habitt but was not to advance further to never so long tell some one dy'd. only this promiss was given her, as it might be many years before any place was void so not to be refuss'd when the time came for her age, if we have no other exceptions against her.

the 14 of desember Sister Perpetua Errington departed this life in 81 of her age & 59 since her profession[.] the account of her going out & her appostancy is to be found in the year 1696 & her return in the year 1707 which mercy of God to her may be attributed in part to the ardent prayers of the Community.[1] she arrived here the 14 of november 1707 having spent a 11 years wanting a month in that wicked condition & part of it great want & pouverty, & as she herself told one of our religious sometimes in fear of her life & forced to run out in the street & cry murder.

allmighty God made use of those meanes to compell her to return, as he did to the prodigal Child, & with no less a goodness did he receive her as we may believe since he gave her the grace to come in the spirit of pennance which was very apparent at her first coming in so much that what ever was brought her for her meals she esteemed [*illeg.*] to good for her, & would put by the bear she left at dinner for supper in place of having fresh, & her chousing to come back here was a great marke of it since she might have gone to a nother monastery where her fault not being known she would have avoided the confussion she must suffer in the place where it was. all which shews she came in the spirit of pennence with a desire of repairing the fault where she had commit'd it. the parson which supply'd the Bishops place (he being dead) came to her, & was very well satisfy'd with her intier submission & repentance. by him the excumunication was taken off in presence of all the Community she kneeling in the middle of the Choir, & no othere pennence by him injoyned her but the exact obsorvance of order[.] a greater fidelity in it might have been expected then appear'd, but those humble sentiments of humility **[p. 68]** & pennance with which she came soon chang'd by an unhappily contracting a friendship with some about her own age & profession which was not very regular, but Gods mercys which was so singular in her, in her [*sic*] convertion removed the obsticals by their deaths which was some years before hers, which being taken away & her sight allso in part forced her in a manner to seek & find her Comfort but in God, she being by it render'd uncapable of doing little works which she took a pleasure in, & all so of all imployments, which blindness she bore with great patience & resignation tho according to her

[1] Dorothy Errington, in religion Perpetua (BA076); see also vol. 1, **[pp. 113, 121, 128, 129, 131, 132, 183–92, 244–52, 442]**.

nature no cross could have equal'd it, & as she had neglected her spirituall duties in her younger years made prayer & recolection much hearder to her, not withstanding some years before she dy'd she keept close to her cell except times of meals, which she took in the infirmary & as she could not benefitt her self by reading, one of our religious did dayly read some good book to her, & before confession & communion the prayers or what might dispose her for them[.] she was from her return most constant in going to the sacrements from whence she drew grace to moderate & over come her temper which was both heard & disagreeable & a true tryall of patience to the officers which had anything to do with her, which could not eassily content her, tho they truly indevor'd it, & what ever apear'd less kind or considerat from others she judged as a design'd contempt for what she had been guilty of, which was a reale sufference to her, tho undesigned, & tis to be hop'd of equal merit by her acts of resignation to it[.] she suffered much with rumatizen & other infirmitys, but did not lay in the infirmary tell october before her death.

she had all ways a tender devotion to the passion of our saviour & she told one of the religious that when she reflected on the crucifix in the middle of our Choir, she found her heart moved. after her return she got a Lanthorn made & every year she bought such a quantity of Candles as would suffice for to burn on for every Friday in the year, which was lighted after Complin before the Crucifix in the garden. she had allso a tender devotion & a great Confidence in our Ladys protection & intercession hoping [for] her salvation by her all powerfull mediation, & even when she was in her misserable condition she never omitted to performe some little devotion in her **[p. 69]** honour. after God had afflicted her with blindness the greatess part of the day her imploy was saying her [*word missing*], she told us that she imputted in great part the grace of her return to saints whose relicks she had a bout her, & had never left of during all her absence, & what was most wonderfull tho they often search'd about her for popery yet they never found them. God by her blindness having deprived her of the satisfactions of this life disposs'd her for his concluding mercy of a happy death which proceeded from a decay of nature, she had & no wonder frequently great terrorrs & apprehentions concerning her past life, yet when she came nerer to her last end she often say'd she placed her hopes in the merits of our saviour & in the intercession & protection of our Blessed Lady. she received all the sacrements with a great sence of piety & in a great calme & tranquility render'd up her soul between 11 & 12 at night, she was the first that was burry'd in our new church the 16 instant in the bottom oven next the stairs on the left hand in going downe. *Requiescat in Pace.*

the 15 of desember mis Mary Tachburn took the first habitt & is call'd Sister mary ignatia.[1]

---

[1] Mary Tichbourne professed as Mary Ignatia (1741–81) BA200.

on the 30 mis julia Fitz Gerald was receiv'd for a Convictress[.] her motive was to see & larne what a religious life was before she embraced it which she came with a designe of doing having got her friends consent.

a gentelwoman by name mrs Dorothy Orick some years ago left at her death between Lovain & us the sum of three hunder'd & six pound english[.] the occation of this was the kindness & Charity we show'd to her nephew when in these parts[,] seventy pound of which was left in the hands of one mrs Prichard & she was yearly to pay the intrest of it which was three pound ten shillings between Lovain & us, but as [her] poverty was represented to us to be very great both our Community & that of Lovain remitted her both intress & the principal this year. our share of the remmainder of the above mention'd summ which was a 118 pound was joyn'd to other moneys of ours & put in the south sea stocks[1] which rents we afterwards sold in england & drew the money here & with it bought rents at bruges which will remaine to our house for ever being perpetuall rents[,] for which reason as long as our stands there is ~~yer~~ yearly to be a mass said for her in june, in which month she dy'd but we know not forsarten the day, & all the Community to hear it for her **[p. 70]** & the Chantress to give notice of it by a little bill on the Choir door as she dos for the othere anniversarys that we sing mass for.

our Choir & Church is now finish'd except some plastering work in the Church[.] our disapointment in this was the death of the plasterer, his father in law has undertaken to finish it upon the same agreement as all so what is wanting to be done of the same work in the new speak houses.

we have not yet got the Communicating bank[2] which parts the Sanctuarium from the body of the Church nor have we our Organ but in dayly hopes of both.

the expences of building the Choir & Church was taken from our Arke & it amounted to the sum̃ of sixty thousand eight hunder'd gilders permission [*word pasted in*] the marble Altar was from mr Chichester[3] pay'd on his Sister's account, the buying the two little houses which were necessary to make the Choir long enough, the little rome at ^the^ end of the Choir with the conveniences that are under it, & likways the wash house galery & little pant came not out of the Arke but was pay'd for in this manner[.] our procuratrix gave towards it what she had saved from time to time which was 4000 gilders, & our Reverend Mother[4] gave

1 The reference is to the South Sea Company, whose shares had been subject to the inflationary bubble and subsequent catastrophic collapse in 1720. It is not clear from the reference here at what time the convent had shares in the company.

2 This refers to the rail in the church where communicants would kneel to receive the host.

3 John Chichester (d. 1783) had two sisters who were choir nuns at Bruges: Catharina, in religion Teresa Joseph (BA052); and Ursula, in religion Frances Xaveria BA053.

4 Reverend Mother in 1739 was Prioress Lucy Herbert (BA101). 'Permission' refers to the regulation which allowed monetary gifts to be allocated to community projects or shared among the community instead of remaining for the sole use of the recipient.

7725 gilders permission which she had by the exchange & high moneys pay'd in england & presents from her own relations.

the first stone of our building was lay'd on St Gregory's day[1] 1736, & the first peg was struck in by our Reverend Mother in the Carpenter's work the 24 of september of the same year, which day is keept the feast of Lady of mercy in whose all powerfull protection we place our hopes.

1740

We begun this year with so severe & sharp ^a^ cold, that the like has not been known of many years, & all provissions very dear, & a scarcite of Corn.[2]

the 9th of february Sister mary xaveria Gage made her Holy profession[3]

the 5 of march mis julia Fitz Gerald took the first habit & is call'd Henerieta[4]

the 31 of march mrs Tasbrough whose husband was gone for england about buisiness enter'd our inclosure we having obtain'd leave for her to remaine during his absence in our house

[p. 71] the 8 of Aprill madamoisell jacobus one of antwerp was receiv'd for a convictress.

on the 20 of april mrs Gage with her two sons came to be present at Sister mary frances Tasbourgh Cloathing & with her mis Willis who had formerly been a Convictress here came in order to be religious, mrs Gage lodg'd with in our enclousur during her stay.[5]

the 21 of april Sister mary Frances Tasbourgh was Cloath'd & two days after mrs Gage with her sons return'd back to dunkerke.

the 16 of may mary Hunt sarvant to Mrs Tasbourgh came here from england & brought with her a little one for lier[.][6] we got leave for both to be in our enclosur tell the Child went for Lier which was six days after.

Sister Frances xaverius Simnor Mother sent five pound for prayers for her happy death.[7] Reverend Mother order'd each to hear three masses & for three days to offer the cross prayers for her.

the 11 of june mis willis took the first Habitt & is call'd Sister mary catherin.

---

1 The feast of St Gregory the Great is 12 March.

2 The winter of 1740 was the coldest for three hundred years, creating enormous problems for the supply of food across Europe.

3 Mary Xaveria Gage (BA084).

4 Julia Fitzgerald (BA080) did not continue to profession.

5 Mrs Gage was Elizabeth née Rookwood (1683–1759) who had arrived at Nazareth as a convictress in 1689 and left in 1695; see vol. 1, **[pp. 148, 178–9]**. She had two sons, Thomas Rookwood Gage (later 5th Baronet of Hengrave) and John Gage SJ. Maria Frances Tasburgh (BA192). Both families came from Suffolk and belonged to the same social circle of Suffolk recusant gentry. Winefrid Willis, in religion Mary Catherine (professed 1742) BA221.

6 Reference to the English Carmelite convent at Lierre.

7 Frances Xaveria Simner (BA174); see vol. 1, **[pp. 401, 406, 408, 421]**.

the [*blank*] of june mrs Tasbourgh with her sarvant parted from hence.

the 18 of june mis Frances Bettem & mis Elizabeth Darill came for convictrisses mis Bettem was about 16 & mis Darill about nine years old.

the 26 madamoiselle Kyken one from Ostend came & was receiv'd for a convictress

mrs Faire Child came over to fetch her two daughters for england which were at Lile to larne french she brought them & the two mis Blundells which were all so there on the same account they all arrived here the 24 of iuly.

on the same day mis Biddy more came & was received for a convictriss she was about 15 & a half year old[1]

the 4th of august Sister mary ignatia Tichbourn was Cloathed[2]

on the 8 mis Edwardina jernegan came & was receive'd for a Convicttriss she was past seven years old[3]

the 23 mrs Fairchild with her two daughters went for england they both exprest a great desire of being religious.

the 29 mis mary & mis dorothy Riddels came the eldest was past 13 & the other past 11 years of age they were neeces to Sister Widdrinton[4] **[p. 72]** which was their great Aunt they were both received for convictrisses.

on the 10 of october my Lord Bishop[5] celibretated his half jubily of being Bishop & all so of bruges great preparations by the towne was made to express their joy for this solemnity, not only as being the first that had arriv'd to those years, but all so for his own personall merits & the Fatherly ^love^ he had shewn for his flock, which gain'd him the love of all, so that each endevour'd to shew the share they took in so genneral a joy. our Reverend mother was unwilling to be wanting there in, & so made inquiery what our neighbouring monasterys did to shew their respect & joy, being unwilling to do less, yet not desirous of doing more. they sent us word what they pretended to do [which] was to ring from eight tell nine for three nights & to have severall illumination with in their court, we follow'd their example in ringing, but out did them in the number of lights, for the front of our Church with out was full of light in lanthorns made of oyle paper, which were fixt on the wall from our Fathers house to the end of the new building, & in the nich over the portal there was a piramid of wax lights, & my Lord Bishops name & *jubilate* at the tope which was Crown'd with a Crown composs'd of 25

---

1 Biddy More was the daughter of Thomas More of Barnburgh and Catherine Gifford of Black Ladies.

2 Mary Ignatia Tichbourne (BA200).

3 Edwardina Jerningham later professed as Francis Joseph (1752–96) BA121, musician.

4 Mary and Dorothy Riddell were daughters of Thomas Riddell of Swinburne Castle and Mary Margaret Widdrington of Cheeseburn Grange, Northumberland. Mary Widdrington, in religion Ann (BA219).

5 The Bishop of Bruges was Hendrik Josef van Susteren, Bishop 1716–42.

lights, but the wether not favoring our ^designe^ permitted them not to remaine lighted. what my Lord seem'd most pleas'd with was a letter which our Reverend mother wrote & ^sent^ by our Confessor in the name of our Community to my Lord, in which after the usuall Compliments on such an occation, she sayd "If my Lord we don't with so much exteriour pomp & luster as others dos celebreat this feast, tis with more respect, obedience & submission to your greatness, that we beg your acceptance of our sincere congratulations, & humble present of a hunder'd masses & as many Communions for the intention your Lordship shall forme & all so a partisipation of all the merits & good works of the whole Community for an intier year & this to obtaine of allmighty God to continu to singulise his power in favour of you & to grant your Lordship a long life glorious to yourself & advantagious to your flock, which how ever long it may be will still apear too short to us which expects of God by your Lordship's means all our happiness[.]" this was the subject of the letter, which we heard afterwards from several that my Lord took most kindly, & exprest a greater satisfaction & to be better pleas'd with that present then with any that had been made him & he came him self some time after to our Reverend Mother to return thanks

[p. 73] the 19 of october mis Salvin parted from hence by order of her father to go to marquet to larn french.

on the 15 of november Sister Henrietta Fitzgerald was Cloathed.[1]

My Lady Nitzhdail[2] Sister to our Reverend Mother sent her from Rome several Relick amongst which was a large pice of the Holy Cross made in a Cross & sett in a Cristal Cross, a relick of St Peter another of St Francis xaverious with their authentication which we sent to the Bishop & he aproved them & brought them back againe him self to us & in our Choir fix'd them in the places they are now in & put his seal to them.

the 5th of desember mis mary Sanderson neice to our Sister Widderington was receiv'd for a Convictriss.[3]

the 26 mademosell Rykes return'd home to her friends at ostend

the 29 Sister mary Baptest Salvin departed this life in the 31 of her age & 13 of her Holy profession[4] tho she was proposs'd here for a confictress by her father, not withstanding the parson that brought her had orders to carry her to the dames of Gant, but her aunt[5] which then was here would

---

[1] Julia Fitzgerald left before profession; see also **[pp. 69, 70, 75–6]**.

[2] Lady Nithsdale: Winifred Herbert, sister of Prioress Lucy Herbert (BA101).

[3] Mary Widdrington, in religion Ann (BA219). Her sister Elizabeth married George Sanderson of Heales; see Stirnet, Family Tree, Widdrington 02.

[4] Mary Baptist Salvin (1728–40) BA170.

[5] Mary Baptist's aunt, Elizabeth Browne (OB014), led a somewhat peripatetic religious life as a demanding member of the convents she chose to join. Originally professed at a French convent in Rouen, she lived at Nazareth 1721–23, before leaving to rejoin a Benedictine convent. No evidence has yet been found to link her directly with the English Benedictine convent at Ghent.

not let her go tell she had writ to her father saying ^she^ [had] more right to her then other, her mother having before she dy'd recommended her to her, upon which he concented to her remaining here. when she was of fitt age, she made known her vocation of being religious, which her ^Father^ then opposs'd, & would have her go for england, but her perseverent entreaty so far prevail'd that he would not force her home, only to a seperation from us, thinking it might be some affection she had for some one in the monastery that moved her to settle amongst us rather then God's call. that he might be sattisfy'd he order'd her to be sent to the english poor Clares at dunkerke where by his orders she was to be by the Confessor there of examined concerning her vocation, her answers was so satisfactory as to obtaine her return & leave all so to be religious[.] soon after she took the first habit & with it the name of mary Baptist, her behaviour in the time of tryall gave all hopes of her being a good religious woman as well as a sarviciable one but after her profession she did not answer our expectation by not proving so regular as we hop'd she would have been having both good sence & vertue, but a most unacountable temper, most heard to manage[,] for mildness did not gain her & severity made her worce, which was no smale affliction to our superiour which had a tender concerne for her[.] she had a great propention to opposs such as she thought remark'd & complain'd of others, & if of her she would a purposs do what they blam'd her for, to shew she valued not their **[p. 74]** blame nor yet their prayse, & did the worce for either, not careing for what any thought of her, she concealed what made to her advantage, & made appear what was not, for she was more pious & better then she appear'd to be, which tho done out of humility, yet had been better she had done, othere ways, & have shin'd by good example by which God would have been more Glorify'd & her neighbour benefitt'd & she would have had a share in ^the^ good done by her example in place of drawing on her self the faults committed by her ill example. she was mistress of severall good parts which would have made her very valiable to the Community had she made use of them as desir'd but her little humour did not allways permitt her to do it. on all saints of the year before her death she was taken with violent paine [a]t [the] time of the durge, which both doctor & surgeon judg'd to be the stone, but they were mistaken for it prov'd not so[.] from the begining of her illness she complain'd of a swelling at her namble which was as heard as a stone which swelling so increas'd that she could not ly in bed for a considerable time before she dy'd[.] nothing was neglected towards her recovery nor any expence spar'd advice was had both from england & other parts[.] mr Salvin to whome her father left his estate at his death sent her twenty guineas to procure what ever might be a solace to her & it was spent in that use[.] many devotions was perform'd by severall of the Religious for her recovery but that petition she would not joyn saying since God had heard her petition & freed her from the cancer in her breast which she fear'd & had so great a horror of she would not desier to be freed from the sufferings he now sent her which she suffer'd with a vast deel of courage & patience making her merit of what she suffer'd. her body was swelle'd to an increediable bigness & for a considerable time before she dy'd could not have the solace of going to bed which to a sick body is so great an ease. yet [she] did not omitt going to the sacrements those days that they Religious went if possible she could, & communicated in the sick Chapel tho in her condition it was very heard, & even pernishtious to fast so long yet she under went it. her comportment in her sickness was very different from what was before & truly made amends for all her former faults. she express'd much gratitude to the Community for the tender concerne which each one shew'd for her in this her illness & said she thought she could never do enough if God gave her life to acknowledg it nor her obligation to him for calling her to religion which she look'd upon as a far greater favour then if he had made **[p. 75]** her queen of the world. she had allways a singular love & confidence in our Blessed Lady, making recource to her as a child to her mother in her necessitys & took a great pleasure to be imploy'd in any thing for her sarvice[.] therefore with reason may we believe that she obtain'd for her the grace to attone in her last sickness by her eddifying comportment for the little good example she had given in her life as well as a safe passage out of this life. she was sensible to the last moment & said gest before she dy'd, I dye sweet Jesus I dye, & made a signe to Father Confessor for the last absolution which she bow'd & receiv'd ^and^ a few minets after she expier'd[.] she was bury'd the following day in the 2^d oven from the colling on the left hand as you ^go^ downe. *Requiescat in Pace.*

this whole year continued after the manner it had begun with a scarcity of corn, barley & all other provissions[.][1] the frost & colc wether continued so long that in the month of may there was little or no grass nor where with all to feed their ketle which dy'd for want, which made meat very dear[.] wheat & barley was above two parts in three as dear again, nor were we permitted to buy it with out a bill from they lords of the towne & were all so oblig'd to give in our number not withstanding our usuall Charity was not only continu'd but increas'd for the poverty of our poor neighbours was so great that they might have perish'd had it not been for our Charity to them assisting them in what we could.

we end this year with the Comfort of having finish'd our building & our Communicating reals up & our Organ made fitt for use, but the damps being yet to great tis not yet perfected but the factor has promiss'd

1 The severity of the frost and cold, together with a prolonged wet period, had a devastating impact on harvests, with high prices and scarcity leading to numerous deaths from starvation across Europe.

to come & finish it. few days pass without numbers, coming to see the Altar & Church & is admir'd by all, the Altar is judg'd without equal in these contrys.

our old building to witt our old Choir & Church, which we have made into severall conveniences fully answers the expence we have been at being of use to us[.] may God be pray[s]e'd for so good a conclution.

1741

this year begun with a cold not less sever then the former tho not so lasting on the 15 of january Sister ^Winifred in Religion^ mary Catherin willis was cloathed[1] [*in margin*] professed Aprill the 18 1742

the 20 of march Sister Henrietta Fitz Gerald having been novice **[p. 76]** about fore months but not having her health & many doubting of her vocation it was proposs'd to her parents (which were then in towne) her change of air for her recovery as all so to prove if her vocation was good & solide which they consented too. she was sent to the ursulins at Lille to remainc ther tell parfectly recover'd.

the 23 of aprill Sister Mary Frances Tasbourgh made her holy profession.[2]

on the 30 the towne steeple was sett a fire by a flash of lightting[3] which seem'd to us inconsiderable as all so the thunder which preceded it, but we were soon appriz'd of the Contrary by the bells ringing & we all so could see it from severall windows in our house[.] it was a most dreadfull sight, it begun about 12 at noon & was not extinguish'd tell the following day tho all indevors was us'd[.] the steeple was fine & had in it about 70 bells besides the clock. but the greatess loss was the Chimes which were esteem'd one of the best in e[u]rope[.] the expence they must be at to it, will be vastly great, it being a generall loss to all tis mightily lamented by all. every one even the poor & day laboures shew their willingness to contribute towards the reparation of it, by offering to give a penny or more out of what they gain. there was printed papers offer'd to such as had where with all to see what they would give towards it but nothing was exacted from any. they brought us one, & it was thought that in this occation some thing hansome would be kindly taken & of great credit to our house, so we sign'd for to give three hunder'd florence that is fifty pound grot permission,[4] & my Lady Montaigue[5] to whome they all so

1 Winefrid Willis, in religion Mary Catherine (BA221).

2 Maria Frances Tasburgh (BA192).

3 A wooden steeple had been added to the belfry after a fire in 1493. Following the 1741 fire, the belfry was rebuilt in stone.

4 Pounds grot or grote were Flemish pounds; florence were florins.

5 Lady Montagu was Mary Herbert, sister of Prioress Lucy Herbert (BA101). She had been married to Francis Browne, 4th Viscount Montagu (d. 1708) and continued to use the title even after her third marriage.

presented their petition gave 30 pistols, neither is to be pay'd at present but at three different times as they shall require it, at each time a third part

the 5 of may Sister victoria Canningh selebreated her half jubily of fifty years of profession.[1]

the . . madmoisel jacobs returned to her friends at antwerp.

the 24 of may mis Salvin return'd from Lille.

the 25 m[rs] Tasburgh enter'd our inclosure & lodg'd in the appartment in the scoole.

the 26 mis Salvin & mis Frances Betham went from hence for england

the 2[d] of june mrs Tasbourgh parted from hence.

the 7 of june mis Pickering which was about 18 years old was receiv'd for a convictress.[2]

the 3[d] of july Elizabeth jernengan went from hence to the ursulins at Tounney to larne french.[3]

the 4th miss moor about 18 year old was receiv'd for a convictress.[4]

[p. 77] My Lady Montaigue Sister to our Superiour, whose kindness to our Community was such that tho she had given us severall marks of her kindness & severall donations towards our Church yet not content with that was desirous to perpetuat for ever a mark of her affection to all which she thought she could ^not^ better do, then by giving five hunder'd pound english to be put out to rent, for a dayly mass which is to be said in our Charch & at the time that we would have it, by the Carmes, for the soules in purgatory (besides some that she owes obligations too) tis for all those that are deceas'd or will decease out of this community. the intention for which it is to be offer'd by the priest, as all so those that hear it, is for the poor souls according to the intention of the giver, & for self after her death, which gratitude requires from us to do since by it we receive not only a spirituall but a temporall advantage for it spares us 18 pound grot a year which we pay the Carmes for our secound Mass with out having the intention. the intentions mention'd need no ways hender you from offering for other intentions besides, but those must be the first. this foundation begun the 16 of july & the mass is said in her Chamber & will be so tell after her death.

the 21 of july mis Pordage was receiv'd for a convictris, she was a bout 16 years old.[5]

the 25 of july mis Harcout went from hence to her parents which then lived at Boulen.[6]

---

1 Elizabeth Victoria Canning (1691–1750) BA044.

2 Cicily Pickering, in religion Isabella Cecilia (1745–56) BA155, musician.

3 Elizabeth Jerningham (1745–1807) BA122.

4 Probably Ann Moor; see **[p. 86]**.

5 Probably Arabella Pordage; see **[p. 86]**.

6 Probably Boulogne.

the 26 of july m[rs] Brevarious enter'd our inclousure leave having been obtain'd[.] she was housekeeper to m[rs] Blondell & was sent by her to fetch over her two daughters.

The 2[d] of august it pleas'd allmighty God to call to him self our dear Sister winefrid Jernengan[1] she came young to our monastery & was of a very pious dispostion, which pious disposition soon made her susceptable of the grace of a vocation to corespond with which she tho young whilst in the scoole begun even then to practiss little mortifications & to be very exact in all the orders of the scoole, & not only prompt in rising as soon as call'd, but often before to make tryall of what she hop'd here after to do when religious. she had so great an esteeme & respect for the house of God, that when not seen would kiss the walls esteeming it a happiness to dweel with ^in^ them. as soon as her age permitted her she beg'd the habitt, & from first putting it **[p. 78]** on she so behav'd herself as to give grounds to think she would be a very good religious woman & so indeed she was. she ever shew'd both in her readiness to comply with all the duties requir'd of they young ones how ever disagreeable the[y] might be & her chearfullness in performing them the love & esteem she had of her religious vocation[.] she was a great lover of pease & all so of neatness keeping all they things she had to do with all both neatly & order'dly, she was very obsarvant of they orders given in Chapter & even scrupulous there in, she was very timourous in the divine ^office^ & making her morning oblation even to a fault, she apear'd most anxious in those two duties, & could not bare to be interupted in them with ^out^ shewing an uneaseness in her looks[.] othere ways she look'd allways chearfull as became a good religious to do that was sensible of the happiness of her state, for which reason she was appointed to go for a Companion to those that was call'd for to the great. her comportment did both please & eddify secalers,[2] but it was a great trouble to her to be forced to spend so much of her time there which to her satisfaction she would have imploy'd in othere things especially in advancing pleane song & musick for which she had a great zeal[.] she was perfect in the skill of both, she effected the change of the pleane song which before was very crabit & heard to performe the great desire of having it well perform'd made her often to force her voice othereways she would not be heard by all, for she had but a weak breast her desire to strength it, made her often to take those solaces that she thought would norish & strengthen it which othere ways she would not have done & which she seemmed some times with regret to do. on St ignatious day[3] she went to communion with the rest for tho no holy day yet it was a Communicating day & she was constant in going

[1] Winefrid Jerningham (1698–1741) BA119, musician.

[2] Seculars: that is, people who were not vowed religious.

[3] The feast of St Ignatius is celebrated on 31 July.

to the sacrements[.] that evening it was remark'd she was particulary gay & had practiss'd a new peice to play on the organ that night after *Salve regina* which accordingly she did, seeming as well as usuall when she went to bed but in the night was rais'd ~~but~~ at what hour we know not between one & too she went to her Sister whose cell was next to hers & told her that her head was in so violent a way that she had never felt the like before[.] twas a speice of an apperplex & lethargi which soon deprived her of her senses no time was lost for proper remides which were made use of but all in vaine she continu'd so tell next day, which was the feast our Blessed Lady of prochoncula[1] she ever had a tender love & great confidence to our Lady, making recourse to her in all her necessitys. about 7 a clock in the morning of this her feast, she ^render'd^ up her dear soul to God, she only could receive extremuntion but the day before **[p. 79]** she communicated & very likly by way of *viaticum*[.] twas obsarved that she was saiz'd with her illness on the feast of St Peter's chaines[2] she had a little before express'd her concerne that [the] relick we have of him in the Choir ^was not^ in a better chrine to comply with that pious inclination of hers our Reverend imploy'd the little money she had of hers after her death in procuring one so that what she desir'd was effected by her meanes[.] no doubt but the Blessed Saint by his all powerfull intercession obtain'd her a more speedy admittance into ever lasting bliss where I confide through the mercy of God she now is. she was about sixty years of age & forty three since her profession, she was burry'd in the bottom oven of the 2^{d} row. *Requiescat in pace.*

the 28 of august Mrs Lloyd came & was taken into our inclousor for the time she stay'd.

on the 29 mis Constancia Dicoson was receiv'd for a Convictriss[3]

the 3^{d} of september mis mary & mis Anne Blundell with m^{rs} Breverious return'd to england. on the 10 m^{rs} Lloyd went from hence

the 29 october mis Titchborn with her little brother ^which^ came here by the desire of their Father to stay tell the ship came that was to come from yorrk[.] twa's judg'd proper whilst they stay'd that she should be with our Chilldren in our schoole [*illeg.*] & so she was.

on the 8 of november it pleas'd allmighty God to take from us Dear Sister Gertrud Stanley[4] in whose life & proctisses our Rule & Statues might faithfully be read. she had the blessing of perfect good health & an excelent voice for the choir, which she most zealously imploy'd in the divine sarvice[.] for neer 30 years she was subchantress, she was allso a

---

[1] The feast of Our Lady of Portiuncula is celebrated on 2 August.

[2] The feast of St Peter in Chains is celebrated on 1 August.

[3] Constancia was likely the daughter of William Dicconson (d. 1742), former Treasurer to Queen Mary of Modena at St Germain-en-Laye. His wife was Juliana Walmesley (d. 1751). See *ODNB* and **[p. 85]** below.

[4] Mary Gertrude Stanley (1704–41) BA184, Chantress.

great help to the musick having the skill as well as a good voice nature seem'd in her so to concur with grace that she had little to overcome in her self[.] she was an example of regularite & much esteem'd & lov'd by all for her sweet & ease dispossion, seeming allways to injoy pease of mind, & no wonder since discourcing with othere of scruples she owned she had non, for she would not do what she thought was a fault, & if she did it, & thought there was non[,] there could be no sin, & therefore she had no scruple which shews the purity of her soul she was constant in any duty Committ'd to her how frivolus so ever it was looking on it as Gods will & doing ^it^ for his sake[.] she ever obsarved the practiss requir'd of novisses of going to the Choir a quarter before compline, which she continu'd to do tell she was confin'd to the infirmary, whatever company she was in did ^not^ hender from it. her death like her life was most pious her patience in her sickness was **[p. 80]** most edifying no complaints but that too much care was taken of her when they ask'd her towards her end if she suffer'd much she reply'd a little but if allmighty God is glorify'd by it twa's no matter what she suffer'd his will & glory was all she desir'd[.] these were her last dispositions & in appearence those of her whole life she was sigularly emine[n]t in her exactitude of smale things that we have cause to hope according to the promiss of our Lord being faithfull in smale things she now is placed over great. her desease of which she dy'd was a consumption, which consum'd all the flesh of her bones so that she was a meer skilleton[.] she receiv'd all the last sacrements on her knees in her perfect senses with great Tranquility & devotion[.] for two or three days before she dy'd we expected that each minet would have been the last, but to our surprise 4 hours before she dy'd she fell into convolitions with a heard agony she expir'd about eleven at night on the a bove mention'd day & the 57 of age & 38 of her Holy profession & was bury'd the 10 in the upermost oven of the first row. *Requiescat in Pace*

on the 11 of november our dear Sister Clementina Conyers departed this life,[1] she was a women of very good sense & of such parts as might have render'd her most serviceable had not want of health joyn'd to her continual anxietys of mind been a hendrence, her timorosity was so great that without an equal sumission twa's impossible to injoy pease of mind which she was wanting in, by aiming at a sartingty seeking it where it was not to be had, & refussing it where she might have found it, which was in a blind obedience to derectors, for want of which she seem'd on a rack in the performance of the divine office, & frequenting the sacrements she often & in a manner dayly repeated her office over again not think[ing] she had perform'd it so ^as^ to fulfill her obligation, which depriv'd her of the Comfort & benefitt she would othere ways have drawn from those

[1] Clementina Conyers (BA062).

duties. at the beginning of this month she was seaz'd with the fever that raign'd in town of which many dy'd, it deprived her of her senses which render'd uncapable of the last sacrements. her Sister desir'd she might get a mass said at the jesuites in honour of St Francis xaverious[1] to whome she had a most sigular devotion to beg he would obtaine that she might be able to receive her *viaticum*, & it pleas'd God that same morning to grant her to come so much to her self as to be capable to receive it & she did & she ask'd if she was to receive then the holy oyles, but that not pressing twa's thought better to deffer it. about five o clock in the after noon the fever again seiz'd her head, & she remain'd so tell she fell into her agony upon which extremunction was immediatly given her, & a hour after she expir'd **[p. 81]** in the 37 of her age & 18 since her holy profession. her disease was judg'd so infectious that by orders of doctor & surgion she was to be bury'd in the earth & that as soon as possible for she turn'd black before [she] was cold[.] the next morning she was accordingly bury'd in the earth in time of our lauds in our new Church yeard under the organ loft windors. on the 13 her mass & all as usuall was perform'd. *Requiescat in pace.*

[*change of hand*] on the 11 of December Sister Ann Gladin was cloathed having been two years Schollar[.][2] the reason was because the number of lay Sisters was more than we ought to have & the community was resolved not to cloath any more till it should please God to take one to himself, but many of our Religious having compassion of her, beg'd she might be cloathed, she having comported her self so as to give content to the community. She has 60 pound which mrs Sykes left at her Death, for portion, & judged not to have sufficient strength, to be either cook or baker she was dispenced from these two offices not doubting but in other things she may be very Serviceable.[3]

on the 14 of December Mis Pikering received the Schoolar's kerchief & name of Cicily.

the 15 mis Eliz: Tichbourn & her Brother went for England.

---

1 St Francis Xavier (1506–52), co-founder of the Society of Jesus. His feast day is 3 December.

2 Ann Gladin, lay sister (BA087).

3 Mrs Mary Sykes (d. 1738), mother of Mary Michael (BA189) and Ann Augustine Sykes (BA188), left money for a number of educational causes, here providing money for a dowry to enable Ann Gladin to profess as a lay sister; see also **[pp. 19, 53–5, 66, 128]**.

1742

on the 1st february it pleased God to call to himself our Dear Sister monica Trafford,[1] a true good Religious woman, & very Serviceable in many imployments, she did not come young to Religion, yet shew'd a great value for the Smallest observances, & was most Singularly exemplar in her zeal for the common work, & constancy to the work Chamber, nor was She less faithfull to the choir Duties as allso of good Service to it[.] She was heartily friendly & of a good nature, but Somewhat hott but it Soon past, which notwithstanding was to her an occation of humility & to others of patience[.] her love for the community appear'd preferable **[p. 82]** to that of nature, as was evident in regard to her Sister, who for some time was mad, which was a most Sencible cross to her, yet She was the person when She saw She was past management to Desire her confinement & Seperation from the Community Shewing more concern for the trouble it gave the Religious, then from the pain She must naturally have felt. for many years She had been troubled with a cough which suddenly Stop'd which joyn'd with a great cold in a few days carry'd her off She received all the rights kneeling with much piety & Devotion, had her Sences to the last, & so perfectly resigned, that She never Shew'd the least desire of either life or Death. She expired between one & two a clock in the affternoon the 77 years of her age & 47 of her holly profession she was bury'd on the 3d instant in the 2d oven of the 2d row. *Requiescat in pace Amen*

The Same day that we buryed Sister monica which was the 3d of february it pleased Allmighty God to call to himself Dear Sister Ann Markham who we did not think so near her end as She proved to be[.][2] She came to Religion young, & put on the Schollar's kirchief as Soon as her age would permitt, She was from the begining exact in Religious observances, Shewing to have a great esteem & value for them, She Served the community in many imployments, & out of what was allow'd her for her own use & Solace She gave what She could Spare to improve those imployments She was put into, Spending so little of the pention given her by her friends for her use, as to make at different times very considerable Guifts to the monastery[.] the last & greatest was a hundred pound Sterlin for a new Alter for our old Church which upon the building of a new one was given to the Seminary Built by the Bishop,[3] tho She was when in health Sparing to herself yet She was very liberal to others & so considerate of the common, that when wine or any extraordinary medesin was appointed by any Docter for her health She would pay

1 Monica Trafford (1695–1742) BA204.

2 Ann Mechtilda Markham (BA137).

3 In 1738 Bishop Hendrik Josef van Susteren bought the Hof van Pittem to establish a seminary in Bruges. It later became the episcopal palace.

[p. 83] them out of what her friends allow'd which was 5 pound a year, Saying pentions was allow'd Religious to Solace them when Sick, & Spare the Community not to regal them in health[.] the last office she had was Subprioress but finding her health & Strength decay She used all endeavours to be discharg'd nor would She Celebrate her whole jubily tell freed[.] tho She was very Charitable & Compationate yet her words & cariage shew'd an air of imperiousness & Sufficience Seeming to be more knowing than others which made her less loved than esteemed, being valu'd for a good & exempler religious woman for when in health She never complain'd for having no consideration given her on whit-meat days She not being allow'd to eat fish but contented with 2 boiled eggs & a mess of porage as was Served in common. She had ever been Subject to a weakness in her Limbs which much encreased with age so that she could not sometimes drag her Self to places of order & therefore it was judg'd necessary that She Should lye & be all together in the infirmary which She was about two or three years before She dyed, from which time she endeavour'd to Supply that want by recollection & prayer & preparation for Death hoping that when fitt God would take her to himself[.] a great cold which Seassed her joyn'd to her age Soon accomplishd her desire, with great content She received all the Rights of the church & had her Sences to the last, & expir'd about three a Clock in the affternoon on the 3^{d} of february in the 73 of her age, & 55 of her holy profession[.] She was bury'd on the 5 instant in the upermost oven of the 2^{d} row. *Requiescat in pace. Amen*

the 22 of february being the compleat 50 years Since the arrival of our Reverend Mother Lady Lucy Herbert,[1] the Religious being desiorous to express their love & esteem for her by a little pious [*~~illeg~~.*] action, had a peramade made & erected in the work chamber, affter the half hour of medidation affter Vespers lighted Candles being prepared for all the religious unknown **[p. 84]** to Reverend Mother they placed themselves choir ways in the Galary a Seat being before prepar'd at the uper end of the Galary for her[.] as Soon as she was Sett down one of the Religious representing the Guardian Angel of the house, having made an adress to her, they lead her to the work Chamber & all the religious went & two before her with lighted Candles Singing the *Te Deum*[.] our Reverend Mother Seem'd mightily confounded at the honour & great kindness they Shew'd her the Pyramade was illuminated with a great many Candles, on one Side form'd Lucy Herbert her worldly name, on the other her name in Religion Teresa Joseph, & on the 3^{d} was Superiour, round her seat was faith, hope & Charity, they having Congratulated, explain'd & apply'd each vertue, the Action ended with her being Crown'd, from whence it being time for Collation we went to the Refectory where the Procuratrix

---

[1] Lucy Herbert (1693–1744) BA101.

had p[re]par'd a very good one[.] our Reverend Mother Seem'd to take all that was done exceeding kind & not content to express it by words must do it by deeds taking hold of the first Convenient day to Shew her gratitude by treating the Community & by her many expressions of kindness made it doubly wellcome to us all.

on the 24 it Pleased Allmighty God to take out of this life the most holy & renown'd Henry Joseph Van Susteren our most worthy Bishop,[1] who was greatly Lamented as a loss to the publick both for his great Charityes & other vertues by which he was a light to his flock & much loved & esteem'd by all *Requiescat in pace Amen*

April ^the 24^ mis Mary Darell went for Tourcoin[2] to learn french

on the 28 mis Pickering quitted the Schollars habit to goe for England **[p. 85]** the reason given was to secure her fortune[3]

in June our Allter Step arrived Safe from Rome, & with a kind presant from Lady Neezdall[4] to each of our Community of an *Agnus Dei*, with a pair of beads trimed & brass Crucifix, to which was granted an indulgence[.] her Ladyship sent also a box in which was 14 pictures of the Passion, Stiled the Stations of the holy Cross, to which great indullgences is given, but as we have not conveniency to place each at their proper distance the latter is lost[.] these pictures hangs in our new Gallary[.] from the Same kind hand [from which] not long before we had a parcel of Gold & Silver Galloons & Edgings very usefull to our Church ornaments, & Sufficient to repare those that before had false triming, the lace also of our 4 best Allbs; 2 point 2 flanders lace was also her guift, they belong'd to the Prince of Wales's Cradle & cost near £1000;[5] the Dutchess her mother being Governant to the princc caused them to be at her Ladyships Disposal;

on the 26 of June m^is^ Mary Sanderson return'd to her parents; Lady Montague having been at the whole expence of her being here;[6]

on the 26 of June Mrs Collingwood with her Servant Margaret wood enter'd our enclosure as boarders, they Table in the fathers house & lodge in the Schooll appartment.

on the 26 m^r^ Bruce brought his daughter to be Religious she was past 23 years of age.[7]

---

1 The bishop died on 24 February 1742.

2 Tourcoin: Tourcoing, near Lille, France.

3 Cicily Pickering, in religion Isabella Cecilia (BA155).

4 Lady Nithsdale: Winifred Herbert, sister of Prioress Lucy Herbert (BA101).

5 The Duchess of Powis, Elizabeth Herbert née Somerset, mother of Prioress Herbert, was governess and governor of the Prince of Wales at St Germain-en-Laye 1689–91; see Corp, p. 365.

6 Lady Montagu: Mary Herbert, another sister of Prioress Lucy Herbert.

7 Elizabeth Bruce, in religion Mary Ann (1744–1800) BA036, Procuratrix 1776?–1782; Novice Mistress.

on the 29 m[is] Constantia Dicconson[1] by her fathers orders parted hence to the great joy of our Community, her conversation having been very prejudicial to many then in our Schooll, for too worldly an Education with an unhappy turn of thought towards romances & Entreagues was a dangerous bail to youth, & this her misfortune, which being joined with a good temper excellent voice, & many other engaging qualities insensibly draws the love of her Companions & without designing harm instill'd her principles, which our Superiour being inform'd off Sent to her friends to remove her[.] She went to her parents then at Paris **[p. 86]** & M[is] Arabella Pordage to Lille to learn french, thus far our Confessor conducted them

on the 3[d] of August M[is] Eliz: Bruce took the Schollar's habit, & is called in Religion Sister MaryAnn

on the 11 of August M[is] Lucy Pool about 14 years of age was receiv'd a convictress, & with her came mis Moston, & mis Parry, both for Lovain, but was taken into the Enclosure, till our Religious there could have notice & send for them;[2]

on the 14 M[is] Sallvance was received Convictress to learn English;

on the 16 M[is] Ann Moor parted hence for Paris;

on the 17 Sister Barbara a lay Sister from Lovain[3] came for the 2 yound [*sic*] ladys above mention'd but their cloaths being not yet come, she was obliged to make some stay, during which she remain'd in our Enclosure;

on the 21 M[is] Bridged more returned from Doway;[4]

on the 29 Sister Barbara return'd to Lovain with mis moston & M[is] Parry & Caried also with her the writing by which this month was resigned to Lovain all right to the remaining monies left (as mention'd) by m[rs] Sykes for the perpetual Education of youth;[5]

on the Same day the 29 of August our Dear Sister Letitia Huddleston Departed this life;[6] She had ever bin of an innocent & most Pious Conversation, truly exact in each Religious observance, & very Servicable in the different imployments obedience Charged her with, for She never spared her Self, but was ready to help & assist all, which justly gain'd

---

[1] Constantia Dicconson was possibly the niece of William Dicconson (d. 1742) of Wrightington, Jacobite courtier. See *ODNB*. His wife, Juliana Walmesley, was the daughter of Edward Dicconson and Mary Blount and later married Charles Jerningham, a general in imperial service. See B. Burke, *Genealogical and Heraldic History of the Landed Gentry* (London: Harrison, 1875), vol. 1, p. 343.

[2] Lucy Poole professed as Mary Aloysia (1747–99) BA158. She was the daughter of Rowland Poole and Bridget Huddleston.

[3] Probably Elizabeth Barbarina van Doornem, lay sister (1727–88/9) LA084.

[4] Bridget More later returned to England; see **[p. 92]**.

[5] Probably Jean Parry, in religion Teresa (1763–1816) LA197. She was 38 when she professed: she had to wait for her dowry because her inheritance was shared between two brothers and eight sisters. Miss Moston/Mostyn did not proceed to profession. For Mrs Sykes, see **[pp. 19, 53–5, 66, 128]**.

[6] Laetitia Huddleston (1706–42) BA111.

the love & esteem of each. She was, she [*sic*] eminent in many vertues, & never lost her first fervour, but So Singular in Cheerfulness & Sufferings that it Seemeth her Caracter, for she had Constantly great infirmities[,] as Rupture, fistula, & violent pains in the head besides so many other ailments, that it may be truly said from her first year of profession till Death She was never one day free from Suffering **[p. 87]** yet ever So Cheerfull that those that did not know her illness would Scarce immagin what she endured[.] when Reverend Mother has Sometimes pitty'd her Painfull life, she would answer t'was indeed disagreeable to nature, but when Death came She Should not grieve for having Suffer'd it, nor was her hopes decieved by the joy[,] comfort & happiness She express'd to feel the day before her Death[.] She was not long confin'd to the infirmary, & received all the last Sacraments with an edifying Devotion had her Sences to the last & Expired about two of the Clock in the afternoon, the 56 of her age, & 37 since her holy profession. She was buried on the 30 in the bottom oven of the 3d row. *Requiescat in pace Amen*

on the 20 of September Mis Mary Newlin arrived here being by her sister Teresa Augustin invited over for a visit[.] the motive was hopes of her Conversion, & for the same admitted into our Enclosure & lodg'd in the Schooll;[1]

on the 29 of September we were all Surprized with the Sudden Death of Sister Mary Magdalain Coffee[2] about 2 years before She was Seased with a dead palsey, but by proper application So far recover'd Sence as to receive all the last Sacraments, after which she grew so much better that in a Short time She could with a Stick walk about the infirmary & even goe to the Sick chapell; till by a Second attack of the Same illness She was wholy confin'd, no more able to help her Self than an infant & in appearance had no more Sence, being then judged in Eminent danger, the holy Oyles was appointed, not thinking her capable of more, but Father Confessor who better knew her Conscience & great piety gave also her *viaticum*[.] She continued many months in the Condition like an innocent, & unlucky Child for whenever left allone, she would tear to peices whatever was in her reach, to prevent which, they bounds her hands & ty'd her in the chair, tis fear'd the manner in which she was that day ty'd caused her Death[.] She was left well before the Hours & at the end of Refectory found dead She had allways a Singular devotion to St Michaell in whose protection **[p. 88]** we confide, She exchanged

---

1 Mary Newlin (for Elizabeth Newlin, see vol. 1, **[p. 419]**) had been the subject of some correspondence between her father John Newlin, Lady Mary Caryll and Philip Caryll in 1726–7. He was vicar of Harting and accused the Caryll family of subverting her religion, encouraging her to travel to France and Bruges and convert to Catholicism. Elizabeth Newlin, in religion Teresa Augustine (BA147). See archive.org/stream/historyofharting-00gordiala/historyofharting00gordiala_djvu.txt, pp. 146–52, accessed 25 February 2016.
2 Magdalen Coffee (1694–1742) BA060.

a Suffering for an Eternal rest, the 73 year of her age, & 48 Since her holy profession She was buried the 1 of October in the 2d oven of the 3d row. *Requiescat in pace*.

on the 13 of october mis Mary Newlin returned for England having had the happiness during her Short Stay here to be received into the Church, admited to Communion[.] the Lady Montague was at all expence of her journey.

on the 26 of November it pleased Allmighty God to deprive us of Dear Sister Winifred Placida Stanley[1] a no less Servisable than truly good Religious, her perfect Skill in musick made her very usefull both in Choir & organ house, her good Sense, prudence & other talents made her fitt for most employments but her weak State of health permitted not such as was labourious[.] She was ever most exact in Religious observances, & for many years so exempler in recollection & interiour union with God that the very Sight of her moved to Devotion; towards the latter end tho she ever retain'd the Same Serene modest air: yet Shew'd dispositions to the active life, but a Consumption (to which She had bin long inclined) being joyned with a cancer in her breast hasten'd her end, She enjoy'd perfect Sences to the last, received all the last Sacraments with much piety & Devotion, was resigned to Dye, yet great as her Sufferings was Shew'd desiorous to live[.] She expired between 2 & 3 in the afternoon, the 57 year of her age, & 39 Since her holy profession, She was buried on the 28 in the uppermost oven of the 3d row. *Requiescat in pace. Amen*

on the 12 of December Sister Ann Gladin made her holy profession.[2]

1743

on the 14 of January Sister Mary Anne Bruce was cloathed[3]

on the 16 Mis Etiene came from Doway to be a convictriss to learn English

on the 19 Mis Betty Jernegan return'd from Tourney & Mis Pordage from Lille.

[p. 89] on the 8 of Aprill mis Peggy Tasburgh return'd from Bruxelles.[4]

on the 30 of May Mis Eliz: Wheeler Aged 24 & Mis Eliz: Bertin Aged 23 arrived here, their intention to be Religious so was received into our Enclosure.[5]

the 5 of June which was that year on Whitson Eve, was the Jubely of our Dear Reverend Mother,[6] we begun in May to prepare for the same,

---

1 Winifred Placida Stanley (1704–42) BA186, musician.

2 Ann Gladin, lay sister (BA087).

3 Mary Ann Bruce (BA036).

4 Margaret Tasburgh (BA193).

5 Both later professed: Elizabeth Wheeler, in religion Ann Joseph (1745–99) BA218, and Elizabeth Barton, in religion Mary Baptist (1745–94) BA015.

6 Reverend Mother was Prioress Lucy Herbert (BA101).

in making our house neat & clean, mending & repairing all places that wanted, whiten'd our refectory, kitchen[,] infirmary, work house, & all our windows on the outside of the garden Side, & all our boards at our windows new painted. every one was desiorous of Shewing their duty & respect to Lady Lucy by a Small token, Some gave works, Some money, as 2 guineys, Some 3, Some more, Some gave plate for the church, a Crucifix 5 foot high, the ground brass guilt[,] al the work Sillver, given by Sisters Stanleys, 2 large Sconces the ground black[,] the work all Sillver given by Mr Tasburgh[1] her profession day falling on Whitson-eve, no great matters could be done, we all put on our clean habit as on holy Saturday, & the day before we Swept our cells & places; her Reverence perform'd her devotions after the Convents mass; that being done we Sung the *Te Deum*; but no bell rung, our Confessor[2] Sung the prayer a quarter after that the whole Community came to the Gallery with lighted Candles, which we had from our church; the Subprioress[3] handed her out of the choir & so along the gallery & Dormitryes Singing the *Veni creator*, to her Chamber, then we all asked Blessing, & made our Compliments of Congratulations[.] She had a handsome Canopy in the choir, Refectory & her chamber, at dinner we had recreation, which the procuratrix[4] gave, whole Lobsters, Cramboly, & a good glass of mountain wine, at collation **[p. 90]** we talked, but kept silence at 6 & a half. Sunday was spent in devotion till night, for at supper we had a very pritty recreation & a good glass of mountain wine, munday we had recreation at dinner portions of neats toungs & half pints of white wine,[5] Tuesday the ceremonies was perform'd, we rung our bell after Compline for an hour, only munday night; next morning we read our office but sung Prime & after prayers was done we had no more silence that day. The high mass was at ten, perform'd by the ArchPriest having no Bishop;[6] our own Religious with the best musitians we could get in town perform'd all in Musick. Our Jubilarian went attended with two of the elldest Religious into the church at the begining of Mass, her candle was carryed by one of our pentioners & brought back by her again; when all was done & mass was out the ceremony was perform'd; when done the *Te Deum* was sung in musick; we rung our bell as did all our neighbours, when we went down to take her Ladyship in we had lighted candles in our hands & conducted her to choir where she saluted all; & so to dinner where we ware very

---

1 Mr Tasburgh: possibly Francis Tasburgh of Bodney, Norfolk, father of Margaret Tasburgh (BA193).

2 The Confessor was Fr Caryl Gerard, Confessor 1723–79; Anstruther 4, p. 110.

3 The Sub-Prioress was Mary Teresa Jerningham (BA118).

4 The Procuratrix in 1745 was Dorothy Stanley, in religion Mary Xaveria (BA183).

5 Neats tongues: cow tongues (OED). Mountain wine: a type of wine formerly produced in Malaga (OED).

6 Bishop Hendrik Josef van Susteren had died on 24 February 1742; his successor, Jan-Baptist de Castillon, did not take office until 20 May 1743.

merry. We had pigion-pie & wine; the pentioners both dined & sup'd in the refectory, our neighbours shott at proper times, our workmen sent a letter of compliment to her Reverence to beg they might have audience & wait on her at one o'clock, which was permitted. we all attended her Ladyship to the speak house above which was full of our workmen; they first saranaded her with Musick, then one read alowd the verses & presented them to her Reverence, they were printed on silk with her coat of arms, & then they presented us all with a coppy of the same on paper, & then Musick again, all was very handsome & oblidgingly done, from us they went down to the company below then at table **[p. 91]** & perform'd the Same, making such Gentellman a present of a paper of verses; we read our Vespers & Compline then *Salve*; we had recreation at Super, raw Candles, & Some things that was left at the father's house dinner; we Set up as late as we would to See the fire works which was very fine; great illumination in all our Neighbour-hood, our workmen could not get leave to come in, so erected a Scaffold in the Street on the garden Side, & threw in their Squibs, we had recreation all the week, Dinner & Supper which the Procuratrix gave, we invited to Dinner on the day of the Jubely the 2 burger masters, the Scout, the Treasurer, Arch Priest, Docter. the following Thursday all our workmen, was invited to dinner, & Staid till 9 at night; & very merry they were; her Reverence gave 200 Loaves of bread to our poor neighbours, & 15 or 16 Barrells of bear in the Streets.

a week after all this our Dear Superiour or Jubelarian treated the Community most generously noble & kind, in the morning she begun & gave us a Breakfast of Tea, Coffey, & hot bread; when She was brought into the refectory, there was musick at her entrance, we all found at our places, a pound of Tea, a Suggar loaf, a book & a thin vail; the lay Sisters had a p[oun]d: of Tea, a pair of gloves, & half a nine Shilling peace; no Silence that day, at dinner her Reverence treated us with whole Chickens, green peas, Strawburies; & half a pint of frountinack,[1] & a glass of good Languidock wine to drink then we talked at Supper, but had nothing in particular; we Sat up till 9, on the 26 of June our dear Jubelarian or Superiour treated us again, with a dinner & gave us pigg, Goosbury tart, & Strawbury, with half pints of Languidock, the day after we had a play perform'd for her, on the 6 of July her Reverence treated us a third time with Pidgions, cream-cheeses, Cherryes, & half pints of frountignack, we had in all 3 plays & one opera perform'd for her, & our pentioners acted an opera also in the work-chamber, from the first putting up of the Stage, it **[p. 92]** remain'd so till all was done, & we made the warm chamber our workroome, the third recreation, we Sat up at night, & her Reverence gave us Lemmonade, wine, punch, Buisquets & bitter puffs,

---

[1] Frontenac: muscat wine made in Frontignan (OED).

this night concluded all. [*in margin*: june the 23d miss Eliz. Wheeler & mis Eliz Barton took the Scholars habit, mis Weeler the name of Sister Ann Joseph, & miss Barton the name of Sister Mary Baptist]

August the 17th mis Bridged more went for England.

August the 20th Mary wood an English Girl of about 14 years of age was permitted to come into our inclosure in the day time to be instructed in her Religion, but was lodged in town;

August the 26th Mrs Cumberford come for a visit with her maid & was lodged in the new apartment without the inclosure

September the 11th mrs Cumberford return'd back to Dunquerque;

October the 3d mis Molly & mis Dolly Riddles went for Lille to learn French, mis Lucy Poole with them for Tourcoin, & mary wood for Lille;

Ocober the 5th mis Molly Darell returned from Tourcoin,[1]

November that 25 mis Frances Burrell was received for convictrix, Aged 16.[2]

1744

Jan: the 19th The Right Hon[oura]ble Lady Lucy Herbert, our Dear Superiour, Departed this life,[3] Leaving the whole Community in true Affliction for so great a loss, & Example of all vertues, she was indued with all Religious vertues, an extream piety & Devotion, most Exact in all Religious Duties, a well grounded mortification, a profound Humility, a most ardent Devotion to our Redemer in the holy Sacrament of the Allter, her feelling devotion to our Saviours passion was Such as many be reacon'd among the vertues of the primitive Christians, & made her suffer **[p. 93]** all pains both Corporal & Spiritual with exceeding patience; her meekness & Sweetness of temper render'd her aimiable to every one both Equalls & inferiours, an heroic courage to over-come all Difficulties in any thing she undertook for the Glory of God; She improved our inclosure by the Addition of Building from the Refectory quite to the End; the last work in her time was the Church the new Father's house, & Speak house, the trouble & fatigue of which She went thro with invincible Courage; Soon affter She was chosen prioress she allter'd our Statutes, Leaving out & putting in what She thought more proper, in which she met with much opposition, having many Aged & Different Tempers to Deal with, they thinking themselves injur'd by not being consulted before her Reverance had procur'd my Lord Bishops consent & approbation, it gave her much to Suffer, She also with the consent of the Community chainged the fassion of the vailes, Leaving notwithstanding all the Ellders free to change or not, which some never did to their Dying day, looking upon it not so

1 Tourcoin: Tourcoing, near Lille, France.

2 Frances Burrell, in religion Mary Magdalen (1747–1803) BA039.

3 Lucy Herbert (1693–1744) BA101, Prioress 1709–44.

Religious, & to much like worldlings to change the fassion of our habit in any kind, She also with the consent of the Community changed the plain Song; She being ever of a mild Disposition Desired to see every one easy, & indeavour'd to make each one so, acting notwithstanding with resolution in which she undertook, & with the authority Suitable to the post she was in; She had been for above 2 years in a Lingering weak State of health but could by no means be perssuaded to stay from the Choir & Refectory, till Subprioress[1] Sent to the Arch Priest to use his authority; he obliged her to Stay from mattins, & to use such helps as was judg'd absolutly necessary to keep her alive, She being almost exhausted & worn out She was prevailed upon to lye in her Chamber, which was much against her inclination for She had a true love for her Cell & Solitude, in all things she was perfectly resign'd **[p. 94]** to Gods will, & her Confidence in his Divine providence made her goe thro the greatest Difficulties with cheerfulness, offten Saying in her last illness when she could hardly be heard to Speak being near her End, <u>who can distrust in Gods mercy</u>; when the Doctor by by reason of her excesive weakness judg'd She could not hold out long, order'd her all the holy rights of the Church, the Subprioress with great Difficulty, being moved with a tender concern for our approaching loss told her of it, She smiling answer'd Gods will be done then She desired that when She had received them she might be left alone as much as possible the remaining time she was in the world, but that being to hard a task for her Chilldren to be deprived of her before it pleased God to make the seperation She cheerfully submitted to our going to her as often as we could.

She received the holy rights from the hands of our Reverend Father Confessor who assisted her to the last moment of her life, which She ended in all peace about 11 a Clock at night on the 19th of Jan: the feast of the Name of Jesus to which she had a particular devotion. She was 75 years of age, 51 professed, & 35 Superiour, during which time She professed 26 Religious for the choir, 15 Lay Sisters, & left 25 nuns, one Novice & 3 Schollars for choir Nunns & 12 Lay Sisters, She buried 45 nuns & 11 Lay Sisters;

On Teusday the 23 She was buried, my Lord Bishop & the Abbot of Echoute being present,[2] both had their places in the *Sanctuarium*, the Archpriest Sung the mass with 2 assistants & received the offering both of men & women, & our Reverend Father Confessor[3] buried her in the 2d oven of the first Row on the right hand; *Requiescat in pace*.

[p. 95] My Lord Bishop having ordain'd the 3 days of fasting & Silence for the happy Success of the Election of a new Prioress, we

---

[1] The Sub-Prioress was Mary Teresa Jerningham (BA118).

[2] My Lord Bishop: Bishop Jan-Baptist de Castillon (1743–53). The Abbot of Eeckhoute was Abbot Albert Folque.

[3] Father Confessor was Fr Caryl Gerard, Confessor 1723–79; Anstruther 4, p. 110.

perform'd the Same, with the prayers as our institutions appoints, The Reverend Father Roberts then Rector of Gant[1] was Sent for for anyone to apply to for advice that would, on the 25th of the same month was the day appointed for the Election, my Lord Bishop having Sent word he would be here at 8 of the clock in the morning, we begun mattins at 4 to be ready for that time, our Reverend Father Confessor Sung the mass which was of the holy Ghost, at which we all Communicated; My Lord Bishop came at the time appointed, attended by the Arch priest, his Secretory & a Cannon of his Church who Spoke English, all assisted at the Election our Reverend Father Confessor distributed the schedules to all the Religious, my Lord Bishop Collected all the voices with his own hands, Sister Mary Olivia Darell was Legally chosen for Prioress,[2] which his Lordship declar'd & confirm'd, She then made before my Lord Bishop her solemn vow of obedience to the Bishop of Bruges for herself & Community, & being conducted by the 2 chief Ellders to her Seat, all the profess'd nuns & Lay Sisters made their vow of obedience to her;

On the 27th of the Same month the new Prioress order'd an other Solemn Service for the late Superiour; perform'd by our Selves, that we might not be wanting in performing for our Superiour what we do for all our Religious; the first being done by the town musitions; our Reverend Mother Darell from her first coming to Religion shew'd a dislike to seculars living with Religious, & having now for Some years seen the inconveniences which attend it, resolved at her first being elected to Declare against it as Soon as anyone offer'd which hapen'd but 2 days affter her Election when twas proposed to her Reverence a young Ladys Boarding here, her Reverence answer'd she would turn none out of the house who was then in it, but that **[p. 96]** She would never bring any more in; She Saw the Discontent it caused in the Community, therefore as they had chosen her tho unworthy to be their mother, She thought her Self bound to ~~ack~~ act the part of one, by Seeking their content & Satisfaction in which lay in her power, being convinc'd this would make them happy by Seeing which would contribute much to hers, that as she begun She could with ease goe on, for to accept of Some & refuse others was to Disoblige many, these & the like reasons her Reverence made use off; my Lord Bishop highly approved her proceeding, & order'd her to Continue her resolution; notwithstanding some few relations & friends of that young Ladys family ware much Disatisfy'd & took up the cause so hottly as to give her Reverence a good deal to Suffer, the Subprioress being a relation, the procuratrise a friend,[3] proved the most Troublesome, alledging it was not in her Reverence power to put an end to having

---

[1] Fr Roberts SJ (1677–1758), alias Stephen Swindall, was Rector of the Jesuit College, Ghent (1742–46) and also served as extraordinary confessor to the convent; Holt, p. 240.
[2] Mary Olivia Darell (BA071), Prioress 1744–66.
[3] The Procuratrix was Dorothy Stanley (BA183).

boarders without the consent of the convent, that She ought at least to have consulted her councell Sisters, that it was the way to ruin the house, for we had not Sufficient income to live without Boarders therefore they privately adress'd to the Bishop, who stood by her Reverence, Said She had done a prudent action, & what he approved of that in case of want he was obliged to assist them, this caused Some uneasiness for a time, which Soon wore off, & leaves the community in perfect peace & union;

February the 4th Sister Mary Ann Bruce made her holly profession which had been Differ'd on account of Reverend Mother Herbert's illness & Death.[1]

February the 26 Mr Tasburgh[2] return'd from Bruxells with his Daughter Margaret, She lodg'd & tabled in the School, & Mr Tasburgh in the new Father's house, which apartment he had inhabited some time. **[p. 97]** March the 23d our Reverend Mother being inform'd of the Death of Lord Neezdall[3] & the family having been benefactors to our house, ordered the hearing of one mass which was Said for him, & the cross prayers for 5 days from each of the community.

Aprill the 7th Sister Ann Joseph Wheeler, Sister Mary Baptist Barton & Sister Cicily Pickering were cloath'd.[4]

Aprill the 11 Mis Eliz Jernegan took the Schollars habit, & the name of Mary Agness.[5]

Aprill the 13 Mr Tasburgh & his daughter Margaret went to Gant;

Aprill the 20th Mrs Collingwood & her maid went to Gant;

May the 16th Mis Harcourt came back from Marquett, & Mis Lucy Poole from Tourcoin.

May the 17th Mr Tasburgh & his Daughter come from Gant Staid here till the 1st of June then went for England.

June the 2d Mis Molly Darell & Mis Harcourt went for England.

[*There is a gap of six months in Chronicle writing here, with no space allowed for additions. The text is continuous*]

1745

January 17th which was the feast of the name of Jesus[6] we Solemnised the whole Jubily of Sister Angella Huddleston, the Lauds nor hours ware not Sung that day.[7]

---

1 Mary Ann Bruce (BA036).

2 Francis Tasburgh of Bodney, Norfolk.

3 William Maxwell, 5th Earl of Nithsdale (d. 2 March 1744) was the brother-in-law of the late Prioress, Lucy Herbert (BA101). His wife was a benefactor of the convent.

4 Ann Joseph Wheeler (BA218); Mary Baptist Barton (BA015); Cicily Pickering (BA155).

5 Elizabeth Jerningham (BA122).

6 The feast of the Holy Name of Jesus was celebrated at varying times in January.

7 Angela Huddleston (1695–1756) BA112.

on the 19th of the Same month being the anniversary day of Lady Lucy Herbert our late Dear Superiour, it was kept with a late mass with Deacons, our Reverend Father Confessor Sung the mass, the herse was placed in the church, & the last Responsary of the Dead office Sung in the choir affter the mass;

January the 31st dyed mademoiselle Dubois a flemish pentioner, in our School of a worm fever as it was Judg'd by the Physitions, during her illness her father, who was a shop keeper in our town, obtain'd leave of my Lord Bishop to come into the inclosure, & finding her so ill beg'd leave to bring another Physition besides our own, they both judg'd her in Danger, & the next day ordain'd her the *Viaticum*, she grew much worse, & at about 6 at night she received the holy Oyles, & about 11 the Same night dyed, attended by **[p. 98]** a Carme who was her confessor, much regreted by all that knew her, being of a Sweet obliging temper & very pious; the next morning as Soon as the convent mass (which was said for her) was finish'd, we said the commendations in the Choir as for our Religious;

On the 2d: of Feb: at 6 in the Evening her corps was cary'd into the church Father Confessor came into the School pant where the corps was placed all the Religious present, said the *miserere & de profundis*, & then attended it to the church, the pentioners caryed the pall; we Staid in the Lay Sister's chapel till the coach come for her corps; then our whole Community assembled with lighted Candles, Sung the responsory while they cary'd her out of our church, our Bell rung till she was got to the Carms,[1] where she was buryed. *Requiescat in pace.*

Tis not to be Said the greatfull thanks her Father gave for all our kindness to his Daughter, & would not be Satisfyed without giving a pistole[2] for a Glass of wine for the community who had had so much trouble as he said with his Daughter.

February the 3d Monsieur Beaugard, a gentellman of our Town was mary'd to Mr Damarins Youngest Daughter, which was desir'd by the family might be done in our church, our Reverend Mother consented to it & made them the Compliment of playing the mass her Self which was perform'd in musick,[3] the Pastor of St Anns[4] mary'd them, affter Mass they with all the company they brought (which was very numerous) breackfasted in the new Fathers house, then come up to the Speakhouse,[5] where Reverend Mother & some of the Religious were ready to make

[1] The Carmelites were neighbours of the convent in Carmerstraat: see Marc Ryckaert, *Historische stedenatlas van België: Brugge* (Brussel: Gemeentekrediet, 1991), pp. 195–6.

[2] Pistole: a coin of small value.

[3] Special permission had to be obtained to perform a marriage in the convent chapel; it was a very rare occurrence.

[4] St Anne's was the local parish church.

[5] Speakhouse: see Glossary.

them their Compliments, all which they took so kind, that Mr Damarin Sent that day a Dozen Bottles of Champaign wine for the community to drink their Healths & the young couple could not be put of from giving the **[p. 99]** community a handsome recreation in the Same weeke,

February the 8th Mis Margaret Standfield was received for convictrix aged about 10 years her Parents are English, but inhabitants of this town many years & keep a Shop;

February the 25th Our Dear Sister Mary Widdrington Departed this life;[1] about 3 years before her Death upon the feast of All Saints,[2] she found her Self as She Said in a great Disorder but could not well describe it, we perceived She hardly knew what She did, in time of the musick mass at which She play'd the Bassviol, She Surprized every one in the organ house, for instead of playing, She knelt down & Said She could not See[.] we Sent for the Doctor & Surgion, they both agreed it was a kind of Pallsey & Aperplex which had Seased her head & all one Side, but not wholy taken away the use of her limbs, except one hand which she never recover'd, She was cary'd to the sick house & ordain'd the *viaticum* with great Devotion, all proper remedys ware apply'd but she never perfectly recover'd her Judgment from the time She was confined to the infirmary, growing more & more insencible, to that Degree as by her looks, drevelling faultering speech she appeard like a natural which was a concern to all, She having been a woman of extraordinary Good Sence, all the Sence She now Shew'd was of piety, which corresponded to the life she had allways led, never loosing her first fervour, most exact in all religious observances, her darling vertue was that of Charity towards her neighbour, in which She was so nice, that She was never heard to Say the least slighting word or reflecting of any one, the fear of which made her very reserved, & a few words in company; not withstand agreeable too and beloved by all for their great esteem of her sanctity, She was of so quiet a Disposition that she gave offence to none, never Seem'd to know, nor concern her self with what past in the house, when at her prayers Seemingly perfectly united **[p. 100]** to God, remained immovable, & as it was wholy absorb'd in him her thoughts so taken up with God & heavenly things had no roome for Earthly objects; yet She being of very timorous make & more inclined to the part of Mary than Martha,[3] it led her into the errour of thinking She could not Save her Soul if imploy'd in any office, which render'd her less usefull to the community than otherways she might have been; t'was so much against her inclination to be imploy'd in any exteriour occupation that She even Shew'd such

---

[1] Mary Widdrington (1687–1745) BA219.

[2] The feast of All Saints is celebrated on 1 November.

[3] On the role of Martha and Mary in the convent, see for example the discussion in Claire Walker, 'Combining Martha and Mary: Gender and Work in Seventeenth-Century English Cloisters', *Sixteenth Century Journal* 30 (1999), pp. 397–418.

a Stiffness in complying with her Superiour will, that when put into any office, she could not rest till by tears & much untreaty Superiours was forst to consider her weakness by taking her off from any imploy during the 3 years she was confin'd to the Infirmary, she was Judg'd capable of going to the Sacraments once a week, which she did with most Singular Devotion, till about a fortnight before her Death, after receiving her *viaticum* & holy Oyles she grew much more Stupid & insencible but not wholy confin'd to bed till 3 days before her Death, when she fell into a kind of Lethargy in which she expired about 3 in the afternoon on the 25th of February in the 77th year of her age & 59th of her holy profession, She was buried on the 27th in the bottom oven of the 4th row on the left hand. *Requiescat in pace*

Aprill the 21st was the whole Jubily day of Sister Anastasia Trafford[1] no notice was taken of it on account of her having been out of her Self many years, but as she was not then confined the community gave that day a recreation & her niece gave the community a breakfast;

On the 23d of Aprill which was Fryday in Easter week, Sister Elizabeth Ann Joseph Wheeler, Sister Elizabeth Mary Baptist Barton, & Sister Isabella Cicilia Pickering made their holy Professions.[2]

[p. 101] Aprill the 25th Sister Isabella Joachim Enoo departed this life,[3] She was ever very pious, of a timorous Conscience; a mild peacable temper, & zealous to Serve the community in the most laborious imploys, for almost 2 years before her Death she had very ill health, having had a great Cold which fell upon her breast that she could never Speak out but like one which a fresh cold, notwithstanding She went through the hardest offices as Sick house & kitchen; all remidies proved ineffectual, but the Doctor did not judg her illness dangerous till about 3 months before her Death, when She was taken with a violent oppression up on her breast in the night, She thought Death had Seazed her & with much Difficulty went to one of the Lay Sisters who lay the nearest to her, could not Speak but making a Strange noise like one in their agony frigh[t]ed her[.] She got her to bed again & call'd for help Father Confessor come in immediatly to her, finding her so bad we sent for a Syrgion to bleed her, which made her breath easier, the next day the Doctor found her in great danger, Said her lungs ware touch'd & had they not blooded her She would have Dy'd in the night, he order'd her the holy rights which she received with great Devotion; a little before her Death She Spit vast quantities of blood, with a great cough and Shortness of ~~Blood~~ Breath, found no relief but by opening a vain from time to time, She had her Sences to the last moment, & tho all her life had express'd a great terrour

---

1 Ann Trafford, in religion Anastasia (1695–1759) BA202.

2 They had arrived in May 1743 and were clothed the following April: see **[pp. 89, 97]**.

3 Isabella Vendow, in religion Mary Joachim (1726–45) BA210.

of Death, when she drew near to it was perfectly resign'd to Gods will, & with all peace & tranquillity expired about 3 in the afternoon the 25th of Aprill in the 43d year of her age & 19th of her holy profession, She was buried on the 27th in the 2d oven of the 4th row on the left hand. *Requiescat in pace;*

[p. 102] May the 30th Mis Barbara Herbert Daughter to Lord Edward Herbert & niece to Lady Lucy our late Superiour, come here with their priest & her maid, She and her maid ware Lodg'd in the new fathers house, the priest & maid went for England the 23d of june, the same day we took mis [*name not supplied*] in for pentioner;[1]

we being now under the french, the king of france was received into our town with great rejoicings;[2]

the 30th of june the Dauphin of France come to see our Church affter compline; we all put on our Surplices, & went to the Lay Sisters' Chapell, after he had veiw'd the Allter he come up to the gate to us, behaved in a very familiar obliging manner, the Chapell gates ware open'd for him which he seemed to Expect he come in with about half a Dozen of his followers, but gave orders no more Should enter, he would goe no farther than the Chapell where he stood & talked to us about a quarter of an hour, & then went away, our Bell was order'd to be rung from his first coming into the Street till he was quite out of it;

August the 14th our Dear Sister Christina Markham[3] departed this life much regreted by us all she having been a most pious good Religious & Serviceable member, & tho of a weak constitution her Sweet agreeable temper togather with her zeal to Serve the Community, made her goe thro all offices with cheerfullness & to the Satisfaction of every one, She was taken with a great cold and cough which never left her for above a year before she Dyed & which wore her away for a perfect Schelleton, she was taken wholy to the infirmary, all that could be thought of for her recovery was procur'd **[p. 103]** but had no Effect, so that for some months she lived a Dying life, during which time She gave vast Edification by her patient Suffering, never Shew'd the least Change of temper, took whatever was given her but ask'd for nothing, often Saying her only concern was to see She gave the community so much trouble in tending her, but Gods will be done. as she grew nearer her End so her cough

---

1 Barbara Herbert was the only child of Lord Edward Herbert and Henrietta Waldegrave; she left the convent in 1747: see **[p. 108]**.

2 France occupied parts of the Austrian Netherlands during the War of Austrian Succession, 1740–48. This is the first mention of the war in the chronicles. The French had conquered much Austrian territory by the end of 1746 but this was returned to Austria by the terms of the peace treaty in 1748. The allied army supporting Austria was led by the Duke of Cumberland, who was in charge at the battle of Fontenoy, 1745, when the territory was lost to France. The King of France was Louis XV, who ruled 1723–74. The Dauphin was Louis, who was born in 1729 and died in 1765 before becoming king.

3 Christina Markham (1717–45) BA138.

increased that She was often near choaking with the quantity of fleam She Spit which the Doctor Said was from her lungs, She was Sencible to the last moment and answer'd to our Ladys Littanies[1] which our Reverend Mother was Saying for her at her Bed Side, till about the middle of it She fell a coughing & expired about 5 in evening of the 14th of August in the 50 year of her age & 29th of her holy profession, on the 16th she was buried in our vault. *Requiescat in pace*.

August the 19th the 2 mis Riddles come from Lille

on the 20 mis Lucy poole, & mis Frances Burrell took the Schollars Kerchief, mis Pool the name of Mary Alloisia & mis Burrell the name of Mary Magdalen[2]

September The Nunns of the order of our Ladys conception at Ostend[3] being obliged to leave their inclosure by reason the french besieged that town, was order'd by our Bishop to come to our Neighbours at Bethania,[4] were they ware accomodated till they could fitt up their own house tollerable to goe into which was much indamaged by the Siege, our community had great compassion of them in their affliction & Shew'd them all kindness possible, we gave them in charity 12 ducatts which made 10 pound grot & 14 Shillings, our Confessor gave them one pistole, & 2 more one of our Religious gave out of her Spending mony; they had leave of our Bishop to come once into **[p. 104]** inclosure, they Dined at a round table set for them in the middle of our Refectory, & at night took collation with us it being one of the Ember days[5] on the 17th of September the Abbess with the 2 next Elldest, Sat with our Reverend Mother & Subprioress, they ware much obliged with all our kindness to them as well as for the Almes we bestow'd on them;

September the 24 the 2 mis Riddles went for England

October the 8th Sister Mary Agness Jernegan made her holy profession[6]

October the 30 departed this life the Right Honourable Lady viscountess Montague, Sister to Lady Lucy Herbert our late Superiour;[7] She was a Lady of extraordinary piety & Devotion, charity to the poor she look'd upon as her obligation, often Saying why had God bestow'd upon her a plentifull income but to relieve those in want, therefore never more concern'd than when She could not Satisfye every one that petition'd her charitable Succour; her Ladyship lived with us 7 years & half, much pleased with the company of the Religious whose little innocent recreations and Divertions She had a pleasure to partake of, her conversation

---

1 Our Ladys Littanies: see Glossary.
2 Lucy Poole (BA158) and Frances Burrell (BA039).
3 The siege of Ostend in August 1745 was part of the War of Austrian Succession.
4 Bethania Convent: see Appendix 1.
5 Ember Days: days set aside for penance four times a year.
6 Mary Agnes Jerningham (BA122).
7 Lady Montagu (d. 1745) was Prioress Lucy Herbert's sister Mary: see Herbert family tree.

was most Edifying & cheerfull; she often frequented the holy Sacraments with great Devotion, her confidence in God was so great that she was offten heard to say she did not wish to live nor fear to dye, for She wholy trusted in the mercys of God that he would Save her poor Soul; perfectly resign'd to Gods will, for she deprived of the use of her limbs so as not to be able to walk for many years which according to nature must have been a great cross **[p. 105]** to one of so active a make as She had all her life been, was never heard to complain or repine at it

The preventing civility & respect shew'd her Ladyship by the community was most obligingly receiv'd, & all content & Satisfaction appear'd in my Lady & family, She had all her Sences perfectly till about a year before She Dyed when her memory began to fail her & she grew perceptably weaker, Some months before her Death turn'd quite like a child, on Xmass eve she received all the holy rights from the hands of our Confessor whome she had allways made use off while she lived with us, affter which as she grew weaker & not able to fast, She obtain'd leave to communicate by way of *viaticum* from time to time, till the 2d of July following which was the last time she was judg'd capable of it; when She drew near her end Reverend Father Confessor[1] for her comfort was often with her in the Day time, & having Satt up two nights with her & She not Sencible to make use of a Confessor we sent for a Carme to release Father Confessor in the night, which night she gave 2 or 3 groans & expired, between Eleven & twelve in the 90th year of her Age. *Requiescat in pace*

The next morning affter the Convents mass we said the Comendations; She was kept 3 days all which time we took our half hours to pray by the corps as we do for our Religious, 2 & 2 reading Dierges for her Soul, all Soules night[2] affter Compline we all went into the great pant in our mantles with lighted candles in our hands, accompanyed the corps to the church where the Gentellmen of the Town ware expecting it, we Sung the Burial as we do for our Religious, She was buried in our Vault by her own Desire, in the first oven over Lady Lucy Herbert, her own Sister; The next day we sung a solemn Mass; on the 11th of November we said a long dierge and the next day we Sung the commendations in the choir, & a High mass follow'd, perform'd in musick by the Town musitians, our Reverend Father Confessor celebrated assisted with 2 deacons, the chief of the Town ware invited; the church & Seats there in ware **[p. 106]** intirely covered with black, a herse erected in the middle with Scutchions & all that is usual for one of her quality done by the undertakers:

---

1 Fr Gerard (Confessor 1723–79) was not entirely well himself.

2 All Souls' night, 1 November, when the Community said prayers for the departed following the Vespers for All Saints.

Tho her Ladyships living with us was an advantage so far as her giving us £500 for a mass to be said daily in our Church as may be seen in page 77 & for the iron railes of the *Sanctuarium*, & Some other things amounting to about £180 yet as her age & infirmities increased so did our expences having for near 2 years had the addition of an other woman to Sett up every night, whose Diet we found, as we did for the helps her Servants had for their washing & ironing, & for a year & a half left a Lay Sister wholy to be a help to her Ladyship & family, for the which & many other inconveniences, her Ladyship did not in any kind consider us, except paying some part of the coals they burnt, which by reason of the war ware double their usual price,[1] but as her Ladyship express so much Satisfaction in being with us, & the regard we had for her Sister our late Superiour, nothing was thought to much that we could do for her Self & family, therefore when She was in that Declining condition, & again at her death, our Reverend Mother very kindly told Mrs Delahoy'd (who was her Ladyships companion) & the 2 maid servants, that they ware welcome to Stay till a more convenient time for travelling, which at that time was very troublesome, by reason of the war & hard Season of the year, they readily accepted of the offer & staid, Mrs Delahoy'd 4 months, & the 2 maids 6 months, only 3 of which their Board was paid for, I promised her Ladyship to have a mass said on her anniversary day yearly & doubt not but my successors will continue the Same;

[p. 107]

1746

March the 1st Mrs Delahoy'd went from hence to Paris, mis Elizabeth Darell for Tourcoin, & mis Eddy Jernegan for Lille to learn french went with her;

Aprill the 25 my Lady Montagues 2 servants Mrs Martha Coleman & Mrs Catherin King went hence to England; now we are intirely without Boarders, much to the Satisfaction of the whole Community;

June the 2^d^ Sister Mary Alexia Tattlock's father leaving us at his death 5ll[2] for prayers, & he having given his Daughter a Sufficient fortune had she chose rather to be a nun than a lay Sister, we sung a Mass for him & each offer'd one Communion & the Cross prayers for 5 days;[3]

---

[1] The War of Austrian Succession led to much disruption of trade, causing price rises.

[2] 5 livres or pounds.

[3] Mary Alexia Tatlock (BA194) became a lay sister because she was unable to learn Latin. The dowry for a choir nun was much greater than for a lay sister. Her father was Thomas Tatlock of Lancashire.

June the 9th Corpus Christi Day, in time of the hours a message was Sent us by the Duke of York[1] (who the night before come to town), to Desire in place of a musick mass we would have only a low one which he would hear, accordingly at the end of the hours we Staid for his Royall highness who in about half an hour come, t'was most edifying to see with what Devotion he heard mass; he would admitt of no ceremony, not so much as to knell at the place prepared in the Sacristy for him, but knelt the whole time in the church, at the End of the mass he come into the Sacristy, & desired to see the whole Community, the Blessed Sacrament being exposed, he would not goe to the chapel gates for fear of causing distraction, we all went to the Sacristy door where his highness Spoke to us in a very familiar way and permitted us to kiss his hand, he would not come into the inclosure saying it would occation trouble & confusion, but like a private person recommended himself to our prayers & took leave;

September the 26 mis Lucy Pool and mis Frances Burrell ware cloath'd in the 19 year of their Age;[2]

[p. 108]

1747

February the 8th Mis Herbert went from hence to Gant, to be under the care of Mrs Collingwood, Sister to Lord Montague, who was appointed Guardian to Mis; She staid there 3 or 4 months, then to a french monastry at Paris, now we having none in our School but Mis Peggy Stanfield whose parents ware inhabitants of our town, we Sent her home to them till Such time as it pleased God to send us pentioners[3]

March the 14th Mis Eddy Jernegan come home from Lille;

Aprill the 5th Mis Margaret Tasburgh[4] having buried her father at Gant where she had lived with him Some time, resolved to follow her vocation to religion which she had had some years but was advised not to leave her father, he being in an ill state of health, he Dyed in february & in the aprill following she enter'd our inclosure to be religious, Lodged in the Apartment in the School and tabled in the father's house;

The same day Mis Peggy Stanfield return'd to our School;

Aprill the 29th Mis Margaret Tasburgh took the first habit and the name of Mary Margaret, in the 20th year of her age;

---

[1] The Duke of York was James III's second son, Henry Benedict Stuart (1725–1807), created Cardinal in July 1747. He had arrived in France to assist in preparations for the 1745 Jacobite invasion of England, remaining with the fleet in Dunkirk until after Culloden in 1746. He then joined the French fleet.

[2] Lucy Poole (BA158); Frances Burrell (BA039).

[3] Barbara Herbert, niece of Prioress Herbert; see also **[p. 102]** and Herbert family tree.

[4] Margaret Tasburgh (BA193). Her father was Francis Tasburgh of Bodney, Norfolk (d. Jan. 1747), who was buried at the English Benedictine convent, Ghent; see *Annals of the English Benedictines of Ghent* (East Bergholt: privately printed, 1898), Appendix The Third, p. 195.

September the 26th Sister Mary Margaret Tasburgh was cloathed;
October the 8th Sister Mary Alloisia Pool, & Sister Mary Magdalen Burrell made their holy profession

1748

february 17th Mis Mary[,] Usebia & Eliz: Pickerings ware received for convictrix's, the Elldest 11, the 2d 9, & the 3d 7 years of Age,[1] they ware Brought by their maid & a marchand of porto[2] where their parents are Settled, their maid was obliged to Stay till june, by reason of the war their was no free passage; **[p. 109]** May the 24th Mis Margaret Stanfield went home to her friends in Town; june the 5th Mademoiselle Lemettre was received for convictrix aged 16 her parents are inhabitants of Gant.

june the 28 Sister Mary Alexia's mother having left us at her Death ll 5 for prayers, we Sung a mass for her, & each offered one Communion & the Cross prayers for 5 days;[3]

August the 5th it pleased All God: to deprive us of Dear Sister Mary Joseph Lloyd[4] in whome we lost a perfect good Religious & Servicable member, her Death tho in manner Sudden, we have all reason to hope,was not unprovided, ^she^ being of a very pious Disposition from her infancy, & most of her devotions tended to that of begging & preparring for a happy Death; from her tender years shew'd a most humble complying temper, & of a more Sollide judgment than often appears in one of that age, which increasing with her years render'd her a very valuable member, tho allmighty God did not bless her with Good health, yet her fervour & Desire to Serve the Community carry'd her thro the most laborious offices, on the 2d of August She went to the kitchen, (she being Selleress) affter Vespers to prepare for Supper, & as she was speaking to one of the Lay Sisters, she put her hand to her head, & said Sweet Jesus, my head, She Sat down for 3 or 4 minutes, then Said She must goe a little way. one of the Lay Sisters would goe with her, & led her but before she could get to the kitchen door, her limbs fail'd her, the Lay Sister call'd for help as she could not hold her up, She never Spoke more, nor shew'd the least Sign of Sence but by her groaning express'd excesive pain, She was cary'd to the infirmary & had all help of Sirgions & Doctors but to no effect about 5 of the clock She received the holy Oyles, was put into bed, & fell into violent convultions all on one Side the other quite dead, the Doctors declared they had never Seen nor read her case, She continued so till the 4th at night when the convultions left her & her

---

1 Eusebia Pickering (1758–1810) BA156. Mary and Elizabeth did not profess.
2 Oporto, Portugal.
3 The name of Sister Mary Alexia Tatlock's mother is not currently known. Cross prayers: see Glossary.
4 Mary Joseph Lloyd (1726–48) BA129.

Strength failing, She expir'd on the 5 about 11 at noon, ^in the 39th year of her age, & 22d of her holy profession,^ She was buried on the 7th in the 2d row & 2d oven on the right hand; *Requiescat in pace.*

[p. 110] August the 7th Mis Loissia Lyttleton[1] was received for convictris aged 12 her mother being Dead who was a roman Catholick, she was in Danger of being bread up a protestant, all father & all his family being perverse ones, but Allmighty Gods providence was so great in her behalf as to raise her friends amongst Strangers the chief of which was my Lord Teynham, who promis'd her father in case he would let him choose the place of her education She Should be no longer upon his hands, which as soon as he consented to my Lord Sent her here with Mr James Darell;[2]

August the 14th Mis More niece to Mr Gifford of Chillington was received for Convictrix aged 16[3]

August the 21 Mis Ellizabeth Darell come home to us from Tourcoin,

August the 29th Sister Mary Teresa Jernegan was taken of from the office of Subprioress, & Sister Stanislaus Gage chosen in her place;[4]

August the 31 Mis Annastatia Tichbourn ag'd 17 Mis Henrietta Havers aged 13 & Mis Catharin Bedingfield aged 11 ware all received for convictrix's[5]

September the 14th Mis Edwardina Jernegan took the Scollars habit & the name of Francis Joseph aged 16[6]

October the 8th Sister Mary Margaret Tasburgh made her holy profession;[7]

November the 20th Mr Gerard our Reverend Father Confessor[8] Celebrated his half Jubily of living with us, his handsome way of proceeding was most kindly taken by the whole community, who to Shew their esteem of & value for him, made him presants out of their little Spending mony, we had musick mass, which he Sung himself, but as he desir'd it might be kept ^as^ private as possible we had no Deacons nor the **[p. 111]** *Te Deum* Sung in musick as we had Design'd, he Desired rather to have it Sung by the Community which was done at the end of mass & the Bell rung the whole time, the church was adorn'd the Same as on the chief

1 Miss Lyttleton was the daughter of Launcelot Lyttleton of Lichfield. The family relationship between the Lyttletons and Lord Teynham has not been firmly established. However links existed and a marriage was later arranged between his son Francis and Mary Lyttleton of Lichfield.

2 Probably Fr James Darell SJ (1707–85), brother of Rev. Mother Mary Darell (BA071). Elizabeth Darell (below) was their sister.

3 Miss More was Elizabeth More, who later professed as Mary Augustina More (1753–1807) BA145; see frontispiece portrait. Her parents were Thomas More of Barnburgh Hall, Yorkshire, and Catherine Giffard.

4 Mary Teresa Jerningham (BA118); Stanislaus Gage (BA085).

5 None of these three proceded to profession.

6 Edwardina Jerningham, in religion Francis Joseph (BA121).

7 Margaret Tasburgh (BA193).

8 Fr Caryl Gerard, Confessor 1723–79; Anstruther 4, p. 110.

feasts of the year that day being confession day we only recreated till Silence in the affternoon on the monday following he gave a handsome recreation, Breakfast, dinner, & Supper, with a bottle of wine at each ones place, choice of either good old french Clarett, or Spanish wine, & the afternoon, Coffey & tea for all, & affter Compline Burnt wine & Buisquits, for which the whole community assembled at 8 a clock in the refectory, & Sat up till 9 or 10 a clock much obliged with his Reverences kindness, & he much pleased in the company of the Community the greatest part of which he had Seen profess'd;

December the 10 M[is] Anastatia Tichbourn went to a flemish monastry at ostend;

1749

March the 6 M[is] More went to l'Abbey de Pretz to learn French;[1]

March the 15th Sister Elizabeth Moody Departed this life in the 38th year of her age & 15th of her holy profession,[2] She was ever laborious & Servicable of a cheerfull temper, yet Soon moved to anger which so much took place of reason as to bury the Talents God had given her, & made her less beloved amongst her companions, about 3 years before her Death, She fell into a consumption, after being confin'd to the infirmary some few months her Strength much failing the Doctor order'd her the *viaticum* on the 24th of february on the 9th of march the holy Oyles, & Dy'd on the 15th most peacably & happily. *Requiescat in pace*;

May the 24 M[is] Elizabeth Darell went for England to her friends,

june the 9th M[is] Catharin Darell Daughter to Mr Georg Darell of Scottney was received for convictrix aged 12,[3]

July the 5th M[is] Molly Smithson Daughter to Mr Smithson apothycary of London was received for convictrix aged 12;[4]

[p. 112] September the 2[d] Sister Frances Joseph Jernegan was cloathed;[5]

October 8th Sister Mary Teresa Jernegan celebrated her whole jubilee of 50 years in Religion[6]

November the 11 our Dear Sister Dorothy Stanley Departed this life in the 67th Year of her age & 49th of her holy profession,[7] She come here at

---

[1] Abbaye des Pres de Douai was a Cistercian community of nuns who had a well-known boarding school. They fled to England at the French Revolution. See Pierre A. Plouvain, *Souvenirs à l'usage des habitans de Douai, ou notes pour servir à l'histoire* (Douai, 1822), pp. 59–61.

[2] Elizabeth Moody, lay sister (1734–49) BA143.

[3] Catherine Darell later professed as Mary Olivia (1754–1802) BA070.

[4] There were a number of London apothecaries in the Smithson family in the eighteenth century.

[5] Francis Joseph Jerningham (BA121).

[6] Mary Teresa Jerningham (BA118) professed on 8 October 1699.

[7] Dorothy Stanley, in religion Mary Xaveria (1700–49) BA183.

the Age of 13 at which time She even Shew'd a genious for management in household affairs which increased with her years & render'd her most Servicable to our Community in the office of procuratrice which She had been imploy'd in for 19 years, She was ever a most fervorous, good religious, her zeal for the choir was Such that She would never exempt her Self from the Divine office but when the Affairs of her office could not possibly be cary'd on without her which time allways Seem'd long till she could return again, She had a good voice & had been chantress several years, She would often Say of the young people coming on, that She could wink at most faults in them provided they had a zeal for the choir; She was the last of 5 Sisters all profess'd in the house, She ever bore a greatfull remembrance of the favour God had done her in calling her to Religion having a true esteem of her vocation; She had for some years been troubled with a Soar leg which from time to time, confined her wholy to the infirmary & of which She had suffer'd much for Some months before she Dyed; on friday the 7th She complain'd she was ill all over, She was put to bed with a Shaking fit like an ague, the next day the Doctor come, who aprehended her illness mortall, She having Symthoms of Lethargy, her Speech & Sences failed, all remidies ware apply'd by the Sirgion to make her leg run which was dry'd up (& twas thought the humour fluwe upwards which occation'd her illness) but took no **[p. 113]** Effect, on the 9th she received the holy Oyles, on the 10 Shewing Some Signs of Sences she was judg'd Capable of receiving the *viaticum*, which she did with great devotion & Dy'd on the 11, She being very fatt & no long illness to purge her She remain'd with a coulour & warm the next day which made some think She was not Dead, therefore for greater Satisfaction Reverend Mother order'd She Should be kept a Day longer than usual, She was buried on the 14th. *Requiescat in pace*

November the 20 our Convent Sisters assembled to choose a procuratrix, Sister Mary Michael Sykes was chosen[1]

1750

January the 25 Departed this life our Dear Sister Victoria Cannyng on the 79th year of her age & 59th of her holy profession,[2] She had been very Servicable in many offices, particularly in the case of the Linnen Habitt for 20 years She was of a cheerfull temper, which made her agreeable & beloved by all her beheaviour when young was more than ordinary giddy & odd yet not so as to be guilty of any Essential fault which could hinder her profession She ever Seem'd Sencible of the favour God had done her in calling her to religion, & apply'd her Self Seriously to her Spiritual duties, particularly in preparing for the Sacrament, She had

---

1 Mary Michael Sykes (BA189).
2 Elizabeth Victoria Canning (1691–1750) BA044.

been some time confin'd to the infirmary, occation'd by a weakness all on one side by a fit of the palsy; notwithstanding She would imploy her time in the common work for which She allways had a great zeal, Some months before She Dy'd She had a little return of the palsy which went on weakening her so much that in December She was ordain'd the *viaticum*, the January following the Doctor finding her fervourish & much weaker with an oppression upon her breast she received the holy Oyles & *viaticum* again, the next day which was the 25 She render'd up her Soul between 11 & 12 at night. *Requiescat in pace*

February the 19 Mis Elizabeth Greenwell Daughter to an upholsterer in London was received for convictrix aged about 11 **[p. 114]** Aprill the 2^d^ Mademoiselle Van Zullen Daughter to the post master of our town was received for convictrix;

June the 6th Mis Barbara Clavering Sister to Mr Clavering of Callaly was received for convictrix aged 12;[1]

Mr Percy Markham having sent ten pounds for Prayers for his Sister Pool's Soul, we Sung mass for her, & Reverend [Mother] in chapter order'd each one to offer one Communion & the Cross prayers for 5 days for her Soul;[2]

July 18th Mis Molly Huddleston Daughter to Mr Huddleston of Saus[t] on was received for convictrix aged 12;[3]

November the 9th Mademoisell Lemetter return'd home to her friends at Gant;

1751

January the 2^d^ Sister Mary Michael Sykes was taken off from the procuratrixship, & Sister Ann Teresa Jernegan chosen in her place;[4]

March the 1st Mis Ann Ancker one of our town was received convictrix,

Aprill Sister Lucy Smithson[5] being in an ill state of health & fearing Death would deprive her of the indulgence granted for celebrating the whole jubily, obtain'd leave of my Lord Bishop to take in her year of noviship, which he consenting to She kept it on her profession day the 23^d^ of Aprill the 49 year of her profession, which being uncommon amongst us was not liked;

£5 being given us for prayers for Mis Anastatia Tichbourns Soul we Sung Mass for her & each was order'd to Say the Cross prayers for 5 days for her,

---

1 Barbara Clavering later professed as Mary Gertrude (1757–94) BA057.

2 Cross prayers: see Glossary.

3 Mary (Molly) was the daughter of Richard Huddleston of Sawston (1716–60) and his wife, Jane Belchier. She later married Richard Bostock.

4 Mary Michael Sykes (BA189). Ann Teresa Jerningham (BA120).

5 Lucy Smithson (BA177).

May the 7th Mis Havers come from the french house

June the 30th Mis Huddleston went for England with her papa & mama who come over to bring their Sons to St Omers & take Mis [*name missing*] home[1]

[p. 115] August the 2d Miss Loisia Littleton went to Doway to learn french

August the 14th Miss Bedingfield come from Lille

August the 20 Miss Havers, Mis Bedingfield and Mis Molly Smithson went of England

October the 10th Miss Barbara Riddle was received for convictrix aged 19

November the 8th Miss Barbara Riddle went to L'Abbey de Pretz to learn french

November the 12th the two ^Sisters^ Mis Briget & Mis Lucy Ferges ware received for convictrix's Miss Brigit 13 & Miss Lucy 11 years of Age, they are of irish parents born in the west indies;[2]

November the 30th Miss Eliz Wayett was received for convictrix aged 15 her parents are trade people of London all prodestants

1752

January the 21 Miss Molly Yates was received for convictrix aged 12 She goes by the name of mousley on account her parents are protestants & not willing it should be known where she is

May the 25 Miss Greenwell went for England with her father;

May the 27th Miss Olivia Darell Daughter to Mr Darell of Cailhill was received for convictrix Aged 9

May the 29th Sister Francis Joseph Jernegan made her holy profession;[3]

june the 14th Miss Molly Pickering, Miss Kitty Darell, & Miss Waylett went to learn french, Miss Pick[ering]: & Miss Darell to Lille, & Miss Waylett to Tourcoin;

june the 30th Miss Ann Ancker went home to her friends in Town;

july the 8th Miss Molly more having perfected herself in the french toungue at L'Abbey de Pretz,[4] went into England to Settle her affairs in order to return to Settle with us, arived on the 8th & brought her **[p. 116]** 2 Couzens Miss Molly & Miss Nanny Watertons who the Same day we

1 Mary Huddleston had three brothers – Ferdinand, Thomas and Richard – who all attended the Jesuit College at St Omer.

2 Bridget and Lucy Fergus were daughters of Patrick and Lucy Fergus and granddaughters of James Farril. Bridget (or Brigitta) later professed as Mary Monica Teresa (1757–64) BA078. They were born on the island of Montserrat.

3 Francis Joseph Jerningham (BA121).

4 Abbaye des Pres de Douai: see **[p. 151]**.

received as convictrix's & M[iss] more[1] in order to take the habit which with great fervour She Desired might be in a very Short time, her Elldest Brother accompanied her to Bruges Stay'd a few days to See his Sister in the habit then went to Watten to be a Jesuit;[2]

july the 10th M[iss] More took the habit & the name of Mary Augustin;

August the 17th M[iss] Ann Waterton went to L'Abbey de Pretz to learn french, her Elldest Sister M[iss] Molly being of a weak constitution & in an ill State of health chose to Stay the Winter here;

October: the 8th M[iss] Charlot Blundel Daughter to Mr Blundel of ince, come here with her Elldest Brother, her design is to be religious but could not obtain that leave of her Father till she had been some time as pentioner, on the Same day we received her as convictrix aged 20[3]

October the 20 M[iss] Molly Waterton was taken ill about 3 in the afternoon of a violent cholick, all remidies ware used but in vain any further than from time to time gave her a little ease but could not wholy remove the pain, 3 Satt up with her the whole night about 7 the next morning the Doctor found her so weak that he order'd her the *viaticum* but said there was no Such pressing danger as to give her the holy Oyles unless he found her worse about one in the Affternoon when he would come with out fail, he was not gone a quarter of an hour before when those who watch'd by her found a great change in her countenance, they Spoke to her & found she fallter'd in her speech, they call'd Father Confessor who had only time to give her the last absolution before she expired without **[p. 117]** the least Struggle about 8 of the clock on the 21st of October: *Requiescat in pace*; her Short illness & Death was no less concern than Surprize to the whole Community, She being of a sweet temper, pious & extraordinary good Sence, She seem'd quite happy here, & grew so much better in health that She was quite Surprized at her self Saying She had never remember'd to enjoy Such; She was beloved by the whole house[.] as Soon as She was Dead we Said the commendations for her, on the 23d she was buried in our vault, we Sung mass & the burying & rung our bell the 3 hours the Same as for our Religious;

December the 3d Sister Mary Augustine more was cloathed;[4]

---

1 Elizabeth More, in religion Mary Augustina (1753–1807) BA145, Procuratrix 1766; Prioress 1766–1807. The Misses Waterton were cousins through the marriage of Mary More (b. 1703, daughter of Cresacre More) to Charles Waterton of Walton Hall in 1733. They had three daughters, Mary, Anne and Catherine. Anne later married one of the Irish Daly family of Demerara, Guyana and Montserrat: see **[p. 206]**.

2 Two of Elizabeth More's brothers became Jesuits. Thomas was the eldest (1722–95); he went to Watten in November 1752. See Wood, pp. 250–3, 265; Holt, pp. 169–70.

3 Charlotte Blundell, in religion Mary Joseph (1754–1813) BA027.

4 Mary Augustina More (BA145).

1753

January the 19th M[iss] Kitty Darell come from Lille;[1]

February the 9th M[rs] Blundell of ince the widdow having left us £5 sterling for prayers, we Sung mass for her; & each was ordain'd to Say a Short Dierge a pair of beads & offer one communion for her;

March the 25th Lady Stourton[2] Sent £10 Sterling: for prayers for the Soul of Lord Stourton her Spouse, we Sung mass for him, & each was ordain'd to hear 3 masses, offer one communion, & the cross prayers 5 days for him;

Aprill the 21 & Easter Eve, M[iss] Charlot Blundell, & M[iss] Cath: Darell took the Schollar's Habit, M[iss] Blundell the name of Mary Joseph, & M[iss] Darell that of Mary olivia,

May the 7th M[iss] Barbara Clavering went to the Garden of our Lady at S[t] Omers to learn French;[3]

june the 5th M[iss] Pickering & M[iss] Waylet come home;[4] **[p. 118]** June the 21st Lord & Lady Teynham brought their 2 daughters for pentioners, M[iss] Kitty in the Eleventh year of her age and M[iss] Winy in the tenth of her age; at the same time his Lordship also brought M[iss] Alsworth for pentioner she is daughter to Mr John Alsworth, a tennant of Lord Teynhams aged about 10.[5]

The 26th it pleased God to take out of this life our most worthy Lord Bishop John Baptist de Castilon;[6] tho no prayers was ordain'd for his Lordship our Reverend Mother thought it our duty to sing a Mass for him the first free day which was done, & the Prayer at gracc said 8 days for him. *Requiescat in pace.*

july the 20th M[iss] Molly Pickering return'd to her friends at Oporta, with her Father by the way of England.[7]

[*Two lines crossed through: illeg.*]

August the 27th M[iss] Elizabeth Waylet took the Schollars habit and the name of Eliz: Joseph,[8] her parents of London, sent her with no thought of Religion, but to be out of the Dangers that young peopel are offten

---

1 Kitty (Catherine) Darell professed in October 1754, taking the name Mary Olivia (BA070).

2 Lady Stourton, née Catherine Walmesley (1697–1785), widow of Lord Petre, married Charles Stourton, 15th Baron Stourton (d. 1753). There were no children of the marriage.

3 The Ecole du Jardin de Nôtre-Dame was founded by Bishop Blaise in 1615 for poor girls to teach reading, writing, sewing and spinning. Later a boarding house was added. See Jean Derheims, *Histoire de la ville de St Omer* (St Omer, 1843), p. 636.

4 See June 1752, **[p. 115]**.

5 Mary Catherine and Winifred Roper were the daughters of Henry Roper, 10th Baron Teynham (d. 1781) and his wife, Catharine Powell of Sandford (d. 1765). Winifred Roper joined the Sepulchrines at Liège (1770–96) LS186.

6 Jan-Baptist de Castillon, Bishop of Bruges 1743–53.

7 Miss Pickering had grown up in Oporto, where her father was a merchant. See **[p. 108]**.

8 Elsewhere in the Chronicle she appears as Elizabeth Willeck (BA220), clothed and left in 1654.

exposed to in the world when to much liberty is given them of choosing their companions, She come with no dislike to the place but seemingly with a resolution of returning back in the same persuation she was when she come, but Gods providence was so great over her that she had not been 3 months here when she felt exceeding trouble and uneasiness of mind about Religion, which in a short time she declared to her mis-stress, was instructed and taken into the Church by our Reverend **[p. 119]** Father Confessor, which her parents ware not avers'd to saying it did not depend upon the Religion but the leading a good life to save the soul; Soon affter her conversion she had a great desire to be a religious which increased daily so much that she could injoy no peace. At last by her frequent impertunity, our Community was moved with compassion, and knowing the danger she was into of being forced to Church if she went to England by her Father who tho at first was easy about what Religion she was of, now so changed as to shew a great dislike to it and to her for the change, and more when he understood she had a mind to be fix'd in a religious state which for some time he absulutly refused his consent to, all which consider'd we consented to take her, looking upon it the greatest of charities to contribute to the saving a soul, as in all appearance, this was she has no fortune to recommended her, only £50 sterling which some friends procured her, notwithstanding we hope the good Dispositions that appears in her & her seeming desire to serve the Community will supply for the want of fortune.

August the 29 Mademoiselle Kemp aged 19 was received for convictrix her parents are of Ostend.

September the 14th the 2 Mesdemoiselles van de Ker ware received for convictrixes one aged 15 the other 13 their parents are of Dunquerque.

October 4th Sister Mary Joseph Blundell and Sister Cath: Mary Olivia Darell ware cloathed.[1] December the 4th Sister Mary Augustina More made her holy profession.[2]

[p. 120] December 13 Sister Lucy Smithson departed this life in the 71 year of her age and 51 of her holy profession;[3] She had for several years been in a weak declining state of health, but not wholy confin'd to the infirmary till about a week before her Death, when she found herself much weaker, but no appearance of presant Death till the Day before she dyed, She then allter'd so much that all persuations ware used to make her receive her *viaticum* which the Doctor had order'd 3 days before on account of her great weakness, cough, & shortness of breath, but as she was still able to walk about, she thought the more mild weather would recover her again, therefor would deffer it a while longer, but a short

1 Mary Joseph Blundell (BA027); Mary Olivia Darell (BA070).
2 Mary Augustina More (BA145).
3 Lucy Smithson (1702–53) BA177.

time made appear that there was no hopes of her recovery for on the 12th she could no longer help herself, & the next morning both the *Viaticum* & holy oyles & dyed peacably about 9 in the morning; she was ever zealous for all Religious observances, had ever a great esteem & value for her Religious vocation, She suffer'd much by her unhappy violent temper & from which she mett with many occations of humiliation She was sencible of it & sometimes would say ["]happy those of a good temper, they know not what I have to suffer from mine["] she was but weak in judgment & at the same time had so good an oppinion of it that she thought all weak but herself, which made her on many occations so stiff even with divines that she got little good by the numbers she spoke too. Superiours ware forced to yield to her in what they could to keep her in moderation, all which we may hope did not appear so bad in Gods sight as to those she lived with & as it was not only others that suffered by her unhappy **[p. 121]** buisy temper, but no doubt herself greatly, we may hope that made some atonement & that she now enjoys the reward of her suffering life, she render'd up her soul as is said above on the 13th & was buried on the 15th. *Requiescat in pace*

1754

January the 29th Sister Eliz: Joseph Waylet was cloathed.[1]

Aprill the [*blank*] Miss Barbara Lyttleton, Sister to Miss Loisia Lyttleton mention'd in the year 1748 was receiv'd for convictrix aged 7.

May the 4th Miss Olivia Darell went to Dunquerque by her Fathers orders to meet him & her Mama who cary'd her to the Ursulines at Lille.[2]

May the 7th Miss Barbara Clavering come from the french house at St Omers.

june the 1st Miss Charlot Bond Sister to Sir Charles Bond was received for convictrix, aged about 22 she was newly converted & come to be more settled in the true Religion;[3]

june the [*blank*] Miss Cath: Clavering come to make her Sister a visit in her way to England, leave was obtain'd for her to come into the inclosure for the time she stay'd which was about a fortnight;

August 16th Miss Barbara Clavering went to Bethania to learn ~~french~~ flemish;[4]

August 29th Mademoiselle Kemp went home to her friends at ostend.

---

1 Elizabeth Willeck (BA220).

2 Olivia Darell was possibly Olivia who entered the Benedictines at Cambrai in 1760, CB051: see **[p. 115]**. A number of English girls went to Ursuline convents to learn French in this period.

3 Sir Charles Bond (1734–67), 4th Baronet of Peckham, had an unnamed sister who died unmarried in 1760. She left the convent in 1756; see **[p. 125]**.

4 Barbara Clavering (BA057): she later translated the 'Eight-Day Exercise' from Flemish. Bethania was the convent adjacent to Nazareth: see Glossary and map.

September the 8th Sister Eliz: Joseph Waylet having pass'd about 7 months of her noviship very much to the satisfaction of the Community, with cheerfullness & semingly all ease of mind, exact in every religious duty; her brother made her a visit,[1] pretended he come for the pleasure of seeing his Sister so happy as she declar'd to all her friends she was, particulary in one occation, when some **[p. 122]** of her friends & relations who ware all prodestants come to see her & examin if she realy was happy & thought she should remain so in this state of life, she answer'd them with great resolution that nothing could make her happyer that if we turn'd her out she would lye & dye at the door which answer so satisfy'd them that they return'd home full of joy, convinced from her own mouth she was that happy creature they had heard & assured her father & mother as much; However her Brother ^was^ not of the oppinion that anyone shut up & seperated from the world could be so therefore resolved to use all means to compass his design & as we heard affterwards that at his first coming to town at the inn where he lodg'd he said he had a Sister in a monastry but he was resolved to get her out & to cary on his design the better pretended to be much struck with seeing the practice of our Religion appear'd thoughtfull & desired to be instructed & to make the best use of the time he had to stay in these countrys towards being converted the which he would execute as soon as he got to England, whether he realy was touch'd or talk'd so to gain more credit the easier to carry on his design he cant best tell, 'tis certain when he saw his Sister so changed & taken the resolution to return to England, he either felt or pretended the deepest affliction & in the greatest passion of tears protested to our Reverend Mother[2] that he repented he had taken the journey since it had made so great a change in his Sister for he own'd he found her quite happy but could not say she was so now, as indeed appear'd for she began to look like one loosing their sences, & what before was most to be admir'd in her to witt a cheerfull, easy temper changed into a sullen sourness **[p. 123]** could hardly give a civil answer when Spoke too, none immagin'd what she had in her head the eve of our Ladys Nativity then she confided to one or 2 of her chief friends that she had taken the resolution to put of the habit & goe with her Brother to England in a day or two, they told her 'twas absolutely necessary to acquaint Reverend Mother and her misstress[3] with her design, which she seem'd to have some difficulty in, but however the next day which was our Ladys Nattivity[4] she told her misstress who acquainted Reverend Mother with it[.] she sent for the Novice who had little to say but that she understood by his Brother that her Father was so unhappy with her change & settleing in Religion

[1] Elizabeth Willeck's brother has not been identified.
[2] Reverend Mother in 1754 was Mary Darell (BA071).
[3] 'Her misstress' refers here to the Novice Mistress.
[4] The feast of the Nativity of Our Lady is celebrated on 8 September.

that 'twas likely to be his death which to hear would make her for ever miserable, therefore was resolved to goe to him with her Brother who was to set out in a day or two, our Reverend Mother spoke to her in a kind manner, representing to her the danger she was putting herself in of leaving also the true Religion by this large step; she still insisted upon going with her Brother, to which our Reverend Mother answer'd she would no ways goe about to persuade her to stay longer than could get an answer from her parents when & where to send her, till then she should not positively goe out of the house, but that she might put off the habit & goe to the School pentioner as before, at which answer she seem'd much disapointed & displeased & beg'd her change might not be known till she was sure when to goe, as soon as we found it was whisper'd about even in the town Reverend Mother order'd her to take off her habit & goe to the School which she did on St Mathew's eve[1] in her cell & went with the misstress of the School amongst the pentioners very gay, Shew'd a dread of any thing being spoke or read for fear of being touch'd, thus that poor creture went on till the 16th of october: when Captain Burchet by her parents orders come for her, She rejoiced to hear the news that he was come & went out of the house without shewing the least concern for any one tho she had been so kindly used.

[p. 123] [*sic*] October the 15th Miss Bridget Fergus went to the Ursulines to learn french.

1755

April the 12th Miss Mary Farrill & Miss Ann Fergus ware received for convictrix's, Miss Farrill aged 15 & Miss Ann Fergus 12.[2]

April the 16th Miss Bridget Fergus returned from Lille.[3]

May the 31 Miss Barbara Clavering return'd home from the Magdalens.

july the 9th Miss Lucy Fergus went to Lille to learn french.

july the 26th Miss Bridget Fergus took the habit & name of monica.

july the 29th Miss Christina & her Sister Molly Stuart ware received for convictrix's Miss Christina aged 13 & Miss Molly 12 they are nieces to Lord Traquair in Scottland;[4]

july the 30th Miss Elizabeth Freeman grandaughter to Mr Smithson apothycary in London was received for convictrix aged 12,[5]

August the 11 Miss Farrill went to Lille to learn french.

---

[1] The feast of St Matthew is celebrated on 21 September.

[2] Mary Farrell, in religion Teresa Clare (1758–1820) BA077, School Mistress in 1783.

[3] Brigitta Fergus, in religion Mary Monica Teresa (BA078).

[4] Christina and Molly Stewart were the daughters of John Stewart and Christiana Weir, née Anstruther (d. 1771). Lord Traquair inherited the Traquair title in 1764 from his brother Charles, 5th Earl of Traquair, who died without heirs.

[5] Bernard Smithson was an apothecary in London.

August the 11th Mademoisell Pelechy daughter to the Barron Pelechy of our town was received for a convictrix.

August the 13th Miss Usebia & Miss Betty Pickering return'd from Lille.

August the 27th Miss Barbara Clavering took the habit & name of Sister Mary Gertrud.[1]

September the 8th Miss Catherine Roper & Miss Nanny Alsworth went to England.

December the 11th Mademoiselle de Ghendt was received for convictrix. She is one of Gand.

1756

January the 6th Ann Fergeson took the habit for a lay-Sister & the name of Martha,[2] She was one in whom Gods providence appear'd very particular, her father ^& mother Scotch & her Father^ was a soldiar in the English service which brought him into these countrys in the war, this girl **[p. 124]** sometimes runing to the Churches & offten to our monastry was moved with such a desire to know & be of the true faith that she would frequently say (tho but a child for she was then but about 6 years old) I'll be a Catholick, I'll be a nun; in a short time the Regiment in which her Father was, was call'd up further in the country, Lady montague who then boarded with us, offer'd the girls mother to take care of her for which the Mother was very greatfull & pleased, the girl was put to a carefull woman here in town, Lady montague allowing sufficient for her meantenance & learning, but, when her mother came back in her way to England, she demanded her daughter only for 2 hours which was granted her, when she had her would not part with her & resolved to cary her to England to breed her up a prodestant, which the girl resisted as far as she could, but her mother being resolute, she could find no means to escape but by runing away to a poor woman in the neighbourhood for shellter who kept her private till her mother was gone to England then Lady montague gave a sufficient maintinance till she became of an age to get her bread, as soon as able to be of service to us, we took her as a servant which she remain'd about 6 years when by her great importunity, & the Community well satisfyed with her behaviour and good dispositions she was admitted to the habit on the first of January aged 19.

February the 5th Sisters Monica Fergus & Sister Gertrude Clavering ware cloath'd.

february the 23d Sister Angella Huddleston departed this life,[3] for 3 years she had been confin'd to the infirmary with a weakness & decay she was ever a pious exact good Religious, zealous for the choir service, & had

---

1 Barbara Clavering (BA057).

2 Ann Fergusson (1757–1802) BA079.

3 Angela Huddleston (1695–1756) Procuratrix 1723–30, BA112.

given great satisfaction in the most important **[p. 125]** offi^c^es of the house, these 3 last years of her life she in a particular manner prepar'd herself for death, about a year before her death she fell into a Dropsy with which she suffer'd greatly & with most edifying patience. on the 23d about the half hour affter 4 in the morning, beging herself for absolution (having her perfect senses) to the last moment she expired in the 78 year of her age & 61 of her holy profession she was bury'd on the 25th. *Requiescat in pace.*

February the 25th Miss Lucy Fergus & Miss Farrill return'd from Lille.[1]

March the 4th Miss Lucy Fergus went to her friends in England.

March the 10th Sister Justina Huddleston was chosen arcaria[2] in place of her Aunt Angella who had that office from the year 1733 till her death.

May the 11th Miss Peleche went for some weeks to her father in town.

june the 2d Miss Bond went to England.

june the 7th Sister Teresa Augustin Newland was couch'd by a famous occolist of france.[3] She had had for some years cartracts upon both eyes, which growing worse and worse, she become so blind as not able to see her way about the house. a Lady in our town lying under the same misfortune sent for the occolist, which our Community being inform'd of was willing to be at the expense for the recovery of Sister Teresa eyes out of charity to her & hopes of a servisable member we paid ten guineas in specie & hope the success will prove to our wish.

the 7th Catherine Forshaw was received a servant on tryal for a lay Sister, recommended by Miss Blundell of Ince[4]

[p. 126] june the 25th Prince Charles, Brother to the Emperor & whose representative he is at his court at Brussells, come to town with his Sister Charlot Abbess of Remiremont,[5] they with all their attendants ware lodged at the Bishop's palace all came one morning about 9 of the clock to see our Church. the noise, their number & great retinue were such as frightened the Carme who was just going to begin Mass so much that the server was obliged to tell him who it was, no less was we in the Choir surprized, having had no notice given of their coming; they soon went

---

1 Mary Farrell professed in 1758 (BA077).

2 Arcaria: see Glossary. Mary Justina Huddleston (1727–87) BA113. Angela Huddleston (1695–1756) BA112.

3 Teresa Austin Newlin (BA147). Couching was an ancient technique performed by specialists in an attempt to cure cataracts.

4 Catharina Forshaw, in religion Joachim, lay sister (1759–1821) BA083. The Blundell family, associated with two properties in Lancashire (Little Crosby and Ince Blundell), were strong supporters of the English convents during the exile period.

5 Prince Charles Alexander of Lorraine (1712–80) governed the Austrian Netherlands on behalf of his brother. His sister, Princess Anne Charlotte of Lorraine (1714–73), became Abbess of Remiremont in 1738, Mons in 1754, Thorn in 1756 and Essen in 1757, living externally while she held office. After her brother was widowed she became influential in court politics in Brussels.

away as we thought & hoped, for good; but in time of our dinner my Lord Bishop[1] come & sent to the Refectory to our Reverend Mother word that her Royall Highness was coming with him to see our inclosure, that he would stay in the parlour till she come to conduct her in accordingly in about a quarter of an hour her Royall Highness with my Lord Bishop, the Grand Maitre and several Ladys of her court enter'd. her Highness behaved very courtiously, at her first entrance our Reverend Mother asked the Honour to kiss her hand, which she immediatly permitted as also to Subprioress who accompanied Reverend Mother they seem pleased, & went away in about half an hours time & I as much when they ware gone:

July the 5th Mademoiselle de Ghendt went home to her friends at Gant.

july the 18th Miss Freeman went to Dixmieu to learn french.

july 18th Mademoiselle Pielegie returned to us again.

August the 7th Sister Cecily Pickering departed her life.[2] She was recommended to us by Mrs Gastalldi for a woman of good sense, a perfect musician & in case she took to **[p. 127]** Religion might prove of great service & in all appearance at her fathers death would have the fortune of the house. She was received for convictrix[3] affter some time that she had been in the School, she declar'd her mind to be Religious & was admitted to the first Habit which affter about 4 months she quitted to goe to England as it was said to settle her affairs, but as the community ware rather inclin'd to think she had changed her mind was not desiorous to receive her again though she beg'd it when she had been in England above half a year, & very much advised to goe to another house by our Reverend Mother[.] but she persisting in her desire she was received again, but not to the habit till she had been some time in the School, from that time forward she behaved to the satisfaction of the Community and prov'd as servicable as her health would permit, of a peaceable quiet temper rather inclin'd to malencholy; & want of good health made all Religious duties appear hard to her notwithstanding being very pious would do as far as she was able; She was a perfect mistress at the Organ which she had learn'd from 7 or 8 years old, & had so fine a hand that the greatest massters had a pleasure to hear her play. She suffer'd extreamly with a cancer in her breast about a year and half before her Death she complain'd, of a pain in her breast & found there a lump which startled her, her Mother & Aunt having dy'd of that illness. She told one of our Religious she feared it was so, her mothers having begun in the same manner; the Surgion was sent for who **[p. 128]** imediatly judged it to be so, in a short time it sprede all over her body swelling out in great lumps, she suffered a great deal & wore away to skin & bone,

---

[1] The Bishop of Bruges in 1756 was Jan-Robert Caimo, Bishop 1754–75.

[2] Cicily Pickering (1747–56) BA155.

[3] The use of the term 'convictrix' here suggests that she came to the convent with a view to trying out the religious life.

about a week before she dy'd her breast broke, attended with a fever soon caryed her off, on the 5th she received all the last Sacraments & on the 7th dy'd. She was buried in our churchyard, her disease being so inveterate, the Surgion & Doctor was of oppinion t'was not safe to keep her body above ground longer than the next morning, therefore as soon as the office was out the next morning we went down to the great Pant (where the corps was placed ready) & conducted it to the churchyard, singing the *Subvenite* as usual & at the grave we sung *in paradisa &c*[1] in the afternoon we said the Dierge & the next morning the ceremonies & Mass. *Requiescat in pace*

September the 17th Miss Gifford, Daughter to Sir John Gifford[2] come here with a design to board with us till some affairs she had in France ware finish'd, but finding we took no boarders she went to Spermalle[3] that she might be near us, retaining a vast affection to the house where she had been bred from the age of 4 years till 14 or 15.

Miss Pelechy returned home to her Father.

october the 1st Miss Molly Stuart went to the Ursulines to learn french.

october the 15th Sister Ann Teresa Jernegan being in an ill state of health & no longer able to do the office of procuratrix was taken off & Sister Mary Catherine Willis chosen in her place;[4]

october the 26th Sister Ann Gladin departed this life.[5] She was servant to Mrs Sykes who she served here till her Death, she was pious but not of a strong constitution, on which account Mrs Sykes left at her Death £60 sterling the intrest of which she was to have the use of for little necessaries, & at her death to the Community.[6] She was dispensed with from Baker & Cook, not having strength for it, she was very **[p. 129]** handy about the sick & at her needle. On the 19th she found herself much out of order, which appeared like a great cold, towards the evening she complained of an inward trembling & a violent pain in her head, the Doctor being then in the house felt her pulse & said she had a high fever, he ordered that was proper to swett her, she was immediately put to bed & grew worse & worse. The next day the Doctor declar'd it the scarlet fever which took so much to her head & throat that she was not capable of receiving the *viaticum* but on the 24 received the holy oyles & on the 26th expired about ten in the morning in the 47th of her age & 14th of her holy profession, as the Doctor declar'd it dangerous to keep

---

1 The *Subvenite* begs the saints of God to come to the assistance of the dead soul. *In paradisum* prays for angels to lead the soul into paradise.

2 Mary Anne Gifford (1706–59), daughter of Sir John Clifford, Baronet (d. 1707) and Catherine Middleton (1685–1763). See also **[pp. 140–2]** and vol. 1, **[pp. 283–4]**.

3 Spermalie, a Cistercian monastery for women situated immediately behind Nazareth.

4 Ann Teresa Jerningham (BA120); Mary Catherine Willis (BA221).

5 Ann Gladin, lay sister (1742–56) BA087.

6 For other benefactions of Mrs Sykes, see **[pp. 19, 53–5, 66, 86]**.

her body above ground longer than the afternoon, she was cary'd out the same day & bury'd in the churchyard. *Requiescat in pace*;

November the 3[d] our Reverend Mother being inform'd that a young gentellwoman was coming over to settle in some monastry in these parts was advised by Father Francis Cliffton of the Society[1] & great friend to our house to shew her all civility that perhaps she might take here, on the 3[d] she come with a companion or servant & brought a Letter of Recommendation from the said Father Clifton; she soon shew'd an inclination to fix here & proposed it, but as we take no boarders & she being but newly converted, t'was not advicable to admit her of some time to the habit, but rather than leave us she chose to be in our School, where she had a room to her silf, after being here a fortnight she told our Reverend Mother that she found some Difficulties which she could not surmount therefore chose to try some other place, on the 22[d] she went away in order to board for the winter at Lier, but soon left Lier & com to Gant,[2] where she is at present still retaining such an affection to us that she has more than once declared that she has never been easy since she left us, yet seemeth to **[p. 130]** want sufficient Resolution where she will fix God only knows, she is an agreable woman, behaved extraordinary well, & liked by everyone here, has a handsome fortune, for a nun £700 sterling in mony, besides some jewells, plate & a great stock of cloaths, linnen & other things of value;

November the 21 Sister Martha Ferguson was cloathed.[3]

November the 22[d] M[rs] English left us.

1757

January the 17th M[iss] Eusebia Pickering & M[iss] Mary Farrill took the Scholars habit, Miss Pickering the name of Sister Eusebia & M[iss] Farrill that of Sister Teresa Clare;[4]

february the 8th M[iss] Winny Roper having been ill some time in danger of going into a consumption our Reverend Mother[5] acquainted my Lord Teynham her father,[6] who sent his valet de chambre for her, she left us on the 8th;

---

1 Reverend Mother was Mary Olivia Darell (BA071). Father Francis Clifton SJ (1702–57), Rector of St Omer, later Rector at Ghent 1756–64; Holt, p. 60.

2 Her name is not revealed in the Chronicle. Lier refers to the English Carmelite convent at Lierre, Ghent to the English Benedictine convent at Ghent.

3 Martha Fergusson, lay sister (BA079).

4 Eusebia Pickering (BA156); Mary Farrell (BA077).

5 Reverend Mother was Mary Olivia Darell (BA071).

6 Winifred Roper was the daughter of Lord Henry Roper, 10th Baron Teynham. She left Bruges and in 1770 professed at Liège as a Sepulchrine, LS186.

the 9th Sister Monica Fergus, & Sister Gertrude Clavering made their holy profession;[1] the 21 Mademoiselle Fyes was received for convictrix She is Daughter to a head mason of our town who maid the vault of our choir She being the only child her father at his death left her a considerable fortune & to the care of her uncle who placed her hear both for the advantage of Learning the Language & to be out of Danger of marrying till of a more proper age;

March the 19th Our servant Catherine Forshaw took the schollars habit for a Lay Sister & name of Sister Joachim aged about 24[2]

Aprill the 2d Our servant Holobeck went to her friends at Lopam;

Aprill the 23d Miss Freeman returned from the french house;

May the 8th Monsieur Stoppens then Scout of our town, was mary'd in our Church to the daughter of Mr Damarin & widdow of **[p. 131]** Monsieur van de Beaugar, to whom she was also mary'd in the year 1745 in our Church;[3] they ware mary'd in time of our office about 5 in the morning, had their Breakfast in the new fathers house with all their company in number 18 or 20 then set out for Lille in their way to Paris where they staid some weeks, & at their Return come to return thanks for all the trouble they had given, & gave a soveraign to the Community to drink their healths, in [*sic*] being a communicating day, their wedding day our Reverend Mother excused herself from making her compliments in person that morning which was very well taken by them;

May the 27th Sister Mary Teresa Jernegan departed this life,[4] She had been of service in many imploys of the house, ten years Subprioress, She was a good Religious & example of patient suffering in the Racking pain of the Stone, which from her youth she had been subject to, but for some years had been quite free till about 2 years before she dyed she had frequents attacks of it, for 3 years before she dyed had been confin'd to the infirmary with a pain & stiffness in her Limbs, that she was not able to walk but upon plain ground, nor to get out or in bed without help, which according to her nature was a hard tryall, being allways unwilling to give trouble, & in her last sickness expressed so much gratitude for the Charity & service done her as even to move them about her to tears; on St Michaels day[5] at night she was particulary out of order, the next morning had a shaking fit like an ague, follow'd with a fever; the Doctor order'd her all the holy rights, our Confessor being abroad we sent for

---

1 Mary Monica Teresa Fergus (1757–64) BA078; Mary Gertrude Clavering (1757–94) BA057.

2 Catharina Forshaw (BA083).

3 See **[p. 98]**.

4 Mary Teresa Jerningham (1699–1757) BA118.

5 The feast of St Michael to celebrate the apparition of St Michael (as here) was celebrated on 8 May; Michaelmas was 29 September.

the Confessor of princenhoof,[1] who judged it not necessary for her to make her confession she having done it but the day before she fell ill, & fearing a stranger might raise **[p. 132]** difficulties in her mind, a Carm[elite] who we ware used to gave her the *viaticum* & holy Oyles, on the 13th our Confessor being come home she made her confession to him; her fever renewing every night left no hopes of her recovery, thus better & worse she continued to live till the 27th about 4 in the morning Expired in the 74 year of her age & the 55th of her holy profession; the next day being pentecost eve, she was cary'd out affter ^we had sung^ Vespers, & Exposed the time of the Dierge which we then said, then went down & sunk her, the Mass & ceremonies ware all perform'd on the munday affter the octave of Penticost or Whitson munday we begun our Psalter. *Requiescat in pace*.

June the 1st Mr Stuart & family come, brought their youngest daughter Miss Lucy, for pentioner aged about ten, they boarded here 6 days, then went to the Millers where they lodgid & boarded themselves;

june the 20th Sister Eusebia Pickering & Sister Teresa Clare Farrill ware cloathed;

june the 28th Miss Freeman went to England,

july the 3d Miss Betty Pickering went to L'Abey de Pres at Doway[2]

August: our Bishop having resolved to approve none to hear confessions in his Diocess with^out^ his first Examining them, required it also of the Jesuits, whom we had always had for our Extraordinary, but they refusing to Submit to any other Examin than what they pass in their own order, his Lordship refused to give faculties to Father Thomas Clifton then Rector of the English College at Gant,[3] who come to help us, so was forced to return back again to gant, without our making use of him, my Lord said we might procure who we liked that would stand the Examin, or he would get us one; this gave our Reverend Mother & the community great concern, & not finding anyone willing to come we had no Exercises [~~*illeg.*~~] this year;[4]

September the 15th Mrs Gifford went to Gand

---

[1] Prinsenhof was the convent of the English Fransciscans in Bruges; their Confessor in 1757 was Joseph Needham OFM (d. 1791).

[2] Seven girls were sent from the convent to the school at the abbey to learn French: see **[p. 111]**. Betty Pickering returned in 1759 but finally left the convent the following year. See also **[pp. 146, 147]**.

[3] Fr Thomas Clifton SJ; see Foley, vol. 7, p. 141. Regarding faculties see also pp. 418–19.

[4] The Spiritual Exercises were normally undertaken on an annual basis in those convents which followed Jesuit spirituality. In some communities, the Exercises were led by the Superior or other senior members of the community, who developed their own texts for this purpose. Here we have an example of some of the complications in relationships between the Bishop as Visitor to the convent, with the right of overall supervision, and the Jesuits, who supplied spiritual direction to individuals in the community.

[p. 133] September the 21st Mademoiselle vanhoock come & was received for convictrix, daughter to a sort of marchand at Gant

November Miss Molly Stuart returned to us again;

November Miss Christina went to her Papa & Mama at St Omers;[1]

November the 22d Sister Ann Martha Fergason made her holy profession;[2]

December the 17th Sister Mary Barbara Huddleston departed this life in the 50th year of her age & 33d of her holy profession,[3] she had always been infirm tho naturally of a strong constitution, but her unhappy temper put her upon a continual rack, made her troublesome to herself & the whole community, She had a good voice both for choir & organ house, besides other tallents that would have made her a very valuable member, had her temper corresponded, with the Bishops leave & the consent of the Community she went twice to Spa[4] as is said (page 39) in the year 1737, having not taken the proper means to correct her temper when young, it become more troublesome both to herself & others as she grew older, & the irregularities it lead her into rendered her contemptable in the community which she perceiving was a great humiliation to her, & we may in some measure hope atoned for her faults & moved God's mercy to bestow his grace upon her at her Death. She had been near 2 years waring away in a consumption, she received all the rights of our Holly Mother the Church & with perfect resignation peacably departed this life about 10 of the clock at night, & on the 19th was buried. *Requiescat in pace.*

[p. 134]

1758

January the 4th Mademoiselle Fyrts being recover'd, return'd to us again,

February the 30th [*sic*] Sister Ann Clare Fornby[5] departed this life affter suffering extreamly for several years divers infirmities of body but still more in those of her mind, having an uneasy resenting temper to menage, she was ever very pious, has so religious a comportment that drew the eyes & edifyed all that saw her ^for which &^ she having the French toungue she was judged the properest of all our lay-Sisters to send abroad in occations of bringing or sending our pentioners or the like; she had been bread up at Gravlin,[6] partly pentioner, & partly servant, & her first vocation was there, but perswaded by her Uncle & other friends

---

1 Christina and Molly Stewart were daughters of John Stewart and Christiana Weir, née Anstruther (d. 1771). Lucy, who arrived on 1 June this year, was the third daughter. See also **[p. 123]**.

2 Ann Martha Fergusson, lay sister (BA079).

3 Mary Barbara Huddleston (1725–57) BA114.

4 Spa, near Liège, a popular town to take the waters.

5 Ann Clare Formby (1726–58) BA082.

6 Gravelines at the house of the English Poor Clares.

to be here, which may be a warning never to admit anyone who does not come intirely by her own choice, since, in all appearance that order ever run in her Head, which render'd her less happy & content, about 7 or 8 years before her Death she fell into a great malencholy & disorder of her head, but by proper remidies recover'd so as to give no trouble, nor was she ever so bad as to be confined, she continued to do the hard works till about 3 years before she dyed, she had a sort of Dropsy, & offten for several days togather, violent purgings which weaken'd her to the point of Death; she was perfectly sencible to the last & most piously render'd up her soul to her creator about 8 at night in the 54 of her age & 32 of her holy profession. *Requiescat in pace.*

March the 4th Mademoiselle Genyn was received for convictrix aged 17, daughter to a marchand of Gand;

The 25th Madelle Fyrts went home to her friends in town;

April the 22d Elizabeth Hamson come in order to be a lay-Sister, recommended by Miss Blundell of ince.[1]

in this month of Aprill when allmost a year was past without an extraordinary, my Lord Bishop sent us word that he had one in **[p. 135]** view who knew the English toungue, whom he required we should make use of, since we could not procure one for ourselves, for according to the Councell of Trent, we was obliged to have an Extraordinary at least once or twice in the year, our Reverend Mother understanding that the person his Lordship designed to put upon was an irish Oritorian, was much concerned, therefor wrote to Mr Willis, Confessor to the English Benedictines at Bruxelles & brother to our Sister Mary Catherine Willis[2] to ask the favour of him to help us, who obligingly answer'd he would with all pleasure, & stand any examin my Lord Bishop should require, which he did, & render'd us that piece of service as extraordinary towards the end of this month, his Lordship give him faculties for 3 years,[3]

May the 5th Sister Joachim Forshaw was cloathed[4]

the 9th Miss Mary Egan was received for convictrix aged 12 recommended by Mr Clavering of Callali whose Sister he maryed[5]

The 9th Miss Ann Fergus went to Marquette to learn French;

---

[1] Elizabeth Hampson, in religion Thecla (1761–92) BA097. Miss Blundell has not yet been identified.

[2] Fr Thomas Willis, Chaplain at Brussels 1748–68; Anstruther 4, pp. 304–5. Winefrid Willis (BA221).

[3] See also **[pp. 149, 236, 284]**.

[4] Joachim Forshaw, lay sister (BA083).

[5] Ralph Clavering (b. 1727) of Callaly, Northumberland, married as his first wife Eliza Egan (Stirnet, Family Tree, Clavering2). For Miss Egan see **[pp. 146, 147]**.

May the 14th Sister Allipia Conyers departed this life.[1] She had long been in a very suffering condition with a scurvitick umour[2] which from time to time broke out in her leggs even from her Noviship she was subject too, & confined to the Infirmary months together, with the addition of a complaint in her throat that gave her so great an aprehendsion of swallowing that she was forced to have something particular prepar'd for her; as she advanced in years, so did the aprehention or infirmity increase, that for above a year before she dy'd she could not be perswaded to eat the least morcell of bread nor any thing that **[p. 136]** was not liquid, all she took at meals she only suck'd & spitt out in a pott she had for that purpose; she had been some months wholy confined to bed with a sore leg, about a week before she dyed had a fever & St Anthony's fire in her face & Head to a great degree, & not being able to take the nourishment requisit was soon judged in such danger as to receive the Rights of our holy Mother the Church, remained sencible till the day she dyed when she fell into a doze & thus expired in the 58th year of her age & 42nd of her holy profession, She was of a peacable quiet temper, and had been very servisable in the choir having a strong voice she was Chantress several years, as she dyed on Whittsunday about 4 in the morning, we could do no more than say the Commendations affter the halfhour affter Communion with out ringing, on munday at the quarter before Prime we come down to the great pant where the corps was placed and accompany'd it as usual to the vault where she was inter'd but no ringing the same day begun the Psalter, on Trinity Sunday affter we had said Vesper's we said the Dierge, the next day perform'd the burial and Mass as usual. *Requiescat in pace.*

May the 17th Eliz Hamson went to oscam[3] to learn Flemish

june the 21st Sister Eusebia Pickering made her holy profession[4]

june the 24th Mademoiselle Genyn went home to her friends for a time,

jully the 11th Madlle Vanhoock went home to her friends at Gand,

Jully 14th Miss Molly & Miss Lucy Stuart went to their pa: & mama at St Omers

The 23 Madlle Genyn come back again to us,

September the 4 th Miss Molly & Miss Fany Taunton was received for convictrixes, recommended to us by Mr Wright the Banker,[5] Miss Molly

---

1 Alipia Conyers (1717–58) BA063.

2 Scorbutic humour: for discussion about the theories of humours and their effects on the body and illness, see, for example, Andrew Wear, *Knowledge and Practice in English Medicine, 1550–1680* (Cambridge: Cambridge University Press, 2000), pp. 37–40 and elsewhere.

3 Elizabeth Hampson (BA097). Oostkamp in West Flanders.

4 Eusebia Pickering (1758–1810) BA156.

5 The Wright family were owners of a Catholic bank in Covent Garden which acted for the conent. From 1729 the business was managed by Anthony Wright.

in her 12th year of age & M[iss] Fany in the 9th year of her age, their eldest Sister M[iss] Dolly was to have come with them, but fell ill at that time,

the 17th M[iss] Dolly Taunton being recover'd come & was received for Convictrix,

September the 24th Sister Teresa Clare Farrill made her holy profession[1]

October the 13th M[iss] Eliz: Hamson come from the Dutch house,

November the 6th M[iss] Babby Lyttleton went to Lille to learn French,

December the 14th Mad[lle] Genyn went home to her friends at Gand

[p. 137]

1759

February the 9th our Reverend Mother Darell[2] Solemnised her half jubily of profession, which tho it fell on a fryday was kept in the manner following, her seat in the Choir, Refectory & chamber ware adorn'd, affter her Reverence had been at Communion which was at the end of the Convent Mass & half an hour of Recollection, the Community ware all ready at the choir door to conduct her to her chamber, where the Subprioress place a crown on her head, in the mean time the musitians perform'd some musiek, affter the community had made their compliments, she took her tea with the subprioress, it being not a day for breakfast in the Refectory; at ten was high Mass sung by the archpriest with deacons our own musitians only the addition of a houtboy[3] in time of the offer: Elevation and Communion, the Cannons[4] both in our own garden & the neighbourhood went off; at the end of Mass the *Te Deum* was sung the neighbouring monastrys all join'd with us in Ringing their Bells & again the cannons; then a little quarter & to dinner, eal pye and boiled cavillo[5] over the tables & a glass of wine given by the com[ty] in time of Dinner a coppy of Verses was presented in the name of the whole Community, printed & coppyes of them to Each, a handsome dinner in the fathers house at which was the Scout & several other gentlemen of the town besides the archpriest and Deacons, in times of which the cannons playd again at the drinking her Reverences health, flags ware hung out in the Street & on the windmills, the shops in the neighbourhood shut up, & the people walking about in the street in their best cloaths, at night we had for collation princes bread to the butter & cheese usualy given, & Bishop;[6] all had leave to sit up as long as they pleased to see the fireworks which went on till very late, Every house in the neighbourhood illuminated,

---

1 Teresa Clare Farrell (1758–1820) BA077.
2 Mary Darell (1734–66) BA071.
3 Houtboy: oboe.
4 Cannons here refer to fireworks.
5 Possibly cavally; described in OED as a kind of mackerel.
6 Bishop here meaning a drink, similar to mulled wine (OED).

sky rocketts, & squibbes & Cannons both in our own garden & the town; **[p. 138]** thus ended the day; on the 13th Reverend Mother gave a handsome Recreation, a breakfast of tea, cofey & chocolate & cracknals[1] & cream, at dinner a large turkey rosted & a wild Duck at each table, large sausage & collard veal, a Bottle of frontinack[2] at each ones place, a pound of Behe tea & 3 pound loaf of sugar, and a handsome glass of either Spanish or Burgandy wine, affter Compline we come down to the Refectory for rum punch or Bishop, with buisquetts, during which each was presented with a pair of tan leather gloves and a pair of thread knitt gloves of her Reverence own knitting; all had leave to set up till ten to see the fireworks which ware that night repeated, as her Reverence had offten declared her aversion to any formall plays being acted, there was only an action perform'd in time of supper that night; the regard and affection that all the Community Express'd was most gratfully received by her Reverence

we did not ring to work all that week; every one in a most obliging manner presented her Reverence according to their ability some with fine works others with mony, her Reverence gave to the poor in the street near 300 loaves of bread, design'd only 200 but by mistake t'was near 300 distributed on her profession day, by our portresses & our 2 bakers who baked them, & £5 grot[3] devided according to the number of each family in our own street, also beer but not to cause any disorder would not give that till some days affter; the first convenient day the Community gave another Recreation, Cracknalls & cream for breakfast, for Dinner half Chicken roasted, Ham, tart, each ten oisters & half pints of wine, at night supper portions of burn'd wine, in Lent her Reverence gave another recreation, Salmon, orange tart, each a bottle of Burgandy wine, and a glass of either Burgandy or frontinack.

February the 16th Mrs Bevarius housekeeper to Mr Blundell of ince[4] having left us £5 for prayers, the Convents Mass was said for her, and Reverend Mother order'd the hearing of 2 Masses more, one Communion and the cross prayers for 3 days,

[p. 139] february the 20th Mr Rookwood Gage of Coledame having given us 5 guineas for prayers for his Mothers soul, & she having been pentioner here, the Convents Mass was said for her & Reverend Mother

---

1 Cracknell was a light crisp biscuit (OED).

2 Frontenac is a sweet wine made from muscat grapes, made at Frontignan, France (OED).

3 Here the use of 'grot' denotes that the currency is Flemish pounds rather than sterling.

4 The Blundell family of Ince Blundell Hall, Sefton, Lancashire, were strong supporters of the convents, with several daughters as members. Household servants were likely to be Catholics during the recusant period.

order'd also the hearing of two more, one Communion & ^each^ a short dierge;[1]

[*sideways in margin*] ^Aprill the 15th Elizabeth Hamson took the Schollar habit for a lay Sister and name of Sister Thecla^[2]

Aprill the 16th Sister Annastatia Trafford departed this life in the 88th year of her age and 64th of her holy profession,[3] she had been several years in the infirmary, but was able to goe about the house till on maundy Thursday[4] when she had a sort of fainting fitt, from which time she kept her bed She was of a most agreable civil temper that made her beloved by all it pleased God to take from her her sences when she was not above 10 or 12 years profess'd which she never perfectly recover'd, sometime at the begining so bad as to be confined, but for many years had her liberty except at nights she was bolted up in her cell, the chief trouble she gave was by taking things from out of the cells or any where else that she could find, particulary books and would cut them to pieces, sometimes only the margin saying t'was to make them the lighter to hold in the hand, but when she found she had given offence to any, she would seek the first occation to render them some particular piece of service, She was remarkable for piety, if any thing hindered her from Communion she seem'd quite uneasy; she was ever most gratefull for the least kindness show'd her allways affraid of giving trouble, she was sencible to the last, & with great resignation & piety gave up her happy soul to her Creator about 6 in the morning on Easter munday. affter the Convents Mass we said the Commendations & rung as usual, on Tuesday as we only read our vespers we did not put on our surplices a choir *salve* follow'd the vespers affter which we came down to conduct the corps as usual, then said the Dierge, the next day the burial & Mass as usual. *Requiescat in pace*

[p. 140] Miss Gifford mention'd in the year 1756, & september the 15 1757 went to Gand boarded at the English Dames[5] that winter & spent some weeks at Bruxelles, went home to her house at Paris, with seemingly a resolution to settle her affairs in france, then to come & take a house at Bruges, where she wish'd to live and dye, Soon affter her arrival at

---

1 Elizabeth Rookwood (mother of Rookwood Gage) died on 30 January 1759. See F. Young, *The Gages of Hengrave and Suffolk Catholicism, 1640–1767*, CRS Monograph 8 (Woodbridge: Boydell and Brewer for the CRS, 2015), p. 147. She first came to Nazareth as a convictress in 1695: see vol. 1, **[pp. 148, 179]**.

2 Elizabeth Hampson (BA097).

3 Anastasia Trafford (1695–1759) BA202.

4 Thursday of Holy Week.

5 The English Benedictine convent at Ghent. Mary Anne Gifford (1706–59) was the daughter of Sir John Clifford, Baronet (d. 1707) and Catherine Middleton (1685–1763), daughter of Charles Middleton, 2nd Earl Middleton and Catherine Brudenell. Michael Rothe, an Irishman and later a Lieutenant-General, was Lady Clifford's second husband, whom she married in 1710.

Paris she fell dangerously ill and on the 23d of Aprill 1759 dyed; made her will not long before her Death, and left her Mother (the Right Honble the Lady Catharine Roth Daughter to the Earl Middleton & relict of Sir John Gifford Father of the said Miss Gifford and affterwards maryed to Coronell Roth) her Executrix, She having a large fortune by her Brother Dying without an air,[1] was not unmindfull of this Community where she had her Education from the age of 4 years till 14 or 15 & to which she was ever attach'd, a convincing prooff of which was her desire that her heart should be bury'd in our Church, also left to the Monastery at the Death of her Mother two contracts in the Townhouse of Paris[2] amounting yearly to about two thousand one hundred and fifty livers[3] yearly for a fund & on the obligation of maintaining three nunns who are not able to pay the fortune required by the house; the which as she know the laws of France did not favour such donations, she had it writ by way of a private Direction sign'd with her own hand, & obliged her Mother to promiss her to comply with her will & intention specify'd in her private directions, & also her promiss so to secure the said two contracts to us in her life time that we may have no difficulties therein affter her Decease; now whether her Ladyship **[p. 141]** will think herself obliged to comply with her Daughters intention is very uncertain, having never taken the least notice to us that her Daughter had left such Directions, nor should we have known it but by a friend of ours who writ them by Miss Giffords desire, in the same private paper was her desire that her heart should be sent here, which she taking no notice off affter about 4 or 5 months our Reverend Mother wrote to her Ladyship to beg she would not longer deprive us of that treasure as we esteemed her daughters Heart her answer was that France as well as England gives the Executrix a year for fullfilling a will, therefore she thought herself not faulty as yet, that she believed before the year was out she should send the Heart if she could meet with a good occation; till which time it remains in the vault where her body lyes at Paris.

October the 7th 1759 Miss Gifford Heart was brought by one Mr Buttler an irish Priest sent by Lady Catherine with fifty Louis Dores[4] which her Ladyship desired our Reverend Mother to imploy as she thinks fitt, the Heart was in Lead, with a Copper or Brass plate with the following inscription in french by Gyst[:] *La Coeur de Haute et Puissante Demoiselle Marie Ann Gifford, fille du Haut et Puissant Seigneur Messire Jean*

---

1 Miss Gifford's brother was John Gifford, 2nd Baronet (d. 1736).

2 Investments arranged by the Hôtel de Ville (Municipal Authority), Paris: these were held by several English convents.

3 Livers here means pounds.

4 Golden Louis coins.

Gifford, Chevalier Baronet en Angleterre et de Haute et Puissante Dame Catherine Middleton, morte a Paris le 23ᵈ Avril 1759, Agée de 53 Ans.[1]

Requiescant in pace

[p. 142] & that put in a Coffin or box of plane oakwood, lined with white Silk; thus it come from Paris, which our Reverend Mother took in & immediatly placed it within the Sanctuarium of our Church till the place could be made ready to fix it in on the 11th of October: we said the long Dierge & rung as for our own Religious, we also rung the 3 hours, on the 12th we sung Mass and performe'd all the burial, except the *in paradisi*, during which time the Heart was placed under the Hearse which was erected in the Church then placed in the Oven made for it between the two Pillars near to the Sanctuarium, before which a Marble Stone to be seen with the following inscription in Latin, *D:O:M: Hic Manet Depositum Cor Generosa Domina Domina Mariae Annae Gifford Filiae Ioanis Gifford Equitis aurati et Illustrissima Domina Catharina Middleton, Aetatis suae 53, obiit Die 23 Aprilis An. Dom. 1759. Requiescat in Pace.*

Our Reverend Mother also ordered each of the Religious to say a short Dierge, offer one Communion & the hearing of 3 Masses that was said for her. Out of the 50 Louis Dores sent with the Heart Reverend Mother gave one to Father Confessor for performing the ceremonies, to Each of the [~~Comunity~~] Community a bottle of frontinack, a pound of sugar & a Stiver Loaf of Bread[2] in the Refectory. to the work men who made the oven for her Heart to repose in, for the tombstone, for the Alter & Hearse & Candles, for Masses, and in Charities for her Soul, in all about £12 Sterling.

As we dont yet know what Lady Catherine Rothe will do I shall leave places in this book to add what more may be said on the subject[3]

1763

[p. 143] in this year the Right Honble Lady Catherine Rothe departed this life,[4] as soon as our Reverend had notice of it, she wrote a Civil letter

---

[1] Translation: 'Here lies the heart of the High and Mighty Miss Mary Anne Gifford, daughter of the High and Mighty Lord, John Gifford, Gentleman Baronet of England and High and Mighty Lady Catherine Middleton, died in Paris, 23 April 1759, Aged 53'. A similar inscription is given in Latin below. For the Giffords at the court at St Germain-en-Laye, see Corp, p. 141.

[2] In around 1670 a loaf of brown bread weighing 1lb cost about 1 stuiver 8 pennies; see John Michael Montias, *Vermeer and his Milieu: A Web of Social History* (Princeton: Princeton University Press, 1989), p. 217.

[3] The arrangement of the pages here appears to confirm the explanation that the author was waiting to add detail about what Lady Catherine Rothe would do about the substantial legacy expected by the convent.

[4] Catherine Rothe died in Paris on 10 July 1763.

to her son[1] whom her Ladyship had left her executor and Heir to all she had; to remind him of his Sister M[iss] Giffords kind design to this house, by a private direction a few days before she died, in answer to which he sent me the coppy of his mother & Sisters Will: wherein not [what?] she mention'd in the private direction for this house, is there appointed for him & family by which we must suppose she was advised to change her mind;

[*half page left blank; pp. 144–5 left blank*]

[p. 146]

1759

May the 5th Sister Joachim Forshaw made her holy profession.[2]

The 9th M[iss] Betty Pickering and M[iss] Nany Fergus come from the french ^house^

june the 5th Mademoiselle vanzandyke was received for convictress: she is of the ^town^ affter being here a few days went to make a visit to her friends & that same night was taken ill of the small pox, which we look'd upon a particular providence of God, we having at that time several of the Religious and pentioners that had not had it, and it being much in town, likly would have spread, had she been taken with it ^here^

july the 9th M[iss] Egan went to the Ursulines at Lille to Learn french;[3]

August the 18th Mad[lle] vandenbroukes was received for convictress she is of Dunquerque;

September the 28th Mad[lle] vanzandyke being recover'd of the small pox & now about 3 months since she had it we received her again;

December the 9th M[r] Blount of Maple durham[4] wrote to our Reverend Mother[5] to acquaint her that his wifes mother, M[rs] Mary Strickland who was daughter to M[r] Wright of Kelverdon Hall in Essex,[6] had order'd him her executor by a private direction affter payment of her debts & funeral charges, that ten pound should be remitted to us, and requested that we

---

1 By her second marriage to Lieutenant-General Michael Rothe (1661–1741), Catherine Middleton had one child, Edward Charles Rothe, Comte de Rothe (d. 1782).

2 Joachim Forshaw, lay sister (1759–1821) BA083.

3 For Miss Egan, see also **[pp. 135, 147]**.

4 Michael Blount (1719–92) of Mapledurham, Berks, married Mary Eugenia Strickland (1723–62). Her mother, Mary (d. 1744), was daughter to John Wright, goldsmith and banker of Henrietta Street, Covent Garden, London, whose family appears several times in these chronicles.

5 Reverend Mother was Mary Olivia Darell, Prioress 1744–66 (BA071).

6 For the relationships here, see WWTN. Henrietta Strickland (DB170) professed with the Benedictines, Dunkirk in 1751; she was the daughter of Mannock Strickland and Mary Wright of Kelvedon.

would annually pray for her and her husband, Mr Mannock Strickland[1] the words of her said directions are as follows, I give to the Augustines at Bruges in Flanders, where all my Relations ware nuns[2] £10 on the condition that they put the Anniversary day of my late Dr Mr Strickland who dyed November 19th 1744 old stile, & mine when the day comes in their register for the Dead, & pray for our Soules, the day of her decease Was March the 4th 1749–50, upon those conditions Reverend Mother accepted of the £10 & perform'd all as desired, and Sung mass for her;

[p. 147]

1760

february the 7th Sister Mary Catherine Willis was taken of from the procuratrixship & Sister Ann Teresa Jernegan was choesen in her place;[3]

july the 23st M^iss^ Betty Pickering and M^iss^ Nanny Fergus left us to goe home to their friends,

the 21st Mademoiselle vanzandyke went home to her friends

the 27th M^r^ and Mrs Rookwood Gage of Coledame brought their 2 elldest daughters for pentioners the same day we took them in, M^iss^ ^Lucy^ the Elldest past 12 years of age, and M^iss^ Betty past ten;[4]

August the 7th M^iss^ Egan comes from the french house staid about six weeks than on the 25th ^of September^ left us to goe to her friends ^in^ England;[5]

August: our confessor[6] complaind of a gathering like a whitlow the inside of his thumb, which grew so painfull as to put him in a fever, the surgion Launced it, nothing but blood follow'd, nor did the pain diminish, his hand & fingars swell'd to a vast Size & proves very Dangerous tho the fever left him in a few days, tis feard he will lose the use of his hand; in this his illness our Reverend Mother applyed again to the Society for help & was absolutely refused the provincial, (then Father Hen: Corbie[7]) said they had none to Spare, in this distress Father Mathew Diconson then

1 Mannock Strickland, Catholic lawyer (1688–1744); see *ODNB* and R. G. Williams (ed.), *Mannock Strickland (1683–1744), Agent to English Convents in Flanders: Letters and Accounts from Exile*, CRS 86 (Woodbridge: Boydell and Brewer for the CRS, 2016).

2 Three of Mrs Mary Strickland's aunts had professed at Bruges: Barbara Wright (BA226), Frances Wright (BA227) and Ann Victoria Wright (BA225).

3 Mary Catherine Willis (BA221); Ann Teresa Jerningham (BA120).

4 Lucy and Elizabeth were daughters of Thomas Rookwood Gage, 5th Baronet of Coldham Hall, Suffolk, and Lucy Knight; see WWTN.

5 See also **[pp. 135, 146]**.

6 The Confessor in 1760 was Fr Caryl Gerard, Confessor 1723–79; Anstruther 4, p. 110.

7 Father Henry Corbie SJ (1700–65) Provincial 1756–62, Rector at Ghent 1764–65; Holt, p. 69.

Confessor at Princenhooff[1] with our Bishops aprobation had the charity to come & hear our Confessions the day before he heard **[p. 148]** his own Community, thus we went on for about 6 weeks when Father Confessor grew to have less pain, so heard all our Confessions making 2 days of it, the Carmes supply'd all the rest except the helping to dye which the said Confessor of Princenhoff did to whom we have great obligations;

1761

february the 13th Martha Randall come in order to be a Lay Sister,[2] Recommended by her aunt Mrs Lauronson formerly servant to Lady Montague when here;

March the 9th Martha Randal went to a shop in town to learn Duch;

March the 12th Miss Dolly Taunton took the schollars habit & name of Clementina[3]

April the 18th Miss Molly Markham was received for Convictrix aged nine on that day;

April the 21st Sister Thecla Hampson made her holy profession aged 23[4]

May mr Willis Confessor to the Benedictin Dames at Brux:[5] who for 3 years had helped us as Extraordinary declared he could no longer do it, we therefore apply'd to the confessor of Princenhoff who had the charity to help us in that quallity of extraordinary

june to the surprize of Everyone our Confessor Mr Gerards hand is so far recover'd as to be able to say mass & do all his duties, affter suffering with it Burning, cutting & with uncommon patience, resignation & courage which edifyed extreamly his surgion & all that knew the dangerous condition he was in, & the pain he must have suffered;

[p. 149] june the 21st Sister Frances Borgia Trafford celebrated her jubily of fifty years of profession;[6]

August the 22nd Miss Sally Farrill was received for Convictrix aged 14 she is sister to Sister Teresa Clare Farrill whose elldest Brother brought her out of the west indies;[7]

september the 22d Sister Clementina Taunton was cloathed;

---

1 Father Matthew Dickenson OFM, Confessor 1757–61 (d. 1767); Bellenger, p. 54. He is recorded as Confessor to the nuns at Prinsenhof in *Franciscana*, although he does not appear in the necrology in that volume.

2 Martha Randall, in religion Eugenia, lay sister (1764–1815) BA159.

3 Dorothy (Dolly) Taunton, in religion Clementina (1763–66) BA195.

4 Thecla Hampson (BA097).

5 Fr Thomas Willis, Chaplain at Brussels 1748–68; Anstruther 4, pp. 304–5.

6 Francis Borgia Trafford (BA203).

7 Sally Farrill (BA237) left Bruges after clothing and entered the Sepulchrines at Liège briefly in 1776. She is probably the same as Sarah Farrell, who became a pensioner at the Conceptionists in Paris because her health prevented her from becoming a religious. Teresa Clare Farrell (BA077); her father was Richard Farrill.

Mr Gerard[1] growing old & infirm desired our Reverend Mother[2] to seek for one to supply his place, that he had no thoughts of leaving us, but would pay his board, say the foundation mass & if the Bishop approved of it would be our Extraordinary, affter 9 months seeking for one, Mr millner[3] recommended by Father Corbie Provincial of the Jesuites and Father John Darell,[4] the said Mr Millner began his studies at Doway & ended at the English Semenary at Lisbon, he come here on the 19th of october, on the 24th was presented to our Bishop who not satisfyed in the private conference with him, defer'd as he said giving him faculties for three weeks, upon which Mr Millner left us & went to the English Teresians at Hoogstrat was examined by the Bishop of Antwerp & approved for Confessor there;

November the 3d madll Mary vanzandyke was receved for Convictrix:

November the 22nd our Servant Man John having been ill for some days, his illness flew to his head he become quite mad & was cary'd to the Hospitall, where he remaind about a month & when quite recoverd we took him again;

[p. 150] December the 18th Mr Francis Hinde, recommended by Bishop Talbot and Mr Tichbourne Blunt come for our Confessor was Examin'd and next day approved by our Bishop, he began his studies at Doway ended and was made priest at Paris[5]

1762

february the 2d Martha Randal took the schollars habit and name of Eugenia.[6]

March we having now had 3 months experience of our new confessor Mr Hind above mention'd, found him a most holy man, but with all so Scrupulous[7] that render'd him by all that knew him upon the mission (even a Bishop of England with whom he had lived some years) very unfit for a directer of Nunns, which our Reverend Mother was ignorant

---

1 Father Gerard retired at this point as Confessor, although he continued to live in the convent and to contribute as much as he was able to its religious life.

2 Reverend Mother in 1761 was Mary Olivia Darell (BA071).

3 Fr John Milner (d. 1782), ordained priest Lisbon, 31 May 1749, left for the mission 28 January 1750; Confessor to the English Carmelites at Hoogstraten, November 1761–June 1762. See archive.org/stream/lisboncollege00crofuoft/lisboncollege00crofuoft_djvu.txt, accessed 16 November 2016; Anstruther 4, p. 190.

4 Fr Henry Corbie SJ: see **[p. 147]**; Fr John Darell SJ: see Holt, pp. 76–7.

5 Fr Francis Hinde, Confessor 1762–67; Anstruther 4, p. 138. Fr Henry Tichborne Blount (1723–1810) became second Chaplain at the Poor Clares, Rouen in 1752; Anstruther 4, p. 39; Harris, pp. 340–79. The Bishop of Bruges in 1761 was Jan-Robert Caimo, Bishop 1754–75.

6 Martha Randall (BA159).

7 The terms 'scruplous' and 'scrupulosity' as used in convent documents appear to record an over-exact approach to the observation of rules and regulations; OED refers to 'punctilious exactness'.

off, till affter he had been examin'd an aprouv'd by our Bishop; his proceedings caused so great allarm, in the house, many of the Religious in the greatest agitation of mind, terifyed & sent away without absolution in cases judged by other Learned men rather triffles, and seeing no appearrances of things going better under his extraordinary conduct; Reverend Mother civily spoke to him, told him that she realy had a great esteem of him but that she thought him too Scrupelous for a confessor of Nunns, at which he was much displeased said I was unjust to him & the like, but however Since I was not satisfy'd with him, desired I would provide one in his place, desired I would consider well of it; a few days affter I told him I had considerd of it, but that as I **[p. 151]** could not provide an other in his place without acquainting my Lord Bishop,[1] I had apply'd to his Lordship who promiss'd he would be here in a few days & see into it himself; but his Lordship having other business, unluckly for us, was forced to put off his visit for some weeks in the mean time, the Sanctity that appears in Mr Hind & his zeal as he asured them for perfection gaind the Hearts of more than half of the community;

March the 26th my Lord Bishop made a formal visitation 2 days before, he Sent the archdeacon to acquaint Reverend Mother that it was the day his lordship fix'd for his visit, & order'd every one should be left to their liberty & no one Byas'd, on the 25th his Lordship sent word he would be here at 7 & say mass of the holy Ghost;[2] for which our church was prepar'd by Dress, the same as on great feasts; on the following day as design'd his Lordship come, said Mass visited the tabernacle & Sacristy, then went to the confessor's apartment & took Tea, than come to the speakhouse with the Archdeacon, his Secretory & Mr vanacre as intirpreter, Sent for Reverend Mother made through examin into all points of Regularity from most Chapters of our Statutes, which he had ready prepar'd & held in his hand for that Effect, the archdeacon looking on the Statutes at the same time, all which his Lordship was quite pleased to find so well observed; than he examined about the confessor; many things in his regard his Lordship **[p. 152]** did not like & said he should see further into that; then he sent for the Subprioress, affter he had done with her, it being very cold wether his Lordship come into the enclosure to the fire in Reverend Mother chamber & everyone of the profess'd in order of profession went to him, he went home to dinner & about 2 of the clock come again & finished hearing everyone, affter a short consult with the archdeacon, his Secretary & Mr vanacre a cannon of St Dona's who he brought for interpretor;[3] his Lordship sent for Reverend Mother, told her he found the greatest part of the community satisfyed

1 The Bishop of Bruges in 1762 was Jan-Robert Caimo, Bishop 1754–75.

2 A Mass of the Holy Ghost was generally sung before visits or important meetings.

3 Mr Vanacre was a Canon of St Donatus' Cathedral, Bruges.

with M[r] Hinde above the half most pressing for his stay therefore could not think of Dismissing him, but that he would speak to him & change in him what I disliked, so that he should be intirely to my Satisfaction; his Lordship asured me he was much edifyed & pleased with what he had found & wish'd me joy for that he thought me the happyest superiour in the world, that he found but one thing here to redress, which he would rather have given 30 pistoles than should have happen'd meaning the discontent with our new Confessor, but that he hop'd & did not doubt but a little more experience & knowledge of the community would set all right, in the mean time he would allow some who had real Difficulty with M[r] Hinde to confess to an other for some time, but as for me, his Lordship said how necessary it was for a Superiour to give good **[p. 153]** example for that reason he looked upon it my obligation to Confess to M[r] Hinde, in a kind manner bid me resigne to it, to which I answer'd his Lordship, to know his will & inclination was Sufficient, I would do so, accordingly went again to M[r] Hinde which for some times before I had not, the next confession day I went to M[r] Hinde tho with great Difficulty, did all in my power to be easy with him but all in vain, for which reason affter a time his Lordship give me leave to Confess to the Archdeacon, which I did for some time, till he could not longer conveniently come, then I was permitted to go to the Confessor of Princenhoff,[1] whom his Lordship had appointed extraordinary in places of M[r] Gerard[2] who had refused to hear the confessions of any, in this uneasy situation we go on till Allmighty God is pleased to allter things,

his Lordship made no alteration but at Reverend Mother['s] request give leave for *Salves* on the octave day of the feast of our holy Father[3] & the Subprioress to be continued in her office tho ^near^ ~~past~~ her jubily.

june the 3[d] mademoiselle Brower one of this town was received for Convictrix

june the 4th miss Goldfrass was received for convictrix, she is of London of prodestant Parents, who in all apearance sent her here to be out of harmsway;

[p. 154] july the 12th the Subprioress then Sister Stanny Gage Celebrated her jubily of fifty years of profession;[4]

july the 18th M[iss] Fany & M[iss] Dolly Dalton ware received for convictrix, M[iss] Fany aged 17 & M[iss] Dolly 15[.] they are daughters to M[r] Dalton of Thurnham in Lancashire;

---

[1] Fr Felix Cox OFM (d. 1788), Confessor at Prinsenhof 1761–5; Bellenger, p. 51, and *Franciscana*, pp. 72, 75, 76, 165, 218.

[2] Fr Caryl Gerard, Confessor 1723–79; Anstruther 4, p. 110. Ill-health led him to resign as Confessor, although he continued to live in the convent.

[3] The feast of St Augustine is celebrated on 28 August.

[4] Stanislaus Gage (1712–72) BA085.

july the 27th the 2 Miss Rookwoods & Miss Markham went to Lille to learn french;

july the 30th Miss Fany Taunton went to the Dames of Gant for change of air;

August: the English Jesuites being Banish'd France,[1] come into the queen's Dominions being much invited by the magistrates of this Town, they come a few at a time, their students in different companies at different times, judged more safe to seecure them, before even they could provide for them house board or beding; we helped them all we could by sending several beds, chairs, tables, & what else we could pick up through out the house for their presant conveniences & suffering persecution, we also let them have 3000 florins ex: demanding only what security they could give & for one year free of interest.

September the 24th Sister Frances Xaveria Simner[2] departed this life in the 85 year of her age & 37th of her holy profession, she had suffer'd much for many years great pains & infirmities with great courage & resignation to the Divine will of God in which she had great confidence & made frequent acts thereof under the surgians hands with a sore leg, she was extream pious, her ardent devotion to the passion of Christ moved her to begin all she undertook **[p. 155]** upon a fryday, allways wished to Dye on that day our Dear Redeemer did, he was pleased to hear her prayers for on a fryday she happily departed up life & was buryed on the 26th *Requiescat in Pace*

October: the English Jesuites now being like settled in our town our Reverend Mother was in hope of having the Spiritual Excercize given by them as ware used to have when they ware our Extraordinaries, which our Bishop would not consent to, but order'd we should do it as at other houses in town, viz by 2 or 3 at a time & the confessor the Director of it [~~*illeg*~~.]

November: the 13th Miss Mary Ann & Miss Teresa Greniers ware received for convictrix, they are of Lisbon & couzin to Sister Eusebia Pickering the Elldest aged 12 & the youngest [*blank*][3]

November Mrs Boddenham having order'd £5 for prayers for the soul of Mr Boddenham her spouse the Convent Mass was said for him, each to hear 2 mass more, one Communion & each a short Dierge for his soul

December: we end this year as we begun, with great uneasiness on account of our New confessor Mr Hinde,[4] & no less to my Lord Bishop

---

[1] The Jesuits were expelled from France in 1763–4. For an account of the expulsion and their coming to Bruges, see Maurice Whitehead, *English Jesuit Education* (Farnham: Ashgate, 2013), Chapters 3–5; and Foley, vol. 5, pp. 168–83.

[2] Frances Xaveria Simner (1726–62) BA174.

[3] Eusebia Pickering (BA156) was one of five daughters of Edward Pickering (d. 1761) of Oporto and Eusebia Aylward.

[4] Fr Francis Hinde, Confessor 1762–67; Anstruther 4, p. 138.

upon the frequent application made to his Lordship both by Reverend Mother & Several of the Religious who cannot yet make themselves easy with him.

[p. 156]

1763

january the 29th Sister Eugenia Randal[1] was cloathed in the choir with all the usual Ceremonies, but in place of Reverend Mother performing it, the confessor did by Reverend Mother['s] Desire, her Reverence allways had great Difficulty in it, it appearing to her a ceremony more belonging to a priest, prevail'd upon our new confessor to do it;

january finding our man John much impared by his illness mention'd in the year 1760 not able to apply himself to anything we dismissed him.

february the 7th we took John Saron for under Gardiner;

the 10th Mademoiselle Brower went home to her friends;

march the 24th Miss Fany Taunton return'd from Gand in order to goe to England with her Sister Molly by her friends order;[2]

March Miss Semmes was received for convictrix she is of Merryland, come with her 2 sisters,[3] hoped by presenting herself as pentioner she in time might get admittance to the habit here in which we encouraged her.

April the 13th Miss Molly & Miss Frany Taunton went to England;

~~April~~: the 16th Miss Semmes went to Ostend to learn flemish;

the 24th Miss Suliard was received for convictrix aged 18,

May the 4th Mademoiselle de Bien, one of Courtray was received for convictrix

May the 29th Sister Clementina Taunton made her holy profession;[4]

July the 15th mademoiselle La Vrijne one of this town was received as convictrix

the 25th Miss Fany Taunton return'd again to our school with her 2 youngest sisters Miss Nanny aged [*blank*] & Miss Betty

[p. 157] july Sister Mary Xaveria Gage[5] lying now under the rights having been administered by Father Cox confessor of princenhoff,[6] who as mention'd before was appointed by mi Lord Bishop for extraordinary & ordinary to those who could not make use of Mr Hinde, she being one of them, & desierous to have her Confessor frequently with her twas

---

1 Eugenia Randall, lay sister (BA159).

2 Four Taunton sisters, daughters of Samuel Taunton of Axminster Devon and his wife, Elizabeth Chapman, tried out at Nazareth; two of them professed: Dorothy in 1764 (BA195) and Elizabeth in 1770 (BA196).

3 The Semmes family of Maryland have a genealogy which is tangled: five Semmes nuns are listed as from one family. Miss Semmes left the following year; see **[p. 161]**.

4 Clementina Taunton (BA195).

5 Mary Xaveria Gage (1740–63) BA084.

6 Fr Felix Cox OFM, Confessor 1749 and 1761–65; Bellenger, p. 51.

necessary to apply again to the Bishop for help, as at that time one also at princenhoff was near Dying so that their confessor could not be with Sister Xaveria, nor could he (as he declared to the Bishop) longer help our monastry, his Lordship appointed one of the English Jesuites now in town, both for Extraordinary & to help those who had made use of the Confessor of Princenhoff.[1] Twas Father Angier[2] whom his Lordship chose as a very Learned, humble, pious & good religious, August: the 8th Sister Mary Xaveria Gage departed this life. She had suffer'd great pains caused by a complication of diseases, which ended in a Dropsey all which she suffer'd with extream patience, sencible to the last, answering to the aspiration which Father Angier above mention'd repeated to her, who attended her to the last moment, she was remarkable for her eminent piety & devotion & charity to all, from the first to the last none but experienc'd it in need, she offten express'd **[p. 158]** with great sence of gratitude to god for her vocation to Religion, She Suffer'd a great deal all her life with scrupulls, yet cheerfull & agreable to all, which made her Death much regreted, tho doubt not but she will soon enjoy the reward of her suffer[ing] life; she dyed on the 8th between 3 & 4 in the affternoon & was buried the next day affter vespres, by reason of the corps purging & the vast quantity of watter that burst from the body & leggs, the funeral services was perform'd on the 11th by reason that the corps not being in the church it could not be perform'd on St Laurences day being a secunda class.[3] *Requiescat in Pace*

October: our Reverend [Mother] petition'd again my Lord that since His Lordship allow'd us a Jesuite for our Extraordinary[4] we might have the Spiritual Exercises as we ware used to have, but his Lordship would not concent to it but said the Jesuit who help us might do with those who belong'd to him as he pleasd so might expound the meditation to them but not in the choir, in the speakhouse & none of the rest to be presant, nor make it at the same time, all which was very afflicting to Reverend Mother but being his lordship orders must submitt, so twice a day Father Angier expounded the meditations in the Speakhouse to Reverend Mother & the rest that belonged to him;

---

[1] Prinsenhof, the English Franciscan convent in Bruges.

[2] Fr Thomas Angier SJ (1730–88), Bruges College 1764–73 (Holt, p. 20); Rector of the English College, Bruges in 1773; see Foley, vol. 5, pp. 176, 180, 184, 561.

[3] The feast of St Lawrence is celebrated on 10 August; a second-class feast was for apostles or a special celebration.

[4] Reverend Mother was Mary Olivia Darell (BA071). Jesuits were not permitted to become confessors in convents, although they could serve as spiritual directors or extraordinary confessor to individual nuns. Here the problem for the community was compounded by the difficulty that some of them had with Fr Hinde, the Confessor, and they wished to undertake Spiritual Exercises under the direction of a Jesuit.

[p. 159]

1764

january the 22d[1] Sister Monica Fergus[1] Departed this life. She had for some months suffered greatly both exteriorly & interiorly, she was naturally of a timourus conscience & mett with great Difficulties from the direction of our new confessor Mr Hinde which having declar'd to my Lord Bishop[2] he consented to her confessing to the archdeacon, which she did for some time, till the archdeacon advised her to try with Mr Hinde again he being the ordinary confessor of the house, she did so & seem'd easy with him till a little time before her death declar'd she must have help elsewhere or she must dye misserable, she applyed to the archdeacon who heard her confession & at her request made her case known to the Bishop who was a good deal surprised at it & give her leave for the future to make use of the Jesuit, who was Father Angier, by whom she was assisted at her Death to her great comfort; she had for above half a year before spit blood from time to time, her illness soon shew'd that her lungs ware touch'd by the vast quantity she spitt & wore away to skin & bone, she received all the rights of our holy Mother the Church & dyed most happily on the 22d in the 25 year of her age & 6th of her holy profession, *Requiescat in Pace*

february the 3d Sister Eugenia made her holy profession[3]

february the [*blank*] Miss Goldfrass went to the Ursulines at Lille to learn french

April the 25 Miss Semmns return'd from ostend with the hopes of **[p. 160]** being soon admitted to the habit which she was desiorous of if she might have the liberty of making use of an other confessor rather than Mr Hinde[4]

April: the 25th my Lord Bishop having such frequents complaints of the uneasiness amongst us on account of our confessor Mr Hinde was resolv'd to come & give every one the hearing again on the subject, he sent to our Reverend Mother the night before to acquaint her he should be here the next morning at 8 of the Clock; at that same hour come, sent for her to the uper Speakhouse, told her he would come in, & ask'd if there was no room that had another over against it, for he would have none know the questions he should put to each one, to prevent which he would have the whole communitty call'd together & one by one call'd to him & not to return to the rest, as we had not a room over against

---

1 Monica Teresa Fergus (1757–64) BA078.

2 Fr Francis Hinde, Confessor 1762–67; Anstruther 4, p. 138. The Bishop of Bruges in 1764 was Jan-Robert Caimo, Bishop 1754–75.

3 Eugenia Randall (BA159).

4 For Miss Semmes, see **[p. 156]**.

another, his Lordship satt in the great pant faceing the workchamber with the archdeacon his secretary & M[r] Van Dr Herst for interpretor, the religious all shutt up in the work chamber, a disagreable confinement as it lasted 4 hours, nor would his Lordship let them be releas'd even for the Divine office so no choir was kept that morning; his lordship give to every one the choice of going to an other confessor if they ware not easy with M[r] Hinde, & of 27 religious 20 declare'd they were easy with him, God no doubt so permitting for a further trial ^& [*illeg.*]ert^ for our Reverend Mother who suffers great uneasiness by the indiscretion & extraordinary direction of M[r] Hinde, as it soon appear'd for in a short time affter his Lordship had given them their choices & they declared for him they could not go on with him their reason ware heard by his **[p. 161]** Lordship & have to make use of Father Angier, many things in Mr Hinds way of direction his Lordship condemn yet tollerate since more than the half of the community choose to have him continue our confessor.

April the 26 the 2 M[iss] Dalltons went to Courtray to learn french

June the 4th we were allarm'd & terrify'd with a rash attempt of Sister Mary Bernard Forth[1] to Drown herself, she had all her life been very Labourious & tho weak of judgment very serviciable to the community till Allmighty God was pleased to afflict her with the loss of sight so far as scarcely to see her way about the house, which render'd life tedious to her, offten found her self in others way; which inclined her to malencholy; this accident was providentially prevented by one of the lay sisters going into the new washouse saw some bodys cloaths, frighten'd went & call'd one of the Nunns who with a lay sister ran & found her in a tub of watter allmost dead which she own'd she had pump'd at 2 or 3 different times till she found there was sufficient to affect her design, she was immediatly put to bed, blooded & proper means used that in a few hours brought her intirely to her self; may God be ever praised & blessed for preventing such a terrible accident

june the 20th M[iss] Semm's left us to go to pontoise where in a short time she was admitted to the habit;[2]

jully the 12th M[iss] Canvane was rec[ed] for convictrix going 7 years of age, her parent are irish of West-indies but **[p. 162]** settled some years in England at Bath;

jully the 16th M[iss] Mary Ann Grienie having for some time been in an ill state of health, it was thought proper she should change air we sent her to the English dames at Gand

july the 30th M[iss] Mary Bond was received for convictrix going 7 years of age she is daughter to Mr Hary Bond;

---

[1] Mary Bernard Ford, lay sister (1725–64) BA081.

[2] Probably Mary Catherine Semmes, who professed at Pontoise in 1765, PB074.

september the 18th the archdeacon & my Lord Bishop[s] secretary come to present to Reverend Mother & community some ordinations which his Lordship had design'd from his first visit in the year 1762 all the community being assembled in the uper speakhouse, when the Archdeacon made a short speech in his Lordships name requiring obedience & submission to what his lordship now ordain'd, than the Secretary read his Lordships pastoral letter & ordinations in french & our confessor Mr Hind (whom his Lordship had order'd to put them in English) read them in English,

october the 6th Miss Terry Grienie appearing to be quite discontent to be separated from her Sister we sent her also to Gand to her

December the 9th Sister Mary Bernard Forth[1] fell into an apperplexi from which time she could never speak more than yes or no, she received the holy oyls, in a few days she shew'd so much sence as to be judged capable of the holy *viaticum*, which she had the happiness to receive, she was ever very pious, much devoted to our Saviours Passion & to our Blessed Lady & very labourious & servisable to the community & to each in particular till Allmighty God was please'd to deprive allmost intirely of sight, she dy'd on the 22d aged 71 & in the 40th of her holy profession. ([*along the margin*] She dyed about 3 in the morning & on account of its being So near Xmas she was carry'd out the same Day at the usual time & burry'd on the 23d) *Requiescat in pace*

[p. 163]

1765

january the 28th Miss Sulyard went to Courtray to learn french

february the 5th Sister Margaret Linny dyed in the 68 year of her age & 48th of her holy profession,[2] She had been a most servisable member, imploy'd not only as market Sister, but in the most important affairs of the house both at home & abroad having a solid judgment more than common of her rank & a civil address could speak upon Business to the chief of the town & to their great satisfaction & our advantage was naturally of a compassinate good temper, ready to assist & to do for all & generally beloved; but age & infirmities coming on render'd her in a manner incapable of further service, she grew very infirm for some years[.] on the 25th of January: she was seazed with violent inward pains, which brought on her strong convulssion fitts, which continu'd & very frequent as she drew nearer her end, & on the 5th of february she expired about five in the evening, she had for some time with the Bishops leave made use of Father Angier (our Extraordinary for Confessor)[3] who assisted

---

1 Mary Bernard Ford, lay sister (1725–64) BA081.

2 Margaret Linny, lay sister (1717–65) BA128.

3 Fr Thomas Angier SJ (1730–88); Holt, p. 20.

her during her illness, but being obliged to goe home upon business, during which time she fell into her agony & we was forced to call our Confessor who give her the last absolution; she expired in a quarter of an hour[.] she was ever very pious & particularly devoted to our lady she was buried on 7th *Requiescat in pace*

[p. 164] March the 11th Sister Nelly went to Gent to take the 2 Miss Grienies from there to Lille to learne french[1]

April the 18th Miss Angier niece to Father Angier of the S:J: was receiv'd for convictrix in the 8th year of her age;

May Mr Rowland Stanly[2] bring in our town the hearing of his mothers death, give us 5 guineas for pr[ayer]s for her soul, we sung a Solemn Mass & as he would be presant we perform'd it at ten of the clock;

july the 2nd Miss Nanny Gage niece to Sister Mary Xaveria Gage was received for Convictrix in the 12th year of her age.[3]

September the 8th we ware all inrol'd in the confraternity of the Sodality of our Lady[4] at the English Jesuites then in our Town, Father John Darell brother to Reverend Mother was ^then^ prefect[5]

October the 17th Mademoiselle Odonoheu was received for convictrix

November the 21st Madlle vanoye one of the town was received for convictrix

December the 8th Miss Paston of Norfolk was receiv'd for convictrix aged [*blank*]

December the 26 Madlle Odonoheu went to her friends to keep her Xmass, was there taken ill & return'd no more;

1766

~~June the 6th being the fryday after the Octave of Corpus Christi the feast of the heart of jesus almost all of the Community were enroled in the Association of the Heart of Jesus, established at the College of the English jesuits in our Town by Father Thomas Lawson then Rector.~~

[unpaginated] ~~The 14th of June Miss Barbara Darell Daughter to Mr Darell of Calehill~~

[*Rest of this page and following page blank*]

[p. 165] we began this year with the Afflicting Distemper of the Small pox, the first that had it was Miss Betty Taunton pentioner, She was taken

1 Probably Helen Blevin, lay sister (1734–88) BA026.

2 Probably Sir Rowland Stanley, 4th Baronet (1707–71); his mother was Catherine Eyre of Hassop Hall, Derbyshire.

3 Anne ('Nanny') Gage did not profess; Mary Xaveria was Catharina Gage (BA084).

4 Sodalities were societies or guilds with particular devotions closely connected to Jesuits. Up to 1751 they were only open to men.

5 Fr John Darell SJ (1705–68), brother of Prioress Mary Olivia Darell (BA071), was at Bruges College 1762–66. Foley, vol. 7, pp. 194–5; Holt, pp. 76–7.

ill on the 18th of january: as soon as the Doctor declared her illness to be that we removed the 2 Mistresses who had not had them, but they being both with her till affter they ware broken out their was little hopes of their Escapeing them, Especially as one of them viz: the 2nd Mistress was Sister Clem her own Sister, she had them favourably & soon recover'd.[1]

January the 25th Sister Mary Margtt Tasburgh began with the Small pox, had them very much but recover'd.[2]

february the 1st Miss Fany Taunton pentioner[3] was taken ill of the Small pox in a violent & very dangerouss manner & on the 3d little Miss Canvan about 8 years old, both recover'd, & thank God no more in the School to have it.

the 26th Sister Clementina Taunton began to be much out of order, which as we had reason to fear, proved the Small pox, with such ill symtoms that gave little hopes of her recovery, on the 28th they began to appear follend [*sic*] with violent convulsion fitts, that 4 or 5 Strong people could scares hold her, thus she lived till the 3d of march about 11 on the 2d She fell into a kind of dozy sleep and about one in the morning on the 3d, happily & peacably **[p. 166]** expired in the 23d year of her age, & 3d of her holy profession, much regreted by all, She was Naturally of a Sweet, ^pious^, civil peacable temper, & from her first putting on the Religious habit, gave her self wholy to the practice of Solid vertues, exact in all Religious duties, most nice in her obedience to Superiours & Director; to purifye her the more God was pleased to try her with great Desolations & fears under the Direction of our Confessor Mr Hind which would have proved a great hindrance to her Spiritual advancement, but as she knew sufficient of french to make her case known to the Archdeacon, he procured the Bishops leave for her to make use of Father Angier of the Society then our Extraordinary, under whose direction she recover'd her peace of mind & made great progress in perfection, he assisted her during her illness & at her Death, as She dyed of that distemper her body could not be kept longer than about 9 the same morning, the friars who said Mass that day at the penetents over the way[4] buried her, our Confessor having not had the Destemper, She was bury'd in the Church yard. *Requiescat in pace*

February Sister Ann Teresa Jernegan was taken off from being procuratrix & Sister Mary Augustina More chose in her place[5]

[p. 167] April the 22 Miss Fany & Miss Dolly Dalton return'd from the french house at Courtray.

---

[1] Elizabeth Taunton later professed as Mary Aurelia (1770–71) BA196; her sister was Dorothy Taunton, in religion Clementina (1763–66) BA195.

[2] Margaret Tasburgh (BA193).

[3] Fanny Taunton was clothed in 1771 but was withdrawn by her aunt later that year.

[4] The Penitents across the street were the Grey Sisters or Penitents of Aardenburg.

[5] Ann Teresa Jerningham (BA120); Mary Augustina More (BA145).

the 20th Miss Fany Taunton went to the ursulines at Tournay to learn french

June the 6th being the fryday after the Octave of Corpus Christi the feast of the Heart of Jesus[1] almost all the Community was enrolled in the Association of the Heart of Jesus established at the College of the English Jesuits in our Town, by Father Tho' Lawson then Rector.[2]

The 18th Miss Barbara Darell Daughter to Mr Darell of Calehill was received for Convictrix in the 10th year of her age.[3]

On the 4th of July in the Evening our dear Superiour, Reverend Mother Olivia Darell[4] complain'd of a pain in her back, which she supposed the Stone or Gravel that she had been afflicted with at different times for several years; She grew much worse in the night & the next morning was taken with a vomitting shaking & fever, we still thought it proceeded from the same desease, & the Physician seem'd of that opinion, but as his prescriptions failed of the desired success, except for once or twice at some short intervals, when she found herself a good deal better, he with another joined to him in consult, apprehended the Gout in her **[p. 168]** Stomach (which effectively appear'd to be the cause of her Death) her family being very subject to it, & she herself having had it often in her feet, which they endeavour'd in vain to draw there again, She supported the great pains of her illness with a most edifying patience, expressing a perfect conformity to the will of God either for life or Death as was most pleasing to him, & being declar'd in danger received the last sacraments with much devotion from her Confessor Reverend Father Angier of the Society of Jesus,[5] having her senses of speech to the last, & on the 25 about 2 in the morning sweetly resigned up her soul to her Creator in the 61 year of her age, 33d of her religious profession & 23d of being Superiour. She left 26 Choir Nuns & 9 Lay Sisters. [~~*Hleg*~~.] Had professed 17 for the Choir & 4 Lay Sisters, & buried 15 Religious for the Choir & 7 Lay Sisters.

She was buried on the 27th the funeral Service was performed by Musicians from the Town, the Arch-Priest sung the Mass; with 2 Assistants received the Offerings both of Men & Women, & buried her in the upper oven next the Cross on the right hand.

---

1 The feast of the Heart of Jesus (Corpus Christi) is celebrated nineteen days after Pentecost.

2 Fr Thomas Lawson SJ (1720–1807), Rector of the English College, Bruges 1766–69; Foley, vol. 5, pp. 709–12; Holt, p. 144.

3 Barbara Darell was daughter to Philip Darell of Calehill, Kent and his wife, Mary Constantine, and cousin to Prioress Mary Darell. She left before profession because of the presence of Fr Hinde as confessor. See **[p. 188]**.

4 Mary Olivia Darell (1734–66) BA071.

5 Fr Thomas Angier SJ (1730–88), Rector of the English College, Bruges in 1773. See Foley, vol. 5, pp. 176, 180, 184, 561; Holt, p. 20.

Reverend Mother Darell retired from the World at the age of 29 recommended to this House by Father Joseph Wright of the Society of Jesus.[1] Her great progress in vertue, her regularity in each Religious duty, her Sense & capacity soon convinced the Community of her being capable of rendering great service **[p. 169]** to it. Her Humility soon shone forth in performing with pleasure & eagerness the meanest offices in the house. A few years after her Profession she was made Mistress of the Sick, in which station she attended every one with care & tenderness, always solicitous to procure to each those Helps & Consolation which their circumstances requir'd, & this still more particularly appear'd after she was Superiour. Young in Religion but old in vertue, she was chosen Prioress by the greatest part of the Votes of the Community, at a time when it was requisite to have a Person resolute & firm to correct the several abuses crept in, & which were unavoidable through the great number of Boarders permitted to live in the House. Zealous therefore for the maintenance of Regular discipline, tho' she did not exclude those that were already established here, yet she positively refused to admit any others for the future, which although it raised her some persecutions from abroad, & within, still firm in her good resolutions, the good order that soon followed, convinced the Community of the necessity of the step she had taken. See page 95.

Her Piety & Prudence soon made her to be respected & esteemed at home & abroad. Being extremely well versed in Business & good management, she soon put the affairs of the House in good order, which had been greatly damaged by the continual expenses in Building the Church & part of the Monastery begun & finished by her Predecessor. In her conduct she was rather severe than mild, of a serious turn, of an edifying **[p. 170]** & agreeable behaviour both within the House & at the Grate. Her constant Charities to the poor shewed the tender dispositions of her Heart towards them. She was also particularly kind & tender in helping comforting, & assisting without exception, any of the Religious under any trials or afflictions. Her own chearfullness & exemplary courage under them were a true model worthy of her Subjects imitation. Beloved & esteemed by all in her own House, her good sense & perfect understanding render'd her the admiration of all Strangers that conversed with her. Various were the proofs she gave of a noble disinterested & Generous heart in the several occurrences that offer'd during the time of her being Superiour, which was upward of 22 years.

Her latter days were greatly embitter'd by many afflicting circumstances, & which as she had them constantly before her eyes, must have greatly contributed to increase her sufferings, & render life a burden to her, had not a fund of vertue of a great resignation to the Will of God

---

[1] Fr Joseph Wright SJ (1698/9–1760); Holt, p. 272.

made these very sufferings an enjoyment & a pleasure to her here & an encrease of merit to her in the next life. In her afflictions she had recourse constantly to the Powerfull help of St Joseph, to whom she had a tender & solid devotion. At last worn out with fatigue, & by a lingering & painfull Sickness, supported with true Christian courage, full of the greatest sentiments of Piety & confidence in God, amidst the Prayers & tears of her afflicted Subjects, after having received all the Rites **[p. 171]** of the Church by the hands of the Reverend Father Angier of the Society of Jesus, her Ordinary Confessor, she chearfully & quietly resigned her Soul to her Creator.

It is no easy matter to describe the situation of our affairs during the last five years of Reverend Mother Darell's Superiority. The Reverend Mr Gerard our Late Confessor, being worn out with age & corporal Infirmities, was desirous of procuring a little rest to himself in order that he might wholly spend the few remaining years of his life in peace & quietness.[1] Several attempts were made in order to procure some one or other fit for & willing to accept of the Charge. But after many fruitless attempts the Reverend Mr Tichbourne Blount at last hearing of our necessity recommended the Reverend Mr Hinde, a man whose solid Vertue & Learning made him immediately be accepted of by the Bishop & Superiour, & he consequently took his place as Confessor in the latter end of December 1765.[2] The many encomiums given him, his great capacity & Understanding, his extreme facility in speaking on any Religious subject, & an unfeigned Piety made him be looked upon by every one as the most proper Person to succeed Mr Gerard in that delicate & difficult Employment. With these good beginnings every thing seemed to forbode happiness to this Community under such a Director, had not his prejudices in regard of the Religious, To wit that their morals were very Lax, & that a thorough ignorance of every Religious Duty reigned throughout the house; notions imbibed before **[p. 172]** his arrival here, frustrated all the hopes which every body had conceived of him. Whereas at his first coming he found a Community far from being irregular in the essential duties of their State, peace & concord reigned among all, a confidence in one another, & a perfect Obedience & Submission to every Will & Command of their Superiour, & there were Several to be found in it who were truly desirous of arriving to that Perfection which their state required of them. These [~~*illeg.*~~] false notions & Wrong Impressions

---

1 Fr Caryl Gerard, Confessor 1723–79; ill-health led him to resign as Confessor in 1761, although he continued to live in the convent and act for the canonesses occasionally. Anstruther 4, p. 110.

2 Fr Henry Tichborne Blount (1723–1810) became second Chaplain at the Poor Clares, Rouen in 1752. Anstruther 4, p. 39; Harris, pp. 340–79. Fr Francis Hinde (d. 1810) replaced Fr Blount at Rouen 1759–61. He was appointed chaplain at Nazareth in 1762 and left in May 1767; Anstruther 4, p. 138.

which he had received concerning the Community were the Principles he acted upon, & in which he was still more confirmed by the Religious themselves, who being naturally of timorous & tender consciences failed not to make the most of every thing, & he judging of them by the accusations they made without examining any farther whether or no they were founded, inferred from thence that what he had heard before was but too true. These were the unhappy causes & Sources of all the confusion that soon followed, which however was far from being intended by him, who being full of zeal for the honour & Glory of Almighty God, designed only to correct, to the utmost, of his power whatever he thought amiss, & to establish among them a fervorous Religious Spirit.

Several in the Community being averse to any thing that was new & different from the method of the former Confessor (which was certainly very peculiar **[p. 173]** allowing no other liberty or time than barely to make their Confession, & at no time any opportunity of asking one word of advice) Mr Hindes severe method in point of Direction began to cause great uneasiness among the Religious, & put the greatest part on making General Confessions, which tho' he did not require of them, yet his manner of acting made it appear necessary to almost every one. From thence, under the specious pretext of wanting time to examine their Consciences, they spent hours upon hours without advancing one jot farther. Of Consequence their common duties were greatly neglected; those of a Scrupulous turn frequently left the Sacraments, & some went even so far as to deprive themselves of the benefit of them for several weeks, nay months. This method was greatly disapproved of by many both at home & abroad, & drew upon him most severe Censures from every quarter. The Bishop of Bruges[1] being made acquainted with the Situation of affairs, made a Visitation in the House, which instead of being disadvantageous to Mr Hinde rather served to encrease the esteem he had of him, & approve of the methods he had taken. Altho' at the same time (which seemed inconsistant) he gave leave to several to go to different Confessors. The affairs went on in this manner, the Community being greatly divided in point of a Confessor, some against him, the greatest number for him, so that it may easily be imagined that the uneasiness wou'd not cease by this first Visitation; & in fact it was so, for fresh applications **[p. 174]** were made to the Bishop for another, which the most Sanguine against him were fully persuaded wou'd turn out to his disadvantage. The Event however shewed how much they were mistaken, for the greatest part then declaring for him assured the Bishop they were content & happy with him. Notwithstanding this did not hinder several of his own people from being at times very uneasy under his Direction: once more applications were made to the Bishop for some

---

[1] The Bishop of Bruges in 1766 was Jan-Robert Caimo, Bishop 1754–75.

of his Penitents to go to a different Confessor, which with reluctance was granted to them. The English Jesuites being banished from France came at this time to settle in Bruges,[1] & Mr Hindes shewing but little civillities to them, doubtless served to alienate the minds of some of his people from him, & might innocently contribute to encrease the desorder in the House. The Superiour, Reverend Mother Darell, seemed to follow no other advice but what came either from the Jesuites or Mr Gerard, each of whom were averse to any thing that had the appearance of new tho' ever so good. If a Person was sick in the House, or cou'd not go through with her duties, the blame was immediately cast on the then Ordinary Confessor, for permitting them to make such long examinations of conscience, & so many repeated General Confessions. Indeed it is a difficult matter to determine upon whom to throw the blame, each party tho' in perfect union of charity with one another, were always partial to their own side, & directed according as **[p. 175]** their minds were for or against him; & by speaking to any of them, it was an easy matter to discover which party they were of. It is certain that the many Confessors which it was necessary to have & frequently obliged to change, might contribute without designing, to that Confusion; Each naturally partial to his own ways might disapprove what was not according to his notions, or the Ideas each had of his Penitents.

In the mean time, both Superiour & Confessor met with many a mortification from each party; Obedience to their lawful Superiour seemed to be greatly diminished, & some even went so far, that tho' they were not guilty of an open breach of it, near border'd upon it; arguing that by obeying the Confessor they obey'd their head Superiour. The Bishop in a manner authorized all their Proceedings; which tho' the Confessor by the great sway he had over his own people, might easily have put at stop to, yet he seemed to let them go on quietly in this way, either not looking upon it as of any consequence, or not sensible that by this method of proceeding the Community was as it were divided under two Heads: The one party acknowledged the Bishop & Confessor, & the other looked upon the Prioress to be more their immediate Superiour. Unfortunately every Religious plainly saw the disagreement between the Superiour & Confessor, for neither of them concealed their sentiments of each other: hence those that were discontented with him found a Shelter in her; & those that were displeased with her found a Friend in him. These are the unhappy **[p. 176]** consequences of a Superiour & Confessor not going hand in hand, & not mutually helping one another. Her greatest Friends were no more so to her, or she to them some time after his Establishment here; & they even sacrificed her to the satisfaction of having a Confessor

---

[1] The English Jesuits expelled from France settled in Bruges in 1762, establishing a college with a junior section there.

that was willing with patience to hear them, & give them proper advice; & at any time they were ready to forfeit all her regard of esteem, provided they might enjoy that satisfaction without any molestation.

This made the Adverse Party stigmatize Mr Hindes People with a violent attchment to him, & that in their frequent conversations with him, it was not at his Instructions or their own spiritual improvement which they sought after, but the company of the Man. How far these suspicions concerning them might be true, God only knows, the corruption of Mans heart is without doubt very great; yet their declaring constantly that the spiritual good of their souls was the only & sole motive of frequenting so often the Confessional, charity ought to incline us to believe them. The Event shewed certainly the imputation to have been false in regard of some, since they manifestly found great benefit both by his method & Instructions; & their present edifying behaviour & conduct is an evident proof of it. It was to have been wished that he had used milder means with some tremorous Spirits, who were driven almost to Despair by his harsh & severe treatment of them. Full of an indiscreet zeal & wanting to extirpate at once all the **[p. 177]** Evil he imagined he saw in every Religious, made him go deep to the root, without considering the Temper, Constitution, & Vertue of each of his Penitents: like those unskillful Gardiners who for want of experience lop-off every branch that to them may seem too exuberant, & which pruned by a skillfull hand, wou'd bring forth abundance of fruit. Such was in some measure his case, for want of knowing well his Community, he fell into indiscretions, pardonable only in unexperienced Persons; nothwithstanding all that Men of the most consummate Learning & solid Piety, cou'd say to him, had no effect, in regard of making him alter his method.

But at last his Severity towards a Community that had the name of being very Pious & extremely regular, making a great deal of noise abroad, the friends of the House, wrote to the Bishops in England, begging of them to try to remove him, but all without effect, & more pains were taken to bring it about than Persons can imagine. Others to render the Man odious every where Stigmatized him (though very unjustly) with the name of Jansenist.[1] Several letters were written to him, to desire he wou'd quietly quit the place; which he wou'd easily have comply'd with, had not his People persuaded him to the contrary: Nay some malicious Persons went even so far as to write to him a most scandalous

[1] Abbot Geoffrey Scott of Douai Abbey comments on this situation: 'It is a bit late to be calling Hinde a Jansenist, but the pro-Jesuit part of the Bruges community would have been happy to do so because the Society of Jesus and the Jansenists were sworn enemies. The issue at stake was confession. The Jansenists had criticized the Jesuits for being lax in the confessional, while the Jansenists had a very rigorous approach to the sacrament of Confession. However, calling someing a Jansenist in the mid-eighteenth century was equivalent to calling someone a communist in the 1950s.'

letter, the contents whereof neither agreed with common civility, Charity, Justice, Reason, nor truth. To his great commendation, he never retaliated **[p. 178]** on such occasions; & the surest way of obtaining a favour from him, was to disoblige him. These proceedings of the fiery Zealots against him, instead of obtaining their ends, made things a great deal worse; & several medling in this affair that were neither asked nor desired, brought things to a much greater Confusion than they wou'd otherwise have been, & served only to sour the minds of each Party, whereby that confidence which once reigned in every individual was entirely banished out of the house. The Prioress tried many ways & means to get him removed from the House, but all her attempts proved fruitless, & contributed greatly to the Bishops taking such a dislike to her, as to be near upon the point of accepting the Voluntary renunciation which she offer'd to make of her place of Prioress. Every thing now seemed to be carried on with great heat & violence, both Partys Caballing to get their ends, one side his removal, the other his continuance, & no wonder that no Novices presented themselves,[1] for every one so dreaded the severity of Mr Hindes conduct, as to require an exemption from going to Confession to him if they took the Habit ~~here~~ which the Bishop absolutely refusing, one person went to be Professed in another House, who had asked the Habit here.[2] The steps that were taken by the Bishop & his people (tho it is not to be doubted every one acted with an upright intention) portended nothing less than the Destruction of the House. For the Friends of it **[p. 179]** were absolutely resolved to trust, no more of their Children with us, if he was not removed. So that it was much to be fear'd that the obstinacy of all sides might prove extremely prejudicial to the Community. Nothing seemed to weigh with the Bishop & the arguments used to obtain of his Lordship to dismiss him from his Employment were of no effect, he fearing that it might prove detrimental to Mr Hindes Character if he shou'd be sent away in that manner; which it certainly wou'd have been as several thought him a Janseniste. In this situation were affairs of this House when Almighty God was pleased to call to himself to receive the reward of all her sufferings our Dear Superiour Reverend ~~Mary~~ Mother Darell.

Upon the Election of the new Prioress, Sister Mary Austine More,[3] Mr Hinde & all his penitents seem'd in a manner to triumph & exult, since from her being strenuously included for him, they concluded that now he was established here for ever, & the adverse party seemed now

---

1 No professions took place between 1764 and 1769, and only four in the whole decade, whereas there had been ten in the previous decade, and there were another ten in the ensuing one.

2 Sir Thomas Gage's youngest daughter, intended for Nazareth, withdrew and tried out at the Sepulchrines, Liège: she did not profess. See **[pp. 190–1, 203]**.

3 Mary Augustina More (1753–1807) BA145.

to give over all hopes of ever seeing him removed. The Event shewed how different are the ways of God from those of men, by disposing things quite differently from the expectations of both sides. Almighty God seemed to have his designs accomplished by Mr Hindes coming here; some loose notions & maxims both in regard of perfection & also of the essential duties of a Religious State were entirely banished out of the house, which a person who wou'd have used milder means perhaps **[p. 180]** might never have performed. He render'd tis true many of the Community very uneasy, but then the Religious might give themselves thoroughly to God without fear of incurring any censure or disapprobation for it, whereas before his coming, for any young Persons to be seen giving themselves in a more particular manner to Prayer, Recollection or Mortification, was enough for them to incurr some reflections from one or other & the least faults or defects in those Persons met with more sharp & cutting taunts, even from the Superiour herself than much greater committed by such who thought all secure & sufficient if they only followed Regular Order. These good notions being only by these means established, it was time that Peace & tranquillity shou'd once more reign in the House, in order that the good Instructions received, might work in each one the good effect to be wished for, & doubtless intended by the Infinite Goodness of God. The new Prioress being Elected, Almighty God in imposing on her the obligations of a Mother, had been pleased to give her the heart of one towards each one of her Community indiscriminately. She therefore greatly suffered to see & hear some express themselves to be downright unhappy on account of Mr Hindes being here: Moreover she found his conduct most surprizing in regard of some under his direction, whose healths & heads were not a little enda^n^ger'd by it, notwithstanding their attachment to him; She also greatly fear'd that **[p. 181]** his conduct wou'd never satisfy new Comers who wou'd never be able to continue long with him on account of his extreme strictness & severity; all which wou'd certainly contribute to perpetuate divisions, both in the House, & between two Confessors. In this situation of affairs, she being anxious for the welfare of the House, & very desirous to see the Community united & sincerely seeking the real satisfaction, inward peace & progress in vertue of each Particular, She was resolved to take the most proper steps, in order to bring it about. The Task was hard, the undertaking in the situation of affairs very difficult; still as her desire was only the greater Honour & Glory of Almighty God; he helped & assisted her in it. She therefore exposed the whole state of the Community to an Impartial & good Judge, & one no ways byassed by inclination or Interest to one side or the other: & to do it in the most quiet as well as equitable manner. She procured in writing the sentiments of the most violent Persons of each Party, who freely & without constraint, wrote down pro & con according as things appear'd to them in the sight of God. The perusal of these

Papers had this effect, that the affair which was by almost every Body looked upon to be only a Party affair, now turned upon this, To wit, whether Mr Hindes removal was necessary for the Spiritual & Temporal good of this House. The Judgment formed upon them was what might be expected, & in consequence thereof it was resolved that to restore **[p. 182]** peace & quietness to the Community, it was absolutely necessary that another Confessor should be sought after, for Mr Hindes method of Direction & conduct was judged improper for a Community of Nuns. Thus Almighty God was pleased without any noise or confusion abroad, & with the help & assistance only of a few Persons to bring about that happy change, which many & powerfull Friends of this House, their Superiour also, & a great part of the Nuns all combining together for several years, cou'd never effect, but which perhaps they might have done, had they not taken the violent means they did.

N.B: As Reverend Mother was a party concerned in these affairs regarding Mr Hinde, She desired an Impartial Person to pen the account of them, who had every opportunity to examine each Religious of both Parties & as often as he pleased. Time was also allow'd for cool reflexion, & for Prejudices to abate on all sides, as it was not committed to writting till December 1770 three years & seven months after Mr Hindes departure. And to be wanting in no precaution of giving a just Idea of these affairs to Posterity, She shewed the Copy to another Impartial disinterested & good Judge, who sent her in writting the following opinion of the manner in which it was done: "As to the manner of treating the affairs, it seems to me to be done with the utmost Good sense, exact Truth, Propriety **[p. 183]** Judgment, Charity & Impartiality; nor do I think it can be amended. This is my real Sentiment & opinion."

My Lord Bishop Caïmo having ordained the 3 days of Fasting & Silence for the happy success of the Election of a new Prioress, we performed the same with the prayers as our Constitutions appoint. The 4th of August was the day fixed ^upon^ by his Lordship for the Election who sent word he wou'd be here at 9 of the clock in the morning. Our Reverend Father Confessor Mr Hinde sung the Convent Mass which was of the Holy Ghost at the usual time, at which we all communicated. My Lord came at the hour appointed attended by the Archdeacon, his Secretary, & another Secular Priest from the Seminary who spoke English & came for Interpreter. They all with our Confessor assisted at the Election. On entering the Choir his Lordship made an offer to the Community of having the Prioress for the future a trienial Superiour, but whom they might choose over again as often as they pleased, he added that it was in his power to establish it thus by his own authority, but he would rather leave it to our choice, & therefore wou'd have it decided by Votes, upon which he called for & there was brought black & white Beans, which his Lordship distributed giving one of each to every Religious.[1] This sudden unexpected proposal threw Several of them into perplexities, especially as they saw the Bishop's inclination towards a Trienial Superiour.[2] However his Lordship collecting the Votes, to which were witnesses all his Attendants, our Confessor, the Subprioress, the Arcaria & the Procuratress **[p. 184]** it was decided by a majority of above half, for a perpetual Superiour. His Lordship was so exact that each one shou'd give by their own free choice, that he sent one of his Attendants down to the Infirmary twice to hear what side Sister Ann Austine Sykes gave hers,[3] (who being lame cou'd not come to the Choir) not depending on what her Sister assured him was her intention.

After this our Reverend Father Confessor Mr Hinde distributed the printed scedules to all the Religious. My Lord Bishop collected all the ~~Votes~~ Voices with his own hand, & found out of 25 Votes 21 were for our Procuratress Sister Mary Austine More, who thus Legally chosen for Prioress, his Lordship declared & confirmed her. She then made before My Lord Bishop her Solemn Vow of Obedience to the Bishop of Bruges for herself & Community; & being conducted by the 2 chief Elders to her Seat all the Professed Nuns & Lay Sisters made their Vow of Obedience to her. The Bishop himself entoned the *Te Deum*. This almost unanimous concurrance of Voices in the Election, was an evident proof the Community was realy united, notwithstanding all our troubles concerning the Confessor.

The new Prioress appointed Sister Ann Teresa Jernigan[4] to supply for Procuratress till the year was elapsed for the Election of a new one.

July the 26th Miss Molly Ley was received for Convictress, Daughter to an Irish Merchant ^settled^ here in Town.

July the 28th Mademoiselle Moorzelle was received for Convictress Daughter to a Gentleman in town.

August the 5th Sister Nelly went to Tournay to bring **[p. 185]** back Miss Fanny Taunton whom her Uncle order'd immediately for England.[5]

August the 6th Miss Sulyard returned to us from Courtray.

August the 7th the new Prioress order'd another Solemn Service for the late Superiour, to be performed by our selves, that we might not be wanting in performing for our Superiour what we do for all our Religious, the first being done by the Town Musicians.

---

1 Black and white beans were widely used in the English convents to record votes in secret ballots during Chapter meetings.

2 Augustinians elected their superiors for life in this period.

3 Ann Augustine Sykes (BA188).

4 Ann Teresa Jerningham (BA120).

5 Sister Nelly was most likely Helen Blevin, lay sister (BA026).

August the 14 Mr Berkeley of Spitchley gave us 5 guineas for prayers for his Lady deceased.[1] We had a Solemn Mass performed, & 4 low ones said, which each of the Religious heard for her.

August the 29 Ann Stevendale, a young widow enter'd the Enclosure in order to become a Lay Sister.[2] Mother Darell accepted her tho a Flemming, we having lately for some time had very ill luck with our English Sisters, who soon after their Profession grew sickly and infirm.

September the 3d Miss Fanny & Miss Dolly Dalton & Miss Fanny Taunton returned to England.

September. Our Reverend Mother thinking it contrary to Uniformity that the Community shou'd have 2 different methods for the Spiritual Exercise,[3] & having reason to believe the Bishop only allowed it, thro condescension, to the Late Superiour ^Reverend^ Mother Darell, she consulted his Lordship upon it, who order'd Reverend Father Angiers Penitents to conform to the method he had established for the rest of the Community.[4]

November Reverend Mother, hearing of Father Diconson's Death, had a Mass said for him, & order'd each Religious **[p. 186]** to hear 2 more in gratitude for the extraordinary kindness he had shewn us in our Distress at different times, as mention'd in the years 1760 & 1761.[5]

November the 21. Sister Mary Baptiste Barton[6] appear'd much indisposed & shewed some symtons of the Small Pox, which in 2 or 3 days was declared to be that distemper: it proved extremely favourable to her, & she soon recover'd. As our Confessor Mr Hinde[7] had not had it, & the Jesuits were then free from it, Our Reverend Mother was affraid of endangering their students if our Extraordinary, Reverend Father Angier assisted Sister Mary Baptiste, She therefore with the Bishop's approbation and leave obtained that favour of Reverend Father Anderton Confessor of Princen-hoff,[8] who did it in the most charitable & obliging manner.

In December Reverend Mother was thrown into great perplexities from Mr Hindes having discover'd to ~~her~~ several of his Penitents her intention of laying the state of the Community before an Impartial Person,

---

1 Probably Mr Robert Berkeley (1713–1804) of Spetchley, Worcestershire, political writer (see *ODNB*). He married three times: to Anne Wyborne of Flixton, Suffolk, Catherine FitzHerbert of Swinnerton, Staffordshire, and Elizabeth Parry of Twysog, Denbighshire. No dates are given for the deaths of his wives.

2 Ann Stevendale, in religion Austin (clothed 1767, left 1768) BA239.

3 Spiritual Exercises: see Glossary.

4 Fr Thomas Angier SJ (d. 1788), extraordinary Confessor from 1763; Holt, p. 20.

5 Fr Matthew Dickenson OFM (d. 1767) had supplied as extraordinary Confessor from the Franciscan convent, Prinsenhof, while Fr Gerard was ill; Bellenger, p. 54.

6 Mary Baptist Barton (BA015).

7 Fr Francis Hinde, Confessor 1762–67; Anstruther 4, p. 138.

8 Fr John Anderton OFM (d. 1795), Confessor at Prinsenhof 1764–76; *Franciscana*, pp. 76–80, 166, 167, 218–22, 233.

to procure a Decision whether his staying here was for the advantage of the Community or not, which she had undertaken with his consent & approbation: the Papers she had demanded from the most violent, had given them allarms, & finding from his discourse that the affair inclined counter to their desires, they began to give Reverend Mother some trouble by their uneasiness of complaints, & except 2 or 3 all the rest wholly withdrew ~~the~~ their former Confidence in her. On the other side Mr Hinde communicated to her that he had taken a resolution to leave us immediately, which wou'd have thrown things into the utmost confusion, as the greatest part of **[p. 187]** his Penitents had an unconquerable repugnancy to make use of Reverend Father Angier our Extraordinary. Therefore to prevent Mr Hindes taking such a step till we cou'd be provided, Reverend Mother wrote to Mr Wilkinson Vice President of the English ^College of^ Secular Clergy at Doway,[1] who was the person to whom She had exposed the state of the Community, & who was his peculiar Friend, & begged him to come over & prevail with Mr Hinde to stay till things were settled, which request he comply'd with immediately. He spoke to Mr Hinde, & also to several of both parties, likewise to the Bishop, who appear'd inclined for Mr Hindes removal, if his own choice but he wou'd not dismiss him. After Mr Wilkinson left us he apply'd to Mr Alban Butler president of the English College at St Omers[2] to accept Mr Hinde as Vice President there, which he agreed to, & he then prevailed on Mr Hinde to acquiesce to the change. It was a great comfort to Reverend Mother to have him so honourably provided for. Mr Butler wrote to her giving her the choice of two for his Successor here; after mature consideration she fixed upon Mr Wyndham,[3] whom it was judged wou'd be the most proper Person to give satisfaction to both Parties. In the uncertainty of success, whether his Bishop wou'd permit him to come to us, or his own acceptance of the Post ended this year.

[p. 188]

1767

January the 3^d^ M^iss^ Bab Darell returned to England.[4] Her Parents removed her on account of Mr Hindes being here. She left us with extreme regret.

---

1 Fr William Wilkinson (1722–1803), President of Douai College 1770, later President at St Omer 1773–87; Harris, pp. 342, 430. In Anstruther 4, p. 104, he appears under the name of Fletcher.

2 Fr Alban Butler (1709–73). After the suppression of the Jesuits, the college at St Omer was handed over to the secular clergy and Fr Butler became President. *ODNB*; Anstruther 4, pp. 52–3.

3 Fr Philip Wyndham (d. 1825), Confessor 1767–72; Anstruther 4, pp. 311–12.

4 Probably Barbara Darell, daughter of Philip Darell of Calehill and Mary Constantine, and cousin of Prioress Mary Olivia Darell (BA071). See also **[p. 167]**.

February the 3d Sister Ann Teresa Jernegan was chosen for Procuratress,[1] She had only supply'd from the Election of the Prioress in August.

In the month of February Mr. Wyndham came over to look himself into the State of the Community, ~~whose~~ our late troubles having made a great noise in the World. After some conversation with Reverend Mother, he promised to accept the charge, but assured her he cou'd not leave his Mission till May, with which She was obliged to be content. He returned to England in a few days.

February the 17th The Bishop[2] came to our Grate accompanied by the Archpriest, the Archdeacon & Mr Alban Butler the President of the ^English^ College at St Omers. After some discourse with Reverend Mother, his Lordship called for all the Choir Nuns, to whom he declared that as Mr Hinde[3] chose to remove, he had accepted his Successor. He spoke strongly against Religious Persons having private Pensions, exhorted us to throw them in common, yet left it to each ones liberty to resign them or not, but order'd no one shou'd be allowed to have one who settled here for the future. As Reverend Mother knew many were desirous of having them in common, on the Chapter following his **[p. 189]** Lordship's Visit, she desired those who were willing to resign them & live wholly in Common conformable to our Holy Rule, wou'd give her their names before the 28th of the same month.

February the 20th The Bishop sent Mr Alban Butler to be our Extraordinary, & required each of the Religious Nuns & Sisters to go to him in her turn. One of the Choir Nuns displeased at the proposed change concerning the Pensions, shewed Mr Butler our Constitutions in which they were authorized by the approbation of My Lord Van Susteren,[4] & begged him to acquaint the present Bishop of it, which he did, his Lordship immediately relented, but after some reflection, he order'd his archives to be sought to find the Latin copy of this approbation, which not being found, he sent to Reverend Mother to seek among the Papers of the Convent, which was likewise without success. His Lordship also finding several other things to be different in our English Constitutions from the Lattin Copies he had of them, he resolved to have a new translation made by Mr Butler, which was effected & given to us in the following year.

February the 28th being the Feast of the Translation of our Holy Father,[5] Reverend Mother, Eleven Nuns & three Lay Sisters, with a Servant who was upon Trial for one, began to live wholly in Common according to the Regulations Reverend Mother had made to bring every point of

---

1 Ann Teresa Jerningham (BA120).

2 The Bishop of Bruges in 1767 was Jan-Robert Caimo, Bishop of Bruges 1754–75.

3 Fr Francis Hinde, Confessor 1762–67. Anstruther 4, p. 138.

4 Hendrik Josef van Susteren, Bishop of Bruges 1716–42.

5 The feast marks the traditional date of the removal of St Augustine's bones from Sardinia to their final resting place at Pavia.

Our Holy Rule on that head into Practise, & before the end of the year 3 more Nuns & as many Sisters joined to them. Several of those who did not enter made for a long time great opposition to this change, but Reverend Mother being resolute, tho' it **[p. 190]** cost her many severe trials, yet by degrees it got a quiet footing to the great interiour Peace & Contentment of those who embraced it. These Religious sentiments in the greater number were under God owing to Mr Hindes Instructions.

May the 10th Mr Wyndham a Roman Priest arrived here for Confessor, recommended by the President of the English College at St Omers Mr Alban Butler.[1] He was Examined & approved on the 18th & took the charge on the 23d.

May the 11th Miss Lievens was received for Convictress.

May the 23d Mr Hinde left us to the extreme regret of the greatest part of the Community who were his Penitents, & to the no less joy of the rest.

June the 6th Miss Molo was received for Convictress, Her parents are of the Gentry in this Town, but as we found her subject to fits, we sent her home on the 12th of the same month.

June the 10th Mademoiselle La Meyer was received for Convictress. Her Parents are of Antwerp.

July the 20th Miss Beeston was received for Convictress.

July the 20th We Solemnized the Anniversary day of Reverend Mother Darells ^death,[2] our late Dear Superiour^. not being allowed to do it on its own Day being Secunda Classis, it was kept with a late Mass with Deacons, Our Reverend Father Confessor Mr Wyndham sung the Mass, the Herse was placed in the Church, & the last *Responsorium* of the dead Office sung in the Choir after the Mass. In the month of July Mr Hinde in passing through the town intended to stay with us on a Visit for a few days, but was seized with an ague which detained him some weeks. Whilst he was here Sir Thomas Gages youngest Daughter[3] arrived from England **[p. 191]** whose Father was very Strenuous against him, & from his being then actually at the House, Sir Thomas fear'd he had still influence in the Community, & therefore wou'd not permit her to come to us, but sent her to Liege.

July the 31st Miss Wheeler was received for Convictress.

August the 18th Miss Beeston went to a French House.

August the 28th Ann Stevendale took the Schollars Kerchief, which she obtained by importunity & fair promises, for her conduct whilst a

---

1 Fr Philip Wyndham (d. 1825), Confessor 1767–72; Anstruther 4, pp. 311–12. Fr Alban Butler (1709–73) became extraordinary Confessor to the nuns in 1757; following the expulsion of the Jesuits from France, he was made President of the English College at Omer in 1766; see *ODNB* and Anstruther 4, pp. 52–3.

2 Reverend Mother Mary Darrell died on 25 July 1766.

3 Probably Sir Thomas Rookwood Gage, 5th Baronet of Hengrave (d. 1795). His youngest daughter was Mary; she did not join the Sepulchrines at Liège and later married.

Servant did not give satisfaction in regard of Religious duties. She took the name of Austine.[1]

October The Spiritual Exercise was given us by M[r] Butler our established Extraordinary,[2] half the Community taking the first week, & the other half the 2[d], the Bishop having left it to Reverend Mother to appoint the manner she judged this the most conformable to Regularity & Uniformity. The Extraordinary remained here the whole time, & gave a different Exercise to each Company.

October the 17th Miss Goldfrass returned to us for Convictress.

November the 7th Miss Terry Grenier returned to us for Convictress.

November the 9th Sister Mary Michael Sykes celebrated her whole jubilee.[3]

November the 22[d] Sister Mary Green celebrated her whole Jubilee.[4] She was the first Lay Sister in this cloister that lived to it.

December We having now had seven months trial of our new Confessor M[r] Wyndham, the Community appear'd satisfied with him. Having acted with an extraordinary prudence & great moderation, he gave no umbrage to either Party, but gained the Confidence of several **[p. 192]** in both, which he made use of to extinguish that Spirit & procure the reunion of hearts & minds, he labour'd equally on both sides, supported Reverend Mother in all her Proceedings regarding the Regulations she had made, but exhorted her to concur with him by her Conduct & Example in words & deeds to banish the party prejudices that had reigned during our late troubles. He had the comfort to see his labours blessed with success beyond expectation.

1768

January the 9th Sister Mary Green[5] departed this Life in the 78th year of her age, & 6 weeks after her Jubilee. She died of a pure Decay. The day before her death appearing rather worse than usual, she was sent to the Infirmary, the Confessor went to her after Compline, but found her so stupified that he cou'd not be of any service to her, the next morning he went again & found her sensible, therefore thought fit to give her the Holy *Viaticum*, after which not judging her so near her end, he went out to hear Confessions, but about an hour after was hastily called for, but she was dead before he arrived. The Doctor had been with her about a quarter of an hour before, who apprehending no immediate danger order'd the Holy

---

1 Ann Stevendale, in religion Austin (BA239). See also **[p. 195]**.

2 As extraordinary Confessor, Alban Butler was not officially appointed by the external Visitor, although approved by him. He was able to hear confessions and give advice. Anstruther 4, pp. 52–3.

3 Mary Michael Sykes (BA189).

4 Mary Agathe Green, lay sister (1717–68) BA091.

5 Mary Agathe Green (1717–68) BA091.

Oyls to be given her in the afternoon. To compensate the loss of them & the last Absolution, Reverend Mother[1] procured 2 Masses extraordinary for her. The day after **[p. 193]** her death being Sunday, Vespers was read follow'd by a short Choir *Salve*, & then the Corpse carried out. Sister Mary Green had been a very Serviceable laborious Religious, & appear'd to tend truely to the spirit of her holy State, of which she seem'd to have better notions than those of her Rank commonly have. She was fervorous & signalized herself by being constantly at Mattins, to which Duty she called the Religious for Several years, even to decrepit old age. She was naturally of a hard temper, but the 2 or 3 last years of her life, she seem'd to apply herself wholly to prepare for death, kept herself quiet & meddled with nothing, but became an edifying example of Piety & Patience, spent much of her time in prayer, & was exceeding gratefull for the least kindness or charity shewn to her. *Requiescat in pace.*

January the 23d Miss Ley went home to her Parents.

March the 10th Miss Mary Norris came from England for a Choir Nun in the 21st year of her age.[2]

March the 14th Ann Hyde came in view of being a Lay Sister in the 20th year of her age.[3]

March the [*blank*] Miss Moorzelle went from hence.

March the 19th Miss Norris took the Schollars Kerchief & the names of Sister Catherine Joseph.

Aprill the 5th Mademoiselle Lievens of Ostend was received for Convictress.

Aprill the 8th Our Bishop Lord Robert Caimo came to our Grate accompanied with his Secretary, Mr Butler our Extraordinary, & Mr Wyndham the Confessor of the House.[4] His Lordship called for Reverend Mother & the Community, when all were arrived, he presented us the Rule newly translated & review'd by the Learned, the Constitutions **[p. 194]** likewise corrected & reviewed, not much different from the old Statutes, except the article of Pensions being omitted & some few alterations his Lordship thought fit to make.[5] After Mr Butler had read My Lords pastoral Letter to us, the Bishop made a little Speech, gave us his Benediction & dismissed the Community. On the same day Reverend Mother appointed us to meet,

---

1 Reverend Mother in 1768 was Mary Augustina More, Prioress 1766–1807 (BA145).

2 Mary Norris, in religion Catherine Joseph (1769–1828) BA148.

3 Anne Hyde, in religion Anne Maria (1771–1806) BA103.

4 Jan-Robert Caimo, Bishop of Bruges 1754–75. Fr Alban Butler (1709–73), extraordinary Confessor 1767–73; Anstruther 4, pp. 52–3. Fr Philip Wyndham (1732–1825), Confessor 1767–72; Anstruther 4, pp. 311–12.

5 In 1768 a new version of the *Rule of St Augustine* in English, written for nuns with a Preface by Right Reverend Nicholas Loes, Bishop of Bois-le-Duc (1615–25), was published. The volume also contained The Constitutions written for Nazareth with the mandate of the Bishop of Bruges, Jan-Robert Caimo, printed at St Omer in 1768.

the Rule was first read, ~~then~~ with one reading of the Constitutions, the 2 following days they were read twice each day, at the end of which, her Reverence informed us that Several at the first Visitation of Lord Caimo had requested of his Lordship that we might have half an hour of Silence in the afternoon in Lent, which the Bishop wou'd not insert in the Statutes, but left it to be decided by the Votes of the whole Community. Her Reverence made a 2d proposal, viz to have the Holyday of Holy Innocents[1] taken off, & the Pensioners excluded from the Choir that day, but to retain all their other usual Priviledges, as also the Elders to keep Mattins & stay from the Office that day, which Reverend Mother desired might be ~~also~~ likewise decided by the Votes of the ^whole^ Community. We were assembled the next morning the 11th of Aprill, & both points were concluded for the Affirmative.

Aprill the 15th Mademoiselle La Veine went from hence.

Aprill the 19th Mad'lle Van Oye went home to her Parents in Town.

Aprill. Reverend Mother thought fit to have that point of our Constitutions put in practise, which requires asking Mercy in the Chapter,[2] to which **[p. 195]** all submitted with great docility, tho' it had never been before exacted. Several were Elders, one past her Jubilee, another afflicted with a palsical indisposition & 4 of the younger Religious. Two who had been professed with a Dispensation from wearing woolen were exempted from it.

May the 17th Miss Nanny & Miss Betty Taunton returned here from Tournay.

June the 11th Mademoiselle Lievens went from hence.

June the 27th Our Flemish Schollar Sister Austine was Voted tho' a month before the usual time.[3] As she did not give more satisfaction than when she took the Kerchief, nor shew proper dispositions for a Religious State, being also of a hard temper, Superiours often advised her to leave the Habit, but always strong in her own Ideas she insisted upon its being decided by the Votes, by which she was turned out. From the Voting till she left the House she behaved exceeding well. She appear'd to have a great struggle, & went from hence with much regret on the 29th of the same month.

September the 18th Sister Catherine Joseph Norris was Clothed.[4]

September the 25 Miss Sulyard returned to England.

September the 30th Miss Kitty Gage niece to Sister Mary Xaveria Gage was received for Convictress in the 12th year of her age.

October the 19th Miss Goldfrass returned to England.

---

1 The Holy Innocents massacred by Herod are commemorated on 28 December.

2 The Constitutions of 1629 required faults to be confessed in Chapter meetings and specified what punishments should be imposed.

3 Austin Stevendale (BA239). See also **[p. 191]**.

4 Catherine Joseph Norris (BA148).

October the 28th Ann Hyde returned to England not having her health here, tho otherwise she seem'd excellently well qualified for a Lay Sister.[1]

November the 8th Miss Betty Taunton went to the Grey Sisters in Town to learn Flemish.[2]

[p. 196] November the 22d Mademoiselle Keuchelinck was received for Convictress. Her parents are of this Town.

November the 25th Miss Dolly Allam was received for Convictress being 12 years old the same month.

December the 10th Ann Currell arrived here from England for a Lay Sister in the 22d year of her age.[3]

One side of our garden wall being near falling, we ~~rebuilt~~ rebuilt it this year, the greatest part from the Foundations. We sent to Mr Tilleghem Treasurer of the Town for leave to build it strait for which end it was necessary to take in some part of the Street, which he readily granted & wou'd have given the permission under his hand if it had been needfull. By making a wooden wall within with boards, before the other was pulled down we had the happiness to have no breach of Inclosure & of consequence no trouble or irregularities from the entrance of Seculars.

December Our new Confessor[4] continuing to give satisfaction, the Community appears united & easy.

1769

January the 14 Mademoiselle Lievens went from hence.

January the 15th being the Feast of the most Holy Name of Jesus, Mrs Henley an English Lady, was taken into the Church by Mr Wyndham our Confessor. We neither sung Lauds nor Prime. The Church was adorned in the most handsome manner, a Place was prepared **[p. 197]** for the Lady within the Sanctuarium, where She knelt. The Ceremony began by the *Veni Sancti Spiritus*, which was sung by the Choir, after it she made her Profession of Faith the Choir repeating each article. At the end *Te Deum* was sung in Fauxbourdon.[5] The Bishop having order'd it to be done in private, we neither rung the Bell nor open'd the Church door. It was talking in the Refectory at both Meals: by the Ladies desire She gave portions of Spanish Wine at Supper.

---

1 Anne Hyde returned in 1770 and was clothed as a lay sister in September that year (BA103).

2 Betty (Elizabeth) Taunton was one of the few choir nuns who learned Flemish. Both the Sisters of St Elizabeth (or hospital sisters) and the Penitenten von Aardenburg in Camerstraat were otherwise known as the Grey Sisters.

3 Ann Currell, in religion Mary, lay sister (1771–1827) BA069.

4 Fr Philip Wyndham (d. 1825), Confessor 1767–72; Anstruther 4, pp. 311–12.

5 See explanation in Kate Van Orden, *Materialities: Books, Readers, and the Chanson in Sixteenth-Century Europe* (Oxford: Oxford University Press, 2015), p. 262. Fauxbourdon was intended to facilitate singing by allowing singers to sing polyphony by ear.

January the 17th Mademoiselle Lybaert was received for Convictress, Daughter to a merchant in Town.

February the 22d Miss Ann Byrne arrived here from England, for a Choir Nun, being in the 26th year of her age.[1]

February the 27th Sister Teresa Joseph Chichester departed this life in the 64th year of her age, & 45th of her Holy Profession.[2] She was naturally of a morose humour & weak judgment, yet was pious & very exact in Regular duties according to her understanding. During her Noviceship the under Mistress perceived something that argued a desorder in her head, which to satisfy her Conscience She impartted to the Confessor & Superiour, the latter being prepossessed in her favour, seemed willing to believe it wou'd prove of no consequence, however soon after her Profession the misfortune of her Family manifestly appear'd, so that she was confined, & several times ~~was~~ set at liberty, till a continual madness oblig'd her to be constantly confined the last 30 years of her life, where she was tended with great charity by one of the Religious. Some years before her death in a fit of Illness she received the Holy Extreme-Unction, but having never after any use of her Reason it cou'd **[p. 198]** not be reiterated. The last day of her life in the morning she fell into an apoplective & Lethargic fit ^in^ which She remain'd till about 10 at night. The Confessor gave her Absolution conditionally. She calmly expired. *Requiescat in pace.*

March the 17th Miss Betty Taunton returned from the Grey Sisters.

March the 18th Miss Betty Taunton & Miss Ann Byrne took the Schollars Kerchief, the former being 16 years of age, [~~*illeg.*~~] & took the names of Mary Aurelia, the latter in the 26th year of her age, & the names of Mary Teresa.[3]

March the 29th Miss Wheeler went from hence to a French house at Tourcoin.

Aprill the 6th Mr Wyndham our Confessor went with Miss Nanny Taunton for England.

Aprill the 26th He returned with Miss Kitty & Miss Polly Havers whom he brought for Convictresses the Eldest being past 12, the youngest in the 11th year of her age. Also Miss Sweetman being about 13 years old. Nanny Hyde likewise returned with him having recover'd her health.[4]

Aprill the 29th Mad'lle Le Meyer went from hence.

June the 24th Nanny Hyde & Nanny Currell took the Schollars Kerchief for Lay Sisters, the first the names of Anna Maria, the other that of

---

1 Ann Byrne professed in October 1770 (BA043).

2 Teresa Joseph Chichester (1724–69) BA052.

3 Elizabeth (Betty) Taunton, in religion Mary Aurelia (1770–71) BA196; Ann Byrne, in religion Mary Teresa (1770–1829) BA043.

4 Neither of the Miss Havers nor Miss Sweetman remained to profess. Nanny Hyde professed in 1771 as a lay sister (BA103).

Mary.[1] July the 4th Our Subprioress Sister Stanny Gage[2] having been for some months confined to the Infirmary by lameness, & never likely to recover it at her great age being past fourscore, was very desirous **[p. 199]** of being discharged from her Office, which the Community readily consented to, for her sore leg had for some years render'd her unable to comply with it. She was a Person of Exemplary Vertue, but her great Humility & natural timidity caused her to be easily influenced by others, however she kept the office near 21 years, but inconveniences arising from it, at the meeting for a new Election, Reverend Mother proposed a trienial one, to which all readily agreed. Sister Mary Catherine Willis was canonically chose, a Person of eminent vertue great zeal & discretion.[3] As She was then actually Mistress of Novices, Reverend Mother was perplexed to find a proper Person for that Employ, therefore with the consent of her Cou[n]cil Sisters, the said Sister Mary Catherine was confirmed in both offices.

August the 28 Miss Isabella Angier was received for Convictress in the 7th year of her age.[4]

September the 12th Sister Mary Aurelia Taunton & Sister Mary Teresa Byrne were Clothed.

September the 24th Sister Catherine Joseph Norris made her Holy Profession.[5]

October the 17th Mad'lle Lybaert went from hence.

October the 23d Miss Terry Grenier went from hence to a French house at Lille.

November the 26th Miss Sweetman went from hence to a French house at Lille.

October the 29th Mad'lle Keuckeulinche went from hence.

December the 1st Mad'lle De Ronquier Daughter to a great merchant in Town was received for Convictress, & on the same day Mad'lle Vandenberg Daughter to a great Inn-Keeper in Town was also received for Convictress.

[p. 200]

1770

January the 22d Sister Mary Joseph Blundell was chose Procuratress.[6]

February the 3d Sister Catherine Aspinal a Lay Sister celebrated her whole Jubilee of Religion.[7]

---

1 Anne (Nanny) Hyde (BA103); Ann Currell (BA069).

2 Stanislaus (Stanny) Gage (BA085).

3 Mary Catherine Willis (BA221).

4 She later professed as Mary Regis (1788–1837) BA005.

5 Catherine Joseph Norris (BA148).

6 Mary Joseph Blundell (BA027).

7 Catherine Aspinal, lay sister (1720–86) BA006.

February the 16th Mad'lle Van Viure was received for Convictress, her Parents are great Inn-Keepers at Ghent. She went from hence on the 8th of Aprill.

May the 11th Sister Frances Borgia Trafford departed this life in the 80th year of her age & 59th of her Holy Profession.[1] She was a person of eminent Piety, who never seemed to have lost her first fervour, & tho confined to the Infirmary for several years before her death, & even when she kept her bed, she nevertheless observed all the Regular hours of Recollection & never omitted the 8 days anual Retreat, yet very much advanced the Common work being never Idle. She was Humble, Charitable & of great Mortification, & had been very Serviceable in most of the Laborious offices. She Died of a pure Decay, & met Death with joy & vehement desires of enjoying Almighty God; She had little or no Agony. Her Death seem'd indeed to be Precious in the sight of God. _Requiescat in pace_

May the 17th Miss Plunket was received for Convictress. Her Parents are Irish, but she was born & wholly bred up in these Countries. On the same day Mad'lle **[p. 201]** Peterinck was also received for Convictress. Her Parents are of Tournay. These 2 young Ladies were of the same age, viz about 17.

May the 30th Miss Wheeler returned here from the French house.

June the 1st Miss Hamilton a Scotch young Lady of good birth, but a Protestant was received for Convictress, being about 17 years of age.

June the 20th Mad'lle Smydth Daughter to our Mason was received for Convictress, being about 17 years of age.

July the 1st Mad'lle Vandenberg returned to her Parents in Town.

July the 31st Miss Dove a Protestant was received for Convictress about 20 years of age. Her Mother being a Catholick was desirous she shou'd also embrace the true Faith.

August the 7th Miss Wheeler Niece to Sister Ann Joseph Wheeler[2] returned to England.

August the 16 Miss Bond went from hence to a French house at Bruxelles.

August the 28th Miss Molly & Miss Nelly Langton came here from Spain, & were received for Convictresses, the Eldest in the 10th year of her age, the youngest in the 8th. Their Father is a younger Branch of the Langtons of Low in Lancashire, settled at Cadiz in Spain.[3]

---

1 Francis Borgia Trafford (1711–70) BA203.

2 Ann Joseph Wheeler (BA218).

3 Langton family of Lowe Hall, Lancashire, Ireland and Cadiz, Spain. Some of the family moved from Ireland to Spain as merchants. Nicholas Langton of Kilkenny (d. 1779) married (1737) Frances Carew of Cadiz. Nicholas and his father-in-law, Lorenzo Carew, established a wine business in Cadiz. Nicholas and Frances had four daughters and four sons. The ages of these two suggest that they are the daughters of the eldest son, Michael Langton, who had three daughters with Mary Ellen Wadding: Frances, Mary and Ellen. See lostlangtons.co.uk/LoweHallPart1.shtml, accessed 28 April 2015, and **[pp. 249, 322]**.

September the 9th Sister Anna Maria Hyde & Sister Mary Currell were Clothed for Lay Sisters.[1]

September the 12th Mrs James Angier was taken into the Church by her Brother in Law Reverend Father Angier, who performed the Ceremony in our Church. he began it by saying a Low Mass which was served by his 2 Nephews **[p. 202]** Students at the College.[2] after it, we sung the *Veni Creator* in the Choir, the Priest sung the Prayer, then Mrs Angier made her Profession of Faith, when finished she left her Place to her Brother Reverend Father Angier who repeated the last Article of it, Mr Gerard our ancient Confessor did the same,[3] the Ceremony was concluded by the *Te Deum* sung in the Choir, & by the Prayer after it sung by the Priest. The Church was handsomely adorned, & a Place prepared for Mrs Angier before the High Altar within the Sanctuarium, where she knelt during the whole time, except when her Brother & Mr Gerard made their Profession of Faith.

September the 19 Mad'lle D'andreis de Haselberg was received for Convictress about 17 years of age. Her Parents live near Tournay.

September the 21st Miss Molly & Miss Hester Goodsons, Cousins to Sister Mary Aurelia Taunton, were received for Convictresses. The Eldest in the 11th year of her age, the youngest in the 10th.

September the 29th Miss Hamilton returned to England.

October the 1st Sister Mary Aurelia Taunton & Sister Mary Teresa Byrne made their Holy Profession.[4] On the same day Mad'lle De Ronquier (Elder Sister to the former received in December 1769) was received for Convictress.

October the [*blank*] Mad'lle Smyth returned to her Parents in Town.

October the 9th Miss Fanny & Miss Nanny Tauntons enter'd the Inclosure in quality of Boarders, which Reverend Mother permitted from the assurances She had from their Brother Mr Samuel Taunton, that he judged **[p. 203]** the Eldest young Ladys view in asking it was to deliberate quietly on the choice of a State of Life, but as she wou'd not own it publickly, Reverend Mother insisted on their ~~only~~ staying only 3 Months to which they agreed.[5]

September the 29th Miss Kitty Gage went from hence to Count Gage's at Ghent.

November the 23d Mad'lle Peterinck returned to her Parents at Tournay.

---

1 Anne Maria Hyde (BA103); Mary Currell (BA069).

2 Fr Thomas Angier SJ (d. 1788), extraordinary Confessor from 1763; Holt, p. 20.

3 Fr Gerard became Confessor at Bruges in 1723, intending to stay only a short time. He remained for 56 years and died there in 1779. Anstruther 4, p. 110.

4 Mary Aurelia Taunton (BA196); Mary Teresa Byrne (BA043).

5 The community had reached a decision at the death of Prioress Herbert not to take in lay boarders because of the disruption they caused to life in the enclosure. The Prioress here expresses concern about the intentions of the two girls. Samuel Taunton of Axminster had a connection with the Arundell estate in 1757.

December the 4th Mad'lle Pigou was received for Convictress being about 17 years of age. Her Parents are French but settled at the Hague in Holland where she was born & bred.

December the 19th being Ember Wednesday,[1] there was such a Storm of wind in time of the High Mass, that one pannel of the Window over the Organ House was blown into the Sanctuarium, the Confessor narrowly escaped being cut with the glass, having at the end of the Creed just rose from the place where it fell, the Server had a blow from it & was cut on the forehead which obliged him to withdraw; the wind continued with such violence that the Priest had difficulty to finish the Holy Sacrifice, which however he did without harm. After we left the Church part of one of the Choir Windows was also blown in; the Clattering of glass & that of Tyles from different parts of the House frighten'd the most courageous. Reverend Mother assembled several of the nuns to the Work-chamber, where she said Littanies & other Prayers, & had the Pascal Candle light-up for about an hour. We suffer'd some damage but very small in comparison **[p. 204]** with many Places in the Town. We were obliged to keep Choir in the Work Chamber & Chapter-house till the damages were repaired. Five days after this Storm, the Divine Providence shewed its mercy to us again on another occasion. The Murrain among Cattle[2] being then in Town, the Magistrates had order'd under a Fine of above £50 cur: that whoever had any Cattle ill shou'd inform them of it. We not knowing this order till too late, had procured the usual helps to our Cow which was sick after Calving, but in spight of remedies she died, which exposed us to the Fine, & our 2 Gardeners & the Cows Doctor to be put in Prison. In this Perplexity Reverend Mother consulted Mr Cotteaux the Bishop's Overseer & a true Friend to the Monastery, by whose Dexterity in managing this business we were preserved from trouble of expense. Reverend Mother procured 2 Masses to be said in Thanksgiving for these 2 benefits, for such considerable extraordinary Charges wou'd have hurt our Temporals greatly this year.

December the 21st St Thomas's day compleated Reverend Mr Gerards whole Jubilee of Priesthood.[3] Reverend Mother had designed a ~~Musick~~ Mass & *Te Deum* &c in Musick, & also to have made an Entertainment ^in^ the Fathers house, but the old Gentleman wou'd not allow it, judging through his great Humility that he had not comply'd with that Sublime Dignity, tho to every one else he appears of an uncommon Vertue, & a most worthy Ecclesiastick esteem'd by all that know him; however her Reverence made him a handsome present from herself & another from the Musicians he having Taught most of them, **[p. 205]** & also

---

1 Ember Days: see Glossary.

2 Murrain was a serious infection, generally fatal in cattle, and it spread rapidly.

3 Fr Gerard was ordained on 21 December 1720. Anstruther 4, p. 110.

a present from some others who desired it. At all which the good old Gentlemans gratitude & Humility caused him to shed abundance of tears. The Procuratress gave a little Recreation & a glass of wine.

1771

January the 2d Miss Molly Daly a West Indian was received for Pensioner in the 6th year of her age.[1]

January the 19th being the Feast of the Holy Name of Jesus, Miss Nanny Taunton took the Schollars Habit, & the names of Aloisa Joseph.[2] She was in the 19th year of her age.

January the 21st Mr Gerard gave a handsome Recreation to the Community for his Jubilee of Priesthood.

February

The 9th Miss Fanny Taunton took the Schollars Habit & the names of Mary Clare.[3] She was in the 21st year of her age.

The 19th Mademoiselle Peterincke returned here again for Pensioner, having recover'd her health.

The 23d Mademoiselle Van Vergelo a Merchands daughter of Antwerp was received for Pensioner in the 19th year of her age.

Aprill

The 28th Miss Kitty & Miss Molly Havers went from hence to a French House at Bruxells.

[p. 206]

May

The 9th being Ascension day Mr Daly was married to Miss Waterton in our Church by Mr Wyndham our Confessor.[4] As it was perform'd in time of the Office Lauds were not sung.

The 21st [*sic*] being Whitsunday Miss Dove was taken into the Church by Mr Wyndham our Confessor. He first enton'd the *Veni Creator* which the Choir went on with, then she made the Profession of Faith, the Confessor, the Nuns & Pensioners repeating each article after her: he then enton'd the *Te Deum*, which the Choir finished, after it he sung the prayer of Thanksgiving & made a short Speech to the new Convert. Neither Mattins nor Lauds were sung that day.

---

1 Miss Molly Daly is likely to have been of Irish descent, with parents who went to the West Indies as traders and planters in Montserrat and Demerara.

2 Nanny Taunton, in religion Aloisa Joseph, was clothed in November 1771 and left in August 1772. See also **[pp. 208, 210]** below.

3 Fanny Taunton, in religion Mary Clare, was clothed February 1771 and left in July that year: see **[p. 207]** below.

4 Marriage ceremonies in convents were rare, and needed special authorisation. For Miss Waterton, see **[p. 116]**.

June

The 10th Miss Mary James was received for Pensioner in the 6th year of her age. Her Father is a broken London Merchand now settled in Bruges, he was then a Protestant but afterwards Converted.

The 20th Miss Canvane a West Indian returned here from the French House in the 14th year of her age.

The 26th Miss Molly Hughes was received for Pensioner in the 10th year of her age.[1]

The 29th Miss Fanny Angier, Miss Allam & Miss Dove went from hence to England.

July

The 3d Miss Paston went from hence to her Parents at St Omers, Miss Molly Darell also left us on the same day. She came on the 4th of May on a visit **[p. 207]** to us, She Lodged at the Millers & tabled in Our Fathers House.

The 4th Sister Mary Clare Taunton Schollar went from hence; Her Aunt who was her Guardian requiring of her to return to England.[2]

The 7th Mademoiselle Peterincke a Flemish Pensioner went from hence.

The 23d The 2 Miss Greniers returned to us.

The 30th Miss Teresa Tichbourne was received for Pensioner in the 12th year of her age. She is Niece to Sister M. Ignatia Tichbourne.[3]

August

The 1st Miss Atkinson a young Lady of a Good Family came here with a view of seeing something of a Religious Life. She was in the 19th year of her Age. She eat with our Pensioners.[4]

The 27th the youngest Mademoiselle De Ronquier returned home to her Parents.

The 29th Sister Mary Aurelia Taunton departed this life in the 18th year of her age & the first of her Profession.[5] She died of a lingering Illness or Consumption which she bore with extraordinary patience. She was very Pious & of a peaceable disposition & promised to be an excellent Religious, by the solid practises of vertue to which she gave herself. She had a most sweet death, & I doubt not but it was precious in the sight of God. *Requiescat in pace*. Amen.

---

1 Molly Hughes was the daughter of Mr John Hughes of Deptford, Kent.

2 Her mother, Elizabeth Chapman, had predeceased her father.

3 Mary Ignatia Tichbourne (BA200). Teresa Tichbourne did not enter the convent.

4 Spending time within the community allowed women to experience the religious life and test their vocation before deciding whether they wished to join the community; it was the only reason given for admitting women into the convent at this time. See also **[pp. 202–3]**.

5 Mary Aurelia Taunton (1770–71) BA196.

[p. 208]

September

The 16th The 2 Miss Talbots were received for Pensioners. Miss Kitty in the 14th year of her age, & Miss Betty in the 12th. They are Nieces to Lord Shrewsbury.[1]

The 25th Miss Atkinson went from hence to a French Convent at Tourcoin.

The 26th Miss Canvane went from hence to England.

October

The 14th Mademoiselle Pattemans was received here for Pensioner in the 16th year of her age. Her Father is a Merchand at Antwerp.

November

The 5th Sister Aloisa Joseph Taunton was Clothed.

The 12th the 2 Miss Greniers went from hence to Monsieur D'Acquettes at Furnes.

The 12th Sister Anna Maria Hyde, & Sister Mary Currell made their Profession for Lay Sisters.[2]

December

The 16th Miss Plunket returned to her Parents.

1772

Aprill

The first Mademoiselle De Ronquier went from hence.

The 4th Mademoiselle Pigon went from hence.

May

The 14th Laetitia Garnet came here for a Lay Sister in the 21st year of her age.

[p. 209]

May

The 16th Miss Lucretia Havers was received for Pensioner in the 13th year of her age.

The ~~16th~~ 22d the 2 eldest Miss Havers returned here from the French House. They were taken into the Enclosure, & left us for England on the 29th of the same month.

The 30th The 2 Miss Langtons went to the Monastery at Ostend.

---

[1] Two sisters appear in the WWTN family tree for Talbot: Catherine (Kitty), who professed in 1780 as Alicia (BA190), and Barbara, who left the convent. Betty Talbot died in 1787; see **[p. 305]**. Their father was Charles Talbot (d. 1766), brother of George, 14th Earl of Shrewsbury (d. 1787), and their mother Mary Mostyn.

[2] Anne Maria Hyde (BA103); Mary Currell (BA069).

June

The 12th Miss Harriot Havers was received for Pensioner in the 10th year of her age. She is Daughter to Mr William Havers, & first Cousin to the 3 Miss Havers just mention'd.[1]

July

The 16th the 2 Miss Bodkins West Indians were received for Pensioners, Miss Molly in the 16th, & Miss Nanny in the 11th year of their ages.[2]

The 23d Mr Thomas Berington came here for Confessor recommended by Mr Alban Butler President of the English College at St Omers, & Mr Tichbourne Blount President of the English College of Clergy at Doway where Mr Berington was brought up & finished his Studies.[3]

On the 29th Mr Wyndham[4] left us. He had been our Confessor 5 years, 2 months & 19 days. Tho' he quitted his post by his own choice, yet it was with very great regret.

On the 30th Miss Betty Homes a West Indian was received for Pensioner in the 13th year of her age.

August

The 16th Mademoiselle D'Asselberge a Flemish Pensioner went from hence.

[p. 210]

August

On the 17th Sister Aloisa Joseph Taunton Novice put off the Habit, & the next day went out of the Inclosure to her Brother & Sister who came over for her, & she returned to England with them.[5]

On the 26th the 2 Miss Langtons returned here from Ostend. Mrs Paston, (Sister to our Sister Chichester) at her death left us £5 for Prayers.[6] There was a Solemn Mass sung & 3 Low Masses said for her Soul.

Mrs Maire (who was Beddingfield) Counsellor Maires Lady sent us £20 for Prayers for her deceased Husband.[7] Reverend Mother order'd for him a Solemn Mass & 2 Low Masses, with the addition of one Communion & the hearing another Mass from each one of the Community.

---

1 It has not been possible to identify this group of Havers girls; the family hailed from Thelveton, Norfolk.

2 The Miss Bodkins were of Irish descent and merchant interests.

3 Fr Thomas Berrington was Confessor at Bruges 1772–75; see Anstruther 4, p. 30. Fr Alban Butler (1709–73); *ODNB*. Fr Tichbourne Blount (d. 1810) became president of the English College at Douai in 1770; see Anstruther 4, p. 39.

4 Fr Philip Wyndham (d. 1825), Confessor 1767–72; Anstruther 4, pp. 311–12.

5 Aloisa Joseph Taunton (BA197).

6 Teresa Joseph Chichester (BA052) of the family from Arlington in Devon; another sister, Ursula (BA053), had died in 1723. Their sister Mary had married Mr William Paston of Horton, Gloucestershire.

7 Mary, née Bedingfield (d. 1784) was the widow of John Maire of Lartington, Co. Durham, a leading Catholic conveyancer, who died on 30 September 1771.

October

On the 27th Sister Stanislaus Gage departed this life in the 85th year of her age & 61 of Religion.[1] She had always been an exemplary Religious, & never seem'd to have lost her first fervour. She was remarkably Humble & Meek: ^In^ the latter years of her life, she gave herself much to Prayer & Solitude, & tho then unable to be serviceable in Employments, yet her vertue, & chearfull patient suffering very painfull sores in her leg & the Infirmities of old age made us sincerely regret the loss of so great an example of Religious Perfection. *Requiescat in pace*. Amen.

[p. 211]

November

On the 3d Laetitia Garnet left us, not having health or other qualifications for being a Lay Sister.

1773

February

On the 2d Sister Ann Austin Sykes departed this life in the 72d year of her age & 47th of her Profession.[2] It was said her entrance into Religion was occasion'd by her having been crossed in love, however she appear'd happy in her State, tho' she seem'd to have a great repugnance to Regular Observances. She was not of an easy temper, & of infirm health. The last 15 years of her life she was confined to the Infirmary with a Palsey & very humbling and mortifying Infirmities, which she bore with remarkable patience. She had a particular charity in offering her Prayers & Sufferings for the Solace of the Souls in Purgatory. *Requiescat in pace*. Amen.

On the 23d Miss Bates a Pensioner from Cambray came here: She was taken into the Monastery till one of our Sisters cou'd conveniently conduct her to Louvain where she was designed. She was here 8 days, & being Cousin German to Mr Berington the Confessor, she eat in the Fathers House.[3]

[p. 212]

Aprill

On the 28th Mademoiselle Van Vergelo went from hence.

---

1 Stanislaus Gage (1712–72) BA085.

2 Ann Augustine Sykes (1726–73) BA188.

3 Miss Bates was probably Anne Marie Bates, in religion Mary (1787–1844) LA022. She was clothed in March 1780, aged 19, seven years before her profession. She was affected by changing regulations regarding age at profession: in the Austrian Netherlands this was raised first to 25 and then reduced to 24, and there must have been additional reasons for delay. Fr Thomas Berrington was Confessor at Bruges 1772–75.

May

On the first Mary Webster came here for a Lay Sister in the 20th year of her age.[1]

On the 14th Miss Paston returned here, & took the Schollars Habit on the 20th, which was Ascension day, & the names of Mary Bernard.[2] She was in the 18th year of her age.

On the 24th Miss Jenny Bates from Wales was received here for Pensioner, being about 12 years old.

June

On the 4th Miss Mary Jane Huddleston was received for Pensioner in the 9th year of her age. She is Daughter to Mr Richard Huddleston & Little Niece to Sister Justina.[3]

On the 16th Sister Mary Alexia Tatlock a Lay Sister departed this life in the 62^{d} year of her age, & 37th of her Profession.[4] She was of Substantial Parents who were able to give her a good Education. They sent her here, where she was Pensioner for 3 years, but as she cou'd not learn to read latin, it proved an impediment to her being admitted amongst us as a Choir Nun. Tho she might have been received in that quality by another House, as her parents gave her a Nuns fortune, yet she insisted upon being a Lay Sister here. Her Brother came on purpose to examine her on the Subject, & finding she had a sincere desire of it, he consented but upon condition that she shou'd be exempted from the hard works, which was granted. She was so humble that if any **[p. 213]** Sister said she had brought a Nuns Fortune, she wou'd shed tears, & say it was very hard she shou'd be ~~reproached~~ reproached with it. She had a peaceable temper & a great ~~shate~~ share of holy Simplicity, & appear'd of great innocency of life. She had been many years very infirm, & was the picture of a walking Ghost. She bore all her infirmities with great patience. For some weeks before her death, she had been an Inhabitant of the Infirmary, but walked about the House even the day before she died, & was not judged in any immediate danger, however rising on the 16th she fell down, they ran ~~to~~ to her assistance, but she never spoke more. The Confessor gave her the Holy Oils with all speed, yet doubtfull whether she was alive or dead. She had been at Holy Communion a few days before, so that tho' her death was sudden, we have reason to hope it was not unprovided. *Requiescat in pace*. Amen.

---

1 Mary Ann Webster, in religion Monica, lay sister (1778–82) BA213.

2 Henrietta Paston, in religion Mary Bernard (1780–1837) BA150.

3 Mary Jane's great aunt was Mary Justina Huddleston (BA113). Mary Jane left the convent and later married Basil Eyston of East Hendred, Berkshire, a family with many connections to the English convents.

4 Mary Alexia Tatlock (1736–73) BA194.

In the beginning of June a Lay Sister was sent with the Bishops leave for 3 months to Blackenberge to attend & wait on Miss Nelly Langton, who was order'd to bathe in the Sea.

July

On the 6th Miss Usher came here to be Religious, in the 33d year of her age, recommended by Mr Alban Butler. She took the Schollars Habit on the 16th & the names of Agnes Austin.[1]

August

On the 9th Miss Ann Patterson came here to be Religious in the 22d year of her age, recommended by Mr Alban Butler.[2] She took the Schollars Habit on the 14th & the name of Alban.[3]

[p. 214] On the 12th of August Miss Betty Dillon was received for Pensioner in the 16th year of her age. She is of Irish extraction.

On the 16th Sister Agnes Austin Usher put on Secular to go to bathe in the Sea at Ostend for her health.

September

On the 8th Miss Usher went from hence to England to consult a Physician there.

On the 13th Miss Ann Green, Niece to Sister Ann Joseph Wheeler,[4] came here to be a Nun in the 25th year of her age. She took the Schollars Habit on the 18th & the names of Ann Austin.

October

On the 9th Miss Nanny Bodkin went for England.

His Holiness Clement the 14th having this year published a Bull for the Suppression of the Order of the Society of Jesus; in consequence of it, the 2 English Colleges here at Bruges were seized by the Government at Bruxells on the 20th of September. Mr Berington our Confessor was appointed President of the Little College; which disagreeable Commission he accepted purely out of friendship to Mr Aston who was Principal of that House.[5] The Bishop & Commissaries required of him to ^Lodge^ [~~ladge~~] there every night, which he did till the 14th of this month. About 6 o'clock in the evening of that day, without a moments warning, all the Superiors & Masters were removed out of both **[p. 215]** Colleges. Those who were not in Orders had the choice of being confined with

---

1 Miss Usher left before profession.

2 Anna Charlotte Paterson, in religion Albana (1777–1828) BA151. In religion she took the name of her sponsor, Alban Butler: his support would have smoothed the path for her acceptance, particularly since both her parents were Protestants. For details of the miraculous cure with which she was associated, see **[pp. 275–9]**.

3 Two pages cut out here, although no text is missing.

4 Anne Austin Green (1775–1833) BA090; Ann Joseph Wheeler (BA218).

5 Little College, Bruges: Fr William Aston SJ (1735–1800) was Superior of the school 1767–73, when it was suppressed. See Holt, p. 22; Foley, vol. 5, p. 183.

the Rectors & Priests or to leave the Town in 24 hours. In this distress, Reverend Mother sent to offer Bed & Board to all those who chose to withdraw, which they accepted. We hired all the Rooms at the Millers, & filled all our outward apartments with beds on the floor as we had no better convenience: Mr Berington kindly allowed the same in his Chamber. He behaved in the most handsome manner in the whole affair, & joined with Reverend Mother in giving all the Succour & comforts possible both to the distressed Gentlemen & to their Students: for which kindness Mr More the Provincial (who was Reverend Mother's Brother) & Parents expressed the warmest gratitude.[1] Two old Lay Brothers viz. Brother Tucker & Brother Thomas Padbury[2] being allowed to stay in Town, they table with us till they can be disposed of.

November

On the 20th Mr Gerard compleated his Jubilee of being here.[3] But as he had laid down his Post of Confessor many years before, he wou'd not allow the least notice to be taken of it. However Reverend Mother made him a present of 48 Bottles of Spanish wine & 6 of Rum: & She with several others presented him prayers. The Procuratress gave a little Recreation & a glass of Wine.

[p. 216]

December

On the first of this month Sister Mary Michael Sykes departed this life in the 79th year of her age, & 57th of her Profession.[4] She possessed Talents not usual to Persons of our Sex, understood Painting & drew several Pictures for our Refectory & other places: She had an insight in Architecture & had a great hand in the Plan & in the direction of the Building of our Church: She had likewise a pritty turn for Poetry if she had been in the occasion of improving it: She was in general very ingenious & of a lively active disposition, She had read a good deal, & was agreeable in conversation, but having a peculiar kind of humour she was not much liked in Employment. For some time after her Profession, she did not seem to have a right notion of Religious Duties, but for several years before her death she applied herself to the practise of them, & was very zealous of Regular Observance, especially the Choir, which (tho' deprived of her sight) she constantly attended as well at Mattins as all the other parts of the Office, till about a year before her death. She was much addicted to penance & Mortification, & very submissive to Superiours. She supported

---

1 Mary Augustina More's brother was Fr Thomas More SJ (1722–95). See *ODNB*; Holt, pp. 169–70.

2 Br Robert Tucker (1700–90), lay brother, died at Liège; Br Thomas Padbury (1714–92) died at Bruges. Holt, pp. 249, 183.

3 Fr Gerard had arrived at the convent in 1723, but had retired as Confessor in 1761.

4 Mary Michael Sykes (1717–73) BA189.

with great vertue some very sensible mortifications, & her blindness with an edifying patience & chearfulness: and **[p. 217]** in all occasions of suffering expressed an entire conformity to the Will of God. She died of a Decay, & not being judged in present danger, she suddenly departed without the benefit of the Sacraments; but as the Confessor visited her daily for some time before her death, there is reason to hope it was not unprovided. *Requiescat in pace*. Amen.

Mr Alban Butler who had been our Extraordinary from the year 1767 died on the 15th of May this year.[1] In his Will there was found the following Paragraph. "I desire a Cross or a Plate of Metal or small Marble Stone be set up near the Doors of the Church in the English Colleges at Doway, & St Omer with this or the like Inscription. *Deus Pater Omnium Sanctificetur nomen tuum ab Omnibus in omnibus in Æternum, Fiat Voluntas tua perfectissima ab Universis, Et Fidelium Animae. requiescant in pace.*[2] *Amen.* The like in the Choir of the English Austin Nuns at Bruges." For the Expense, he left us Six Guineas, part of which Sum or the whole to be employ'd for it. Mr Wilkinson[3] his Successor at St Omer paid this money into Reverend Mothers hands in the month of December this year. At Mr Butlers death he had at her request most obligingly accepted the Charge of being our Extraordinary. About Xmass Brother Thomas Padbury[4] being turned out of his College in Bruges we received him & gave him a room in the Gardiners quarters.

[p. 218]

The Year 1774

January

On the 27th Sister Alban Patterson & Sister Ann Austin Green were clothed.[5] As the times appear'd very ~~unfa~~ unfavourable to Religious People, it was judged the most prudent to have it done quite in private, therefore the Church door was not open'd. The Arch Priest said a Low Mass, & performed all the ceremonies without singing or Musick except the *Veni Creator* which he entoned as usual. The Brides & Musicians also sung the *Eructavit* with the Organ only, which played likewise whilst they were

1 Fr Alban Butler (1707–73); see *ODNB* and Anstruther 4, pp. 52–3.

2 Translation: 'God, Father of all, may your name be hallowed by all in all things for ever. Your will be fulfilled throughout the whole world and may the souls of the faithful departed rest in peace.' I am indebted to Michael Shaw for this translation.

3 Fr William Wilkinson (1722–1803), President of St Omer. Anstruther 4, p. 104.

4 The Jesuit lay brother had been required to leave the premises following the closure of the college in Bruges in 1773.

5 Albana Paterson (BA151); Anne Austin Green (BA090).

dressing.[1] We had no Deacons. On the 30th Sister Martina Bambridge a Lay Sister departed this life in the 70th year of her age, & 45th of her Profession.[2] She was a very wild young Girl, & extremely ignorant when she came to us, therefore Superiours thought proper to give her good trials. She had a violent temper, but with it many good qualities, & was laborious even to the end. She was particularly charitable in rendering every service in her power to those who were disabled through Age or Infirmity without distinction of Persons, & when at her Prayers she appear'd to be very attentive to them, to which holy Exercice she was rema[r]ked to give herself more than usual a little before her death. She was seized by an apoplexy on the 28th, received **[p. 219]** the Holy Oyls on the same day, & expired peaceably on the 30th. *Requiescat in pace.*

March

On the 19th Mary Webster took the Schollars Habit for a Lay Sister, & the name of Monica in the 22d year of her age.[3]

Aprill the 18th Sister Ursula Clough celebrated her whole Jubilee of Religion.[4]

May

On the 19th Miss Lucretia Havers went from hence to a French house at Tournay.

On the 21st ^Miss Tichbourne^ left us to board in Town.

June

On the 3d Madlle D'Heere a flemish young Lady Daughter to one of the Magistrates of the Town was received for Pensioner in the 13th year of her age.

On the 14th Mr Talbot Nephew to the Earl of Shrewsbury with his Preceptor & 3 Sisters arrived here: They all boarded with us: The young Ladies laid in the School, but eat at the Confessors Table.[5] Miss Julia Talbot left us on the 27 & returned to Louvain where she was Pensioner.

---

1 The brides were those being clothed, wearing their wedding dresses which they gave up to put on the novices' habits. In the past it would have been a ceremony for celebration, and neighbours would have witnessed the occasion. *Eructavit cor meum*: 'My heart overfloweth …', from Psalm 44, which begins, 'For them that shall be changed …' – a reference to the ceremony when the candidate left the world and entered the religious community. It was also sung as part of the daily liturgy.

2 Martina Bambridge (1729–74) BA011.

3 Mary Ann Webster, in religion Monica (BA213).

4 Ursula Clough (1724–89) BA058.

5 Charles Talbot (b. 1753) was nephew to George Talbot, 14th Earl of Shrewsbury, who had no children. Charles had three sisters, Barbara, Juliana and Theresa Talbot. Some elite Catholic families in the period sent their sons travelling in Europe, accompanied by young priests, as part of their education.

July

On the 9th Mad[lle] D'Heere returned home to her Parents.

On the 21st Mr Talbot his Preceptor & 2 Sisters set off for England.

August

On the 4th Mad[lle] Guitard Daughter to a Merchand at Bruxells was received here for Pensioner in the 11th year of her age.

On the 24th Miss Molly Bodkin went from hence to the Ursulines at Lille.

On the 30th Miss Eliz: Daly Sister to Miss Molly Daly was received here for Pensioner in the 6th year of her age.

[p. 220]

September

On the 13th Mad[lle] Maret Daughter to a French Merchand at Dijon came from her Sister at Lille to be Pensioner here in the 16th year of her age.

On the 22d Sister Mary Bernard Paston was clothed privately in the same manner as Sister Green & Sister Patterson were ^in^ last January this same year.[1]

On the [*blank*] M[r] Berington our Confessor went for England on some Family affairs.[2]

October

On the 13th Miss Tichbourne returned here for Pensioner she came from the Convent at Ostend.

On the 24th Mad[lle] Coopman was received for Pensioner in the 16th year of her age. She is Daughter to an attorney in Town.

November

On the 14th Mademoiselle Caimo Niece to our Bishop was received for Pensioner in the 20th year of her age.

December

On the 3d Miss Molly Bodkin returned to us from Lille.

On the 18th M[r] Berington returned from England. His Place of Confessor was supplied during his absence by Reverend Father John Anderton the Confessor of Princen-hoff.[3]

On the 20th Miss Hughes went from hence to the Ursulines at Bruxells.

---

[1] Mary Bernard Paston (BA150). See **[p. 218]**.

[2] Fr Thomas Berington (1740–1805), Confessor 1772–75; Anstruther 4, p. 30.

[3] Fr John Anderton OFM (d. 1795), Confessor to the English Franciscans at Bruges 1764–74. See *Franciscana*, pp. 76–80, 233.

1775

February the 13th By the Bishop's consent & that of the Comunity Reverend Mother received Master Tomy Daly into the Inclosure for 2 years with a Maid to attend him: he **[p. 220]** was then 2 years old.

February the 9th Sister Ann Austine Green made her Holy Profession. Sister Albina Patterson was not allow'd to make hers on account of the Empresses Edict forbidding under great penalties any one to be admitted to Profession before the age of 25:[1] but she was consented by the Community with Sister Green, & performed all the Penances with her till the Profession eve. She was not examined by the Arch Priest, nor admitted in Chapter, nor was her Cell dressed. Seven days after viz on the 16th the Bishop allowed her all the Priviledges of the Professed, except wearing the black veil; giving her vote in Chapter; or being put into any of the Principal Offices ^of the Community,^ but this latter might be done with his consent. He also ordered that she shou'd not be present when the Superiour had any particular correction to give in Chapter or when the Statutes are read. The same is to be observed in regard of all others who for want of age cannot be Professed, & they are to take their own Rank after it.

March

On the 8th Miss Coopman returned to her Parents in Town.

On the 25 Miss Kitty & Miss Betty Talbots went from hence to L'Abbathe des Pretz at Doway.[2]

On the 29th Miss Joanna Caimo Niece to our Bishop was received for Pensioner.

May

On the 1st Sister Monica Webster was clothed for a Lay Sister.[3] A Singing Mass followed the Ceremonies, & the 2 last Hours were read.

On the 25th Miss Eliz: Green was received for Pensioner in the 12th year of her Age.

---

1 Albana Patterson would not be 25 until 1777. Empress Maria Theresa of Austria (1717–80) imposed a number of reforms on the religious life in her territories, including the Southern Netherlands. The restriction on age at entry was passed partly in order to keep labour available for use outside convents. Here Albana is being granted most of the privileges of the professed, without the convent appearing to challenge the new edict, in order to avoid controversy.

2 Abbaye des Pres de Douai: see **[p. 151]**.

3 Monica Webster (BA213).

[p. 222]

June

On the 10th Miss Charlotte & Miss Harriott Jenison [~~illeg.~~] 2 Protestant young Ladies were received for Pensioners. The eldest was in her 15th year, the youngest in her 14th.

On the 13th Miss Homes went from hence to the Ursulines at Lille.

On the 16th the two Miss Langtons left us for England.

July

On the 26th Sister Teresa Clares[1] Sister, Miss Sally Farrill came here to be Religious in the 28th year of her Age. & on the same day Miss Nanny Bodkin returned for Pensioner.

On the 27th Miss Tichbourne went from hence to the English Monastery at Liege.

August

On the 2d Mademoiselle D'Huet Daughter to a Merchand at Mecklin was received for Pensioner, in the 16th year of her age.

On the 3d Miss Harriott Jenison returned to her Parents.

On the 28th Miss Sally Farrill took the Schollars Habit & the names of Mary Xaveria.

On the 29th Madlle Rouget Daughter to one of our Magistrates was received for Pensioner about 19 years of age.

September

On the first Mr Ball a Doway Priest arrived here from the Mission in England to supply the place of our Confessor Mr Berington.[2]

On the 4th Madlle Maret returned to her Sister at Lille & Miss Bell Angier went on the same day to a french Convent at Tourcoine.

[p. 223] On the 11th Mr Berrington our Confessor by the consent of the Community left us to travel for 2 years as Preceptor to Mr Plowden.[3]

On the 21st Miss Charlot Jenison returned to her Parents.

October

On the 1st Sister Mary Bernard Paston having compleated her years Noviceship was allowed the Priviledges of the Professed in the same manner as Sister Albina.[4]

On the 12th Miss Nanny Bodkin went to the Dames at Dunkerk.

---

1 Teresa Clare Farrell (BA077).

2 Fr John Ball (1722/3–81), Confessor 1775–78; Anstruther 4, pp. 15–16.

3 This is not mentioned in Anstruther 4, p. 30. A number of elite Catholic families sent their sons on a Grand Tour accompanied by a young priest to act as guardian, arrange their programme and introduce them to the right people.

4 Mary Bernard Paston (BA150). This is a second example of a novice being allowed to proceed to profession according to convent rules, but in contravention of the imperial edict on age at profession.

On the 17th Miss Dillon & Miss Bates went to a French House at Tournay.

On the 29th Miss Frances Henrietta Jernimgham arrived here. Daughter to Mr Henry Jernimgham of Maryland, & Niece to our 3 Sister Jerninghams. She was in the 30th year of her age:[1] & on the same day Mrs Bella Sparling came to wait on Master Tomy Daly.

November

On the 4th The Negrow Woman Nurse to Master Tomy Daly set off for England.[2]

On the 6th Madlle Van Oye was received for Pensioner the Daughter of a Merchand in Town in the 19th year of her age.

On the 21st Madlle Vandenberge was received for Pensioner, Daughter to a Lace Merchand in Town in the 17th year of her age.

December

On the 22d Reverend Mother & the Community lost a great Friend by the death of our worthy Bishop Lord John Robert **[p. 224]** Caimo, who was universally regretted by his whole Diocess.

1776

January

On the 13th Miss Frances Henrietta Jerningham took the Schollars Habit in the 31st year of her age, & the names of Mary Frances Sales.

February

On the 2d Mad'lle Rouget went from hence.

On the 7th Sister Mary Xaveria Farrill quitted the Habit, & left us to go to Liege, not having health or other dispositions proper for us.[3]

On the 16th Miss Bates returned to us from Tournay.

March

On the 21st Miss Julia Talbot was received for Pensioner, being 17 years of age the same month.[4]

---

[1] Frances Henriette Jerningham, in religion Mary Francis of Sales (1777–1824) BA123, Sub-Prioress. Her parents were Henry Jerningham of St Mary's County and Catherine Rozer, born in St George's County, Maryland. Her aunts were Ann (BA120), Edwardina (BA121) and Elizabeth (BA122) Jerningham.

[2] The black nurse must have been appointed to accompany young Tommy Daly from the West Indies; a local replacement had been found to look after him while he was in the convent community. Several groups of young Catholics from Maryland and the West Indies travelled together to Europe for their education without their parents in this period because of a lack of Catholic schools in America.

[3] Sally Farrill, in religion Mary Xaveria (BA237), did not profess with the Sepulchrines.

[4] Julia or Juliana Talbot (b. 1759) was the sister of Barbara and Theresa Talbot, daughters of Charles Talbot and Mary Mostyn.

Aprill

On the ~~26~~ 16 Miss Betty Dillon & Miss Lucretia Havers returned here from Tournay.

On the 20th Miss Lucretia Havers left us to go to England.

On the 30th Miss Bates went from hence to the Ursulines at Ghent.[1]

May

On the 5th Miss Peggy Ley came here for Pensioner in the 15th year of her age. She is Daughter to an **[p. 225]** Irish Merchand settled in the Town.

On the 18th Miss Betty Dillon took the Schollars Habit in the 18th year of her age, & the names of Mary Aurelia.[2]

June

On the 15th Miss Kitty & Miss Betty Talbot came here from the French House on a visit expecting their 2 younger Sisters arrival from England. they were in the School on the same footing as the Pensioners.

On the 18th Sister Frances Sales Jerningham was Clothed.[3]

On the 22d Miss Teresa & Miss Charlotte Talbot came here for Pensioners. Miss Teresa in the 15th year of her age & Miss Charlotte in the 10th. And on the same day Miss Biddy & Miss Conny Dalton Nieces to Reverend Mother More.[4] Miss Biddy in the 15th year of her age, & Miss Conny in the 10th.

On the 27th Miss Caimo went from hence.

July

On the 7th Miss Kitty & Miss Betty Talbot returned to the French House at Doway.

On the 30th Miss Mary Ball came here for Pensioner in the 20th year of her age. She is Niece to the Gentleman who supplies Mr Beringtons Place.[5]

August

On the 17th Miss Mary Mawhood came here as Boarder **[p. 226]** in the 24th year of her age to see our method of life.[6]

---

1 Miss Bates was here deciding to join not one of the English convents in exile but a local community.

2 Elizabeth Dillon, in religion Mary Aurelia (1780–1803) BA073, Sub-Prioress from 1794, Novice Mistress from 1795, musician.

3 Mary Francis of Sales Jerningham (BA123).

4 Bridget and Constance Dalton were the daughters of Robert Dalton (d. 1785) of Thurnham Hall, Lancashire, and Bridget née More (d. 1797), sister of Prioress Mary Augustina More. See **[pp. 233, 237]**.

5 Fr John Ball (1723–81) was supplying as Confessor 1775–78; see Anstruther 4, p. 16. John Ball's father came from Scale Hall, Lancaster. Mary Ball has not yet been identified.

6 Maria Mawhood professed as Louisa Austin in 1779; see below **[pp. 227, 230]**.

September

On the 16th Madlle Maricourt of Lille came here for Pensioner in the 15th year of her age.

On the 27th Miss Kitty Talbot returned here from the French House.

October

On the 10th Miss Kitty Talbot took the Schollars Habit & the name of Alissia in the 19th year of her age.[1]

On the 26th Miss Mary Bodkin took the Schollars Habit & the name of Stanislaus in the 20th year of her age.

November

On the 19th Sister Mary Aurelia Dillon was Clothed, privately on account of the Queens Edict which forbids a Profession before the age of 25 compleat.[2]

On the 21st Joanna De Court of Flemish Parents from the Country, took the Schollars Kerchief for a Lay Sister & the name of Benedict in the 29th year of her age.[3] She had lived ^with^ us 10 years as Servant.

December

On the 3d Madlle Maricourt returned to her Parents at Lille.

[p. 227]

The Year 1777

January

On the 3d Miss Mawhood left us to enter the Noviceship at the Ursulines at St Omer. Miss Julia Talbot & Miss Ball went with her to be pensioners at the same French House.

February

On the 9th being Shrove Sunday Sister Justina Huddleston celebrated her whole Jubilee.[4]

On the 15th Miss Bell Angier returned to us from the French House.

On the 21st Madlle Vandenberge went from hence.

Aprill

On the 4th Madlle Van Oye went from hence.

On the 10th Miss Tuite a Pensioner from Louvain was taken into the Inclosure to wait an occasion for England, which occurred on the 20th of the same month.

On the 21 Madlle D'Huet went from hence.

---

1 Catherine Talbot, in religion Alicia (1780–1822) BA190, Procuratrix from 1788.

2 See **[p. 220]**.

3 Joanna De Corte, in religion Godoliva Maria Benedicta (1778–1829) BA066.

4 Mary Justina Huddleston (1727–87) BA113.

On the 21 Miss Julia Talbot ~~returned~~ ^came^ here from the French House at St Omer ~~for~~ to be present at her Sisters Clothing.

On the 28 Sister Alissia Talbot & Sister Stanny Bodkin were Clothed privately.[1]

On the 30 Miss Julia Talbot returned to St Omer.

May

On the 2d Miss Bates returned to us from the French House at Ghent.[2]

[p. 228]

May

On the 3d Miss Elizabeth Morris was sent here by Lady Powis for Pensioner, being 9 years old the precedent month.[3]

On the 21 Madlle Proost of Bruges came here for Pensioner, being 17 years of age.

On the 22d Sister Benedict De Corte a Flemming was Clothed for a Lay Sister.[4]

On the 26 we sent Charles Teborier our upper Gardiner to England with Master Tommy Daly, who had been here 2 years and about 5 Months.

June

On the 10th Miss Betty Talbot came here on a Visit to her Sister She ~~tabled~~ ^tabled^ with the Pensioners.

On the 16th Madlle De Vaux Daughter to our Physician came here for Pensioner in the 13 year of her age.

July

On the 2d Sister Albana Paterson & Sister Francis Sales Jernimgham made their Holy Profession.[5] On the 7th Miss Betty Talbot returned to the French House at Doway: & her Sister Teresa went with her.

On the 14 Miss Biddy Dalton went to the Ursulines at Lille.

September

On the 14 Miss Molly Havers (Sister to Miss Harriott) came here for Pensioner in the 13 year of her age.

---

1 Alicia Talbot professed in 1780; she later moved to join the Poor Clares from Gravelines after their move to England. See M. J. Mason, 'Nuns of the Jerningham Letters: Elizabeth Jerningham (1727–1807) and Frances Henrietta Jerningham (1745–1824), Augustinian Canonesses of Bruges', *Recusant History* 22(3) (1995), pp. 360.

2 Miss Bates was the daughter of Mr Bates of Stock Hall, Essex, and a cousin of Fr Thomas Berington. See also **[p. 211]**.

3 In 1777 Lady Powis was Barbara, widow of the 1st Earl, who died in 1772. Their son, who inherited the title, did not marry.

4 Benedicta De Corte (BA066); see also **[p. 226]**.

5 Albana Paterson (BA151); Mary Francis of Sales Jerningham (BA123).

[p. 229]

September

On the 19th Miss Sally Powell ^a Convert^ came here to be Religious in the 23d year of her age.[1] Miss Carpenter a Protestant came with her being about 24 years of age they both Tabled with the Pensioners.

October

On the 5th being the Feast of Our Blessed Ladys Rosary, Miss Powell was taken into the Church by Mr Ball.[2] She had been Pensioner at a French House in Boulogne, which was the happy cause of her Conversion, but her Parents being Protestants, She did not dare after her return to them to be received into the Church, but delayed it till she came here.

On the 10th The Arch Bishop of Mechlin, our own Bishop, & the Bishop of Ipres came to see the Church which was adorned with all the Plate.[3] The Nuns were placed Choir ways on each Side the Sisters ~~Chapplle~~ Chapel, the Novices & Lay Sisters in the Chapter House, & the Pensioners in the Church: By his Lordship's orders the Chapel doors were open'd, & the 3 Bishops, Mess'r Gerard & Ball,[4] with some other Ecclesiastics & Secular Gentlemen attending the Prelates came in and walked through the lower parts of the Monastery only. As our Bishop had acquainted Reverend Mother of their coming & appointed the hour, Vespers was differ'd till 4 o'clock.

[p. 230]

October

On the 22d Madlle Stevens the only Child of a great Baker in Town came here for Pensioner being about 17 years old.

On the 25 Miss Nanny & Miss Fanny Rooper came here for Pensioners, Daughters to the Honble Mr Phill ~~Rop~~ Rooper. Miss Nanny being 9 years old; Miss Fanny in her 8th year.[5]

November

On the 4th Miss Carpenter went from hence to a French House at Bruxelles.

On the 18th Madlle Proast returned to her Parents.

On the 24 Madlle Vandewoostyne of a Gentlemans Family in Ghent came here to be Pensioner, between 15 & 16 years of age.

---

1 Sally Powell left before profession.

2 Fr John Ball (1723–81), Confessor 1775–78; Anstruther 4, pp. 15–16.

3 The Archbishop of Mechelen was Cardinal Johann Heinrich von Frankenberg (d. 1802); the Bishop of Bruges from May 1775 was Feliz Brenart (d. 1794); the Bishop of Ypres was F.-J. H. de Wavrans, 1762–84.

4 Fr Caryl Gerrard, Confessor 1723–79. A second confessor was needed because of the illness and age of Fr Gerard. Fr John Ball (1723–81), Confessor 1775–78; Anstruther 4, pp. 15–16.

5 Philip Roper, fourth son of Henry, 10th Lord Teynham and his wife, Barbara Lyttleton, had five daughters.

On the 29th Miss Powell took the Schollars Habit, & the names of Elizabeth Austine.[1]

1778

January

On the 1st Sister Monica Webster a Lay Sister made her Holy Profession.[2]

On the 20th Miss Maria Mawhood returned here to be a Nun. She took the Schollars Habit on the 24th & the names of Louisa Austine being in the 25th year of her age.[3]

February

On the 10th Miss Daly & Miss Green went to the Ursulines at Lille.

[p. 231]

February

On the 11th Sister Stanny Bodkin our Novice went for England: Our Upper Gardiner conducted her.

On the 12th Miss Shee of Irish Parents came here for Pensioner in the 14th year of her age.

March

On the 11th Madlle Haerts a Fleming from Ghent was received for Pensioner in the 18th year of her age.

Aprill

On the 15th Madlle De Waele Daughter to ^the Master of^ the Ghent Barge [~~*illeg.*~~] was received for Pensioner in the 14th year of her age.

On the 20th Miss Bates went from hence to England.

May

On the 7th Miss Carpenter returned to us from the French House at Bruxelles.

On the 13th Madlle De Roo was received for Pensioner about 17 years of age. Her Father is an Echevin of the Countries.

On the 20th Miss Julea & Miss Betty Talbot returned to us from Doway.[4]

June

On the 1st Madlle Vandewoostyne went from hence.

On the 2d Sister Benedict De Courte made her Holy Profession.[5]

---

1 Miss Powell left before profession.
2 Monica Webster (BA213).
3 Maria Mawhood, in religion Louisa Austin (1779–1832) BA140, Procuratrix from 1799; Prioress 1807–10.
4 Julia and Betty Talbot were daughters of Charles Talbot and Mary Mostyn.
5 Benedicta De Corte (BA066).

On the 2d Miss Harriett Havers went from hence to the Ursulines at Antwerp.[1]

[p. 232] On the 8th Sister Martha Fergusons Mother was Baptised conditionally in our Church with all the Ceremonies by Mr Ball.[2]

On the 16th Mr Ball left us, being recalled to the Mission in England by his Bishop.

On the 23d Miss Kitty Blundell the eldest Daughter of Henry Blundell Esqr of Ince was received for Pensioner in the 16th year of her age. She is Niece to our Sister Blundell.[3]

July

On the 1st Madlle Taillieu Niece to our Doctor De Vaux was received for Pensioner about 14 years of age.

On the 9th Miss Julia & Betty Talbot left us to go to England.

On the 16th Sister Louisa Mawhood was Clothed.

On the 17th Madlle De Vaux went from hence.

On the 18th Miss Molly Huddleston Daughter to Ferdinand Huddleston Esqr of Sawston was received for Pensioner in the 9th year of her age. She is little niece to Sister Justina Huddleston.[4]

On the 24 Miss Peggy Ley left us. On the same day Miss MacGuire of Irish Parents was received for Pensioner about 14 years of age.

~~July~~ August

On the 30th Miss Betty Mawhood was received for Pensioner in the 14th year of her age. She is Sister to Sister Louisa Mawhood.[5]

[p. 233]

August

On the 31st Miss Carpenter left us to return to England.

---

1 Harriet Havers, probably daughter of William Havers, was cousin to the three Havers sisters, Lucretia, Kitty and Molly.

2 Fr John Ball (1723–81), Confessor 1775–78. Anstruther 4, pp. 15–16, suggests that he went to England to act as chaplain to the Bishop family rather than being recalled by the bishop.

3 Catherine Blundell, daughter of Henry Blundell and Elizabeth Mostyn (d. 1767) of Ince Blundell, Lancashire; later married Thomas Stonor (WWTN family tree). Her aunt was Charlotte Blundell, in religion Mary Joseph (BA027). See also Janet E. Hollinshead, *Women of the Catholic Community: The Blundells of South Lancashire during the Seventeenth and Eighteenth Centuries* (Wigan: North West Catholic History Society, 2010).

4 Molly Huddleston was one of two daughters of Ferdinand Huddleston and Mary Lucas; her great aunt was Mary Justina Huddleston (BA113): see **[pp. 303–4]**. See also Stirnet, Family Tree, Huddleston03.

5 Elizabeth Mawhood (bap. 1763) was the daughter of William Mawhood and Dorothy Kroger of London; her sister was Maria Mawhood, in religion Louisa Austin (BA140); see *Mawhood Diary*, p. 11.

September

On the 12th Mr Burgess came here for our Confessor from the Mission in England on which he had been a few months.[1] He began his Studies at Rome, but finished them at Doway at the English Clergy. He was only 27 years of age when he came to us.

November

On the 27th Miss Biddy Dalton[2] & Miss Green, & Miss Daly returned to us from the French House at Lille.

December

On the 4th Reverend Mother More Solemnized her half Jubilee of being Religious.[3] It fell on Fryday a Communicating day being the first Fryday in the Month, & Fasting day by the Church because it was in Advent. On the Eve nothing was done, except adorning several parts of the House, particularly the Choir Refectory & her Chamber where she then laid being in a poor State of health: which obliged her the next day to communicate in the Sick Chapel before Mass, & She took her Breakfast in the Infirmary which was also decorated. Half an hour after the Community had left the Choir, the Subprioress rung the Refectory Bell, & all the Nuns assembled in the passage near her **[p. 234]** Chamber where she then was: when she came out of it they conducted her to the Upper Speak House & placed her in a great arm chair before a Table cover'd with a Carpet upon which stood a large Japanned Tea Board which held a Glass Pyramid: On the board & each row of the Pyramid were laid Flowers, Purses, & several sorts of Works, & a large crown of Silver Flowers at the top: These works which the Community presented to the Bride, as well as the Crown which was very noble were done by some few, but by their desire offer'd from all, & tho' there were then three of the Nuns who had not embraced the Reform of having all things in Common, yet they wou'd have their Presents mingled with the rest, which gave a great satisfaction to Reverend Mother. It was then about 12 years since she had happily introduced this Regulation. We were in Community including 10 Sisters, 41.

When the Bride was seated Mr Burgess our Confessor on the outside of the Grate accompanied our Musicians on the Harpsicord ^& all sung the Base to^ a piece of Musick composd by himself for that occasion whilst they performed it, the Subprioress put the Crown on her Head. When the Musick finished the Community attended her through the Dormitory to the Choir the Pensioners were placed on each side the Gallery as she

---

[1] Fr Matthew Burgess (1752–86), Confessor at Bruges from 1778, but considered himself 'ill-used' by Prioress Mary Augustina More and left in 1782. Anstruther 4, pp. 50–1.

[2] Bridget Dalton, daughter of Robert Dalton of Thurnham and Bridget More; see **[pp. 225, 237]**.

[3] Mary Augustina More (BA145); she professed on 4 December 1753.

passed. The *Te Deum* **[p. 235]** was sung in Fauxbourdon, M[r] Burgess play'd and sung the ground, & then came into the Choir & sung the Prayer. When finished she was conducted to the Nuns Musick Room where She received the compliments of the Pensioners, & being seated in an arm chair, their Presents ^of fine works ^were ~~offered~~ ^presented in baskets^ by 5 or 6 of the least dressed in their best, during which her Eldest Niece Miss Dalton accompanied a Motette composed in her honour & sung by 2 of the Young Ladies. We had then 23 Pensioners & they dined in our Refectory. The Procuratress ^gave a very handsome dinner.^ In the afternoon an Ode was performed by M[r] Burgess & our Musicians in the Work Room.

At Collation her Health was drank in hot Liquor, & during the time of it, the Cloisters & other places of the House were Illuminated. It was Recreation till 7 & no longer. Mother More kept her half Jubilee a secret from the Town: She wou'd not allow a Musick Mass, nor permit the Neighbours to do any thing in her honour. None of her Relations were here, so that we enjoyd it entirely amongst ourselves to her great satisfaction. It did not ring to work the whole Octave.

On the 6th a Lay Sister came from Louvain, She was taken into the Inclosure, slept in the Purple Room & eat in the Infirmary. She left us on the 9th of the same month.

[p. 236]

The Year 1779

January

On the 2[d] Mad[lle] Mean was received for Pensioner about 17 years of age. She is Daughter to a Gentleman of Bruxelles.

On the 22[d] Mad[lle] Haerts went from hence.

On the [*blank*] Reverend Mother gave a handsome Recreation for her half Jubilee, & a present to each of the Nuns of 2 particular Aprons 2 p[r] of Gloves & a Spiritual Treatise. The Sisters had ~~only~~ one fine blue Apron, with the Gloves & Spiritual Treatise. Her Reverence gave a 2[d] Recreation in Lent.

March

M[r] Burgess our Director having discovr'd that one of our former Confessors (who was with us 5 years & odd months) had not Faculties, to satisfy his conscience he obliged all those who had been his Penitents to make a general Confession of those years:[1] As the greatest part of the Com-

[1] Fr Matthew Burgess (1752–86), Confessor at Bruges 1778–82; Anstruther 4, pp. 50–1. Confessors to convents of nuns were required to have faculties granted to them by the bishop or his representative in order to hear confession: without them his role was unauthorised and invalid. I am indebted to Fr Luke Beckett OSB of Ampleforth, for his explanation of this point.

munity were involved in the case, it caused no small trouble & allarm, but Mr Burgess acted in the affair with such an extraordinary Prudence & Charity that without noise he made it easy, by taking the immense fatigue on himself of helping each one. {^As Reverend Mother knew the case mentioned above in the year 1782 ^& 1783^, She consulted 4 Learned Men upon it, who unanimously declared that the Confessor had not lost his Faculties, & of consequence that the Repetition of Confessions from his Penitents was not necessary. Mr Burgess acted to the best of his judgment, but did not then think it prudent to consult other Divines^}[1]

Aprill

On the 14th Miss Biddy Dalton went from hence to the Ursulines at Ghent.

[p. 237]

May

On the ~~17th~~ 7th Madlle Joanna Caimo went from hence.

On the 10th Madlle Stevens went from hence.

On the 28th Miss Biddy Dalton & Miss Harriette Havers returned to us from the French House.

June

On the 12th Sister Joachim Forshaw[2] set off for England with Miss Biddy & Conny Dalton: the youngest being in a very ill State of health a proper Person was requisite to tend her on the Road. Miss Green went by the same [~~illeg.~~] occasion.

On the 13th Miss Blundell left us to go to a French House at Bruxelles.

On the 15th Mr John Giffard Cousin German to Reverend Mother desired to place his Daughter of 4 years old with a maid in our Inclosure.[3] He had fled ^secretly^ from England with this Child to prevent her being brought up a Protestant by his Lady: As her admission with a Maid was not approved of by the Council Sisters, & Reverend Mother would not determine on it herself, being her own Relation, the Community desired it might be put to a general Voting, which was done, & it was concluded in the affirmative.

---

1 Added later in the same hand, but different ink.

2 Joachim Forshaw (BA083).

3 John Giffard (d. 1797) of Plas Ucha, Nercwys, North Wales married Elizabeth Hyde (1730–1805), daughter of Robert Hyde of Nerquis Hall. They had two daughters, Eleanor (probably 'Nelly' in the Chronicle) and Elizabeth (b. 1765). Archives Wales in their introduction to the Nerquis Hall Estate Papers (held at Flintshire Record Office) records a dispute over the education of the daughters because Elizabeth Hyde was Protestant. See a http://arcw.llgc.org.uk/anw/get_collection.php?coll_id=1114&inst_id=28&term=Deeds%20%7C%20Wales%20%7C%20Flintshire, accessed 20 March 2017.

On the 20th Ann Wheeler Niece to Sister Mary Currell took the Schollars Kerchief for a Lay Sister **[p. 238]** in the 20th year of her age[1] & with her Elizabeth Sargeant in the 26th year of her age: the first took the names of Ann Clare, the other Lucy Austine.

On the 26th Sister Joachim returned to us from England.

On the 28th Miss Nelly Giffard & her Maid left us to go into France: As Mr Giffard was apprehensive that his Lady wou'd procure the Court of England to apply to that at Bruxelles for her, he carried her to Paris, for the French being then at War with England he judged her secure in that Kingdom.

July

On the 8th Miss Powell put off the Habit & left us to go to board at a French House in St Omer.

On the 14th Miss Shee went from hence to Ireland.

On the 20th Sister Louisa Austine Mawhood made her Holy Profession.[2]

On the 20th 2 Miss Hawcourts came here for Boarders ^within the Inclosure^ to see our manner of life, they ~~tabled~~ ^eat^ at the Confessors Table.[3]

August

On the 13th Madlle De Waele went from hence.

On the 14th Miss Nanny Hawcourt took the Schollars Habit in the 25th year of her age, & the names of Mary Xaveria.

On the 14th Madlle De Roo went from hence.

On the 17th Madlle Nanny Taillieu was received for Pensioner being about 10 years of age.

[p. 239]

September

On the 1st Madlle Stapignon was received for Pensioner about 15 years of age. She is Daughter to a Merchant in Bruges.

On the 6th Miss Mary Jane Huddleston left us to go to Paris.

On the 12th being the Feast of Our Blessed Ladys Name, Reverend Mr Gerard departed this life in the 84th year of his age.[4] He had been Confessor here 38 years: finding himself grow Infirm, he gave up his Charge, but remained with us the following 18 years of his life. He paid his Board, & said the Foundation Mass. He was a Man of great Learning, & of an irreproachable life, but of an odd turn of temper, which rather

---

1 Ann Wheeler, in religion Ann Clare (BA217), left in 1785 to join the Carmelites at Lierre as a servant; her aunt was Ann Currell, in religion Mary (BA069). Elizabeth Sargeant, in religion Lucy Austin (1782–1835) BA171.

2 Louisa Austin Mawhood (BA140).

3 The two Harcourts may have been trying out the religious life before deciding whether to enter.

4 Fr Caryl Gerard, Confessor 1723–79; Anstruther 4, p. 110.

diverted, than offended his Friends & Acquaintances by whom he was universally esteem'd. He had a most extraordinary devotion to the Holy Sacrifice of the Altar, constantly saying Mass even in his old age & Infirmities till he was confined to his Chamber, which was about half a year before his happy Death. When Confessor he very much promoted piety & Regularity in the Community & was a singular example of ^both^ in his own daily conduct. Almighty God was pleased to purify him by many Trials, especially during our Disturbances under Mr Hinde[1] & he bore many slights he met with on that occasion both from the Bishop & several in the Community with **[p. 240]** great vertue & without complaint. His Illness was a decay: his judgment was perfect to the last, & he supported his sufferings with extraordinary patience, Resignation, courage & chearfulness of temper even to the very last day of his life. The night before he died, his attendants finding a considerable alteration called on Mr Burgess[2] who was his Confessor, who gave him immediately the Rites of the Holy Church, & after a short, tho sharp Agony he yielded up his happy Soul with great calmness about 4 & a half in the morning. *Requiescat in pace.*

We said the Commendations in the Choir as soon as Breakfast was over, & the Bell was rung during the time of them. He was laid out & vested in an Amice, Alb, girdle, black Manipule, Stole & Vestment: Mr Burgess with the assistance of the 2 Men Servants, performed this charitable act: 4 small Candles were placed by his Corpse, & continued burning till he was removed into the Church. Reverend Mother being desirous that every regard shou'd be paid to him, endeavour'd to procure [~~*illeg.*~~] ^Religious, then^ to pray by him night & day, but being the time of the Vacancy, she cou'd only obtain them the 2 nights the body remained above ground. On the 14th Vespers was said at 2 o'clock, when finished the Corpse was carried on the Bear by 4 Bidders from his Apartment **[p. 241]** through the Sacristy, preceded by the Pensioners & Sisters who walked 2 & 2 with lighted candles weighing one ounce, after these followd the Servant Man carrying the Crucifix & ^Silver^ Holy Water Bucket, then Mr Burgess in the black Velvet Cope & Mr Potts from Doway in a Surplice:[3] the 2 Priests sung the *Subvenite* together. At the half hour after 6 in the evening the Corpse was carried on the Shoulders of 6 Priests to the Grave in our Church Yard: he had many years before fixed on the spot he judged the most proper to remind the Community to pray for him, the Nuns & Sisters follow'd with lighted Candles, the Pensioners were also present.

On the 15th the Solemn Funeral was performed by Mr Burgess our Confessor (being commission'd by the Archpriest to whom it belonged to

---

[1] See **[pp. 150–3, 190]** above. Fr Francis Hinde; Anstruther 4, p. 138.

[2] Fr Matthew Burgess (1752–1786), Confessor 1778–82; Anstruther 4, pp. 50–1.

[3] Probably Fr Thomas Potts, who entered at Douai, was ordained in Arras 1778 and left for the mission in 1782. Anstruther 4, pp. 220–1.

do that Office) the 2 Reverend Friars from Princen-hoff were Deacons by their own desire: the High Mass & Funeral was sung by them Mr Burgess, Mr Potts & Musicians from the Town in the most Solemn manner. We had an Undertaker who took care of every thing from his death till the first Funeral Service was ended.

Reverend Mother recommended to the whole Community to say the Private Dierges as for our own Religious & order'd the *Miserere* & *De profundis* to be said for him 30 days.

[p. 242]

September

On the 14th of September this year we closed the 150th year of our Establishment at Bruges.[1] We Sung the *Te Deum* a quarter after Communion, but no further notice was taken on account of Mr Gerard's death, except a glass of wine at Supper which we drank in Silence.

On the 14th Miss Blundell came here on a visit from the French House at Bruxells.

On the 17th Miss Hawcourt left us to return to England, but returned on the 20th being driven back by a Storm at Sea.

On the 22d at 10 o'clock we had a Solemn Mass with Deacons for Mr Gerard, the Herse was placed in the Church, & the *Responsorium Libera* [*me*][2] sung after the Mass by Mr Burgess & the Deacons.

On the 25th Miss Blundell returned to the French House at Bruxells.

October

On the 7th The Community was assembled to decide by ~~Voti~~ Votes, whether if our Schollar Sister Mary Xaveria Hawcourt[3] gave satisfaction in every other point during her Trial, She might be received with a constant permission of drinking Wine, as beer wou'd not agree with her health, but with the proviso of an allowance made by her for the payment of it, the votes passed in her favour.

[p. 243]

October

On the 25th Mademoiselle Merlin from Antwerp was received for Pensioner about 13 years of age.

On the 25th The Procuratress gave the Cummunity a handsome Recreation ^at Dinner,^ for the 150th year of our Establishment at Bruges. We had ^also^ a breakfast of hot Cracknells Tea, or Coffee, & a Collation after Compline of oysters &c with choice of Punch, Spanish or Red wine: We sat up till 10 o'clock, & had no silence throughout the day except in time of the Office.

---

1 Five nuns had been sent from Louvain on 11 September 1629.

2 The Responsory 'Deliver me from eternal death', sung as part of the Office of the Dead.

3 She had come with her sister in July to try out the religious life; see **[p. 238]**.

November

On the 6th Miss Bell Angier took the Schollars Habit & the names of Mary Regis in the 17th year of her age.[1]

1780

March

On the 16th Madlle Taillieu left us. On the 29th Miss Nanny Hawcourt left the Habit, & returned to England, not having health for our State of life.

[p. 244] On the 31 Miss Blundell came here on a Visit to her Aunt: She Lodged & tabled with the Pensioners.

Aprill

On the 9th Miss Daly & Miss Poly Havers went to Marquette.

On the 20th Mr Wappeler came to board here & says the Foundation Mass.[2]

May

On the 8th Miss Polly Huddleston went to Lille & returned on the 16th.

June

On the 2d Miss Teresa Stapignon was received for Pensioner in the 15th year of her age.

On the 4th Miss Jane Huddleston of Saupon was received for Pensioner in the 10th year of her age.[3]

On the 7th Miss Teresa Talbot returned to us from the French House at Doway.

On the 9th The 2 Miss Fleischman's from Amsterdam were received for Pensioners. Miss Mary in the 13th year of her age, Miss Betty in the 10th.

On the 13th The Bishop gave us leave to have the 40 hours Prayer in our church for our distressed Nation, which then suffer'd extremely from dreadfull Riots.[4] We began at seven **[p. 245]** [*blank*] o clock in the morning & ended at 5 for 4 days. His Lordship granted an Indulgence of 40 days, as often as we or any Extern visited the Blessed Sacrement during that time.

On the 17th Two young Ladies grown up came here as Pensioners for a few weeks, viz Miss Hopton & Miss Kelly, till Mr Hopton (Father to the One & Uncle to the other) had fitted up a House in Town.

---

1 Isabella Angier, in religion Mary Regis (BA005).

2 Fr William Wappeler SJ (1711–1781), Bruges College 1767–9 and later; Holt, p. 258.

3 Jane Huddleston, sister of Polly (above) was the daughter of Ferdinand Huddleston, who married Mary Lucas in 1766. She later married Francis Canning of Foxcote.

4 Forty hours' continuous devotion before the Blessed Sacrament, beginning with a Mass. The practice first appeared in the sixteenth century in a time of crisis. 'Riots' refers to the Gordon riots, which broke out in June 1780 in London following the presentation of a petition to the House of Commons on 2 June claiming that the Catholic Relief Act was a threat to the Church of England.

On the 29th Miss Lelia Havers of Thelton was received for Pensioner in the 12th year of her age.[1]

On the 30th Miss Guitare returned to us & was received as Pensioner.

July

On the 7th Miss Charlotte Talbot left us to go to the English Monastery at Liege.[2]

On the 27th Miss Hopton left us, & Miss Kelly on the 29th.

August

On the 4th Sister Regis Angier our Schollar went to Blackenberghe to bathe & drink the Sea Water, Sister Anna Maria Hyde a Lay Sister went with her.[3] A week after Sister Lucy Serjeant a Schollar for a Lay Sister, **[p. 246]** was sent for the same advantage.[4]

On the 13th a young Widow called Mrs Johnson a Protestant enter'd as Pensioner in the view of being taken into the Church.

On the 13th Miss Lucy Mawhood was received for Pensioner in the 9th year of her age.[5]

On the 14th Miss Feast was received here for Pensioner in order to be taken into the Church.

September

On the 1st Miss Feast was taken into the Church by Mr Burgess our Confessor at 4 o'clock in the Afternoon: The *Veni Creator* was sung with the Organ: after it She made her Profession of Faith, which the Choir repeated, & when finished we sung the *Te Deum*.

On the 2d Miss Teresa Stapignon left us, & on the 5th Mrs Johnson the Protestant widow.

On the 12th being Mr Gerards Anniversary, we had a Solemn Mass with Deacons at 10 o'clock: the Hearse was erected, & after Mass the 3 Priests sung the last *Responsorium*.

On the 30th Miss Daly came here from Marquette, & Miss Blundell from Bruxells.

October

On the first Sister Mary Bernard Paston made her Holy Profession.[6]

[p. 247] On the 8th Miss Guitare returned home.

On the 16th Miss Teresa Talbot left us to return to England.

---

1 Leila Havers was the daughter of Thomas Havers of Thelveton, Norfolk, and Catherine Dutry.

2 There is no record of Charlotte Talbot having joined the Sepulchrines at Liège.

3 Mary Regis Angier (BA005); Anne Maria Hyde (BA103).

4 She professed in 1782 as Lucy Austin (BA171).

5 Lucy was the sister of Mary and Betty Mawhood, daughters of William Mawhood (d. 1797) of London and Dorothy Kroger (d. 1798).

6 Mary Bernard Paston (BA150).

On the 16th Madlle Cante Daughter to a Silk Mercer at Ghent was received for Pensioner in the 16th year of her age.

On the 18th Miss Daly returned to Marquette.

On the 21st Madlle Rose De Roo of Tilt was received for Pensioner about 17 years old. She is Sister to one of that name who came to us May the 13th 1778.

On the 29 Sister Lucy Serjeant was Clothed by Mr Burgess our Confessor:[1] it being Sunday the first Mass was a Low one: the Ceremonies began a quarter before 9: after them Mr Burgess sung the Mass, & the 2 last Hours were read.

November

On the 7th Miss Charlotte Talbot came here from Liege.

On the 8th Miss Blundell returned to Bruxells.

On the 16th Sister Aurelia Dillon & Sister Alissia Talbot made their Holy Profession, tho they were both only 23 years old.[2] This special Grant was obtained of the Empress for them by Mr Swinburne.

On the 22d Miss Charlotte Talbot returned to Liege, accompanied by one of our Lay Sisters.

[p. 248] On the 30th Madlle Stapignon returned home.

December

On the 2d Miss Nanny Hawcourt enter'd the Convent, Lodged in the School, & Tabled at the Fathers House. She left us on the 10th.[3]

The Hon'ble Mr Stourton having left us £5 for Prayers, we had a Solemn Mass, 2 Low ones, & each one said a Short Dierge.

1781

January

On the [*blank*] Sister Regis Angier was Clothed in private.[4]

On the 9th Madlle Mean left us.

At the Death of the Empress Queen, the Bishop order'd one Low Mass to be hear'd by the whole Community, & each one to say a long Dierge privately.[5]

On the 14th of this month we had further orders, viz: a Solemn singing Dierge, on which account (it being the Feast of the Sacred Name of

[1] Fr Matthew Burgess (1752–86), Confessor 1778–82; Anstruther 4, pp. 50–1.

[2] Mary Aurelia Dillon (BA073); Alicia Talbot (BA190). The age at profession had been raised by Empress Maria Theresa to 25 in her dominions. Joseph II continued this policy, although he later reduced the age at profession to 24.

[3] She had left the convent in March.

[4] Mary Regis Angier (BA005). This unusual observation of a usually open occasion was part of the recognition of the need to be discreet in a time of changing perceptions of the religious life in Flanders.

[5] Empress Maria Theresa died on 29 November 1780.

Jesus)[1] neither Lauds nor Prime were sung; we had no *Salve*, **[p. 249]** but our Ladies Littanies were sung at the end of the Dierge. On the next day we had a Solemn Funeral Service performed by Mr Burgess without Deacons, the Herse was exposed. We were order'd to ring every day for 6 weeks from 6 in the morning till the half hour after, from 11 & half till 12, & from 6 in the evening till the half hour. *Requiescat in Pace.*

Mr Crusce of Cadiz having sent us £5 for Prayers for his Lady, who was educated here (her Maiden name was Langton) we had a Solemn Mass for her & each one was order'd to hear 2 more & to say a Short Dierge for her.[2] *Requiescat in Pace.*

February

We had this month a Solemn Mass for the Soul of Mr Ball, who had been 2 years & 9 months Confessor of this Monastery.[3] *Requiescat in Pace.*

On the 3d Madlle Merlin left us.

On the 6th Miss May was received for Pensioner in the 11th year of her age.

On the 12th Madlle Verenocke from Ostend was received for Pensioner, about 17 years of age. On the 23d Miss Daly returned to us from Marquette.[4]

March

On the 8th Sister Aurelia Dillons 2 Sisters, Miss Molly & Miss Nanny Dillon were received for **[p. 250]** Pensioners; the eldest in the 22d year of her age, Miss Nanny in the 17th.[5] & on the same day Madlle Riecx from Ostend, in the 20th year of her age.

On the 14th Madlle Cante returned home to Ghent.

On the 31 Miss May left us.

Aprill

On the 23d Mademoiselle Maertens of this Town was received for Pensioner in the 20th year of her age.

May

On the first Madlle De Chane of this Town was received for Pensioner about 19 years old.

On the 3d Miss Blundell of Ince returned here from Bruxells.

On the 15th Miss Feast went from hence.

On the 19th Miss Morris & Miss Macguire left us to return to England.

---

1 The feast of the Sacred Name of Jesus. Devotion to the Holy Name was introduced in the early modern period, with a special feast celebrated on 3 January; the devotion lasted the whole month.

2 Mary Langton, sister of Nelly and Frances, educated at Nazareth, married Peter Cruise [Crusce] from Rathcool in Ireland, but living in Cadiz. See also **[pp. 201, 322]** and lostlangtons.co.uk/other/langton/humogen/family/humo/F619/1771, accessed 25 June 2015.

3 Fr John Ball (1723–1781), Confessor 1775–78; Anstruther 4, pp. 15–16.

4 Abbaye de Marquette, near Lille.

5 Anne (Nanny) Dillon, in religion Mary Ignatia, professed in 1789 (BA074).

On the 21st Sister Tecla[1] was sent by Reverend Mother & the Community to a famous Oculist at Antwerp for the recovery of her sight, which was almost gone; Sister Martha accompanied her, but Monsieur Sacré the Oculist not finding her eyes fit for the purpose, they returned here on the 25th.

June

On the 9th Sister Ann Clare alias Ann Wheeler quitted the Schollars Habit, & went to Service **[p. 251]** ~~at~~ in an English Family, settled in Town viz Mr Hopton's for She had not health for a Lay Sister.

On the 14th It being the Feast of Corpus Xti the Duke of Gloucester, (Brother to George the 3d, King of England)[2] came to our Church about the end of *Salve*; after it, he desired to see Reverend Mother[3] & the Community at the door of the Sacristy which opens into the Cloister. We all went down in our Surplices, as soon as Reverend Mother unlocked it, he advanced forwards to come in, but her Reverence assuring him it was not in her power to admit His Royal Highness without the Bishops consent, he received the refusal in the most gracious manner & retired immediately: from thence we all went to the Lay Sisters Chappel Grate where he & his Attendants met us; He staid about a quarter of an hour & then took leave: That evening Reverend Mother sent him by Mr Burgess our Confessor a Present of 2 Nosegays, one of Silver Flowers the other of Silk for his Dutchess, also a handsome Watch String & long Purse, which his Royal Highness received in the most obliging manner, & expressed great gratitude for them: The next morning about 9, The Bishop brought him & his Attendants to the Monastery, The Sisters Chappel doors were immediately open'd to em, & they were **[p. 252]** received by Reverend Mother & the Community in their Surplices. The Duke upon seeing Reverend Mother renewed his thanks for the Presents, & behaved the whole time in the most affable Polite manner. At his return to England he spoke in the highest terms of the civillities we had paid him, at which the Catholicks were much pleased, & some assured Reverend Mother of the approbation her conduct had met with from them in general.

July

On the 23d were received for Pensioners Miss Darell of Scotney in the 10th year of her age: Mr Tom Huddleston's eldest Daughter Miss Betty[4] in the 11th & Miss Julea Shee from Ireland in the 13th.

---

1 Thecla Hampson (BA097); Martha Randall, lay sister (BA159).

2 William Henry, Duke of Gloucester (1743–1805) married Maria Walpole, Dowager Countess Waldegrave in 1766. Maria Walpole had convent connections through her extended family: see Walpole family tree in WWTN.

3 Reverend Mother was Mary Augustina More, Prioress 1766–1807 (BA145).

4 Elizabeth was part of the Sawston family with connections to Bruges: Thomas Huddleston of Milton, Cambridgeshire married Elizabeth Mackworth of Normanton (Stirnet, Family Tree, Huddleston 03).

On the 31st Miss Sutton was admitted amongst our Pensioners for 6 months in order to be instructed & taken into the Church. She was a Jew & her parents also, Her Father was a Physician settled in Germany but of English Extraction.

August

On the 6th Miss Blundell of Ince left us to go to England.

On the 7th We had a very handsome Recreation given us by Miss Monington who sent us Ten Pounds Sterling for that purpose on the day she made her Profession at Princen-hoff.[1] Reverend Mother allow'd the Community to set up till ten, & gave every **[p. 253]** priviledge She could, to Shew her gratitude for the unexpected Kindness

On the 19th of August Miss Betty Mawhood left us to return to England.

On the 23d Miss Betty Blundell of Ince was received for Pensioner in the 15th year of her age.

September

On the 23d a Lay Sister from Louvain arrived here just before Compline, & was taken into the Inclosure. The next day being Lot Day,[2] She eat with the Sisters in the Refectory, & the next day in the Infirmary, & left us on the 26th.

On the 30th Miss Charlotte Talbot returned to us from Liege.[3]

October

On the 3d Lord Stourton departed this life:[4] He left us £5 Sterl: for Prayers: We had a Solemn Mass for him, & Reverend Mother order'd each one to hear 3 more, to offer a Communion, & to say one Short Dierge for him. *Requiescat in Pace.* Amen.

On the 7th Madlle Ryex left us, & her Sister was received for Pensioner the same day being about 19 years of age.

On the 11th Reverend Mr Wappeler departed this life;[5] He was an exJesuite, a very Learned & Holy Man: He had been to Confession & said Mass the day before his death: Being taken ill early in the morning he called the Man Servant who gave him what he thought wou'd do him good, **[p. 254]** & finding himself much better, he sent him to Mass: Our Confessor Mr Burgess went to him immediately after it & found him fallen down & expiring, but judging he still breathed, he gave him the

---

1 Ann Monington professed at the Franciscans, Prinsenhof, Bruges on 29 June 1781, BF166.

2 Lot days were four days of relaxed regime to accommodate the practice of bloodletting, which took place three times a year, before Lent, in May and in September. I am indebted to the Community for this reference.

3 See also **[p. 260]**.

4 Lord Stourton: William Stourton, 16th Baron Stourton (d. 3 October 1781); two of his daughters became Sepulchrines at Liège.

5 Fr William Wappeler SJ (1711–81) was at the Bruges College before its suppression. Holt, p. 258.

last Absolution, & he departed: Tho his Death was sudden we confide it was not unprovided but precious in the sight of God. By his Will he order'd his Burial at the Carmes,[1] & left Mr Burgess his Executor, who caused his Funeral to be performed with all possible decency & Piety.[2] He left 5 Guineas to the Community & some few things in his Chamber: We said a Solemn Dierge on the 13th. He was carried on the following day to the Carmes in Procession, our young Ladies follow'd the ~~Corps~~ Corpse 2 & 2, then our Confessor, 6 of our Lay Sisters, & some of the Religious Orders, the poor School Boys walked on each side the Street with lighted Torches: On the 15th we had a Solemen Mass, & Reverend Mother order'd each one to hear 3 more, to offer a Communion, & to say one Short Dierge for him. *Requiescat in Pace*. Amen.

On the 11th Mary Wheeler, Niece to Sister Mary Currell was received for a servant in the 16th year of her age.[3]

On the 18th Miss Polly Dillon went from hence to Ghent to learn French. **[p. 255]** Mr John Livesay an ExJesuite Lay Brother[4] having left us Five ~~pounds~~ Guineas at his Death, we had a Solemn Mass for him this month, & Reverend Mother order'd each one to hear 3 more, to offer a Communion, & to say one Short Dierge for him. *Requiescat in Pace*.

On the 23d Miss Witham a Novice from Louvain came here, & was taken into the Inclosure:[5] That day being Recreation, She eat in the Refectory, on the following day in the Infirmary, & She left us on the 25th.

On the 24th Madlle Andevare of this Town was received for Pensioner about 13 years of age.

Miss Sutton being Instructed & Prepared for Baptisme, Confirmation & Communion, She had the happyness to receive all these Sacrements on the 28th of this month: Our Bishop Baptised her himself in his own Chappel, & Confirmed & Communicated her the same Morning: She returned to us quite over joy'd, expressing the most sensible Comfort, & Gratitude to Almighty God for such singular mercies & favours.

November

On the 13th Sister Mary Margaret Tasburgh departed this Life in the 55th year of her Age & 34th of her Holy Profession.[6] She was a woman **[p. 256]** of very good Sence, but of a most difficult Temper: every Duty appear'd

---

1 The Carmelite fathers, who were neighbours of the convent in Carmerstraat. See Appendix 1 and Map of Bruges.

2 Fr Matthew Burgess (1752–86), Confessor at Nazareth 1778–82; Anstruther 4, pp. 50–1.

3 Mary Currell, lay sister (BA069).

4 John Livesay SJ (1712–81), lay brother, died in England. He was at the Bruges College before its suppression and spent time at the convent. Holt, pp. 151–2.

5 Probably Mary Gertrude Witham, who had an extended novitiate because of the new regulations on age at profession. She was clothed in 1775 and professed in 1782 aged 25, LA305.

6 Margaret Tasburgh (1748–81) BA193.

to cost the utmost violence to her contradictory humour, yet she had so extraordinary a command over it that to strangers She appear'd a most amiable woman: She was extremely Regular, & peaceably forced through every Duty & Employment She was entrusted with beyond her Strength. She suffer'd the violent pains of her last Illness, which was a dropsie, Tympany & Consumption with a most Heroic Patience & courage to our great Edification, & died most sweetly & Peaceably. *Requiescat in Pace.*

On the 29th Miss Nelly Langton returned to us, to Lodge & Table with the Pensioners for 6 months.

December

On the 4th Miss Sutton ~~& Miss Sutton~~ & Miss Nanny Dillon went to Ghent, & on the 11th the 2 Miss Dillons returned to us from thence.

On the 13th Miss Mary Young was received for Pensioner in the 15th year of her age. Her Father is a Presbyterian Settled in the Grenada Islands.

On the 19th Sister Mary Ignatia Tichbourne departed this life in the 59th year of her age, & 41st of her Holy Profession,[1] She had always very poor health, but ~~being of~~ having a Strong Constitution, & ~~having~~ a great courage **[p. 257]** She was very Serviceable in many Employments; being Clever in whatever She undertook, but of a terrible bad Temper, so curious & Artfull that no body cared to have dealings with her, & was by Nature Sharp & Censorious: but in the latter years of her Life she corrected herself very much & generally repaired her faults by acknowledging them in a very humble manner to the Persons she had offended, & often ~~spoke~~ in those occasions spoke very feelingly of the badness of her Temper. She had for many years an outward swelling in her Throat, which was judged the Kings Evil;[2] for some months before her Death, it appear'd to have broke within, by the quantity of Blood she Spit. It gradually prevented her Swallowing, so that for many days, she was nourished only by Glisters: it was a sensible pain to the Community to see one of its Members Starving to death. She suffer'd extreme Thirst & Inward heat with extraordinary Patience & even chearfulness, so that we hope it might in some measure have been her Purgatory. She had her Senses to the last, & died most peaceably. *Requiescat in Pace.*

On the same day Sister Ignatia died, Reverend Mother & the Community were allarmed beyond measure at **[p. 258]** the Reports brought to them

---

1 Mary Ignatia Tichbourne (1741–81) BA200.

2 King's Evil: a skin disease which was thought to be cured if the sufferer was touched by the king. For an example of this happening in the convent in 1708, see vol. 1, **[p. 253]**. For the medieval origins of the practice in France and England, see Frank Barlow, 'The King's Evil', *English Historical Review* 95(374) (1980), pp. 3–27. Barlow concludes by stating that the practice died out suddenly in 1714 in England with the arrival of the Hanoverian monarchy. I am indebted to Dr Francis Young for his information that, although the practice died out in England, the exiled Stuarts continued it down to the death of Cardinal Henry Benedict Stuart in 1807.

from all their Friends in Town, that the Emperor Joseph the 2d was resolved to suppress all Convents of Women, except the Ursulines & those of the Order of Saint Elizabeth.[1] The utmost concern was expressed for us, but no hopes given of our being Excluded tho English. Reverend Mother deposited in the hands of her Friends some watches & other things of value which belonged to different Secular Persons lest they shou'd be seized with what belonged to the Convent: Sorrow & Grief was painted on the Countenance of each Member, & the fear of being separated from each other appear'd in the most lively manner. Reverend Mother was pierced to the heart, & in the utmost concern for each one, especially for the Infirm, & those who had not a Friend left in the World: We were kept in this cruel Situation till Xmass day, when our Physician Doctor De Vaux relieved us by bringing the real Edict, which was of a very different Tenor, containing many wise Ordinances for the Regulation of Convents.[2] The concern & Solicitude the Doctor expressed for us in this occasion, gave us convincing proofs of his regard. From this time we receive continual assurances from all Hands that tho' probably many Womens Convents in the Low Countries, that are not useful to the Publick will be Suppressed, yet ours will not be Included, on account of our School[3] which through **[p. 259]** the Goodness of Almighty God has been very flourishing these many years & is so full that for want of Place we were obliged to refuse about thirty Pensioners this year.

1782

January

On the 10th Miss Charlotte Talbot of Hore Cross died in our School in the 16th year of her Age.[4] She returned to us from Liege in a Consumption, & was too far gone in it to recover. She was always very Pious, & suffer'd her lingering Illness with edifying patience, & also very severe pains for some days before her Death. She expressed a fear of recovery, & a

---

1 Emperor Joseph II wished to see all contemplative cloisters suppressed in his lands. Only convents carrying out useful work would be allowed: the Ursulines provided schooling for girls and the Order of St Elizabeth cared for the sick.

2 Rumours had circulated about the intentions of Joseph II regarding religious reforms. He ordered the closure of all contemplative monasteries except those caring for the sick, in education, agriculture or trades. Their income was to be sequestered and administered by a Religious Fund answerable to the state and used for education and similar purposes. The life of the Augustinian Canonesses, combining both contemplative and active elements of religious life with a focus on education, enabled Nazareth to survive these regulations.

3 The presence of many local girls in the school encouraged the nuns to think that they would be included among useful establishments and escape suppression.

4 Charlotte Talbot was the daughter of Charles Talbot (d. 1766) and Mary Mostyn. The latter received Hore Cross, Staffordshire and lands in Berkshire as part of a marriage settlement in 1752. Stirnet has Charlotte erroneously as Caroline. Her brother Charles was 15th Earl of Shrewsbury.

desire of being buried amongst us: She had a very sharp & long Agony, enjoy'd her Senses to the last & died most calmly. The Corpse was laid out in the Nuns Musick Room, & two poor Women hired to watch it by Day & Night. It was carried into the Church on the 12th, Six of our Little Pensioners dressed in white, 3 on each side held the Pall. As **[p. 260]** She was Niece to Lord Shrewsbury, & her Brother Heir apparent to that Title & Estate, Reverend Mother was desirous the Burial shou'd be suitable to her Rank, especially as it cou'd be done at a very reasonable expence, therefore three Steps were erected in the Middle of the Church, on which the Corpse Stood Shut up in the Coffin, surrounded by 18 Candles, her Eschuteon [escutcheon] fixed on each of them, & also on the 12 ~~the~~ at the Altar, the Benches & Pavement cover'd with White: A Crown was laid on the Coffin when removed to the Church, & continued till her Burial. Mr Burgess sung the Mass with 2 Deacons: it was performed in the most Solemn manner as well as the Funeral by Musicians from the Town. She was buried in the Vault on the 13th. *Requiescat in pace*

We said the Commendations for Miss Charlotte Talbot in the Choir, & the long Dierge on the Day she was carried out, & rung during both, & also the 3 Hours for her the same as for our own Religious.

Sister Mary Ann Bruce having been 6 years Procuratress was discharged from that Office in this month, & Sister Ann Teresa Jerningham chose in her Place.[1]

February

On the 3d Sister Lucy Scrjeant made her Holy Profession.[2]

On the 10th Our Novice Sister Regis Angier left us for England to recover her health.[3]

[p. 261] On the 10th of February Madlle Verenocke returned to her Parents.

March

On the 3d Madlle Verloge from Ghent was received for Pensioner about 18 years of Age.

On the 18th Madlle Maertens left us.

Aprill

On the 3d Madlle Vermersch from Ipres was received for Pensioner about 15 years of Age.

On the 4th Madlle De Chaine left us, & on the same day Madlle Marouse of this Town was received for Pensioner, in the 22d year of her age.

On the 11th Miss Polly Havers returned to us from Marquette.

---

1 Mary Ann Bruce (BA036); Ann Teresa Jerningham (BA120).

2 Lucy Austin Sargeant (BA171).

3 Mary Regis Angier (BA005).

On the 13th Miss Fanny Rooper Daughter to the Hon'ble Mr Phill Rooper departed this life about 2 in the morning in the [*blank*] year of her age. She received her *Viaticum* which was her first Communion: Suffer'd extremely in her last illness with edifying Patience, & gave us all reason to believe she died in her Baptismal Inocence. The Doctor judged that Water in her Head was the cause of her Death. *Requiescat in pace.*

We hired 2 Women to watch by the Corpse which was exposed in the Nuns Musick Room. On the 14th which was the Feast of the Dedication of our Church[1] we read Vespers, a Short *Salve* followed, after which the Corpse was carried into the Church, & we immediately began the Dierge: She was **[p. 262]** buried on the 15th in the same manner as one of our own Religious.

May

On the 24th the 2 Miss Dillons & Miss Polly Havers left us to return to England, & on the same day Madlle De Roo returned home.

June

On the 7th Madlle Dc Vaux returned to us.

On the 7th Mademoiselle Maertin Cousin to the former was received for Pensioner, about [*blank*] years of age.

On the 24th Madlle Scheppers of Ghent was received for Pensioner between 12 & 13 years of age.

July

On the 7th Miss Nanny Rooper went from hence to the English Monastery at Liege.[2]

On the 8th We had a Solemn Mass for the Soul of Mrs Mary Weston:[3] Her Executors sent us £5. Reverend Mother order'd each one to offer one Communion, & 3 Masses, & to say one Short Dierge for her. Two of her Aunts had been Nuns here. *Requiescant in Pace.*

On the 16th Mrs Fallon a Widdow entered the Inclosure in quality of Teacher to our young Ladies. She had the Strongest Recommendations from several Priests, & we found her excellently qualified by her Talents for that Purpose, but upon Trial her Temper was so extraordinarily Imperious that we were obliged to dismiss her. She left us on the first of August.

---

1 The ceremony of dedication, which took place on 7 April 1639, is described in detail in vol. 1, **[pp. 60–3]**.

2 Anne was one of five daughters of Philip Roper (1739–1831) and Barbara Lyttleton (d. 1805).

3 Melior Mary Weston (1703–10 June 1782), only child of John Weston of Sutton Place, Surrey and Elizabeth Gage. Mrs Weston died unmarried. Her aunts were Elizabeth Weston, in religion Delphina (1699–1721) BA216, and Paula Weston, in religion Ann (1699–1738) BA215.

[p. 263]

August

On the 1st Madlle Sunaert of Ghent was received for Pensioner, about 18 years of age; & on the same day Madlle Lightvoet of Bruges about 17.

On the 3d Mad'lle Cosyn of Ostend about 12 years old was received for Pensioner.

On the 21 Miss Daly left us to take Shipping at Ostend for Demarary.[1]

September

On the 3d Miss Nelly Langton left us.[2]

On the 18th Mr Anthony Wright our Banker departed this Life:[3] As our Community has extraordinary Obligations to him for his Charity in receiving & paying all our monies in England without any profit to himself, Reverend Mother order'd a Solemn Mass for him, & each one to offer a Communion & 2 Masses, & to say a Short Dierge for him, & also to be wrote down amongst our Deceased Benefactors. *Requiescat in Pace.*

On the 20th Miss Huddleston of Sawson went from hence to Paris.

On the 21st Mr Oliver a Scotch Secular Priest passed this way in order to retire to his College at Doway, his health being impaired by too hard a Mission at Aberdeen in Scotland: We were glad to retain him for some months to say the Foundation Mass; having accepted our offer, we fitted up Mr Wappeler's Apartment for him.

[p. 264] On the 26th Miss Kitty Mostyn was received for Pensioner in the 9th year of her age, & on the 27th her Sister Miss Winny who was only 5 the precedent month.[4]

October

On the 2d Madlle De Turck was received for Pensioner about 17 years of age.

On the 15th Madlle Schatellyne a Hollander was received for Pensioner about 17 years of age.

On the 30th Miss Rutledge of English Parents settled in these Countries was received for Pensioner in the 12th year of her age.

November

On the 25th To shew our regard to Mr Burgess our Confessor, we sung a Solemn Mass of Requiem for his deceased Father in Law.

---

1 The Daly family were involved in trade and plantations in the West Indies. Demerara was in the Dutch colony of Guyana.

2 Nelly Langton had arrived at the school in 1770; see **[p. 201]**.

3 Anthony Wright, banker of Henrietta Street, London, died on 18 October 1782, aged 79. He was connected to the Wright family of Kelvedon Hatch, Essex. They provided financial services to a number of Catholic institutions and individuals.

4 Possibly daughters of Sir Roger Mostyn, 5th Baronet of Mostyn, married to Margaret Wynne.

December

On the 2d Mad[lle] De Turcke returned home to Ghent not having her health here.

On the 7th Sister Monica Webster a Lay Sister departed this Life suddenly.[1] She had been a Laborious Usefull Member, particularly in the service of the Sick: but about 3 years after her Profession, She was desorder'd in her head, yet not so, as to be confined: She gave herself much to Prayer & Fasting, was naturally extremely Obstinate, loved Singularity, & ^was^ of a weak Judgment. Having a Quartan Ague She was an Inhabitant of the Infirmary for some **[p. 265]** months, where She gave a great deal of trouble as she wou'd not eat unless it was forced into her Mouth: About a fortnight before She Died, She every now & then Stripped herself Stark Naken, on which account on the 3[d] we were obliged to Confine her, & on the 7th the Sister who took care of her found her about 5 in the morning ~~found her~~ Prostrate in that Situation, & without the least symtom of Life. Reverend Mother fearing she might be Buried alive, had the Doctor & Surgeon frequently to visit her & every means used to prevent it, so that her Funeral was differ'd till the 11th of the same month. She was in the 30th year of her age, & 5th of her Holy Profession. *Requiescat in Pace.*

On the 11th Miss Harriott Havers the youngest Daughter of Tho' Havers Esq[r] of Thelton was received for Pensioner in the 9th year of her Age.[2]

On the 11th M[r] Burgess left us.[3] He was reckon'd a good Schollar, & the first year gave general Satisfaction to the Community, by his Regularity, Impartiallity, & discreet conduct in the Confessional: But being unfortunately given to Liquor he exposed himself in Town at a great Entertainment given for the Primus at Louvain, at which were present many English Protestants: This Publick Scandal made his removal absolutely necessary. The Bishop intended to do it without noise, but two of the young Nuns who were his **[p. 266]** Confidents, were so violent & artfull in their Proceedings that to prevent more disturbance in the House his Lordship was obliged to send him Suddenly on the 11th to the Seminary in Town, & in a Paternal manner exhorted him to make a Spiritual Exercise & a General Confession: Another view in sending him there was probably on the Account that the Bishop of London[4] knowing his Character, absolutely refused to receive him unless he spent some time in the retirement of a good Seminary. He Staid there till the 21st, & during that time frequently attempted to send letters to his two Confidents here, tho the Bishop had Strictly forbid him to keep Correspondence

1 Monica Webster (1778–82) BA213.

2 Harriet or Henrietta Havers was the daughter of Thomas Havers and Catherine Dutry.

3 Fr Matthew Burgess (1752–86), Confessor 1778–82; Anstruther 4, pp. 50–1.

4 The formal title was Vicar Apostolic of the London District; in 1782 the position was held by Bishop James Talbot (1726–90).

with any one in the Convent except Reverend Mother: These letters were always Intercepted, chiefly by the Strict watch his Lordship order'd to be kept over him: this Indiscretion on his Side, & the violent Temper & Proceedings of the two young Nuns in the Monastery made the Bishop resolve he shou'd never return to it; but his Presence being necessary to arrange his Papers & Pack up his Clothes, His Lordship on the 20th order'd his Secretary & a Priest from the Seminary to come with him at 8 in the Evening, at which hour all the Community wou'd be retir'd, & no **[p. 267]** one to be acquainted of it unnecessarily; moreover to keep it more secret the Bishop gave leave for the Lay Sister who was to attend him to Sleep at a Neighbours House that night. He was not allowed to speak to any one within except Reverend Mother, & not even to Louis, the Man Servant belonging to his Apartment, because by his means he had endeavour'd to send & receive letters from the 2 young Nuns his Confidents. He staid about two Hours, & returned to the Seminary that night, the next morning the Bishop order'd him to go to Ostend with the Curate of that Town, & to stay at his House till he took Shipping for Margate: He set sail on Christmass Day. Reverend Mother & Community were much mortified that his own & 2 Confidents Indiscretions had obliged the Bishop to act in a manner so different from what was intended for His Lordship, Reverend Mother & each one wished to see him removed honourably. The People in Town who were ~~better~~ better acquainted with his misfortune than Reverend Mother were much surprized that he was allowed to stay with us so long. Mr Hiver the Scotch Priest was so good as to supply his Place till we cou'd be provided.

[p. 268]

1783

January the 31st Mr Chichester departed this Life.[1] His Lady having informed Reverend Mother of it & sent us Ten pounds, She order'd a Solemn Mass for him, & each one to offer one Communion & 3 Masses, & to say 2 Short Dierges for him. & also to be wrote down amongst our Deceased Benefactors as we look on him in that light.
See page 43 in this Volume.

---

[1] Mr John Chichester, father of Catherine Chichester, a Sepulchrine nun at Liège (LS040) and brother of Catharina Chichester, in religion Teresa Joseph (BA052). See **[pp. 43, 44]** for the problems relating to an inheritance due to Catharina in 1737. An amicable solution had been reached whereby John Chichester paid the convent £500 and an additional £50 as a gift from him and his wife, Mary, towards the cost of the altar in the new church.

Aprill

As the Suppression of Bethania our Neighbouring Monastery was expected during the course of this summer:[1] & it being uncertain what use their Convent wou'd be put to; Our Friends in Town judged it necessary to raise the Wall higher that separates theirs & our Garden which was extremely low, & being very old, we found ourselves obliged to build the new one from the Foundations: this making a Breach on the 13th of this month Reverend Mother procured the Bishop's leave to admit Miss Joanna Caimo who had been Novice amongst them, & all their Lay Sisters into our Inclosure, being glad of an opportunity of shewing the esteem & affection of our Community for those cordial **[p. 269]** neighbours before their threatened Dissolution. The Superiour & Nuns were extremely obliged for our civillities to their Sisters, who Supped in our Refectory, & recreated with our Lay Sisters till the half hour after 8 in the Evening. Her Reverence gave to each of em a pair of English Mittens, & sent 2 pair to their Superiour with which they were extremely pleased.

June

Upon the Suppression of the English Carthusian Convent at Newport, Mr Williams their Holy Prior accepted Reverend Mothers Invitation to an apartment here & boarding with us, which he gratefully accepted, & arrived here on the 30th of this month.[2] He continues to practise his Rule as far as circumstances will permit, & as he never eats meat, we provide Lenten Diet for him: He gives great edification by his Retirement & assiduity in the Church, where his recollected behaviour is very exemplary & is much remarked by Seculars.

^July on the next page^

August

On the 20th Mr Marroucks an Imperial Commissary came by orders of the Court, & called for Reverend Mother whom he examined most Strictly concerning the Effects of the English Jesuits Colleges that were suppressed

---

[1] The suppression of enclosed contemplative orders had been decreed by Joseph II as part of his reforms of the religious life. See **[p. 258]**.

[2] The Carthusian Monastery was the descendant of the Charterhouse of Sheen Anglorum, which had settled in Nieuport, Flanders, in 1626. It was suppressed in March 1783 by Joseph II as part of his rationalisation programme. Fr Francis Joseph Williams (1729–97) left Bruges later that year, moving first to the Dominicans at Bornhem and then, from 1789 until they departed for England, with the Augustinian Canonesses at Louvain. For further details of the suppression of the English Carthusians, see Dom Lawrence Hendriks, *London Charterhouse, Its Monks and Its Martyrs with a Short Account of the English Carthusians after the Dissolution in March 1783* (London: Kegan Paul, 1889), pp. 336–41; Jan De Grauwe, *Histoire de la chartreuse Sheen Anglorum au continent: Bruges, Louvain, Malines, Nieuport (1559–1783)* (Salzburg: Institut für Anglistik und Amerikanistik, Universität Salzburg, 1984).

at Bruges in the year 1773,[1] for She **[p. 270]** was accused to have sent off for them to a very considerable value: She denied the Charge with a firmness that Inocence alone cou'd inspire, He tried to intimidate her, but to no effect. He also required a new Inventory of our Rents to be sent to him that very night. This unexpected visit, Accusation, & Demand allarmed us extremely, & also our Friends; but thank God we have hear'd no more of that Business except that the Accusation came from a Woman who was then Prisoner at Bruxells, whom it is supposed hoped to retrieve her own Affairs at our expence.

July

On the 1st Mrs Collins took the Schollars Habit & the names of Mary Xaveria.

September

On the 6th Sister Regis Angier reassumed the Novices Habit.[2]

Mrs Tasburgh having sent us five pounds for Prayers for her Husband's Soul, we had a Solemn Mass for him, & Reverend Mother order'd each one to offer a Communion, to hear 3 more Masses & to say one Short Dierge. *Requiescat in pace*

On the 24th Two Magistrates of the Town accompanied by the Bishops Secretary paid Reverend Mother a Visit, which they acquainted her was in consequence of an Imperial Edict that they read to her, & which amongst other other things required **[p. 271]** all Schools to have an Inspector taken from the Magistrates or Clergy, to see that they were properly Instructed, Taught & kept in due Order.[3] Reverend Mother with great freedom told them that if such a Person was appointed for us, The English Parents wou'd immediately remove their Children, for they were too much allarmed & had not forgot the Treatment their Sons & Relations had met with at the Suppression of the English Jesuits in Bruges. These Gentlemen answer'd that her reasons against it were just, & that she shou'd receive only a visit at the Grate once a year from the Person appointed to which she readily assented. They then required to see the School & all of them enter'd the Inclosure accompanied by our Confessor Mr Oliver.[4] When within, the Bishop's Secretary told Reverend Mother privately not to shew them any part of the Convent, for their Commission only extended to the School. As we that day celebrated the half Jubilee of Sister Teresa Clare Farrill who was Mistress of ~~the school~~ it, all the young Ladies to the number of 22 were genteelly dressed, & the School being adorned in a most handsome manner appear'd to advantage:[5] These Gentlemen admired the fine works

---

1 For the impact of the suppression on the convent, see **[pp. 214–15]**.
2 Mary Regis Angier (BA005).
3 Part of Joseph II's reform to ensure the regulation of monastic schools.
4 Fr Andreas Oliver, from Scotland, Confessor 1782–1812.
5 Teresa Clare Farrell (1758–1820) BA077.

the young Ladies had wrought & presented to their Mistress, behaved with great politeness **[p. 272]** refused to see the apartments above Stairs, asked many questions, & declared themselves highly satisfied. They sent to Court a most favourable & honourable account of our method of Education, & asked for us the Priviledge of Professing our Novices at the age of 21 years.

October

On the 2d Brother Thomas Carfoot a Carthusian Lay Brother of Newport came to settle with us in quality of a Servant. As he knows the Carpenters Trade he will be of great use to us.[1]

November

Mr Williams the late Prior of the English Carthusians of Newport left us on the 22d of this month to pay a visit to the English Dominicans at Bornhem, & finding it a very retired Situation, he resolved to Lodge & Board with them, & acquainted Reverend Mother of his Intention.[2]

December

On the 8th Nanny Wheeler reassumed the Schollars Habit for a Lay Sister.[3]

Pensioners &c that came this year
1783

February the 6th Madlle Van Zeeveren of Bruges about 15 years of age.
March the 10th Madlle Beubroucke of Tourroute about 14.
Aprill the 17th Madlle Derdyn of Ostend, about 11.
The 23d Madlle Lees of Ostend about 17.
[p. 273] May the 6th Madlle Mary Vermersch of Ipres about 15.
the 7th Miss Cecily & Miss Louisa Webbe Daughters to the famous Musician, the Eldest about 19 the youngest 16.[4]
the 11th Miss Bell Angier returned to us, but by her Parents orders not to reassume the Habit till the end of Summer.[5]
the 22d Madlle Mary Pollet from Blackenberge about 19.
June the 6th Mrs Mary Collins a Convert originally a Quaker came to take the Schollars Habit For a Choir Nun in the 37th year of her age.
the 11th Mad'lle Ann Audevare of Bruges about 13.
July the 5th Madlle Coutteau of Tourroate about 37.
the 12th Miss Norris of Colney in the 11th year of her age.[6]

---

1 Thomas Carfoot, one of two lay brothers at Nieuport at the time of its suppression by Joseph II. He died at Nazareth in 1786.
2 Fr Francis Joseph Williams (1729–97).
3 Anne Wheeler left without professing.
4 Daughters of Samuel Webbe the elder (1740–1843), musician, and Anne Plumb; see *ODNB* and **[p. 283]**.
5 Isabella Angier, in religion Mary Regis (BA005). Her parents were James and Isabella Angier or Augier. She professed in 1788.
6 Miss Charlotte Norris was a granddaughter of Richard Norris of Colney.

the 20th Madlle Conii from Ostend about 15.
August the 16th Madlle le Grand from St Omer in her 13th year.
September the 29th Madlle Van Outrive of Bruges about 16.
November the 3d Madlle De Pauw of Bruges about 12.
December the 15 Mad'lle Van Tieghem of Ghent about 18.
August the 31st Nanny Wheeler returned to us for a Servant.

Pensioners &c that left us this year
1783

January the 2d Madlle Chateleyn.
the 31 Madlle Lightvooet.
February the 28 Madlle Verloge.
March the 2d Madlle Monica Rycx.
[p. 274] Aprill the 17th Madlle Maertens the Doctors Daughter.
the 23d Miss Betty Blundell & Miss Julea Shee went for England.
May the 6th The Eldest Mad'lle Vermersch.
the 12th ~~The 2~~ Madlle ~~Fleischmanns~~ Scheppers.
13th The 2 Madlle Fleischmanns.
June the 14th Miss Young.
24th The Eldest Madlle Aadevare.
August the 9 Miss Webbe left us to go to Princen-Hoff.[1]
the 16th Mrs Collins our Schollar returned to England for the recovery of her health
the 18th Madlle Cosyn.
September the 26th Madlle Van Zeeveren.
28th Madlle Coutteau.
October the 26th Madlle Sunaert.
November the 25th Miss Lucy Mawhood went for England.[2]
December the 1st Madlle Mary Pollet.
7th Madlle Beesbrouck.

1784

January

On the 10th Miss Nanny Dillon returned to us, from England, & took the Schollars Habit on the 17th for the Feast of the Holy Name of Jesus & the names of **[p. 275]** Mary Ignatia.[3] She was in the 20th year of her age.

---

[1] Cecilia Webbe was clothed in April 1784, but left in March 1786, being 'unwilling to submit herself', BF261.

[2] Lucy Mawhood was the daughter of William Mawhood and Dorothy Kroger; her older sister Maria had professed at Bruges as Louisa Austin in 1779 (BA140). For William Mawhood, see *ODNB*.

[3] Anne Dillon, in religion Mary Ignatia (BA074).

February

On the 25th being Ash Wednesday Sister Albana Paterson began at Mattins all her Religious Duties after an interruption of About 6 years occasion'd by very ill Health.[1] Having hear'd the Fame of the Miracles wrought at the Tomb & by the Invocation of the Venerable Benedict Joseph Labre a Voluntary ~~Hol~~ Holy Beggar who died at Rome on the 16th of Aprill 1783;[2] She felt a strong Confidence of her cure, if She performed a Novena in his Honour: She obtained the consent of her Director (viz Mr Oliver) & her Superiours. She finished it on Ash wednesday, & tho' she suffer'd extremely during the time, She felt herself on that day perfectly well full of Strength and vigour, performed every duty of it without [~~illeg.~~] difficulty, fasted the Whole Lent without any dispensation whatever either of the Church or Order, & complied Strictly in the same manner with all the Observances of her State. In June Reverend Mother procured our Physicians attestation of his opinion on this cure, which here follows in French copied from his own Hand writting. *Je Soussigne, Medecin pensionné de la Ville De Bruges, declare:*[3]

1. *D'avoir depuis 5 a 6 ans vue assidûement* **[p. 276]** *et observé en qualité de Medecin Dame Albana Paterson, Religieuse Angloise de la Communauté de La Rue Des Carmes de cette Ville, qui pendant tout ce tems a eté constamment affligée de differentes infirmités, telles que cardialgie presque continuelle, constipation des plus opiniatres, extintion de voix, defaut d'appetit, douleurs de Gravelle*

---

[1] Albana Paterson (BA151).

[2] Benedict Joseph Labre (1748–83), described as a beggar saint, tried several orders including the Carthusians at Montreuil, was refused permission to enter and decided to follow the most austere way of life as a pilgrim in Italy. He was canonised in 1881.

[3] 'I the undersigned, salaried doctor of the town of Bruges, declare that in my role as doctor for the past 5 to 6 years I have visited Dame Albana Patterson, English nun of the Community on Carmerstraat in this town. During all this time, she has constantly suffered from different infirmities such as almost continual cardiac pain, persistent constipation, loss of voice, lack of appetite and pain caused by stones which threw her into such a state of exhaustion through lack of nourishment that it made me fear for her life. When I examined her again before Lent last past at her request, in order to establish how far she would be able to observe fasts and abstinences, I found her in such a state of wasting and exhaustion that I judged it necessary to dispense with not only the requirements of the church, but also the other obligations that her life as a nun imposes on her, such as attending choir, reading Divine Office, etc. Having seen her again towards the end of Lent, I was amazed to find her very alert and also having put on weight, assuring me that she did not feel the least discomfort, but she had been able during the period of penitence to undertake all her obligations with as much ease as one of her Sisters. The same Dame Albana, her Superiors and the whole house, have assured me that the wonderful change all happened in the space of a few days immediately after she invoked the help of the celebrated B. J. Labre, who died at Rome on 16 April 1783. I have to bear witness that this striking cure is not due to any remedy, either pharmaceutical or dietary, both of which she has foresworn for several months. Given at Bruges this 17 June 1784. J. Devaux. Doctor' (Editor's translation).

&c. &c, ce qui l'avoit jettée dans un etat d'inanition qui faisoit craindre pour ses jours.

2. *que l'ayant, pour sa Satisfaction, examinée de nouveau, immediatement avant Le Careme dernier pour juger jusqu'a quel point elle auroit pu observer le jeune et les Abstinences je l'ai trouvée dans un tel Etat d'epuisement et de ~~Langueur~~ Langeur, que j'ai jugé necessaire de la faire dispenser point seulement des Lois de L'Eglise, mais aussi des autres devoirs que Son etat de Religeuse lui imposait, comme frequentation du Choeur, la Lecture des Offices divins, &c.*
3. *que L'ayant revue vers la fin due Careme, j'ai été stupefait de La trouver tres alerte et disposé ayant meme un certain degré d'embonpoint; m'assurant q'elle ne ressentoit plus La moindre incommodité mais qu'elle s'*étoit acquitée pendant tout ce ~~*tem*~~ *tems de penitence, de tous ses devoirs, avec autant de* **[p. 277]** *facilité qu'aucune de les Consoeurs.*
4. *que La ditte Dame Albane, ses Superieurs, et generalement toute La maison m'ont assuré, que ce changement merveilleux s'etoit operé dans l'espace de quelques jours, immediatement apres qu'elle avoit invoqué le Secours du Celebre B: J Labre, decedé a Rome le 16 Avril 1783. Du moins dois-je attester que cette frapante guerison, n'est due a aucun remede, soit pharmaceutique, soit dietetique, auxquels elle avoit renoncé depuis plusieurs mois. Donné a Bruges ce 17 Juin 1784.*

J DEVAUX MED.

An English Dominican of Borhnem who understood Physick, gave his Attestation also, as follows.

This to testify that in August 1782, passing by Bruges I was desired to See Sister Albana Patterson Born in London 1752, who for the Space of four years had continually complained of most violent Cholicks, loss of appetite, frequent privation of Sleep. The Obstructions difficulty in the passages, declared, as afterwards appear'd by the evacuations of a great quantity of Gravel, her Cholics to be entirely Nephritick, tho complicate, as She never was without a Slow Fever: such a continual dejection of Spirit as to be able to do no **[p. 278]** one Duty to signify; & frequently obliged to take Nourishment, as much by night as by day. Hence it naturally appears that not ^only^ Wasting, but even the fasting diet proved no better than a poison. Such was her complaint in the year 1782. By Medecine She found for a time a temporary relief: but in 1783 & ^beginning of^ 1784 her complaints Returned with more than common violence, which had never totally ceased, & brought such a dejection, that I attest I thought her cure impossible, & even fear'd for the loss of her head. The Patient continued in this

Situation till reading the Life & Miracles of the B: Benedict Labre, She found herself moved with an extraordinary confidence, & tho She scarce dared to ask health, She thought she might at least beg through his Intercession, that Providence wou'd find some means whereby She might sanctify her Soul & perform her Religious Duties most according to his Divine Will. She thought of performing a *Novena*[1] & proposed the same to her Director & Superiour, who at first received the Proposal with indifference: She however undertook it with Confidence on the 17th of February 1784: on the 3d day She began to perceive herself better, but on the 8th was in a great deal of pain: On the 9th found herself perfectly cured; this was on Ash Wednesday, She began the Fast with the rest, & applied from that day to this to all her Duties, observing the Lent **[p. 279]** without difficulty, & frequenting the Choir both Night & Day with the rest; her Voice which before was lost, now is the loudest in the Choir. In a word through the Goodness of God & the Intercession of the Saint, the cure is so compleat that from my knowledge of Medecine, I can attest no Medecine within that space of time cou'd have worked such wonderfull effect.

Signed Henry Chappell Surgeon & Apothecary[2]

He gave this attestation March the 29th 1784 when he passed this way in his road to England.

Aprill

The 2d Councellor Maires Widow alias Mary Bedingfield departed this Life.[3] She was educated here, & besides considerable Charities to us during Life, She left us £50 at her death. Reverend Mother order'd a Solemn Mass, & long Dierge, also a Low Mass, each one to hear 2 more, to offer one Communion & to say 2 Short Dierges for her, & likewise to be wrote down as [*~~illeg~~*.] amongst our Benefactors.

June

The 25th Sister Helen Blevin a Lay Sister ~~kept~~ celebrated her whole Jubilee of Religious[4] **[p. 280]** In the course of this Month our 2 Neighbouring Convents of Bethania & Penitents were Suppressed & dispersed to different Places.[5] Reverend Mother did all in her power to solace &

---

1 *Novena*: see Glossary.

2 Henry Chappell, in religion Francis Xavier OP (d. 1825). In 1784 he was sent on mission to Sawston, Cambridgeshire, and must have been on his way there when he stopped at Bruges. See *Dominicana*, pp. 135, 162, 166, 254.

3 Mary Bedingfield (d. 2 April 1784), daughter of Mary (d. 1770) and Henry Bedingfield, had married John Maire of Lartington (d. 1771) as her second husband: Stirnet, Family Tree, Maire; T. D. Dunham and J. M. W. Turner, *History of Richmondshire* (London: Longman, 1823), p. 132. See also **[p. 210]**.

4 Helen Blevin (1734–88) BA026.

5 For Bethania and Penitents see Appendix 1.

comfort them, for which they were exceeding gratefull. Three of the poor Penitents were in the most distressed situation from the House they had taken not being ready for them. One was a Jubilarian with a sore Leg, the 2^{d} a Cripple from Palsey brought on her by the dread of Suppression, & the 3^{d} was Sister Francisca Keyser the Infirmarian who from a pure motive of Charity dedicated herself to tend them, for that end renouncing to the most ardent desire She had of going into another Monastery. They were turned out of their Convent to a small House in their own Court in which their Maid lived, & where the Confessor had also a Chamber to Lodge in. when any of the Community were dying: they had only the use of the latter, & another small place joining to it, where they lived cooped-up for about 5 weeks. During their stay there, the Goods of their Convent were publickly sold at it. The 6th of July being the first day of the Sale, to spare them so afflicting & affecting a Scene before their own eyes, Reverend Mother procured the Bishop's leave for them to spend it within our Inclosure. His Lordship consented & seem'd much pleased with Reverend Mother's intention. They enter'd after the Convent Mass, by **[p. 281]** their own desire they eat together & alone. ~~Aft~~ After dining in the Sisters Work Chamber, they came to ours & Recreated with the Nuns, & gave us great edification by their truly Religious Sentiments & comportment. Till the Sale was over they spent the other days in Mr Gerard's Room below Stairs.[1] During their 5 weeks Stay in their Court the Commissaries allowed them as a great favour & a Secret to Lodge altogether in one Room in the Infirmary. Reverend Mother obtained the Bishop's leave to take them into the Inclosure on Sundays, which was the greatest comfort we cou'd give them, & for which they expressed the most feeling gratitude, & promised to remember us in their Prayers during Life. After they left this Neighbourhood the Bishop with great pleasure granted Reverend Mother's Petition that the good Infirmarian might Spend the High Feasts within our Inclosure. She sat up with our Subprioress Sister Mary Catherine Willis[2] (whose yearly custom it is) on Xmass Eve, all the remaining part of the Night after ~~after~~ the Office &c is over. And whenever She comes, She spends all the time she can in the Choir with great fervour & Piety. She eats with us in the Refectory sitting by the Subprioress. The Abbot of the Dunes[3] was so pleased with our Charity to these good Religious, that he allows his Monks to serve us, by saying the Foundation Mass, which we found extremely difficult to procure elsewhere. & they do it in the most exact obliging manner.

---

[1] Fr Gerard had been Confessor at Nazareth 1723–79; latterly he had lived in the convent without being able to act fully as Confessor because of his health.

[2] Mary Catherine Willis (BA221).

[3] The Abbot of the Dunes was Robert Van Severen, Abbot 1748–92.

[p. 282]

July

On the 13th Sister Mary Ignatia Dillon was Clothed.[1]

August

On the 9th Mrs Catherine More Sister to our Reverend Mother departed this Life.[2] She left Reverend Mother £50. Our Subprioress order'd the Same publick & private Prayers for her as for Mrs Maire, & also the favour of being wrote down amongst our Benefactors which was not her due. She had for some years contributed £4 towards paying for Sister Regis Angiers board. *Requiescat in pace.*

November

Sister Mary Currell a Lay Sister appear'd very ill for some days, & on the 25th of this month the Doctor declared She had the Small Pox.[3] Sister Albana Patterson kindly offer'd herself to be shut up with her as her Nurse, which Reverend Mother accepted:[4] but being unexperienced procured an old Woman out of Town to be her Aid, who was used to this dangerous Distemper. Through God's mercy it proved a very good Sort, & no one either in the Monastery or School catched the Infection.

Pensioners &c: that came this year
1784

January the 10th Miss Nanny Dillon as mentioned page 274[5]
March the 8th Madlle Meulemestre from Ghent. age 19
June the 12th Madlle Van Remoortere from St Nicholas. Agc 18
[p. 283] June the 25th Miss Betty Blundell returned to us from England.
June the 25th Miss Kitty Dillon. aged 22
July the 24th Madlle Beesbrouck returned.
the 26 Madlle Aerts from Bruges. Age 17.
the 26 Madlle Ocket from Ostend. Age 14.
the 26th Miss Rutledge returned.
August the 15th Miss Lomax. age 17.
September the 29th Madlle De Gruytlers from Ostend. age 18.
October the 4th Madlle Sola from Bruges. Age 17.
November the 10th Madlle van Damme of Bruges. Age 14

---

1 Mary Ignatia Dillon (BA074).

2 Catherine More died unmarried in 1784. See Martin Wood, *Family and Descendants of St Thomas More* (Leominster: Gracewing, 2008), p. 265.

3 Mary Currell (BA069).

4 Albana Paterson (BA151).

5 Nanny Dillon is also mentioned on **[pp. 249, 256]**. The reference noted here is to her return from England.

the 14th Miss Kitty Fielding & Miss Betty Nieces to Sister Eugenia Randall,[1] the Eldest 16. the Youngest 13 years of Age.
December the 20th Madlle Derdyn returned to us.
November the 14th Miss Ann Moore from Staffordshire. age 17.

Pensioners &c that Left us this Year
1784

Aprill the 14th Miss Teresa Darell of Scotney went to Tourcoin.
May the 3d Madlle Vermersche the youngest.
the 14th Miss Jenny Huddleston of Saupon went to the Austines at Paris
June the 6th Miss Louisa Webbe went to Princen-hoff.[2]
The 13th Madlle Leep.
July the ~~28th~~ 28th Miss Betty Blundell of Ince went to Barlaimont Convent at Bruxells.[3]
[p. 284] July the 28 Madlle Audevare the Youngest.
August the 17th Miss Betty Huddleston went to Barliamont Convent at Bruxells.
September the 29th Madlle Van Outrive.
The 30th Miss Lomax.
October the 10th Miss Lizey Daly went to Middlebourg to take shipping for Demarary.[4] November the 20th Miss Rutledge.
The 21st Madlle Derdyn.
The 29th Madlle De Gruytters

An Article for January 1784 forgot in its proper place.

The Community being very well satisfied under Mr Oliver, The Bishop established him for our Confessor about the [*blank*] of January 1784. Upon Mr Burgesses departure, his Lordship allowed a Flemish Dominican to assist Mr Oliver in Hearing Confessions, his health being then very weak.[5] Mr Burgesses 2 Confidants & one other Choir Nun were all the Penitents the Dominican had. On Xmass Day 1783 The Bishop acquainted Reverend Mother, that if the 3 Nuns that went to him, wou'd not make use of Mr Oliver, he had appointed a Carm for them, & that the Dominican had no longer Faculties to hear them.[6] This was dreadfull

---

1 Eugenia Randall (BA159).
2 Louisa was the sister of Cecilia Webbe, who tried out Prinsenhof but left in 1786, BA262.
3 Berlaymont Convent, Brussels, an Augustinian convent with a boarding school for girls. The site is now Berlaymont Buildings, headquarters of the European Union. Betty is probably Elizabeth Blundell (1766–1845), daughter of Henry Blundell and Elizabeth Mostyn of Ince, who in 1789 married Stephen Tempest.
4 Demerara in the Dutch colony of Guyana.
5 Fr Andreas Oliver, from Scotland, Confessor 1782–1812. Fr Matthew Burgess, Confessor 1778–82; Anstruther pp. 50–1.
6 Carm: Carmelite. On faculties, see **[p. 236]**.

news to 2 of his Penitents who appear'd equally attached to him, as they had been to M[r] Burgess. However through God's Grace to Reverend **[p. 285]** Mothers great satisfaction they behaved very well, & begged her to decide for them. Tho' they were violently prejudiced against M[r] Oliver, She appointed him for them, being convinced it was more for their own good, as well as that of the Community, & its comfort which was now again united under one Pastor, to Reverend Mother's great joy, & the satisfaction of the whole.

1785

January

On the 18th Miss Nelly Langton returned to us, willing tho 22 years old to Lodge & Board in the School, as she cou'd not be received or remain here on any other footing.[1] She has an ardent desire to be a Nun, but has not Strength of body or Sight sufficient for it.

February

Sister Ann Austin Green who had been for some years intirely incapable of Saying the Divine Office **[p. 286]** or of any regular observance, by making a *Novena* to Venerable B: I: Labre,[2] which She began on Our Lady's Purification, was wholly restored by the Annversary day of her Profession, the 9th of the same month; & returned to every Religious duty without the least dispensation in any kind even during the whole Lent. Her indisposition was brought on her by too close an application ~~to the~~ attempting a constant attention to the Actual Presence of God, even whilst teaching in the School, or learning any thing herself, & in every other duty, which by degrees weakned her head so considerably that for about 6 years she was totally incapable of the least application: to which was added Scruples & their usual attendant Obstinacy: also Histerics to a very great degree. So that tho' her cure in itself was not perhaps miraculous, yet the courage She shew'd in beginning & continuing to frequent the Choir, to fast, & to perform every regular Duty, was not natural to her own disposition, & so contrary to her extreme Nervous Complaint that we piously presume to attribute it to the Intercession of Venerable Benedict Joseph Labre.[3]

---

1 Nelly Langton had arrived in the school in 1770 and left in September 1782. See **[pp. 210, 263, 287–8]**. It was important that candidates had good health when they entered the community in order that they could fully participate in the religious life of the convent. If they suffered from ill-health later, they were looked after by the community.

2 Anne Austin Green (BA090). She followed the example of Dame Albana Patterson, who made the Novena in 1784 starting at Candlemas; see **[pp. 275–9]**.

3 By 1785 the process towards canonisation had already started. See also **[p. 275]**.

March

The 15th Sister Ann Clare Wheeler after having been about 2 years Schollar, & 11 months Novice, left us to go to the English Teresians at Lierre in quality of Servant.[1]

[p. 287] At the beginning of Lent Miss Kitty Dillon was attacked by a feverish disorder, which turned to raging Madness. Two Women were hired to attend her night & Day. Her Brother Robert came from London for her, & She returned with him on the 28th of this month.

Aprill

On the 16th we received two Protestant Pensioners, viz Miss Sarah Parish from Norfolk about 17 years old, who was strongly recommended to us by Mr Tasburgh, & by whom we were assured that if her inclinations turned to become a Catholic, she wou'd not meet with opposition from her Friends; & Miss Eliza Mootham, Daughter to a Wealthy Distiller in London.[2] Her Father ought to be a Catholic, but married an Inveterate Protestant who having nursed all her Children, except this girl, She took a dislike to her, & used her very differently from the rest. Doctor Savage a Catholic Physician in London, being witness of it, proposed her being sent over to us, which the Mother most readily agreed to, & added that She might also be a Nun too, which was the greatest proof she cou'd give of her dislike to this poor Child, who is only 5 years old.

June

During the Course, ^viz on the 3d^, of this month, Miss Nelly Langton went to Amette, & made a *Novena* there **[p. 288]** in honour of Venerable Labre to obtain strength of health & Sight to be a Religious, but returned much the same as She went.[3] Venerable Labres Mother, with whom she Lodged & Boarded, exhorted her to continue her confidence & that Almighty God wou'd at last grant her request. As she has excellent dispositions, is extremely pious, & has a very good temper, She wou'd be a welcome Member to the Community. Sister Joachim Forshaw[4] accompanied & staid with her the Whole time: they were much edified with the Xtian Simplicity, & Piety of Mrs Labre & her Children. In returning through Aire they found Miss Eliza Webster at the English Convent,[5] who was coming ^to us^ to be Pensioner about 11 years old, Daughter to a Protestant Parson settled in Derbyshire, who being a Learned Man, had by reading the Holy Scriptures & Holy Fathers discover'd his own errors,

---

1 Ann Clare Wheeler (BA217). She went to the English Carmelites at Lierre.

2 Her father, John Mootham, and Philip Booth were partners in the Cow Cross distillery business in London until 1772. Miss Parish has not been identified.

3 Amettes, Artois, France was the birthplace of Benedict Joseph Labre in 1748.

4 Joachim Forshaw (BA083).

5 Poor Clares, Aire-sur-la-Lys. Elizabeth Webster was clothed at Nazareth in 1791, but decided to leave in November 1794, BA234. See also Chronicle, vol. 3, **[p. 40]**.

& tho he had a ^wife &^ large family, sacrificed every consideration to his own & their Salvation. Mr Wyndham one of our former Confessors, sent this Child to us.[1] Sister Joachim took the charge of her from Aire, & they all arrived here June the 18th

July

On the 16th Miss Ann Moore of Wolverhampton took the Schollars Habit in the 18th year of her age **[p. 289]** & the names of Mary Clare.[2]

September

Mrs Pickering having by her Will left to her Daughter Sister Eusebia Pickering £55 Sterling,[3] we had a Solemn Mass, ^also a Low one^, & Dierge for her, & each one of the Community offer'd a Communion, 2 Masses & 2 Short Dierges for her. *Requiescat in pace.*

December

On the 4th Sister Ann Teresa Jerningham solemnized her whole Jubilee, being then actually Procuratress.[4]

The Pensioners we received in the Year 1785

January the 18th Miss Betty Langton of Cadiz.	22 years old
Aprill the 16th Miss Parish a Protestant from Yarmouth	18
the 16th Miss Eliza Mootham from London	5
May the 22d Mademoiselle Balbart from Ostend	14
June the 18th Miss Webster from Derbyshire	11
August the 3d Mademoiselle Van Outrive from Ostend	15
December the 18th Mademoiselle Pieters from Ghent	

The Pensioners that left us in the year 1785

January the 24 Mademoiselle Ochet
24 Mademoiselle Beesbroucke
February the 10 Mademoiselle Le Grand
[p. 290] March the 15 Mademoiselle Vantieghem.
28 Miss Kitty Dillon.
June the 16 Mademoiselle De Gruytters.
~~Sep the 12~~ July the 27 Mademoiselle Aerts.
September the 12 Mademoiselle De Pauw.
12 Mademoiselle De Gruytters for good.

---

1 Fr Philip Wyndham (d. 1825), Confessor 1767–72; Anstruther 4, pp. 311–12.
2 Anne Catherine Moore, in religion Mary Clare (1790–1845) BA144.
3 Eusebia Pickering (BA156). She was one of five daughters of Edward Pickering (d. 1761) of Oporto and his wife, Eusebia Aylward.
4 Ann Teresa Jerningham (1735–96) BA120.

1786

January

On the 1st Miss Parish was called upon by an Uncle from England,[1] who pretended business in these Countries. As She had acquainted her Mother & Friends of her Intention to become a Catholic, they were immediately allarmed, & determined on her return to England. Her Friends in London held a Council about her, & called to it an Apostate Ex Jesuite who had studied at the College here: He persuaded them it would be difficult to get her out of our hands, advised Mr Parish to secure her Person before he acquainted her or us of his Commission: & for greater Security he had **[p. 291]** a letter to Lord Torrington the English Envoy at Bruxells to desire his assistance if necessary.[2] As soon as Mr Parish appear'd both She & we suspected his errand. He desired She might go with him that Evening to Mr Edwards a zealous Protestant Gentleman settled in Bruges to whom he was recommended: to our great surprize She returned that night to the Convent, & told us her Uncle had not said a word to her upon Religion, & that She hoped other business had brought him over: begged of Reverend Mother[3] to procure him leave of the Bishop to see the Convent the next day, which was granted. He accepted it, but appear'd fearfull of entering, & during his Stay in it was very thoughtfull & meloncholly, yet seemed much obliged at our civillities. Miss Parish went out with him to dine at Mr Edwards. About 5 in the evening Mr Parish came to the Convent & desired a private conference with Reverend Mother: he appear'd much perplexed, & with some difficulty acquainted her that he was commissioned to take Miss Parish to England; Reverend Mother replied that as She had received her from her Uncle Mr Woodbine, She hoped he would not find any impropriety in her asking if he had letters from that Gentleman with those orders, he seem'd quite satisfied with her question, & immediately put into her hands letters to himself from Mr Woodbine & Mrs Parish requesting him to come over for her: **[p. 292]** after Reverend Mother had perused them, She told him Miss Parish was at his command. He still appear'd perplexed, & at last upon Reverend Mother's enquiry if Miss Parish was come back to the Convent, he acquainted her that he was commmission'd not to allow her to return even to pack up her Clothes, he produced her keys, & begged we wou'd send her Trunks to Mr Edwards. He told Reverend Mother he was very sensible the precautions he was order'd to take were unnecessary, made

---

1 The family can be identified from the name of the uncle, named later in this account as 'Woodbine'. Woodbine Parish (1768–1848) is described in *ODNB* as a well-connected London merchant trading with the Netherlands.

2 The envoy in Brussels was George Byng (1740–1812), 4th Viscount Torrington, envoy 1783–92.

3 Reverend Mother in 1786 was Mary Augustina More (BA145).

many excuses, & even ventured to exceed his Commission by bringing her to the Grate the next day to take leave of us. He said his Niece was much hurt & wept bitterly when he open'd the affair to her: we were therefore the more surprized to find her behaviour very cool at her taking leave, for She had appear'd attentive to her Instructions, & ^expressed^ that her ^desire^ of changing her Religion was from absolute conviction: for she had been very firm in her own for 4 or 5 months. She had given such entire satisfaction in every part of her conduct, her behaviour was so modest, & her temper so pleasing that She was universally beloved & admired both in the School & Convent, & appear'd much attached to us. She wrote to Reverend Mother from London, & told her, that She hoped by the grace of God to shew that the advice She received in the Convent was not lost or thrown away. We **[p. 293]** hear her Uncle Woodbine (on whom She chiefly depends) has desired she may be left at liberty in point of Religion: but whether She lives with her Mother at Yarmouth or with her Uncle Woodbine at Rainham, there are no Catholics of fashion near her, & of consequence She will have no means of further Instruction. She was far advanced in making a General Confession before her Uncle came for her, but the Bishop would not allow her to be taken into the Church, as She would be immediately exposed to imminent danger by returning amongst her Friends.

January the 17th Sister Mary Clare Moore was Clothed.[1]

March

Sister Eusebia Pickering[2] having received £35 Sterling from her Sister Betty's Effects, we had a Solemn Mass for her, & each one offer'd one Communion, 4 Masses & one Short Dierge.

Aprill

On the 9th Mr Anthony Wright Junior departed this life.[3] As he kindly undertook to do our business in the same manner his Father had done, we performed the same for him, & he is also wrote down amongst our Deceased Benefactors.

May

On the 9th Sister Margaret Catherine Aspinal departed this life in the 89th year of her age & 67th of her **[p. 294]** Profession.[4] She was a Convert & had much to suffer from her Protestant Father, from ^whom^. she stole away. Divine Providence brought her here, where she became an exemplary Religious in quality of a Lay Sister, & gave great edification

---

[1] Mary Clare Moore (BA144).

[2] Eusebia Pickering (BA156).

[3] Anthony Wright, banker of London. The obligations of the community to his father (Anthony) are recognised on **[p. 263]**, where his death in 1782 is recorded.

[4] Margaret Catherine Aspinal (1720–86) BA006.

to the whole Community by her extraordinary regularity even in the most minute Observances. About half a year before her death, she was rather superannuated, yet was capable of the Sacrements: She was very exact in approaching to them, as well as in all her ^other^ Spiritual duties, & employ'd the rest of her time in some work for the Common as far as She was capable. She died of a pure decay: received the last Sacrements in great peace, & calmly resigned her Soul into the hands of her Creator. *R: I. P.*

The Emperor Joseph the 2^d^ having forbid any one whatever to be Buried in the Towns of his Dominions,[1] Reverend Mother did not choose her Religious shou'd go to the Common Church Yard, & applied to the Curate of the Parish of St Croix in The Country, who very obligingly appointed a particular place in his Spacious Church Yard for us. Sister Catherine Aspinal was the first we buried there: The Community was so affected with grief when the Corpse was taken out of our Church door that tears prevented our being able to pursue with decency what we were there to sing viz. **[p. 295]** *In Paradisum*. The People in the Church remarked it, & shewed great compassion of us. Six of our Lay Sisters & the young Ladies accompanied the Corpse, & when arrived at the Parish, the former carried it into the Church, & from thence after the Obsequies to the Grave, the Pensioners walking 2 & 2 in Procession before it both times.

On the 16th Sister Elizabeth Teresa Austine Newlin departed this life in the 71st year of her age & 49th of her Profession.[2] She was Daughter to a Protestant Clergyman who had a numerous Family, Lady Mary Caryll offer'd him to provide for one of his girls if he wou'd consent to have her educated as her Ladyship thought fit, he agreed to it, & Sister Teresa Austine being the happy one She chose. her Ladyship sent her to this Convent being then about 10 years of age. She was designed to have remained here a year, & after that, to wait on her Ladyship at Paris. It is supposed that her Father met with threats from a Protestant Bishop, which made him resolve to have her home again: he therefore order'd her back at the end of the Year: & She suffer'd much from her Parents during the 6 years she lived with them: Notwithstanding the Impressions of Religion She had received here made her firm in her resolution of living & Dying in the true Faith. **[p. 296]** Wishing to return here She consulted Lord Caryll on the means of making her escape, & by his

---

1 The decree, made out of concern for public health, had been extended to the Austrian Netherlands in 1784. The new regulations prevented religious from being buried within their convents. The parish of St Croix is just outside the town limits, across the canal from Nazareth; see map of Bruges.

2 Elizabeth Teresa Austin Newlin (1737–86) BA147. One of nine daughters of a Protestant vicar, she grew up in Harting, Sussex, and was sent to the Catholic Caryll family at the 'big house' at Harting for her upbringing. She was converted to Catholicism while there.

assistance She left the Country & arrived safe in London, & from thence came here with only the Clothes on her back. She was kindly received into our School, & being very desirous of embracing a Religious State, the Community had the charity to receive her, for such a miracle of Grace cou'd not be rejected. She appear'd vigorous for health & Strength, but it pleased Almighty God to dispose otherwise, for when young Professed she became quite blind, but by means of a famous Oculist, she recover'd her sight. Some Employs were committed to her, but her health soon failed, & She became a complication of Infirmities, which she bore with singular patience & uncommon chearfulness. She was of a rash, morose, resenting, difficult temper, which made her very improper for offices, yet She was generally beloved, being of a chearfull facetious humour. Her attract to corporal mortifications, & her extravagant rash practises of some in her youth was judged to have hasten'd her Infirmities. She was very fervorous in all her Spiritual duties even to her last Illness, & was of great service for the Common work. Her last Illness was short tho' she had had so many severe ones, that the **[p. 297]** Holy Oyls were then given her for the 8th time, & the *Viaticum* the 25th. Her Death was most calm & peaceable. *R. I. P.* She was buried at the Parish of the Holy Cross, & laid next to Sister Catherine Aspinal.

May

On the 19th Brother Thomas Carfoot departed this life.[1] He was born at Little Crosby in Lancashire.[2] His Father who was a Carpenter brought up to that Trade. He left his Country to enter as a Lay Brother at the English Carthusian Convent at Newport where he arrived the 5th of September 1766 being 23 years of age. He made his Engagement to that Community in September 1768. He was the last Religious received in that Charter House before the Suppression of it. At its Dissolution in June 1783, he came to our Convent, but soon after went to the English Austines at Louvain, where he only staid a short time, & returned to us October the first the same year. We found him very serviceable by his Trade, & exceeding usefull in every occasion. He Lodged in the Father's House, & waited on the Confessor whose affection & esteem he justly acquired as well as that of the Community, in general by his Religious, modest, Humble, behaviour. His character is comprized **[p. 298]** in the 2d Stanza of the Hymn for a Confessor viz.

---

1 Thomas Carfoot died aged 43. For further details of the suppression of the English Carthusians, see Dom Lawrence Hendriks, *London Charterhouse, Its Monks and Its Martyrs with a Short Account of the English Carthusians after the Dissolution in March 1783* (London: Kegan Paul, 1889), pp. 336–41. The Chronicle here adds significantly to knowledge of Br Carfoot's last years.

2 Little Crosby was one of the Blundell properties in Lancashire. See also Janet E. Hollinshead, *Women of the Catholic Community: The Blundells of South Lancashire during the Seventeenth and Eighteenth Centuries* (Wigan: North West Catholic History Society, 2010).

His humble Prudence & his thoughts on High.
His pure & unpretending piety
By blameless Steps a Sober life convey'd,
Till last it center'd, where at first was made.

He died in his 44th year of a Consumption, from which he had Suffer'd much for some years. He had made a Spiritual Retreat with great fervour & piety the November before his Death. He received the last Sacrements on the 18th of May, & expired with great calmness & tranquillity between 11 & 12 at night on the 19 in the Confessors Quarters, universally regretted by the Community & all that knew him. He was buried at the Parish of the Holy Cross next to Sister Teresa Austine Newlin. He left us by Will a small Rent of thirty Shillings English a year in the Funds in England 3 per Cents Consolidated & also all the furniture of his Room, & other small Things. Reverend Mother has appointed a low Mass for him yearly on his Anniversary. *R. I. P.*

On the 20th Jane Harrish came here for a Lay Sister being 28 years of age.

June

On the 2d Miss Laelia & Miss Harriott Havers were sent into the Country to be innoculated.[1] **[p. 299]** The Abbot of Eckoute was so obliging at our Physicians request, to lend them his Country House for that purpose.[2] They were attended by Sister Joachim Forshaw a Lay Sister,[3] & Mary Robey, a clever English Servant Maid, & returned quite recover'd on the 12th of July.

June

On the 18th Mr Frank Wright departed this life.[4] As he had kindly undertaken our business after his Brother Anthony's death in May we performed the same for him, as for his Father & eldest Brother, & he is also wrote down amongst our Deceased Benefactors.

July

On the 11th Sister Tecla Hampson who was quite blind kept the Feast of her half Jubilee.[5] Reverend Mother procured leave for her 5 Cousins Lay

---

1 The practice of innoculation against smallpox was widely known in the eighteenth century. As early as 1718, when living in Turkey, Lady Wortley Montagu had her son innoculated. However, the practice was relatively uncommon, difficult to carry out and not without risks. Edward Jenner was developing his practice of vaccination in this period in England. Leila and Harriet Havers were daughters of Thomas Havers and Catherine Dutry; see **[p. 245]**.

2 The Abbot of Eeckhoute was Emmanuel II Prisie, Abbot from 1776 to the suppression.

3 Joachim Forshaw (BA083).

4 He was part of the family which owned Wright's Bank, Henrietta Street, Covent Garden, which acted for a number of English Catholic families and institutions.

5 Thecla Hampson (1761–92) BA097.

Sisters[1] at Princen-hoff to enter our Inclosure at the end of our Convents Mass & to stay till 7 in the evening, which very much obliged their Mother Abbess & Community & also themselves, who left us highly satisfied with their days diversion & the civillities we had shewn them.

At the beginning of this month Brother James Orford an English Carthusian Lay Brother of Newport came to settle here with us.[2]

[p. 300] On the 17th Jane Harrish left us. We found her quite improper for a Lay Sister, shewing even some Symptoms that her head was disorder'd.

October

On the 18th St Lukes Day, Sister Ursula Clough arrived to her quarter Jubilee, which no Choir Nun had ever done since the Foundation of the Convent.[3] We had a Musick Mass, the 2 last Hours were read before it. The Procuratress gave a handsome Recreation, & Reverend Mother gave another in the Jubilarians name, & allowed one Sitting up night.

December

On the 6th Reverend Mother procured secretly from the Under Commissary at the Suppressed Convent of Penitents, the Head & all the Bones that remained of Mother Stamford our first Superiour who died March the 7th 1635, & was buried in their Church.[4] & by the same means, on the 27 of the same month, She procured a few bones, the only remains of Sister Mary Best one of our Foundresses, who was buried at Bethania in the year 1631.[5] We interred them very privately in our own Church Yard on the same days we procured them. *Requiescant in Pace.*

These two Convents were sent to Sale a few days after.[6]

[p. 301]

The Pensioners we received in the year 1786

	years old
February the 10th Miss Stuart from Scotland	16
27th Madlle Meurant from Ostend	16
May the 11th Mad'lle Cornelis from Ghent	17

---

1 Five Ainsworth lay sisters (BF007, 008, 009, 010 and 011) can be identified at Prinsenhof, although it has not been possible to establish the family connection with Thecla Hampson. She had been recommended by Miss Blundell of Ince Blundell.

2 One of two lay brothers from Nieuport, he remained in Flanders in the hope of participating in the restoration of the community.

3 Sister Ursula professed on 18 April 1724. It appears that the quarter jubilee was 60 years.

4 The Penitents (Grey Sisters, Carmerstraat) had agreed to bury some of the first nuns who died at Nazareth before they had their own burial site: see vol. 1, **[p. 17]**.

5 Mary Best (LA031) died in Bruges in 1631. Bethania was the convent nearest Nazareth in Carmerstraat.

6 The sale was enforced as a result of the edict of Joseph II to close enclosed contemplative monasteries in the Habsburg dominions.

21st Miss Manby[1] 14
21st Miss Ann Manby 10
23d Madlle Mene from Ghent 17
29th Miss Deacon from Manchester a Protestant 12
June the 6th Miss Hudson,^alias Nappier^, of Protestant Parents 5
July the 11th Madlle Vanden Clooster of Bruxells 14
11th Madlle Ann Vanden Cloosters of Ditto 13
13th Miss Teresa Darell & Miss Betty Fielding from Tourcoine
15th Miss Monica Clavering of Callaly 9
19th Miss Masterson Daughter to an ^English^ Protestant Merchant in Bruges 15
19th The 2 Madlles Van Hoorícks from Bruxells 19 & 16
August the 3d The 2 Miss Gibsons from Northumberland 14 & 13
17th Madlle Subaert of Bruges 12
17th Miss Fielding from Tourcoine
21st The 3 Miss Sulyard's of Haughley Park[2] 12, 10, 9
October the 8th Madlle Van Ipheghem from Ostend 14
23d Madlle Vanden Bruggen from Ghent 14
November the 13th The 2 Miss Hans from Ipres. Their Mother is English, their Father a Flemming 15, 12

As Miss Nappers Parents are separated, & She is placed here unknown to her Father, to conceal her from him she goes by the name of Hudson. Her Mother when she brought her gave Reverend Mother half a Card cut in Scollops & kept the other half herself. & the Child is to be deliver'd **[p. 302]** only to the Person who ^brings^ the half card from her Mother that will join with the half left with Reverend Mother.[3] This Child will probably be Heiress to a large Fortune.

The Pensioners that left us in the Year 1786

January the 2d Miss Parish.
18th Madlle Sola.
19th Madlle Derdeyn
February 18th Madlle Van Remortere.
20th The 2 Miss Fieldings to Tourcoine.

---

1 Frances and Ann Manby were daughters of Thomas Manby Esq. of Beads Hall, South Weald, Essex.

2 The Sulyard family of Haughley Park, Suffolk, had long-standing links with Nazareth. These three sisters are Sophia, Lucy and Frances, daughters of Edward Sulyard (c. 1725–79) and his wife, Susanna Ravenscroft (1751–78). All three went on to marry.

3 This practice replicates that of indentures, where a document was cut creating an irregular shape: both parts would have to match exactly to prove that the document was a true copy.

Aprill 13th Madlle Meurant.
June 27th Madlle Van Outrive.
July 24th Miss Laelia Havers to Tourcoine.
August 8th Miss Teresa Darell to England.
14th Madlle Van Hoorieck.
September 16th Madlle Cornelis.
August 10th The 2 Miss Mostyns.
October 20th The 2 Miss Fieldings to England.

1787

January

Reverend Mother being informed of the Death of Mr Burgess our last Confessor[1] we had a Solemn Mass for him on the 16th. He died in sentiments of penance on the 4th of December 1786 at La Bassée a **[p. 303]** Convent of Augustin Monks between Lille & Doway, where his Bishop in England had sent him, not finding him proper for the Mission.

On the 25th Sister Mary Clare Moore was placed in the Rank of those who wait for the age required for making their Solemn Vows, having finished her Noviciate & been consented by the Convent to her future Profession.[2]

February

On the 9th Sister Justina Huddleston departed this life, between 8 & 9 in the morning, being the Anniversary of her Profession, on which day She completed her 60th year, & 78th of her age wanting 4 days.[3] She had suffer'd a long course of Infirmity with resignation for above ten years. She always expressed the highest esteem & love of her Vocation, & the greatest gratitude to Almighty God for it, for having embraced it in the very early part of her life. Being Little & difformed, she was inclined especially during the first years after her Profession to think herself slighted in the Community. She had a good understanding, a Solid Piety, perfectly obedient to her Directors, sincere, & remarkably exact in regular Observance. She was by nature very timorous & of a delicate conscience, which was often the cause of interiour sufferings. She was strong & constant in her affections & dislikes, which if they **[p. 304]** might sometimes influence her judgment with regard to Particulars, had never any effect when Duty was concerned. She had been for many years at different times Mistress of Novices, & acquired the respect & love of those under her Charge. For several years before her death, she was

---

1 Fr Matthew Burgess (1752–86), Confessor 1778–82, died 4 December 1786; see Anstruther 4, pp. 50–1.

2 Mary Clare Moore (BA144). She was one of those affected by Maria Theresa's regulations requiring 25 as the minimum age for profession.

3 Justina Huddleston (1727–87) BA113.

unable to fast, Abstain, or to keep order, but was assiduous at the common work. She required a great deal of attention, & did not refuse, but even expected the lowest services from the Nuns, not from Pride, but self love, because their hands & assistance were more kinder than the Lay Sisters. Her temper was indolent, peevish & resenting, the 2 latter afforded her many ^combats &^ victories. A Melancholly disposition made her wish for company, which exposed her when old, to the caresses of the young & relaxed, who often made a Dupe of her for their own ends. She had a very religious air, & was carefull even to the last to keep her hours of reading & Meditation. As death was always in her thoughts, we have all reason to believe she was well prepared for it. She received all the last Sacrements, & calmly expired without any Agony, which she had a great apprehension of, but joined with a perfect resignation to suffer it, as long as it shou'd please Almighty God: these sentiments she expressed to her Confessor about 2 hours before she died. *R. I. P.* She was buried at the Parish **[p. 305]** of the Holy Cross next to Brother Thomas Carfoot.

February

On the 26th The Convent Sisters were assembled for the Election of the Arcaria,[1] the Place being vacant by the death of Sister Justina: at the meeting Reverend Mother proposed a triennial one for the future, to which the Convent readily agreed. As no one had the requisite number, viz two thirds of the votes, the first & 2d time, they proceeded to a 3d, when Sister Mary Oliva Darell was chose.[2]

Aprill

On the 25 Sister Regis Angier set off for England for the recovery of her health.[3]

May

The 19th being the Anniversary of Brother Carfoot we had a Solemn Mass of Requiem for him.[4]

June

On the 12th The Carmes came in Procession to our Church as usual, but by the Bishop's ^orders^ on the Tuesday within the Octave of Corpus Christi instead of the Octave day as formerly. It was omitted last year on account of an Edict from the Emperor for reducing the number of Processions, but the **[p. 305]** Archdutchess Christina having on the 30th of May this year ratified the Priviledges of the Countries, many things

---

1 The Arcaria was responsible for the documents relating to the community; see Glossary.

2 Mary Olivia Darell (BA070).

3 Mary Regis Angier (BA005).

4 Thomas Carfoot was one of two Carthusian lay brothers who stayed at Nazareth after their monastery at Nieuport was closed. See **[pp. 297–8]**.

were again reestablished for a short space, for the Emperor wou'd not confirm what She had done.[1]

Our good Friend & Benefactor M[r] Taunton having sent us a Present of Ten Pounds & recommended to our Prayers, his Family & other Intentions, Reverend Mother order'd each one of the Community to offer 2 Communions, 4 Masses & once the Divine Office.

July

On the 13th Mr John Blyde an Ex Jesuite Lay Brother died & left us Five Pounds:[2] Reverend Mother order'd a Solemn Mass to be sung for him, & each one to hear 3 more, to offer one Communion & to recite one Short Dierge for the same Intention.

On the 24 Miss Eliza Talbot died, & left us fifty pounds.[3] We had a long Dierge said for her in the Choir, a Solemn Mass sung, & a Low one said, & Reverend Mother order'd each one to hear 2 more, to offer one Communion, & to say 2 Short Dierges.

Sister Regis Angier[4] expressing a great desire of returning here & her Physician declaring ~~that her~~ **[p. 306]** that he did not look upon her Indispositions & Humours as an essential impediment to her engaging in a Religious State, & performance of the Duties annexed to it: Reverend Mother assembled the Convent Sisters to acquaint them of it.[5] A second voting was not judged proper as She had been already consented to her Profession after her Years Noviceship was expired, before she returned to England, & ^had^ only waited for the Age of 25 required by the Imperial Edict. As her health did not promise to be strong, some of the Convent Sisters were inclined to have her pass the votes again, but Reverend Mother opposed the motion, & acquainted them of the following particulars that had happen'd a few years before at the English Convent of Princenhoff. A Novice was voted to her Profession, after the votes had passed in her favour, it was discover'd that she was illegitimate, upon which the Community refused to Profess her, alledging that circumstance was not known before the voting: the affair was laid before the Bishop who [~~*illeg.*~~] insisted the Novice had a right to make her Profession which was accordingly granted to her in the same Convent. Upon this information no further objection was made to Sister Regis Angier. On this **[p. 307]** occasion Reverend Mother acquainted the Convent Sisters that for the

[1] Archduchess Maria Christina, Duchess of Teschen (1742–98), ruled as Regent of the Austrian Netherlands between 1781 and 1793 with her husband, Prince Albert of Saxony, although, as we see here, her powers were effectively limited by Joseph II.

[2] John Blyde (1715–87), lay brother, spent some time at the Jesuit College, Bruges; Holt, pp. 35–6.

[3] Betty Talbot had arrived at Nazareth in 1771; see **[pp. 208, 231, 232]**.

[4] Mary Regis Angier (BA005).

[5] Reverend Mother in 1787 was Mary Augustina More (BA145).

future whoever was received to Profession by the Votes in her favour wou'd never be put to them again.

August

On the 25th Sister Regis Angier arrived from England & the next morning reassumed her Habit and Religious duties.

September

On the 21st The Emperor having at the earnest Solicitations of the States of the different Provinces given a Ratification of the Ancient Priviledges of these Countries (except those of the Secular & Regular Clergy) on the 23d, the Bishop sent us orders to ring from 7 to 8 o clock that evening.[1]

October

On the 9th Sister Mary Catherine Willis was reelected Subprioress for the 6th time.[2]

The Pensioners we received in the Year
1787

Aprill the 24th Miss Lelia Havers from Tourcoine
May 22d Miss Ibbetson from Arundell aged 20, the 3 Miss Byrnes aged 12, 11–10, & Miss D'Eveline 14.

[p. 308]

August

4th Miss Maria Hawkins from Knash in Kent aged 7

September

10 Miss Assiotti from London aged 10
17 Madlle Winclemann from Bruges aged 15.
20 Madlle Leep from Ostend aged 18
30 Mad'lle Columbet from Graveline aged 19

The Pensioners that left us in the Year
1787

February 10 Madlle Van Damme.
10 Madlle Subaert.
June 16 Miss Laelia Havers to England.
22 Madlle Menne.
July 10 The 2 Mesdomoiselles Vanden Cloosters.
August 15 The 2 Miss Hans.

[1] Joseph II responded to opposition to his reforms by granting concessions and, as here, recognising local rights and privileges belonging to the estates, while maintaining his reforms of the Church.

[2] Mary Catherine Willis (BA221).

16 Miss Masterson
October 8 Mad[lle] Van Hooriech the youngest.

1788
January See page 311

February
On the 20th Sister Alissia Talbot was chosen Procuratress at the 3[d] Voting.[1]

[p. 309]

March
On the 9th We had a Long Dierge said in the Choir for Prince Charles Stuart, & a Solemn Mass sung for him the next morning. He died at Rome on the 31st of January this year.[2]

On the 12th We had the same Service for Lord Caryll, & a Solemn Mass on the 13th.[3] He died on the 7th of this month. He had been so great a Benefactor to our House that his name is recorded amongst those Deceased.

On the 26th Our Dear Sister Helen Blevin departed this life in the 81st year of her age & 54th of her Religious Profession.[4] She had served the Community faithfully in quality of Lay Sister, & by her assiduity in laborious employments, & exact discharge of what was committed to her, render'd herself a valuable Member of it. She was much beloved & esteem'd of Her companions. Her life passed in peace & tranquillity being seldom or ever afflicted with interiour trials, which probably proceeded from the great confidence she had in Almighty God & an entire conformity to his Holy will. On the 5th of March she was much indisposed, on the following days she cou'd not be taken out of bed without swooning, & on the 21 was seized with an Apoplectic fit accomanied by a Palsey which deprived her of speech till she died, but she appear'd sensible, & calmly expired, terminating a **[p. 310]** pious life as we firmly hope by a happy Death. She was buried in our own Church Yard, the Edict for a common burial place being recalled by the Patriots.[5] *Requiescat in Pace.*

May
On the 8th Sister Mary Regis Angier made her Holy Profession in the 26th year of her age.[6]

---

[1] Alicia Talbot (BA190).
[2] Prince Charles Edward Stuart (1720–88), known to Jacobites as Charles III, died in Rome following a stroke on 30 January 1788. See *ODNB*.
[3] Lord John Caryll (Jacobite peerage) died in Dunkirk on 7 March 1788. He was Secretary of State to Prince Charles Edward Stuart; see M. H. M. Ruvigny et Raineval, *The Jacobite Peerage, Baronetage, Knightage…* (Edinburgh and London: T. C. and E. C. Jack, 1904) p. 29.
[4] Helen Blevin (1734–88) BA026.
[5] Joseph II had decreed that burials should take place outside the city in designated cemeteries. See **[p. 294]**.
[6] Mary Regis Angier (BA005).

October

On the 31st Miss Eliza Houel took the Schollars Habit for a Choir Nun in the 16th year of her age.[1]

November

On the 18th Mary Robey returned to us from England to be a Lay Sister.

The Pensioners we received in the year
1788

February 12 Miss Fanny Clavering of Callaly age 14.[2]
28 Madlle Barbara Leeps from Ostend aged 16
Aprill 21 The 2 Miss Wakemans from Essex age 13 & 14.
21 Miss Cruse from Essex age 13.
June 5 Miss Howe from Kent age 14
5 Miss Lane from Wolverhampton age 15
19 Miss Burlton to teach French.
July 25 Miss Winny Mostyn returned to us. age. 11
25 The 2 Miss Doodies from Wolverhampton. age, 15 & 19.
August 28 Miss Deacon returned to us.
September 27 Madlle Segaert of Bruges ~~returned to us~~ age 14.
October 24 Miss Houel for a Choir Nun.
November 18 Mary Robey for a Lay Sister.[3]

[p. 311]

The Pensioners that left us in the year
1788

January 22 Madlle Vanderbrugghen.
24 Miss Ibbetson to learn French at Rousselaer.
February 18 Miss Stuart to Tourcoine at the Ursulines.
March 2d Miss Deacon to the Ursulines at St Omer.
13 Madlle Columbet.
August 5 Miss Mary Byrne to the Ursulines at Tourcoine.
September 11 Miss Sulyard to the English Dames at Bruxells.[4]
21 Madlle Leep the Eldest.
October 4 The eldest Madlle Van Isseghem.
7 Miss Fanny Clavering to the English Austines at Paris[5]

---

1 Elizabeth Howell (1795–1825) BA110.
2 Probably Frances Clavering, daughter of John Clavering of Callaly, Northumberland and his wife, Christina Swynburne. She did not remain in the convent and went on to marry.
3 Mary Roby, in religion Mary Antonia (1791–1850) BA163.
4 Miss Sulyard does not appear on the membership lists at Brussels.
5 Fanny Clavering does not appear on the membership lists in Paris.

January 1788

On the [*blank*] between 8 & 9 at night we were disturbed & allarmed by hearing the Pensioners in the Dormitory, who cried out that the School was on fire. Some of the Nuns ran down immediately, & found the Smoke violent in the Cloister that leads to it, but at their arrival the fire was extinguished by the Sister of the School. One of the Pensioners had deliberately set fire to some Clothes that were drying on a Horse, which soon communicated to the whole, the guilty Person did not intend it to go far, called on the Sister herself & was very busy in putting it out, yet feigned as much fear **[p. 312]** as the rest. We took the Pensioners from the Dormitory into the Infirmary, where a fire was made, & refreshed them with Wine & Cakes, & after the School was clear'd from Smoke they returned to bed, from whence several had run without Shoe or Stocking. One or 2 who were asleep were near being suffocated by the Smoke & in going down stairs were for some time not able to proceed, being beat back again by its violence: however, thanks to the Divine Mercy, no cold or harm came to any of them. We had a Mass said in thanksgiving for their preservation. Some few days after this accident, the guilty Person began to be suspected, & tho' she persisted in denying it to different Persons, yet she at last owned it to Reverend Mother, who immediately took measures to have her removed without her suspecting it, till she was out of the House, lest revenge or vexation might prompt her to renew seriously the same scene. According to every appearance her only motive was to be taken notice of & to be thought the Saviour of the House. We found out at the same time that She was the Person who had stoln a small sum of money, & many other things that were missing, & in buying Lace, had even taken of a whole piece privately. She acknowledged the greatest part of these things before she left us, **[p. 313]** & as her Parents were in good circumstances, upon information they repaid all the Damages both by Thefts & Fire. Her Friends had sent her over to screen her from the contempt she had drawn on herself by her Thefts in England, & in hopes of her reformation, but she was thoroughly harden'd & no motives of Religion seem'd to make any impression, tho M[r] Oliver our Confessor,[1] & some of the Nuns used every means to bring her to a sense of her duty. Before this accident of Fire she had feigned a great delicacy of conscience, & had all the arts of a real Hypocrite. As we sent her to a ~~french~~ Convent, that had only very low people for Pensioners, poor diet &c: & was threatened with a total neglect from her Parents, who notwithstanding were extremely fond of her: She began to enter into herself & became so true a Penitent that She gave uncommon edification to the whole Community. As her Abode was little more than 9 miles from hence, M[r] Oliver visited her from time to

[1] Fr Andreas Oliver, Confessor 1782–1812.

time. She made a general Confession to him, & he was perfectly satisfied with her dispositions & Conduct from that time forwards. She soon declared her inclination to do pennance in a Religious State, refused to return Home, & being sensible of her own weakness, she ardently wished to settle here, where she was known & of **[p. 314]** consequence would be more suspected & watched over.

On the Night the Fire happen'd & the following one, we had a Person to watch ~~lest~~ in the School lest any hidden fire might break out.

1789

January

On the 5th Miss Harriott Ibbetson took the Schollars Habit, & the names of Teresa Austine in the 23d year of her age & is to remain Schollar for a whole year.[1]

On the 6th Mary Robey took the Schollars Habit for a Lay Sister, & the names of Winefride Anthony in the 22d year of her Age.[2] As she had lived with us before, the year required as a Secular Servant in her trial was dispensed with at her earnest request.

February

On the 22d Sister Mary Ignatia Dillon made her Holy Profession in the 24th year of her age.[3] On the 20th the Bishop informed us that the Emperor had now fixed the age to 24, She therefore immediately **[p. 315]** & earnestly petitioned she might make her vows the following Sunday, which was Shrove Sunday, the 22d of this month.

Aprill

On the 26th Sister Ursula Clough departed this life in the 83d year of her age, & 66th of her Religious Profession.[4] She was not a Person of extraordinary capacity, but very pious: by nature neat & warm in her temper, but full of vivacity, pleasant & chearfull: affectionate, but inconstant in her friendship. She had a very strong constitution, but not good health, was laborious, being always ready to help in the Garret in wash weeks, to sit up with the Sick, & for many years was constantly one that watched at the Sepulchre on Maundy Thursday night.[5] She had no turn for her ~~M~~ Needle, bore many painfull infirmities with great patience & was very mortified in her diet: tho' confined to the Infirmary for several years

---

1 Harriet Ibbetson, in religion Teresa Austin (1791–1809) BA117.

2 Mary Roby, in religion Mary Antonia (BA163). The change in age was part of the concessions made by Joseph II in his attempt to reduce opposition in the Austrian Netherlands. The name in religion is Mary Antonia at all other mentions, rather than Winefride, as given here.

3 Mary Ignatia Dillon (BA074).

4 Ursula Clough (1724–89) BA058.

5 Maundy Thursday is the day before Good Friday.

before her death, she would only ^have^ a Mess of Pottage on Good Fryday, & on other days avoided taking what was particularly good at Table. A considerable time before she died, she was reduced to almost a 2ᵈ Infancy, partly from age & some attacks of a Paralytic desorder, yet was still judged capable **[p. 316]** of the Sacraments: In her last Illness which continued about a fortnight she seem'd to enjoy her reason much better than before. She received all the last Sacrements, & tho' she appear'd to suffer much pain, ~~her mind y~~ yet her mind was calm & peaceable till as we have reason to hope She happily expired. *Requiescat in Pace.*

August

In this month our Convent Sisters met twice to give their Votes whether our Church Plate shou'd be sold or not. As we have been these 7 years in continual apprehensions of being Suppressed, we sent off secretly our Plate & Papers into French ^Flanders^, partly in 1786, & partly in 1787, viz to the French Ursulines at Tourcoine, & the English Poor Clares at Dunkerk, who very kindly received them in trust for us. As a great Revolution in France began last month which threatened the Clergy & Religious Houses we fear'd for its security.[1] Having little prospect of tranquillity for ourselves in these Countries, the votes the first time concluded for its being sold, & the money arising from it to be put out to Interest in England, by which we hoped in some years to recover the loss we must have suffer'd by Selling it only for its weight. The **[p. 317]** Capital with all its Interest to be employ'd in purchasing new ^Church^ Plate, when we were settled with Security either here or elsewhere if obliged to leave these Countries. Upon this determination Reverend Mother wrote to Mʳ Dourlen a French Gentleman at St Omer, a very particular friend of hers, & begged he would meet Sister Eugenia[2] (whom we sent from hence) at Dunkerk on the day she specified which he did accordingly, approved our resolution & expressed the utmost readiness to assist her by every means in his power: but when he saw the beauty of the Plate, & consider'd the great loss we must suffer, he refused the Commission till he had wrote again to Reverend Mother which he did in the Strongest terms, & assured us he would answer for the Security of the whole both at Dunkerk & Tourcoine. Reverend Mother therefore assembled the Convent Sisters a 2ᵈ time, & upon hearing Mʳ Dourlen's objections, the votes decided for a delay. Sister Eugenia returned with the greatest part of our Papers, but according to orders presented the Poor Clares with the Silver altar bell as a mark of our gratitude for their kind care. We received the rest of our papers October the 15 the same year. Mʳ Dourlen has removed all

---

[1] July 1789 saw the Storming of the Bastille on 14 July, following the decision of the National Assembly to write a new constitution for France. At the same time, tension had also risen in the Austrian Netherlands in opposition to Joseph II, who sent in troops to quell dissent.

[2] Eugenia Randall, lay sister (BA159).

our Plate ~~that~~ from Turcoine, & deposited it very secretly in the House of a trusty Friend **[p. 318]** of his at Lille & has sent us the direction as follows: *Deux Coffres contenant plusieurs pieces d'Argenterie travaillée, montée et demontée, le tout provenant des Dames Augustines Angloises a Bruges sont actuellement deposés dans une Chambre haute, aiant vue sur la cour, chez Mr Charles le Perre Negociant, demeurant pres Les Dominicains, vis a vis la rue de la ~~grand~~ Grande Chaussee en la Ville de Lille.*[1] The date of his acknowledgement with the Above direction is September the 27 1789. We presented the Ursulines at Tourcoine with a Silver Dove we had amongst our Church Plate, & Reverend Mother added a very handsome Reliquary adorned with flowers of Silver plate: also a Silver Nosegay, & a long purse knit with Gold & Silver to Mrs Atkinson an English Nun there, who had been extremely usefull to us on this occasion. Amongst the Donations made us in Plate formerly, Mr Tasburgh of Bodney in Norfolk, Father to Sister Mary Frances, & Sister Mary Margaret presented Lady Lucy Herbert Superiour at that time with 2 Silver Sconces on black that cost Sixty pounds Sterling.[2]

September

We being in want of a Gardener Levinus Verhulst was recommended to us, but was taken **[p. 319]** ill about a fortnight after he came with a violent fever which took him off in a few days: he died on the 12th after having received all the last Sacraments from our Confessor commission'd by the Pastor of St Ann's Parish. Two Women prayed by him day & night till he was buried. We said the Commendations for him, but did not ring. The Body was attended to St Ann's Church by the Children from the Charity School; we went to the Gate, & all the Sisters & Maids that cou'd be spared follow'd & was present at the Service: We rung till the Corpse arrived at the Church, from whence after the Service it was carried to the common Burying Place. As he died without a Will, Reverend Mother was advised to be very cautious ~~not~~ of spending much even for Masses, as his Heirs might call her to account for it. He had a decent Funeral which cost f54.16-6 cur: & after that expence paid & all others, his Heirs had f209-9-3 cur: besides his Clothes, Watch & Buckles. *Requiescat in Pace.*

1 Translation: 'Two chests containing several pieces of worked silver, both mounted and unmounted, all coming from the English Augustinian Ladies at Bruges, are currently placed in a high room which looks out over the courtyard, at Mr Charles le Perre, merchant, living near the Dominicans, opposite the rue de la Grande Chaussée in the town of Lille.' I am indebted to Amanda Haste for this translation.

2 Francis Tasburgh (b. 1686) married Mary Symonds; Mary Frances (BA192) and Margaret (BA193) were sisters.

November

In this month Miss Nelly Langton was taken ill of the small Pox:[1] The 13 of December following Sister Mary Ann Bruce & Sister Mary Oliva Darell were attacked by the same Desease:[2] tho the first was in the 71st year of her age, she had it in so favourable a manner that she was wholly ignorant of it herself till the Physician declared **[p. 320]** it: Sister Oliva tho a great many years younger had it very severely: they were both nursed together, & thro' the goodness of Almighty God all three are happily recover'd.

December

On the 10th by an order from the Bishop to implore the divine Mercy for appeasing the troubles of the Country,[3] the most Blessed Sacrament was this day exposed before the Convent Mass, to be continued during 4 days, upon each ten hours & terminated at 4 & half with *Salve*. On the last day we had a Solemn Mass in Fauxbourdon at 10 o'clock & the *Salve* in Musick except the first Blessing. On the 2 preceding days *Salve* was in Fauxbourdon. It did not ring to work during these 4 days, nor was there recreation till after Supper. All the Convents in the Town & Country of this Diocess 2 at a time had the 40 hours prayer for the same intention. We & Princen-hoff were put together. Zeal for the ^Religion & freedom of the Countries^ [~~*illeg.*~~] made those Nuns in the Sick House (that were able) to take their half hours: Our 2 Schollars were also allowed to do it.

The Pensioners we received in the Year
1789

January 5 Miss Ibbetson for a Choir Nun.
Aprill 28 Madlle De Pauw the Youngest. Age. 14
[p. 321] May 13 Madlle Solvins from Antwerp. aged 19.
16 Madlle Van Isseghem from Ostend the Youngest aged 14
27 Miss Stuart, Miss Ann & Miss Mary Byrne returned from Tourcoine.
June 18 Madlle Segaert of Bruges aged 14.
July 3 Miss D'Eveline from Tourcoine.
August 3 Madlle Meresse from Lille aged 13.
10 Madlle Custos of Bruges aged 15.
18 Miss Stuart from Bruxelles.
September 19 Madlle Reymenants from Bruxells aged 15.

---

1 Nelly Langton had been unwell for some time and had undertaken a *Novena* to Benedict Joseph Labre. See **[pp. 287–8]**.
2 Mary Ann Bruce (BA036); Mary Olivia Darell (BA070).
3 The troubles in Flanders, which by then had troops involved in open fighting, were the result of opposition to the reforms of Joseph II. These were perceived by many as an attack on the Catholic Church and local customs. The leaders of the revolt were known as the Patriots.

20 Miss Julia Browne Cap'n Brownes Daughter from Aire aged 8.
27 Mad[lle] Rose Solvins from Antwerp aged 12.
October 22 Miss Winny Doody from W.hampton aged 19. Miss Ann Houel from W.hampton aged 16.
30 Miss D'Eveline returned to us from Bruxells.
November 27 Miss Sulyard returned to us from Bruxells.

The Pensioners that left us in the Year
1789

January 21 Miss Byrne & Miss D'Eveline to Tourcoine.
March 31 Mad[lle] Barbara Leep.
Aprill 15 Miss Lane to Lille.
May 29 Miss Stuart to Bruxells.
June 18 Miss Hawkens, Miss Ann & Miss Mary Byrne to England.
July 5 Miss D'Eveline to Bruxells.
5 The 2 Miss Gibsons to England.
August 5 Miss Doody to England.
15 Miss Deacon to England.
September 2 Miss Stuart Miss Mootham & Miss Howe to England.
October 26 Miss Harriott Havers & Miss Norris to Liege.
November 10 Mad[lle] Custos.
December 18 Miss Browne to her Mother at Aire.

[p. 322]

1790

On the 5th Miss Ann Houel[1] took the Schollars Habit for a Choir Nun, & the names of Teresa Joseph in the 17th year of her age.

On the 26th Sister Mary Elizabeth Houel was Clothed.[2]

On the 28th Sister Anthony Roby was clothed for a Lay Sister.[3]

February

On the 16th Four Gentlemen from the States of Flanders called upon Reverend Mother, begging She would contribute to a Collection they were making for the Poor who had suffer'd at the Siege of Ghent & its Castle in the month of November 1789: Reverend Mother gave them 4 Louis d'ors which were paid by the Procuratress.[4]

---

1 Anne Howell, in religion Theresa Joseph (1795–1840) BA108.
2 Mary Elizabeth Howell (BA110).
3 Mary Antonia Roby (BA163).
4 The siege of the castle in Ghent was part of the protest against the policies of Joseph II. By the end of 1789 the Austrians had been driven out of the Southern Netherlands. However, the revolution was shortlived as the revolutionaries (the Patriots) failed to gain external support and Austrian authority was reimposed, but with concessions to their territories.

On the 18th Miss Nelly Langton died Suddenly about 7 in the morning.[1] She had been attacked a few days before by Epileptic fits, which joined to an Apoplexy was judged the cause of her death. The sweetness of her Temper & dispositions which only breathed Peace & Charity, with the most sincere Piety render'd her aimable to the whole Community. She was born in Spain of English Parents, & sent here when very young for Education. After her departure from hence, she remained some years with her Friends, but her inclinations being strong for retirement & much attached to us, she obtained their leave to return here. As we do not take Boarders we received on the footing of a Pensioner, **[p. 323]** it being then advantageous for us to have many to prevent our being Suppressed during those trouble-some times for Convents.[2] She gratefully & readily accepted the condition, & being remarkably prudent the peace of the Community never suffer'd the least alteration from her, but each one was very much edified at her steady vertue on every occasion. She had great desire to enter amongst us, but the defect of her sight not allowing her to say the Divine Office was an obstacle to it. She died in the 27th year of her age, & according to her desire was buried in our Habit & Church Yard exactly the same as one of our own Religious. Her Father gave us Ten Pounds Sterling. *Requiescat in Pace.*

March

On the 5th Sister Mary Clare Moore made her holy Profession in the 22d year of her age, by a dispensation from the States of Flanders at Reverend Mother's request.[3] She not having attained the age of 25 required by an Edict from the Emperor, which the States had not annulled.

On the 25th & the 2 following days we had the Blessed Sacrement exposed again, which was performed for the same Intention, & in the same manner as in December last year, except that *Salve* was at 5 & only for 3 days.

Aprill

A Patriotic Subscription being open'd in Flanders for the Maintenance of Soldiers for the Army, Reverend Mother **[p. 324]** & the Convent Sisters judged it proper we shou'd contribute handsomely to it, we therefore

---

[1] Nelly Langton first arrived in 1770 and was very anxious to profess. Her ill-health prevented this. See **[pp. 201, 256, 263, 286, 287–8]**.

[2] After the death of Prioress Lucy Herbert in 1744, it was decided that no more boarders would be taken into the convent. Only those wishing to try out the religious life would be taken in. Here the Chronicler is aware of a fine line between providing a service to women in need of shelter and appearing too inward-looking at a time when contemplative convents were being closed.

[3] Mary Clare Moore (BA144).

engaged to pay for 3 Soldiers during one year at ten pence cur: a day for each, which was at the expence of the Ark.[1]

May

On the 4th Miss Harriott Burlton took the Schollars Habit for a Choir Nun, & the name of Placida in the 28th year of her age. ~~On the 20th three gentlemen came for Reverend Mother to desire we would give to a Patriotic Subscription in Bruges for the expense of 3 canons This town was to offer to the Congress: Reverend Mother Presented them 8 Louis d'ors from her own purse, In gratitude to Almighty God ^& the Magistrates^ for the unalterable peace & quiet we have enjo'd by their vigilance & the constant fatiguing guard the Burghers have kept from the beginning of the Revolution that began last November.~~[2]

On the 21st we were much allarmed in the Evening by the appearance that our Garden dog was going Mad: most providentially the Gardiner had tied him up only about an hour before he became raging: he was shot immediately, & as he had bit a little dog we had belonging to the 2 Miss Hawcourts, tho' not to blood, yet the Physician insisted on its being killed which was done.[3] The Doctor advised that all those who had touched our Dogs slaver **[p. 325]** during that day to bathe in the Sea immediately, we therefore sent our 2 Men & 3 Maids in a Diligence[4] to Blankenburg about 8 o'clock that same evening, another Maid who cou'd not then go, we sent some days after to Ostend for the same purpose: & thank God no bad consequence has ensued to any of them.

June

On the 6th being the Sunday within the Octave of Corpus Xti, the most Blessed Sacrament was brought in Procession to our Church from that of St Ann, which was the first time that Parish had done so.

On the 10th Sister Mary Oliva Darell was reelected Arcaria at the first voting.[5]

On the 10th Three Gentlemen came to Reverend Mother to desire we wou'd give to a Patriotic Subscription in Bruges for the expense of 3 Canons this Town was to offer to the Congress: Reverend Mother presented them 8 Louis d'ors from her own purse, in gratitude to Almighty God & the Magistrates for the unalterable peace & tranquillity we with the rest of the Town have enjoy'd by their vigilance & the constant fatiguing Guard

---

[1] The Patriots had to find money to pay troops to continue the struggle against Joseph II. Ark: see Glossary.

[2] The same passage appears under June, suggesting that a re-writing of the sources was taking place.

[3] The transmission of rabies through the bite of a mad dog was clearly understood by the nuns. Here precautions were being undertaken with care.

[4] Diligence: the public stage-coach. Blankenburg and Ostend were both close to Bruges on the coast.

[5] Mary Olivia Darell (BA070).

the Burghers have kept from the beginning of the Revolution, which began last November.

[p. 326]

July

On the 8th Sister Teresa Austine Ibbetson & Sister Teresa Joseph Houch [Howell] were Clothed.[1]

August

On the 3d Sister Eugenia Randal[2] set off for St Omer, that in her return ~~from~~ ^by^ Dunkerk she might prepare & help to bring back part of our Church Plate which was deposited there with a Friend of Mr Dourlens, ^we sent^ Sister Martha & Brother James Orford the Suppressed Carthusian with 2 Pensioners in a Coach from hence to assist her:[3] Thank God they all returned safe without accident or Suspicion of what they concealed.

On the 12th we placed the bones of Mother Stamford & Sister Mary Best mentioned December 1786, the first at the foot of the middle Pillar under the Organ House, & those of Sister Mary Best at the foot of the first Pillar next to the great Pant.[4]

September

Reverend Mother obtained the Bishop's leave to admit into the Inclosure for a whole day the Penitent Nuns & Sisters who were to re-enter their Convent at soon as it was sufficiently repaired.[5] Only 4 Choir Nuns & one Sister came in. They all dined in the Infirmary with Reverend Mother, the Infirmarian & Sister Gertrude Clavering **[p. 327]** & Supped in the Refectory:[6] they went to Choir with us, & seem'd vastly gratefull & pleased with every thing. On the 8th of the same month one of their Choir Nuns Sister Francisca Keyser celebrated her half Jubilee in our Convent. She communicated with us in the Choir, after Mass Reverend ^Mother^ crowned her, She dined in the Refectory kept Silence & Recollection, & follow'd all our duties the whole day till Supper, when we talked & after it recreated with her till Compline.

---

1 Teresa Austin Ibbetson (BA117); Theresa Joseph Howell (BA108).

2 Eugenia Randall, lay sister (BA159).

3 Martha Fergusson, lay sister (BA079). James Orford was one of the two Carthusian lay brothers who associated himself with Nazareth following the suppression in 1783; see Dom Lawrence Hendriks, *London Charterhouse, Its Monks and Its Martyrs with a Short Account of the English Carthusians after the Dissolution in March 1783* (London: Kegan Paul, 1889), p. 336.

4 Frances Stamford (1619–35) LA242 Prioress 1629–35; Mary Best (1615–31) LA031. The bones had been brought home to Nazareth for burial in December 1786 just before the sale of the convents where they had formerly been buried: see **[p. 300]**.

5 The Penitent sisters here were probably the Grey Sisters of Aardenburg. Those at Bethania were also known as Penitents and were also neighbours.

6 Gertrude Clavering (BA057).

October

On the 16th Miss Eliza Webster took the Schollars' Habit for a Choir Nun, & the names of Augustina Clare.[1]

November

On the 17th We had by the Bishop's orders a Solemn High Mass & *Te Deum* in Thanksgiving for the Revolution, it being the Anniversary day of this Town's being ^given^ up to the Patriots.

The Mass only was in Fauxbourdon.

December

On the 16th we were obliged to Illuminate & there were other Rejoicings in the Town for these Provinces being again returned to the Obedience of the Emperor.[2] The Reverend Mr Thomas Berington sent us 2 Guineas & recommended his deceased Eldest Brother to our prayers:[3] Reverend Mother order'd a low Mass **[p. 329]** for him, which each one hear'd, & also the hearing of another, & to add one Short Dierge.

The Pensioners we received in the Year
1790

February 28 Madlle Aerts of Bruges, aged 16.
March 9 Miss Hawkens returned from England.
May 15 Madlle Kercove of Bruges, age 18.
16 Miss Murphy from London, age 9.
June 10 Miss Patty Masterson of English ^Protestant^ Parents settled as Merchants in Bruges. age 11.
July 5 Madlle Holm from Ostend age 12. & Mad'lle De Lieu from Mons, age 13.
17 Madlle De Gruytters the Youngest from Ostend, age 13.
August 10 Madlle Peneranda of Bruges, age 17.
28 Miss Webster returned from England.
28 Miss Warner from London, age 9.
^31 Miss Ann Manby^
September 26 Miss Julie Browne returned.
30 Madlle Weerbrouck from Antwerp, age 15. & Madlle Josephine Meresse from Lille, age 11.
October 5 Madlle Balbaert from Ostend the Youngest, age 16.

---

1 Elizabeth Webster did not continue to profession. See also Chronicle, vol. 3, **[p. 40]**.

2 The celebrations marked the return to the authority of the emperor. Joseph II died on 20 February 1790 and was succeeded by Leopold II, who issued an conciliatory manifesto to the rebels. However, they ignored it. Leopold's situation was transformed when he made peace with Prussia and was able to deal with the rebels and restore his authority.

3 Fr Thomas Berington (1740–1805), Confessor 1772–75; Anstruther 4, p. 30. His eldest brother was William of Moat Hall, Shropshire, who died in 1790; see Stirnet, Family Tree, Berington01.

The Pensioners that left us in the Year
1790

~~January~~
March 18 Mad[lle] Segaert.
May 29 Miss Fanny Manby & Miss Webster to England.
31 Miss Ann Manby to Dixmude.
[p. 329] June 10 Miss Letty Byrne to England.
21 Miss Winny & Miss Mary Doody to Tournay.
August 21 Mad[lle] Raymenans.
September 18 Miss D'Eveline to London.
November 10 Mad[lle] Peneranda.
27 Mad[lle] Meresse.

1791

January

On the 14th We had a Solemn Mass for the Soul of M[r] John Massey Stanley,[1] Reverend Mother order'd each one to hear it, & also 2 more & to say one Short Dierge for him. Sir W'm Stanley sent us 5 Guineas.

February

On the 3[d] Sister Mary Antonia Roby made her Holy Profession in the 26th year of her age.[2]

On the 9th Sister Elizabeth Houell was placed in the Rank of the Professed, the Edict not being revoked that fixes the age of Profession to 25, She could not make her Solemn vows.[3]

On the 16th of January being the Feast of the Holy Name of Jesus, our worthy Neighbours the Penitents had a High Mass, *Salve & Te Deum* in Musick to thank Almighty God for their happy & so long desired return to their Convent.[4] As they had then no Church Bell we rung every thing for them.

---

1 John Massey-Stanley died on 30 December 1790. He was the son of Sir John Stanley, 6th Baronet of Hooton and his wife, Mary Clifton (d. 1770); see Stirnet, Family Tree, Stanley07. Sir William Stanley, 5th Baronet, died in May 1792.

2 Mary Antonia Roby (BA163).

3 Elizabeth Howell (BA110).

4 The Penitents: probably the Grey Sisters of Aardenburg.

[p. 330]

February

M[r] Weld having recommended to our Prayers the Soul of M[r] John Massey Stanley & presented us 5 Guineas, we performed the same for him, as on the 14th of last month.[1]

On the 22[d] Sister Mary Joseph Blundell was chosen Procuratress at the 3[d] Voting.[2]

Aprill

On the 23[d] Sister Mary Frances Tasburgh compleated her Jubilee of 50 years from her Profession, but falling on Holy Saturday the celebration was differ'd till the following Tuesday.[3]

June

On the 14th Sister Placida Burlton & Sister Augustina Clare Webster were Clothed:[4] the first about the 29th year of her age, the other in the 17th

July

On the 20th Sister Teresa Augustina Ibbetson made her Holy Profession, in the 26th year of her age: & on the same day Sister Teresa Joseph Howell was placed in the Rank of the Professed.[5]

August

On the 4th Reverend Mother More[6] compleated the 25 years of her Superiority, which was celebrated by the Community with the most lively expressions of gratitude & affection, her Reverence was **[p. 331]** perfectly sensible of it, & was sometimes even moved to tears at the cordiality & multitude of the tokens she received from all in general & each one in particular. The account of the whole is as follows:

It fell on a Thursday the 4th of August. A Mass was said a quarter before 6 We put on our clean Habit & Sunday Veils. We communicated at the end of the Convent Mass, no other Mass followed: when the half hour after Communion was finished, we conducted her Reverence to the Work Chamber, the best voices going first singing the 99th Psalm in parts, 2 of the least Children strewing the way, & a third carried the crown,

---

1 John Massey Stanley's sister Mary was married to Thomas Weld (d. 1810) of Lulworth Castle. They had a daughter Juliana (BF263), who professed in 1795 at Prinsenhof, where a relative, Mary Gertrude Simeon-Weld (BF221), was abbess. The family were also benefactors at Prinsenhof.

2 Mary Joseph Blundell (BA027).

3 Maria Frances Tasburgh (1741–93) BA192.

4 Harriet (Sister Placida) Burlton (BA232) left before profession in 1793, see **[pp. 359, 368]**. Elizabeth (Sister Augustina Clare) Webster left in 1794 before profession; see also **[p. 288]** and Chronicle, vol. 3, **[p. 40]**.

5 Teresa Austin Ibbetson (BA117); Teresa Joseph Howell (BA108). The latter was affected by the regulations requiring candidates to be 25 before professing.

6 Mary Augustina More was elected Prioress in 1766 (BA145).

all the Community follow'd. There was a Throne erected in the Work Chamber, on which She was seated & Crown'd by the Subprioress, & the Eldest Religious, during which the Musicians performed a piece of musick in parts accompanied by a Forte Piano, when finished we all went to the Refectory which was extremely adorned: All the Elders breakfasted at Reverend Mothers Table, there was choice of Coffee or Tea **[p. 332]** with hot Cracknals & cream. It rung Silence at 9, which we kept being Communion day. It rung Mass at [*blank*] as Reverend Mother wou'd not have a high one it was only a low one with Musick, & ^being Thursday^ the 2 Benedictions were performed in musick, & the *Te Deum* sung in Fourbadon[1] with the Organ.

The Pensioners dined in the Refectory. After the 2d Table we all met in the Work Chamber, when Reverend Mother was seated on the Throne, one of the pensioners repeated a copy of Verses, then they presented her with their works, which were very handsome; after which they danced, & then went by one by one to her, & received a book for hearing Mass collected by Lady Lucy Herbert.[2]

In the afternoon it rung silence at 3. We sung Vespers: Supper a quarter before 5, we only recreated till 6 & half being Communion eve.

It did not ring to work during the 8 days following except on Saturday at one o'clock to ask forgiveness.

The Procuratress gave 3 Recreations both at Dinner & Supper: the first on the day itself, the 2d the Munday, & the 3d on the Octave day. On Munday it we did not keep silence, but it rung in the afternoon at 3 & half, at which time those that pleased might keep their Meditation. **[p. 334, *sic*]** Compline follow'd Vespers: It rung to Supper at 6 & half, we said Grace as usual, but after the Martyrologe[3] & Gospel were read, & the Supper served in, every one was free to rise, & go into the Pants or where they pleased, as on other sitting-up nights: for Grace after Supper each one took care to say it in the Sick Chappel when they retired, which might be any time they chose before 9. All the Elders sat at a round Table in the middle of the Refectory.

The 3d Recreation was like other great Recreations both at Dinner & Supper.

Reverend Mother's Seat in the Choir, & Chapter House were much adorned. The Lay Sisters hung the Pants in Festoon & Garlands from one end to the other, & also the Kitchen: the 2 Gardiners embelished most curiously the Court before her Room windows, & her Chaplain

---

1 Fauxbourdon: see Glossary.

2 *Several excellent methods of hearing Mass*..., by the Right Honourable Lady Lucy Herbert of Powis (Bruges: John de Cock, 1722).

3 The martyrology contained the names and anniversaries of saints, martyrs, early members of the community and benefactors so that they could be prayed for on their anniversaries.

adorned her Room in a most elegant Style. When dark the Pants were illumenated, which made them appear most beautiful.

On the 16th we had a Solemn Mass of Requem for the Soul of Mrs Webbe Weston, each one was order'd to hear 2 more, & to say one Short Dierge for her; Mr Webbe Weston sent us 5 Guineas.

[p. 335]

September

On the 5th Reverend Mother treated the Community with the best things she cou'd get. The day & evening were regulated as on the 4th of August.

December

On the 19 The Bishop ^had^ order'd us by a Printed paper to send a Deputy to a meeting of the Clergy on that day, who were to concur to the National Debt contracted by the Patriots who rose in the Year 1789 to regain the Priviledges of the Countries which the Emperor Joseph the 2d had deprived them of.[1] Mr Oliver our Confessor[2] went to the Palace at the hour appointed, but nothing was then agreed on. It is supposed every Convent will be taxed according to the Statement of their Revenues, given up to Court by order of the Emperor Joseph the 2d in the Year 1781.

The Pensioners we received in the Year
1791

January 28 Mad'lle De Brugghe from Ghent. Age 16.
March 10 Miss Ann Norris from London age 16.
14 Mad'lle Simons from Bruges age 18.
May 13 Miss Charlotte Norris from Liège.
18 The 2 Miss Doodies from Tournay.
24 Miss Kitty Dillon.
[p. 336] June 11 Miss Yates from Manchester, age 7.
July 12 The 3 Miss Leslies of Fetternear in Scotland, the Eldest 14, Miss Harriott 13 & Miss Teresa 8.
18 Miss Patty Masterson returned.
August 1st Mad'lle De Vaux of Bruges our Phisicians Daughter, Age 14.
23d Miss Kitty & Miss Betty Kerwan from Lille, the Eldest 15, the Youngest 11.
23d Miss Mary Hawkers returned from Lille.
September 19 Mad'lle Marcellin from Aire in Artois. Age 15.
27 Mad'lle Leveringhem De La Faille from Antwerp Age 15.
November 2 Mad'lle De Becker from Bruxells Age 15.

---

1 The clergy hoped that the Patriots would restore their taxation rights and privileges lost under Joseph II.
2 Fr Andreas Oliver, Confessor 1782–1812.

The Pensioners that left us in the Year
1791

January 3 Mad'lle Holm.
7 Mad'lle De Lieu.
26 Mad'lle Van Isseghem.
February 19 Miss Lucy Sulyard to England.
20 Miss Sophie Sulyard to the Dames at Bruxells.
28 Mad'lle Marie Ann De Pauw.
Aprill 5 Mad'lle Aerts.
12 Mad'lle Kercove
13 The youngest Mad'lle De Gruytters.
16 Miss Patty Masterson.
20 Mad'lle Weerbrouck.
May 22d Mad'lle Teresa Soloyns.
June 8 The 2 Miss Doodies to England.
6 Miss Mary Hawkens to Lille.

[p. 337]

The year
1792

June 20 Miss Assiotti to Dixmude.
14 Mad'lle Simons.
25 Mad'lle De Brueg.
26 Mad'lle Balbaert.
29 Miss Kitty Dillon to England. Miss Assiotti from Dixmude to England.
November 21 Miss Charlotte Norris to Ditto.
December 6 Miss Patty Masterson.

1792

With the leave & Approbation of our Bishop we this year began to keep the English Saints in the Divine Office.

February

On the 20th Sister Tecla Hampson departed this life in the 54th year of her age; & 31st of her Religious Profession.[1] As long as health permitted She was serviceable to the Community in her quality of Lay Sister, but for a great many years was subject to a most painfull indisposition which was incurable to Physicians: to this was added for about the last 12 years of her life the privation of sight, so much the more sensible as she loved reading. Her natural disposition was rough & harsh, but without malignity; & her sufferings seem'd much augmented, by a fearfull uneasy **[p. 338]**

[1] Thecla Hampson (1761–92) BA097.

situation of mind, proceeding probably at least in part from her corporal infirmities & the perplexities of a very timorous conscience. Her last Illness was painfull, but short: She received all the last Sacraments, & expired as we humbly confide in the arms of her Divine Redeemer; in whose infinite Mercy we hope, her many sufferings in this life, will be accepted in attonement for the faults incurred by human frailty. *Requiescat in pace.*

March

On the 25th by the Bishops orders we began a Novena to obtain Almighty God's blessing on our young King Francis the 1st.[1] He appointed the *Veni Creator* to be said before the Convent Mass, & our Ladies Littanies after it with the *Sub tuum* & prayer; & at *Salve* the 19 Psalm with the Verses & prayer to be sung.

On the 29th Brother Thomas Padbury departed this life about the 78th year of his age:[2] after the Suppression of the Society being turned out of his College in Bruges about Xmass, in the year 1773, we received him to bed & board, giving him a Room in the quarters of our Gardiners. He lived with us above 18 years in quality of Domestic, but with the same considerations allowed to our Lay Sisters. **[p. 339]** He was faithfull to a degree nicety in the discharge of Commissions intrusted to him: Exact as much as circumstances permitted in complying with the duties of piety annexed to his former State: of a peaceable disposition, never complaining of the mortifications he received from others, nor was ever complained of. His last years passed in a State of langour & infirmity, supported with patience & resignation. The Illness which terminated his holy life was not long, he was perfectly sensible to the last, received all the last Sacraments with that piety & devotion, which gives us an humble confidence that we may apply to him. *Beati mortui qui in Deo moriuntur.*[3] He was buried at St Anns the 1st of April, being Palm Sunday, the Funeral Rites were performed before the ceremonies of the day.[4] The first free day after Low Sunday, we recited a Dierge of 9 Lessons in the Choir, & had a Solemn Mass the day following, & each one was appointed to hear 3 more, to offer one Communion & to say 2 Short Dierges for him. As his Superiours in England allow'd him £5 Sterl[ing] a year, for Clothes & little necessaries, he left ^by will^ what he had saved & all his small possessions to the Convent, which answer'd the expences of his Funeral, a Present **[p. 340]** of £5 to Mr Oliver, & £10 to the Community, besides the Retribution for 100 Masses, & some charities to the Poor, to whom

---

1 Francis I (1768–1835), nephew of Joseph II, who had no children. As Francis II, he became Holy Roman Emperor on the death of his father, Leopold II (d. 1 March 1792).

2 Brother Thomas Padbury SJ, lay brother (1714–92); Holt, p. 183.

3 Translation: 'Blessed are the dead who die in the Lord'.

4 St Anne's church was the local parish church.

also his Clothes were distributed by Reverend Mother & Mr Oliver[1] who were his Executors.

Aprill

On the 15 being Low Sunday, by orders from the Bishop we said a long Dierge in the Choir for the Emperor Leopold the 2^d.[2] We read Vespers, a Short *Salve* follow'd, & then began the Dierge. The next day a Solemn Mass was sung for him, but without a Herse or other ceremonies. Tho the Dierge ^& burial^ was prescribed by the Publick ordinance to be sung, the Arch-Priest decided it was sufficient for Religious Communities to perform the same they did for their own Members. From that day viz Low Sunday till Whitsunday which was 6 weeks, we had orders to ring 3 times a day from 6 till the half hour after in the morning, from 12 till the half hour after, & from 6 in the evening till the half hour. *Requiescat in pace*. On the 18th Our Subprioress Sister Mary Catherine Willis compleated her Jubilee of 50 years.[3] She had obtained leave, & we celebrated it on the 10th, which was Easter Tuesday, on account of **[p. 341]** some inconvenience occurring the following week. His Holiness Pius the 6th has been pleased to grant a Plenary Indulgence in perpetuity, to each one of our Community on the day they shall attain to the 25th or 50th year of their Religious Profession, performing the ordinary duties prescribed on such occasions.[4]

Aprill May

On the 16 The Secretary of the Clergy wrote to all the Convents desiring them to send to him the same Statement of their accounts that they gave up to Government under Oath in the year 1786. Reverend Mother receiv'd the same orders from him. She answer'd his letter in as civil terms as possible, but told him she thought it hard we shou'd be included being Strangers: that all our Revenues come from England, that we have no immoveables except the ground on which our Convent & Church is built: that we have a large Family maintain'd by english money: that we draw Strangers to the Town who spend the same. That in the overthrow of Religion in France our English Convents are exempt from all their new pecuniary **[p. 342]** charges, & have even the Protection of the National Assembly, & therefore she hoped the same justice from the Clergy here

---

1 Fr Andreas Oliver, Confessor 1782–1812.

2 Emperor Leopold II (1747–92) was Holy Roman Emperor 1790–92. He died on 1 March 1792.

3 Mary Catherine Willis (1742–97) BA221.

4 Pope Pius VI (1717–99).

as yet Catholic.[1] That since our Foundation in 1629 we have only been twice asked for a *Gratuite* gift, which we only gave once in gratitude for the Peace & tranquillity we enjoy'd many years under this Government, that by the same motives we now offer'd a Sum once paid, & their acceptance of it under this free denomination would give us pleasure & to our Friends in England also. We received no answer, & heard no more of this affair.

July

On the 26th Ann Stoker took the Schollars Habit for a Lay Sister in the 25th year of her age, & the name of Frances.[2] She had been 6 months in the same Habit at our Mother House at Louvain, but passing by here in her road to that Convent last June, she took a great liking to us & returned to Bruges on the 19th of January this year.

[p. 343]

August

On the 14th Miss Margaret Wharton took the Schollars Habit for a Choir Nun in the 21st year of her age, & the names of Mary Gonzaga.[3]

September

On the 4th Mr Hiccq Curate of Longuenisse near St Omer arrived here, being ancient & lame Reverend Mother sent Brother James Orford[4] to meet him at Dunkerk, & to attend him on the Barges from thence, for She had offer'd him an azylum from the persecution of the Clergy in France, which he gratefully accepted, & being driven out, he fled to us, & occupies the 2 Rooms on the Ground floor of the Apartment on the outside of the Convent.

On the 30 we received into the Inclosure Sister Agnes Moore an English Nun who had settled amongst the French Capucinesses at St Omer.[5] She

---

1 The French decrees applied to French foundations; the English convents were unaffected at first, although they feared the extension of the decrees to their convents after war broke out in February 1793. For a detailed discussion see Carmen Mangion, 'Avoiding "Rash and Imprudent Measures": English Nuns in Revolutionary Paris, 1789–1801)' in C. Bowden and J. E. Kelly (eds), *The English Convents in Exile: Communities, Culture and Identity* (Farnham: Ashgate, 2013) pp. 247–63, particularly pp. 248–58. In pre-revolutionary France the *don gratuit* was the taxation given by the Church to the crown. Here the term is being applied to the Habsburg Empire, suggesting that the money given by the convent was an offering from the convent rather than formal taxation owed to the emperor.

2 Ann Stoker did not proceed to profession.

3 Margaret Wharton had a complex convent history before finally leaving in 1798, BA233. See also Chronicle, vol. 3, **[pp. 34, 65–6, 113–14, 116, 118]**.

4 Br James Orford was one of the two Carthusian lay brothers who associated himself with Nazareth following the suppression in 1783; see also **[p. 269]**. Mr Hicq was Antoine Hubert Hiecq (1730–1800), an ex-Jesuit, formerly Principal of the College of St Omer; see Bellenger, *French Exiled Clergy*, p. 202.

5 Sr Agnes Moore: no further details found as yet.

Staid with us till the 29th of October the same year, then she went to the Capucinesses here in Town where she pays a Pension of 200 flo cur: a year, whilst with us, she follow'd the Community in all its Observances, kept Choir with us **[p. 344]** when she served the Same Saint. She sat next to the Reverend Mother both in the Choir & Refectory, wore her own Habit, & laid in a Cell in the Dormitory.

In this month 3 Choir Nuns & a Lay Sister ~~turned out~~ ^Benedictines^ turned out of their Monastery at Montargis[1] arrived here from England where they were obliged to land in order to get to Bruxelles: they staid one night, laid in the Infirmary & set off the next morning for Ghent in their road to the English Benedictines at Bruxelles. They were of 4 different Nations, viz. English, Irish, Scotch & Flemish.

October

On the 24th we Lodged a Nun from the French Austines at Paris: she left us the next morning, to enter into a Convent of the same order at Ghent. She was a Native of St Omer.

On the 25th we Lodged a Flemish Capuciness from Bergs, she went the next day to the Capucinesses here in Town.

On the 30th we received as a Servant, but without wages, Alice Skark an English **[p. 345]** Protestant to be instructed in the Catholic faith.

November

On the 5th three of the Nuns of Montargis returned here from Bruxelles in their road again to England to join their Community which was going to found a Monastery of Benedictines there: they set off for Ostend on the 7th of the same month; & at Reverend Mother's request took Mr Hiccq with them, for as the French were then expected here, she wished to have the old Gentleman in security. He was recommended to & received by Mrs Corney to bed & board, that Lady is Sister to our Sister Louisa Mawhood.[2]

In the course of this year during the Persecution, Massacre & Banishment of the Secular & Regular Clergy in France, many fled to this Town. Our Community fed 9 ^constantly^ at its Confessors Table, ^for about two months^, besides several others from time to time: Beds were put up in the Outward Apartment for as many as we cou'd Lodge. Our Revenues not being sufficient to answer such an expence, to **[p. 346]** help towards

1 The convent at Montargis, south of Paris, was founded in 1630 as a reformed Benedictine convent by nuns from Montmartre. A few English women joined and by 1791 there were four from Britain, three of whom are mentioned here. They were the earliest community to leave France, avoiding the worst effects of the French Revolution. By October 1792 the community of 34 was in transit. See Elphege Hind, 'Princethorpe Priory', *Ampleforth Journal* 11 (1905), pp. 192–204.

2 Louisa Austin Mawhood (BA140). Louisa's sister Dorothy (1752–1806) married Thomas Corney, a laceman, in 1791. See *Mawhood Diary*, p. 14.

it, there was not one in the Community who was not only willing but even desirous to give up their money for Lot day,[1] with the Wine & better food of other Recreations that fell during that time, & they did it most cheerfully, contenting themselves with talking as usual on such Recreations, to Reverend Mothers great edification & satisfaction. On the 9th of this month all the French Priests left us for fear of the Troops of that new Republic, who had then possession of these Countries,[2] Several of them went to England: Reverend Mother procured one of them to be received at the Nuns at York,[3] & 3 more by her own Relations or Friends, viz her Nephew Mr Metcalfe, her Cousin Mr Waterton, & Mr Sulyard. The Van Guard of the French came to Bruges 2 days after their departure.

December

About the middle of this month the Magistrates sent Workmen to build stables on the outside of the North Wall of our Garden **[p. 347]** for the French Marseillois Dragoons who were expected; the Bishop gave leave for their entering the Inclosure, but they only came as far as the half way on the Grass plot. If there had been time, & Reverend Mother had reflected on it, she would have procured a partition of Boards to have separated that part of the Garden till the Workmen had finished, they only were allow'd to enter, & one of our Men guarded the Gate whilst they were at work, which lasted about 14 Days, they at first proposed to go on even on Sundays & Holydays, but they only worked on one Sunday. The Magistrates promised to repair the wall, to leave it as they found it, & to take away the dirt without any expence to us.

On the 27th We Lodged Dame Dillon the only remaining Montargis Nun at Bruxells:[4] she arrived here in her way to England in order to join her Community then settled at Bodney in Norfolk. She set off the next day with her Sister Lady Jerningham.[5]

---

1 Lot Days originated when, for health reasons, blood was taken three times a year; generally before Lent, in May and in September. The community was granted rest days with better fare for four days. I am indebted to Sr Mary Aline and the community for this reference.

2 The French Republic was declared on 10 August 1792. Dumouriez led French troops into the Austrian Netherlands on 27 October 1792.

3 The Mary Ward Sisters had opened the Bar Convent in York in 1686.

4 Dame Dillon: Catherine Dillon (d. 1797), daughter of Henry, 11th Baron Dillon and his wife, Catherine Lee; see Stirnet, Family Tree, Dillon02.

5 Lady Jerningham, née Frances Dillon: see WWTN family tree.

[p. 348] After the French had taken possession of these Countries ^& this Town^[1] one of their Generals an Irishman, by name Omoran,[2] sent one of our Burghers to acquaint Mother Abbess of Princen-hoff,[3] & also our Reverend Mother, that if they did nothing against the French Nation, he wou'd protect them: as he had left the Town, Reverend Mother wrote to thank him, & desired he wou'd give orders that none of the Soldiers who had Stables at our Garden Wall might break into the Inclosure, or any wise molest us, which according to every appearance he really did, for tho' some of the Marseillois Dragoons broke into the Convent of Springmaille,[4] they, nor any others attempted the least thing against us, & we were informed they were forbid even to approach to our gate.

We had another singular marck of the Divine Protection, for the Commissary from Paris having received orders to seal up the Plate & all the Valuables of every Convent, Almighty God raised us up a friend in Mr Barrell **[p. 349]** a Burgher of this Town who being of the Jacobin Club here had more influence on the Commissioner: he prevailed on him by strong intreaties not to include us, as being English without writting to, and waiting an answer from the National Convention, he even allowed Mr Barrell to dictate the letter. In the mean time other Commisssaries arrived, one of which Mr Oliver our Confessor was acquainted with, he called ^upon^ him, recommended us to his Protection, & in conversation mention'd, that we had sent away our Plate in the time of the Emperor Joseph the 2^{d}.[5] In time Divine Providence so governed matters, that we were never molested by Seals, visits, call for Contributions, or in any other manner, except by just fears & alarms, which induced us us to hide or send off, our 6 best Pictures, Account Books, Papers of Importance, & all we cou'd spare of Vestments & linnen &c belonging to the Church & Convent. On this occasion we made use of all our hiding places, viz, in the workroom **[p. 350]** near the Altar, the Sick House Closet in the bed Chamber below, in the little Dormitory over against the House of Office, the Surplice cell, & the Small one that has the Warmroom Chimney in

---

1 Following victory at Jemappes on 6 November, Dumouriez and his army were able to invade the rest of the country and move north into the Netherlands.

2 General James O'Moran (1739–94) entered French service in Dillon's Irish Regiment in 1759 and rose through the ranks. By 1791 he was commandant of Berwick's Irish Regiment and fought in the Southern Netherlands. He was known for his wise administration of Tournai and became commander-in-chief of French Flanders. Sadly, he, like others, was accused of disloyalty, tried and guillotined in Paris on 6 March 1794. See Richard Hayes, *Biographical Dictionary of Irishmen in France* (Dublin: Gill and Son, 1949), pp. 246–7.

3 Mother Abbess of Prinsenhof was Mary Gertrude Simeon-Weld (1759–1801) BF221, elected abbess seven times 1782–1801.

4 The Spermalie convent was the near neighbour of Nazareth: see Appendix 1 and map.

5 Emperor Joseph II, ruler of the Austrian Netherlands 1780–1790. The convent sent away plate in 1789: see **[pp. 316–17]**.

it, then occupied by Sister Catherine Willis our Subprioress:[1] these were filled with our Silver Table & tea Spoons, with those belonging to the Chaplain, Portress & the Confessors apartment, nothing but pewter ones were made use of either within or out of doors. All these things were concealed till near Penticoast, as the French were still on our Frontieres: nor cou'd the Procuratress give up her accounts for 1792 till [*blank*] as will be mention'd next year.

Charities given us this year.

In March for Mrs Ann Stanley £5. We had a Solemn Requiem Mass for her, each one hear'd 2 low ones, added one Communion, & said one short Dierge for her.

Brother Tho[mas] Padbury £10, as mention'd page 339.

In July for Sir W[illia]m Stanley 5 Guineas, **[p. 351]** for whom we performed the same as for Mrs Ann Stanley.

In September for Mr Charles Stanlcy £10: we had a Solemn Requiem Mass. Each one hear'd 3 Low ones, offer'd one Communion & said 2 Short Dierges for him.

The Pensioners &c we received in the Year
1792

January 19 Ann Stoker from Louvain, for a Lay Sister.
February 22 Miss Lucy Howell age 15.
March 20 Miss Field from London. age 12.
Aprill 18 Thc 2 Miss Byrnes one from the Ursulines at Lille, the other from those at Tourcoine, the eldest 14, the yongest 12.
May 13 Miss Wharton to see our practices. age 21.
August 13 Mad'lle Le Clerk from Ostend. age 13.
17 Mad'lle Lybaert from Ditto. age 14.
18 Mad'lle Vandemeeren. age 16 daughter to an innkeeper at Ghent
19 Mad'lle Bess, from Ghent. age 16.
22d Miss Sophie Sulyard from Liege.
September 4 Mr Hiccq a french Curate from Longuenisse
4 Miss ^Mary^ Howe from London. age 12.
6 Miss Anna Maria Stapleton from Paris age 15.
16 Miss Holm & Miss Mary Helier from Ostend the first 12, the other 16
November 8 Miss Coppinger. age 18 & Miss Ellis a Black [*sic*], age 9.
[p. 352] November 13 Mad'lle Rappaert from Bruges. age [*blank*]

Pensioners that left us in the Year
1792

Aprill 21 Miss Ann Manby to England.

[1] Mary Catherine Willis (BA221).

May 16 Miss Mary Hawkens to England.
25 Miss Rosa Solvyns to Antwerp.
30 Miss Field to England.
June 19 Mad'lle Becker.
July 9 Miss Monica Clavering to Dunkerk.
28 The 2 Miss Wakemans to England.
August 24 Mad'lle Josephine Meresse.
September 14 Miss Sophie Sulyard to England.
October 3 Miss Cruse to England.
25 Miss Anna Maria Stappleton, Miss Fanny Sulyard & the 3 Miss Leslies to England all sent over on account of the French Troops expected here.
November 11 Mad'lle Lafaille returned to Antwerp.
28 Miss Winny Mostyn to Cambray.
30 Mad'lle De Paun.
December 5 The 2 Miss Kerwans to Dunkerk.
17 Miss Helyer to Ostend.
28 Mad'lle Vandermeeren.
31 Mad'lle Bess.

1793

January

We began this year with little comfort & many fears as the French shew'd themselves very despotic, & had numerous Troops in this Town, which the Burghers **[p. 354, *sic*]** & Convents were obliged to Lodge or pay for them elsewhere. Almighty God shew'd a peculiar mercy to us on this occasion, for the Person called the Wickey Master who had the billetting of the Soldiers always spared our Convent, so that we never had one during the whole time, tho the English Nuns of Princen-hoff, & every other Community had their share.

By the proceedings of the French in regard of Convents & Religion itself, we had just reason to fear the being obliged to leave these Countries, we therefore resolved in that case to seek Shelter in England: in consequence Reverend Mother wrote to Mr Blundell of Ince,[1] begging him to find out a House in Lancashire large enough to contain us all, then 42 in Community, besides the Confessor & Servants we shou'd want, in all 51: He answer'd in the most obliging terms, & took the affair entirely to heart. He proposed Moor Hall or Puddington, both belonging to the Stanley Family; & as he imagined they would themselves inhabit the latter, he secured Moor Hall for us. Upon our release from the French

---

[1] The French government had suppressed religious houses including nursing and educational orders and required priests to take an oath of support. Robert Blundell of Ince (d. 1773) was half-brother to Charlotte Blundell, in religion Mary Joseph (BA027) and married as his first wife Catherine Stanley of Hooton.

& return of the Austrian Government. I enquired what we owed for the time he had hired it, but he so kindly managed it with the Family that we had nothing to pay. Mr Blundell is Brother to our Procuratress Sister Mary Joseph Blundell. The security he obtain'd for us of a Shelter in case **[p. 355]** of need, was a comfort & cordial to Reverend Mother & the Community that those only can conceive who have experienced a similar anxiety. We hope & pray that Almighty God's blessings may attend him for it both in Life & Death.

Reverend Mother being apprehensive that the French Commissaries would visit us, & require her to draw money from England, She gave orders to our Bankers there, Mr Tom Wright & Co not to honour any Bills she might send or he receive from these Countries.[1] This obliged her to take up £300 Ex: here, as mentioned in the Ark book in March this year, see January page 259.

March

On the 22d we were assured the French Troops had left the Town for good, & that it had narrowly escaped being plunder'd before they departed: this news revived our Spirits, & those of the Inhabitants in general, who impatiently expected the arrival of the Austrian Troops: in the mean time we thought ourselves secure & happy. On the 29th being Good Fryday about 8 in the morning we hear'd a Drum on the Ramparts near us, which chear'd our hearts, supposing it to belong to the Imperialist Troops: part of them marched through our Street. Our Church door being open as usual on that morning: we were soon informed they were French, & that all the Churches of the Town were immediately shut for fear of prophanations. **[p. 356]** these Troops, took possession again of the Town, seizing the Gates, Bridges &c: they were about two Thousand in number, & required a Contribution of 2 Million florins, or the Plunder of the Town for 4 Hours: Our Jacobin Magistrates, who were friends to them, had sufficient honour to refuse the latter, & sign for the first; for which many of them were carried off by the French as Hostages. During the night they let into the Town two thousand more of their own Troops, & notwithstanding the aforesaid agreement, they intended to pillage the whole Town but by God's special providence, the Commandant of the last Troops told the first that they ^had^ not a moment to loose, as the Austrians were advancing, upon which they made their preparations in great haste. The day before they had loaded some butters with part of the immense Magazines they had laid up here, worth 2 Million of florins, but the Populace would not suffer them to depart, abused the French, & threw dirt & stones at them. They left the Town about 2 o'clock on Holy Saturday morning. About 9 the following morning, being Easter day, the Austrian Van Guard of only 9 men enter'd the Town to the inexpressible

[1] Wright & Co., Bankers, Henrietta Street, Covent Garden.

joy of its Inhabitants, the Bells were rung & illuminations order'd for night, but about 2 in the afternoon our joy was damped by the notice, given that the French were returning upon us breathing Vengeance, & the fixed resolution of reducing the Town to ashes. The Churches were **[p. 357]** were again Shut up, & all the Burghers under arms. A great part of em went out to assist the Peasants, who with about 200 Austrians were driving them back, which they effected as far as Newport, but having no Cannons, the French turned & fired upon them, which drove our people back again: in the mean time news was brought of the first retreat of the French, on which the rejoicings & Illuminations went on, they lasted till 11 & half: Our Nuns & Sisters that sat up to attend the Candles, had just extinguished them, & were preparing to go to bed, when they were very much terrified by the toling of all the alarm-bells, both in the Town & Country; ^&^ a report soon reached us that the French were at the Gates. About Midnight some of our Friends, who lived in that part of the Town where the French were expected to enter took refuge at our Convent. The People began to unpave the Streets, & orders were given to throw Stones at them if they enter'd: But by God's mercy about 5 in the morning we had the comfortable news that they were drove back, a 2[d] time as far as Newport, where they staid till after Low Sunday, & were then chaced off our Territories by the brave Austrians.

Aprill

On the 19th The Duke of York honour'd us with a visit, he was accompanied by our Bishop & **[p. 358]** Colonel St Leger.[1] We received him in our Surplices at the Sisters Chappel grate. At his entry into the Church, the Bell rung & the Organ play'd. Reverend Mother conducted him through the Chapter House to the Workroom, all the Nuns following: a genteel Desert was prepared there from the Confectioners & arranged by one of their people, which was also adorned with flowers. It stood about the middle of the room, & at the bottom of it, there were smaller side tables, with Liquors, Glasses & other proper necessaries for the Desert. He staid only about half an hour, having the night before received unexpected orders to set off with his fine Troops that very day: he left us to head them on the Market place, where they were ready waiting for him. About 2 hours after, the same Colonel St Leger, & the Dukes Secretary came from him with a present of 25 Louis d'ors. These 2

---

[1] Frederick, Duke of York (1763–1827), second son of George III and Queen Charlotte; see *ODNB*. In 1793 the Duke was sent to Flanders as commander of the British contingent to fight the French. After some initial successes, by the end of 1794 the British army had fallen back and York was nearly taken prisoner. He returned to England at that point. Colonel John Hayes St Leger (1756–1800) accompanied the Duke on his special mission to Berlin. He saw action in Flanders in 1793, returning home with the Duke in 1794. See historyofparliamentonline.org/volume/1790-1820/member/st-leger-john-hayes-1756-1800, accessed 29 July 2015.

Officers also came in, & seem'd much pleased with their visit, but we did not put on our Surplices for them, the Community attended them also. We hear'd afterwards that His Royal Highness was very well satisfied with the reception we gave him. Reverend Mother not having then any fine Works worth his acceptance, our Nuns made for him afterwards a very handsome Sword-knot, & Bouquets of Silver & Silk flowers for his Dutchess which were most graceously received.[1] As we were informed he was **[p. 359]** coming to the Convent whilst we were saying Sext, the Choir broke off at the end of it, & we said None after Dinner, which we did not go to till about 1 o clock. On the 24th we put off our Mantles, for the weather was too cold to do it at Easter as usual, which this year fell on the 31st of March.

May

On the 25th Miss Lucy Howell took the Schollar's Habit in the 17th year of her age, & the name of Clementina.[2]

Forgot in January
1793

On the 2d Sister Barbara Heetvelde was Clothed for a Lay Sister in the 24th year of her age.[3] On account of the times it was performed privately with a Low Mass & the Church doors shut: Her Parents were not even invited, tho they are of the Countrys, & in it, She being a Native of Blackenburghe.

On the 20th Miss Harriott Burlton (alias Sister Placida) put off the Habit, not having health to persevere, or a temper proper for a Community. She set off for England on the 26th of the same month.

June

On the 13th Sister Gonzaga Wharton was Clothed.[4] As her eyes are very weak, the Bishop granted her a **[p. 360]** dispence to say a common Office when the Choir kept a proper one: Also from reading in the Refectory, but instead of it to serve 2 weeks every turn.

July

On the 6th Mrs Atkinson an Ursuline of Tourroine took refuge in our Community, by the invitation of Reverend Mother, her Convent being

---

[1] The Duchess of York was the Duke's cousin Frederica Charlotte of Prussia, whom he married on 29 September 1791 in Berlin. They travelled to London to repeat the ceremony. The marriage was not a success and the couple separated.

[2] Lucy Howell, in religion Clementina (1796–1832) BA109; she was the sister of Anne Howell, in religion Theresa Joseph (BA108).

[3] Barbara Hetvelde (BA240) left before profession.

[4] Margaret (Gonzaga) Wharton eventually left in 1798. See also Chronicle, vol. 3, **[pp. 34, 65–6, 113–14, 116, 118]**.

then dispersed by the French.[1] She fled from Lille through many dangers. During the Reign of the Emperor Joseph the 2d, She & her Community had render'd us many services in regard of our Church Plate as mention'd page 316. She Lodges & boards in the Infirmary & pays us a Pension of £16 Sterl[ing]

On the 18th Mrs White an Annunciate of Boulogne was also received. She likewise eats & sleeps in the Infirmary, but for some time before she left us came to the Refectory, & to all the Day office from her first entrance. She pays us at the rate of £18 a year, Sterl[ing]

On the 20th Mrs Anderton a Dominicaness of Calais, & Mrs Stubbs a Benedictine Nun of Paris came here & remained one day: they eat and slept in the Infirmary, & set off for Ghent on the 22d.

August

In this month the Magistrates gave orders to Illuminate for the taking of Valenciennes, but left it to every one to do as they pleased, **[p. 361]** their view was to discover the Partizans of the French, for many of the Inhabitants were for them. We Illuminated.

September

As the war between our Emperor & France prevented us from having from Mr Daniel from Doway[2] as Our Extraordinary, Mr Wallet Chaplain to Mr Hawkens of Nash passing here in his return to England, our Bishop gave him leave to supply for him.[3] He did the same to Mr Greg Stapleton in October 1792, as Mr Daniel was then detain'd by necessary business at his own College.[4]

The Bernardin Monks the Dunes our near Neighbours having lost their Abbot, at the blessing of the new one, Reverend Mother order'd our Bell to be rung at their *Te Deum*, & to put up lights at night, which was done with Pitchpots (to the value of a crown) 3 at each of the Garret windows facing their Convent: & She gave leave to her Community to sit up, but did not allow eating or drinking. These Monks had served our Convent for some years very diligently by saying our daily Foundation Mass for Lady Mountague.[5]

October

---

1 The nuns who arrived at Nazareth in July 1793 were English women who had all professed in French convents. When their convents were suppressed they had no family immediately to hand to provide shelter.

2 Mr Daniel, their new Confessor; see Anstruther 4, although it is not clear which Daniel he is.

3 Fr Lewis Wallet (d. 1812), supply Confessor 1793; Anstruther 4, pp. 287–8. He became chaplain to the Hawkins family at Nash in Kent.

4 Fr (later Bishop) Gregory Stapleton (d. 1802). Anstruther 4, pp. 257–8.

5 The Bernardine monks were Cistercians. Lady Montagu (d. 1745) had left £500 for saying daily Mass, which obligation the community had arranged with the monks at the Dunes; see **[pp. 104–6]**.

About the middle of this month we began to be extremely allarmed at the progress the French made towards us by the taking of Menin & Furnes, **[p. 362]** where they seized all the English & their Effects, which they said, they had orders to do in every Town they shou'd take. Our Forces being then very weak in these parts, they also made a furious attack upon Newport, & were expected immediately at Bruges if they succeeded. Colonel Doyle who was Commandant of the Town, & the English Troops then with us, was most extremely kind to us.[1] On the 26th as every body was flying the Town, we consulted him on the danger we were in, he acknowledged it was great, but promised to give us some hours notice for our departure: & wished us to have all our Goods packed up ready, that we cou'd carry with us, which we put upon Carts, & every moment expected to mount them ourselves, for other Carriages were not to be had, & in that bad Season we intended to fly to Sluys in Holland: thus were we situated from noon till 10 at night: during that interval we frequently sent Sister Eugenia Randall[2] to the Colonel, who tho overwhelmed with affairs of the greatest importance, always received her with the tenderness of a Father. Sometimes he sent us word we had 8 hours to prepare for our departure, at another only 4, & the last time only 2. Whilst in this cruel dilemma, Reverend Mother concluded if we were spared till morning, that all the Infirm shou'd set off for Ghent **[p. 363]** in their road to Antwerp, & there to take Shipping for Holland, as it was not safe to go by Ostend, but by God's great mercy we were saved the affliction of leaving our Convent, by the arrival of new Forces from England, who repulsed the French, when the Troops in Newport were reduced to their last charge of Shot, & were only 8 Hundred against many thousands of the Enemy. The Col^n both sent us the joyfull news, & came himself to confirm it to us that the present danger was past: however we still live in fear. Our Goods as far as possible are packed up in large Chests & Trunks, & are all about the lower part of the House, to be ready for the Carts on a new allarm. We kept 3 Waggons within the Inclosure for 3 nights: for when the People of the Town are frighten'd, & every body seeking to fly, other carriages are exorbitantly dear, & even Carts are hard to be got. Except in the case of a sudden flight it is not allow'd to use to use other Waggons for carrying off Goods, but such as are appointed by the Town.

On the 30th Mrs White the Annunciate set off for England.

On the 26th Reverend Mother had appointed Sister Frances (alias Ann Stoker who was Sick Sister) to attend the Infirm to Ghent, to which she made no **[p. 364]** objection, but as they did not go, to our great surprize

---

1 Colonel Welbore Ellis Doyle (1758–98) of Kilkenny became Colonel of the 14th Regiment of Foot in Flanders, several times acting heroically in difficult circumstances. He was made commandant of Bruges and was known to the Duke of York. See *ODNB*.

2 Eugenia Randall, lay sister (BA159).

& inconvenience, she acquainted Reverend Mother she did not intend to settle with us, but wished to have time to prepare her Clothes & pack up, which obliged us to make a change of the Lay Sisters immediately. She left us on the 30th. She was pious but obstinate, & inclined to Scrupulosity, & seem'd to have a defect in her Judgment, so that ^there^ was little prospect of her being received by the Community.

November

On the 26th Sister Peter De Gui, & Sister Josephine 2 Nuns from St Catherine's of St Omer were admitted into our Inclosure. We gave each of them a Cell as soon as possible, & they joined the Community in every duty, even Mattins. We found them most excellent, pious quiet Religious Women.

December

On the 11th Sister Mary Frances Tasburgh departed this life in the 76th year of her age, & 53d of her Religious Profession.[1] For several years before her death, she was so blind as not to be able to read, & only worked by feeling, but getting others to thread her Needles, she was always constantly at it in the hours appointed. She bore her blindness with that chearfull edifying patience that cou'd only proceed from a solid vertue. She had an anxious scrupulous & uneasy mind in regard of Spirituals, but was **[p. 365]** naturally full of courage, of a very high temper and a decisive tone; She had a great deal of good sense nature & good sense, but of a very singular turn in her Ideas & opinions. She was very zealous for frequent Communion, & spent much time in prayer, practised many mortifications & suffer'd much in her diet, especially when it was Fish on account of the bones, not being able to see what she put into her mouth: but tho so old, she never asked nor wou'd allow the Cellaress to serve her with a particular portion, but eat the common diet. Tho' a Jubilarian & Blind she made her own bed & swept her Cell till a little before her death, when a young Nun would absolutely sweep it for her. She was very exact in keeping Silence, & went very litle to the fire.

She fell ill with a cold, which she caught by living with her window open unknown to herself. She went to the Infirmary on the 6th, on the 9th received the Holy *Viaticum*, the Holy Oyles on the following day, & on 11th between 8 & 9 in the morning she expired without any Agony. *R. I. P.*

On the 12th we sent to Sluys in 7 Chests or trunks all the writtings the Church stuff we cou'd spare, some Plate, & our best Habits & surplices to the care of Mr Cornette the **[p. 366]** Vice Curate of Sluys who hired a room for them, for which we paid half a crown a week. The Emperors Head Commis of his Countoir in Bruges came into the Convent to plumb

[1] Maria Frances Tasburgh (1741–93) BA192.

the Trunks & Chests, & gave us a *Passavant*,[1] which we received back from West Capelle, & we must shew it there when the same Goods return. He order'd us to keep the keys.

The French Priests whom we had maintain'd (mention'd in November 1792) remained in England except Mr Stordeur who upon the Countries being again under the Emperor, returned to us. Some others petition'd also to be admitted. We receiv'd Lodged & Boarded Mr Saingevin ~~& Stordeur~~ Principal of the French College at Doway & his Professor Mr Stordeur. The Canon Dourlen brother to our great Friend at St Omer arrive'd here Aprill the 20th, Reverend mother was too sensible of our obligations to that Gentleman to allow his brother to seek an Asylum elsewhere.[2] He was about 70 and lame: he declined the offer, having then sufficient to maintain himself any where, but as Reverend Mother insisted on his stay with us, he absolutely would pay her at the rate of 32 Louis d'ors a year: however circumstances obliged him to keep what he had for his own use, as he cou'd not get any remittance from St omer. Besides these 3 who lodged with us, several others came daily to the Confessors Table & to concur to their maintenance the Community was content to live more poorly in diet, & continued to give up their own douceurs as mention'd in November 1792. Messieurs Saingevin[3] & Stordeur taught some of our Nuns the french Grammar, & the latter gave lessons of French to several of our Pensioners, by which he gained a triffle for himself. Mr Oliver our Confessor was exceeding kind & charitable to all these Gentlemen, by giving & procuring them great succours in money which tho small to each ^one^ was considerable in the whole. He almost stripped himself in shirts, stockings &c to clothe them.

The Pensioners &c: that we received in the year 1793.

Aprill 20 The Canon Dourlen from St Omer.
26 Mad'lle De Breucq, the youngest from Ghent, age [*blank*]
May 2d Mad'lle Van Emerie from Holland, a Protestant. age [*blank*]
June 13 Mad'lle Goudin of Bruges. age [*blank*]
20 Mad'lle Poublon of July
2 Miss Parker of English Protestant Parents settled at Ostend. Age [*blank*]
[p. 368] July 6 Mother Xaviera Atkinson an English Ursuline Professed at a french Convent of that Order at Tourcoine.

[1] *Passavant*: permit for the goods to proceed.

[2] Fr Charles Joseph Stordeur of the Diocese of St Omer died at London on 4 March 1828 (although Bellenger gives his date of death as 1831). Canon Louis Dourlen (1756–1839) of the Diocese of St Omer went to the Carmelites at Lanherne, where he died; see Bellenger, *French Exiled Clergy*, pp. 175, 247.

[3] Fr Nicolas Jean Saingevin (1748–1813) of the Diocese of Arras, went to Bodney Hall to the Montargis nuns when in England. See Bellenger, *French Exiled Clergy*, p. 244.

17 Mother St John White, an English Annunciate Professed at a French Convent of that Order at Boulogne in France.
Augustt 1 Mad'lle Marannis of Furnes. age [*blank*]
27 Mad'lle Delvoy of Bruges. age [*blank*]
October 21 Mad'lle Deutz from Holland. age [*blank*]
November 2d Two french Nuns from St Catherine's at St Omer viz Sister St Peter de Gui, & Sister Josephine

Pensioners &c that left us in the year
1793

January 15 Miss Hudson, alias Gapper to England.
26 Miss Burlton, & Miss Ellis, the Black West Indian to England.
March 9 Mad'lle Marcellin to Aire.
14 Miss Harriott Holmes to Ostend.
May 3d Mad'lle Teresa De Vaux Daughter to our Physician.
[p. 369] Oct 18 The 2 Miss Byrns to England.
30 Mother St John White the Annunciate to England.
30 Ann Stoker alias Sister Frances our Schollar for a Lay Sister.

[*note in pencil; twentieth-century hand*] Reverend Mother's Lucy Herbert half jubilee of being Superior … p. 21

GLOSSARY

This glossary defines words found in the Chronicle as they were understood at Bruges in the period under discussion, unless otherwise specified.

Arcaria: A nun elected to help the Prioress, Sub-Prioress and Procuratrix with the convent financial accounts. Responsible for the keys to the chests and their contents (mainly convent papers). From the root word 'arc/ark'.

Ark: A locked chest or room in which the nuns kept their important documents, money and material goods.

Augustinian Rule: Composed by St Augustine c. 400, his Rule was the first ever manual for communal Christian life.

Augustinian habit: The habit at Nazareth consisted of a white habit, leather belt, white linen rochet or over garment, surplice on great feasts, black veil, white stockings and plain black leather shoes. Lay sisters wore a coarse black or dark woollen habit, an upper garment with buttons, a leather belt and white linen veil, stockings of coarse grey cloth and leather shoes.

Burial practices: The first Canonesses at Bruges were buried either at Bethania or the Grey Sisters, their neighbours, then from 1637 in what is now the courtyard and later from 1651 in vaults or 'ovens' built of brick under the church. From 1783, as a result of an imperial edict, burials were outside the town in St Kruis (St Croix). From 1845 burials took place in the town cemetery, where every convent has a burial plot.

Canonesses: Canonesses followed the Augustinian Rule and combined elements of the active and contemplative religious life. At Bruges they were (and still are) part of the Windesheim tradition, a reform movement with the spirituality of the *Devotio Moderna* originating in the Netherlands initiated by Geert Grote (1340–84), who founded the Sisters and Brothers of the Common Life, some of whom became religious and took the Rule of St Augustine as Geert Grote had seen it lived by Jan van Ruysbroeck (1293–1381) in Groenendaal. Thomas à Kempis (1379–1471) was a significant author associated with the Windesheim tradition whose books have been of great importance at Nazareth.

Cellaress: The nun responsible for all food and drink in the convent, including the Father's house, preparation, keeping, purchasing, etc.

Chantress: The nun responsible for the performance of the liturgy, selecting music, choosing cantors and readers, supervising singing practices and ensuring that all the correct books are in place and in good order.

Chapter: A weekly meeting (normally held on Fridays) of Choir nuns, in which the Prioress catechized and taught the nuns in her community. The Chapter also discussed and voted on potential members and punished transgressors of the Rule after the sisters had confessed any faults.

Choir nun: Choir nuns brought a substantial dowry before profession; they could vote in all convent elections in Chapter and on business matters. They had to know Latin in order to sing the Divine Office.

***Clausura*:** Perpetual enclosure within the convent, confirmed for women religious by the Council of Trent in 1563. Enclosure restricted movement into the convent as well as out.

Clothing: A highly symbolic ceremony usually attended by a postulant's parents and family, in which the postulant moved from the world to the cloister, becoming a novice. Postulants for the Choir arrived at the ceremony dressed as brides of Christ. During the ceremony the candidates moved into the enclosure, receiving the habit and veil of the novice. At Nazareth they followed the custom started at St Monica's, Louvain of not having a ring. Following the ceremony a feast was held, to which family and friends were invited.

Confessor: A priest who heard confessions at all stages of a nun's life. Appointments of confessors required the agreement of the Mother Superior of the convent, or they were selected by her. Occasionally they were imposed from outside by the Visitor and as a result were the cause of disputes. Confessors were of great importance in the spiritual life of the convent. They might also say Mass and act as spiritual director. Sometimes, if the confessor was called away or in the case of sickness, an extraordinary or supply confessor might be appointed.

Chaplain: A priest who said Mass in a convent, but might be also called upon to carry out other functions requiring a priest.

Constitutions, also known as Statutes: Detailed regulations for daily life in a community; instructions for office holders, etc. The first copy at Bruges was brought from Louvain and survives in manuscript; it was first printed in 1717.

Convictress: Someone, generally quite young, who had expressed a desire to become a nun when she was old enough to take formal steps in the process towards profession.

Cross Prayers: Said by individual nuns at three o'clock in the afternoon, the time of the crucifixion. The nun raised her arms in the shape of a cross and said five *Pater Nosters* and five *Ave Marias*. [I am indebted to the Community for this explanation.]

Customs and Officers Rules: Small volumes of rules and guidelines developed by the nuns for the organization of daily convent life, based on the Constitutions.

***Devote* or *Beata*:** A devout woman who felt called to lead a consecrated life but without taking the full vows of a nun. They sometimes lived in small communities following simple rules and often served local people.

Devotion of Ten Fridays: A devotion performed to seek improvement in health. It was particularly associated with Fr Louis Sabran SJ and one explanation appeared in print, *An instruction to performe with fruit the devotion of ten Fridays in honour of S. Francis Xaverius apostle of the Indies* (1690). The text is a translation of an Italian work, and dedicated to Abbess Mary Caryll (1650 Ghent–1712 Dunkirk) of the Dunkirk Benedictines, who had been suffering from breast cancer and who experienced a miraculous cure in 1670. It described the devotion thus: 'Ten Fridays are ordained, and, if convenient, without intermission, on each of which he that will perform this Devotion must confess and communicate, and before some altar or picture of the Saint, or wherever else it is convenient, must also say ten *Pater Noster*s, and ten *Ave Maria*s, and ten *Gloria Patri*s, &c, offering to God the merits of this Saint, to obtain the favour he desires.' [I am indebted to members of the History of Women Religious of Britain and Ireland List-serv for this note.]

Discreets or Councillors: Senior members of the convent either elected or appointed to manage the convent and assist the Mother Superior.

Divine Office: The daily round of services in the Breviary for each of the canonical hours, held in the Choir and performed by the Choir nuns.

Examination: These were held before both clothing and profession by a representative of the Visitor, to test whether the candidate made her decision to enter without any pressure, that she was free from any worldly ties such as betrothal or marriage and that she fully understood the nature of her commitment. The records were kept by the diocese.

Fauxbourdon: Mentioned in the Chronicles as a new way of singing Divine Office in the eighteenth century. It was intended to facilitate singing by allowing participants to sing polyphony by ear, based on plain chant, with one part written out and additional parts supplied by the singer(s).

Grate sister: A nun, also known as Portress, who acted as guardian of access to the cloister, making sure that only those with special permits could enter the enclosure and that time spent in the speakhouse was monitored to avoid gossip and social gatherings. The grate or grille sealed the aperture in the wall where lay people including family members came to talk to members of the community.

Jubilee: Fifty years of profession were celebrated with jubilee festivities, often consisting of a sumptuous meal, followed by musical and dramatic entertainments. Convents also had jubilees and double jubilees to celebrate their foundations.

Lay or converse sister: A female religious who served the convent by carrying out practical work and brought a much lower dowry than a Choir nun. She could not vote on most matters. In houses of Augustinian Canonesses, she did not take vows of enclosure and so was able to act as escort on external journeys and carry out other outside tasks. Lay sisters did not have to know Latin and recited either the Little Office of Our Lady daily or said a prescribed number of *Pater Nosters* and *Ave Marias*, usually 150.

Monastic Office: The Divine Office as prayed by Choir nuns in contemplative convents. The Canonesses differed slightly but still followed a daily cycle. The services were: Matins, the office of Readings; Lauds; Midday office; Vespers; and Compline.

***Novena*:** A cycle of nine days of prayers, often to a particular saint, which are repeated daily as a supplication.

Novice: The second step (following postulancy) in a nun's formation process, generally lasting one year. At her clothing a candidate was officially accepted as a member of the religious community and received the holy habit and a new name. During the novitiate, the new member learned the Rule and constitutions, as well as undergoing a more intensive study of the order's spirituality and, for Choir nuns, of Latin. The noviceship or novitiate period for the Augustinians lasted for at least one year. The community voted in Chapter on whether or not to admit a candidate to profession. Equally, some novices concluded that religious life was not for them and decided to withdraw before profession.

Novice Mistress: The nun responsible for implementing the education and daily routine of the Choir novices; considered to be a senior role in the convent as she played an important role in setting standards for the community.

Our Ladies' Litanies: A series of prayers to Our Lady, often recited as a call and response chant in a group setting.

Pant and hanging pant: 'Corridor', from the Flemish word. Pants served as a cloister area at Nazareth. The hanging pant was where laundry was hung to dry.

Penitential Psalms (following numbering of the Vulgate): Psalm 6, *Domine, ne in furore* ('Lord, do not reprove me'); Psalm 31, *Beati quorum* ('Blessed are they whose offences are forgiven'); Psalm 37, *Domine, ne in furore* ('O Lord, do not rebuke me in your anger'); Psalm 50, *Miserere* *mei* ('Have mercy upon me'); Psalm 101, *Domine, exaudi* ('O Lord, hear my prayer'); Psalm 129, *De profundis* ('Out of the depths have I cried to you'); Psalm 142:1–11, *Domine, exaudi* ('Lord, hear my prayer'). These seven Psalms of penitence and forgiveness were particularly associated with Lent.

Pensioners: Refers to both girls and adults who boarded at the convent. Generally the context makes clear which is referred to. They were expected to lead quiet religious lives. Having pensioners was one way for the convent to earn money and also to build relationships with outsiders which might lead to benefactions.

Postulant: The first step in a nun's formation process. A postulant learns the basic elements of convent life and the spirituality of the convent.

Prioress: For Canonesses, the most senior office holder. She was elected by the community in secret ballot and served for life or as long as her health allowed. After 1807 Prioresses were elected for a three-year period. The Prioress was responsible for the community, setting standards, keeping discipline, choosing senior officers, and taking care of all temporal and spiritual matters, including the relationship with the Visitor and the Confessor.

Procuratrix/Procuratress: A nun chosen to manage the convent finances and accounts, in consort with the Arcaria, Prioress and Sub-Prioress. The Procuratrix was responsible for securing funds received from benefactors, dowries from the parents and guardians of professed nuns, and interest accrued from investments or rents. She was also responsible for keeping accounts and reporting everything to the Prioress. At the same time, she was to take as much care as she could with her spiritual life.

Refectress: A nun responsible for the refectory and its administration.

Rites for the Dying: These are recorded in the Chronicle for most nuns at Nazareth. Following the ritual was important, with the Confessor being sent for at the appropriate moment. The sacrament of Extreme Unction (Holy Oils) was meant to help and comfort the dying sister. The *viaticum* (lit. 'food for the journey') was Holy Communion for the dying.

Sacristan: A nun who would prepare the necessary items for Mass to be celebrated by the priest. Responsible for the candles, for the flowers in the chapel and for laying out the vestments worn by the priest and the linens placed on the altar, as well as for setting out the communion hosts and wine. Also responsible for seeing that everything, including the silver, was kept in good order and repaired.

Scholar: Generally the entry level for young women hoping to become nuns, this rank was one step below that of postulant. The term might also be applied to girls who did not join the community: intended future nuns were not always treated separately from lay girls when they were young. *See also* Convictress.

School Mistress or Mistress of the Pensioners: The nun who organized the pensioners' daily routine. She would help them get ready in the mornings, chaperone them to Mass and class, read to them at mealtimes, teach one or more subjects (e.g. languages, mathematics, geography) and offer spiritual guidance. Other tutors, often men, were hired to teach dancing, music and art.

Speakhouse or Parlour: A room where nuns could receive visitors, whether they were family, friends or members of the local community, and conduct business. Nuns were separated from the visitors by a grille or grate and hidden behind a curtain so they could not be seen, and were chaperoned.

Spiritual Director: Priest who advised individual nuns; there might be several at any one time. Although Jesuits were not able to serve as confessors, a number were linked to the English convents, including Nazareth, as spiritual directors carrying out Spiritual Exercises on the Ignatian model.

Spiritual Exercises: Devotional activities based on *The Spiritual Exercises devised by Ignatius Loyola*, translated into English in 1618, were followed in many of the English convents in exile. Other versions appeared subsequently and a number of convents wrote their own manuscripts. Led by the Spiritual Director or a senior member of the convent, nuns took part in an annual retreat, generally for a period of ten days. They focussed their meditations on texts chosen by the retreat director.

Statutes: A list of rules and prescriptions drawn up by male clerics (usually an archbishop or bishop) with the nuns, formally voted upon and implemented by the convent community. *See also* Constitutions.

Sub-Prioress: Second in command to the Prioress. She was permitted to admonish the Prioress if she committed a fault.

Tabernacle: A vessel designed to house consecrated hosts outside Mass.

Temporals: Money, property and goods associated with the convent.

Turn or wheel: The device through which goods were passed into the convent. It could be locked to secure it and had inner partitions that closed it when not in use. Other entry points were supplied for priests to come for Mass or for goods for the kitchen or for building.

***Viaticum*:** *See* Rites for the Dying.

Visitor: In most convents, the local bishop or his representative was the Visitor. He was responsible for good order and the supervision of management in a convent. Visitations were generally carried out every three years. Nuns had the right to write directly to the Visitor if they were troubled. At Nazareth, the Visitor was the Bishop of Bruges.

Vestry: Room where the nuns made habits, under the supervision of the Vestiarian. The Vestiarian had custody of all the garments of the sisters and of all fabric for making the habits.

APPENDIX 1

BRUGES MONASTERIES MENTIONED IN THE CHRONICLES

Abbey of Spermalie or Niew Jerusalem: Located on Snaggaertsstraat, behind Nazareth. A Cistercian Abbey for women. Moved to Bruges after a serious fire destroyed its buildings during religious troubles of the sixteenth century, and built on land purchased from the Abbey of the Dunes. Church consecrated 1634. Suppressed in 1796.

Abbey of the Dunes (Ten Duinen): Located at Potterierei, a Cistercian Abbey for men; dedicated to Onze-Lieve-Vrow. Like the nuns at Spermalie, the monks moved into Bruges during religious troubles of the sixteenth century. Suppressed in 1796; the site became the diocesan seminary.

Bethania: Penitenten van Maria-Magdalena or Maagdendal; separated from Nazareth only by a wall. They were Augustinian contemplatives, also known as Penitenten because they followed a life of penitential piety. Founded originally as a house for reformed prostitutes in 1460 by Dominicans, the convent soon attracted other aspirants and by the sixteenth century its membership was like other cloisters in the town. The name came from Mary of Bethany, sister of Lazarus, who saw herself as a penitent sinner. Suppressed in 1784 when there were 16 Choir nuns and 6 lay sisters.

Carmelite friars: Onze-Lieve-Vrowbroeders, located on Carmersstraat, near Potterierei. Suppressed in 1796.

Eeckhoute Abbey: An abbey for Augustinian Canons Regular. Suppressed in 1796 and demolished after suppression; site now occupied by the Groeninge Museum.

Penitenten van Aardenburg or Grey Sisters: Located on Carmersstraat, across the street from Nazareth; on the site from 1609. They had arrived from Aardenburg in 1604, affected by a siege. The Grey Sisters were Third Order Franciscan contemplatives and, like Bethany, they followed a life of penitential piety and prayer. Their foundation took inspiration from the life of Clare of Assisi. Suppressed in 1784.

Prinsenhof: An English convent of Third Order Franciscans in a former aristocratic house in Bruges. The nuns moved there in 1662, remaining until 1794, when they moved to England. They were contemplatives and fully enclosed.

APPENDIX 2

A NOTE ON CURRENCY

Money of account

To solve the problem of the many currencies in circulation in the Spanish and Austrian Netherlands, bookkeepers and accountants used a standard money of account for their financial records. This was the pound flemish (£fl) or pound grote. It was divided into sub-units of 20 schellings or shillings and each schelling was worth 12 grooten, so that there were 240 grooten to the pound. Convent accounts generally refer to florins which are equivalent to two shillings. It was modelled on the old Carolingian monetary system and was identical to the pound sterling (£st) in pre-decimal Britain, although the value of the two pounds, flemish and sterling, fluctuated in relation to each other according to current exchange rates. A second money of account was used in areas bordering France including the Southern Netherlands. This was the livre tournois (pound from Tours), again divided into 20 sols (sous after 1715), each sol being worth 12 deniers, with 240 deniers to the pound.

I am grateful to Professor James Bolton for his comments on currency.

Coins mentioned in the text

Florin or guilder = 20 stuivers; 120 stuivers = one pound Flemish

Louis d'or (from 1640) – of varying value until 1726, when it was fixed at 6 livres tournois

Livre tournois (written as ll or ŧŧ) = 20 sols = 240 deniers

Pattacon = 8 flemish schellings or 48 stuivers

Pistol or pistole = one Louis d'or but varying in value until 1726, when the Louis d'or was fixed at 6 livres tournois

English pounds are generally written as pounds sterling or have £ attached to the figures.

APPENDIX 3

CALENDAR OF FEASTS AND SAINTS' DAYS AT NAZARETH MENTIONED IN THE CHRONICLES

6 January	Epiphany
2 February	Candlemas Day, celebrating the presentation of Christ in the Temple. Also called the Feast of the Purification of the Blessed Virgin
28 February	Translation of St Augustine: the second move of the relics of the saint, from Sardinia to safety in Pavia
12 March	Pope Gregory the Great (c. 540–604)
19 March	St Joseph
25 March	(unless falling in Holy Week) Feast of the Annunciation
Maundy Thursday	Thursday before Easter Sunday, commemorating the Last Supper
Low Sunday	First Sunday after Easter
23 April	St George
24 April	Conversion of St Augustine (sometimes celebrated on 5 May during this period)
28 April	Dedication of the church of St Vitalis in Rome
4 May	St Monica, mother of St Augustine
8 May	Apparition of St Michael on Mount Gargano
Whitsunday/Pentecost	A moveable feast 50 days after Easter, celebrating the moment when the Holy Spirit visited the followers of Christ and they began to convert many others to follow Christ
11 June	St Barnabas, apostle
Corpus Christi	A moveable feast celebrating the real presence of Christ in the Eucharist, celebrated on the Thursday following Trinity Sunday (occasionally translated to the next Sunday); otherwise known as the Feast of the Blessed Sacrament
29 June	St Peter and St Paul, apostles
2 July	Visitation of the Blessed Virgin Mary, celebrating the visit of Mary to her cousin Elizabeth

22 July	St Mary Magdalene
26 July	St Anne, mother of the Blessed Virgin Mary
31 July	St Ignatius Loyola (1491–1556), founder of the Jesuits
1 August	St Peter in Chains
2 August	Our Lady of Portiuncula
10 August	St Lawrence, martyr
15 August	Assumption of the Blessed Virgin Mary
20 August	St Bernard
28 August	St Augustine of Hippo
8 September	Nativity of the Blessed Virgin Mary
11 September	Saints Protus and Hyacinth, martyrs
14 September	Feast of the Exaltation of the Holy Cross commemorates the recovery of the cross in 629
21 September	St Matthew, apostle and evangelist
29 September	St Michael and All Angels (Michaelmas)
4 October	St Francis of Assisi
11 October	Translation of St Augustine, celebrating the removal of his bones from North Africa to Sardinia
15 October	St Teresa of Avila
18 October	St Luke, evangelist
19 October	St Peter of Alcantara, mystic
1 November	All Saints Day; the evening was known as All Souls night, when prayers for the departed were said
2 November	All Souls Day
11 November	St Martin of Tours
21 November	Presentation of the Blessed Virgin Mary in the Temple
23 November	St Clement
30 November	St Andrew, apostle
3 December	St Francis Xavier
8 December	Immaculate Conception of the Blessed Virgin Mary
21 December	St Thomas, apostle
28 December	Holy Innocents
29 December	St Thomas of Canterbury
Rogation Days	days set aside to ask for mercy and to seek blessing on fields for planting at the end of April and just before Ascension
Ember Days	days of penance, fasting and abstinence set aside four times a year

APPENDIX 4

CITATION INDEX FOR MEMBERS OF THE NAZARETH CONVENT BEFORE 1800

The spreadsheet for this index was created from the WWTN database by Victoria Van Hyning and Alyn Still; I am grateful for their permission to reproduce its contents here. Dates indicate year of profession and year of death. Where there is only one date, this indicates that the nun died in the year of her profession.

Mary Amscotts, in religion Bernard (1695). BA002.
Ann Andrews, in religion Ann Joseph (1675–1724). BA003.
Helen Andrews, in religion Helen (1682–1728). Procuratrix from 1709; Novice Mistress 1716–17; Sub-Prioress 1717–20; Procuratrix 1720–23; Sub-Prioress from 1723; School Mistress. BA004.
Isabella Angier, in religion Mary Regis (1788–1837). BA005.
Margaret Aspinal, in religion Catherine (1720–86). Lay sister. BA006.
Mary Atwoode, in religion Mary (1631–40). Lay sister. BA007.
Ursula Babthorpe, in religion Monica (1642–62). BA009.
Ursula Babthorpe, in religion Ursula (1670–1719). Infirmarian. BA010.
Elizabeth Bambridge, in religion Martina (1729–74). Lay sister. BA011.
Margaret Barker, in religion Agnes (1656–91). BA012.
Mary Barker, in religion Mary (1656–82). BA013.
Catherine Bartlett, in religion Catherine (1646–83). Lay sister. BA008.
Elizabeth Bartlett, in religion Elizabeth (1653–91). Lay sister. BA014.
Elizabeth Barton, in religion Mary Baptist (1745–94). BA015.
Agnes Bedingfield, in religion Agnes Genoveva (1687–1725). BA016.
Mary Bedingfield, in religion Mary (1678–1712). BA018.
Mary Bedingfield, in religion Mary (1652–1693). Novice Mistress from 1655; Prioress 1661–93. BA019.
Josepha Bentall, in religion Josepha (clothed 1651, left 1654; did not profess). BA021.
Mary Berington (Schippe/Skippe), in religion Xaveria (1684–1704). BA022.
Ann Bessbrown, in religion Mary Ann (1687–1717). Lay sister. BA023.
Helen Blevin, in religion Helen (1734–88). Lay sister. BA026.
Charlotte Blundell, in religion Mary Joseph (1754–1813). Procuratrix 1770–?76; Sub-Prioress 1791–1806. BA027.
Helen Bowes, in religion Catherine (1633–79). Lay sister. BA029.

Catherine Darell, in religion Mary Olivia (1754–1802). BA070.
Mary Darell, in religion Mary Olivia (1734–66). Prioress 1744–66. BA071.
Barbara Devery, in religion Ann Barbara (1694–1733). Lay sister. BA072.
Elizabeth Dillon, in religion Mary Aurelia (1780–1803). Sub-Prioress from 1794; Novice Mistress from 1795; Musician. BA073.
Anne Dillon, in religion Mary Ignatia (1789–1814). Apothecary from 1803. BA074.
Grace Eddows, in religion Grace (1651–74). Lay sister. BA075.
Dorothy Errington, in religion Perpetua (1681–1739). BA076.
Mary Farrell, in religion Teresa Clare (1758–1820). School Mistress in 1783. BA077.
Sally Farrill, in religion Mary Xaveria (scholar's habit 1775, left 1776; did not profess). BA237.
Brigitta Fergus, in religion Mary Monica Teresa (1757–64). BA078.
Ann Fergusson, in religion Martha (1757–1802). Lay sister. BA079.
Julia Fitzgerald, in religion Henrietta (clothed 1740, left 1741; did not profess). BA080.
Mary Ford, in religion Mary Bernard (1725–64). Lay sister. BA081.
Ann Formby, in religion Ann Clare (1726–58). Lay sister. BA082.
Catharina Forshaw, in religion Joachim (1759–1821). Lay sister. BA083.
Catharina Gage, in religion Mary Xaveria (1740–63). BA084.
Penelope Gage, in religion Stanislaus (1712–72). Sub-Prioress 1748–69. BA085.
Ann Gladin, in religion Ann (1742–56). Lay sister. BA087.
Anne Green, in religion Anne Austin (1775–1833). BA090.
Mary Green, in religion Mary Agathe (1717–68). Lay sister. BA091.
Mrs Halsall (arrived 1692, left 1693; did not profess). BA092.
Mary Hall, in religion Mary (1632–69). BA093.
Elizabeth Hamilton, in religion Augustina (1674–83). BA094.
Lucy Hamilton, in religion Laurentia (1656–93). BA095.
Mary Hamilton, in religion Ann (1682–99). BA096.
Elizabeth Hampson, in religion Thecla (1761–92). Lay sister. BA097.
Mary Hannoye, in religion Mary Anne (scholar's habit 1655; remained in convent but did not profess; died 1668). BA098.
Mary Havers, in religion Mary (1681–1733). BA099.
Elizabeth Heath (clothed 1690, left 1691; did not profess). Lay sister. BA100.
Lucy Herbert, in religion Teresa Joseph (1693–1744). Procuratrix 1699–1709; Prioress 1709–44. BA101.
Mary Heton, in religion Mary (1657–1713). Sub-Prioress 1699–1710. BA102.
Barbara Hetvelde (clothed 1793, left 1794; did not profess). BA240.
Emerentiana Higgonbottom (1700–03). Lay sister. BA104.
Catharine Holland, in religion Mechtildis (1664–1720). Arcaria from 1713. BA106.

Ann Howard, in religion Dominic (1693–1734). BA107.
Anne Howell, in religion Theresa Joseph (1795–1840). BA108.
Lucy Howell, in religion Clementina (1796–1832). BA109.
Mary Howell, in religion Elizabeth (1795–1825). BA110.
Dorothy Huddleston, in religion Laetitia (1706–42). BA111.
Elizabeth Angela Huddleston, in religion Angela (1695–1756). Procuratrix 1723–30. BA112.
Frances Huddleston, in religion Mary Justina (1727–87). Novice Mistress. BA113.
Mary Huddleston, in religion Mary Barbara (1725–57). Musician. BA114.
Brigitt Hughes, in religion Margaret (1665–82). Lay sister. BA115.
Anne Maria Hyde, in religion Maria (1719–33). BA116.
Anne (Nanny) Hyde, in religion Anne Maria (1771–1806). Lay sister. BA103.
Harriet Ibbetson, in religion Teresa Austin (1791–1809). BA117.
Mary Jernegan, in religion Mary Teresa (1699–1757). Sub-Prioress 1738–48. BA118.
Ann Jernegan, in religion Winefrid (1698–1741). Musician. BA119.
Ann Jerningham, in religion Ann Teresa (1735–96). Procuratrix 1751–56, 1760–66, 1782–?88; Chantress. BA120.
Edwardina Jerningham, in religion Francis Joseph (1752–96). Musician. BA121.
Elizabeth Jerningham, in religion Mary Agnes (1745–1807). BA122.
Frances Henriette Jerningham, in religion Mary Francis of Sales (1777–1824). Sub-Prioress. BA123.
Clare Johnson, in religion Clare (1683–1720). Lay sister. BA124.
Magdalen Kemp, in religion Mary Magdalen (1656–87). BA125.
Diana Keynes, in religion Mary Joseph (1677–1707). Chantress; Portress. BA126.
Teresa Lauraine (Byrhaut), in religion Antonia (1662–91). BA127.
Margaret Linny, in religion Margaret (1717–65). Lay sister. BA128.
Elizabeth Lloyd, in religion Mary Joseph (1726–48). Cellarer in 1748. BA129.
Elizabeth Loveden, in religion Elizabeth (1695–1701). BA130.
Ann Lovegrove, in religion Mary Gertrude (1799–1816). BA131.
Dorothy Mannock, in religion Angela (1662–91). BA134.
Teresa Mannock, in religion Augustina (1665–98). Novice Mistress. BA135.
Ann Delphina Markham, in religion Christina (1717–45). BA138.
Ann Mechtilda Markham, in religion Ann Matilda (1687–1742). Sub-Prioress 1732–37. BA137.
Henrietta Markham, in religion Melior (1696–1733). BA136.
Maria Mawhood, in religion Louisa Austin (1779–1832). Procuratrix from 1799; Prioress 1807–10. BA140.
Agnes Mildmay, in religion Agnes (1662–91). BA141.

Elizabeth Momsey, in religion Alloysia (1652–91). BA142.
Frances Montack (clothed 1712, left 1712). AD017.
Ann Moody, in religion Elizabeth (1734–49). Lay sister. BA143.
Anne Catherine Moore, in religion Mary Clare (1790–1845). Sub-Prioress 1806–10; Prioress 1810–20. BA144.
Elizabeth More, in religion Mary Augustina (1753–1807). Procuratrix 1766; Prioress 1766–1807. BA145.
Margaret Moss, in religion Margaret (1662–79). Lay sister. BA146.
Elizabeth Newlin, in religion Teresa Austin (1737–86). BA147.
Mary Norris, in religion Catherine Joseph (1769–1828). BA148.
Ursula Palmes, in religion Ursula (1631–79). Procuratrix from 1655; Sub-Prioress 1673–79. BA149.
Henrietta Paston, in religion Mary Bernard (1780–1837). BA150.
Anna Charlotte Paterson, in religion Albana (1777–1828). School Mistress. BA151.
Mary Petre, in religion Mary (1665–92). BA153.
Cicily Pickering, in religion Isabella Cecilia (1745–56). Musician. BA155.
Eusebia Pickering, in religion Eusebia Joseph (1758–1810). BA156.
Lucy Poole, in religion Mary Aloysia (1747–99). BA158.
Martha Randall, in religion Eugenia (1764–1815). Lay sister. BA159.
Frances Reading, in religion Frances (1634–72). Lay sister. BA160.
Susan Reynoldson, in religion Susan (1670–1730). BA161.
Dorothy Risdom, in religion Eugenia (1701–05). BA162.
Mary Roby, in religion Mary Antonia (1791–1850). Lay sister. BA163.
Frances Rookwood, in religion Apollonia (1685–1717). Sub-Prioress 1716–17. BA164.
Mary De Rope, in religion Constantia (1681–1719). BA165.
Dorothy Rows, in religion Clare (1654–83). BA166.
Mary Rows, in religion Mary Ignatia (1654–83). BA167.
Milburge Russell, in religion Milburge (1688–1730). BA168.
Elizabeth Sales, in religion Elizabeth (1713–24). Lay sister. BA169.
Catherine Salkeld, in religion Mary Bernard (clothed 1720, left 1721; did not profess). BA238.
Dorothy Salvin, in religion Mary Baptist (1728–40). BA170.
Elizabeth Sargeant, in religion Lucy Austin (1782–1835). Procuratrix; Sub-Prioress. BA171.
Clare Saunderson, in religion Clare (1687–1731). Procuratrix from 1713; Sub-Prioress 1720–23, 1728–31. BA172.
Catherine Simner, in religion Frances Xaveria (1726–62). Lay sister. BA174.
Penelope Simons, in religion Ignatia (1656–1717). BA175.
Ann Smith, in religion Ann (1661–99). Novice Mistress; Procuratrix from 1693. BA176.
Catherine Smithson, in religion Lucy (1702–53). BA177.
Dorothy Smithson, in religion Mary Augustine (1700–37). BA178.

Frances Standish, in religion Mary Theresa (1684–91). Lay sister. BA180.
Agnes Stanley, in religion Mary Xaveria (1711–23). BA185.
Charlotte Stanley, in religion Mary Ignatia (1703–25). BA182.
Dorothy Stanley, in religion Dorothy Mary Xaveria (1700–49). Procuratrix 1730–49; Chantress. BA183.
Elizabeth Stanley, in religion Mary Gertrude (1704–41). Chantress. BA184.
Winifred Stanley, in religion Mary Placida (1704–42). Musician. BA186.
Ann Stevendale, in religion Austin (clothed 1767, left 1768; did not profess). BA239.
Margaret Sulyard, in religion Alexia (1658–99). BA187.
Anne Sykes, in religion Ann Augustine (1726–73). BA188.
Mary Sykes, in religion Mary Michael (1717–73). Procuratrix 1749–51. BA189.
Catherine Talbot, in religion Alicia (1780–1822). Procuratrix from 1788. BA190.
Margaret Tasburgh, in religion Margaret (1748–81). BA193.
Mary Tasburgh, in religion Mary Bernard (1700–15). BA191.
Mary Tasburgh, in religion Maria Frances (1741–93). BA192.
Margaret Tatlock, in religion Mary Alexia (1736–73). Lay sister. BA194.
Dorothy (Dolly) Taunton, in religion Clementina (1763–66). BA195.
Elizabeth Taunton, in religion Mary Aurelia (1770–71). BA196.
Fanny Taunton, in religion Mary Clare (clothed 1771, left 1771; did not profess). BA236.
Nanny Taunton, in religion Aloisa Joseph (clothed 1771, left 1772; did not profess). BA197.
Mary Taylor, in religion Agatha (1713–15). Lay sister. BA198.
Ann Thirwall, in religion Benedict (1684–1739). Procuratrix 1716–20. BA199.
Mary Tichbourne, in religion Mary Ignatia (1741–81). BA200.
Mary Timperley (clothed 1633, left 1634; did not profess). BA201.
Ann Trafford, in religion Anastasia (1695–1759). BA202.
Anne Trafford, in religion Francis Borgia (1711–70). BA203.
Monica Trafford, in religion Monica (1695–1742). BA204.
Ann Tremaine, in religion Ann Teresa (1722–29). Lay sister. BA205.
Ann Vaughan, in religion Mary Joseph (1709–14). BA207.
Mary Vaughan, in religion Mary Teresa (1687–92). BA208.
Teresa Vaughan, in religion Teresa Augustine (1709–31). BA209.
Isabella Vendow, in religion Mary Joachim (1726–45). Lay sister. BA210.
Frances Webb, in religion Augustina (1651–70). BA211.
Elizabeth Webb, in religion Winefrid (1652–96). Procuratrix. BA212.
Elizabeth Webster, in religion Augustina Clare (clothed 1791, left 1794; did not profess). BA234.
Mary Ann Webster, in religion Monica (1778–82). Lay sister. BA213.
Elizabeth Weston, in religion Delphina (1699–1721). Novice Mistress 1717–21. BA216.

Paula Weston, in religion Ann (1699–1738). Sub-Prioress 1737–38. BA215.
Margaret Wharton, in religion Mary Gonzaga, later Aloysia Joseph (clothed 1793, left 1795, returned 1797, left again 1798; did not profess). BA233.
Ann Wheeler, in religion Ann Clare (scholar's habit 1779, left 1781, returned 1782, left for Lierre as a servant 1785; did not profess). Lay sister. BA217.
Elizabeth Wheeler, in religion Ann Joseph (1745–99). BA218.
Mary Widdrington, in religion Ann (1687–1745). Sub-Prioress 1710–13. BA219.
Elizabeth Willeck, in religion Elizabeth Joseph (clothed 1654, left 1654; did not profess). BA220.
Elizabeth Willis, in religion Mary Xaveria (1730–35). Musician. BA222.
Winefrid Willis, in religion Mary Catherine (1742–97). Procuratrix 1756–60; Sub-Prioress from 1769; Novice Mistress from 1769. BA221.
Jane Wollascott, in religion Mary Magdalena (1652–65). BA223.
Martha Wollascott, in religion Martha (1651–93). BA224.
Ann Wright, in religion Ann Victoria (1685–91). BA225.
Justina Wright, in religion Barbara (1685–91). BA226.
Mary Wright, in religion Frances (1681–1730). Musician. BA227.
Frances Wright, in religion Mary (1657–1709). Novice Mistress; Sub-Prioress 1683–93; Prioress 1693–1709. BA228.
Mary Wyatt, in religion Mary (1653–84). Lay sister. BA229.
Elizabeth Young, in religion Elizabeth (1646–69). BA231.
Lucy Locker, in religion Teresa Magdalene (clothed 1797, left 1798; did not profess). BA241.

Louvain nuns who died in Bruges

Mary Altham, in religion Mary (1616 Louvain–1661 Bruges). School Mistress; Novice Mistress from 1629; Sub-Prioress 1635–55. LA004.
Helen Bedingfield, in religion Augustina (1622 Louvain–1661 Bruges). Prioress 1640–61. LA023.
Mary Best, in religion Mary (1615 Louvain–1631 Bruges). Procuratrix 1629–31. LA031.
Lucy Brereton, in religion Elizabeth (1626 Louvain–1646 Bruges). LA044.
Jane Clapton, in religion Lidwine (1622 Louvain–1669 Bruges). LA052.
Joyce Clapton, in religion Barbara (1622 Louvain–1674 Bruges). LA051.
Grace Constable, in religion Grace (1625 Louvain–1673 Bruges). Procuratrix 1633–42; Novice Mistress 1642–55; Sub-Prioress from 1655. LA069.
Mary Gifford, in religion Mary (1625 Louvain–1675 Bruges). Procuratrix 1642–55. LA107.
Elizabeth Lovell, in religion Elizabeth (1621 Louvain–1634 Bruges). Procuratrix 1631–33; Chantress 1633–34. LA172.
Mary Pole (1622 Louvain–1640 Bruges). Prioress 1635–40. LA203.

Frances Stamford, in religion Frances (1619 Louvain–1635 Bruges). Prioress 1629–35. LA242.

Anne Tremaine, in religion Anne (1601 Louvain–1637 Bruges). Sub-Prioress 1629–37. LA272.

SELECT BIBLIOGRAPHY

Manuscript sources

'Registre abrégé', Bénédictines anglaises de Pontoise, 68H3, Archives départementales du Val d'Oise, France

Chronicles of Nazareth, vols 1 and 2, Community of Nazareth, Bruges, Belgium

Louvain Chronicles, Box W.M.L.C., MS C2 'Louvain Chronicle', Douai Abbey, Berkshire

Printed primary sources

Annals of the English Benedictines of Ghent (East Bergholt: privately printed, 1898)

Augustine, *The Rule of the Great S. Augustin Expounded ... now Publish'd in English for the use of the English Augustin Nuns at Bridges* (Bruges: John de Cock, [1737])

Bowden, Caroline (ed.), *English Convents in Exile 1600–1800. Vol. 1: History Writing* (London: Pickering and Chatto, 2012–13)

Daemen-de Gelder, Katrien (ed.), *English Convents in Exile 1600–1800. Vol. 4: Life Writing 2* (London: Pickering and Chatto, 2012–13)

Dominicana: Cardinal Howard's letters, English Dominican friars, nuns, students, papers and mission registers, CRS 25 (London: CRS, 1925)

Durrant, C. S., *A Link Between Flemish Mystics and English Martyrs* (London: Burns, Oates and Washbourne, 1925)

Foley, Henry (ed.), *Records of the English Province of the Society of Jesus, 8 vols* (London: Burns and Oates, 1875–83)

Gillow, J., and Trappes-Lomax, R. (eds), *The Diary of the Blue Nuns, or Order of the Immaculate Conception, at Paris, 1658–1810*, CRS 8 (London: CRS, 1910)

Hallett, Nicky, *Lives of Spirit: English Carmelite Self-Writing of the Early Modern Period* (Aldershot: Ashgate, 2007)

——— (ed.), *English Convents in Exile 1600–1800. Vol. 3: Life Writing 1* (London: Pickering and Chatto, 2012–13)

Hamilton, Adam (ed.), *The Chronicle of the English Augustinian Canonesses Regular of the Lateran, at St. Monica's in Louvain 1548–1644*, 2 vols (Edinburgh: Sands and Co., 1904–06)

Herbert, Lucy, *A daily exercise and devotion for the gentlewomen pensioners* (Douai: M. Mairesse, 1712)

———, *Several excellent methods of hearing Mass* (Bruges: John De Cock, 1722)

———, *Several Excellent Methods of hearing Mass ... collected together by the Right Honourable Lady Lucy Herbert of Powis, Superiour of the English Augustin Nuns, At Bruges* (Bruges: C. De Moor, 1790; reprinted 1816)

Kelly, James E. (ed.), *English Convents in Exile 1600–1800. Vol. 5: Convent Management* (London: Pickering and Chatto, 2012–13)

Harris, P. R. (ed.), *Douai College Documents 1639–1794*, CRS 63 (London: CRS, 1972)

Marconi, G. L., *Account of the Life of the Servant of God, Benedict Joseph Labre, Frenchman* (London, 1785)

Neville, Abbess Anne, 'English Benedictine Nuns in Flanders: Annals of Their Five Communities, 1598–1687', wwtn.history.qmul.ac.uk/publications-static/pdfs/Annalsof5communitiesJan09.pdf

Reynolds, E. E. (ed.), *The Mawhood Diary*, CRS 50 (London: CRS, 1956)

The Rule of S. Augustin as also the Statutes & Constitutions of the English Regular Canonesses of the Order of St Augustin Established at Bridges in Flanders (Bruges: printed with permission in the year 1717)

Skeat, F., *Life of Sir Edward Widdrington, Knt., & Baronet of Cartington, in Northumberland: with an account of his piety in the practice of the Catholic faith* (London: Burns, Oates and Washbourne, 1923)

Trappes-Lomax, R. (ed.), *Franciscana: The English Franciscan Nuns, 1619–1821 and the Friars Minor of the Same Province, 1618–1761*, CRS 24 (London: CRS, 1922)

Williams, R. G. (ed.), *Mannock Strickland (1683–1744), Agent to English Convents in Flanders: Letters and Accounts from Exile*, CRS 86 (Woodbridge: Boydell and Brewer for the CRS, 2016)

Young, F. (ed.), *Rookwood Family Papers, 1606–1761*, Suffolk Records Society 59 (Woodbridge: Boydell and Brewer for the Suffolk Records Society, 2016)

Secondary sources

Anon., *A History of the Benedictine Nuns of Dunkirk* (London: Catholic Book Club, 1957)

Anon., 'Some Althams of Mark Hall in the Seventeenth Century', Part 2, *Essex Review* 17 (July 1908), pp. 134–46

Allanson, Athanasius (ed.), *Biography of the English Benedictines* (Ampleforth: Ampleforth Abbey, 1999)

Anstruther, G. (ed.), *The Seminary Priests: A Dictionary of the Secular Clergy of England and Wales, 1558–1850*, 4 vols (Ware: St Edmund's College, 1969–77)

Arblaster, Paul, *Antwerp and the World: Richard Verstegan and the International Culture of Catholic Reformation* (Leuven: Leuven University Press, 2004)

Barlow, Frank, 'The King's Evil', *English Historical Review* 95 (374) (1980), pp. 3–27

Bedingfield Papers, Genealogical Supplement in Miscellanea VI, CRS 6 (London: CRS, 1909)

Bellenger, Aidan (ed.), *English and Welsh Priests 1558–1800* (Bath: Downside Abbey, 1984)

——— (ed.), *The French Exiled Clergy in the British Isles after 1789* (Bath: Downside Abbey, 1986)

Berlière, Ursmer, et al. (eds), *Monasticon belge*, 7 vols (Maredsous: Abbaye de Maredsous, 1890–1993)

Berry, W., *County Genealogies: Pedigrees of the Families in the County of Sussex* (London: Sherwood, Gilbert and Piper, 1830)

Biographie nationale de Belgique, 44 vols (Bruxelles: Académie royale de Belgique, 1866–1986)

Burke, B., *Genealogical and Heraldic History of the Landed Gentry* (London: Harrison, 1875)

Corp, Edward, *A Court in Exile: The Stuarts in France, 1689–1718* (Cambridge: Cambridge University Press, 2004)

De Grauwe, Jan, *Histoire de la chartreuse Sheen Anglorum au continent: Bruges, Louvain, Malines, Nieuport (1559–1783)* (Salzburg: Institut für Anglistik und Amerikanistik, Universität Salzburg, 1984)

Derheims, Jean, *Histoire de la ville de St Omer* (St-Omer, 1843)

Dunham, T. D., and Turner, J. M. W., *History of Richmondshire* (London: Longman, 1823)

Durrant, C. S., *A Link Between Flemish Mystics and English Martyrs* (London: Burns, Oates and Washbourne, 1925)

Gailliard, J., *Recherches historiques sur la Chapelle du Saint-Sang à Bruges* (Bruges, 1846)

Hayes, Richard, *Biographical Dictionary of Irishmen in France* (Dublin: Gill and Son, 1949)

Hendriks, Lawrence, *London Charterhouse, Its Monks and Its Martyrs with a Short Account of the English Carthusians after the Dissolution in March 1783* (London: Kegan Paul, 1889)

Hind, Elphege, 'Princethorpe Priory', *Ampleforth Journal* 11 (1905), pp. 192–204

Holt, G. (ed.), *The English Jesuits, 1650–1829: A Biographical Dictionary*, CRS 70 (London: CRS, 1984)

———, *The English Jesuits in the Age of Reason* (London: Burns and Oates, 1993)

Hollinshead, Janet E., *Women of the Catholic Community: The Blundells of South Lancashire during the Seventeenth and Eighteenth Centuries* (Wigan: North West Catholic History Society, 2010)

Keats-Rohan, K. S. B. (ed.), *English Catholic Nuns in Exile 1600–1800: A Biographical Register*, Prosopographica et Genealogica 15 (Oxford: Unit for Prosopographical Research, Linacre College, in press 2017)

McCoog, T. M., *English and Welsh Jesuits, 1555–1650*, 2 vols, CRS 74–5 (London: CRS, 1994–95)

Mason, M. J., 'Nuns of the Jerningham Letters: Elizabeth Jerningham (1727–1807) and Frances Henrietta Jerningham (1745–1824), Augustinian Canonesses of Bruges', *Recusant History* 22(3) (1995), pp. 350–69

Montias, John Michael, *Vermeer and His Milieu: A Web of Social History* (Princeton: Princeton University Press, 1989)

Mangion, Carmen, 'Avoiding "Rash and Imprudent Measures": English Nuns in Revolutionary Paris, 1789–1801' in C. Bowden and J. E. Kelly (eds), *The English Convents in Exile: Communities, Culture and Identity* (Farnham: Ashgate, 2013), pp. 247–63

Newman, P. R., *Royalist Officers in England and Wales: A Biographical Dictionary* (New York: Garland, 1981)

Nolan, P., *Irish Dames of Ypres* (Dublin: Browne and Nolan, 1908)

Oliver, G., *Collections towards Illustrating the Biography of the Scotch, English and Irish Members* (Exeter: Featherstone, 1838)

Parmentier, J., 'The Irish Connection: The Irish Merchant Community in Ostend and Bruges during the Late Seventeenth and Eighteenth Centuries', *Eighteenth-Century Ireland* 20 (2005), pp. 31–54

Payne, J. O. (ed.), *Records of English Catholics of 1715* (London: Burns and Oates, 1889)

Plouvain, Pierre A., *Souvenirs à l'usage des habitans de Douai, ou notes pour servir à l'histoire* (Douai, 1822)

Questier, M. C., *Stuart Dynastic Policy and Religious Politics, 1621–1625* (Cambridge: Cambridge University Press, 2009)

Rommelse, G., *The Second Anglo-Dutch War 1665–7* (Hilversum: Verloren, 2006)

Ruvigny et Raineval, M. H. M., *The Jacobite Peerage, Baronetage, Knightage …* (Edinburgh and London: T. C. and E. C. Jack, 1904)

Ryckaert, Marc, *Historische stedenatlas van België: Brugge* (Brussel: Gemeentekrediet, 1991)

Smith, Geoffrey, *The Cavaliers in Exile* (Basingstoke: Palgrave, 2003)

Tayler, Henrietta, *Lady Nithsdale and Her Family* (London: Lindsay Drummond, 1939)

Trenqualion, Max de, *West Grinstead et les Caryll*, 2 vols (Paris, 1893)

Van Dycke, F., *Recueil héraldique* (Bruges, 1851)

Van Hyning, Victoria, *Convent Autobiography: English Nuns in Exile 1609–1807* (Oxford: British Academy and Oxford University Press, forthcoming)

Van Orden, Kate, *Materialities: Books, Readers, and the Chanson in Sixteenth-Century Europe* (Oxford: Oxford University Press, 2015)

Walker, Claire, 'Combining Martha and Mary: Gender and Work in Seventeenth-Century English Cloisters', *Sixteenth Century Journal* 30 (1999), pp. 397–418

Wear, Andrew, *Knowledge and Practice in English Medicine, 1550–1680* (Cambridge: Cambridge University Press, 2000)
Whitehead, Maurice, *English Jesuit Education* (Farnham: Ashgate, 2013)
Wood, Martin, *Family and Descendants of St Thomas More* (Leominster: Gracewing, 2008)
Young, F., *English Catholics and the Supernatural, 1553–1829* (Farnham: Ashgate, 2013)
———, *The Gages of Hengrave and Suffolk Catholicism, 1640–1767*, CRS Monograph 8 (Woodbridge: Boydell and Brewer for the CRS, 2015)
———, 'Mother Mary More and the Exile of the English Augustinian Canonesses of Bruges in England, 1794–1802', *Recusant History* 27 (2004), pp. 86–102
———, 'The Tasburghs of Bodney: Catholicism and Politics in South Norfolk', *Norfolk Archaeology* 46 (2011), pp. 190–8

Unpublished PhD thesis

Van Hyning, Victoria, 'Cloistered Voices: English Nuns in Exile, 1550–1800', University of Sheffield, May 2014

Online sources

The Art World in Britain 1660 to 1735, artworld.york.ac.uk
British History Online, british-history.ac.uk
Douai–Rheims Bible, online edition, drbo.org
The Hierarchy of the Catholic Church, catholic-hierarchy.org
The History of Parliament, online edition, historyofparliamentonline.org
Oxford Dictionary of National Biography, online edition, oxforddnb.com
Oxford English Dictionary, oed.com
Stirnet (genealogy website), stirnet.com
'Who Were the Nuns?' database, wwtn.history.qmul.ac.uk

INDEX OF PEOPLE AND PLACES

Page spans may indicate repeated mentions rather than continuous discussion.
Sr before a name indicates profession as a nun: place name in brackets following a name denotes convent where professed if not Bruges. Some novices were given names in religion at clothing.
Mrs before a name does not imply marriage in this period.

INDEX OF SUBJECTS

Page spans may indicate repeated mentions rather than continuous discussion.

The Catholic Record Society

The Catholic Record Society was established in 1904 in order to publish editions of primary sources relating to Catholic individuals and ecclesiastical institutions in the British Isles, including registers, chronicles, letters and diaries. The Society's motto, *Colligite fragmenta ne pereant* ('Gather up the fragments lest they perish'), reflects the aim of the Society to make primary sources available to posterity and a general readership.

Over ninety volumes have been published so far and they form a unique collection of primary source material indispensable to all those with an interest in the history of Catholic dioceses, parishes, religious communities, schools and colleges. The Society has also published a number of scholarly monographs dealing with particular topics or with Catholic individuals prominent in public life.

British Catholic History, formerly titled *Recusant History*, is the official journal of the Catholic Record Society, published twice annually in May and October by Cambridge University Press. The journal acts as a forum for innovative, vibrant, transnational, inter-disciplinary scholarship resulting from research on the history of British and Irish Catholicism at home and throughout the world. It publishes peer-reviewed original research articles, review articles and shorter reviews of works on all aspects of British Catholic history from the fifteenth century up to the present day. Central to its publishing policy is an emphasis on the multi-faceted, national and international dimensions of British Catholic history. The journal welcomes contributions on all approaches to the Catholic experience.

The Catholic Record Society welcomes new members, whose membership entitles them to receive *British Catholic History* as well as new Catholic Record Society volumes. The Society hosts an annual conference.

catholicrecordsociety.co.uk